Lecture Notes in Compι·

28

Commenced Publication in 1973
Founding and Former Series Editors:
Gerhard Goos, Juris Hartmanis, and Jan ·

Maria A. Wimmer   Jean-Loup Chappelet
Marijn Janssen   Hans J. Scholl (Eds.)

Electronic Government

9th IFIP WG 8.5 International Conference, EGOV 2010
Lausanne, Switzerland, August 29 - September 2, 2010
Proceedings

 Springer

Volume Editors

Maria A. Wimmer
University of Koblenz-Landau, Institute for IS Research
Universitätsstr. 1, 56070 Koblenz, Germany
E-mail: wimmer@uni-koblenz.de

Jean-Loup Chappelet
IDHEAP Swiss Graduate School of Public Administration
1015 Lausanne, Switzerland
E-mail: jean-loup.chappelet@idheap.unil.ch

Marijn Janssen
Delft University of Technology, Faculty of Technology,
Policy, and Management
Jaffalaan 5, 2628 BX Delft, The Netherlands
E-mail: m.f.w.h.a.janssen@tudelft.nl

Hans J. Scholl
University of Washington, The Information School
Mary Gates Hall, Seattle, WA 98195-2840, USA
E-mail: jscholl@uw.edu

Library of Congress Control Number: 2010932132

CR Subject Classification (1998): C.2, J.1, H.4, K.4.2, H.3, H.2

LNCS Sublibrary: SL 3 – Information Systems and Application,
incl. Internet/Web and HCI

ISSN   0302-9743
ISBN-10   3-642-14798-4 Springer Berlin Heidelberg New York
ISBN-13   978-3-642-14798-2 Springer Berlin Heidelberg New York

springer.com

© IFIP International Federation for Information Processing 2010
Printed in Germany

Typesetting: Camera-ready by author, data conversion by Scientific Publishing Services, Chennai, India
Printed on acid-free paper   06/3180

Preface

For almost a decade the International Federation for Information Processing Working Group 8.5 (Information Systems in Public Administration), or IFIP WG 8.5, has organized the EGOV series of conferences, which has solidly established itself as one of three core conferences in the research domain of e-Government, e-Governance, and e-Participation. Until last year, EGOV was hosted within the DEXA cluster of conferences. For the first time in 2010, the IFIP WG 8.5 organized the conference on its own, which was also reflected in the slight name change to IFIP EGOV 2010.

Like its predecessors, the IFIP EGOV 2010 conference attracted scholars from around the world as a venue of high reputation. In 2010, the conference brought together scholars and practitioners from four continents and 40 countries.

Like in 2009, IFIP EGOV was co-located with ePart, the International Conference on eParticipation. ePart aims at presenting advances in both social and technological scientific domains, seeking to demonstrate new concepts, methods, and styles of eParticipation. ePart is closely aligned with the IFIP EGOV conference. The chairs of both conferences maintain close links and are committed to co-locating the two events in the years to come, which intentionally allows for exchange and cross-fertilization between the two communities.

The IFIP EGOV 2010 Call for Papers attracted 111 paper submissions, which included 81 full research papers and 30 work-in-progress papers on ongoing research as well as project and case descriptions, and 9 workshop and panel proposals. Among the 81 full research paper submissions, 36 papers (empirical and conceptual) were accepted for Springer's LNCS proceedings. These papers have been clustered under the following headings:

- Foundations
- Transformation
- Evaluation
- Adoption and diffusion
- Citizen Perspectives and Social Inclusion
- Infrastructure
- Business Process Modelling

As in past years, Trauner Druck, Linz/Austria, published accepted work-in-progress papers and workshop and panel abstracts in a complementary proceedings volume. This year, the volume covers approx. 45 paper contributions and 7 workshop and panel abstracts from both conferences, IFIP EGOV and ePart.

Also in 2010 and per the recommendation of the Paper Awards Committee, led by Committee Chair Ralf Klischewski of GUC, Cairo/Egypt, the IFIP EGOV 2010 Organizing Committee granted outstanding paper awards in three distinct categories:

– The most interdisciplinary and innovative research contribution
– The most compelling critical research reflection
– The most promising practical concept

The winners in each category were announced in the award ceremony at the conference dinner, which is a highlight of each IFIP EGOV conference.

Many people make large events like this conference happen. We thank the 98 members of the IFIP EGOV 2010 Program Committee and dozens of additional reviewers for their great efforts in reviewing the submitted papers. Olivier Glassey of IDHEAP was a major contributor who tirelessly organized and managed the zillions of details locally. Andreas Jeworutzki of the University of Koblenz-Landau (Germany) supported us in the administrative management of the review process and in compiling the proceedings of IFIP EGOV 2010.

The host of IFIP EGOV 2010 was the Swiss Graduate School of Public Administration (IDHEAP) in the University of Lausanne/Switzerland. IDHEAP is an institution of postgraduate education that prepares students for senior functions in Switzerland's public administrations. IDHEAP is a renowned institution accredited on national and international levels. Leading in interdisciplinary research, IDHEAP provides advice and expertise to administrations, political leaders, and the national government of Switzerland. Finally, the City of Lausanne, capital of the Swiss canton Vaud, is situated on the shores of Lac Leman (Lake Geneva) in the middle of a wine region and provides a formidable site for holding IFIP EGOV 2010. The city's long and at times turbulent history beginning with Celtic and Roman settlements has created a rich heritage and a cultural setting with numerous sites of interest. Lausanne is also the headquarters of the International Olympic Committee (IOC), which officially recognizes the city as its Capitale Olympique. It was a great pleasure to hold IFIP EGOV 2010 at such a special place.

August/September 2010

Maria A. Wimmer
Jean-Loup Chappelet
Marijn Janssen
Hans J. (Jochen) Scholl

Organization

Executive Committee

Maria A. Wimmer   University of Koblenz-Landau, Germany
Jean-Loup Chappelet   IDHEAP, University of Lausanne, Switzerland
Marijn Janssen   Delft University of Technology,
     The Netherlands
Jochen Scholl   University of Washington, USA

Program Committee

Ashraf Hassan Abdelwahab	Deputy to the Minister of State for Administrative Development, Egypt
Suha AlAwadhi	Kuwait University, Kuwait
Vincenzo Ambriola	University of Pisa, Italy
Rex Arendsen	University of Twente, The Netherlands
Yigal Arens	Digital Government Research Center, USA
Karin Axelsson	Linköping University and Örebro University, Sweden
Molnar Balint	Corvinus University, Hungary
Frank Bannister	Trinity College Dublin, Ireland
Karine Barzilai-Nahon	University of Washington, USA
Victor Bekkers	Erasmus University Rotterdam, The Netherlands
Lasse Berntzen	Vestfold University College, Norway
John Bertot	University of Maryland, College Park, USA
Melanie Bicking	University of Koblenz-Landau, Germany
Dana Maria Boldeanu	Bucharest Academy of Economic Studies and University Politehnica of Bucharest, Romania
Bojan Cestnik	Temida d.o.o., Slovenia
Jean-Loup Chappelet	IDHEAP, Switzerland
Yannis Charalabidis	National Technical University of Athens, Greece
Sergey Chernyshenko	Dnipropetrovsk National University, Ukraine
Wichian Chutimaskul	King Mongkut's University of Technology Thonburi, Thailand
Flavio Corradini	University of Camerino, Italy
Jim Davies	University of Oxford, UK
Sharon Dawes	University at Albany, USA

Rahul De	Indian Institute of Management Bangalore, India
Marco de Marco	Catholic University of Milan, Italy
Elsa Estevez	UNU Macao, China
Enrico Ferro	Istituto Superiore Mario Boella (ISMB), Italy
Leif S. Flak	University of Agder, Norway
Iván Futó	Corvinus University of Budapest, Advisor for E-Government, Hungary
Andreás Gábor	Budapest University of Economic Sciences and Public Administration, Hungary
Rimantas Gatautis	Kaunas University of Technology, Lithuania
José Ramón Gil-García	Centro de Investigación y Docencia Económicas (CIDE), Mexico
Olivier Glassey	IDHEAP, Switzerland
Dimitris Gouscos	University of Athens, Greece
Åke Grönlund	Örebro University, Sweden
Luis Guijarro-Coloma	University of Valencia, Spain
M.P. Gupta	Indian Institute of Technology Delhi, India
Jan Pries Heje	Roskilde University, Denmark
Helle Zinner Henriksen	Copenhagen Business School, Denmark
Zahir Irani	Brunel University, UK
Tomasz Janowski	United Nations University IIST, Macau, China
Arild Jansen	University of Oslo, Norway
Marijn Janssen	Delft University of Technology, The Netherlands
Luiz Antonio Joia	Brazilian School of Public and Business Adminstration, Getulio Vargas Foundation, Brazil
Ralf Klischewski	German University in Cairo, Egypt
Trond Knudsen	Research Council, Norway
Helmut Krcmar	Technical University of Munich, Germany
Herbert Kubicek	University of Bremen, Germany
Christine Leitner	Danube University Krems, Austria
Katarina Lindblad-Gidlund	Mid Sweden University, Sweden
Miriam Lips	Victoria University of Wellington, New Zealand
Euripides Loukis	University of the Aegean, Greece
Ann Macintosh	Leeds University, UK
Alexander Makarenko	Institute for Applied System Analysis at National Technical University of Ukraine (KPI), Ukraine
Josef Makolm	Federal Ministry of Finance, Austria
Gregoris Mentzas	National Technical University of Athens, Greece

Additional Reviewers

Dimitris Apostolou, Greece
Gaston Concha, Chile
Ciprian Dobre, Romania
Marleen Haase, Austria
Bernhard Hitpass, Chile
Herbert Leitold, Austria
Jianwei Liu, The Netherlands
Nikos Loutas, Ireland
Ulf Melin, Sweden

Ansgar Mondorf, Germany
Barbara Re, Italy
Francesca Ricciardi, Italy
Sabrina Scherer, Germany
Daniel Schmidt, Germany
Amirreza Tahamtan, Austria
Silke Weiß, Austria

Table of Contents

Evaluation

Adoption and Diffusion

Citizen Perspective and Social Inclusion

Infrastructure

Business Process Modelling

Towards an Understanding of E-Government Induced Change – Drawing on Organization and Structuration Theories

Anne Fleur van Veenstra, Marijn Janssen, and Yao-Hua Tan

Faculty of Technology, Policy and Management, Delft University of Technology,
Jaffalaan 5, 2628 BX Delft, The Netherlands
{a.f.e.vanveenstra,m.f.w.h.a.janssen,y.tan}@tudelft.nl

Abstract. E-government research deals with 'wicked' problems that require multidisciplinary approaches to gain a full understanding. One of the main challenges of e-government is to induce change in the structure of public organizations to realize its full potential. This paper investigates e-government induced change using two complementary theoretical lenses applied to an e-government case study. We use organization theories to explore aspects of organizational structure that may change when implementating e-government and structuration theory to investigate how these aspects are affected by human action within its social structure. This combination allows us to investigate the discrepancy between the ambitions of e-government induced change and the actual changes accomplished in practice. Our analysis shows that using these two frames gives us better insight into the thorny subject of e-government than using a single theory. Further research should look into how these theories can be used to deepen our knowledge of e-government.

Keywords: E-government, organizational change, organization theory, structuration theory, multidisciplinary approach.

1 Introduction

Over the past decades the research field of e-government "has advanced past the stage of infancy" [1, p. 2]. A recurring theme in studies of the e-government research field, however, is that most e-government research is empirically based, lacking theoretical foundations [2-4]. One reason for this lack of common foundations is that e-government is essentially a multidisciplinary research field dealing with 'wicked', unstructured problems, and "[i]ntegration and interdisciplinarity has proved to be more and more difficult as more disciplines with different paradigms and standards begin to interact" [1, p. 23]. To advance interdisciplinary understanding of e-government, this paper explores the use of different theoretical lenses for explaining challenges e-government implementation encounters in practice.

One of the main challenges for e-government is to realize organizational change to realize the full potential of information technology (IT), thereby improving operations [5-7]. For public agencies, this means that previously stove-piped organizations will

M.A. Wimmer et al. (Eds.): EGOV 2010, LNCS 6228, pp. 1–12, 2010.
© IFIP International Federation for Information Processing 2010

need to break down the silos in which departments operate and change from hierarchical – vertically oriented – organizations into network-centric – horizontal – organizations [6]. However, empirical studies suggest that, in reality, the introduction of IT not often changes institutions and, rather, often reinforces current work practices and organizational structures [8-10]. This has resulted in a gap between the promises and actual realization of e-government induced change. This paper aims to understand this gap and to deepen our knowledge on how these organizations may reap the full benefits of e-government. E-government induced change is among the complex and unstructured research problems that have been mentioned to benefit from using a multidisciplinary approach [11]. To understand the differences between the objectives and promises of e-government induced change and its achievements in practice, we use two different theoretical strands.

One theoretical strand encompasses theories on organizational structure. Aspects of organizational structure and IT-induced change will be identified. The other strand of literature that is used is structuration theory. Structuration theory can be used to study the complexity of a change process by looking at it as the result of the duality of agency behavior and social structure. We will apply these two theoretical lenses to a case study in the Netherlands to see how they enhance our understanding of e-government. This paper continues with introducing aspects of organizational structure. Then, structuration theory will be discussed. Next, the research approach of applying this combination of theories to a case study of e-government in the Netherlands is presented, followed by the case study description and its findings. Finally, we present conclusions and recommendations for future research.

2   Theories on Organizational Structure

Since the emergence of the information society, networks and organizations adopting a network approach are on the rise [12]. Effective e-government also requires public organizations to adopt a network orientation [6], governed by interdependent relations that collaborate to achieve mutual benefits [13]. Traditionally, however, government organizations are organized as bureaucracies: functional hierarchies that are made up of stove-piped departments supported by fragmented information systems. Characteristics of bureaucracy include a specialization of labor, a hierarchy of authority, a system of rules limiting discretionary power of individuals and written records of activities. Although, according to Weber [14], bureaucracies represent the most efficient organizational form, nowadays, they are most often linked with concepts such as red tape and inefficient decision structures: "the very structures that ensure continuity and stability are major inhibitors of change" [6, p. 66]. To make a shift from a hierarchy to a network-oriented organization requires changes that will alter work practices and organizational structure. The increasing use of IT is generally considered as one of the main drivers of this shift in organizational structure. In this section we indentify from literature which organizational aspects likely change supporting e-government implementation.

Researching which organizational characteristics fit certain circumstances, Galbraith identified three characteristics of the structure of an organization under uncertainty: rules and procedures, decentralization of decision making, and professionalization of the work force [15]. Another aspect of organizational structure is the (set of) mechanism(s) coordinating activities. Mintzberg distinguishes five different mechanisms defining five structures [16]. While informal coordination mechanisms are used in very simple as well as in very complex organizations, direct management is used in smaller organizations. As soon as organizations grow further, standardization is used as the main coordinating mechanism. Mintzberg distinguishes standardization of tasks, outputs and abilities. In addition to specialization of labor, centralization of decision-making and formalization of tasks, organizational size and coordination mechanism can, thus, be considered as aspects subject to change.

Next, we look at which of these may be changed to support e-government implementation. However, there are few conclusive studies on changes in organizational structure as a result of IT-implementation. IT has been said to change managerial structure by cutting out the middle management [17], thereby increasing centralization of decision-making [18]. Pfeffer and Leblecici, on the other hand, found that IT-implementation correlates with decentralization of decision-making while it negatively coincides with the degree of formalization of decision rules [19]. There is one main aspect that has been identified as determining organizational structure and being influenced by IT and that is the height of transaction costs.

Transaction costs are those costs involved in coordinating economic transactions. Among the factors influencing the height of the transaction costs are information-uncertainty and complexity, frequency of the transaction and asset specificity. When transaction costs are high it may make more sense to incorporate certain activities into the hierarchy, whereas when they are low, they may be best left to the market [20]. For a shift towards a network structure, lower transaction costs are, thus, considered a prerequisite – otherwise, activities may best be incorporated [14]. Transaction costs are widely found to decrease dramatically as a result of diminished asset specificity and complexity of product information [21]. IT, thereby, allows for room for outsourcing activities and further specialization of organizations into defining their core activities [22]. This, in turn, will affect the formation of networks of specialized organizations.

Yet another aspect of organizational structure is considered influential in determining change. Some claim that the structure of organizations may not be so much influenced by rational decisions or economic measures as held by the theories described in the previous section. DiMaggio and Powell explain the abundance of bureaucratic forms in organizations not as a result of them being the most efficient organizational structure, but as a result of a consensus on bureaucracy being the most common form of organizations [23]. Instead of the rationale organizations functioning in the most optimal form, these authors consider institutions to play a large role in determining organizational structure. *Institutions* are the formal and informal rules that constrain human economic behavior, such as actor behavior and interactions, legal rules and culture, values and attitudes. So far, IT has been observed to change institutions only indirectly [24-26].

Although much research has been done on how IT affects organizational structure, findings regarding which organizational aspects change are still inconclusive and sometimes contradictory. A second line of research is, therefore, used to further investigate the impact of IT on organizational aspects in practice.

3   Structuration Theory

The organization theories mentioned in the previous section incorporate an implicit teleological assumption that changes in structure occur as a result of purposeful actions, seeing change "as a repetitive sequence of goal formulation, implementation, evolution, and modification of goals based on what was learned" [27]. A different way of looking at organizational change is by taking a dialectic perspective [27, 28]. This perspective understands change, instead of as an objective, discernable sequence of action, as a mutually influential process of action and structure [27, 28]. Change occurs, in this view, as a result of human actions shaping social phenomena as well as them being shaped by social structure. Hence, this theory is referred to as structuration theory [29, 30]. The best-known work on structuration theory is that of the sociologist Anthony Giddens. In his view, structure is reproduced by ongoing human action either reinforcing or changing structure. At the same time, structure enables and constrains human action. "Thus, social phenomena are not the product of *either* structure *or* agency, but of both" [31, p. 129]. In Giddens' view structure and agency are a mutually constitutive duality and the two cannot be examined separately.

Many authors writing on information systems have used structuration theories to explain changes in organizations that occur as a result of implementing IT [31, 32]. These authors have both sought to apply the theory as well as extend it to fit studies of technology, something Giddens did not write about extensively [31]. Orlikowski, for instance, was concerned with understanding the role of the social structure in the adoption and use of IT "as a process of enactment" and extended theory to the domain of information systems [31, p. 404]. She distinguishes different forms of interplay between technology and structure, which she called the duality of technology. This duality can be conceptualized as follows:

> "[T]echnology is physically constructed by actors working in a given social context, and technology is socially constructed by actors through the different meanings they attach to it and the various features they emphasize and use. However, it is also the case that once developed and deployed, technology tends to become reified and institutionalized, losing its connection with the human agents that constructed it or gave it meaning, and it appears to be part of the objective, structural properties of the organizations." [32, p. 406]

Others have sought to apply structuration theory to understand and explain the adoption of new information systems in practice [33-38], e.g. to study the influence of e-government policies on IT-systems or the use of prototyping in implementing a standard for data exchange. This type of changes affecting organizations share similarities to the type of phenomena Giddens aimed to understand, as "he was particularly interested in large-scale change episodes" [35, p. 3].

A concept worth mentionng for understanding how the processes of structuration and enactment takes place is *appropriation*, which refers to technology not being implemented in an organization in a predestined manner, but rather through ongoing human action [32, 37], appropriating technology "faithfully or unfaithfully" [31, p. 141]. Whether structure can be embodied in technology is, however, still contested; according to Giddens, structure cannot be *embedded* in technology, as, by his definition, it cannot be separated from human action [31], but others hold that that "many institutions preserve structural "traces" in physical artifacts" [38, p. 585]. While this represents one part of the duality, the other part is represented by the use of technology as an enabling and constraining influence on the structuring of human action.

For explaining organizational change as a result of IT implementation, structuration theory holds that the social structure influences – through human action – IT development and implementation, as well as it, in turn, reinforces or transforms structure, again through human action. For e-government, this means that organizational change occurs as a result of IT changing work practices, and at the same time, IT-implementation is influenced by the social structure through the process of human action appropriating technology. Change is no longer an objective process that can be discerned and predicted by identifying forces that influence change, but it also needs to be looked at from a perspective of human action giving meaning to technology. Technology is, thereby, no longer *independently* influencing organizations and institutions, but it is, rather, produced by organizations and institutions through human action. In the same line, it is argued that e-government policies enact with public sector IT [39] by influencing information systems' functionalities. In practice, a result of the process of structuration is that changes of organizational structure often have unintended outcomes.

4 Research Method

The basic premise of this paper is that the combination of both theoretical lenses presented in the previous sections will allow us to investigate e-government induced change by investigating changes in (aspects of) organizational structure. We use organizational theory to project expected changes and structuration theory to investigate how these changes take place in practice. To find out how these two theoretical lenses can be used to deepen our understanding to e-government, we examine a case study from the Netherlands. This case study concerns the adoption of the international financial reporting standard XBRL (acronym of eXtensible Business Reporting Language) for legally required financial reports of businesses. It is considered an appropriate case for investigating e-government induced change, as it captures the involvement of many stakeholders, new technologies and the need to change structures and adapt to new roles. Furthermore, a change in organizational structure was a specific goal of implementing the standard. Although one case study is generally considered to be insufficient for making generalizations [40], our objective is to explore the explanative power of these two theoretical strands in the field of e-government.

A retrospective view on the case was created by carrying out fifteen semi-structured interviews over the course of January and February 2010. Such a perspective allows us to understand the forces and factors that were in place for realizing organizational change as well as how the process of change took place. The fifteen interviewees included three project managers of government organizations involved in implementing and maintaining the government infrastructure and systems for XBRL, five representatives of businesses from different sectors and varying size for understanding the user perspective, three accountants, two software companies developing software packages for financial reporting, and two banks that are currently implementing XBRL in their organizations. All interviews lasted between one hour and an hour and half. Most interviews were conducted by two researchers comparing results afterwards; some were conducted by one interviewer only.

To get new insight into the very process of e-government implementation, we investigate how aspects of organizational structure are influenced by IT-adoption and the process of structuration. Rather than trying to test hypotheses, the interviews were aimed at gathering qualitative data. We started out by asking about the objectives and intentions for implementing the standard and (if mentioned) for changing the organization. Using organization theory, we enquired after specific aspects of organizational structure, such as decision-making authority and the degree of standardization and how they are to be changed. Then, based on structuration theory, we formulated questions on how different actor groups appropriated and shaped IT and its implementation. We enquired after the values attached to the information system and the changes in work practices, and we set up a timeline of actions undertaken by different action groups influencing implementation of the standard that was adjusted after each interview. The purpose of these questions was to compare the intensions of implementation with the outcomes in practices. By using these two theoretical lenses at the same time, we sought to get greater insight into how e-government implementation determines the structure of public organizations.

5   Case Study

The introduction of the international XBRL standard in the Netherlands was set out to change the process of legally required financial reporting by businesses. Instead of all government agencies defining their own requirements for financial reports, a taxonomy was created to harmonize definitions used by the Dutch government in the financial domain. Furthermore, a common process infrastructure under development were to be used for submitting all financial reports. Although the XBRL standard can be used for financial reporting across many sectors, the current project set-up includes a few specific legally required reports: (profit) tax filing at the Inland Revenue Service (IRS), the submission of financial year reports at the Chamber of Commerce and the submission of data to the national bureau for statistics (CBS). The process infrastructure developed to facilitate data exchange consists of a unified gateway for bulk data to government information systems. While the current structure of organizations concerned with financial reporting can be defined as a hierarchical command-and-control situation in which the government agencies enforce their standards onto the market, XBRL implementation is expected to allow for the creation of value chains. As generating financial reports will be done using an open standard, organizations are able to innovate and new applications may emerge as well as new organizations developing new services. This likely results in a new situation in which government agencies remain in control of the interpretation of financial data and the decision-making process, but the process of creating reports will take place within a value chain that enables innovation.

Implementation of XBRL started in 2004 with the set-up of the Dutch Taxonomy project (NTP). This project set out to harmonize all definitions and items used by the government in the financial domain in their contact with businesses. Two years later, also a generic infrastructure project was carried out drawing up requirements for the functionalities necessary for a new process infrastructure for financial reporting based on XBRL. When both the development of the taxonomy and the process infrastructure requirements were published (first version) in 2006, three (semi-)public agencies (IRS, Chambers of Commerce and CBS) signed an agreement that they will implement XBRL. This agreement was also signed by representatives of businesses, accountants and software vendors to stimulate the use of XBRL for financial reporting. Then, as a result of political priorities, the project was appointed to contribute to the central government agenda to achieve a decrease of the administrative burden of businesses. In 2007, the central government estimates that around 350 million euro's worth of administrative tasks of businesses can be cut and around a million tax filings using XBRL will be achieved yearly by 2008. Also in 2007, the first versions of the process infrastructure developed for exchanging data based on XBRL are ready. It had been decided that it should be maintained by the central government IT maintenance agency (Logius) and from 2008 onward the old process infrastructure for financial data exchange based on XML is phased out slowly. Furthermore, a novel authentication mechanism is included in the process infrastructure (AuSP), a step that was not part of the process before.

In 2009, however, it appeared that none of the above mentioned goals were met or will be met any time soon. The administrative burden will not be diminished and few yearly reports or tax filings were submitted using XBRL. Furthermore, while the unified gateway is still under development, no new applications or service developments are emerging yet. Besides the objectives not being met, another problem encountered is that for filing profit taxes a local version of the taxonomy is implemented, thereby not complying with the international XBRL standard. The reason for this diverging standard is that it would be easier to implement, spurring adoption of XBRL in the future. Generally, businesses and government agencies claim that they are not yet ready for implementing the XBRL standard or for building an extension to the process infrastructure. They say that they are waiting for the central government to make decisions before they will invest. Therefore, in 2009 the project was handed over to Logius altogether and a steering group consisting of senior representatives of all Ministries involved was appointed. This means that instead of the expected value chains emerging, change and implementation is still policy-driven, carried out by the public sector. Although the emergence of value chains is still likely to happen eventually and organizations in the new situation work within a network, only limited changes to adjust to their new role in the network can be seen.

6   Findings and Discussion

Based on the case study in the previous section, we now take a look at aspects of organizational structure and the process of change. Findings from the case study are summarized in Table 1. The factors from organizational theory are used to predict the type of organization structure that is expected to emerge. These are shown in the left-hand column. Some of these predictions proved to be correct, but most of them were not realized. Explanations based on structuration theory are shown in the right-hand column to explain why predictions from organization theory were (not) realized.

Table 1. Aspects of organizational structure predicted to change and their behavior as a result of the process of structuration

Aspects of organizational structure influenced by IT-implementation	Degree of change as a result of process of structuration
Standardization is likely to spur the emergence of a network structure as a result of diminishing transaction costs through the use of a single standard for financial reporting (XBRL) as well as specialization into core activities of organizations.	Network structure did not emerge, nor was more specialization observed; the appropriation of technology results in the creation of a diverging standard (for the purpose of simplifying a single process), thereby reducing the degree of standardization across sectors and inhibiting reduction of transaction costs.
The more transparent nature of standardized reporting is likely to change the **authority structure**. Hierarchical levels will likely be cut down and a greater degree of horizontalization is likely to emerge in the form of value chains of specialized organizations.	The authority structure was hardly changed, only an additional control step was added, by adding an extra step to the process: an authorization functionality that requires businesses to identify themselves in a way that was not necessary before. Furthermore, the steering committee did not have the power to steer across organizations, as a result of the current siloed structure.
Institutions (either a law or a common practice) should spur and accelerate uptake of the XBRL-standard and allowing for it to spread throughout different sectors.	Appropriation of the new standard is unlikely to take off as long as the government does not set the right example and facilitate uptake by firmly institutionalizing the standard in its own work practices.
The main **coordination mechanisms** changes from informal mechanisms (before introduction of IT) to standardization of data (previous data standards for each government organization) to standardization of procedures (by standardizing all financial reporting and they way it is exchanged).	A common data standard has emerged; XBRL will become the one standard for financial reporting. Before standardization emerged, however, a long period of negotiation took place on the scope of the implementation, the maintenance structure and the process architecture. For strategic reasons, organizations still try to influence these 'secondary' processes that are the conditions for standardized reporting.
Centrality of decision making is likely to increase as a result of standardization. A central organization is in charge of maintenance as well as implementation.	As long as the process infrastructure is not fully implemented, this leaves room for decentralist forces and decision-making and individual agencies decide to use the standard or not based on their own criteria, as happened in the case of the diverging standard for profit taxes. At the same time, the process of structuration has also led to a central role of the government in implementing XBRL.

The main driving force of implementation of the XBRL standard was its ability to enable the formation of value chains or value networks as a result of diminished transaction costs and a standardization of data exchange and procedures. New services, such as benchmarking, were expected to emerge on the basis of XBRL and the administrative burden of businesses was supposed to be decreased. In reality, however, most of the organizational structure remains as it is and very little of an emerging network structure can be observed yet; the central government still remains in control of the process and has even gained tighter control than before. As a result of tensions in the implementation process, this is currently endorsed by many of the parties involved. Even though all parties claim they are committed to the standard, in reality they do not change as a result of the promise of decreased transaction costs alone. Instead, they adhere to the current structure in which they operate and to which they are used. Businesses we interviewed said they would wait with adopting XBRL until it would become legally required (and thereby firmly institutionalized).

Coordination mechanisms in the past were mainly informal, involving all major stakeholders. Therefore, for the implementation process to be successful, appropriation will have to take place in a manner in which all parties are involved in the decision-making process and a solution will need to be acceptable to all actors having the power to block the implementation process. In the future, the far-reaching implementation of the XBRL standard will give rise to new types of coordination mechanisms as tasks will be shifted towards the maintenance of the taxonomy and a standardization of procedures is likely to emerge. This can be seen as the second part of Orlikowski's duality, where the use of technology in human action shapes renewed social structure. The case study shows that the lack of collaboration among stakeholders is part of the siloed social structure at the start of the implementation which reinforces the existing social structure instead of resulting in change, as decision makers are not allowed to take decisions concerning multiple organizations. This can also explain why the elements developed are optimized within their own organizational context, but could not be integrated as dependencies between these elements were not addressed.

Factors determining organizational structure that were relevant in this case study most often led to different outcomes than predicted by organizational theory. Using structuration theory, we gained insight in the change process where enactment and appropriation of technology leads to different outcomes as a result of the mutual influence of human action and social structure. At the same time, we did not find evidence that the changes in the aspects of organizational structure that were identified may never become reality. By the time e-government implementation becomes part of the social structure, it may well be possible that a greater degree of horizontalization emerges. Thus, we found structuration theory to be powerful in explaining outcomes of government induced change that is enabled and constrained by human action within its social structure and, thereby, powerful for explaining individual cases. At the same time we found that it cannot be used to make any general predictions concerning changes in organizational structure like organizational theory may well be able to.

Therefore, we suggest that further research focuses on combining both theoretical strands to deepen our understanding of how e-government induced change takes place in practice, as well as to be able to make better predictions on how this change will occur. Our case study research shows that using the combination of these two complementary theoretical lenses explains better the practice of e-government implementation than using one theoretical strand. By investigating how the forces influencing e-government induced change identified from organization theory interfere with the process of structuration, we are able to give some explanation on why the achievements of e-government lag behind the objectives and promises. Further research should find out whether these theoretical lenses can also be applied to other e-government implementation processes. A limitation of this research is that a retrospective view was created instead of carrying out a longitudinal study. While this did not hinder our purpose of determining the power of these two theories, we suggest to use a longitudinal approach in further research on e-government implementation.

7   Conclusion

E-government implementation requires organizational change to realize its full potential by changing public organizations from hierarchies into having a networor-orientation. Change in public organizations, however, is a complex and unpredictable process. Current literature on e-government is trying to grasp the complexity of the matter and is in search for multidisciplinary approaches for further investigations. This paper explores the gap between the promises and achievements of e-government induced change. Using two complementary theoretical lenses, we investigate how they can be used to gain greater insight in this gap. We combine organization and structuration theory by using the former category to identify how aspects of organizational structure change under influence of IT and the latter to be able to explain the working of these factors under the process of structuration. This allowed us to investigate the differences between the outcomes of change and the objectives of the change process.

By investigating a case study of e-government implementation in the Netherlands we found that while organization theories are useful for predicting change, they often fail to give insight into why certain predictions do not materialize. And while structuration theory can explain how IT shapes and is shaped by human action within its social structure, it does not allow generalizations to be made on the use of IT in the public sector. In our case study we saw the promised decrease of transaction costs severely curbed by a social structure unable to understand or materialize this decrease and, instead, decided to diverge from the design to meet the project deadline. The process of appropriation, in this case, led to the adoption of different technologies, instead of to a greater degree of standardization as expected by organization theory. We, therefore, conclude that combining these theories can be used to deepen our understanding of the challenges e-government implementation encounters in practice.

References

1. Scholl, H.J.: Electronic Government: A study Domain Past its Infancy. In: Scholl, H.J. (ed.) Electronic Government: Information, Technology and Transformation. M.E. Sharpe, Armonk (2009)
2. Heeks, R., Bailur, S.: Analyzing e-government research: Perspectives, philosophies, theories, methods, and practice. Government Information Quarterly 24, 243–265 (2007)

3. Gronlund, A., Horan, T.A.: Introducing e-Gov: History, Definition, and Issues. Communications of the Association for Information Systems 15, 713–729 (2005)
4. Yildiz, M.: E-government research: Reviewing the literature. limitations, and ways forward. Government Information Quarterly 24, 646–665 (2007)
5. Gregor, S., Martin, M., Fernandez, W., Stern, S., Vitale, M.: The transformational dimension in the realization of business value from information technology. Journal of Strategic Information Systems 15, 249–270 (2006)
6. Bannister, F.: Dismantling the silos: extracting new value from IT investments in public administration. Information Systems Journal 11, 65–84 (2001)
7. Hazlett, S.-A., Hill, F.: E-government: the realities of using IT to transform the public sector. Managing Service Quality 13, 445–452 (2003)
8. West, D.M.: E-Government and the Transformation of Service Delivery and Citizen Attitudes. Public Administration Review 64, 15–27 (2004)
9. Fountain, J.E.: Building the virtual state: information technology and institutional change. Brookings Institution Press, Washington (2001)
10. Kraemer, K., King, J.L.: Information Technology and Administrative Reform: Will E-Government Be Different? International Journal of Electronic Government Research 2, 1–20 (2006)
11. Scholl, H.J.: Central research questions in e-government, or which trajectory should the study domain take? Transforming Government: People, Process and Policy 1, 67–88 (2007)
12. Castells, M.: The Rise of The Network Society. Blackwell Publishing, Malden (2000)
13. Powell, W.W. (ed.): Neither Market nor Hierarchy: Network Forms of Organization. Sage Publications, London (1991)
14. Weber, M.: Wirtschaft und Gesellschaft, Tubingen (1972)
15. Galbraith, J.: Designing Complex Organizations. Addison-Wesley, Reading (1973)
16. Mintzberg, H.: Structure in Fives: Designing effective organizations. Prentice Hall Business Publishing, New Jersey (1983)
17. Leavitt, H., Whisler, T.L.: Management in the 1980s. Harvard Business Review 36, 41–48 (1958)
18. Schwarz, G.M., Brock, D.M.: Waving hello or waving good-bye? Organizational change in the information age. The International Journal of Organizational Analysis 6, 65–90 (1998)
19. Pfeffer, J., Leblebici, H.: Information Technology and Organizational Structure. The Pacific Sociological Review 20, 241–261 (1977)
20. Williamson, O.E.: Markets and Hierarchies: Analysis and Antitrust Implications. Free Press, New York (1975)
21. Malone, T.W., Yates, J., Benjamin, R.I.: Electronic Markets and Electronic Hierarchies. Communications of the ACM 30, 484–497 (1987)
22. Pralahad, C.K., Hamel, G.: The core competence of the corporation. Harvard Business Review 69, 81–93 (1990)
23. DiMaggio, P.J., Powell, W.W.: The Iron Cage Revisited: Institutional Isomorphism and Collective Rationality in Organizational Fields. American Sociological Review 48, 147–160 (1983)
24. Gascó, M.: New Technologies and Institutional Change in Public Administration. Social Science Computer Review 24, 6–14 (2003)
25. Fountain, J.E.: Building the Virtual State: Information Technology and Institutional Change. Brookings Institution Press (2001)

26. Kraemer, K.L., King, J.L.: Information Technology and Administrative Reform: Will e-Government be Different? International Journal of Electronic Government Research 2, 1–20 (2006)
27. van de Ven, A.H., Poole, M.S.: Explaining Development and Change in Organizational The Academy of Management Review 20, 510–540 (1995)
28. Robey, D., Boudreau, M.-C.: Accounting for the Contradictory Organizational Consequences of Information Technology: Theoretical Directions and Methodological Implications. Information Systems Research 10, 167–185 (1999)
29. Giddens, A.: Central Problems in Social Theory. Social Analysis. University of California Press, Berkeley (1979)
30. Giddens, A.: The constitution of society: Outline of the theory of structuration. Polity, Cambridge (1984)
31. Jones, M.R., Karsten, H.: Giddens's Structuration Theory and Information Systems Research. MIS Quarterly 32(1), 127–157 (2009)
32. Orlikowski, W.J.: The Duality of Technology: Rethinking the Conept of Technology in Organizations. Organization Science 3(3), 398–427 (1992)
33. Pozzebon, M., Pinsonneault, A.: Challenges in Conducting Empirical Work Using Structuration Theory: Learning from IT Research. Organization Studies 26(9), 1353–1376 (2005)
34. Orlikowski, W.J.: Using Technology and Constituting Structures: A Practice Lens for Studying Technology in Organizations. Organization Science 11(4), 404–428 (2000)
35. Gil-Garcia, J.R., Canestraro, D., Costello, J., Baker, A., Werthmuller, D.: Structuration Theory and the Use of XML for Web Site Content Management in Government: Comprehensive Prototyping as an Induced Change Episode. In: Proceedings of the American Society for Information Science and Technology (2008)
36. Chu, C., Smithson, S.: E-business and organizational change: a structurational approach. Information Systems Journal 17, 369–389 (2007)
37. Poole, M.S., DeSanctis, G.: Structuration Theory in Information systems Research: Methods and Controversies. In: Whitman, M.E., Woszcynski, A.B. (eds.) The Handbook for Information Systems Research (2002)
38. Cordella, A., Iannacci, F.: Information systems in the public sector: The e-Government enactment framework. Journal of Strategic Information Systems 19, 52–66 (2010)
39. Poole, M.S.: Response to Jones and Karsten, Giddens's Structuration Theory and Information Systems Research. MIS Quarterly 33(3), 583–587 (2009)
40. Yin, R.K.: Case Study Research: Design and methods. Sage, Thousand Oaks (1989)

Ten Years of E-Government: The 'End of History' and New Beginning

Åke Grönlund

Örebro University, Swedish Business School
Fakultetsgatan 1, 701 82 Örebro, Sweden
ake.gronlund@oru.se

Abstract. This paper argues that although there is no lack of eGovernment "frameworks", both governments and research are both in need of better guiding models in order to address contemporary and future challenges. This argument is pursued by reviewing a decade of eGovernment development and research in terms of the guiding values as expressed by influential maturity models and relating them to the eGovernment domain, as defined by formal definitions and practice in combination. We find that development so far has overall been too narrowly guided by a technical focus and economic and administrative values and too little informed by public sector values. While there is no lack of broad frameworks there is scarcity as concerns structured research and evaluation models that encompass such values.

Keywords: Maturity model, eGovernment, electronic services, organization, values, public values.

1 Introduction

In the 2007 EU benchmarking report on eGovernment Austria achieved 100 % on online availability and 99 % for online sophistication (meaning full electronic case handling), the two measures considered by the EU to measure eGovernment success [1], closely followed by several countries. Even if Europe as a whole scored only 70 % and 84 % on the two measures respectively it seems we are rapidly approaching the end of eGovernment history, as defined by the EU. Austria has com there, other countries will follow, sooner or later; the trend is positive over the years since the measurements started in 2000. Soon eGovernment will be fully implemented and then what? Is today's Austrian model the final say on e-government practice? Of course not, most would say (as we shall demonstrate below), but this is as far as the EU eGovernment measurement model reaches, and it is not alone. To guide the efforts onwards we need new models able to cater for future developments. What goals, beyond online availability and full case handling can there be for governments' use of ICT? The eGovernment literature provides many suggestions, but the point to be made in this paper is that research and development are both guided by the models we use to describe and analyze the world. The fact that the EU model hit the ceiling early on is in this perspective a measure of limited vision which has meant limitations to what has been done so far, both in research and practice. While it is easy to point at

M.A. Wimmer et al. (Eds.): EGOV 2010, LNCS 6228, pp. 13–24, 2010.

very creative exceptions (as we will below), eGovernment research is largely a collection of descriptive case studies [2]. There is little theory involved and very little of the theory that is actually there involves both "electronic" and "government", as this paper will demonstrate. Two reasons for this, the paper argues, are that IS researchers have focused too much on technology and even though there is quite some discussion about organizations we have largely ignored government, which is not just any organization. Note that the point of this paper is that structured models are missing, not identification of factors. There is quite some literature on "important factors", but there is so far too little ambition to model relations among factors in ways that sufficiently well cover the problem domain. According to Dawes [3], "Research into relationships among government, society and technology has grown substantially over the past 30 years. However, most research and most advances in practice address narrowly defined categories of concern such as government organization, citizen services, interoperability, or personal privacy."

This paper argues that although there is no lack of eGovernment frameworks, government organization and research are both in need of better guiding models in order to address the step change that is necessary to meet many of the contemporary and future challenges.

The research question of this paper is, what requirements are there for eGovernment maturity models able to guide us over the coming years of new eGovernment challenges and developments? How well do existing models meet the criteria, and what are their shortcomings?

2 The eGovernment Domain

There is no explicit eGovernment theory, but there are several definitions. There are numerous things that researchers and practitioners do under the label of eGovernment or some synonym. None of these things can be discarded so long as they fall within one or more of the many explicit definitions existing. Non-controversial examples of the latter would include privacy, accountability, trust and many more. Controversial ones would address government organization and public values.

The eGovernment domain can be defined by a combination of two approaches. One is to consider all the explicit definitions that organizations and researchers use to delimit and specify the field. The other, complementary, approach is to consider what is done under the label of eGovernment, in research and in practice and analyze the implications. In this section we will do both. We will then combine the two results and define the eGovernment domain in terms of both breadth and depth. Breadth will mean to what extent models cover all the issues and stakeholders involved, and depth will mean how well they deal with the issues involved; the relation with government.

Explicit Definitions

OECD [3] reviewed eGovernment definitions and arrived at four types of definitions:

Type 1. "Internet (online) service delivery".
Type 2. "E-government is equated to the use of ICTs in government. While the focus is generally on the delivery of services and processing, the broadest definition encompasses all aspects of government activity".

Type 3. "E-government is defined as a capacity to transform public administration through the use of ICTs or indeed is used to describe a new form of government built around ICTs. This aspect is usually linked to Internet use".

Type 4. "The use of ICTs, and particularly the Internet, as a tool to achieve better government". This is the only perspective taking a fundamentally external perspective; "better government" must be measured from outside, in terms of what good it does for society.

The categories differ in terms of both domain definition (breadth) and ambition (depth). Breadth, because "better government" (type 4) is clearly a wider problem, involving more issues and more stakeholders, than "electronic service delivery" (type 1). Ambition, because type 4 definitions explicitly relate to government values while type 1 ones does not necessarily. By all accounts, eGovernment involves stakeholders both in politics, administration and civil society [5]. However, the different OECD definition types focus distinctly on different parts of the e-government social domain [5]. For example, while certainly even electronic services may require legal change, this does not necessarily mean a transformation of public administration. Making internal administration more efficient (type 2) does not necessarily involve either policy change or affect customers/users/citizens directly. At the other end of the OECD definition spectrum, "Better government" does not necessarily involve e-services directly. For example, introducing "cyber laws" protecting privacy broadly across all activities people and organizations may undertake could well be seen as making government a bit better in a country where such legislation previously has been missing. Type 4 definitions include the policy making domain, politicians, and consequently also citizens although not necessarily directly. The OECD taxonomy is useful for our purposes because it relates technology to government. These relations are quite different for each category and the integration is the highest for type 4 definitions where technology is directly related to better government; there is no limitation neither in social scope, technology use, or organizational change. In contrast, the type 1 definitions have a limited social scope, do not measure neither organizational nor policy change, and do not include measures of better government. They might of course include measures of better services which may indirectly be a part of improving government. However, the point to be made – which will be illustrated below – is that government is not only the sum of its services, it also includes other aspects of citizen-government relations such as accountability, trust, fairness, etc.; aspects that not pertain to service delivery alone but also to service specification, audit, legal rights and responsibilities etc. Definitions of types 2 and 3 define intermediate levels of relations between technology and government. The OECD taxonomy hence defines the "depth" of eGovernment.

Implicit Definitions: Activities and Issues

Implicit definitions concern what eGovernment in practice and research is about. Here we look in particular for the "breadth" of eGovernment, what issues are involved, but as we shall see, depth is also highly involved if not clearly specified.

eGovernment conferences are typically designed to reflect both developments in practice and researchers' own ideas about what might be interesting now or in the future. Hence the calls for papers typically include comprehensive overviews of what is considered to be the contemporary contents of the field. The following examples are taken from the calls to two main conferences, EGOV 09[1] and dg.o 09[2] which are respectively the main European and US eGovernment conferences. For reasons of space and focus we will not here exhaustively list topics but only submit examples to make three points important for our argument, namely, (1) A comprehensive social domain involving all stakeholders and all government activities is today generally understood as the correct focus of eGovernment study. Limitations, such as focusing on e-services, should be considered as sub-domains and be contextualized within the total domain; (2) The technical eGovernment domain is today seen to include any technology that can be applied to interactions within that social domain; and (3) The OECD definition taxonomy serves as a useful benchmark to analyze maturity models as it can contain any and all of the issues covered by the conferences.

The dg.o conference call supports these three points already by its very structure. It contains four categories, (1) Digital Government Application Domains, (2) IT-enabled Government Management and Operations, (3) Information Values and Policies, and Information Technology, and (4) Tools to Support Government. Category 1 defines the social domain widely in terms of all sorts of government operations, ranging from courts, education and health to natural resources management, transportation systems, and urban planning. In short: any social area where interaction between government and citizens is organized and/or regulated. Theme 2 defines the organization of government operations, pertaining to OECD definitions type 2 (for example "IT service architectures" and "cross-boundary information sharing and integration") and 3 (for example "decision making processes" and "IT adoption and diffusion"). Theme 3 directly matches the OECD type 4 definitions as it focuses on government values to society, such as participation, transparency, trust and openness. Finally, theme 4 addresses the technology domain in an open way, by means of categories not limited to specific technologies but application areas which can be related to government values, such as "collaboration tools".

The EGOV 09 conference themes also suggest OECD type 4 definitions (depth) as well as a wide technical and social domain definition (breadth). For example themes like "e-participation, e-citizenship and digital democracy", "mass collaboration of stakeholders in government modernization", and "e-policy, e-governance, ethics and law" imply type 4 definitions because they involve citizens, discuss roles of different stakeholders ("governance"), and concern issues at the heart of government, such as participation. They also imply a wide social domain definition. Themes like "crowd sourcing, grid computing, social software" and "mobile technologies" imply a wide technological domain definition not limited to web technologies.

Conference calls give a picture of what researchers and practitioners in the field find worthwhile addressing at a given point in time. A more analytical picture is given by an EU-commissioned research project analyzing expected futures of eGovernment, RTD2020, which analyzed the current state of the art in eGovernment globally and developed future scenarios and research themes based on a series of workshops involving senior practitioners and researchers. One outcome of the research was

---

[1] http://www.egov-conference.org/egov-2009/call-for-papers
[2] http://www.dgo2009.org/index.php/en/call-for-papers/52

thirteen research themes [6] that were represented both in the current state analysis and the scenarios for the future, which together represent researchers' and practitioners' view of the eGovernment field.

Consistent with the conference calls, the themes of RTD2010 outline a field where "better government"-type definitions are necessary (e.g. "government's role in the virtual world"; "performance management"), where a wide social domain is addressed (e.g. "cultural interoperability", "e-participation"), as well as an open mind towards new, not yet developed, technologies (e.g. "cyberinfrastructures", "ontologies", "intelligent information"). This paints a picture of a field with great breadth. As for the depth, many of the themes are far-reaching in terms of the role of government and address change yet unseen; "the role of government" and "the value of ICT investments" being two examples that reach far beyond "full electronic case handling", which is the end-of-history for the EU benchmarking model.

Integrating the RTD2020 results into a comprehensive general eGovernment framework, Dawes [3] suggests six central dimensions that need to be taken into account: the purpose and role of government, societal trends, changing technologies, information management, human elements, and interaction and complexity. These six ideas together suggest a government in a state of change due to its role as a central agent in what Dawes calls a "dynamic open socio-technical system". Within this view there is no real difference between government and e-government. ICT is one out of several areas where the development affects government and where government has some opportunity to influence the development. Governments can not think away ICTs, they are inherently intertwined with most operations. Even though ICTs will continue to develop and governments will continuously have to develop new and more effective ways of operating focus will no longer be on the "e" but on the underlying values, issues and processes which governments need to sustain.

This brief review of two major contemporary conferences and a comprehensive research effort investigating present and future eGovernment themes, corroborate the definition of the eGovernment domain made above. It includes (1) a wide social domain including stakeholders in politics, administration and society, (2) a wide technical domain not limited to any particular technology, and (3) a focus on several issues specifically to do with government values, such as accountability, legitimacy, and responsibility, which concern the very role of government. Even though neither the conference calls nor the RTD2020 or Dawes' framework explicitly define eGovernment, the implication of their framing of the field clearly is in line with the type 4 definitions in the OECD taxonomy; eGovernment needs to be discussed in terms of its role to achieve "better government".

3   Models of E-Government Development

Having defined the eGovernment domain we will now turn to an analysis of some of the more commonly used and/or discussed maturity models. The first purpose of this analysis is to see how well they can serve as guiding visions of future eGovernment development. A second purpose is to provide some empirical basis for discussing the need for better models for the next decade, at least, of eGovernment.

The presentation below is organized by the OECD taxonomy, for two reasons. First, as already discussed this taxonomy is organized by "depth", degree of involvement with issues pertaining to government values. Second, it also provides a rough but adequate time perspective on the development in eGovernment practice.

Type 1: Service Delivery Models

The EU model used for benchmarking across Europe since 2000 contained four steps until 2007 when a fifth step was added. The original four stages sequentially were: information, one-way interaction, two-way interaction, and full electronic case handling [7]. In the latest (2007) measurement, the list was complemented with a fifth step called "personalization" which means proactive and/or automatic service delivery of a service granted by law, for example tax return or unemployment subsidy, without request from the user [1].

The EU benchmarking model is not alone in this definition. Another much cited series of measurements covering the whole globe was done by Brown University in the US, in which eGovernment is defined as "the delivery of public sector information and online services through the Internet" [8]. Seen as limited models focusing on one particular eGovernment issue, this kind of models are not problematic even though they clearly limit vision. When used as the only guiding star they might be detrimental as they avoid the complex issues of eGovernment. They show us what is on the web but do not help us decide if or how this leads to "better government". If models like these are taken to define the eGovernment field we are near the end of its history.

Type 2 and 3: Organizational Change Models

Because many models mix elements of OECD definitions type 2 and 3 – organization and policy is closely related in the public sector – we keep these two together in this account. Models in this category deal with interoperability and integration of services across government department borders. As government departments are heavily regulated by law almost anything concerning extending cross-border integration requires some change of regulation.

The arguably most cited model early on in this category is by Layne & Lee [9]. The four stages of this model concern the "multi-perspective transformation within government structures and functions as they make transitions to e-government", that is both technological and organizational challenges are involved. The stages are cataloguing, transaction, vertical integration, and horizontal integration. The focus is clearly on integrating technology to allow for data transfer. For example the goal of vertical integration is "to seamlessly integrate the state's system with federal and local systems for cross referencing and checking". Associated risks, such as privacy intrusion are mentioned as challenges, however only to the extent they pertain to data. Viewed from a government value perspective, privacy is not an individual challenge, just some technical detail, but part of a trustworthy, and legally regulated, relation between government and individuals where not just data is concerned but credibility, accountability and accountability.

Models of this kind considerabl widen the focus as compared to the type 1 ones as they bring in organizational issues. However, in doing so, they tend to be blind to the depth of issues involved; they tend to avoid policy. Integration and interoperability are positive for management, but they are contested values in government. For example, maximizing integration may jeopardize privacy as data flows freely and without citizen control (which is one part of the very definition of privacy). It increases some risks, e.g. for intrusion and fraud, other (negative) government values. It blurs the borders between government organizations which can reduce accountability. Accountability is strictly regulated in (democrativ) government and is one fundament for (any) government's legitimacy. Cross-department electronic, automated, services require reorganizing the accountability regulation accordingly so that no gaps occur [10, 11, 12]. This is an issue that involves not just management but also policy.

Layne and Lee are not alone. Gil-Garcia [13] reviews a number of stage models of this type (including the Layne & Lee one), summarizing them by the following 7-step resultant ladder. The basic thrust identified behind the models is that of integration of technology: "The evolutionary approach examines e-government stages: from developing a Web page to integrating government systems behind the Web interface " [13].

1. Initial presence: getting on the Internet, static information.
2. Extended presence: more dynamic, specialized information that is distributed and regularly updated in a great number of government sites.
3. Interactive presence: Governments use a statewide or national portal to provide access to services in multiple agencies.
4. Transactional presence: Citizens and businesses can personalize or customize a national or statewide portal.
5. Vertical integration: integration, virtual, physical or both, of similar services provided by different levels of government.
6. Horizontal integration: comprehensive and integral vision of the government as a whole.
7. Totally integrated presence: Defined as full integration horizontally as well as vertically.

This 7-step model is more detailed than the Layne and Lee one but not fundamentally different.

There are models basically belonging to this organizational change category that border to next level in the OECD taxonomy, "better government", because they explicitly include the concept of values. For example Gottschalk [14] speaks of "value interoperability" which is recognized as a precondition for (full) interoperability, but value is not specified in detail, neither related specifically to government values.

A popular contemporary discussion is that of Enterprise Architectures (EA). Although EA emerged as a technical concept it has been extended to cover whole organizations, and whole governments [15]. For example the US Federal Enterprise Architecture (FEA) includes five levels starting at the top from goals, performance measures and outcomes and working downwards detailing and specifying distinct layers; in turn, business processes, service components, data, and technologies [16, 17]. By using this model thoroughly, values will be used at the top level to define goals and performance measures and thereafter logically determine definitions and specifications all the way down the pyramid to the bottom layers, data and technologies. However, EA and FEA models are "empty". They are comprehensive logical frameworks defining process maturity but they do not contain specific government content and they do not specify stages. They do define different levels of maturity, however, and are in this respect less vulnerable to advances in research and practice. While this makes them less well-defined in terms of eGovernment definitions it also makes them very useful. They can be used to guide development towards convergence, provided other models are there to fill them with eGovernment specific contents.

Type 4 – Better Government Models

While there are many dimensions along which government can improve and there is no way to define a "best" government, type 4 models are such that relate ICT use in government to government specific factors. The only evaluation model so far that is explicitly built on a comprehensive eGovernment definition is the EU eGEP (eGovernment Economics Project) model. There are indeed models for assessing enterprise architectures, and specifically the FEA [18], and there are maturity models for assessing capabilities in general, such as Capability Maturity Model, CMM [19]. While well defined to measure maturity of processes, these models are, again, "empty" with respect to eGovernment; they do not address government-specific values specifically.

The eGEP model was constructed by the EU for the purpose of being able to monitor eGovernment more generally than the benchmarking model presented above. The eGEP model is designed after the EU definition of eGovernment, which is an OECD type 4 definition:

> "e-Government is the use of Information and Communication Technologies in public administrations combined with organizational change and new skills in order to improve public services and democratic processes" [20].

From this definition, three "value drivers" are elicited, efficiency, democracy and effectiveness. These are specified by several variables, leading to financial & organizational, political, and constituency values respectively [21]. The project reports both a theoretical model underpinning the choice of variables and specifies measurement of indicators. Although not every government value is specifically addressed the model as such can cover everything.

In terms of OECD match, eGEP specifies better government. However, there are reasons to question the depth of the model. Many measures are shallow and it is questionable how well they indicate positive change with regard to the often complicated issues covered. For example, "participation" is measured by "number of queries submitted online", and "transparency and accountability" is measured by "number of services requiring a two-way interaction with users" [21, p. 48]. The ambition with the model is to use quantitative measures so at least calculation is unambiguous and interpretation minimized. This is laudable but there remains the problem of explaining how well the indicators used reflect the underlying reality, the values pertaining to government. Government values are of different nature as concerns measurability. Some values, such as privacy, can not be defined once for all as there is no absolute measure. What is considered "enough" privacy can at the end of the day only be measured by citizens' preferences. These change over time, and they are different in different countries depending on traditions. Other values, such as accountability, can in fact be measured objectively. For each step of each process accountability can be specified and communicated so that all actors can know what is expected from them. The distribution of responsibilities can be discussed, but as long as there are no "accountability gaps" in the processes – issues or events unaccounted for – the process can be trusted from this point of view. While this is not always the case, and electronic cross-organizational services risk inadvertently creating new such gaps (Smith et al, 2008) the point is that accountability can be specified. It does not seem, however, that it can in any reasonable way be measured by the number of services requiring two-way interaction. And it can not be reduced to "transparency". While transparency is one necessary ingredient in accountability it is not sufficient. Accountability is about someone actually taking responsibility for activities, and non-activities, it is not just about information.

In view of such in-depth analysis of the values involved it is open to discussion how well the EGEP model can measure progress.

4 Discussion

There is no doubt that ICT will continue to develop and that government will become more sophisticated in using it for improvement, and in this paper we took the approach that we should update the eGovernment research field so as to stay in business by being able to follow, and hopefully even lead, the further development.

To that end we started by asking, what can we do to modernize the field so as to be able to understand and guide further development? We first asked how the eGovernment domain should best be defined. This question was answered by reference to the OECD taxonomy of eGovernment definitions in combination with a review of today's state of the art and future expected developments. The review of eGovernment practice showed that the fourth type of definition ("better government") was necessary to cover the depth of the eGovernment domain, as were wide definitions of the social and technological domains involved.

At this point let us briefly introduce our eGD-MAM (eGovernment Domain Match Analysis Model), designed to analyze and compare the kind of models we have presented here. It uses five criteria to assess maturity models' match with the eGovernment domain as discussed above: (#1) Coverage of the social domain, (#2) Coverage of the technological domain, (#3) Domain integration, (#4) Consistency and measurability, and (#5) Government (value) relevance. Analyzing the maturity models by means of the eGD-MAM, we can see that models designed after "type 1" definitions, focusing on implementation of electronic services, are clearly approaching the end of their history as guiding stars for the future as they are too limited in terms of four of the eGD-MAM's criteria (except for #4 where they may score well). Most importantly, they are not able to specify the relation with government and hence they cannot help us see if or how online services improve government. As of today, we have a number of models that are not capable of meeting the requirements ahead of us and hence not suitable as guiding stars for eGovernment. There are, however, a few models that may prove useful candidates for next decade of eGovernment. These include the specifically eGovernment-oriented eGEP model as well as open process maturity models such as EA assessment frameworks, ISO 9000, and similar. All of these score well on criteria #1 - #4. While the latter type of open models are frameworks measuring form rather than content (and hence do not necessarily score well on #5), the eGEP aspires to a comprehensive eGovernment content measurement by thoroughly defining a number of variables related to #5. There are pros and cons with the different types of models. Open models can more easily become standards because they can be used in any country independent of government traditions, and state of development. Models detailing contents, like the eGEP, will face controversy with respect to the indicators. As electronic services continue to develop and replace manual services, ever more values will be "hard-wired" into the processes, such as specifications of accountability, openness, audit trails, etc. This means evaluation of progress in pursuing these values will have to be more sophisticatedly designed to meet legal requirements and build public trust. On the other hand, pursuing models like the eGEP will provide a step further towards understanding eGovernment in terms of the measurable values it brings to governments and, to some extent, citizens. It will lead to more discussion about just what public values are (and hence it may face trouble with a general model quality criterion – simplicity). Pursuing EA or ISO 9000 models, to the contrary, is likely to lead to different countries developing different measures which will likely lead to less focus on contents and more on process. On the other hand, EA and ISO type models have the great advantage that they are consistent across the whole system. Using ISO 9000 leads to standardized products with clearly defined properties, produced by a well-defined process. This means they can be used in modules; each and every part of the production chain will have to adopt the same rules. This is a substantial benefit. Clearly eGovernment maturity models need not encompass the entire field. It is of course necessary to also have more specialized models focusing on steps in the development which are particularly important at a certain point in time. Unlike today's situation where we have seen that the "type 1" models are typically ignoring wider government values, applying EA, ISO and similar approaches will mean that even models with more narrow social or technical scope need to include the "depth" of eGovernment, the relation to government.

To stay in business it is a challenge for the eGovernment field to take up the challenge of constructing better models, starting from where the front line is today. This is, we propose, not among the commonly used technology-oriented models or even the organization-oriented ones limited to technical interoperability and service integration, it is among the policy and government values-oriented ones such as EGEP, EA, and similar. This paper has provided the eGD-MAM model to be used as a test of the quality of existing and new models in the eGovernment field.

5 Conclusion

This paper has shown that there is a need for new models to meet the contemporary and future challenges of eGovernment. We have shown that the most important challenge for these new models is to be able to handle government values. That is, eGovernment research must become "deeper". It must better understand the relation between technology, organization and government values. We find that research and development so far has overall been too narrowly guided by technical focus and economic and administrative values and too little informed by public sector values. We suggest that next generation of eGovernment research must take up the challenge of understanding these values and contributing to defining ways of assessing them so that we can understand how eGovernment can contribute to better government. If we fail to do that, the eGovernment research field will face the end of its history. Implementing "full case handling" is today well understood while using ICT to make government better is still a great challenge; eGovernment researchers should take it up. The eGD-MAM model can be used as a test for upcoming proposals.

References

1. Capgemini: The User Challenge: Benchmarking The Supply of Online Public Services. In: 7th Measurement, European Commission Directorate General for Information Society and Media (September 2007)
2. Grönlund, Å., Andersson, A.: E-government research 2003-2006: Improvements and issues. In: Norris, D. (ed.) Current Issues and Trends in E-Government Research, pp. 247–288. Idea Group, Hershey (2007)
3. Dawes, S.S.: Governance in the digital age: A research and action framework for an uncertain future. Government Information Quarterly 26(2), 257–264 (2009)
4. OECD: The E-Government Imperative. OECD Journal on Budgeting 3(1) (2003)
5. Grönlund, Å.: Introducing e-Gov: History, Definitions, and Issues. Communications of AIS 15 (2005)
6. Codagnone, C., Wimmer, M.A. (eds.): Roadmapping eGovernment Research: Visions and Measures towards Innovative Governments in 2020. MY Print snc di Guerinoni Marco & C, Clusone (2007)
7. DGIM: Online Availability of Public Services: How is Europe Progressing. Web based survey on Electronic Public Services, Report of the fifth measurement (October 2004); Prepared by Capgemini for the European Commission Directorate General for Information (2005)
8. West, D.M.: Global E-government-2003. Center for Public Policy, Brown University (2003)
9. Layne, K., Lee, J.: Developing fully functional E-government: A four stage model. Government Information Quarterly 18(2), 122–136 (2001)
10. Bovens, M.: Public Sector Accountability. In: Ferlie, E., Laurence, J., Lynn, E., Politt, C. (eds.) The Oxford handbook of public management, pp. 182–208. Oxford University Press, Oxford (2005)

11. Smith, M., Noorman, M.E., Martin, A.K.: Accountabilities, automations, Dysfunctions, and Values: ICTs in the public sector. London School of Economics, Working paper series, vol. 169 (2008)
12. Pina, V., Torres, L., Acerete, B.: Are ICTs promoting government accountability? A comparative analysis of e-governance developments in 19 OECD countries. Critical Perspectives on Accounting 18(5), 583–602 (2007)
13. Gil-Garcia, J.R., Martinez-Moyano, I.J.: Understanding the evolution of e-government: The influence of systems of rules on public sector dynamics. Government Information Quarterly 24(2), 266–290 (2007)
14. Gottschalk, P.: Maturity levels for interoperability in digital government. Government Information Quarterly 26(1), 75–81 (2009)
15. Guijarro, L.: Interoperability frameworks and enterprise architectures in e-government initiatives in Europe and the United States. Government Information Quarterly 24(1), 89–101 (2007)
16. CIOC: Federal Enterprise Architecture, USA (2001)
17. CIOC: FEA Practice Guidance, USA (November 2007)
18. CIOC: Enterprise Architecture Assessment Framework, Version 2.0., USA (2005)
19. SEI: Official CMMI web site. Carnegie-Mellon, the Software Engineering Institute (2009)
20. EU: eGovernment Research in Europe. European Commission (2004)
21. EGEP: Measurement Framework Final Version. European Union, eGovernment Unit, DG Information Society and Media (2006)

Siblings of a Different Kind: E-Government and E-Commerce

Karine Barzilai-Nahon and Hans Jochen Scholl

University of Washington, The Information School
`{karineb,jscholl}@uw.edu`

Abstract. This paper reports on the last phase of a longitudinal exploratory study, which aims to compare similarities and differences between e-Commerce and e-Government. In two stages, we collected rich data via focus groups of experts from both public and private sectors. This paper reports on our findings in the areas of Process Management, Information Management, and Stakeholder Relations. We found the trajectories of the two phenomena of e-Commerce and e-Government to be quite distinct such that one can hardly serve as a role model for the other. Yet, comparing the two phenomena still unveils a high potential for cross-pollination.

1 Introduction

When we began this longitudinal exploratory study of similarities and differences between e-Commerce and e-Government in 2006 [3, 4, 31], we discovered that e-Commerce and e-Government had fairly different drivers, priorities, and governing principles, while at the same time certain processes were similar. The main drivers studying the subject were the gap of literature and few studies which exist, that compare the two sectors. Also, a deeper understanding of the similarities and differences between e-Commerce and e-Government may lead to cross-fertilization and reduction of unnecessary reduplication in both sectors.

In this paper we present our detailed findings in three important areas of comparison (1) process management, (2) information management, and (3) stakeholder relations. This paper reports on three of then areas, which we studied in our longitudinal exploratory study. However, this does not imply that the other areas are of lesser importance. It is only due to space constraints that we refrain from presenting results in areas such as digital divides, citizen/customer focus, technology management, standardization, interoperability, human resources, and cost/benefits. We will present and discuss those findings elsewhere. However, the three areas mentioned above are central to the understanding of the similarities and differences of e-Commerce and e-Government.

This paper is organized as follows. First, we briefly update the pertinent literature on e-Commerce and e-Government. Second, we introduce and discuss the study design followed by the presentation and discussion of our findings. We aim at creating a theoretical foundation for a later theory testing-oriented stage of research and present the theoretical development in the form of five topical clusters and sub-clusters. We

M.A. Wimmer et al. (Eds.): EGOV 2010, LNCS 6228, pp. 25–37, 2010.

conclude by discussing the implications of our findings for the better understanding of theory and practice.

2   Review of Related Literatures

The body of comparative literature on e-Commerce and e-Government has not grown much over the past few years. Except our own work [3, 4, 31], we found only one further study engaging in comparative analysis of the two phenomena [23]. However, that study based its analysis on surveying user perceptions of relative performance and functionality of US Federal Government websites versus commercial providers such as Google, Yahoo, MSN, CNN, and USAToday among others. As opposed to those authors, we were interested in identifying the drivers, motivations, challenges, and achievements of e-Government and e-Commerce from an internal and behind-the-scene perspective. For anticipating and isolating potential similarities and differences between e-Commerce and e-Government, we also looked at related streams of literature [5, 27, 28].

On a more general plane, public-to-private differences have been identified in three areas: (1) environmental drivers and constraints, (2) organizational mandates and scope, and (3) internal processes, complexities, and incentives [28]. The private sector has been also praised for its higher agility, greater resourcefulness, less burdensome bureaucracy, and stronger motivation to proactively innovate when compared with public sector organizations [6, 27, 28]. These differences also surfaced in a study, which compared the strategic priorities of Chief Information Officers (CIOs) in both public and private sectors. It was found that public-sector CIOs focused on (a) the implementation of an IT architecture, (b) cultural change, (d) hiring/retaining skilled professionals, (e) and streamlining business processes, while private-sector CIOs emphasized (a) simplifying business processes, (b) improving services, (c) effective relationships with senior executives, (d) preventing intrusions, and (e) the implementation of IT architecture. Process change via streamlining and service improvement were more highly ranked by private-sector CIOs [34].

Further, the business models of e-Commerce and e-Government differ in significant ways: while the e-Commerce business model aims at creating customer value and at generating revenue, the e-Government business model is based on laws, statutes, and regulations providing citizens and firms with access to government information and services, and also delineating intergovernmental relationships, strategies, and interoperation of electronic government information systems (EGIS)[16], see also [32]. Citizens' acceptance of e-Government rests on trust, information access, public accessibility, quality of service, time saving, efficiency of service, and social awareness [25]. Also, in e-Commerce several sub-models may be found [7], which explain certain differences particularly in process management.

Finally, as our previous studies uncovered, similarities between e-Commerce and e-Government were found regarding (1) process improvements, (2) backend (process) integration, (3) cost savings, (4) information sharing, (5) vertical and horizontal systems integration, (6) increased responsiveness and service quality, (7) standardization efforts, and (8) the criticality of senior leadership support. Differences between the sectors were found to prevail regarding (1) the drivers and motivations for e-Commerce and e-Government, (2) stakeholder expectations, and (3) resource availability (4) concern regarding the digital divides [4, 31].

3   Research Questions and Method

Study Questions. Except for the few studies mentioned above, we had to deal with a rather thin base of knowledge in this particular area of research and could only incorporate an emergent theoretical framework, which was mostly derived from our own studies on the subject. This led us to follow through with our originally envisioned, two-stage exploratory research approach [2, 8, 26] addressing the two overarching research questions of

(R1) What is similar in private-sector e-Commerce and public-sector e-Government, and how does it matter?

(R2) What is different in private-sector e-Commerce and public-sector e-Government, and how does it matter?

Both e-Commerce and e-Government projects and implementations are engrained in institutional and social settings [11, 24] leading to a mesh of socio, technical, and organizational complexities, which defy the reduction of the study problem to a few variables. As a consequence, we opted for the empirical format of focus group discussions, which has proven highly effective in study situations of this kind [9, 13, 14, 20, 21]. In focus groups, the interaction between participants can be expected to lead to rich data and high data quality [26]. In our study design, we incorporated two stages of data collection. In the first stage, we had sector experts discuss the overall research questions with other experts from the same sector. We compared the findings in each sector, and identified similarities and differences between the two sectors. The first stage entailed six focus groups with 17 individuals from the public sectors, and 18 from the private sectors. Based on this first stage analysis, we developed a theoretical model represented by a set of 29 propositions [31]. In the second stage, we presented the propositions we developed in the area of process management, information management-, and stakeholder-relations to a focus group which comprised three experts from each sector together. This second-stage focus group approach with experts from both sectors, we expected, would amend our insights and give us further clues regarding the soundness and validity of our initial theoretical concept which was derived from separate-sectored focus groups.

Sampling Method. The sampling had to be purposive [29], since certain criteria outlined below had to be met in order to qualify for meaningful data. We also stratified the sample using Anthony's framework, which distinguishes between professionals, supervisors with operational control, managers, and strategic planners [1] and chose the managerial level for the pilot, since that level appeared to us high enough for capturing strategic aspects and motives as well as low enough to identify specifics of implementation and outcomes. Individuals were selected on the basis of willingness to participate and on the basis of prior involvement in and experience with e-Commerce or e-Government projects. For both sectors, participants were selected from organizations in the US Pacific Northwest, which has been found highly developed in both e-Commerce (for example, Amazon.com, Boeing, Micro-soft, etc.) and e-Government [15, 17, 18]. We recruited participants from different size and type of organizations and government entities. We did not allow any expert to participate twice, in order to get a better variation of perspectives. We required that the projects, in which the participants had been involved, had been of strategic nature to the organization. Also, the project had to contain a major transactional component. In the first stage of the exploration, six focus groups were conducted: three with participants from private sector, and three for participants from the public sector. In the second stage, when we confronted participants from both sectors with our study findings from the first stage, we conducted one focus group with six participants, three from each sector.

Data Collection. In the first-stage letter of invitation to prospective participants from the private sector, we verbally and graphically introduced the concepts of business-to-consumer (B2C), business-to-business (B2B), business-to-government (B2G), business-to-employee (B2E), and IEE. Likewise, we introduced the concepts of G2C, G2B, G2G, and government-to-employee (G2E) as well as IEE in the invitation letters to prospective participants from the public sector. Intentionally, we framed and pre-structured the discussion in that way for systematic comparability. We continue to believe that this framing and pre-structuring would not hamper the expert discussion in any way, on the contrary. For all six groups we introduced the two dimensions of "informational" and "transactional." The six focus groups were conducted in pairs. They were organized as half-day focus group discussions with the selected participants, first with the private sector participants, the next day with the public sector participants. The moderator first introduced the focus group format to the participants; she then re-introduced the e-Commerce and e-Government concepts as already outlined in the invitation letters. She explained to participants that the first session would be dedicated to the "informational" aspects of the five concepts followed by a second session on the "transactional' aspects. The moderator then launched the focus group discussion with an opening question and facilitated the discussion, while three observers took notes and administered the audio recording [20]. In the second stage, we invited experts from both sectors who had not participated in the first stage of this study. As attachment to the invitation letter, we shared our publication [31], and indicated that we would focus on the three areas of process management, stakeholder relations, and information management. The second-stage session format comprised two 90-minute discussion sections spread over a half day. The propositions were read to participants, one at a time. Participants then engaged in discussing the proposition. Again, notes were taken, and the discussions were audio-recorded [20]. The audio tracks were transcribed yielding over 370 pages of transcripts for both stages. Also, over 170 pages of notes were taken.

Data Analysis. In this study we mainly used Strauss and Corbin's coding methodology [33]. In four passes, the transcripts and emerging concepts were analyzed. First, the four researchers independently read the transcripts identifying units of data. Our impression from the collection exercise was confirmed during this phase that we had in fact managed to collect rich and high-quality data in all four sessions. In the second pass, the two researchers read the transcripts again and consolidated the units of data. In an open coding process [33], each unit of data was then assigned to a preliminary category or sub-category whose dimensions and properties were developed from the data. New categories and sub-categories were introduced, in case existing categories did not apply [12]. Convergence and assignment of categories, which the two researchers had identified independently, was performed at each step of the data analysis. In the second stage, we conducted a qualitative convergence and gap/difference analysis between the findings from the first and second stage.

4   Findings

In this section, we present our findings the areas of (1) process management, (2) information management, and (3) stakeholder relations.

4.1   Process Management

4.1.1   Process Streamlining and Process Integration

In the first stage of our exploration, we found that e-Commerce information systems (ECIS) and e-Government information systems alike were more effective when processes were streamlined and new workflows were introduced. Also in both sectors, we found a trend in favor of modernizing and overhauling workflows and processes. Early projects in both sectors obviously only mimicked the existing processes leading to manumation (rather than automation) as some scoffers had put it [22]. However, after some low-hanging fruits had been harvested in this fashion, in both sectors it was recognized that process redesign and creation of new workflows would improve service quality, speed up service and the processing of transactions. As we found in the second stage of our exploration, the two extremes of mere mimicking and window-dressing of old processes, on the one hand, and radical redesigning, streamlining, and inventing of new processes, on the other hand, rarely, if ever, occurred in practice. For either sector, the two extremes should rather be understood as the two end points of a continuum, in which hybrids of some sort emerged with a tendency to move over time from the end of old processes towards the other end of new and streamlined processes and workflows. Time pressures in active projects, lack of resources including skilled labor, perceived high risks, concerns regarding manageability, and high cost were among the most frequently cited factors that were attributed to the fact that most e-projects initially appeared as redressed old workflows. On the other hand, when scouring for streamlining opportunities, in both sectors it was found that a number of workflows would not even require the utilization of technology.

Integration and alignment (see also 4.1.3) of processes and workflows between organizational units and across organizations also emerged as both a side effect, and in some cases, as a prerequisite for successful redesign and the launch of e-projects. In both sectors, we found cases where the redesign and streamlining of a process or workflow hinged upon another party's willingness to also adjust and streamline her processes. It was further reported from both sectors that during times of economic hardships and pressures, process alignment and integration efforts were more easily introduced and established than in times of ease.

Also, in the second stage participants from government confirmed earlier findings that process and workflow alignment was still a challenge due to various factors such as preventive statutes, regulations, and laws, or bureaucratic inertia, turf protection, or unwillingness to collaborate. Some technical obstacles such as media breaks or legal requirements also played a role in this regard. Yet, for successful transaction processing, a certain degree of process alignment and integration as well system interoperability on the basis of backend system integration was seen as indispensable.

4.1.2 Transaction Processing

Electronically processed transactions have become a cost-effective, speedy, and reliable method of conducting the business in both sectors. In government, most electronic transactions are still internal, while external online transactions involving citizens and businesses were believed to be not as sophisticated as in e-Commerce. In the private sector, transaction volumes with customers (B2C transactions) appeared to be much higher than those in the public sector with citizens (G2C transactions). We were not able to compare the actual transaction volumes in the two sectors or even give an informed estimate, since the amount of government-internal transactions (G2G transactions) is unknown at this point in time. In the second stage, participants also discussed in more detail the motivation for increasing the volumes of online transactions such as drastic cost savings, higher profit margins (in the private sector), improved customer/citizen profiling, improved service quality, speedier service provision, improved customer/citizen experience, more accurate and complete data entry, and with more accurate data for analysis.

In terms of a pleasing online service experience on part of the human actor, the private sector still appears to have an edge over the public sector, even though some governments seem to have narrowed the gap. Governments, it was said, cannot easily relinquish certain legacies (information systems as well as statutory and legal frameworks) as easily as private-sector firms can that are able to start a new business from scratch without such heritage.

Participants also remarked that the profiling-based customer-centric perspective, which is capable of singling out individual persons' preferences and dislikes as it has evolved in e-Commerce, might be even undesirable in e-Government. The public-sector equivalent it was said might draw connotations of Orwell's Big Brother ("While you are applying for this-and-that license, we are also finding that you have not yet paid the following traffic citations, which are overdue. Also, your pet license is expiring shortly. We can only service your request after you paid the traffic citations in full.").

However, for example, with reference to e-voting practices, particularly in Europe, or, the introduction of citizen self-services via kiosks, participants attributed to government the capability and successful implementation of innovative concepts. Also, shrinking budgets and citizens' increased service quality expectations seemed to have stimulated EGIS-based innovations in government, much like market competition does based on ECIS in the private sector. In other words, despite different drivers, in both e-Commerce and e-Government strong pressures exist, which force innovation to happen.

Another similarity between the e-Commerce and e-Government was seen in the growing data awareness in both sectors. Data-centric approaches when analyzing, for example, service quality and needs-oriented service offerings have been observed in both sectors. Participants expected that the open government and transparency initiatives, which governments on all levels and around the world began pursuing, would massively add to the data awareness and sophisticated use of data in both sectors.

4.1.3 Alignment and Collaboration

In our first-stage exploration, we found collaboration and alignment in B2B and G2G scenarios to be critical to the success of improved service delivery (see also 4.1.1.). Interestingly, whenever effective intergovernmental collaboration was found it was more effective if voluntary rather than an imposed (hierarchical) collaboration. Also, similar organizational sizes and governance structures appeared to matter a lot. Moreover, the development of formal collaborative governance structures and formal agreements appeared to be essential to success, ideally on the basis of a shared vision and a common strategy. In the private sector, most collaborative endeavors appeared to rest on mutual and shared business interest. Both hierarchical (for example, vendor-supplier) and peer relationships were found in B2B collaboration. However, it could not be determined which type of relationship (hierarchical vs. peer) worked more effectively.

Our second-stage experts fully confirmed the earlier findings and also added important aspects. Independent of organizational sizes and governance structures they maintained data sharing had expanded almost exponentially in recent years in both sectors regardless of any mandates. However, the experts acknowledged the inherent complexity of alignment and collaboration, which permeates both organizational and technology-related levels. Interestingly, when it came to continued electronic collaboration, small businesses appear to be much less ready for system interoperation and electronic information exchanges than government agencies or larger private businesses.

Again we heard that similar organizational sizes and similar governance structures of prospective partners are (at least in government) favorable for collaboration, while dissimilarities in those areas can pose serious obstacles for collaboration. The alignment of strategic priorities was found to become stronger over time the more the collaboration was seen as effective and successful.

Finally, the experts in the second stage presented and discussed a number of examples within and across both sectors where collaboration on a voluntary basis seemed to work more effectively than when coerced like in a quasi-hierarchical relationship. In any case, formal agreements between collaborating parties including memoranda of understanding and service level agreements appear to be an important element of successful long-term collaborative efforts in both sectors. However, even for single projects, we found that a formal agreement defining the scope, timeline, cost, and projected outcome had been negotiated and signed.

4.2 Information Management

The subject of information management drew strong attention and discussions from participants. Particularly two main subjects appeared as significant: i) the impact of information quality on the interactions between companies or government agencies and their clients or citizens respectively; and ii) the role content management plays in the organizational/governmental life.

4.2.1 Impact of Information Quality (IQ)

The literature proposes eight major dimensions of information quality that needs to be addressed (1) accuracy, (2) comprehensiveness, (3) currency, (4) cognitive authority,

(5) assurance/reliability, (6) relevance/precision/recall, (7) timeliness, and (8) perceived value [19]. In this study, we found evidence that indeed all eight criteria were important elements of high IQ. Access to information of high quality along those lines was portrayed as crucial to the success of e-projects in both government and commerce. While both sectors consider IQ as critical, and acknowledged the strong correlation between IQ and effective information management, few differences between the sectors surfaced.

First, maintenance of acceptable levels of information quality appeared to be more challenging in e-Government than in e-Commerce. Not only higher volumes of information appeared as a factor explaining the difference between the sectors, but also the possible error range, the status of the information (mandatory or voluntary) and the impact this information has on people. While in private sector people allow a certain degree of error range to occur (for example – delivery of your product to a different address), in the public sector these errors may have a deep impact on people (for example – a emergency call responder messing up with the location of call). The demand for *ever*-high IQ levels burdens and challenges the maintenance of the information. Also, in e-Commerce, strategic decisions about record keeping, for example, what types of information should be kept, may change according to strategic decisions of the organization. As opposed to the private sector, information may be required to be kept and archived for a long period of time in the public sector. Regulations may create constraints that enforce government agencies to maintain information in a certain way. Therefore, the mandatory facet of information keeping in government has straight implications on the complexity of maintenance. Finally, information quality had a direct major and critical impact on the life of people. Therefore, maintenance of the information will be similar to the careful record keeping process.

Second, the impact of information quality was raised again in the second-stage discussion when we presented our proposition derived from the literature and the first stage of the study that lower information quality affects e-Commerce more negatively than e-Government. This proposition stimulated a long debate, and participants thought that the contrary was true, that is, lower information quality more negatively affects e-Government than e-commerce. Participants perceived lower IQ to impact mainly economical and financial aspects companies in e-Commerce, while in e-Government lower IQ was perceived as impacting the life of people in every possible way, for example, the way our identity is represented in public, reward and punishment of society and physical well-being.

4.2.2 The Role of Content Management

Document Life Management, the management of document flows, as well as the proper archiving of electronic records and removed web content along with previous versions of websites were mentioned repeatedly as major challenges in e-Government content management. We found that participants reported in both stages of the study that content management was more challenging in government than in the private sector due to volume of information and complexity of linked content. The complexity of the content management in the public sector as opposed to the private sector was related to two main aspects: i) the time aspect of keeping the data and its retrieval afterwards. The scope of government record keeping was very long on average. Moreover, in many cases it was not due for deletion. Content management it was said became more challenging due to the changing notions of public/private interests or contexts between the time of archiving and the time of retrieval. ii) the sensitive balance between freedom of information and privacy – in recent years there appeared to be a growing trend towards open government and more transparency. It sharpened the debate of what was considered private and what should be regarded public, and more specifically, which publicly held information would still need to be kept secret in order to balance other rights. Government agencies obviously seemingly tried to strike a balance between citizens' need for information and the extent of government services to provide that information electronically. This juggle made it difficult to strategize about content management, especially when the goal changed frequently and the public/private distinction had become so dynamic.

4.3 Stakeholders Relations

The subject of stakeholder relations appeared in both stages of the study in different variations. Participants agreed that governance of stakeholders was a critical component in the success or failure of projects and that the structure of governance influences ECIS and EGIS designs and deliverables both in e-Commerce and in e-Government. Disagreements appeared as to the effect the structure of this governance has. Moreover, we hypothesized that the process of convincing top-leadership to support and EGIS project is harder than in private sector. Participants from the public sector agreed that this was crucial in EGIS projects and very hard due to diverse needs, different weight and influence of stakeholders, and, in public sector, the difficulty to show a clear return on investments. Nevertheless, there was no consent about whether it was harder to win support from top-leadership for e-projects in either the public or the private sector.

In order to establish lasting governance structures in the public sector, the relationships among different types of stakeholders, elected and appointed officials, political and professional staff, and federal, state, and local stakeholders needed to be balanced according to the experts. This was harder to accomplish when the boundaries of the system were rigidly fixed for a long period, most of the professional staff was retained, the needs were vast and the interests were incongruent, or even pulling into different directions [10, 30]. For example, participants reported the fear to partner with "too big a city", and to create a dependency on that City's resources and governance structure. An important issue that surfaced in the second stage of the study was that although there were diverse stakeholders with whom agencies needed to deal, still the collaboration was more effective between institutions of similar size and similar governance structure. Finally, while diversity appeared as a critical issue also for the e-Commerce sector, we were not able to assess its exact impact.

5 Discussion and Summary

We set out to investigate, identify, and characterize the similarities and differences between e-Commerce and e-Government since we believed that the findings from such a study would benefit academic knowledge and e-Commerce and e-Government practice alike. In the following we discuss and summarize our observations and insights.

5.1 Similarities between E-Commerce and E-Government (Research Question #1)

According to our findings both ECIS and EGIS benefit their respective organizations significantly more when the underlying workflows and processes are not only electronic re-embodiments of their paper-based antecedents but rather streamlined, simplified, or completely discarded and replaced by different workflows and processes, which take full advantage of the technology. This seems to be increasingly understood in both commerce and government. We also found completely new workflows in both sectors, which would not have been possible without ECIS and EGIS.

A great incentive for streamlining and redesigning workflows and processes we found in the increased degree of collaboration within and between the sectors, which has become possible in an instantaneous fashion through ECIS and EGIS.

We further found that collaboration between partners within and across sectors works better when it unfolds on the basis of formal agreements. In government, it was noted that imposed collaboration works poorly as opposed to collaborative engagements based on freedom of choice.

Interestingly, cross-sector collaboration based on ECIS/EGIS reduces cost and speeds up the process on both ends even if the private-sector partner provides systems, infrastructure, and maintenance.

Along with transactional collaboration and integration we found increasing collaboration within and across sectors also in the area of information sharing. If collaboration thrives, we saw even the partial alignment of strategic objectives as a result. Information quality played a critical role in this context. A positive feedback between perceived IQ, information sharing, and the strength of the relationship seemed to exist.

We found in both sectors that similar governance structures of organizations influenced how collaborative ECIS and EGIS were designed. Remarkably, in both sectors the perceived needs of citizens (and customers, respectively) strongly influenced the designs of respective systems. In e-Commerce, organizations were interested in providing a social environment, which was conducive to a positive experience as a customer.

These findings suggest that ECIS/EGIS-related phenomena have important characteristics in common, which go beyond the mere technical resemblance of systems and methods. Process redesign practices might be a worthwhile subject of further study. Likewise, practices and principles of organizational and technical collaboration appear to provide valuable experiences to be shared.

5.2 Differences between e-Commerce and e-Government (Research Question #2)

However, we also found formidable differences in practices, principles, and drivers between e-Commerce and e-Government. Transaction processing was found more sophisticated and of far higher volume in commerce than in government. On the other hand, information processing and management, including the archiving of electronic records we found much more developed in the public sector than with private firms. The drivers of innovation were different in e-Commerce and in e-Government; however, the pressures for organizational change, service innovation, and transformation towards more citizen-/customer centric way of conducting business were similarly strong. As a result, the overall sophistication of EGIS did not appear to lag behind ECIS by orders of magnitude. Both sectors also made increasingly elaborate use of historical data and data from transaction processing in order to optimize desired organizational outcomes. Lower information quality was found to lead to immediate and economically negative effects in both sectors. However, while low information quality directly impacts the bottom line of commercial organizations, in the public sector low IQ could have even more dramatic consequences for citizens and businesses alike. In other words, the impacts of low IQ might be even more devastating in the public sector than in the private sector. Still, governments struggled more than commercial organizations to maintain acceptable levels of information quality leading to far greater challenges, for example, in content management.

Interestingly, leadership in government appeared to be more supportive of (in particular, collaborative) e-projects than their commercial counterparts. It also appeared that collaborative structures in the public sector were markedly stronger than those in the private sector.

Overall, what we found different between e-Commerce and e-Government suggests that the two phenomena follow different trajectories despite many similarities and technical commonalities. One obvious explanation lies in the sector-specific differences, which produce different drivers also in this area. It will be interesting to analyze to what extent Enterprise Resource Planning (ERP) systems, which are increasingly introduced in government, may help align the trajectories between e-Commerce and e-Government to a higher degree than we found in this study.

5.3 Limitations and Future Research

In our samples of participants from the two sectors and after the focus groups were conducted we found that e-Government experts on average were from higher levels in the organizational hierarchy than e-Commerce practitioners who were more technically versed. Our results, hence, may be skewed that they represent more strategic perspectives in e-Government and more operational/tactical perspectives in e-Commerce.

We also recognize that what we present here is the result of an exploratory study based on a limited number of participants. Our study attempts to lay theoretical foundations for more quantitatively oriented research on the subject, which we hope will lead us to more generalizable results. Furthermore in this paper we present results from three major (of eight) areas of analysis.

References

[1] Anthony, R.N.: Planning and control systems; a framework for analysis. Division of Research, Graduate School of Business Administration, Harvard University, Boston (1965)

[2] Arthur, S., Nazroo, J.: Designing fieldwork strategies and materials. In: Ritchie, J., Lewis, J. (eds.) Qualitative research practice: a guide for social science students and researchers, pp. 109–137. Sage Publications, Thousand Oaks (2003)

[3] Barzilai-Nahon, K., Scholl, H.J.: Comparing E-Government with E-Business Challenges. In: Internet Research (IR 8.0) Conference, Vancouver, BC/Canada, pp. 1–10 (2007)

[4] Barzilai-Nahon, K., Scholl, H.J.: Similarities and differences of e-Commerce and e-Government: Insights from a pilot study. In: Sprague, R. (ed.) 40th Hawaii International Conference on System Sciences (HICSS40), pp. 92c(1-10). IEEE, Waikoloa (2007)

[5] Boyne, G.A.: Public and private management: What's the difference? Journal of Management Studies 39, 97–122 (2002)

[6] Bozeman, B., Bretschneider, S.: Public management information systems: Theory and prescriptions. Public Administration Review 46, 475–489 (1986)

[7] Chang, Y.-P., Yan, J.: Positioning In a New Dynamic E-Commerce Business Model. In: 3rd International Conference on Wireless *Comm*unications, Networking and Mobile Computing (WICOM 2007), pp. 3592–3595. IEEE, Shanghai (2007)

[8] Creswell, J.W.: Educational research: planning, conducting, and evaluating quantitative and qualitative research, 2nd edn. Merrill, Upper Saddle River (2005)

[9] Finch, H., Lewis, J.: Focus groups. In: Ritchie, J., Lewis, J. (eds.) Qualitative research practice: a guide for social science students and researchers, pp. 170–198. Sage Publications, Thousand Oaks (2003)

[10] Flak, L.S., Nordheim, S.: Stakeholders, Contradictions and Salience: An Empirical Study of a Norwegian G2G Effort. In: Proceedings of the 39th Annual Hawaii International Conference on System Sciences (HICSS39 e-Government Track), vol. 4, pp. 75a–75tig. IEEE, Kauai (2006)

[11] Giddens, A.: The constitution of society: outline of the theory of structuration. University of California Press, Berkeley (1984)

[12] Gorman, G.E., Clayton, P., Rice-Lively, M.L., Gorman, L.: Qualitative research for the information professional: a practical handbook. Library Association Publishing, London (1997)

[13] Greenbaum, T.L.: The handbook for focus group research, 2nd edn. Sage Publications, Thousand Oaks (1998)

[14] Greenbaum, T.L.: Moderating focus groups: a practical guide for group facilitation. Sage Publications, Thousand Oaks (2000)

[15] Ho, A.T.-k.: Reinventing local governments and the e-government initiative. Public Administration Review 62, 434–444 (2002)

[16] Janssen, M., Kuk, G., Wagenaar, R.W.: A survey of Web-based business models for e-government in the Netherlands. Government Information Quarterly 25, 202–220 (2008)

[17] Kaylor, C.H., Deshazo, R., Van Eck, D.: Gauging e-government: A report on implementing services among American cities. Government Information Quarterly 18, 293–307 (2002)

[18] Kaylor, C.H.: The next wave of e-Government: The challenges of data architecture. Bulletin of the American Society for Information Science and Technology 31, 18–22 (2005)

[19] Klischewski, R., Scholl, H.J.: Information Quality as the Capstone of E-government Integration, Interoperation, and Information Sharing. Electronic Government, an International Journal 5, 203–225 (2008)

[20] Krueger, R.A., Casey, M.A.: Focus groups: a practical guide for applied research, 3rd edn. Sage Publications, Thousand Oaks (2000)

[21] Madriz, E.: Focus groups in feminist research. In: Denzin, N.K., Lincoln, Y.S. (eds.) Handbook of qualitative research, 2nd edn., pp. 835–850. Sage Publications, Thousand Oaks (2000)

[22] Mohan, L., Holstein, W.K.: EIS: it can work in the public sector. MIS Quarterly 14, 434–448 (1990)

[23] Morgeson, F.V., Mithas, S.: Does E-Government measure up to E-Business? Comparing end user perceptions of U.S. Federal Government and E-Buisness web sites. Public Administration Review 69, 740–752 (2009)

[24] Orlikowski, W.J., Robey, D.: Information technology and the structuring of organizations. Information Systems Research 2, 143–169 (1991)

[25] Park, R.: Measuring Factors That Influence the Success of E-government Initiatives. In: Proceedings of the 41st Annual Hawaii International Conference on System Sciences (HICSS '08), pp. 218 (1-10), IEEE Computer Society Conference Publishing Services, Waikoloa (2008)

[26] Patton, M.Q.: Qualitative research and evaluation methods, 3 ed. Sage Publications, Thousand Oaks (2002)

[27] Perry, J.L., Rainey, H.G.: The public-private distinction in organization theory: A critique and research strategy. Academy of Management Review 13, 182–201 (1988)

[28] Rainey, H., Backoff, R., Levine, C.: Comparing public and private organizations. Public Administration Review 36, 233–244 (1976)

[29] Ritchie, J., Lewis, J., Gillian, E.: Designing and selecting samples. In: Ritchie, J., Lewis, J. (eds.) Qualitative research practice: a guide for social science students and researchers, pp. 77–108. Sage Publications, Thousand Oaks (2003)

[30] Scholl, H.J.: Applying stakeholder theory to e-government: benefits and limits. In: Schmid, B., Stanoevska-Slabeva, K., Tschammer, V. (eds.) 1st IFIP Conference on E-Commerce, E-Business, and E-Government (I3E 2001), pp. 735–747. Kluwer, Zurich (2001)

[31] Scholl, H.J., Barzilai-Nahon, K., Ahn, J.-H., Popova, O.H., Re, B.: E-Commerce and e-Government: How Do They Compare? What Can They Learn From Each Other? In: Proceedings of the 42nd Annual Hawaii International Conference on System Sciences (HICSS '09), Waikoloa, Big Island, Hawaii, pp. 141 (1-10) (2009)

[32] Stahl, B.C.: The Paradigm of E-Commerce in E-Government and E-Democracy. In: Huang, W., Siau, K., Wei, K.K. (eds.) Electronic Government Strategies and Implementation, pp. 1–19. Idea Group Publishing, Hershey (2005)

[33] Strauss, A.L., Corbin, J.M.: Basics of qualitative research: techniques and procedures for developing grounded theory, 2nd edn. Sage Publications, Thousand Oaks (1998)

[34] Ward, M., Mitchell, S.: A comparison of the strategic priorities of public and private sector information resource executives. Government Information Quarterly 21, 284–304 (2004)

Inter-organizational Information Systems and Interaction in Public vs. Private Sector – Comparing Two Cases

Ulf Melin[1] and Karin Axelsson[1,2]

[1] Department of Management and Engineering, Linköping University,
SE-581 83 Linköping, Sweden
[2] Swedish Business School, Örebro University, SE-701 82 Örebro, Sweden
{karin.axelsson,ulf.melin}@liu.se

Abstract. This paper compares inter-organizational (IO) interaction and inter-organizational information systems (IOS) in public and private sector. The purpose of the paper is to explore differences and similarities between e-government and e-business focusing IOS and interaction. This is done in order to facilitate learning between the two fields. The point of departure is two case studies performed in private vs. public sectors. A comparative study is made using IO concepts from industrial markets that characterize an IO relationship (continuity, complexity, symmetry, and formality) and concepts that describe dimensions of such relationships (links, bonds, and ties). The results from the comparative study show that there are several similarities concerning interaction in relations between organizations in the two sectors. There are also differences depending on the level of analysis (empirical level vs. analytical level). The study shows the need to be explicit regarding organizational value, end-customer or client/citizen value and the type of objects that are exchanged in the interaction.

Keywords: B2B, G2G, interaction, e-government, inter-organizational, IOS.

1 Introduction

Inter-organizational (IO) aspects and processes are central in all organizational development regardless of sector, with or without information systems (IS) development in parallel. Inter-organizational information systems (IOS) have been identified as a key requirement for effective operation of IO relationships [5, 6] and have several impacts on governance, e.g. on a market level and an organizational level [21] and are therefore important to study when analyzing and developing IO interaction. IO aspects have been focused in organization theory, where interaction in dyads and networks are vital objects for research (cf. Håkansson and Snehota [16], who stated that no business is an island). This statement was later used in order to characterize governments in a network setting – *"no government is an island"* [19, p. 1420]. If we take a look at the private sector, business to business (B2B) interaction is an area of increasing interest when discussing electronic commerce, Internet and ERP.

M.A. Wimmer et al. (Eds.): EGOV 2010, LNCS 6228, pp. 38–49, 2010.

IO relations are also central when analyzing and developing government to government (G2G) interaction in order to achieve, e.g., useful one-stop government arrangements [11, 24]. Schedler et al. [22] claims that there are three central statements that constitute the key to a comprehensive understanding of electronic government: 1) e-government uses IT, especially the Internet, 2) e-government deals with organizational aspects of public administration; and 3) e-government considers the interaction of public administration with its environment (e.g. customers, suppliers, citizens, politicians).

IO interaction is the main theme addressed in this paper. A comparative study of two cases will be presented based on the following main research question: In what ways is private and public IO interaction similar and how does it differ depending on the sector context? The understanding of similarities and differences is useful as a point of departure when learning between private and public sector should take place. The need of comparative studies of e-business and e-government is put forth by Barzilai-Nahon and Scholl [3], who argue that such comparative efforts are necessary but still rare. This paper is a response to the shortage of research focusing comparative (inter sector) studies. This paper contains a comparative case study from the private and the public sectors. The private sector is represented by a business B2B relation between a carpentry and a sawmill – both small and medium size companies (SMEs) located in Sweden. The public sector is represented by a G2G relation between two agencies, one organization is Sweden's County Administrations (SCoA) and the other one is the Swedish Road Administration (SRoA).

When a new research field, like e-government, is entered or in a phase of rapid growth there is a clear tendency that "wheels are reinvented". Researchers as well as practitioners in the field tend to identify "too many" unique characteristics or unique factors related to the studied phenomenon, without learning from history and previous studies. On the other hand, there is another more or less opposite tendency; to take things for granted and, not critical enough, import or export ideas, concepts and lines of thinking from one area, sector or field to another. We believe that the IS field, dealing with e-government and e-business, is no exception in this case. Therefore we argue that it is important to conduct comparative case studies from different sectors.

The purpose of the paper, based on the research question introduced above, is to explore differences and similarities between e-government and e-business focusing IOS and interaction. This is done in order to facilitate learning between the two fields. Our analysis will be made based on the IO concepts from industrial markets [16, 17]. Theoretical concepts that characterize an IO relationship (continuity, complexity, symmetry, and formality) and concepts that describe dimensions of such relationships (links, bonds, and ties) will help us to describe and analyze interaction. The approach and the concepts are presented below. We have applied these theoretical concepts to the e-government field in a previous study in order to discuss challenges in one-stop government [2]. In that study the IO concepts from industrial markets were refined and structured into a conceptual framework of IO agency relationship dimensions (ibid.). We will use this conceptual framework in order to structure our comparative case study analysis.

After this introduction, the paper is organized in the following way: In Section Two we describe the research design, followed by the introduction of the case studies. The theoretical background to IO interaction and its relation to the comparison of IO interaction in e-business and e-government, and IOS are then presented in section

Three. The empirical findings from the two cases are analyzed and compared, using concepts from the introduced interaction approach in Section Four. The paper is concluded in Section Five, together with statements about further research.

2   Research Design and Case Study Introduction

The overall research design in this paper is qualitative and interpretive [26] and based on case studies. The fieldwork that we have conducted has been close to the cases and the actors within. Based on this we had a good access to interviewees, written sources, meetings, etc. The interviews had a semi-structured and semi-standardized design and were recorded. The interviewees have been selected in order to reach a broad view of apprehensions. We have asked open questions about how they understand the notion of e.g. IO interaction, IOS, communication, etc.

   The empirical data has been analyzed in a qualitative, interpretive way, using theory as a lens (central IO concepts from industrial markets [16, 17]) when analyzing. This is in line with a strategy using theory as a "part of an iterative process of data collection and analysis" [26, p. 76]. Besides using the concepts as a part of analysis, we tried to be open minded, investigating aspects and discoveries outside and beyond the theoretical concepts applied. The cases included in this paper represent organizations from the public and the private sectors that have performed extensive work with IO dimensions (IO interaction, IOS, etc.). This makes them interesting to analyze and to compare. The cases have, of course, differences in terms of size, complexity, sector, management, type of IT systems, etc. and should not be interpreted as representing a statistical sample. This is however an asset concerning the variation, and the ambition to maximize the variation. When doing this it is of course limitations involved concerning the comparative analysis; all aspects of the cases are not possible or even interesting to compare.

Introducing the E-government Case Study. The G2G case is focused on driving license issues. We have studied the IO interaction between two government agencies (CoA and SRoA) during the issuing of provisional driving licenses. The overall process and background to this case is that everyone in Sweden who want to get a driving license, first have to apply for a provisional driving license from the regional CoA. The provisional driving license is approved if the applicant is judged by the regional CoA to be able to drive a vehicle in a safe way. The permit application was, until an e-service was implemented, a paper form that was filled in, signed and sent by mail to the regional agency. The application had to be complemented with a health declaration, a certificate of good eyesight, and maybe also an application that, e.g., a parent will be allowed to act as a private instructor. These documents were received and reviewed by a case officer at the agency. The case officer also checked if the applicant had been punished for any crimes. This information was registered in a database, operated by the police, which the case officer had access to through an IOS. When the provisional driving license had been granted, the CoA reported this to SRoA through this IOS. When the applicant has completed a driving test and a theoretical test successfully, she/he receives a driving license from the SRoA.

   We have studied the development project that aimed at developing an e-service for handling the provisional driving license applications. The e-service was intended to make an automated decision in "green cases" (i.e., cases that do not call for extensive handling) and support case officers handling such cases. By achieving this, the agency will in the long run try to save and reallocate resources from handling "green cases" to more complex errands. An e-service like this also provided an opportunity to standardize the application handling across the nation and the 21 county administration boards.

The E-government Case Study Research Design. The empirical data generated in this case has mainly been generated through semi-structured interviews with significant actors within the development project. We have in the beginning of the development project interviewed six persons involved in the project. The interviewees had the following roles: an IT strategist, a development project manager, a system manager, an internal investigator, a case officer and an IT development manager. We have then interviewed seven persons when evaluating progress and results in the end of the development project. Five of these interviewees were within the public sector; four of them were case officers and one of them was a local project manager at a CoA. Two interviewees were external consultants who worked for the public sector related to the studied e-government initiative. One of the consultants was a project manager supporter and the other person was an e-government development manager.

Introducing the B2B Case Study. The B2B case consists of the relation between two private owned firms in the wood industry; a sawmill and a carpentry. The studied sawmill is a family-owned company, established in the early 1900s. The business employs approx. 30 people. The sawmill exists in a volatile and competitive market, where raw materials are scarce and prices increasing. Securing the supply of raw material or logs is in focus. The carpentry manufactures a central component for houses; the stairs. The first product was manufactured already in the 1930s and since then production has continued in various forms of organization. 30 people are employed in the organization today including five administrators and the two joint owners. Since a couple of years, the firm enjoys very good profitability. The carpentry's business concept has remained the same since the beginning. The firm manufactures their product piece by piece, each product being unique.

The B2B Case Study Research Design. The two studied firms are a part of an industrial network that we have studied in a longitudinal multiple case study. The most significant unit of analysis was the firms and their business relations. Altogether 21 people in different positions were interviewed in the two focused firms, generating empirical data that is used in this study. Roles covered are e.g. owners, managing directors, administrators, controllers, production managers and mechanics/carpenters. Besides the empirical interview data we have also studied documents (e.g. firms' business strategies), artifacts (e.g. products, production layouts, logistic and IS) and made observations as empirical means for rich data.

3 Theoretical Background

This section of the paper presents core concepts from the so called Uppsala School – "the industrial/business network approach" (IMP [International/Industrial Marketing and Purchasing] approach) and notions of how IO interaction can be compared in e-business and e-government settings.

3.1 The Business Network Approach

The IMP approach [1, 15, 17], is a mature line of thinking that supports the understanding of interaction in business networks. Interaction is an aspect of reciprocal action or interplay; it is not the case of one organization *acting* and the other organization *reacting* [17]. This is an important standpoint in the network approach. If we take a closer look at the interaction between organizations we can find several characteristics of relationships. (1) *Continuity* refers to the relative stability that tends to characterize supplier and customer relationships. (2) The *complexity* in a relationship can among other things comprise the number, type and contact channels for those from each organization who are involved in relations between customer and supplier. Also, contacts can vary from level to level between organizations. It is typical for relations in industrial networks for customers and suppliers to be *symmetrical* (3) in terms of resources and initiatives on each side. In those cases where asymmetry does occur, the customer tends to be bigger than the supplier is. The relationships often demonstrate a *low level of formality* (4). Even though contracts exist, they are seldom referred to, as it is often pointed out that contracts are an ineffective way of dealing with uncertainty, conflict or crises in relationships which are going to survive for some time. [17]

Another important aspect to study, when looking at interaction between organizations, is different dimensions of relations, such as *links*, *bonds* and *ties*. The various links, bonds and ties between organizations in an organizational network are important to consider when studying relationships [1, 17]. The word *link* refers to the connections that exist in the activities between organizations, so-called activity links. An activity is defined as: "a sequence of acts directed towards a purpose" [17, p. 52]. Activities can be of various types, for example technical, administrative or commercial. The links between activities reflect the need for co-ordination which affects how and when various activities are carried out. Matching one actor's resources with others' and dividing out the tasks are examples of an aim towards purchasing and marketing functions within an organization. This, in turn, has consequences for both the costs for carrying out the activities and their effectiveness [17]. The links between activities make up a certain structure within the respect of organization at the same time as it also creates certain patterns in the network.

Bonds between the actors in a network can be of various types, for example technical, social, time- based, knowledge-based, administrative, economic or legal [17]. Bonds arise in relationships as two related actors mutually acquire meaning in their reciprocal acts and interpretation [17, p. 197]. Bonds can have various aims, an example being to achieve co-ordination as a means of saving resources. To gain access to suitable co-operators and maintain a certain position in the network are other examples of the importance of handling bonds. "Actors act and develop bonds; at the same time they are a product of their bonds" [17, p. 201].

An IO relationship affects the way in which the organizations use their personnel, equipment, know-how, and financial resources, only to mention a few. A relationship between two organizations can comprise pooled resources of these kinds, so-called resource *ties*. The relationships between organizations are not just a way of assuring access to resources, they are also a way of getting various types of resources to meet, confront and combine [17], and to develop, create or refine.

We can identify several motives for applying these theoretical concepts when analyzing and comparing our two cases. The B2B case is obviously an illustration of an industrial network. The G2G case does also possess characteristics of IO interaction. The Swedish model for public administration implies that cooperation between agencies in Sweden relies on similar foundations as cooperation between private organizations, i.e., there is a large amount of semi-autonomous agencies that have to find ways to cooperate and coordinate their joint development projects. Thus, we propose that IO relationships between agencies have some characteristics in common with business relationships in other networks. Another reason is that cooperation in the public sector sometimes involves financial exchange, which makes cooperation similar to cooperation in a business network. This implies that the network approach would be able to extend to the public sector.

3.2 Comparing IO Interaction in E-Business and E-Government

Historically, IS research has been argued to be less successful in developing cumulative research [4]. For most phenomena being studied, a new theoretical frame has been put forward instead of careful analysis of already existing frames. Strong theoretical frames with real value are, thus, rare [17]. This is something Heeks and Bailur [12] also emphasize as weak or confused positivism in e-government research dominated by over-optimistic and a-theoretical work, which do not add much practical guidance to e-government. Our ambition in this paper is to adopt core concepts from the mature IMP approach on the B2B and G2G cases in this paper. It is, thus, an attempt to apply and analyze an already existing theoretical frame instead of inventing a new one.

There are few research studies focusing on comparison between e-business and e-government issues [23]. Instead, these two fields are either seen as *closely related* (if focusing on IT aspects) or *totally different* (if focusing on funding mechanisms, some governance aspects and other organizational drivers). Both these standpoints might be harmful since they imply that knowledge either can be transferred between the fields in an uncritical way or that no lessons can be learned based on comparisons. In this paper we assume that increased understanding of how B2B and G2G interaction are alike and different can help improving both fields. This assumption is confirmed by Barzilai-Nahon and Scholl [3] who argue that both the private and the public sector would benefit from a better understanding of similarities and differences regarding e-business and e-government. They present a study that identifies several areas of similarities between e-business and e-government; i.e., process improvements, back-end integration, cost savings, information sharing, vertical and organizational e-systems integration, increased responsiveness and service quality, standardization efforts, and the criticality of senior leadership support. They distinguish some areas of differences as well; i.e., the drivers and motivations for e-business and e-government, stakeholder expectations, and resource availability (ibid.). All in all, Barzilai-Nahon's and Scholl's [3] findings show that there seem to be many aspects where we can find similarities, but we also need to understand the differences in order to avoid exaggerated knowledge reuse. Their study does, however, not focus on IO interaction in any detail, which implies that our study fills a gap in this respect. Several e-government scholars emphasize that the e-government field has disregarded IO aspects even though these seem to be a major cause for many problems [20, 25]. This supports our objective to explore how knowledge can be transferred between B2B and G2G fields.

3.3 Inter-organizational Information Systems

IOS are information systems that in some sense cross organizational boundaries and are shared by two or more organizations [21]; i.e. support B2B, G2B or G2G interaction. There are several studies covering IOS development and use. Early and seminal studies are performed by different scholars [13, 18, 28]. These and other early studies have been used as point of departure for many following studies of IOS. Kumar's and van Dissel's theory [18] has e.g. been expanded by Fahy et al. [7]. Roles of the organizations cooperating via an IOS are the basis for another framework proposed by Hong [14]. There are also studies of theoretical foundations of IOS [21].

IOS exists in a dialectic relation with business processes and the structure of organization or relationship between organizations. A higher level of structure and formalization can be a result when using IOS in IO interaction [18]. Formalization exists e.g. when there are tightly coupled IOS that require extensive relationship specific investments [9]. Tightly coupled IOS are associated with reduced flexibility [10]. EDI was an early example of this. Internet and extranet solutions on the other hand have made data interchange, interaction and communication easier to perform cross organizations. Enterprise systems are shifting from internal to external focus and IO operations are increasingly important to handle [6]. However, such solutions will require integration with internal IS in order to work efficiently [6, 29].

4 Analysis

In Table 1, below, the overall relationship characteristics will be analyzed in the cases from the two sectors using core concepts from the IMP approach [1, 15, 17] presented earlier in the paper. First we will analyze the overall relationship characteristics (continuity, complexity, symmetry and level of formality) followed by the relationship dimensions (links, bonds and ties). The analysis is structured according to a conceptual framework of IO agency relationship dimensions [2]. IOS is not explicitly highlighted in the central concepts that we have applied based on theory. In the concluding section we will use complementary theory, besides the IMP approach, in order to discuss the IOS dimension of B2B and G2G interaction.

Table 1. Relationship and interaction analysis – a comparative study of B2B and G2G cases

Relationship Dimensions	Relationship Categories	Business (B2B) Case	E-government (G2G) Case
Overall Relationship Characteristics	Continuity	Stable and mature (long term) relationship. The sawmill experiences a certain responsibility as a major supplier of wood to the carpentry.	Stable and mature relationship, which seems to be less challenging than the opposite. The relationship and the division of labor is regulated in law.
	Complexity	There is a low level of complexity in the relation. The communication process and the overall exchange process are uncomplicated and straight forward. A small number of actors have contact with each other between the organizations.	The relationship consists of many agency actors and many citizens' applications. There are diverse conceptions about the components of the complexity but the overall complexity is regarded as high.
	Symmetry	The carpentry has a clear initiative in the relationship and the relation is in that sense asymmetrical. The sawmill has a strategy to adjust to (changing) customer demands and initiatives.	Goal conflicts between several overarching roles, responsibilities and missions exist between the agencies. The SRoA is the dominating part in the relationship in terms of resources, knowledge (concerning e.g. e-services, project management, IT). SCoA is more diversified and divided. The relation is considered as asymmetrical.
	Level of formality	Low level of formality. There are variations in the corporate culture, history, etc., but the companies have a lot in common (the regional relation, the SME character, activity in the wood industry, etc.).	A high level of formality concerning the division of labor exists between the parties regulated by the government. This certainly has an influence on the relationship. Differing apprehensions about division of labor and responsibility occur. Variation in project management approaches/cultures also exists.
Links	Technical	Not an "advanced" IOS. The sawmill has created a view in their stock IT system so that they can expose the products that are unique for the carpentry. These products are also put into a special destined physical space in the factory building.	The SRoA supplies the IOS (the Road Traffic Register [RTR]) that the 21 CoAs use as an important tool for handling the applications. Data from the traffic register is used n the new e-service for handling applications; i.e. systems integration exists.
	Administrative	Rather simple and individual patterns of communication and cooperation. Disintegrated processes within the firms, but (individually) integrated between firms.	Disintegrated process with many contacts and deliveries between agencies. The agencies have responsibilities for different phases in the process of handling provisional driving licenses. Complicated patterns of communication and cooperation exist.
	Activity	Sequential interdependencies between activities in the two companies (e.g., in order and delivery processes). The sawmill, to a large extent, adapt their activities to this customer's needs. Information and goods exchange.	One aspect of activity links identified in this relation is the level of adaptation to the other party. The SCoA has to adapt to the IT system supplied by the SRoA; but has some possibilities expressing requirements on design of the IT system and the use of the system. Information and service exchange.
	Commercial	The sawmill has invested in a dedicated production equipment in order to satisfy demands from this important and demanding customer.	Not applicable in this case.
Bonds	Actor	Flat, non-hierarchical organizations, with few organizational levels. Actor bonds rely more on a personal (social) dimension between the firms, built up from the long-term relationship.	A gap between participants in working groups on different hierarchical levels (so called action groups; one at the operative level and one at the strategic level) within and between agencies. History influences opinions about present and future division of labor between agencies often criticized and discussed. Implicit actor bonds.
	Economic	The sawmill depends a lot on the demand from the carpentry (in production volume and economic terms). The ROI is higher at the carpentry than at the sawmill.	Complex principles for compensation related to the performance of activities; some tasks are resource demanding but uncompensated.
	Legal	Written frame contracts occur, but are seldom referred to. Legal bonds are implicit in the relation and in the interaction between actors from the two firms. Bonds are instead created based on mutual trust and a long-term business relation.	The agencies have several external assignments and both superior and inferior roles towards each other. The SCoA has an explicit mission from the government to develop e-services. The SRoA has the overall responsibility for the national road traffic issues sanctioned by the government. This fact also influences the bonds between the parties and the asymmetry (above) in the relation.
Ties	Resource	A number of pooled resources are jointly connected to the product (the customized wood material) and the production. Know-how is also transferred from the carpentry to the sawmill in order to increase the level of refinement in the product.	The studied parties pool resources (personnel and know-how) in order to develop e-services in a joint development project. At the same time there are an asymmetry in incentives for the joint project influences and the amount of resources spent on the project, e.g., due to the fact that the SRoA has an in-house IT development staff and the SCoA lacks this in-house competence. Knowledge is both a resource used in the project and an outcome from the project; i.e. competence development on individual and organizational level.

5   Conclusions and Further Research

In the introduction of this paper we asked in what ways private and public IO interaction is similar and how it differs. The ambition has been to understand similarities and differences in order to explore when and how the e-business and e-government fields can learn from each other regarding IO interaction. The contributions of our study are both presented as identified similarities and differences in the studied cases and as suggested, explorative, refinements of the conceptual framework used for analytical comparisons of B2B and G2G interaction.

Differences. Our conclusions, based on using the IMP approach [1, 15, 16, 17], show that there are differences between the interaction in the studied cases from the two sectors. If we take a look at the overall relationship characteristics there are differences, at the empirical case level, but the categories that support the analysis work in an appropriate way. Important factors framing the interaction and the relations are, e.g., present in the G2G case where we have the Government that regulates e.g. the present processes, actors, division of labor. In the B2B case we also have laws and regulations, but on another level (e.g., concerning accounting, different types of permits, etc.). From the empirical data we have also identified differences in the level of formality, asymmetry, technical (e.g., the use of an IOS), organizational structure (actor bonds), economic bonds and administrative links (in Table 1). Legal and actor bonds (content) also differ between the cases.

Links, bonds and ties are also possible to use when comparing interaction between organizations in different sectors. The difference in the use of the link category "commercial" between the two sectors made us aware of the need to discuss and analyze the "value" category as an alternative. One can also discuss which role the size of the studied organizations has had when comparing the empirical data. The size of the organizations has some effects on how they organize processes and hierarchy levels. But in the same time the size and structure of the private vs. public sector are given by the market and the overall structure of the public sector on a national level.

Barzilai-Nahon and Scholl [3] distinguish some areas of differences between B2B and G2G sectors; i.e., the drivers and motivations for e-business and e-government, stakeholder expectations, and resource availability [cf. 8]. All in all findings [3] show that there are many aspects where we can find similarities, but we also need to understand the differences in order to avoid improper knowledge reuse.

Similarities. Our conclusions based on using core concepts from the IMP approach [1, 15, 16, 17] show that there are similarities between the cases from the two sectors both at an empirical level and at an analytical level (the used categories). For example, both relations are stable and mature (continuity), have disintegrated processes (administrative link), sequential interdependencies (activity link) and pooled resources (resource link) (see Table 1).Earlier in this paper we assumed that increased understanding of how B2B and G2G interaction are alike and different can help improving both fields. We argue that we now have showed that this is the case, in line with [3]. However, we need to separate the *analytical level* from the *empirical level*. Our study shows that we can use the same set of categories when we analyze B2B and G2G relations and the present interaction. The result of using the same set of categories, however, can differ due to what type of organizations (firms or government agencies) that are analyzed, based on contextual factors. We can conclude that our study also shows that there are several areas of similarities between e-business and e-government, as identified above. There is a reported need to continuously improve intra- and IO processes, back-end vs. front-end integration, cost savings (efficiency), vast communication and information sharing, the need for IT integration, increased responsiveness and service quality, standardization efforts, and the criticality of senior leadership support [3]. The last aspect, however, more implicit in the rather non hierarchical SME's in our empirical data. The reported study [3] does, however, not focus on IO interaction, which implies that our study adds value.

Mutual Learning in B2B (e-business) and G2G (e-government). After having analyzed the interaction in our B2B and G2G cases using the IMP approach, we argue that the use of the relationship characteristics and the relationship dimensions are useful when structuring, describing and analyzing interactions – regardless of focused sector. However, we believe that there are aspects that can be made more explicit. There are also indications that a mutual learning in the two fields can occur when taking its differences and similarities into account [cf. 3]. Based on the comparative analysis we also suggest that the conceptual framework of IO agency relationship dimensions [2] can be further developed. Organizational size, culture and value can be made more explicit as well as the aim to create value for an end-customer (end-client or citizen). We also identified a need to be explicit regarding the exchange object (services, products, information, etc.). If the interaction in is supported by an IOS as an example of a technical, administrative and activity link these aspects are also important in order to create organizational and end-customer or client/citizen value. Such applications can be viewed as back-office systems, but has an effect on what joint value organizations can create. In order to compensate for the weak focus on IT (IOS), will we comment upon that in the following section.

IO Interaction and IOS. In the B2B case, a "non-advanced" IOS was used; the sawmill has created a view in their stock IT system so customer unique products can exposed (a technical link in Table 1). This improves and simplifies the interaction between the two firms, without being expensive and resource demanding as an investment [5, 6]. This type of application is tied to this particular key customer, using a remote login solution, but can, hypothetical be used for several customers. It is not technological issues that limit the IOS; it is more a question of trust. Trust based on a stable and mature (long-term) relationship between the two parties. The IOS is tightly coupled, but we would not argue that it has required extensive relationship specific investments [cf. 9]; at least not in direct IT investment terms – rather in mutual trust.

In the e-government case we have studied a development project that aimed at developing an e-service for handling the provisional driving license applications. The e-service was intended to make an automated decision in "green cases". This system has IO parts and is integrated with systems at several other government agencies in order to exchange data concerning e.g. crime records, residential information, etc. Links to the RTR are important in the daily work handling applications for provisional driving licenses. The IOS improves and simplifies the interaction (even if it is mainly unidirectional) between the studied agencies [cf. 5, 6]. The IOS is tightly coupled, and has required extensive relationship specific investments [cf. 5]. The dependency that the technical link represents will probably decrease flexibility [10].

Further Research. Further research is needed in order to compare different types of organizations in the two sectors. Further research is also needed covering G2B and B2G relations. The sample of organizations, and the relations, can be enlarged and chosen based on differences in business type, industries, local government, state, size, types of services, etc. This would add further understanding of the possibilities to achieve mutual learning about IO interaction in B2B and G2G. Choosing the cases that are present and analyzed in this paper is a limitation, as we pointed out above, but the variation represented here is also an opportunity. Based on the comparative study, we have identified that even if an organization is a part of a particular sector the organizations in a certain sector are not homogeneous. The character of the organization can be made more explicit when analyzing its relations. Our comparison indicates that the identified characteristics that can be made more precise compared to the presented relationship characteristics and dimensions (links, bonds and ties) [15, 17] as well as the conceptual framework of IOS agency relationship dimensions [2]. The identified characteristics concerns: organizational size, value and culture, the exchange object (services, products, information), service level, end-citizen/customer value, and the use of IT or e-services (IOS) as an example of a technical, administrative and activity link. These indications can be related to the existing body of knowledge and analyzed more in detail. However, this is out of the scope of this study and an issue for further research. Another interesting area for further research is how to deal with public-private partnerships (PPPs). Studying PPPs could challenge the categories above further. In such cases, where private and public sectors meet, the kind of results that we report on appears to be valuable. To learn more about IO interaction between a private and a public organization would be beneficial for understanding both sectors. The issue of trust is an important part of the IMP approach [15, 17], but can also be highlighted using research focused on trust as such.

References

1. Axelsson, B., Easton, G. (eds.): Industrial Networks: A New View of Reality. Routledge, London (1992)
2. Axelsson, K., Melin, U.: An inter-organisational perspective on challenges in one-stop government. Int. Journal of Electronic Governance 1(3), 296–314 (2008)
3. Barzilai-Nahon, K., Scholl, H.J.: Similarities and Differences of E-Commerce and e-Government: Insights from a Pilot Study. In: Proc. of the 40th Annual Hawaii Int. Conference on System Sciences (HICSS'07), pp. 92–101 (2007)
4. Benbasat, I., Zmud, R.W.: Empirical Research in Information Systems: The Practice of Relevance. MIS Quarterly 23(1), 3–16 (1999)
5. Breu, K., Hemingway, C., Strathern, M., Bridger, D.: Workforce agility: the new employee strategy for the knowledge economy. Journal of Information Technology 17, 21–31 (2002)
6. Daniel, E.M., White, A.: The Future of Inter-organisational System Linkages: Findings of an Int. Delphi Study. European Journal of Information Systems 14(2), 188–203 (2005)
7. Fahy, M., Feller, J., Finnegan, P., Murphy, C.: Complexity and Context: Emerging Forms of Collaborative Inter-Organizational Systems. Journal of Information Technology Theory and Application 8(4), 1–12 (2007)
8. Flak, L.S., Rose, J.: Stakeholder Governance: Adapting Stakeholder Theory to e-government. Communications of the AIS (16), 642–664 (2005)
9. Goethals, F., Vanderbulcke, J., Lemahieu, W., Snoeck, M., Cumps, B.: Two basic types of business-to-business integration. Int. Journal of E-Business Research 1(1), 1–15 (2005)
10. Goodhue, D.L., Wybo, M.D., Kirsch, L.J.: The Impact of Data Integration on the Costs and Benefits of Information Systems. MIS Quarterly 16(3), 293–311 (1992)
11. Gouscos, D., Kalikakis, M., Legal, M., Papadopoulou, S.: A general model of performance and quality for one-stop e-government service offerings. Government Information Quarterly 24(4), 860–885 (2007)

12. Heeks, R., Bailur, S.: Analyzing e-government research: Perspectives, philosophies, theories, methods, and practice. Government Information Quarterly 24(2), 243–265 (2007)
13. Holland, C.P.: Cooperative Supply Chain Management: The Impact of Interorganizational Information Systems. Journal of Strategic Information Systems 4(2), 117–133 (1995)
14. Hong, I.B.: A new framework for interorganizational systems based on the linkage of participants' roles. Information and Management 39(4), 261–270 (2002)
15. Håkansson, H. (ed.): Int. Marketing and Purchasing of Industrial Goods – An Interaction Approach. IMP Project Group. John Wiley & Sons, Chichester (1982)
16. Håkansson, H., Snehota, I.: No business is an island: The network concept of business strategy. Scandinavian Journal of Management 5(3), 187–200 (1989)
17. Håkansson, H., Snehota, I. (eds.): Developing relationships in business networks. Thomson, London (1995)
18. Kumar, K., van Dissel, H.G.: Sustainable Collaboration: Managing Conflict and Cooperation in Interorganizational Systems. MIS Quarterly 20(3), 279–296 (1996)
19. Persson, A., Axelsson, K., Melin, U.: e-Government challenges – Exploring inter-organisational aspects of e-service development. In: Ljungberg, J., Andersson, M. (eds.) Proc. of the 14th European Conference on Information Systems, pp. 1419–1430 (2006)
20. Punia, D.K., Saxena, K.B.C.: Managing inter-organisatinal workflows in e-government. In: Janssen, M., Sol, H.G., Wagenaar, R.W. (eds.) Proc. of the 6th Int. Conference on Electronic Commerce (ICEC), Delft, October 24-26, pp. 500–505 (2004)
21. Robey, D., Im, G., Wareham, J.D.: Theoretical Foundations of Empirical Research on Interorganizational Systems: Assessing Past Contributions and Guiding Future Directions. Journal of the AIS 9(9), 497–518 (2008)
22. Schedler, K., Summermatter, L.: Customer orientation in electronic government: Motives and effects. Government Information Quarterly 24, 291–311 (2007)
23. Scholl, H.J.: What can e-Commerce and e-Government learn from each other? In: Proc. of the 2006 Int. Conference on Digital Government Research, dg.o '06, San Diego, Calif, May 21 - 24, vol. 151, pp. 454–455. ACM, New York (2006)
24. Tambouris, E., Wimmer, M.A.: Online one-stop government: a single point of access to public. In: Huang, W. (ed.) Digital Government: Strategies and Implementations in Developed and Developing Countries, pp. 115–144. Idea Publ (2004)
25. Tranmüller, R., Wimmer, M.A.: E-government at a decisive moment: sketching a roadmap to excellence. In: Traunmüller, R. (ed.) EGOV 2003. LNCS, vol. 2739, pp. 1–14. Springer, Heidelberg (2003)
26. Walsham, G.: Interpretive case studies in IS research: nature and method. European Journal of Information Systems 4(2), 74–81 (1995)
27. Walsham, G.: Doing Interpretive Research. European Journal of Information Systems 15(3), 320–330 (2006)
28. Webster, J.: Networks of Collaboration or Conflict? Electronic Data Interchange and Power in the Supply Chain. Journal of Strategic Information Systems, 31-42 (August 1995)
29. Yang, J., Papazoglou, M.: Interoperation support for electronic business. Communications of the ACM 43(6), 39–49 (2000)

Information Strategies for Open Government: Challenges and Prospects for Deriving Public Value from Government Transparency

Sharon S. Dawes and Natalie Helbig

Center for Technology in Government
University at Albany/SUNY
{Sdawes,nhelbig}@ctg.albany.edu

Abstract. Information-based strategies to promote open government offer many opportunities to generate social and economic value through public use of government information. Public and political expectations for the success of these strategies are high but they confront the challenges of making government data "fit for use" by a variety of users outside the government. Research findings from a study of public use of land records demonstrates the inherent complexity of public use of government information, while research from information science, management information systems, and e-government offer perspectives on key factors associated with effective information use. The paper concludes with practical recommendations for information-based open government strategies as well as areas for future research.

Keywords: Government Information Strategies, Open Government, Transparency, Public Value.

1 Introduction

In 2009, the Obama Administration outlined a set of open government principles for the US government that encompass three fundamental goals: collaboration, participation, and transparency. This paper examines public access to government information as a strategy for achieving transparency. Transparency initiatives generally serve one of two goals. The first is to provide citizens and other stakeholders with a "window" into what government is doing and how it works in order to hold elected officials and public agencies accountable for their decisions and actions. The second goal is to release government data to the public so that taxpayer-supported information can be used to generate social and economic value.

In order to achieve this second transparency goal, the 2009 Open Government Directive (OGD) [11] requires all federal government agencies to post previously internal electronic datasets on a publicly available web site, Data.gov. In addition, the OGD requires all federal government agencies to create an agency-specific Open Government Plan and to make it available to the public over the World Wide Web. These plans make an agency's mission, activities, and results more visible and understandable to the public. They provide important context and metadata through reports, service summaries, links to major programs, and downloadable datasets.

M.A. Wimmer et al. (Eds.): EGOV 2010, LNCS 6228, pp. 50–60, 2010.
© IFIP International Federation for Information Processing 2010

Recovery.gov is a companion initiative created to track the spending associated with the $787 billion American Reinvestment and Recovery Act. Recovery.gov is the first effort of its kind to collect information about spending and performance across a variety of different program areas and from multiple levels of government, as well as from non-profit and business organizations that receive federal funds.

All of these information-based strategies also incorporate Web 2.0 tools to facilitate online public dialogs to solicit feedback, questions, and recommendations for improvements. Taken together, these initiatives do more than open government data to public scrutiny; they also actively encourage businesses, civic organizations, and individuals to use government information for their own purposes. These uses especially foster the second goal associated with opening government information – to enable and encourage information-rich applications outside the government that generate economic and social value.

The success of these transparency strategies rests heavily on easy access to public information resources. Public information resources are defined as the data, information content, systems, and information services that emanate from the day-to-day administration of government programs [7]. Generally, the use of public information resources extends well beyond the government itself to include a very diverse multi-stakeholder society. These stakeholders represent loosely connected communities of interest, where the object of concern is the information in government systems, not the systems themselves or the technologies that comprise them. The societal value of these public information resources is derived primarily from unpredicted and flexible uses of the data content by all stakeholders [3].

Data.gov and similar initiatives offer public access to information resources that are distributed among different government organizations, locations, or custodians. Data.gov provides electronic access to raw, machine-readable information about government finances, program performance, and decisions. Its goal is to allow people and organizations outside government to find, download, analyze, compare, integrate, and combine these datasets with other information that so that they provide greater value to the public. However, it is important to remember that these datasets are defined and collected in different ways by different programs and organizations. They come from a variety of different systems and processes and represent different time frames and other essential characteristics. Most come from existing information systems that were designed for specific operational purposes. Few were created with public use in mind. Some agencies provide good meta data and other contextual information, others little or none. While quickly getting data out in the open is an important goal of this initiative, the value of the data for any particular use depends on making these characteristics easy for users to find and understand.

While thousands of these datasets are now available and being put to a variety of uses outside the government, a number of valid criticisms have been made in terms of basic usability, weak application of stewardship principles, lack of data feedback and improvement mechanisms, and inadequate metadata [5]. Both the criticisms and the potential benefits of information-based open government strategies are receiving much current attention, but they are not new or unique. Past research on public use of government information resources has much to offer that can help refine, improve, and enhance current efforts.

The remainder of this paper is organized as follows. First, we present the results of a case study about the public use of land records to illustrate and assess the benefits, barriers, and policy choices associated with public access to government information. .Next we discuss the implications of the case findings from the perspectives of information science, management information, and e-government research. We conclude with a discussion of practical recommendations for encouraging value creation and suggest future research directions.

2   Case Study: Use and Value of Land Records and Parcel Data

The following case summarizes an in-depth assessment of the prospects for using a common public information resource, land records, for a variety of public and private purposes [4]. The case holistically examines the challenges that confront information-based strategies to derive social and economic value from government data by looking at the full range of information characteristics and uses by both government and external users. The study was conducted in New York State from September 2004 through February 2005 to assess the uses, users, and value of land records and associated detailed parcel information collected. Parcel information is collected at the municipal (town) level, generally when property is sold or sub-divided, for the primary purpose of maintaining real property ownership laws and tax administration. The data is used for this primary purpose by the town, the county of which it is a part, and by the state government. The most detailed information on all properties is maintained at the town level, a subset of data about each property is reported every year to the county level, and a smaller set is reported annually by the counties to the state The same data also has great utility for many secondary uses. These secondary uses represent the latent economic and social value of the data, beyond the value of its primary use in tax administration. The purpose of the study was to reveal this latent value, identify barriers to its realization, and make recommendations for policies and practices that would encourage its development.

The study data consist of 35 interviews plus official publications and web sites prepared by federal, state, local, nonprofit, and private sector organizations. Interviewees were selected from five demographically, operationally, and geographically diverse counties in New York State to provide an understanding of the range of logical, purposive flows of data from original data collectors to other organizations and users. The study began with the Real Property Tax Official in each County who was asked to suggest people to be interviewed who use or otherwise interact with that county's parcel data. State agencies that collect and use parcel-level data as a major part of their responsibilities were also interviewed. Tape-recorded face-to-face or telephone interviews covered the following topics from the perspective of the organization represented by each interviewee: organizational mission and programs; collection, dissemination, access, and uses of parcel data; value of parcel data to the organization; data management, preservation, and sharing methods; data forms and formats, data flow among organizations; and associated costs; issues and barriers. The data were analyzed using qualitative methods to identify similarities and differences among users and uses of this information, to identify barriers to value creation, and to map the flow of data among the organizations that produce the data and those that access and use it for secondary purposes.

2.1 Definitions, Uses, and Value of Parcel Data

The study began with an attempt to find a common definition of parcel data, however the interviews showed that different users apply quite different definitions. Interviewees usually defined "parcel data" by describing how they use it to support their work. For example, planning departments said that parcel data encompasses the parcel identification number, zoning codes, actual uses, boundaries, and physical characteristics. By contrast, real property tax administration officials referred to parcel data as parcel identification and location, information about structures, the parcel owner, and the assessed value. Taken as a whole, parcel characteristics identified by the interviewees fell into eight categories. identification, location, ownership, occupancy and use, structures and improvements, taxation, physical geography, infrastructure, and taxation. Each category comprises a set of detailed attributes. For example, the category "location" includes 'parcel address', which can be descriptive (i.e., 123 Main Street) or spatial data (i.e., a set of coordinates), or both; ownership attributes identify the owner and historical information about ownership.

Public, private, and non-profit organizations, as well as individuals use parcel data for diverse purposes. Although each use is different, all rely in some substantial way on the core parcel data collected at the municipal level. The following highlights illustrate this broad range of primary and secondary uses, each of which delivers a form of economic or social value to the state or community.

Real property assessment and taxation. Parcel data is the foundation for real property tax administration, which is the primary use of this data. Municipal assessors collect specific data elements to establish fair market value for every property. County real property offices use this data to create countywide tax maps and assessment rolls. The state real property agency uses the data to create final tax rolls and equalization rates that place local tax calculations against a statewide standard.

Buying and selling private land. Private land sales occur daily in every locale. Some are single transactions between two parties, while others are more complex and involve multiple individuals and organizations. The most important documentation of a land sale is establishing and recording the ownership rights to a parcel.

Directing emergency response. Emergency response centers use parcel data for almost every incident including attribute categories such as identification, location, and structural and improvement data.. This information helps with emergency routing, can instruct personnel on how to enter a property safely. and identify who should be notified to turn off utilities like gas or water.

Transportation routing. State and local roadways change frequently, affecting several different sectors. Parcel identification, location, and ownership information is used to handle routing of oversized truckloads to avoid low bridges and limited access highways, create and update bus routes for school districts, and determine priority routes for snowplows. Utility companies use parcel data to coordinate maintenance fleets using infrastructure data, structures and improvements, and parcel location data.

Facilities siting. Municipalities use location information to plan for growth and to increase their ability to attract businesses and jobs. Companies wishing to establish or relocate often have very specific site requirements. Using GIS capabilities and parcel identification, ownership, infrastructure, and physical geography data, localities can provide options that help them compete for these businesses.

Planning and prioritizing environmental initiatives. Environmental restoration of old industrial sites, brown fields, or wetlands are a major economic focus for local governments. For these projects, local priorities must be combined with data about parcel identification, location, physical geography, occupancy and use, and surrounding infrastructure, often in the context of a GIS system.

Infrastructure management. Infrastructure, parcel identification, ownership, location, occupancy and use data, as well as structures and improvements data are all used to plan rights of way, and changes, improvements, or additions to utilities such as electricity and water supply.

2.2 Stakeholders and Their Interests

The study identified a wide range of individuals and public, private, and non-profit organizations that use parcel data. The main stakeholder groups include:

- Assessors – municipal (city or town) officials who collect parcel data.
- County Real Property Tax Services (RPTS) – the hub for real property tax administration at the local level of government.
- State Office of Real Property Tax Services (ORPS) – the state-level office designated to guide tax administration and pursue statewide tax equity
- Other Local Agencies – such as planning departments, emergency response services, public health agencies, and water authorities.
- Other State Agencies – government organizations such as transportation, homeland security, environmental protection, and health and human services.
- Data Re-sellers – private companies that add value to public data and sell it to other entities such as insurance companies, real estate brokers, or consultants.
- Private Sector Users – such as realtors, utility companies, and engineering firms.
- Non Governmental Agencies and Community Groups – provide services such as environmental planning and economic development and civil society organizations such as those that serve senior citizens.
- Property Owners and Occupants – those who own and pay taxes on parcels and people or businesses who live or work on a parcel they may or may not own.

Every interviewee represented an organization that used parcel data to perform particular functions. Each organization's intended use determined the specific data attributes needed. For instance, an emergency response organization must have accurate and up-to-date occupancy and structure information in order to know the number of individuals living on a property and the location and placement of a building; but it may not need to know who owns the parcel or the details of the tax history. Alternatively, an environmental protection organization may need detailed location and physical geography data for a specific region but may not need parcel identification numbers or the sales data. However, the interests of these groups coincided with respect to their mutual desire for accuracy, timeliness, and consistency of parcel information as well as strong consensus among most secondary users for easy one-stop access to authoritative data sources in a variety of formats.. Table 1 shows both the areas of common agreement and the areas of divergence among these key stakeholder groups.

As the table shows, all stakeholder groups have a strong interest in high quality data, which they generally characterized as data that is factually accurate, up-to-date, and consistent from time to time and place to place. These general agreements, however, masked a great deal of variation. The interviews demonstrated that accuracy, timeliness, and consistency were important to everyone, but at different levels and for different reasons. For example, an engineering firm planning a residential subdivision may define "accurate" as highly detailed survey-quality information. By contrast, a town attempting to designate a rough boundary for a new municipal park would say an area bounded by certain streets is "accurate" for this purpose.

Table 1. Agreement and divergence among stakeholder interests

Stakeholders		Interests						
	Type of user	Consistency	Accuracy	Timeliness	Low or no cost retrieval	Online access	Choice of format	One authoritative source
Assessors	primary	X	X	X	X			
County RPTS	primary	X	X	X				
State ORPS	primary	X	X	X	X	X		
Other Local Agencies	secondary	X	X	X	X	X	X	X
Other State Agencies	secondary	X	X	X	X	X	X	X
Data Resellers	secondary	X	X	X		X	X	
Private Sector Users	secondary	X	X	X	X	X	X	X
NGOs & Community Groups	secondary	X	X	X	X	X	X	X
Property Owners & Occupants	secondary	X	X	X	X	X	X	X

Most secondary users also strongly preferred that parcel data be available in electronic form, online, from one authoritative or trusted source, and in a variety of formats which they can select from to meet their particular needs. These features add convenience, flexibility, and efficiency to information search, access, and use. They also add confidence that the data is authentic and well-documented so it can be used in appropriate ways. However, these interests are typically less important or not shared by the primary users, the same organizations that collect the basic data – assessors and county and state real property tax offices – because their needs are met by their own internal activities, organized in a way that supports their main missions.

2.3   Issues Associated with Public Access to and Use of Parcel Data

Almost every person interviewed expressed a desire for better quality data. Most users spent considerable resources obtaining, improving, and standardizing parcel data before they were able to use it for their own needs. Much of this cost is associated with a need to supplement, verify, correct, or integrate basic data collected by others. Even when the data they begin with is of high quality, however, it may not be sufficiently detailed or readily comparable with other sources, or derived from systems that are technically compatible.

Interviewees also mentioned incompatible technologies used by different counties as a barrier to more effective data use. For example, not all parcel maps use the same mapping projection, which is a mathematical model for converting locations on the earth's surface in a way that allows flat maps to depict three dimensional features. Although some technologies convert files originating from different mapping projections easily, there are still others that do not preserve the integrity of shape, or the accuracy of area, distance, or direction. To the extent that comparable data cannot be compiled for the whole state or for regions larger than towns or counties, potential value from data use by both government and private users is diminished or lost.

Data management issues were also prominent. Data management associated with the primary purpose of real property tax functions works in a relatively standard way all over the state. However, data management outside of tax functions varies widely and the typical arrangement is best described as ad hoc. Users of parcel data often make many individual data requests to different data sources. A few local governments have data management strategies in place that address the needs of external users, but in most places requests are handled on a one-by-one basis. At the same time almost no feedback mechanisms exist between data users and data collectors, so that the investments that users make in data improvements are not fed back into improvements in the original data sources. There is a notable absence of update and feedback mechanisms in the typical data flow which nearly always goes in only one direction – from the data source to a requester. Many users who obtain data from municipal, county, and state sources often find and correct errors as they use it, but these users are neither expected nor allowed to return data corrections, enhancements, or other improvements to the data sources. Consequently one clear overall benefit of use, data improvement for everyone, is never realized. Instead, when users obtain periodic updates from their data sources, they can actually make the situation worse because the data they have improved for their own use could be overwritten by some of the same old errors that still exist in the source files. Their difficult choice is then to forgo the updates in order to keep their own corrections, lose some of their corrections in order to obtain updated files for other records, or engage in very costly and time consuming matching and integration processes .

3 Discussion

The current emphasis on opening US government information to the public plus the evolving capability of technological tools for doing so, offer many opportunities to satisfy the value-creation goal of greater government transparency. Public and political expectations for the success of information-based open government strategies are high but as the case above illustrates, significant challenges remain for making government data suitable for uses that generate social and economic value. The parcel data case reveals the complexities of these initiatives by taking a comprehensive view of a single data resource and all of its primary and secondary uses and users. Multiply the findings in the case by thousands of data sets, and the magnitude of the challenge embodied in initiatives like Data.gov becomes more visible. Policies, governance mechanisms, data management protocols, data and technology standards, and a variety of skills and capabilities both inside and outside government are needed if these information-based initiatives are to succeed in creating social and economic value beyond the government itself.

These issues have been explored in the research literature at least since the 1990s. This body of work (which comes from research in informatics, management information systems, and public management), offers a set of considerations and guidelines that can help these newer initiatives achieve better results. .

First, while clearly *more* information is being made available in recent efforts such as Data.gov, the case study above amply demonstrates that the problems of diverse user needs and capabilities [6, 14], the limitations of internally-oriented data management techniques [2, 9,], untested assumptions about information content and accuracy [1, 13], and issues associated with information quality and fitness for use [14]. All of these remain barriers to value creation.

Within mainstream public administration research, the impacts of information and knowledge have received relatively little attention [8] particularly when considering the salience of information for open government. However, research findings from other fields indicate that information-based initiatives are fraught with challenges. Political science, information science, and digital government research all shed some light particularly in the areas of information quality, system design, management, and information sharing. This body of work has shown that high-quality data should be not only intrinsically good, but also contextually appropriate for the task, clearly represented, and accessible to users. In other words, it needs to be "fit for use" [15]. The same information may be fit for some uses, but completely inappropriate for others that have different temporal, security, granularity, or other requirements. Users may need to make choices or trade-offs among these characteristics [1, 12], but they need good data descriptions to help them decide. In order for users to assess data quality, they need to understand the nature of the data and because data producers cannot anticipate all users and uses, the provision of good quality metadata is as important as the quality of the data itself [6]. Moreover, e-government interoperability and information integration research demonstrates high sensitivity to the nature of information and quality factors such as comprehensiveness, authoritativeness, trustworthiness, and perceived value as determined by the information seeker [9].

Research on performance measurement, shows how unrealistic assumptions and popular rhetoric about the nature of information can mask the difficulties inherent in information-based strategies for open government. These assumptions include the commonly-stated beliefs that more information leads to better governance and that information is objective, neutral, and readily available [13]. From a political science perspective, Meijer (2009), for example, asserts that computer-mediated transparency has several characteristics that can actually threaten public trust such as its uni-directionality (i.e., it is not interactive), decontextualization (i.e., it is removed from shared social experience), and its overly structured form (i.e., it is predominately quantitative).

Likewise, research on making government data available to public users has identified the need to understand the processes that produce the data and the development of new skills and services to support data users. Research on designing public access programs pulls together many of these findings into a complex, multi-dimensional framework of information access considerations [6]. All of the foregoing research is useful in understanding the nature of public information resources and the challenges of making them available for use outside the government. The case study above goes a step deeper by tracing the path of a specific information resource, land records and associated parcel data, from initial data collection, to its primary use in tax administration, to a wide variety of secondary public and private uses by many external stakeholders. As such, it gives us a picture of the issues associated with the nature, use, and value of the government information over time and from multiple perspectives.

4 Practical Recommendations and Future Research

Some of the challenges of information-based open government strategies, can be understood as technical problems addressing information storage, access, inquiry, and display. Another way to understand the challenges are as management problems such as defining the rationale and internal processes of data collection, analysis, management, preservation, and access. The challenges also represent policy problems including examining the balance and priority of internal government needs versus the needs of secondary users, the resources allocated to serve both kinds of uses, and the criteria for assessing their effectiveness and public value [5]. Consequently if open access to government data is to generate its potential value for society, then government information policies and practices need to be better aligned with the needs of secondary users.

For most government agencies, providing information for public use is an extra responsibility that may compete for resources with the demands of mission-focused operations. As our case study illustrated, vast amounts of useful information are contained in government data systems, but the systems themselves are seldom designed for use beyond the collecting agency's own needs. With few exceptions, making data holdings available to the public in a meaningful and useable way is a new responsibility of government agencies that will need thoughtful investments in skills, tools, and policies, as well as some changes in processes and practices. One needed practice improvement is the creation of formal feedback mechanisms that connect data users to data sources. Feedback from users could lead to ongoing data improvement as users discover and correct errors in the data. By providing the opportunity and a formal mechanism to communicate data errors and enhancements back to the data sources, improvements in the overall quality and integrity of the data can benefit all future users, including the government itself..

Within government organizations, professionals will need to develop several kinds of skills to support public information access and use. Technical skills for information management, display, and integration need to be augmented by communication skills that serve the needs of a wide user community. New roles may need needed as well to coordinate agency-level and government-wide programs of information dissemination and user support services.

Thinking about government information as a public resource reveals not only its potential public value, but also its vast complexity. Understanding the public value proposition of information-based transparency strategies requires us to look at them from multiple perspectives. The government's own perspective brings into focus information stewardship and management considerations that assure good quality data and metadata that is accessible and usable by people with different intensions and different capabilities [5]. It also encompasses policy considerations, such as giving data access programs appropriate priority for funding and determining how much the government will engage in value-added services itself and how much it will leave to private providers. From a technology perspective, semantic interoperability and data presentation and visualization tools are just two of many topics that need research and which could be studied in the context of research-practice partnerships.

In addition, because the community of information users is clearly not homogeneous, their different needs and capabilities cannot all be served by the same kind of information or the same forms of information [6]. More complete stakeholder analysis could lead to better understanding of users' needs for interfaces, services, and analytical tools. Careful stakeholder analysis and engagement could generate broader appreciation for the many ways different people think about, use, and benefit from government data. Such an appreciation could set the stage for active collaboration and joint investments. This is not to say that every use can be predicted in advance, but that a thorough assessment of the needs and capabilities of a wide variety of users could lead to well-articulated standards for data description and formats, high-quality data, and good data management practices that serve many different needs.

Finally, information-based open government strategies constitute a natural experiment in value creation. Evaluation research could help identify which kinds of information content or formats generate different kinds of value for different communities of interest as well as whether information-based strategies as a whole actually lead to not only economic and social benefits, but also to a stronger democracy.

References

1. Ballou, D., Pazer, H.: Designing Information Systems to Optimize the accuracy-timeliness tradeoff. Information Systems Research 6(1), 51–72 (1995)
2. Ballou, D., Tayi, G.: Enhancing data quality in data warehouse environments. Communications of the ACM 42(1), 73 (1999)
3. Bellamy, C., Taylor, J.: Governing in the information age. Open University Press, Philadelphia (1998)
4. Cook, M., Dawes, S., Helbig, N., Lishnoff, R.: Use of Parcel Data in New York State: A Reconnaissance Study (2005),
   http://www.ctg.albany.edu/publications/reports/
   use_of_parcel_data
5. Dawes, S.: Information policy meta-principles: stewardship and usefulness. In: Proceedings of the 43rd Hawaii International Conference on System Sciences (2010)
6. Dawes, S., Pardo, T.A., Cresswell, A.M.: Designing electronic government information access programs: A holistic approach. Government Information Quarterly 21, 3–23 (2004)

7. Dawes, S., Helbig, N., Cook, M.: Governance of Public Information Resources: Lessons from a field study of land parcel data. Available upon request to the authors (working paper)
8. Dunleavy, P., Margetts, H., Bastow, S., Tinkler, J.: New public management is dead: Long live digital-era governance. Journal of Public Administration Research and Theory 16, 467–494 (2005)
9. Klischewski, R., Scholl, H.J.: Information quality as a common ground for key players in e-government integration and interoperability. Presented at 39th Hawaii International Conference on System Sciences. Big Island, Hawaii (2006)
10. Meijer, A.: Understanding modern transparency. International Review of Administrative Sciences 75, 255–269 (2009)
11. OMB (US Office of Management and Budget), Open Government Directive (2009), `http://www.whitehouse.gov/open/documents/open-government-directive`
12. Pipino, L., Lee, Y., Wang, R.: Data quality assessment. Communications of the ACM 45(4), 211–218 (2002)
13. Radin, B.: Challenging the performance movement: Accountability, complexity, and democratic values. Georgetown University Press, Washington (2006)
14. Wang, R., Strong, D.: Beyond accuracy: What data quality means to data Consumers. Journal of Management Information Systems 12(4), 5–34 (1996)

Defining a Taxonomy for Research Areas on ICT for Governance and Policy Modelling

Fenareti Lampathaki[1], Yannis Charalabidis[2], Spyros Passas[1], David Osimo[3],
Melanie Bicking[4], Maria A. Wimmer[4], and Dimitris Askounis[1]

[1] National Technical University of Athens, 9 Iroon Polytechniou str., 15780 Athens, Greece
{flamp,spassas,askous}@epu.ntua.gr
[2] University of the Aegean, Karlovassi, 83200 Samos, Greece
yannisx@aegean.gr
[3] Tech4i2 ltd., 43B Mill Road, LE7 7JP Thurcaston, Leicestershire, UK
david.osimo@tech4i2.com
[4] University of Koblenz-Landau, Universitätsstr. 1, 56070 Koblenz, Germany
{bicking,wimmer}@uni-koblenz.de

Abstract. As governments across the world provide more and more support to
open data initiatives and web 2.0 channels for engaging citizens, researchers
orient themselves towards future internet, wisdom of crowds and virtual world
experiments. In this context, the domain of ICT for Governance and Policy
Modelling has recently emerged to achieve better, participative, evidence-based
and timely governance. This paper presents a taxonomy classifying the research
themes, the research areas and the research sub-areas that challenge this domain
in order to deal with its diversity and complexity. Taking into account
advancements in research, policy and practice, the taxonomy brings together the
open, linked data and visual analytics philosophy; the social media buzz taming
collective wisdom in decision-making; and the future internet approaches
around cloud computing, internet of things and internet of services, while
embracing the collaborative policy modelling aspects and the safeguarding
against misuse implications.

Keywords: ICT for Governance and Policy Modelling, Taxonomy, Research
Areas, Open Government, Social Computing, Future Internet, Safeguard against
misuse.

1 Introduction

As Governments are committing more effort to understand an increasingly
interdependent and complex world [3], [25], [27], [32], citizens demand more
openness, transparency and commitment to results [8] - within or after the financial
crisis. Moreover, citizens are becoming increasingly vocal in monitoring and
influencing policy decisions, through the new media [31].

Along these ways of evolution, future scenarios in ICT for Governance and Policy
Modelling are promising to reach the target of a better, participative, evidence-based
and timely governance, while taming greater complexity and attracting citizens'

M.A. Wimmer et al. (Eds.): EGOV 2010, LNCS 6228, pp. 61–72, 2010.

involvement. ICT for Governance and Policy Modelling has emerged as an umbrella term for a number of technologies that can be applied in order to achieve the common goal of improving public decision-making in the age of complexity. They aim at making the policy-making cycle more effective and more intelligent, and at accelerating the learning path embedded in the policy cycle. However, this is often characterized as a very diverse, not yet consolidated domain, since:

- It is highly multidisciplinary, involving disciplines such as: information systems, engineering, mathematics, statistics, economics, sociology, design and user interface, political science [20].
- It brings together different cultural approaches to research and development: innovation in the field of policy modelling, forecasting and simulation is theory-led and academic, while the fields of mass collaboration, participation and visualization are more practice-based and user-driven.

In recent years we have assisted to a flourishing of ICT tools to support governments in designing policies [10]. However, such tools are not often adopted successfully, also due to fragmentation between academic fields, application areas and approaches to innovation.

In this context, this paper presents a taxonomy of the research areas related to the domain of ICT for Governance and Policy Modelling. It was created in the context of the CROSSROAD project [15], a Support Action funded by the European Commission in order to deliver a Research Roadmap on ICT for Governance and Policy Modelling. In alignment with its definition as the practice and science of classification, the proposed taxonomy aims to clarify the research areas of interest, deal with their complexity, structure any state of the art analysis attempt in the domain in a more formalized way and guide the future research activities in the years to come. The taxonomy proposed builds on relevant work undertaken in the context of electronic government, such as the eGovRTD2020 [13] or eGovernance in general [17], [29], and other related fields research reports, i.e. the Enterprise Interoperability Research Roadmap [9] and generally the Future of the Internet [16], [18], [19].

The structure of this paper is as follows: Section 2 outlines the methodology followed during the design of the proposed taxonomy. Section 3 gives an overview of the Research Areas Taxonomy extended over three levels and containing more than 100 nodes. Section 4 finally presents the conclusions and future steps towards expansion and sustainability of the taxonomy by the broader research community.

2 Methodology

The overall vision that leads the definition of the Research Areas Taxonomy can be summarized as: "*Forward-looking, innovative research topics and themes emerging from various disciplines, sciences and practices, independently of their existing relation to ICT for Governance & Policy Modelling with a view to present and future needs will be included and investigated in the proposed Research Areas Taxonomy.*"

In order to avoid ambiguity, contradiction and omission and reach consensus among the community, the methodology for building the proposed Research Areas Taxonomy includes the following steps:

1. Definition of a common taxonomy glossary in order to ensure common understanding of key terms:

   - ICT for Governance and Policy Modelling (FP7 2009-2010 Objective 7.3) is defined as the *Research Domain*.
   - The first level of the taxonomy can be also referred to as *Research Theme*, i.e. a broad thematic category, containing a number of research areas (at lower levels), which describes a set of approaches and actions that could be undertaken to advance the theme ICT for Governance and Policy Modelling
   - The second level of the taxonomy is defined as core *Research Area*, compromising of similar and in many cases competitive technologies, tools or methodologies that look into progress in a specific Research Theme
   - The third level of the taxonomy includes *Research Sub-Areas* including technologies, tools or methodologies which target at the same Research Area, yet cannot be directly compared

2. Outlining a set of baseline guidelines and rules that will guide the design of the Taxonomy:

   - The levels in which the taxonomy extends for the CROSSROAD purposes are 3 with each level including from three to seven sub-levels.
   - Each Research Theme (Level 1) is bound to the Research Areas (Level 2) with a 1:N relationship, while the Research Areas (Level 2) are correlated with Research Sub-areas (Level 3) in a M:N relationship. Research Sub-areas (Level 3) can also be M:N related to other Research Sub-areas.

Table 1. Baseline Rules for the design of the Taxonomy

Metrics	Res. Theme	Res. Area	Res. Sub-area
Number of Sub-levels	3-7	3-7	-
Number of Results in academic bibliography search engines	At least 200	At least 100	-
Number of Papers with at least 10 citations	At least 10	At least 5	-
Number of Papers in the last 2 years	At least 20	At least 10	-
Number of Papers mentioning the term and recognizing its importance	At least 10	At least 5	-
Number of Research Roadmaps recognizing its importance	At least 1	-	-
Existence of the exact term in Wikipedia and other online dictionaries	At least 1	At least 1	-
Number of references in a Strategic Document which is available in English at EU and national level in the last 2 years	-	At least 1	-
Number of Good Practices across the world in the last 2 years	-	At least 3	-
Number of papers mentioning its existence under the parent Research Area			At Least 5
No implications to vertical application domains			True

3. *Definition of the Research Themes (1ˢᵗ Level) and the Research Areas (2ⁿᵈ Level) of the Taxonomy* based on the guidelines of the ICT FP7 Work Programme 2009-2010 and on a preliminary analysis of the conferences and journals related to ICT for Governance and Policy Modelling [30]:

- Conferences, i.e. EGOV, HICCS eGovernment Track, ePart, dg.o, AMCIS eGovernment Track and ICEGOV
- Journals, such as Elsevier Government Information Quarterly (GIQ), Inderscience Electronic Government: An International Journal, ACI Electronic Journal of e-Government, IOS Press Information Policy, IGI International Journal of Electronic Government Research, Taylor & Francis Journal of Information Technology and Politics, Emerald Transforming Government: Process, People and Policy

4. *Iterative definitions, discussions and updates of the Research Areas (2ⁿᵈ Level) and mainly the Research Sub-areas (3ʳᵈ Level)* of the Taxonomy based on the information and material collected. It needs to be noted that during the state of the art analysis of the bibliography retrieved, the CROSSROAD Research Areas Taxonomy were continually revisited at the second and third level in order to ensure, on the one hand, its alignment with the research domain and, on the other hand, its completeness and soundness.

Generally, the potential sources of information for the taxonomy constitute a mixture of the research, policy, practice and market aspects. Apart from traditional search engines (Google, Bing, etc.) and academic literature databases (Scopus, ISI Web of Knowledge, Elsevier, SpringerLink, IEEE, Google Scholar, etc.) for searching information, social media such as blogs, Twitter hashtags and delicious bookmarks tags were investigated in order to collect the necessary supportive material spanning: Research papers and thesis; Relevant academic Literature and Books; Relevant Project Deliverables as retrieved from the project websites. Particular emphasis has been given to the recent FP7 projects [16], since the results of most FP6 projects have already been underpinned by FP7 projects; Government Initiatives and Strategies; Directives from the European Union; Policy-making initiatives at pan-European, national and international level, such as i2010, IDABC, ISA; Cases and publications in information gathering portals, such as ePractice; Experts' Positions as expressed in white papers and / or blogs; Industry visions and reports, such as the Gartner hypecycle; Outcomes of forecasting models or other roadmapping projects.

3 CROSSROAD Research Areas Taxonomy

Based on aforementioned methodological approach, CROSSROAD developed the Research Areas Taxonomy to classify the broader domain of ICT for Governance and Policy Modelling into 5 Research Themes, 17 Research Areas and more than 80 Research Sub-areas, as depicted in the following figure.

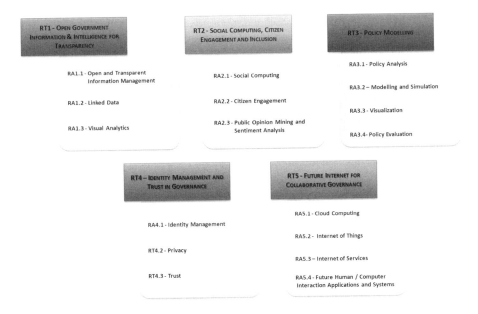

Fig. 1. CROSSROAD Research Areas Taxonomy

3.1 Open Government Information and Intelligence for Transparency

In contrast to the past focus of "making services available online", the current strategic direction in Electronic Governance appears to be transparency and "making public data available for reuse" [24]. In this context, Open Government Information and Intelligence aims at making the long quest for transparency a reality by: Opening up data for public consumption and exploitation; Linking data in advanced applications that allow citizens to browse across datasets and mash-ups; and Visual analyzing and reasoning over public data and facts since government can no longer hide behind analysis and charts they themselves provide due to the combination of open data and visualization tools. Table 2 shows an extract of the research areas and sub-areas of the research theme Open Government Information and Intelligence for Transparency.

Open Data is a philosophy and practice requiring that certain data are freely available to everyone, without restrictions from copyright, patents or other mechanisms of control. The Open Government Working Group [28] has defined a set of fundamental principles for open government data: Data Must Be Complete, Data Must Be Primary, Data Must Be Timely, Data Must Be Accessible, Data Must Be Machine processable, Access Must Be Non-Discriminatory, Data Formats Must Be Non-Proprietary, Data Must Be License-free.

Linked Data, a term coined by Tim Berners-Lee in his Linked Data Web architecture note [4], is about using the Web to connect related data that wasn't previously linked, or using the Web to lower the barriers to linking data currently linked using other methods. The basic assumption behind Linked Data is that the value and usefulness of data increases the more it is interlinked with other data, with the ultimate goal to enable people to share structured data on the Web as easily as they can share documents today[6].

Taking into account that today, data is created and published at an incredible rate and the ability to collect and store the data is increasing at a faster rate than the ability to analyze it, Visual Analytics is characterized as an emerging area of research and practice that aims at integrating the outstanding capabilities of humans in terms of visual information exploration and the enormous processing power of computers to form a powerful knowledge discovery environment [1], allowing them to make well-informed decisions in complex situations [22].

Table 2. Open Government Information and Intelligence Taxonomy Extract

Research Area	Res. Sub-area
1.1 Open and Transparent Information Management	1.1.1 Open Data Publication
	1.1.2 Web Dissemination and Promotion
	1.1.3 Open Data Quality Agreements
	1.1.4 Open Data Communities Building
	1.1.5 Transparency and Reputation Management
	1.1.6 Open Data Legal Implications and Licenses
1.2 Linked Data Management	1.2.1 Capturing and Sharing Linked Data
	1.2.2 Querying and Analyzing Governmental Linked Data
	1.2.3 Browsing and Searching Linked Data
	1.2.4 Government Data Fusion and Mash-ups
	1.2.5 Linked Data Provenance and Evolution
	1.2.6 User Interaction and Linked Data Usability
	1.2.7 Linked Data Quality Assurance
1.3 Visual Analytics	1.3.1 Visual Information Foraging and Design
	1.3.2 Information Visualization and Interaction
	1.3.3 Analytical Reasoning
	1.3.4 Collaborative Analysis and Intelligence
	1.3.5 Visualization Evaluation

3.2 Social Computing, Citizen Engagement and Inclusion

Today, as citizens become more and more engaged in Social Media and vocal in raising their opinion as User Generated Content in the web [31], governments need to look into the following research areas: Social Computing, Citizen Engagement and Public Opinion Mining and Sentiment Analysis as analyzed in Table 3.

Social Computing in the Public Sector is defined as a social structure in which technology puts power in communities, not institutions [11], as well as a set of open, web-based and user-friendly applications that enable users to network, share data, collaborate and co-produce content [2]. Three tenets actually define social computing: 1) innovation will shift from top-down to bottom-up; 2) value will shift from ownership to experience; and 3) power will shift from institutions to communities.

Citizen Engagement is often referred to as eParticipation or eDemocracy. However, a distinction needs to be made among these two terms and the broader concept of citizen engagement and the emerging Wisdom of Crowds, as eParticipation is "the use of information and communication technologies to broaden and deepen political participation by enabling citizens to connect with one another and with their elected representatives" [23].

Finally, Public Opinion Mining and Sentiment Analysis can be defined as a sub-discipline of computational linguistics [5] that focuses on extracting people's opinion from the web. Given a piece of text, opinion-mining systems analyze: Which part is expressing an opinion; Who wrote the opinion; and What is being commented. Sentiment analysis, on the other hand, is about determining the subjectivity, polarity (positive or negative) and polarity strength (weakly positive, mildly positive, strongly positive, etc.) of a piece of text -in other words: What is the opinion of the writer [26].

Table 3. Social Networks, Citizen Engagement and Inclusion Taxonomy Extract

Research Area	Res. Sub-area
2.1 Social Computing in the Public Sector	2.1.1 Social Networking
	2.1.2 Content Syndication in Government Portals
	2.1.3 Collaborative Writing Tools
	2.1.4 Feedback, Rating and Reputation Systems
	2.1.5 Social Network Analysis
2.2 Citizen Engagement	2.2.1 Deliberation
	2.2.2 Consultation
	2.2.3 Argumentation Support
	2.2.4 Polling and Voting
	2.2.5 Petition
2.3 Public Opinion Mining and Sentiment Analysis	2.3.1 Opinion Tracking
	2.3.2 Multi-lingual and Multi-Cultural Opinion Extraction and Filtering
	2.3.3 Real-time Opinion Visualization
	2.3.4 Collective Wisdom Analysis and Exploitation

3.3 Policy Modelling

Policy Modelling aims at including all the necessary pieces required during policy making procedures, such as policy analysis, modelling, simulation, visualisation and evaluation (see e.g.[20]). In this context, this research theme aims at establishing a concrete set of methodologies, which will allow the creation of fair, transparent, well structured and benefit-optimized policies indicatively by:

- Analysing the policy landscape of the present and the past and setting the targets for the future.
- Modelling policies and the various environmental factors in a commonly agreed manner depending on each issue.
- Simulating the policies under discussion for gaining direct feedback from artificial, yet realistic test beds and evaluation in an ex-ante manner the possible options.

- Visualising the various policies, their impacts and their underlying information (from general policy directions to discussion arguments on those) towards increased citizen participation and increased and faster comprehension of complex problems.

Table 4 shows an extract of the research areas and sub-areas of this research theme.

Table 4. Policy Modelling Taxonomy Extract

Research Area	Res. Sub-area
3.1 Policy Analysis	3.1.1 Forecasting
	3.1.2 Foresight
	3.1.3 Back-casting
	3.1.4 Now-casting
3.2 Modelling and Simulation	3.2.1 Multi-level and micro-simulation models
	3.2.2 System Dynamics
	3.2.3 Discrete Event Models
	3.2.4 Multi-agent Systems
	3.2.5 Mental Modelling
	3.2.6 Participatory Modelling and Reasoning
	3.2.7 Models Integration
3.3 Visualization	3.3.1 Virtual Worlds
	3.3.2 Mixed Reality
	3.3.3 Serious Gaming
	3.3.4 Argument Visualization
	3.3.5 Narrative Production
	3.3.6 Legal Corpora Visualization
3.4 Policy Evaluation	3.4.1 Models Quality Validation and Evaluation
	3.4.2 Impact Assessment
	3.4.3 Policy Monitoring

3.4   Identity Management and Trust in Governance

While "Anywhere anytime" computing systems and devices retrieve, validate, process and store personal and business information, identity management, privacy and trust aspects gain more and more momentum within Governance in order to safeguard citizens and public authorities data from misuse. In particular, the Research Theme "Identity Management and Trust in Governance" consists of the following research areas: Identity Management (IDM), Privacy and Trust as depicted in Table 5.

Identity Management (IDM) is the set of processes, and a supporting infrastructure for the creation, maintenance, and use of digital identities. Identity management is an ongoing and evolving strategy that leverages technology to automate and unify existing practices, and provide a consistent service-oriented architecture for applications to access user information securely.

Privacy is the ability of a citizen or a group of citizens to efficiently control the information they make public within a community and to seclude sensitive related personal information. Finally, Trust between two or more collaborating partners, such as citizens and public organizations, is founded on the presence of a robust and efficient legal and statutory framework.

Table 5. Identity Management and Trust in Governance Taxonomy Extract

Research Area	Res. Sub-area
4.1 Identity Management	4.1.1 Federated Identity Management Systems
	4.1.2 Next Generation Access Control and Authentication
	4.1.3 Legal and Social Aspects of eIdentity Management
	4.1.4 Mobility and Identity
	4.1.5 Identity Interoperability
	4.1.6 Forensic Implications of Identity Management Systems
4.2 Privacy	4.2.1 Privacy and Data Protection
	4.2.2 Privacy Enhancing Technologies
	4.2.3 Citizen Profiling
	4.2.4 Privacy Law and Regulations
4.3 Trust	4.3.1 Legal Informatics
	4.3.2 Digital Rights Management
	4.3.3 Digital Living and Citizenship
	4.3.4 Intellectual Property in the digital era
	4.3.5 Trust Services

3.5 Future Internet for Collaborative Governance

Internet is believed to radically change in the next decade and is foreseen as a seamless fabric of connectivity integrating all the different Internet entities – devices, sensors, services, things and people [18]. Future Internet is expected to provide the tools and methods towards an environment of high trust and increased Participation, which in turn are fundamental requirements in order to succeed in a "Co-production of Government". Future Internet is thereby understood in terms of Cloud Computing, Internet of Things, Internet of Services, and Future Human / Computer Interaction Applications and Systems, as depicted in Table 6.

According to [7], a Cloud is a type of parallel and distributed system consisting of a collection of inter-connected and virtualized computers that are dynamically provisioned and presented as one or more unified computing resource(s) based on service-level agreements established through negotiation between the service provider and the consumers. Cloud computing holds a number of advantages for the government, including "reduced cost, increased storage, higher levels of automation, increased flexibility, and higher levels of employee mobility." [12].

Internet of Things (IoT) is also an integrated part of Future Internet and is defined by the EC as: "A dynamic global network infrastructure with self configuring capabilities based on standard and interoperable communication protocols where physical and virtual "things" have identities, physical attributes, and virtual personalities and use intelligent interfaces, and are seamlessly integrated into the information network [19]."

Internet of Services is defined as "... a vision of the Internet of the Future, where organizations and individuals can find software as services on the Internet, combine them, and easily adapt them to their specific context. Users should be able to use software services that do exactly what they need" according to the Software & Service Architectures and Infrastructures initiative [14].

Finally, Human–computer interaction (HCI) is the study of interaction between people (users) and computers. Interaction between users and computers occurs at the user interface, which includes both software and hardware[1]. Future HCI applications and systems in the context of eGovernment portals aim to significantly enhance the interaction with the citizen in terms of usability, learnability and user satisfaction.

Table 6. Future Internet for Collaborative Governance Taxonomy Extract

Research Area	Res. Sub-area
5.1 Cloud Computing	5.1.1 Cloud Service Level Requirements
	5.1.2 Business Models in the Cloud
	5.1.3 Cloud Interoperability
	5.1.4 Security and Authentication in the Cloud
	5.1.5 Data Confidentiality and Auditability
	5.1.6 Regulatory Compliance
5.2 Internet of Things	5.2.1 Communication systems and network architectures
	5.2.2 Device Interoperability Assessment
	5.2.3 Distributed Intelligence
	5.2.4 Standardization
	5.2.5 Business Models for Pervasive Technologies
	5.2.6 Social Impacts and Risks
5.3 Internet of Services	5.3.1 Multi-channel access and delivery management
	5.3.2 Multiple channels coordination and aggregation
	5.3.3 Security and privacy issues on multi-channel service delivery
	5.3.4 Public Service Design and Engineering
	5.3.5 Public Service Aggregations, Mash-ups and Orchestration
	5.3.6 Public Service Level Agreements
5.4 Future Human / Computer Interaction Applications and Systems	5.4.1 Web accessibility
	5.4.2 Future human – computer interaction web interfaces /devices
	5.4.3 Engineering Psychology and Cognitive Ergonomics
	5.4.4 Human-Centered Design
	5.4.5 Augmented cognition
	5.4.6 Digital Human Modeling

4   Conclusions

In an effort to effectively clarify and classify the domain of ICT for Governance and Policy Modelling, the paper presented a taxonomy consisting of research themes, research areas and research sub-areas. Taking into account advancements in research, policy and practice, the taxonomy brings together the open, linked data and visual analytics philosophy (RT.1: Open Government Information & Intelligence for Transparency), the social media buzz taming collective wisdom in decision-making (RT.2: Social Computing, Citizen Engagement and Inclusion) and the future internet approaches (RT.5: Future Internet for Collaborative Governance) around cloud computing, internet of things and internet of services. It also analyzes the collaborative policy modelling aspects (RT.3: Policy Modelling) and the safeguarding against misuse implications (RT.4: Identity Management and Trust in Governance). Utilizing research roadmaps, academic papers and project deliverables, the proposed

---

[1] For extensive literature see the Special Interest Group of ACM under
http://www.sigchi.org/

Research Areas Taxonomy highlights various research questions and challenges that have emerged and must be overcome, while restricting (to the extent that it is possible) mature research areas without many open research issues that have been embraced by market and practice implementations.

Future steps across the CROSSROAD Research Areas Taxonomy include iterative modifications in order to embrace future research challenges (for the years to come) in the domain of ICT for Governance and Policy Modelling which now do not have sufficient background to overpass the methodology thresholds and be included in the current version of the taxonomy. The taxonomy will be further used in the CROSSROAD project to develop a roadmap of future research for ICT for Governance and Policy Modelling. It will therefore help to dig into the state of the art in the research field, and it will be used in the scenario generation and gap analysis to further develop the intended research roadmap.

Acknowledgments. This work has been created in the context of the EU-funded Support Action CROSSROAD (A Participative Roadmap for ICT Research in Electronic Governance and Policy Modelling), Contract No: FP7-ICT-248484.

References

1. Aigner, W., Bertone, A., Miksch, S.: Tutorial: Introduction to visual analytics. In: Holzinger, A. (ed.) USAB 2007. LNCS, vol. 4799, pp. 453–456. Springer, Heidelberg (2007)
2. Ala-Mutka, et al.: The Impact of Social Computing on the EU Information Society and Economy. IPTS Reports (2009)
3. Australian Government 2.0 Taskforce: Engage - Getting on with Government 2.0 (2009), http://gov2.net.au/files/2009/12/Draft-Government-2-0-Report-release.pdf
4. Berners-Lee, T.: Linked data (2007), http://www.w3.org/DesignIssues/LinkedData.htm
5. Binali, H., Potdar, V., Chen, W.: A state of the art opinion mining and its application domains. In: Proceedings of the 2009 IEEE International Conference on Industrial Technology, pp. 1–6 (2009)
6. Bizer, C., Heath, T., Berners-Lee, T.: Linked Data - The Story So Far. International Journal on Semantic Web and Information Systems (IJSWIS), Special Issue on Linked Data 5(3), 1–22 (2009)
7. Buyya, R., Shin, C., Venugopal, S., Broberg, J., Brandic, I.: Cloud computing and emerging IT platforms: Vision, hype, and reality for delivering computing as the 5th utility. Future Generation Computer Systems 25(6), 599–616 (2009)
8. Botterman, M., Millard, J., Horlings, E., van Oranje, C., van Deelen, M., Pedersen, K.: Value for citizens-A vision of public governance in 2020. European Commission (2008)
9. Charalabidis, Y., Gionis, G., Moritz Hermann, K., Martinez, C.: Enterprise Interoperability Research Roadmap, Draft Version 5.0 (2008), ftp://ftp.cordis.europa.eu/pub/fp7/ict/docs/enet/ei-roadmap-5-0-draft_en.pdf
10. Charalabidis, Y., Koussouris, S., Kipenis, L.: Report on the Objectives, Structure and Status of eParticipation Initiative Projects in the European Union. MOMENTUM White Paper (2009)
11. Charron, C., Favier, J., Li, C.: Social Computing: How Networks Erode Institutional Power, And What to Do About It. Forrester Research (2008)

12. Chopra, A.: Cloud Computing in Government. Wired Magazine (2009)
13. Codagnone, C., Wimmer, M.A.: Roadmapping eGovernment Research - Visions and Measures towards Innovative Governments in 2020. Results from the EC-funded Project eGovRTD2020 (2007)
14. CORDIS: Software & Service Architectures and Infrastructures (2010), http://cordis.europa.eu/fp7/ict/ssai/home_en.html
15. CROSSROAD Project (2010), http://www.crossroad-eu.net
16. European Commission: The Future of the Internet: A Compendium of European Projects on ICT Research Supported by the EU 7th Framework Programme for RTD (2008), ftp://ftp.cordis.europa.eu/pub/fp7/ict/docs/ch1-g848-280-future-internet_en.pdf
17. European Commission: European Challenges and Flagships 2020 and beyond, Report of the ICT Advisory Group, ISTAG (2009), ftp://ftp.cordis.europa.eu/pub/fp7/ict/docs/fet-proactive/press-17_en.pdf
18. European Commission: Future Internet 2020, Visions of an Industry Expert Group (2009), http://www.future-internet.eu/fileadmin/documents/reports/FI_Panel_Report_v3.1_Final.pdf
19. European Commission: Internet of Things: Strategic Research Roadmap (2009), ftp://ftp.cordis.europa.eu/pub/fp7/ict/docs/enet/cerp-iot-sra-iot-v11_en.pdf
20. Gilbert, N., Troitzsch, K.G.: Simulation for the Social Scientist (2005)
21. Heeks, R., Bailura, S.: Analyzing e-government research: Perspectives, philosophies, theories, methods, and practice. Government Information Quarterly 24(2), 243–265 (2007)
22. Heer, J., Agrawala, M.: Design considerations for collaborative visual analytics. Information Visualization 7(1), 49–62 (2008) doi:10.1057/palgrave.ivs.9500167
23. Macintosh, A.: eParticipation in policy-making: the research and the challenges. In: Exploiting the Knowledge Economy: Issues, Applications, Case Studies. IOS Press, Amsterdam (2006)
24. Meskell, D.: Transparency and Open Government (2009), http://www.usaservices.gov/events_news/documents/Transparency_000.pdf (retrieved February 15, 2010)
25. Ministerial Declaration on eGovernment (2009), http://www.se2009.eu/polopoly_fs/1.24306!menu/standard/file/Ministerial%20Declaration%20on%20eGovernment.pdf
26. Nasukawa, T., Yi, J.: Sentiment Analysis: Capturing favourability using natural language processing. In: Second International Conference on Knowledge Capture, Florida, USA (2003)
27. Obama, B.: Memorandum for the Heads of Executive Departments and Agencies: Transparency and Open Government (2009), http://www.whitehouse.gov/the_press_office/Transparency_and_Open_Government/
28. Open Government Working Group (2010), http://www.opengovdata.org/
29. Osimo, D., Zinnbauer, D., Bianchi, A.: The Future of eGovernment, an exploration of ICT-driven models of eGovernment for the EU in 2020, IPTS Report (2007)
30. Scholl, H.J.: Profiling the EG Research Community and Its Core. In: Wimmer, M.A., et al. (eds.) EGOV 2009. LNCS, vol. 5693, pp. 1–12. Springer, Heidelberg (2009)
31. Smith, T.: Power to the people - Social Media Tracker Wave 3, Universal McCann (2008)
32. UK HM Government: Putting the Frontline First: Action Plan (2009), http://www.hmg.gov.uk/frontlinefirst/actionplan.aspx

Analyzing the Structure
of the EGOV Conference Community

Nuša Erman and Ljupčo Todorovski

Univeristy of Ljubljana, Faculty of Administration
Gosarjeva 5, SI-1000 Ljubljana, Slovenia
{nusa.erman,ljupco.todorovski}@fu.uni-lj.si

Abstract. The paper applies social network analysis techniques to the task of analysis the dynamics and structure of the e-government research community. From the bibliographic data about papers published in the proceedings of this conference (International Conference on e-Government), we build a co-authorship network representing collaboration patterns among community members in the period from 2005 to 2009. The co-authorship network analysis helps us identify the most productive and central authors in EGR community, as well as delineate the community structures through finding its sub-groups and core parts. In this way, several sub-communities are revealed in sense of the thematic topics, affiliations, and geographical origins of authors.

Keywords: e-government research analysis, social network analysis, co-authorship network, scientific community, e-government research community.

1   Introduction

e-Government research (EGR) as a scientific field has already been a subject of study from different points of view. Authors have considered the maturity [8,9] and the development [10] of the field, have studied the use of different methodological approaches [1], have compared various definitions and limitations of the e-government concept [17], or have profiled the EGR community [6]. A serious common limitation of these studies is that they take a wide variety of different approaches, which often prohibits comparison and/or unification of the obtained results into a single map of the EGR field. In our previous study [7], we proposed the use of social network analysis (SNA) as a general methodology commonly used in scientometrics and bibliometrics and applied to many different scientific fields (see, e.g., [13,3]). Paper presents the results of applying SNA to the study the citation network, induced from the papers published at this (EGOV) conference. The results of the study identify the most influential authors and relate them to the thematic topics that prevailed the EGOV conference through the four years from 2005 to 2008.

In this paper, we continue the work presented in [7] with changing the focus of the analysis from citation networks to networks of collaboration within the EGR community. Let us first define the concept of scientific community. As sociology of science argues, the most significant aspect of every scientific community is the idea of communication between scientists, which represents the foundation of the scientific

M.A. Wimmer et al. (Eds.): EGOV 2010, LNCS 6228, pp. 73–84, 2010.

community. In particular, we can define scientific community as the totality of working, interacting, and knowledge sharing scientists that share common and standardized procedures of scientific communication. The scientific community is often quantified through the analysis of scientific publications, and consecutively through the citation, co-citation, and co-authorship analysis [11]. At this point, the methods of scientometrics and bibliometrics are usually applied. Based on the scientific publications, these methods measure scientific activities through different levels of aggregation, enabling the analysis of research collaborations, evolution of scientific fields, and corresponding scientific networks [15].

In a related study of the EGR scientific community [14], author analyzes the data gathered in the e-Government Master Library of references[1]. Using self-defined criteria, author defines core journals, core conferences, and core researchers in the community. Furthermore, taking into account number of publications, author identifies most prolific researchers, their disciplines, research methods used, and the outlets of core parts of EGR community. In another absorbing attempt of EGR community analysis [6], author identifies the most productive authors, their gender, area of academic expertise, and background, as well as a calculus of papers with different number of co-authors, leading research universities, geographical regions, paper types, paradigm, and research methods which are present in the papers published in the journal "Transforming Government: People, Process and Policy".

In this paper, we introduce alternative approach to the study of scientific communities, which on top of identifying most active individuals, takes into consideration structural properties of whole EGR community. To do so, we apply SNA methodologies to the network of co-authorship in the papers, published in the proceedings of the EGOV conference in the period of eight years from 2002 to 2009. The nodes in the co-authorship networks represent authors and the edges represent joint articles published in the proceedings of the EGOV conference. The analysis of this network helps us identify the most productive but also the most collaborative researches in the community, to delineate the central community parts and main sub-communities, and to identify the main fields of interest of its members.

The rest of the paper is organized as follows. Section 2 introduces the idea of collaboration in scientific communities, presents the data used in the study and the process of establishing the co-authorship network. In Section 3, we present the results of the analysis of the co-authorship network with the emphasis on the community structure. Section 4 discusses the results, putting them in the context of related work. Finally, Section 5 draws conclusions and outlines the directions for further research.

2   Collaboration and Scientific Community

As mentioned in the introduction, the most important aspect of scientific community is the communication among scientists. Although there are several ways in which scientific communication can take place, presumably the most interesting pattern thereof is the collaboration among scientists. Collaboration can be described as a social process in which two or more scientists cooperate and share intellectual ideas.

---

[1] Available at http://tinyurl.com/p5w8vv

In this way, various and quite different situations can be considered to be scientific collaboration; one of them being the cooperation formalized through publishing a joint article. The cooperation of scientists in writing scientific papers, referred to as co-authorship, is in the focus of this paper and is the most frequently used for the analysis of scientific collaboration [2].

The most obvious way to represent the notion of co-authorship is the use of network, where the nodes represent individual researchers, and links among them represent co-authorship relations [2]. Once we have a network, we can apply standard social network analysis to analyze its structural properties, which will reveal important properties and structure of the corresponding scientific community. In this paper, we limit our scope of interest on one part of e-government research community that publishes papers at the International Conference on e-Government (EGOV). The analyzed data include all the papers published in all eight proceedings from the first (2002) to the last one (2009). In the continuation of this section, we introduce the data set and the corresponding co-authorship network.

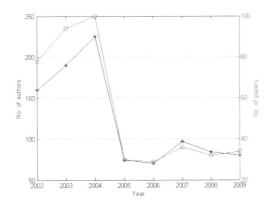

Fig. 1. Number of authors and papers published in the EGOV conference proceedings

2.1 Data Description

For this study, we build up on the data collected in [7], which we extended with the data about papers published in 2009. The complete data set for the period of eight years from 2002 to 2009 includes 433 papers. The total number of co-authors of these papers amount to 980 authors, out of which there are 706 different researchers.

Figure 1 summarizes the data set. It shows the significant drop of the number of published papers from about 100 in 2004 to 30 in 2005; the decrease is due to the improved review criteria and narrowed acceptance criteria. From 2005 onward, the number does not change significantly and it stays close to 30 with minor changes over the years. The change in number of authors resembles the one for papers; while in the first three years the number of authors steadily increased (from 160 to 225), fewer accepted (published) papers lead to the reduced number of authors (from 2004 to 2005 the number dropped from 224 to 74 authors). From 2005 on, it varies between slightly more than 70 to almost 100 (in 2007).

Figure 1 shows a significant change in the data distribution from 2004 to 2005. To avoid analysis artifacts that might be related to this abrupt change, we reduced the time-span of our analysis to the period from 2005 to 2009.

2.2 From Data to Co-authorship Network

The data set, described above, can be transformed to a co-authorship network following a simple procedure. For each paper in the proceedings, we collect the list of paper authors A. For each of them, we add a corresponding node to the network, if one has not been there yet. If the list consists of a single author we proceed with the next paper, since it does not introduces any co-authorship links in the network. Otherwise, for each pair of authors from A, we add an undirected link (edge) connecting the corresponding network nodes. If the link has been already present, we increase its weight by one; if the link is new, we assign weight 1. Thus, the weight assigned to an edge connecting two nodes denotes the number of papers that the corresponding two researchers co-authored.

Following the procedure outlined above, we generated five *weighted undirected co-authorship networks* for each observed year of proceedings from 2005 to 2009. Using the single-year networks, we constructed five "cumulative" co-authorship networks; the first network contains data from 2005 and each successive network is built in the way that to the preceding network data from the following year is added.

Table 1. Number of nodes, edges and density of the five "cumulative" co-authorship networks

	2005	2005-2006	2005-2007	2005-2008	2005-2009
#nodes	74	136	208	262	307
#edges	91	170	295	395	467
weight = 1	91	168	273	364	426
weight > 1	0 (0.0%)	2 (1.2%)	22 (7.5%)	31 (7.8%)	44 (9.4%)
Density	0.0337	0.0185	0.0137	0.0116	0.010

Table 1 presents the general properties of the five cumulative networks. The size of cumulative networks steadily increases, both in terms of the number of nodes/authors and links/co-authorships between them. The increase in size is being strictly followed by density decrease. The density of 0.01 of the final 2005-2009 network denotes that only 1% of all possible edges between nodes are present in the network. And yet, the portion of edges with weight larger than one (that is the number of research pairs that co-authored more than one article) steadily increases from initial 0 to 9.4%. The increase indicates the rising collaboration interest among EGOV researchers. A reason for this trend may be due to the fact that cumulative collaboration tends to be long-term: collaborating once makes collaborating in future more likely. Note however, that individual, non-cumulative, year data (see the last column of Table 2) confirm this cumulative trend.

In the following section, we present the results of the analysis of the dynamic change of the five "cumulative" networks with the emphasis on the structure of the network for the period from 2005 to 2009.

3   Structure and Dynamics of the EGOV Conference Community

Having built the cumulative co-authorship networks, we turn our attention towards analysis of the networks and results thereof. We use Pajek software tool [4] to perform the analysis of the co-authorship network. The results of the analysis are presented in three subsections. In the first one, we quantify and analyze the dynamic change of the community (network) from 2005 to 2009. Second section identifies the most active and most connected (collaborative) authors in the community. In the final, third subsection we analyze the EGOV community structure in terms of subgroups of collaborating (co-authoring) researchers, their geographical distribution, and research topics they are dealing with.

Table 2. Dynamics of the EGOV conference community from 2005 to 2009 in terms of numbers (and portions in %) of authors (newcomers and returning) and papers (single-authored and co-authored)

Year	#authors	#new authors	#existing authors	#papers	#single-authrd papers	#co-authored papers
2005	74	74 (100.0%)	0	30	10 (33.3%)	20 (66.7%)
2006	70	62 (88.6%)	8 (11.4%)	29	8 (27.6%)	21 (72.4%)
2007	97	72 (74.2%)	25 (25.8%)	36	5 (13.9%)	31 (86.1%)
2008	84	54 (64.3%)	30 (35.7%)	32	5 (15.6%)	27 (84.4%)
2009	80	45 (56.3%)	35 (43.7%)	34	3 (8.8%)	31 (91.2%)

3.1   Community Dynamics

Table 2 summarizes the results of the analysis of the EGOV community dynamics. First aspect of community dynamics is the change of the number of new researchers in the community. In the third column of Table 2, we report the number of newcomers for each year, i.e., authors that published a paper at EGOV conference for the first time in a particular year. At the beginning of the observation, in 2005, all authors are considered to be new to the community. As expected, the number of newcomers decreases through the years, from 62 newcomers in 2005 (which represents almost 20% of all the authors of the papers in the proceedings) to 45 in 2009. The later represents only 56% of all the authors of the papers in the proceedings of the 2009 conference. The trend shows that the community reached a stage, where 44% of the authors in 2009 have already published at the same conference before, which proves the EGOV community persistence and stability.

Another aspect of community dynamics is the extent of collaboration between community members. In 2005, one third (10 out of 30) of the papers were written by a single author, i.e., without collaboration. This number monotonically decreased through the years, reaching the minimum of four papers (9%) out of 34. In other words (see the figures in the last column of Table 2) the collaboration between community members steadily increases. The increasingly complex discourse and research issues in e-government community require collaboration of larger research teams, which is reflected in the large portion (91%) of co-authored papers.

In sum, there is a tendency of growing collaboration among EGOV community members through the years. The tendency is accompanied by the process of community convergence and stabilization with researchers that regularly publishes at the EGOV conference.

3.2 The Most Productive and Most Collaborative Authors

The obvious way to identify most productive authors in the EGOV conference community is to perform frequency analysis in terms of number of papers that a community member published in the EGOV conference proceedings in the observed period. In addition, to corroborate this measure, we can also expose in how many proceedings the identified most productive authors published their papers. Table 3 presents the results of the analysis.

Table 3. The seven most productive authors in the EGOV conference community in the period between 2005 and 2009 measured in terms of number of published papers and number of conference proceedings

Author	#papers	#proceedings
Grönlund Å.	6	4
Becker J.	6	3
Van Dijk J.	5	5
Charalabidis Y., Ferro E.	5	4
Andersen K.N., Niehaves B.	5	3

In the period 2005 to 2009, the seven researchers, enlisted in Table 3, co-authored more than four papers in the EGOV conference proceedings. Grönlund Å. and Becker J. published 6 papers, where the first author published his papers in four proceedings, and the latter published in three proceedings (in both cases, more than one paper per single-year proceedings). Each of the other five co-authored five papers. Van Dijk J. published one paper per year (five papers in five proceedings), Charalabidis Y. and Ferro E. in four proceedings, and Andersen K.N. and Niehaves B. in three.

To measure the extent to which authors collaborate with the community, we can use the co-authorship network to observe the degree of connectedness of an individual established to the other researchers in the community. To this end, social network analysis uses centrality measures for individual nodes in the network. There are three centrality measures (degree, closeness, and betweenness) which distinguish in the way the position of individual nodes within the network is referred [4]. In co-authorship network, degree centrality is equal to the number of collaborators an author has, closeness centrality indicates the accessibility (or closeness) of the observed author to the others, and betweenness centrality indicates the number of shortest paths which pass through the observed vertex of the network. Table 4 lists the most central authors of EGOV conference community wrt these three measures.

Table 4. The most central authors in EGOV conference community in the period between 2005 and 2009 measured using degree, closeness, and betweenness centrality. Emphasized (bold) names correspond to the most central authors according to all three centrality measures, while italic names correspond to the most central authors according to two centrality measures.

	Degree centrality		Closeness centrality		Betweenness centrality	
	Author	%	Author	%	Authors	%
1	*Charalabidis Y.*	3.27	*Charalabidis Y.*	3.58	*Tan Y.H.*	0.11
2	**Van der Geest T.**	2.94	**Van der Geest T.**	3.55	Henriksen H.Z.	0.10
3	*Askounis D.*	2.61	**Van Dijk J.**	3.40	**Van der Geest T.**	0.10
4	*Lampathaki F.*	2.61	**Arendsen R.**	3.26	**Van Dijk J.**	0.09
5	**Vintar M.**	2.61	**Vintar M.**	3.07	**Vintar M.**	0.08
6	**Arendsen R.**	2.29	*Askounis D.*	2.99	Andersen K.N.	0.07
7	*Iribarren M.*	2.29	*Lampathaki F.*	2.99	Liu J.	0.07
8	Concha G.	2.29	Jansen J.	2.90	**Arendsen R.**	0.06
9	Valdes G.	2.29	de Vries S.	2.90	Grönlund Å.	0.05
10	Solar M.	2.29	*Gionis G.*	2.76	Flak L.S.	0.04
11	**Van Dijk J.**	2.29	*Koussouris S.*	2.76	Ferro E.	0.03
12	*Gionis G.*	2.29	*Tan Y.H.*	2.74	Tarabanis K.	0.03
13	*Becker J.*	2.29	*Becker J.*	2.61	Sein M.K.	0.03
14	*Koussouris S.*	2.29	*Iribarren M.*	2.61	Todorovski L.	0.02

Despite the differences between the three lists, presented in Table 4, there are four authors, which occupy the central position in the community wrt all three centrality measures: van der Geest T., Vintar M., Arendsen R., and van Dijk J. The listed authors are the most central in view of their collaboration with other authors in the community, they are the most reachable (close) to other authors, and are located on the highest number of shortest paths in the network. Furthermore, van der Geest T. collaborated with 9 other authors and wrote 3 papers, Vintar M. collaborated with 8 authors in 4 different papers, Arendsen R. wrote 3 papers in collaboration with 7 other authors, and van Dijk J. wrote 5 co-authored papers in cooperation with 7 other members of EGOV conference community.

Comparison of these three lists with the list of the most productive authors from Table 3, we can see that there is a high correlation between authors' degree of collaboration with others and her/his productivity in terms of number of publications. Six out of seven authors from Table 3 (all except Niehaves B.) can be also found in at least one of the lists in Table 4, and three of them in at least two lists.

3.3 Community Structure

Until now, the focus of our analysis was on the properties of individual members of the observed network. In this last section, we analyze the structure of the EGOV community network as a whole. To this end, we apply methods for identifying components and cores in the network that help us identify clusters of highly inter-connected (collaborative) subgroups of the EGOV conference community.

The idea of finding components in co-authorship network arises from the presumption that the actors in a network compose a sub-group (component) in which every member of the component can be reached from all other members of the same component. Considering the definition, in co-authorship network components should reveal such groups of authors which collaborate frequently and, presumably, share common research topic(s). On the other hand, the search for cores implies even more restricted conditions under which actors represent the core sub-group of the community, as each of its members is linked with *all the other* members of the same core sub-group. In this sense, one core-group actually represents a set of paper(s) in which *all core members* collaborated [5].

Table 5. The analysis of the nine components of the EGOV co-authorship network. Each component corresponds to a research group that co-authored at least three joint papers.

# authors/ papers		Representative	Geographical distribution	Thematic topics
16	9	Van Dijk J.	Netherlands	citizen-centric e-services; user profiling; delivery channels; e-services adoption and usage
15	9	Andersen K.N. Tan Y.H.	Denmark, Norway, Netherlands	project evaluation; benefits of IT usage; e-customs; super-national e-services
12	7	Vintar M.	Slovenia, Greece	indicators of e-government development; e-services adoption and usage; life events and integration of e-services
10	7	Grönlund Å.	Sweden, Norway	e-government research analysis; misc
9	7	Becker J.	Germany	misc
8	6	Ferro E.	Italy, USA	digital divide and IT literacy
11	5	Charalabidis Y.	Greece	interoperability; meta-data and (semantic) annotation of e-services
5	4	Mentzas G.	Greece	evaluating quality of e-services
7	3	Corradini F. Sabucedo L.A.	Italy, Spain	semantic-driven integration of e-services

In our co-authorship network, we can identify 82 components. Out of these, 13 components contain only one author; the 13 components correspond to isolated authors that never co-authored a paper with others. On the other side of the spectrum is the largest component consisting of 16 authors. Note however, that here we can perceive the impact of papers with significantly higher number of authors compared to other papers: namely, in such a situation a single paper co-authored by many authors would induce a (non-)representative component. To overcome this problem, we augment each component with the list corresponding papers and consider only those components that are induced by at least three joint publications. In addition, we also filter out all the components with less than five researchers.

Table 5 presents the results of the component analysis by enlisting all nine components that satisfy the three-joint-papers criterion explained above. Each community subgroup is described with the leading researcher that is a co-author of majority of the papers in the component, the geographical distribution of authors' affiliations, and the list of thematic topics of the papers in the component.

The results show that most (all but the representatives of the last two components) of the components representatives were already identified as most productive or most central ones. Furthermore, most of the identified sub-groups have narrow geographical distribution: seven out of eight components are entirely from Europe, five are very even tighter, including single region or country, or, in some cases, a single institution. International or trans-Atlantic collaboration is relatively rare. Finally, there is a great variety of thematic topics addressed by the researchers in different groups. Note also that the identified sub-communities are orthogonal in the topics they deal with; each of them develops its own (relatively narrow) expertise area that is different from others. In very rare cases, the identified group covers a wide range of thematic topics marked as miscellaneous in Table 5.

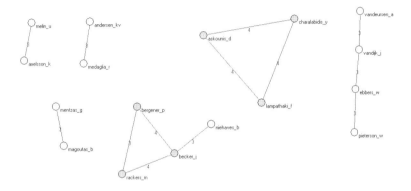

Fig. 2. Six cores of the EGOV co-authorship network

In the continuation of the analysis, we applied the same criterion as above, that is, we took into account only those collaborations that resulted in at least three joint publications. Figure 2 depicts the six cores of the EGOV co-authorship network that follow the three-joint-papers criterion. The identified cores confirm the findings of the component analysis: each of the five cores corresponds to one of the identified components from Table 5. The sixth core (Melin U. and Axelsson K.) identifies a Sweden sub-community of two co-authors of three papers, two of them being citizen participation and involvement in e-government projects. Another fact can be derived from the result depicted in Figure 2: only these 17 authors (out of 307; 5%) have been involved in more than two joint collaboration ventures. This is another piece of evidence that the long-term collaboration within the EGOV conference community is relatively rare.

In sum, the structural analysis of the EGOV community shows that a number of sub-communities has emerged, each of them dealing with topics that are orthogonal to the thematic topics of the other. Virtually all the sub-communities have a representative researcher that is ranked among top active or collaborative community members. Most of the sub-communities have narrow geographical distribution including a single region, country or even institution. The community members are mostly affiliated at institutions in European countries, and large-scale international collaborations are very rare.

4 Discussion

As we emphasized in the introduction, there are number of studies that analyze the state-of-the-art and the dynamics of the development of the e-government research (EGR) field [1,8,6,7,9,10,14,17].

Our study differs from them in several ways. First, it relies on a standard scientometric method widely used to analyze other research fields. Only the study [7] applies the same analysis methodology to the task of analyzing citation networks; in this paper we deal with analysis of co-authorship networks and the EGOV conference scientific community. Note however that other authors have been using the same methodology in various e-government studies, see e.g., analysis of partnership networks for implementing an e-government project [4], implementing local e-government policy [12], or coordination of soft-target organizations [16]. All these studies combine social network analysis with other qualitative and quantitative methods, such as interviews and surveys. In our study, we do not need these, since we collect the empirical data systematically from all the papers published in the proceedings of the EGOV conference in the last five years. The systematic data collection is the second distinguishing property of our study from the others. We focus the analysis on systematic data from a single publication venue instead of using a sample of data about articles and papers from various publication venues. Although this decision makes the definition and the scope of the scientific community clear (as opposed to the vague definition from [14]), it can also be regarded as a main limitation of our study, which we further discuss in the final section.

The present paper offers the findings of co-authorship network analysis which is latterly used as a proxy for the study of collaboration [2]. We should note however, that there exist limitations related to the study of scientific collaboration through publications and to the bibliometric studies in general. On one hand, we should consider the practice of making colleagues or superiors "honorary co-authors" for purely social reasons. On the other hand, scientific collaboration does not necessarily lead to co-authored papers.

Finally, the comparison of our results with the results of our citation analysis [7] provides several insights. First, when comparing the list of authors mention there, we find out that only two most cited authors (i.e., Grönlund Å. and Van Dijk J.) are confirmed to be members of the EGOV community as defined in this paper. Thus, most influential authors and literature come from outside EGOV community. This comes by no surprise, if we consider another result reported in [7], that only 8.5% of citations in the EGOV conference papers refer to other EGOV conference papers. Second, note that the thematic topics identified in this paper match the most influential (most cited) topics identified in [7], i.e., EGR analysis, seamless citizen-centric integration of e-services, interoperability, influence of information technology (IT) on organizational change, digital divide and IT literacy, user profiling and personalization of e-services.

5   Conclusion

Scientific community is a conglomerate of scientists who spread and diffuse their knowledge mainly through the publication of their theories and studies. In the core of every analysis of such communities is the study of communication patterns among scientists on the basis of citation, co-citation, or co-authorship network analysis. In the present paper, we focused on the analysis of EGOV conference community as one relatively small albeit representative part of the whole e-government research (EGR) community. We applied social network analysis to study the co-authorship network and linked the findings with the results of citation network analysis performed on the same data. This enabled us to improve the map of e-government research field with identification of the community most active and central authors, community structure and its core sub-groups. Beside with researchers' membership these sub-communities are characterized with the geographical distribution of the core authors and thematic topics prevailing in the EGR community.

However, we cannot disregard the fact that the data used to perform the analysis is far from being exhaustive. The first obvious limitation is its focus on a single publication venue that is the proceedings of the EGOV conference. Although the use of data on a single publication venue in this paper is well considered since the aim of the present paper was to complete the map of EGR, we are aware of the need for the extension of the data set with data on papers from other e-government conferences (such as the annual conference the Digital Government Society of North America) and journals (e.g., *Government Information Quality* and *Information Polity*).

In the present paper we focused on the co-authorship networks, where nodes represent authors and edges represent joint articles published in the EGOV conference proceedings. Usage of social network analysis methods, however, allows for establishment and analysis of other types of networks as well, on which we will focus in our future work. One possibility is the analysis of the citation networks considering publication venues where the referenced papers come from. Such analysis would reveal the most influential "neighboring" scientific fields and publication venues with highest impact on the development and shape of the EGR field. Furthermore, revising the definition of nodes and the meaning of relations among them opens even more analysis opportunities where other networks (e.g., networks where nodes correspond to publication units or where relations correspond to co-citations) can reveal some other structural patterns and characteristics of the observed EGR field. Note however, that it will be quite a challenge to uniquely identify publication units or co-citations in the rather "noisy" data set of references. Ultimately, there is a challengeable issue of integrating the results of analyzing different networks of relations among scientists and/or publication venues into a unified map of the EGR field.

Acknowledgments. This material is based upon work supported by the Slovenian Research Agency through the funds for training and financing young researchers. Thanks to the four anonymous reviewers for their valuable comments on an earlier version of the manuscript.

References

1. Andersen, K.V., Henriksen, H.Z.: The First Leg of E-Government Research: Domains and Applications Areas 1998-2003. International Journal of Electronic Government Research 1(4), 26–44 (2005)
2. Bordons, M., Gómez, I.: Collaboration Networks in Science. In: Cronin, B., Atkins, H.B. (eds.) The web of knowledge: a festschrift in honor of Eugene Garfield. ASIS Monograph Series. Information Today, Medford (2001)
3. Claussen, H., Wormell, I.: A bibliometric analysis of IOLIM conferences 1977-1999. Journal of Informaztion Science 27(3), 157–169 (2001)
4. Cotterill, S., King, S.: Public Sector Partnerships to Deliver Local E-Government: A Social Network Study. In: Wimmer, M.A., Scholl, H.J., Grönlund, A. (eds.) EGOV 2007. LNCS, vol. 4656, pp. 240–251. Springer, Heidelberg (2007)
5. de Nooy, W., Mrvar, A., Batagelj, V.: Exploratory social network analysis with Pajek. Cambridge University Press, New York (2005)
6. Dwivedi, Y.K.: An analysis of e-Government research published in Transforming Government: People, Process and Policy (TGPPP). Transforming Government: People, Process and Policy 1(3), 7–15 (2009)
7. Erman, N., Todorovski, L.: Mapping the E-Government Research with Social Network Analysis. In: Wimmer, M.A., Scholl, H.J., Janssen, M., Traunmüller, R. (eds.) EGOV 2009. LNCS, vol. 5693, pp. 13–25. Springer, Heidelberg (2009)
8. Grönlund, Å., Andersson, A.: e-Gov Research Quality improvements Since 2003: More Rigor, but Research (Perhaps) Redefined. In: Wimmer, M.A., Scholl, H.J., Grönlund, Å., Andersen, K.V. (eds.) EGOV 2006. LNCS, vol. 4084, pp. 1–12. Springer, Heidelberg (2006)
9. Grönlund, Å.: State of the Art in eGov Research – A Survey. In: Traunmüller, R. (ed.) EGOV 2004. LNCS, vol. 3183, pp. 178–185. Springer, Heidelberg (2004)
10. Heeks, R., Bailur, S.: Analyzing e-government research: Perspectives, philosophies, theories, methods, and practice. Government Information Quarterly 24, 243–265 (2007)
11. Mali, F.: Znanost kot sistemski del družbe (Science as a systematic part of society). Faculty of social sciences, Ljubljana (1994)
12. Medaglia, R.: Local Networking for e-Services: A UK Case Study. In: Wimmer, M.A., Scholl, H.J., Grönlund, Å., Andersen, K.V. (eds.) EGOV 2006. LNCS, vol. 4084, pp. 256–268. Springer, Heidelberg (2006)
13. Otte, E., Rousseau, R.: Social network analysis: a powerful strategy, also for the information sciences. Journal of Information Science 28(6), 441–453 (2002)
14. Scholl, H.J.: Profiling the EG Research Community and Its Core. In: Wimmer, M.A., Scholl, H.J., Janssen, M., Traunmüller, R. (eds.) EGOV 2009. LNCS, vol. 5693, pp. 1–12. Springer, Heidelberg (2009)
15. Scientometrics and bibliometrics, http://www.sciencemetrix.com/eng/methods-_scientometrics_t.htm (accessed, February 2009)
16. Uddin, M.S., Hossain, L.: Towards coordination preparedness of soft-target organisation. In: Wimmer, M.A., Scholl, H.J., Janssen, M., Traunmüller, R. (eds.) EGOV 2009. LNCS, vol. 5693, pp. 54–64. Springer, Heidelberg (2009)
17. Yildiz, M.: E-government research: Reviewing the literature, limitations, and ways forward. Government Information Quarterly 24, 646–665 (2007)

Drift or Shift? Propositions for Changing Roles of Administrations in E-Government

Ralf Klischewski

German University in Cairo
11835 New Cairo City, Egypt
ralf.klischewski@guc.edu.eg

Abstract. As transaction costs of web-based interaction in e-government continue to decrease, the actors involved are forced to reconsider their roles and value propositions. This paper builds on previous research on government transformation and introduces three propositions on how new opportunities opened up by emerging web technologies and methods lead to a paradigmatic change of the role of administrations in e-government. The propositions are developed in the areas of information management, creation of service value, and leadership in administration, based on identifying technology-induced challenges ("anomalies") as well as new opportunities leading to new role conceptions in administrations.

Keywords: government transformation, administrative roles, paradigm shift, web technologies.

1 Introduction

New internet technologies, new methods of designing web applications and new opportunities for online interaction have an impact also on e-government. Previous research has discussed for example the new opportunities induced by web 2.0, and citizens, companies and even government employees are increasingly seizing these opportunities as part of their e-government activities. As starting point of this paper we assume that (1) these emerging technologies, methods and communication channels lead to, economically speaking, a decrease of transaction costs of e-government related interaction, e.g. through less effort for web-based information sharing, service orchestration etc., and (2) therefore all actors involved will (have to) reconsider their roles and value propositions in the e-government networking sphere.

Following these assumptions, we must be able to detect the change of the role of administrations as leading actors in e-government, especially the significant changes. To this end this paper introduces propositions on how new opportunities opened up by emerging web technologies and methods induce a paradigmatic change of the role of administrations in e-government. The contribution to the field of e-government is that these propositions can be further developed for e.g. hypotheses testing in order to collect empirical evidence to what extent administrations do change their behavior and role conception. The practical relevance lies in raising the awareness for

M.A. Wimmer et al. (Eds.): EGOV 2010, LNCS 6228, pp. 85–96, 2010.

stakeholders involved in e-government to reflect about the change of environment, to detect drifts in role implementation and/or to strategically plan for a shift in role definition.

The approach of this research is explorative and conceptual: It develops the propositions for role change based on analyzing the potential for a paradigmatic change. The conception of paradigmatic follows the well-known work of Thomas Kuhn who considered a "paradigm" (or "disciplinary matrix") what members of a scientific community share as a constellation of beliefs, values, and techniques, thus constituting an entire 'worldview' of this community. When phenomena are encountered which cannot be explained by the prevailing (i.e. accepted) paradigm they are considered "anomalies" or non-relevant outliers. However, too many significant anomalies against a current paradigm amount to a significant challenge and can throw the community into crisis, leading to new ideas and eventually a new paradigm.

Based on this understanding the research question is: How do new opportunities opened up by emerging web technologies challenge existing paradigms of administrations' role in e-government and what could be new role paradigms accordingly? After reviewing the literature on government transformation in relation to change of roles and paradigms in e-government (section 2), emerging web technologies are defined and discussed in terms of how governments and government consultants perceive their relevance (section 3). The development of the propositions (section 4) is based on selecting and defining three prevailing role definitions in administrations, identifying current technology-induced challenges ("anomalies") of these role paradigms potentials as well as new opportunities beyond these paradigms, and pointing out possibly new role conceptions in administrations. The conclusion summarizes the propositions for change of the role of administrations in e-government and points to future research.

2   Transformation in (E-)Government?

Change of organization in relation to deployment and use of information systems is an extensively discussed topic in the literature, for example using IS as an opportunity for business process reengineering, but there is no simple and direct alignment between the two concepts. This discussion has reached also the domain of e-government: most authors agree that the use of new information and communication technologies do have an impact on the way e-government is implemented. But there is no causal relationship which can sufficiently explain the phenomena in practice, and there seems to be even little evidence that transformation is taking place [30].

Informatics and computer science tend to perceive organizational change as a sequence of transitions from one state to the next, much alike to the widespread 'unfreeze–change–refreeze' model in change management. However, research in political science has explored the topic of institutional change from many more perspectives. While tracing these perspectives is beyond the scope of this paper, we will follow here the viewpoint of J. Olsen [22] who states that "institutions have a role in generating both order and change and in balancing the two" and "understanding order and change are two sides of the same coin and there is a need to know what processes and conditions may maintain or challenge the status quo" (p. 4f). In view of the debate on institutionalization, Olsen [ibid.] considers the organizational identity to be based on: (a) clarity and agreement about behavioral rules (including allocation of formal authority), (b) consensus concerning how behavioral rules are to be described and justified (with a common vocabulary, expectations and success criteria), and (c) shared conceptions of what are legitimate resources (and who should control them). Such kind of institutional identity frames also the definition and interpretations of roles (on individual and institutional level) which can be considered as part of the shared mindset of government employees.

The literature reflecting on changing paradigms and roles of administrations in relation to e-government is still scarce, but the topic seems to be emerging. Scholl [25] has reviewed the organizational literature and makes use of the distinction first-order changes (incremental, planned, and reaching for minor improvements) and second-order changes (extending to a radical organizational change involving a paradigmatic shift). He concludes that "organizational transformation is of compara-tively slow pace and is mostly first-order change oriented. Organizational 'drift,' 'spread,' 'slippage,' and 'creep' […], that is, evolutionary transformation, are much more likely drivers and embodiments of change in the public sector than second-order or revolutionary transformations." (p. 3) Scholl argues further that for identifying second-order changes the research should be interdisciplinary and also take into account not only G2C but also study phenomena in G2B, G2G and internal affairs.

After reviewing the literature on transformational government, van Veenstra and Zuurmond [29] conclude that transformation points to both process and product, "referring to a paradigm shift of fundamental assumptions and to a gradual change in behavior of individuals within an organization" (p. 235). That means, observation of gradual changes might come along with a 'paradigm shift', i.e. a radical change in the common beliefs of the actors involved. This can be in line with the findings of Scholl [25] proposing that second-order transformations can be observed rather in later stages of e-government development, preceded by a series of first-order changes.

With claiming the difference between e-governance and e-government (e.g. [12, 18]), a new level of abstraction has been opened up, pointing to the need for redefining governance objectives, methods and structures vis-à-vis the changing mode of technically mediated service delivery. More explicitly, Taylor and Lips [27] question the "e-government paradigm" (in particular the mostly shared assumption that e-government per se is 'citizen-centric') and recommend widening the scope of discussing the citizen-government relationship so that the field will become more theoretically informed.

Foreseeing the transformation of public service delivery, research has set out to investigate the transformation of the fundamental relationship between government, community and citizens [14]. Assuming that digital technologies affect functions of direction, control and organization of governments and their dominions, governments have to reconsider their roles to maintain their power in the 'digital state' [33]. In view of the new technical opportunities administrations indeed seem to have choices, for example designing service delivery like an e-government shop or developing an electronic community [26]. Therefore recommendations have been made to consider the (new) role of the government throughout the whole process of e-government development and design [20, 32].

As digitization and virtualization are more and more affecting the government domain, research aims to look ahead to determine the government's role and responsibilities in the future. In the eGovRTD2020 project [4, 31] this had been one of the thirteen research themes, asking e.g. for what kind of virtual citizenship will appear, or whether different legislation is needed for the increasingly non-physical and borderless world and who would define implement the laws. In order to avoid organizational 'drift' or 'creep', some governments try to proactively set the path for a shift. For example the UK Cabinet Office [5] has coined the term 'transformational government' to prescribe the way for achieving more citizen- and business-centric public service delivery, trying to strengthen the link between e-government strategy and implementation. In the same line, van Veenstra et al. [28] identify the "absence of a transformational mindset" as one of the main barriers for transformation (along with a lack of knowledge about necessary changes and a lack of change in the organization structure).

In summary, throughout the last decade some research on transformation in e-government has emerged, but empirical evidence or even propositions remain scarce. From the methodological perspective it seems that transformations can be detected primarily in the change of institutional agreements and in the mindset of the actors involved, usually as a consequence of an accumulation of marginal or gradual changes. This supports the approach chosen here to seek for accumulating challenges ("anomalies") of existing role paradigms in administrations in order to reach for propositions of role changes.

3   Emerging Web Technologies: Challenges and Opportunities

During the last decade several new web technologies and methods have emerged, leading to new opportunities for designing and operating e-government applications. For the remainder of the paper we mean by the term 'emerging web technologies' technologies and methods providing the following internet-based functionalities:

- *Visualization:* Increasing use and integration of maps, pictures, videos for enhanced and/or new services.
- *Interactivity:* Enhanced two-way communication, forums, easy-to-do resource sharing, etc.
- *Semantic structuring:* Use of tagging and ontologies for mark-up and automatic processing of informational and functional resources.
- *Channel and content federation:* Integration of mobile devices, multimedia, mash-ups, crowdsourcing, etc.
- *Smart agency:* Mission-based finding and combining content and services on behalf of users.

Most of the above functionalities are also embraced by the term 'web 2.0' which was originally coined by O'Reilly denoting principles such as the Web as platform, harnessing collective intelligence, data as the next 'Intel inside,' end of the software release cycle, lightweight programming models, software above the level of single device, and rich user experiences [2]. It is important to note that the novel aspects are not the technical specifications as such, but rather the way application developers and end-users make use of these technologies and thereby create new design patterns (i.e. methods) and business models. Often the term 'social computing' is used synonymously, denoting "a set of open, web-based and user-friendly applications that enable users to network, share data, and co-produce content" ([1], p. 15).

Not surprisingly consultants have been the first to point out how to make use of these emerging web technologies in administrations. Gartner [7, 8] has predicted reusability of content and services and a shift of emphasis away from single, one-stop shop portals to more networked solutions; they even expect the establishment of virtual government strategies defining how to participate in a variety of virtual communities, embracing government employees as well as citizens. And the "innovation expert" Anthony Williams (co-author of the best-seller 'Wikinomics') is quoted that "the Web offers the public sector tremendous opportunities to transform service delivery, make smarter policies, flatten silos and reinvigorate government" ([16], p. 30) and that due to institutional rigidity significant changes will take time, but there is an opportunity to change the division of labor for the public good.

Implications of these new technologies and opportunities from the perspective of administrations are now also on the governmental agenda. A research report by the European Commission [22] identifies a set of domains of government activity for which web 2.0 solutions are expected to be relevant: regulation, cross-agency collaboration, and knowledge management as back office domains; and political participation and transparency, service provision, and law enforcement as front office domains (p. 23). The report identifies various user roles (designing and delivering the service, providing comments and reviews, providing automatic attention and 'taste data' by using the service) and points out that such proactive user roles imply that "governments have no power to decide whether or not web 2.0 applications should be adopted and implemented, either by civil servants or citizens" (p. 41). Opportunities provided by web 2.0 applications are considered to relate to strategic objectives such as making government more simple and user-oriented, transparent and accountable, participative and inclusive, as well as joined-up and networked. On the contrary there are many challenges identified because of common risks of web 2.0 with particular relevance in the government context due to its institutional role and universal service obligations: low participation, participation restricted to an elite, low quality of contribution, loss of control due to excessive transparency, destructive behavior by users, manipulation of content by interested parties, and privacy issues.

It seems that the advent of the emerging web technologies creates an unexpected dilemma for governments. On one hand, governments seek to use the new opportunities in line with their strategic objectives; for example the 2009 "Ministerial Declaration on eGovernment" [19], unanimously approved by the European ministers of interior, states as the first shared objective for the period until 2015: "Citizens and businesses are empowered by eGovernment services designed around users needs and developed in collaboration with third parties, as well as by increased access to public information, strengthened transparency and effective means for involvement of stakeholders in the policy process;" and the foreword of EU workshop report on 'Public Services 2.0' points out: "Governments around Europe are aware of these new possibilities and actively started exploring them." ([24], p. 7).

On the other hand, however, analysts have posted numerous blogs indicating that governments have significant problems embracing these emerging web technologies: blurring boundaries and growing tension between hierarchy and collaborative networks are threatening established social barriers (e.g. [13]) and, for various reasons, administrations seem to be unwilling to challenge the status quo (e.g. [9, 10]).

In summary, emerging web technologies have reached e-government, but the self-conception of administrative roles for embracing these technologies and seizing the opportunities seems not yet sufficient: it lacks the 'transformational mindset.' In order to assist administrative change management and support research in following up, the following section elaborates three propositions for administrative role changes.

4 Propositions for Role Change in Administrations

Administrations are the implementers of e-government: they operate the e-government applications and – framed by existing laws and regulations – interact with the constituents and other actors via these platforms according to their interpretation of the governmental mission. In this context we mean by 'role' the actions and activities assigned to or required or expected of a person or group. We consider a role in administration to be 'paradigmatic' when the community of government employees shares the same belief regarding what kind of work they are obliged to perform or not. Given the myriad of specific administrative functions, such paradigmatic roles can only be conceptualized on a rather abstract level, making reference to what government and/or administration as a whole are supposed to do or not (which then prescribes the individual work behavior). Such kind of role interpretations are not necessarily fixed in writing, but can be more importantly considered as part of the institutional identity and as the shared mindset of government employees of all ranks (see above, section 2).

This research is not empirical, i.e. does not validate to what extent any of the role definitions below actually are or will be prevailing in any administration. The purpose is to develop propositions by which future empirical research is expected to advance our knowledge about the impact of emerging web technologies on e-government and/or to assist change management in administrations regarding the strategic use of these technologies.

Based on the web 2.0 user roles and related governance issues pointed out in the previous section, the areas selected for proposition development are information management, creation of service value, and leadership in administration. The proposition development follows the sequence of defining prevailing role in administrations for the selected area, identifying current technology-induced challenges ("anomalies") of these role paradigms, identifying new opportunities beyond these paradigms, and pointing out possibly new role conceptions in administrations.

4.1 From Information Monopolist to Information Provider, Broker, and Consumer

Role definition. The history of administration is also a history of bureaucracy, the heritage of which includes well-established hierarchies, formal division of powers, and a strong sense of leadership. As the executive branch of government, administrations are rule-followers who develop and enact standardized procedures that guide the treatment of (almost) all cases. More often than not this mindset extends to any cooperation with external partners or dealing with its own employees: administrations are the leaders who maintain the core values of bureaucracy for the public good.

Challenges. E-government applications enable the extension of administrative processes into the sphere of citizens and businesses and cut across various agencies. In result we find numerous information providers and managers participating in administrative processes, and information ownership and processing control is increasingly distributed. Furthermore the new emerging technologies allow tapping on completely new sources of information: for example the website mybikelane.com was launched by a New York citizen asking fellow cyclists to post photos of cars illegally parked on bike lanes – with the result that now information on countless regulatory offenses is available, structured and managed without any control by administration (for more similar cases see e.g. [23]).

Opportunities. As governments seek to be more transparent and accountable, websites such as theyworkforyou.com (for keeping tabs on UK parliament activities) or data.gov (for public access to high value, machine readable datasets generated by the US federal administration) open up new venues for sharing relevant information on a large scale. And there are many cases in which participatory large-scale collection of information is for the benefit of administrative performance, for example urban planning or monitoring environmental risks and neighborhood safety, many of these supported by new technologies structuring the information processing by means of maps or other visual concepts [3].

Role change. Since the role of administrations as information monopolists cannot sustain, seizing the new opportunities and alignment with the strategic objectives could be framed by a new role of administrations as information provider, broker, and consumer. This would acknowledge that e-government by default incorporates shared information processing, and it allows setting new specific policies such as focusing on stewardship and usefulness [6] which includes handling information with care and integrity, regardless of its original purpose or source, and promoting access to and use of government information by a wide variety of public and private users.

4.2 From Sole Care Taker to Service Provider and Network Manager

Role definition. When it comes to the question who takes care of the citizens' concerns vis-à-vis the state, for long time the answer could not embrace any significant contributor but the public administration itself. Emerging form the tradition of the kingdoms, citizens were considered entrusted subjects and the administrations are the sole care takers to deal with them.

Challenges. In 2003 the UK Office of the e-Envoy [21] published a policy framework draft aiming at the establishment of 'e-intermediaries' supplementing direct government channels to citizens with additional value-added services built around citizens' needs. While in some areas intermediaries are well established for a long time (e.g. tax accountants), the emerging web technologies enable many new actors ('competitors') to offer admin-related services. The most well-known examples are web portals providing information on and access to public service, operated by companies, public-private partnerships or even by the citizens themselves (see e.g. bccdiy.com, the "community-powered Birmingham City Council site"). Furthermore, the provision of machine-readable service descriptions and interfaces changes the distribution of cost and benefit among service providers, brokers and consumers [17].

Opportunities. As transaction costs are decreasing, governments may indeed reconsider: "What is the best way to divide labor for the public good?" [16]. A well-known example is "Peer-to-Patent" (peertopatent.com), an initiative endorsed by the US Patent Office aiming to improve the process for reviewing patents by allowing voluntary contributions to assess and rate the proposals, thus involving external experts in assessing the current state of the art on the issue addressed by the patent. There are many cases where administrations can benefit from outsourcing and crowdsourcing and/or tapping on new potentials (for more examples and analysis see [23]). And the advent of new electronic intermediaries could support the citizens' development into active consumers of public services [15].

Role change. Restraining the administration's role as the sole care takers of citizens' concerns would deprive administrations and constituents of potential increase in government effectiveness and service quality. Redefining the role as service provider and service network manager allows administrations to focus on their core value proposition as well as to create and manage e-service networks.

4.3   From Bureaucratic Leader to Facilitator and Framework Provider

Role definition. The history of administration is also a history of bureaucracy, the heritage of which includes well-established hierarchies, formal division of powers, and a strong sense of leadership. As the executive branch of government, administrations are rule-followers who develop and enact standardized procedures that guide the treatment of (almost) all cases. More often than not this mindset extends to any cooperation with external partners or dealing with its own employees: administrations are the leaders who maintain the core values of bureaucracy for the public good.

Challenges. As quoted above, "governments have no power to decide whether or not web 2.0 applications should be adopted and implemented, either by civil servants or citizens." Among other, it leads to blurring boundaries between internal and external collaboration, to new methods of processing relevant information and providing services (see above sections). Bureaucracy is mainly challenged by realizing that anticipation of procedures is decaying.

Opportunities. Many issues in e-government need leadership intervention in order to balance values which are on one hand conflicting but on the other hand of equal importance in the public interest, for example the mediating the tension between information privacy and information access [11]. And with respect to emerging web technologies, a social media policy is needed that guides especially admin employee behaviors.

Role change. Identifying leadership with bureaucracy is not compatible with making use of emergent web technologies. Analysts recommend a bottom-up approach, where government agencies should let go control to facilitate engagement empowering employees: "This is the key ingredient, the secret sauce for government 2.0 initiatives to succeed […] 'Let go' means that you cannot plan in advance, you cannot set a future state architecture, you cannot control your employees too tightly, you cannot make assumptions about where and how and when value will be generated." [10] However, this does not mean to subscribe (or surrender) to anarchy. Instead, administrations should resume leadership-related roles where it is more needed and more effective, mainly as facilitators and framework providers.

5 Conclusion

Assuming that emerging web technologies decrease transaction costs of e-government related interaction and therefore all actors involved will (have to) reconsider their roles and value propositions, this research has set out develop propositions that can be further used for collecting empirical evidence on the extent administrations do change their behavior and role conception. These propositions have been developed in the areas of information management, creation of service value, and leadership in administration, based on identifying technology-induced challenges ("anomalies") as well as new opportunities leading to new role conceptions in administrations (see below figure for summary).

From Gov's as	info monopolist	sole care taker	bureaucratic leader
Challenges ("anomalies") based on web technologies & methods	relevant information provided / managed / owned by many, often out of admin control	"competitors" offer (value-added) admin services	empowerment of citizens and admin employees
Opportunities based on web technologies & methods	information dissemination to and consumption from citizens/businesses	specific value creation in a net-work of electronic service providers	setting standards for technical, semantic, organizational, legal, social "interoperability"
To Gov's as	**information provider, broker, and consumer**	**service provider and network manager**	**facilitator and framework provider**

Fig. 1. Drift or shift? Propositions for changing roles of administrations in e-government

The practical relevance of these propositions lies in raising the awareness of stake-holders involved in e-government. Given the change of environment due to increasing use of emerging web technologies, governments and administrations should recon-sider their basic assumptions, i.e. paradigms. The assumptions discussed in this paper are primarily concerned with administrative roles, but the analysis and reconsideration on the institutional level should extend also to the role-related behavioral rules and authorities, to their description and justification, and to the (shared) control of resources. All of these issues are highly relevant for the design and implementation of e-government applications and infrastructures; hence they should be on the agenda of future e-government research, from the technical as well as from the organizational perspective. Will forthcoming studies reveal a strategically aligned shift or rather an unintended drift in administrative role implementation? The answer, of course, depends much on the stakeholders' readiness and willingness to reflect on the challenges and opportunities induced by emerging web technologies, and to what extent this will lead to a proactive approach in re-balancing stability and change of governmental institutions.

Acknowledgments. The above propositions have originally been presented at the Preconference for the EU 5th Ministerial e-Government Conference "e-Government Research and Innovation: Empowering Citizens through Government Services across Sectors and Borders," Malmö, November 18, 2009.

References

1. Ala-Mutka, K., et al.: The Impact of Social Computing on the EU Information Society and Economy. European Commission, Joint Research Centre, Institute for Prospective Technological Studies (2009)
2. Anderson, P.: What is Web 2.0? Ideas, technologies and implications for education. JISC Technology and Standards Watch (2007)
3. Bekkers, V., Moody, R.: Visual Culture and Electronic Government: Exploring a New Generation of E-Government. In: Wimmer, M.A., et al. (eds.) EGOV 2009, pp. 257–269. Springer, Berlin (2009)
4. Bicking, M.: Roadmapping future e-Government research: Government's role and responsibilities in the virtual world. In: Seventh IFIP International Conference on e-Business, e-Services, and e-Society, pp. 469–480. Springer, Heidelberg (2007)
5. Cabinet Office: Transformational Government: Enabled by Technology. e-Government Unit of the Cabinet Office (2005),
   http://www.cabinetoffice.gov.uk/media/141734/
   transgov-strategy.pdf
6. Dawes, S.S.: Information policy meta-principles: stewardship and usefulness. In: Proceedings of the 43rd Annual Hawaii International Conference on System Sciences (HICSS '10), IEEE Computer Society Conference Publishing Services (2010)
7. DiMaio, A.: Government and Web 2.0: The Emerging Midoffice. Gartner Report (2007)
8. DiMaio, A.: The E-Government Hype Cycle Meets Web 2.0. Gartner Report (2007)
9. DiMaio, A.: Why North Americans Will Get Government 2.0 and Europeans Won't,
   http://blogs.gartner.com/andrea_dimaio/ (October 30, 2009)
10. DiMaio, A.: The Government 2.0 Critical Success Factor Is To Let It Go,
    http://blogs.gartner.com/andrea_dimaio/ (November 1, 2009)
11. Duncan, G.T., Roehrig, S.F.: Mediating the Tension between Information Privacy and Information Access: The Role of Digital Government. In: Garson, G.D. (ed.) Public Information Technology: Policy and Management Issues, pp. 94–119. Idea Group Publishing, Hershey (2003)

12. Finger, M., Pécoud, G.: From e-Government to e-Governance? Towards a model of e-Governance. Electronic Journal of e-Government 1(1), 1–10 (2003)
13. Hinchcliffe, D.: Government 2.0: A tale of "risk, control, and trust" (2009), http://blogs.zdnet.com/Hinchcliffe/?p=811 (Posted September 9, 2009)
14. Jones, S., Hackney, R., Irani, Z.: Towards e-government transformation: conceptualising "citizen engagement": A research note. Transforming Government: People, Process and Policy 1(2), 145–152 (2007)
15. Josefsson, U., Ranerup, A.: Consumerism revisited: The emergent roles of new electronic intermediaries between citizens and the public sector. Information Polity: The International Journal of Government & Democracy in the Information Age 8(3/4), 167–180 (2003)
16. Klein, P.: Web 2.0: Reinventing Democracy. CIO Insight/Expert Voices, 30–34 (2008), http://anthonydwilliams.com/wp-content/uploads/web2_reinventingdemocracy.pdf
17. Klischewski, R., Ukena, S.: A Value Network Analysis of Automated Access to e-Government Services. In: Hansen, H.R., Karagiannis, D., Fill, H.-G. (eds.) 9th International Conference on Business Informatics (Part 2), Österreichische Computer Gesellschaft, Wien, pp. 585–594 (2009)
18. Kolsaker, A., Lee-Kelley, L.: 'Mind the Gap II': E-Government and E-Governance. In: Wimmer, M.A., Scholl, J., Grönlund, Å. (eds.) EGOV 2007. LNCS, vol. 4656, pp. 35–43. Springer, Heidelberg (2007)
19. Ministerial Declaration on eGovernment, Malmö, Sweden (2009), http://www.epractice.eu/files/Malmo%20Ministerial%20Declaration%202009.pdf (November 18, 2009)
20. Mofleh, S., Wanous, M., Strachan, P.: Understanding national e-government: the role of central government. Electronic Government, an International Journal 6(1), 1–18 (2009)
21. Office of the e-Envoy: Policy Framework for a mixed economy in the supply of e-government services, UK Cabinet Office, http://archive.cabinetoffice.gov.uk/e-envoy/
22. Olsen, J.: Change and continuity. An institutional approach to institutions of democratic government. European Political Science Review 1(1), 3–32 (2009)
23. Ossimo, D.: Web 2.0 in Government: Why and How? European Commission, Joint Research Centre, Institute for Prospective Technological Studies (2008)
24. Ossimo, D., et al.: Public Services 2.0 - Web 2.0 from the periphery to the centre of public service delivery. In: Report from the ePractice Workshop, European Commission, Brussels (2009)
25. Scholl, H.J.: Organizational Transformation Through E-Government: Myth or Reality? In: Wimmer, M.A., Traunmüller, R., Grönlund, Å., Andersen, K.V. (eds.) EGOV 2005. LNCS, vol. 3591, pp. 1–11. Springer, Heidelberg (2005)
26. Steyaert, J.: Local governments online and the role of the resident – Government shop versus electronic community. Social Science Computer Review 18(1), 3–16 (2000)
27. Taylor, J.A., Lips, A.M.B.: The citizen in the information polity: Exposing the limits of the e-government paradigm. Information Polity 13(3-4), 139–152 (2008)
28. Veenstra, A.F.v., Klievink, B., Janssen, M.: Barriers for transformation: Impediments for transforming the public sector through e-government. In: 17th European Conference on Information Systems, Verona, Italy (2009), http://www.ecis2009.it/papers/ecis2009-0399.pdf
29. Veenstra, A.F.v., Zuurmond, A.: Opening the Black Box: Exploring the Effect of Transformation on Online Service Delivery in Local Governments. In: Wimmer, M.A., et al. (eds.) EGOV 2009, vol. 5693, pp. 234–244. Springer, Berlin (2009)

30. West, D.M.: E-Government and the Transformation of Service Delivery and Citizen Attitudes. Public Administration Review 64(1), 15–27 (2004)
31. Wimmer, M.A., Codagnone, C., Janssen, M.: Future e-government research: 13 research themes identified in the eGovRTD2020 project. In: Proceedings of the 41st Hawaii International Conference on System Sciences (HICSS '08). IEEE Computer Society Conference Publishing (2008)
32. Zappen, J.P., Harrison, T.M., Watson, D.: A New Paradigm for Designing E-Government: Web 2.0 and Experience Designs. In: Chun, S.A., Janssen, M., Gil-Garcia, J.R. (eds.) dg.o 2008: Proceedings of the 9th Annual International Digital Government Research Conference, pp. 17–26 (2008)
33. Zuccarini, M.: Transformation of Government Roles toward a Digital State. In: Anttiroiko, A.-V., Mälkiä, M. (eds.) Encyclopedia of digital government, pp. 1562–1565. Idea Group Reference, Hershey (2007)

An Institutional Perspective on the Challenges of Information Systems Innovation in Public Organisations

Gamel O. Wiredu

School of Technology, Ghana Institute of Management and Public Administration,
Accra, Ghana
gwiredu@gimpa.edu.gh

Abstract. Public organisations are normally overwhelmed with socio-technical challenges of Information Systems (IS) innovation at both organisational and institutional levels. However, most studies of these challenges adopt an organisational perspective, leaving the institutional perspective largely unanalysed. In this paper, the IS innovation challenges faced by a British local authority are analysed to explain the institutional roles of public bureaucracy and information technology (IT). The analysis reveals the tensions between the low-entrepreneurial ethos of public organisations and the efficiency principle of IT. The paper argues that the primary principle of IS innovation should be institutional adjustments of public bureaucracy and information technology. Suggestions on how both institutions can be adjusted are provided.

Keywords: Information systems innovation, public organisations, public bureaucracy, information management, e-government.

1 Introduction

Advances in information technology (IT) development have engendered pressing demands for public organisations to adopt them to consummate information systems (IS) innovation. IS innovation is defined as an organisation's application of IT to make its processes more efficient and effective [34, p.1072]. However, IS innovation in public organisations are confronted by challenges of IT integration [7], as witnessed in the high failure rate of government IT projects worldwide [13]. These challenges have recently engaged the attention of information systems (IS) and e-government researchers. They have attempted to explain and address these challenges, but their models are limited for the following reasons.

Firstly, some researchers mainly focus on the relationship between the public organisation and the public, without much attention to the internal organisational processes [e.g. 11, 8, 18, 6]. For this reason, information management as an important antecedent of the organisation's interface with the public is left unanalysed. Secondly, even if internal organisational processes are focused upon, researchers adopt overly situated perspectives that result in organisational- or micro-level analysis at the expense of institutional- or macro-level analysis [e.g. 20, 29, 4]. A few exceptions are Cordella [8], Henriksen and Damsgaard [19], and Fountain [14]. In so doing, the role

M.A. Wimmer et al. (Eds.): EGOV 2010, LNCS 6228, pp. 97–108, 2010.
© IFIP International Federation for Information Processing 2010

of historical institutional antecedents are excluded in explanations of IT integration in public organisations. Thirdly, many approach IT integration with overly high degrees of IT optimism and determinism [e.g. 18, 13, 31, 24]. IT is so highly privileged that only organisational issues such as people, information, systems and change are problematised. Thus, apart from a few exceptions [e.g. 25], explanations of IT-related organisational change virtually leave the IT as a constant attribute. As a result of all these limitations, extant models preclude explanations of how the *institutional* relationship between IT and public bureaucracy shape information systems (IS) innovation in public organisations.

This paper, therefore, seeks to address these limitations by answering the question: *how can the challenges of IS innovation in public organisations, presented by the interactions between IT and public bureaucracy, be explained and addressed?* It takes an institutional approach to the analysis of organisational-level challenges of IS innovation. One aspect of this perspective is the consideration of IT as an institution in its own right [2]. Yet, the paper, at the same time, focuses on organisational processes. Through the analysis of the information management challenges faced by a British local government authority, it argues that the primary principle of IS innovation should be institutional adjustments of public bureaucracy and IT.

2 Information Systems Innovation and Institutions

Against the backdrop that innovation in an organisation refers to "the adoption of an idea or behaviour that is new to the organisation adopting it" [9, p.197], Swanson [34, p.1072] defines IS innovation as the application of IT to make processes more efficient and effective. But this definition suffers from the problem of IT determinism and optimism because it privileges IT as the unquestioned agent of IS innovation. Avgerou's [3] definition avoids this problem and presents a desirable framework for the analysis in this paper. She defines IS innovation as "IT innovation and organisational change, whereby both the IT items and the individual organisational actors involved are part of institutionalised entities, that are historically formed durable, but dynamic, heterogeneous networks" (p.64). She explains IS innovation by emphasising the interactions between the network of heterogeneous actors involved in the innovation. The heterogeneity in the network is represented by actors such as hardware, software, data, IT developers, vendors, users and consultants [cf. 26].

The mutual interrelations between this range of heterogeneous actors removes any presuppositions or accepted assumptions about the determining capacity of technology or society. Neither the social nor technical determines the other, signifying that socio-technical relationships can be understood in terms of the outer socio-technical context of the network, including its institutional history. The outer socio-technical context refers predominantly to the institutional fields of both IT and the bureaucracy, and also to politics.

The important role of the institutional context as a factor that bears on organisational interactions is a popular argument in institutional and organisational theory [e.g. 27, 10, 30]. An institutional structure is an order which is imbued with time-honoured values. These usually induce specific attitudes among employees in organisations. Furthermore, institutions are "social patterns that, when chronically reproduced, owe their survival to relatively self-activating social processes" [21, p.145]. Institutional structures bear on the details of what happens in organisational interactions – in the operational details which innovation is an instance.

Therefore, understanding the role of the institutional field of IT is important because IT is an institution in its own right [2, 3]. The institutional essence of IT is summarily explained by Avgerou [2] in terms of the established value of technology for post-industrial society; an established array of professional experts devoted to innovating IT the established regulations for IT development and use; and powerful professional associations who promulgate standards of technology development and practice. IT is deemed as an institution because the momentum of its diffusion defies even negative analysis of its organisational value. Thus, IT is ubiquitous in almost all fields of endeavour where it is deemed to be enhancing productivity.

Just like IT, the institution of bureaucracy has acquired its own momentum and has its own norms of good practice in modern organisation. Thus, although post-modern thinkers of organisational governance tout bureaucracy as an institution that degrades human dignity and they celebrate its supposed demise, it remains the best alternative to the market. Both IT and bureaucracy are distinct institutions with their own orders. The foundations of the bureaucratic order are different from the foundations of the technological order, although the two orders interrelate in IS innovation.

3   A Case of Information Management at Lambeth Borough Council

The empirical component of this research, conducted in 2002, focused on Lambeth Borough Council (LBC) as the empirical case. LBC is the local government authority for London Borough of Lambeth (LBL). LBL is one of thirteen Boroughs of the Greater London area and occupies almost a central position in it. By the case study strategy [35], the study was aimed at understanding the IS innovation challenges in public organisations. The study investigated the Council's information management processes in the face of IT and public bureaucracy. The qualitative results, thus, highlight the dynamic behaviours of the main dependent elements of information management – people and information – in response to the institutions of IT and public bureaucracy. In operationalising this strategy, the data were collected through meetings, interviews, documents, the internet and the Council's intranet.

LBC's central aim of public services delivery presented immense challenges. It was in competition with other local councils in terms of Best Value Performance (BVP). BVP indicators had been formulated by the central government to provide a nationally consistent framework for measuring progress in public services delivery. The emergence of the Internet and World Wide Web imposed even greater challenges for BVP. Yet, at the time of this study, the council had not prepared a formal information and knowledge management strategy to guide its information-related decisions and operations. The state of information in the council corroborated a history of *ad hoc* information related decision-making in the council.

LBC was making efforts to accelerate the steps towards meeting these e-government BVP targets, but only as far as *providing information* and *consultation* which were online, with the rest at the rudimentary stages of planning. Even with information provision, interviews indicated that searching for council documents online was frustrating.

With over 10,000 documents scattered on its website, the council seemed to lack the appropriate search software to make online document search easy for its customers. Besides, metadata tagging of the documents was poor. The ability of the Council's website to support smooth documents search by the public was important with regard to accountability, information retrieval and retrieval times, and empowering the citizen with the information resource. Citizens' rights to access documents on the council's website had been given legal backing in the Freedom of Information (FoI) Act 2000. Thus, the council had a significant problem to tackle.

Organisational Processes

LBC's processes reflected personal and political power relations. The political processes thrived in unison and in various degrees of domination within the information handling processes. According to a member of the SMB,

"*[There are] a mix of all of them! Actually, there needs to be another [process] – random – because a lot of the time, decision-making processes have reflected crisis management and expedient solutions. But I would say that the political type is a generally true feature that permeates everything.*"

'Random' processes reflected in senior managers' attitude to IT. Although IT was embraced by them as a useful tool in the Council's operations especially e-governance, it was evident that IT had been isolated instead of being fully integrated into service delivery operations. As a result, a lot of middle managers were either circumspect or, at worst, doubtful about the prospects of IT.

"*[Senior managers] see IT as an overhead. They have a long way to go to recognise the value and power of what is available on the desks of their staff. There are very few areas where process management and automation has been used to improve service delivery and/or cost.*" – Head of IT.

"*We don't have good processes that we could easily automate. We still have lots of paper-based systems. The bulk of work is to make the processes work properly today before we can then automate.*" – a Councillor.

The council had planned to integrate information systems strategy with business strategy. There was sufficient evidence from the numerous BV Review reports and the council's objectives that pointed to attempts at alignment. Besides, its information systems were disintegrated and impliedly did not support collaboration of efforts from various divisions of the council.

"*[There is] too much duplication, too little cohesiveness between departments*" – Head of IT.

"*We had a history of managers spending their money as they wanted and they often did their own thing without thinking about what the person sitting next to them would be doing, and what the department next to them would be doing*" – a Councillor.

Information management and culture

There did not seem to be any formalised mechanisms instituted to facilitate organisational learning at LBC.

"*On organisational learning, my observation is very poor on things like learning from past strategic experience through controlled experiments and executive seminars. We are not really a data-driven organisation.*" – Director of Culture change.

Organisational learning in the council was in this poor state because of its organisational culture. For instance, it was loosely assumed that every section of the council would play some minimum role towards effective and efficient use of information albeit unsystematic and disintegrated. The e-government and BV wind was blowing across the council, apparently because it was being enforced by the central government. But commitment levels were low among some managers and lower level employees, and the roles of various participants seemed disjointed. This was an immense challenge in terms of culture change. It was clear that the new ideology that was required to catalyze the change process within the council was not available, even at the management level.

"I think there is a real historical legacy here. Managers have had to make decisions without having [the required] information. Because there haven't been any information systems in place, they have usually made decisions based on inspiration, talking to few people, and often being quite successful in doing that." – Director of Culture Change.

Besides, fear of redundancy among lower-level staff was a significant factor that impacted negatively on commitment levels to changes in information handling within the council.

There was also a general lack of true understanding of what is achievable through the use of IT in the council. Even though many of the employees had a sense that computers and IT can do a lot of things, there were still many who were just not aware of how they could be used to enhance their activities. As a result, there was low use of IT in the council. It was observed that almost all desks had workstations.

"In terms of internal processes, I think as an organisation, we are not all good at using and sharing information. The fact that e-mail exists helps a lot but that mean that every manager is very heavily dependent on e-mail. We don't have shared drives, and we don't have bulletin board areas or anything like that." – member of SMB.

IT operations were intended to support business objectives. According to the Head of IT, although his department had specific objectives, there were no clearly defined strategies to ensure efficient and effective alignment of IT and business innovation.

4   Public Organisations and Challenges of IS Innovation

The case suggests that attempts at technology integration for information management are fraught with serious tensions between IT and public bureaucracy. The following analysis hinges on the integral components of information management – information and people. Each of these components is further analysed in terms of the institutions of IT and public bureaucracy to show the challenges facing IS innovation and how they can be addressed.

4.1   Relationship between Public Bureaucracy and People

Public bureaucracy as an institution had considerable effects on the employees of the Council and their activities. Public bureaucracies operate with a basic principle of equality and impartiality in their provision of services to citizens, thereby enforcing democratic values [8, p.270]. Grounded in this ethos, local councils operate as low-entrepreneurial bureaucracies [32, 28]. This ethos is a context that affected the employees of the Council. For instance, their exhibition of random or ad hoc processes constituted enactments of political organisation. The employees' political decision-making processes that reflected crisis management and expedient solutions are reactive. According to Moe [28, p.127-127], the necessity for compromise in politics calls for expediency and effectiveness rather than efficiency in the design of public organisations. These processes exhibited by the employees of the Council also reflected their limited knowledge. Limited knowledge is usually caused by information barriers that prohibit information sharing and awareness creation between employees. Their paper-based information moved slowly, was difficult to access, and contributed to the creation of barriers to information. Political processes thrive in environments saturated with information barriers, but they leave employees destitute of shared knowledge.

INSTITUTIONS	Information Technology	Expected • Nature (digital) • Medium (computer) • Knowledge (leaky) • Movement (high speed) • Processing (more efficient) • Systems (innovative/flexible) Finding ○ Poor website design ○ Poor search	Expected • Attribute (entrepreneurial) • Involvement (highly non-inclusive) • Knowledge (expanded) • Actions (transparent, and measurable) • Discretion (expanded) • Impact (highly limited) Finding ○ IT as overhead ○ Poor understanding of the actual value of IT (low use of IT)

	Public Bureaucracy	Existing
		• Nature (analogue)
		• Medium (paper)
		• Knowledge (sticky)
		• Movement (low speed)
		• Processing (less efficient)
		• Systems (customary/routine)
		
		Finding
		○ Poor legacy systems
		○ Poor information sharing
		○ Managers making decisions
		  without adequate
		  information
			Existing
			• Attribute (non-entrepreneurial)
			• Involvement (moderately non-inclusive)
			• Knowledge (limited)
			• Activities (transparent and measurable)
			• Discretion (limited)
			• Impact (limited)
			
			Finding
			○ Ad hoc processes
			○ Poor collaboration between managers
			○ Poor organisation learning
			○ Low commitment levels to BV
			○ Managers make decisions by intuition
			  (without adequate information)

		Information	**People**
		INFORMATION MANAGEMENT ELEMENTS	

Fig. 1. Relationship between the institutions and information management elements

The employees' exhibition of low commitment to the Best Value Practices (BVP) can be explained by the non-inclusive terms by which they were involved in the organisation. The social foundations of the bureaucratic order are the non-inclusive involvement of employees in organisations [22]. Only the individual's role (not the full person) is included in formal organising. The effects of non-inclusivity are over-specialisation, limited discretion and low inclination to initiative-taking. Thus, Özcan and Reichstein [32, p.606] argue that a chief concern among public employees is their "diminished sense of impact." Commitment to BVP would entail employees' initiatives and contingent behaviours, but bureaucratic rules are purported to exclude them. It would also entail employees' efforts to be recognised and rewarded, but their sense of inability to make any changes holds them back.

4.2 Relationship between Information Technology and People

Information technology as an institution was envisioned to address all the problems that employees of public organisations face due to the effects of bureaucracy. IT integration in public organisations aims at their low-entrepreneurial ethos to induce high degrees of entrepreneurship. This has been the predominant philosophy of the new public management (NPM) reform agenda [16, 31] which proposes a radical change in the underlying logic of public organisations, and in the parameters of assessing actions therein. It assumes that public bureaucratic organisations that aim for *effectiveness* must be reformed to aim for *efficiency* [33]. At the time of this research, NPM had highly informed the BVP ideal. But, interestingly, the efficiency or market orientation of the Council's employees through IT did not materialise. This is because those efficiency ideals of IT were challenged considerably by low-entrepreneurial attitudes and expedient actions of the employees.

Thus, employees had poor understanding of the value of IT that caused management to perceive IT as overhead. The envisioned value of IT, informed by NPM-based Best Value Practices, was to make actions more transparent, measurable and efficient. The institution of IT is imbued with an efficiency order borne of the entrepreneurship in its production and consumption. IT production is now a predominant aspect of the global economy [2], as witnessed in the emergence of giant internet and software businesses and their high-valued technology stocks in the international exchange markets. IT consumption is also commonplace in organisations' innovation initiatives aimed at gaining competitive advantage. However, public organisations are not even judged by efficiency but by effectiveness in delivery of services equitably and impartially . Employees' poor understanding of the value of IT, thus, lied in their judgment that it was largely impotent for effectiveness in the public organisational context.

4.3 Relationship between Public Bureaucracy and Information

The low-entrepreneurial ethos of public bureaucracy reflects the nature, media, processing, and systems of information in it. The paper-based media that bear information in public organisations inherently inhibit information sharing. This is because reproduction and dissemination of information with these media are relatively expensive, and therefore prohibitive. Movement of information with these media is slow and cumbersome, inducing the generation of information silos and barriers. Beside the media, the information culture of employees can explain the poor information sharing. Alavi and colleagues [1], for example, argue that employees will share information if their organisation operates a group reward scheme; and vice versa. Individual reward schemes are prevalent in public organisations because of the high degrees of specialisation associated with employees. Skills specialisation coupled with on-the-job training increase the transaction and opportunity costs of leaving public organisations [32]. Employees are, therefore, induced to protect their roles by keeping information tacit instead of sharing to make them explicit. This results in the "stickiness" of knowledge [5] in particular specialisations at the expense of others.

4.4 Relationship between Information Technology and People

IT as an institution is believed to engender efficiency in information capturing, processing, storage, and dissemination. This belief rests on the digital nature of computer-based information which makes it very amenable for easy sharing, for informing citizens through its website, and for enhancing citizens' search for information on the website. Easy information sharing through IT would have resulted in the "leakiness" of knowledge [5] across specialisations in the Council. But the reality was "sticky" knowledge. The poor design of the Council's website and the poor search reflected poor use of internet technology to inform citizens about the various services being offered. Managing information on a website demanded constant updating of the pieces of information and tagging them with the relevant metadata according to established standards of Best Value Practices. These would depend on both responsiveness and initiatives of the employees. However, the dependence on employees' initiatives for providing timely and accurate information to citizens through a website seems to be a monumental challenge. This is because, rewards and promotions are not necessarily tied to employees' contributions in public organisations [32]. Therefore, it is difficult to suddenly turn to depend on employee initiatives for information sharing, and knowledge creation and synthesis. It is likely they will not be motivated to match the demands of IT with their responses.

5   Discussion

The institutional analysis of the challenges of IS innovation induces us to exercise greater circumspection when addressing them. Its central argument is that the primary step of IS innovation is to understand the unquestionable forces behind the orders of IT and public bureaucracy as well as their implications for information management. The primary step is not to think of structuring or restructuring bureaucratic or low-entrepreneurial processes of public organisations with IT, or vice versa. Rather, it is to think of confronting these institutions with the aim of adjusting and aligning them .

Institutional adjustment reflects the old maxim of IS that says 'if you do not sort out your mess before computerizing, you computerize the mess, and end up being worse off.' But this maxim is losing its appeal because of increasing claims in the IS literature that computerization can be used to sort out the mess in high-entrepreneurial organisations [e.g. 17]. Interestingly, IT and high-entrepreneurial organisations share the same efficiency principle and are easily substitutable. Therefore, the claims can be true in that context but may not be true in the context of public organisations. The principle of practice in public organisations is effectiveness in equitable distribution of services to citizens, making IT substitution an imprudent prospect. Therefore, IS innovation should be approached from aligning IT and public organisations according to their institutional realities, not according to the high expectations from substitution, transformation, structuration and reform.

This paper's argument resonates with the works of Cordella [8] and Dunleavy and colleagues [11] who reject the efficiency goals of the NPM agenda. Cordella calls for e-government projects to apply IT to public bureaucracy with the aim of achieving the e-bureaucratic form. The e-bureaucratic form appreciates the enduring role of public bureaucracy in delivering public services effectively, as this paper argues. However, his discussion of this form is limited because it takes IT for granted by refusing to problematise it. This paper, however, problematises both IT and public bureaucracy and provides a more holistic discussion of the relationship between them.

Dunleavy and colleagues' pronouncement of the death of NPM is supported by a critique of its many limitations [11, 12]. Their critique is in harmony with that of this paper. But their proposal focuses on reintegration of various government organisations that were separated or privatised under NPM; on interactions between public organisations and clients in terms of the latters' needs; and on using digitisation as transformative rather than supplementary to organisational processes. Thus, digital-era governance privileges technological determinism and optimism in its tenets while this paper does not do so.

Fountain [13, 15] also approaches IT integration in public organisations from an institutional perspective. In harmony with this paper's argument, she concludes that e-government efforts will not live up to their expectations if organizational and social institutions remain the same. Indeed, she argues, just as this paper, against substitution of social or organisational processes with technology [13, p.80]. However, her approach does not consider technology as an institution, but as an instrument, leaving her institutional change arguments limited to public bureaucracy. With an instrumental, rather than institutional, view of technology, her analysis of it is confined to interpretive flexibility at the organisational level. Moreover, her institutional approach fails to show how institutional obstacles can be overcome to lead to change. But this paper explains it primarily in terms of institutional change, and considers organisational analysis of technology as secondary.

5.1 Suggestions for Adjusting Public Bureaucracy

If any processes in public bureaucracy are perceived to be messy or problematic and need sorting out, then that should be done by adjusting the institution itself rather than depending on IT. One useful approach to institutional adjustment in public bureaucracy is to understand it in terms of constitutive and variable characteristics of the bureaucratic order [22]. The variable characteristics such as standardised and centralised operating procedures can be reassembled, recombined and reshuffled to deal with contingences that emerge. DiMaggio and Powell [10] provide useful insights on the sources of these variable characteristics and how they cause institutional homogeneity in public organisations. Institutional homogeneity refers to those characteristics shared by public organisations to make them so similar. By their insights, public organisations are typical instances of public bureaucracy shaped by external constraints imposed by the state, employee migrations, and the professions. Interestingly, these sources lie outside the influence of public organisations, making it difficult for the changes to be initiated from the organisational level. The external influences make it even more difficult to depend on the instrumental order of IT to change the variable characteristics of the bureaucratic order. Changes in these external sources should be the bases of institutional adjustment in public bureaucracy that will, hopefully, translate into changes in operating procedures and employee roles.

5.2 Suggestions for Adjusting IT

The institutional approach to IS innovation suggests a departure from visions of appropriation of IT by employees and structuration of their processes at the institutional level. It calls for restraining IT commitments and expectations in respect of the various IT projects ongoing or intended in public organisations. This is quite unusual because of the unquestioned momentum of the IT institution in e-government projects, yet it is a prudent choice for public organisations. It suggests a lowering of expectations from IT in terms of efficiency, rationality, and entrepreneurship, as in the NPM agenda. IT also suggests aiming IT projects not at automating all public organisational processes, but only the few that are already reasonably rationalised and efficient. This will substitute those processes with automated versions, thus confining the regulative regime of technology to them only [23]. IT can be programmed to include a very wide variety of functions that can provide options for various users in public organisations. Aiming for technology that has this capability underscores the institutional adjustment argument of this paper because the technology itself becomes the target of transformation. Institutional adjustment of IT aims at making technology amenable and constructible by public organisations instead of making it the determinant.

6 Conclusion

The aim of this paper was to analyse, from an institutional perspective, the labyrinths of IS innovation in public organisations. An important aspect of this perspective is the perception of IT as an institution in its own right. The analysis has revealed that if each of IT and public bureaucracy are adjusted properly at their institutional levels, then their alignment at the organisational level will be less problematic. At the organisational level, their interaction in operations will be more effective and useful for equity and impartiality in the delivery of public services. Taking the institutional approach to IS innovation in public organisations is, therefore, important for analysing the tensions between IT and public organisations.

References

1. Alavi, M., Kayworth, T., Leidner, D.E.: An Empirical Examination of the Influence of Organizational Culture on Knowledge Management Practices. Journal of Management Information Systems 22, 191–224 (2005)
2. Avgerou, C.: IT and Organizational Change: An Institutionalist Perspective. Information Technology and People 13, 234–262 (2000)
3. Avgerou, C.: Information Systems and Global Diversity. Oxford University Press, Oxford (2002)

4. Bellamy, C., Taylor, J.A.: Governing in the Information Age. Open University Press, Buckingham (1998)
5. Brown, J.S., Duguid, P.: Organizing Knowledge. California Management Review 40, 90–111 (1998)
6. Chadwick, A., May, C.: Interaction between States and Citizens in the Age of the Internet: E-Government in the United States, Britain and the European Union. Governance: An International Journal of Policy, Administration and Institutions 16, 271–300 (2003)
7. Chisholm, R.F.: Introducing Advanced Information Technology into Public Organizations. Public Productivity Review 11, 39–56 (1988)
8. Cordella, A.: E-Government: Towards the E-Bureaucratic Form? Journal of Information Technology 22, 265–274 (2007)
9. Daft, R.L.: A Dual-Core Model of Organizational Innovation. Academy of Management Journal 21, 193–210 (1978)
10. DiMaggio, P.J., Powell, W.W.: The Iron Cage Revisited: Institutional Isomorphism and Collective Rationality in Organizational Fields. American Sociological Review 48, 147–160 (1983)
11. Dunleavy, P., Margetts, H., Bastow, S., Tinkler, J.: New Public Management is Dead - Long Live Digital-Era Governance. Journal of Public Administration Research and Theory 16, 467–494 (2005)
12. Dunleavy, P., Margetts, H., Bastow, S., Tinkler, J.: Digital Era Governance: IT Corporations, the State, and e-Government. Oxford University Press, Oxford (2006)
13. Fountain, J.E.: Building the Virtual State: Information Technology and Institutional Change. Brookings Institution Press, Washington (2001)
14. Fountain, J.E.: Information, Institutions, and Governance: Advancing a Basic Social Science Research Program for Digital Government. Kennedy School of Government, Harvard University (2003)
15. Fountain, J.E.: Bureaucratic Reform and E-Government in the United States: An Institutional Perspective 2007, National Centre for Digital Government (2007)
16. Gruening, G.: Origin and Theoretical Basis of New Public Management. International Public Management Journal 4, 1–25 (2001)
17. Gurbaxani, V., Whang, S.: The Impact of Informatuon Systems on Organizations and Markets. Communications of the ACM 34, 59–73 (1991)
18. Heeks, R.: Reinventing Government in the Information Age. In: Heeks, R. (ed.) Reinventing Government in the Information Age: International Practice in IT-enabled Public Sector Reform. Routledge, London (2001)
19. Henriksen, H.Z., Damsgaard, J.: Dawn of E-Government - An Institutional Analysis fo Seven Initiatives and their Impact. Journal of Information Technology 22, 13–23 (2007)
20. Irani, Z., Elliman, T., Jackson, P.: Electronic Transformation of Government in the UK: A Research Agenda. European Journal of Information Systems 16, 327–335 (2007)
21. Jepperson, R.L.: Institutions, Institutional Effects, and Institutionalism. In: Powell, W.W., DiMaggio, P.J. (eds.) The New Institutionalism in Organizational Analysis. University of Chicago Press, Chicago (1991)
22. Kallinikos, J.: The Social Foundations of the Bureaucratic Order. Organization 11, 13–36 (2004)
23. Kallinikos, J.: The Regulative Regime of Technology. In: Contini, F., Lanzara, G.F. (eds.) ICT and Innovation in the Public Sector: European Studies in the Making of E-government. Palgrave Macmillan, Basingstoke (2009)
24. Kim, S., Kim, H.J., Lee, H.: An Institutional Analysis of an E-Government System for Anti-Corruption. Government Information Quarterly 26, 42–50 (2009)

25. Kraemer, K.L., King, J.L.: Information Technology and Administrative Reform: Will E-Government Be Different? International Journal of Electronic Government Research 2, 1–20 (2006)
26. Lanzara, G.F.: Building Digital Institutions: ICT and the Rise of Assemblages in Government. In: Contini, F., Lanzara, G.F. (eds.) ICT and Innovation in the Public Sector: European Studies in the Making of E-Government. Palgrave Macmillan, Basingstoke (2009)
27. Meyer, J.W., Rowan, B.: Institutionalized Organizations: Formal Structure as Myth and Ceremony. American Journal of Sociology 83, 340–363 (1977)
28. Moe, T.M.: The Politics of Structural Choice: Toward a Theory of Public Bureaucracy. In: Williamson, O.E. (ed.) Organization Theory: From Chester Barnard to the Present and Beyond. Oxford University Press, New York (1990)
29. O'Donnell, O., Boyle, R., Timonen, V.: Transformational Aspects of E-Government in Ireland. Electronic Journal of Electronic Government 1, 23–32 (2003)
30. Oliver, C.: Strategic Responses to Institutional Processes. Academy of Management Review 16, 145–179 (1991)
31. Osborne, D., Gaebler, T.: Reinventing Government: How the Entrepreneurial Spirit is Transforming the Public Sector. Addison-Wesley, Reading (1992)
32. Özcan, S., Reichstein, T.: Transition to Entrepreneurship from the Public Sector: Predispositional and Contextual Effects. Management Science 55, 604–618 (2009)
33. Pollit, C., Bouchaert, G.: Public Management Reform. Oxford University Press, Oxford (2004)
34. Swanson, E.B.: Information Systems Innovation Among Organizations. Management Science 40, 1069–1092 (1994)
35. Yin, R.K.: Case Study Research: Design and Methods. Sage, Newbury Park (1984)

Agriculture Market Information Services (AMIS) in the Least Developed Countries (LDCs): Nature, Scopes, and Challenges

M. Sirajul Islam and Åke Grönlund

Örebro University, Swedish Business School
Fakultetsgatan 1, Örebro 701 82, Sweden
{sirajul.islam,ake.gronlund}@oru.se

Abstract. Rural growth is seen as an engine to drive the economy of developing countries and the use of Agriculture Market Information Services (AMIS) is believed to enable this growth. This paper is based on a literature study and investigates the spread and use of AMIS in the least developed countries (n=49) in terms of users, management, funding, infrastructure, and data. We investigate success as well as failure aspects, and discuss the role of new technologies. Findings show that while new technologies can improve dissemination of information, collecting data economically and meeting high quality requirements remains major challenges. The study contributes by providing a comprehensive view of the challenges of AMIS in developing countries and an AMIS project evaluation matrix (IS-PEM) based on the findings, which together contribute to improving the design of future projects.

Keywords: ICT4D, AMIS, agricultural market information systems, LDCs, Rural Development, IS Project Evaluation Matrix (IS-PEM).

1 Introduction

There is a growing consensus that for world poverty to be eliminated, and the Millennium Development Goals to be fulfilled, we need to focus on rural growth [1]. Rural growth is shown to have much higher returns than other sectors and can therefore be seen as an engine to drive the economic growth of the entire nation [2]. One way of facilitating rural growth is through the use of Agriculture Market Information Services (AMIS). AMIS is defined as "A service, usually operated by the public sector (Ministry of Agriculture or a dependent agency or institute), which involves the collection on a regular basis of information on prices, and in some cases quantities supplied, of widely consumed agricultural products, from wholesale markets, rural assembly and retail markets, as appropriate, and dissemination of this information on a regular basis through various means (bulletin boards, radio or television bulletins, newspapers, etc.) to farmers, traders, government officials, policy-makers and others [3, p.1]". According to a FAO survey of 120 countries during 1995 - 1996 [4], there were 53 government operated AMIS, most of which were limited to data collection and had little association to the needs of the farmers and traders.

M.A. Wimmer et al. (Eds.): EGOV 2010, LNCS 6228, pp. 109–120, 2010.

The use of ICT in agriculture especially for information processing is imperative for a country where the economy is dominated heavily by agricultural activities. The need for information is shifting from the use of agricultural technologies towards effective participation and sharing of innovations in national and global markets [5]. This shift is important for economic efficiency, performance, and equity [6]. However, the performance of AMIS upgraded by means of new technologies is yet to be evaluated in a comprehensive and convincing manner. Without such evaluation it is difficult to determine the market efficiency effects, the reductions in transaction costs and the extent of improvement of market integration [7]. This paper therefore contributes to reducing the shortage of such evaluation studies by exploring the nature and presence of AMIS, as well as challenges encountered, in particular among all the 49 LDCs [8]. The research questions addressed in this paper are:

1. What types of AMIS exist in the LDCs in terms of which technologies are used, how they are managed, and what their outreach is?
2. What are the factors critical to success or failure for AMIS projects?

2 Method

In order to achieve a comprehensive charting of AMIS in LDCs two online literature surveys conducted consecutively in May 2008 and December 2009. For locating as many different AMIS as possible, the initial search was very open and conducted by consulting Google (www.google.com) and Google Scholar (http://scholar.google.com/). This search generated many cases of AMIS and useful links to websites and portals on the subject. In order to focus particularly on scientific evaluation papers the second search was conducted by an academic search engine which is hosted by Örebro University (Sweden) and covers several academic databases. In addition to these two search methods, the 'snowball method' [9] was also used to find relevant cases based on the literature we had found. For that search, saturation was used as the stop criterion: the search stopped when no new or special cases were found. We also consulted the online AMIS database [10] maintained by the Michigan State University (MSU). In addition to MSU, this paper used a working paper [11] on market information sources and AMIS-Africa Online database.

Since this study specifically targets LDCs, we started with a search where each country's name was combined with a search term – 'Agriculture Market Information'. In case of unavailability of country specific such services, portals of the related ministries (e.g. agriculture in most cases) of concerned countries had been investigated.

The data from the survey was categorized and analysed based on an evaluation matrix (Table 1) developed by the authors in lack of a commonly used evaluation toolkit in the IS research community. Although AMIS are more or less present in most countries, evaluation or impact studies are yet few [7, 12, 13]. One of the reasons of this lack is the deficiencies in measurement and methodological toolkits. While it is possible to know the number of information recipients, it is difficult to identify their needs and their uses of information. There are indeed some studies that attempt to quantify some benefits, but these are mostly based on limited empirical evidence [6, 13, 14, 15].

Table 1. Research matrix – Information System Project Evaluation Matrix (IS-PEM)

Focus dimensions	Who	What	When	How
Users	(Target) Who are the targeted main user(s) ?	(Needs) What needs are targeted to address?	(Time) When do the users get the service?	(Accessibility) How do the users access the service and how affordable the cost is?
Management	(Managers) Who manages?	(Roles) What are the roles of participants?	(Duration) When did it start and end?	(Strategy) How are the targeted needs planned to address or are addressed ?
Funding	(Sponsors) Who provides the funds?	(Budget) What is the functional allocation of funding?	(Period) What was the period for funding?	(Sustainability) How the fund has been managed; short & long term perspective?
Infrastructure	(Suppliers) Who owns/provides both the supply and demand sides' infrastructure?	(Tools) What infrastructures are considered on both supply and demand sides?	(Availability) When does the infrastructure readily available for targeted operation?	(Use) How the infrastructure is used for targeted operation?
Data	(Providers) Who are the actors in data supply chain?	(Data) What are the data?	(Lead-time) When is the data processed and disseminated?	(Process) How is the data processed for operation?

The research framework used in this study is called the "IS-PEM" model (Table 1). It has five focus dimensions (vertical); Users, Management, Funding, Infrastructure and Data. Each of these dimensions is investigated by means of four strategic and critical questions – who, what, when and how (horizontal). Each cell of the matrix contains a keyword and is associated with queries that would lead to find the most pertinent aspects of a project.

The strategic questions are derived from the well-known 5W2H (Why, What, Who, When, Where, How to and How much) scheme which is frequently used in the discipline of Total Quality Management (TQM). The 5W2H is a systematic root cause analysis technique which is particularly useful when a suspected problem of a project needs to be better defined and reviewed and overall the project process has improvement opportunities [16, 17]. In our matrix, we assume that the aspect 'why' is inherited in all the other aspects while analyzing the situation under a certain context. Furthermore, the 'where' is a 'space' of the object under analysis which is known already. Finally, 'how to' and 'how much' are merged together as only 'how' [17] which explains simultaneously the ways and extent of resolving the problems. This simplification leaves us with the IS-PEM model in Table 1.

We used the model to investigate each project, looking primarily for success and failure factors. Success and failure is measured as stated by either independent evaluations or self-assessment made by, typically, service providers. We hence do not re-assess projects, but look for factors contributing to success or failure, as found in other people's research.

3   Evolution of AMIS: Past to Present

The history of AMIS, at least theoretically, started with the inception of agricultural trade when the farmers used to trade their surplus produce by considering some degrees of spatial and temporal arbitrages. Such trading appeared in ancient Rome during the 1st century BC and in Muslim Caliphate during the 9th century; however the process of the time in accessing price information is not known. During 1200 AD in England and Wales, there was a recorded and organized price information system [18]. The origin of AMIS, by definition, can be traced about 300 years back to the Canterbury Farmers' Club where the farmers of Kent used to have regular meetings with the Club Secretary for exchanging views regarding the agriculture prices [19]. As for the first institutionalized AMIS, it was the Office of Markets which was set up in May 16, 1913, in the USA [19].

With the inception of modern innovation after the World war II, AMIS tend to transform from passive (one way and static) to real-time and interactive services. An early implementation of such active services was found in 1956 in Salinas, California when the USDA Agricultural Marketing Service installed the first machine for Instant Market News (IMN). There the reports for lettuce were disseminated via automatic telephone answering devices on a regular basis [20]. Further in the USA in 1980, the Science and Education Administration of US Department of Agriculture introduced a new system called 'Green Thumb' which was designed for disseminating commodity, weather, and other agricultural information every day from a special computer system which was hooked-up with home telephones and TV [21].

Outside the developed world, organized uses of price information have also been found in several developing countries since the 1950s. These include the Indonesian price monitoring system in the late 1950s [3], the MIS of Nepal in 1960 [12], the MIS of Mali in 1989 and the AMIS of Philippines in 1991 which was designed for female growers and collectors of various non-timber forest products in Quezon province [22].

Nevertheless, the nature and characteristics of MIS have been changing with the de-regularization of economies in 1980s and subsequent changes of market dynamics, progress of information and communication technologies and subsequent changes in farming techniques. In fact, the definition of AMIS has been changing in terms of its contents, geographical factors, technology and management. However despite such progressive trends, the impact and sustainability of AMIS remain the teething issues.

4   AMIS in LDCs: A Critical Evaluation

There have been many AMIS available in the developing countries but their track records are generally not satisfactory as they have most often been about data-gathering for statistical purposes and had very little commercial values to the farming community [23]. Therefore, the following section discusses the success and failure aspects of the contemporary AMIS in the LDCs and subsequently summarizes the major failure factors based on the IS project evaluation matrix (IS-PEM) as discussed (The success factors table had to be excluded for reasons of space).

Table 2. Major Failure Factors of AMIS

Dimensions	Who	What	When	How
Users	Undefined	Inadequate assessment of user needs	After transaction; not on-demand	Inappropriate channel, high cost
Management	Centralized management	Routine work; low commitment, coordination and pro-activeness	Project orientation takes longer time than implementation	Absence of clear strategy , lack of impact evaluation, lack of partnerships
Funding	Relying heavily on external funding	Allocated as a sub-component of a different project; insufficient	Short-term and non-persistent	Poor financial management and unrealistic business model
Infrastructure	Single source; without partnership	Inflexible and un-adapted technologies (e.g. Websites)	Premature (e.g. Websites)	Underutilization and disruption
Data	Inefficient and less committed collectors; Unreliable providers.	Un-updated; time insensitive; sub-standard; Non-qualitative	Long lead time	Non-standardized; delayed collection and dissemination; manual intervention

Users' Perspective

Despite the presence of various forms of market information services, most of the primary stakeholders (e.g farmers, traders) usually obtain the price information through their traditional sources, such as words of mouth from other farmers, neighbors, local schools, price-boards at markets, NGOs and religious or community leaders and network [13, 14, 24]. However, farmers generally perceive that the information from such sources may not be reliable and trustworthy [25].

Garforth [26] finds that the information seeking behavior of farmers apparently depends on the accessibility of information sources and markets, farming systems and livelihoods. The literature reports a lack of assessment and clarity in AMIS requirement specifications, in particular to identifying the primary stakeholders and their needs within a certain socio-economic, technological and behavioral contexts [24, 27, 28]. Insufficient awareness of the value of the services [25, 29] and reluctance towards a user-oriented approach [24] apparently contribute to low or even no sense of ownership [30] for the AMIS. There are many services which are designed in non-native languages (English in most cases) that ultimately create an access barrier to the rural clients [31]. The AMIS of Mali (OMA), a highly regarded service in Africa, was able to make its services available to 70% of Malian population including farmers located in very remote locations [32]. One of the main reasons behind the success of Malian initiative is its ability to satisfy the needs of the diverse clients. This has been achieved through regular contact with the clients, periodic impact evaluation and updating the services as required [33].

There has been a lack of prioritization among the components of AMIS [28, 34]. For example, rather than having wholesale price information (e.g. Agripricenepal.com), farmers seem to be more interested in time specific and reliable maximum farm-gate, off-lorry and retail prices of the nearest and the main neighboring markets [35]. Here, timely dissemination is defined by the availability of information just before or during the time of business transactions [36]. There is also a complementary relation between access to information and access to extension services. Those who are benefitted with price information services would be interested in other information as well such as weather forecasts, advices for crop production, and uses of appropriate seeds and fertilizers [6, 12, 34, 37].

It has been observed that payment for the services by the poor rural people is a critical issue for the sustainability of AMIS [38]. From a user's perspective, delivery methods need to be low cost [37] as the farmers are often reluctant to pay for the services since they do not see far ahead regarding the value of their investment.

Above all, it has been apparent that most AMIS mainly serve the needs of the policy makers [24], researchers and development offices rather than the ultimate target group such as farmers. As in most of cases AMIS are funded by the donors, they become the ultimate clients and accordingly their needs are valued more than those of the farmers [39].

Management Perspective

AMIS is generally initiated by the concerned department of the Ministry of Agriculture [23]. The donors and NGOs in line of their existing agenda of rural development tend to work together or in parallel with the governments in order to make the marketing channel more efficient and effective. However, not all efforts have proven to be successful. In fact, the sustainability of AMIS has always been a challenging issue [38] and the quality of supply-side managerial operation is one important factor in this challenge.

Direct government intervention with the AMIS tends to have limited success [40]. Highly centralized, structured and authoritative governmental administrations in most of developing nations usually work through a complex decision making process and henceforth takes longer time to implement a project. Furthermore, following the lack of accountability and incentives, government officials exhibit inadequate pro-activeness and low motivation to understand the practical contexts of the end users.

As a high degree of managerial autonomy contributes to efficiency in the operational processes [41], AMIS need to be decentralized in the areas where there are regional price differences [12]. The decentralization of Mali's MIS (OMA) in 1998 by moving its control to the Malian Chambers of Agriculture from the government has made it an exemplary service among the West African countries [41].

Carrilho et al. [42] found that the price collectors of AMIS are not adequately trained and there were often irregularities in data collection and tabulation processes. Tollens [7] also found that the officials involved in data collection and dissemination processes are not so efficient. Training is generally required for orienting the unskilled operating staff [26]. On the other hand, as FAO reports [29], there is a shortage of specialized MIS trainers. Overall there has been a lack of institutional incentives [29] and therefore a lack of pro-activeness towards smooth operation of AMIS [33].

Most AMIS are projects in nature and funded for two to five years. However, a significant portion of this duration is spent on project orientation and preparation. For example, Cambodian Agricultural Market Information project (CAMIP) was approved for January 2006 until October 2009. Within this period, actual implementation (FM broadcasting) was started only a year before the completion of the project. Such use of the allotted time leaves little time for the systems to settle so that reasonable evaluation of effects can be made.

Finding dedicated and capable partners to provide quality services seems a challenging task [43]. In particular, cooperation from the private sector is a big challenge [44]. This is mainly for lack of perceived mutual benefits among the prospective parties [45]. This situation leads to challenges in the sustainability of projects especially in the issues like cost and finance, technology, promotion and education, and getting the governments involved in the processes [13].

Lack of information and communication management (ICM) polices at the national or project level [25] and absence of a steering committee in order to manage the processes and monitor the service quality [29] are critical failure factors. These deficiencies bring many undesirable consequences, such as inefficient coordination and non-participation among the various agencies [24], weak content management at the local level [29, 46], and reluctance to carry out periodic impact evaluations [7, 12]. Notably, lack of support from upper management and lack of practical commitment in all levels of administration to facilitate timely and accurate data create many sustainability problems. Trust and reliability issues are not given adequate importance in many services, which is crucial for user acceptance of services. For example the 'terms of use' page of eSoko (former TradeNet based in Ghana) states that 'we have no control over, do not guarantee, and you will not hold us responsible for, the quality, safety or legality of any content on the Service; the truth or accuracy of any contention of the Service'.

Funding Perspective

Most AMIS, unless it has been a regular job of the concerned ministry, are donor dependent. In this regard, donors generally participate with the governments in cooperation with other local partners. Major AMIS donors include FAO, CTA, USAID, ADB, GTZ, IICD and World Bank. National AMIS are funded through the respective national budgets as part of regular activities of the concerned departments of the ministries. Countries who have such AMIS include, for example, Bangladesh, Myanmar, Liberia and Mozambique. Generally, allocation of funds is done by assessment of relevance for mission or policy, economic and social impacts, urgency, scope of operations, modalities, time lengths and degree of short and long-run prospects of the projects. Such funds are allocated either as one sub-components of a project (e.g. part of second component of the project as entitled "Agricultural Productivity and Food Security Project" in Burkina Faso, supported by the World Bank) or as an independent project (e.g. Cambodia-Canada Agricultural Market Information Project or CAMIP).

Having a realistic financial and business model and efficient financial management are the most important aspects of a project's financial sustainability. Therefore, there is a need for a realistic economic model for network extension and continuity of a quality service that would ultimately help to strengthen the socio-economic activities of the rural community [47]. In this regard, Roberts et al. [13] suggest that the financial model should have the right mix of subsidy and feasible user fees. For example, Mali's MIS (OMA) achieves sustainability by having support for its operating cost from the national budget of the government, getting equipments and technical assistances from the donors, and earning revenues through advertisements and selling specialized market information [41, 48].

Lack of, non-persistence, or delayed funding is another root cause of lack of project sustainability [6, 7, 25, 29, 28, 42, 46]. Findings reveal that most projects are discontinued once the funding is phased out (e.g. Lao's AMIS as funded by FAO for 2001 and 2002). After this phasing-out, the principal initiator (e.g. government) either waits for a new source of funding or starts launching or continuing the AMIS as part of regular function of the concerned ministry (e.g. the AMIS of Bangladesh, Myanmar , Mozambique etc.).

Infrastructure Perspective

AMIS infrastructure is defined as the tools required for ensuring uninterrupted connectivity between the content providers and recipients. In general, the quality of infrastructures for AMIS has so far been found poor [25, 29, 38]. For high-quality connectivity, services must be designed in a way so that they can be adapted with the socio-economic and technical profiles of the targeted users [47]. Here 'adaptability' is defined as perceived availability, affordability, and accessibility of services and technologies. In this aspect, there would be a possibility of underutilization of a system if it is launched prematurely in a context where the associated technology is relatively new and difficult to access by the end users (e.g. web-based government AMIS in Bangladesh).

There is a variety of technological platforms used for accessing the AMIS across the world. Large networks (e.g. RESIMAO/WAMIS-NET for the West African AMIS) collects large amount of data for large audience and therefore dissemination of information needs multiple channels. Use of hybrid/multi-channel technologies has been growing in recent time. USAID's LINKS project for East African countries uses multiple platforms: Internet, Satellite, radio and SMS. RASIMAO/WAMIS-Net provides market information via internet, radio, print, email and SMS. Interests for expanding network by the telecommunication companies for rural consumers are also growing. Manobi's Time to Market (T2M) system provides value added services at low cost, uses PDA (Personal Digital Assistant) for collecting market data twice a day, and disseminates real-time information through their specially designed open source Multi-Channel Service Platform (MCSP; web, WAP, SMS, voice). Manobi's 'Xam Marse' ('know your market') service in Senegal uses Wireless Application Protocol (WAP) enabled cell phones which connect to the Internet to check market information and compare the offers of the local buyers in the markets. Mobile handsets and their associated value added services are also getting attention [43]. Nokia has introduced a graphical 'Life Tool' application which is designed for entry-level rural consumers and has been tested successfully in Maharashtra, India.

Radio, especially community/FM band, is historically the most influential medium for information services [3, 13, 14, 23, 48], as it accessible for large populations at a reasonable cost [30, 33]. However, some studies find that radio broadcasting at the local level is often found to be interrupted and unreliable [46].

Though web-based services are used either as the main (e.g. Bangladesh) or compliment to other modes of information dissemination (e.g. Mali), findings show that Web-based AMIS are not accessible by the rural clients because of low internet penetration and lack of ICT awareness and skills [27]. Poor connectivity and low bandwidth in the LDCs are the major technical barriers for web-based services [24, 29, 42, 48]. A study on Africa also finds that web-based AMIS is time consuming and not so user friendly [31].

Moving now to what in effect is the most challenging part, the input side; we devote next section to data collection.

Data Perspective

Data collectors and data providers are the two parties involved in the local level data gathering processes. Generally, the data collectors are local, regional, and central level officials, while the data providers are farmers, traders and retailers. Depending on the nature and types of information, officials from the various agencies may work together. For example, OMA of Mali uses officials from multiple agencies - Malian Livestock and Meat Office (OMBEVI) and the International Institute of Soil Fertility (IISF).

Accuracy of data collection and reliable reporting are critical factors for the success of AMIS [24]. However, the data management process especially at the local level has been found weak [29]. There has been a lack of data standardization [12, 24, 29] and quality control [29] as well in terms of methodology, weights and grades of the produce.

On-time dissemination of such information depends on the data acquisition, transmission and tabulation process, and the characteristics of the associated technology [29]. Use of passive (disk, fax, regular postal and print) media in the data transmission to the central hub and manual intervention for checking and tabulation (e.g. basic spreadsheet or paper) of data delay the final dissemination process [24, 29] and subsequently in long-run reduce the credibility of the services [36]. Regarding the time of data processing and dissemination, there have been huge differences. For examples, in Cambodia information is disseminated every day at 6:00 pm, whereas in

Laos it appears only weekly in a radio program. In Benin (ONSA-Infoprix project), data is collected after business hours. In Ethiopia, data entry and analyses take even for two months. These examples may result in a conclusion that late information loses it value to farmers [6] and decreases the creditability of the project administrators in the long run.

5 Conclusions

Our literature survey among the 49 LDCs found that AMIS quality has imrpoved significantly in terms of needs assessment, processes and technology. Out of 49 LDCs, 25 have web-based services and 20 of these services are integrated with SMS mobile technology. The rest remain using traditional methods like radio, newspapers, bulletin and price board.

Findings show that input rather than output is the major challenge today. While new technologies can improve dissemination of information, collecting it economically and meeting users high quality requirements remain major challenges. Knowledge of the right mix of resource mobilization, needs for localization and perhaps personalization, and the logistics of the agricultural marketing systems at the various levels of the marketing chain are critical for project success. On-time delivery of reliable and high-quality information via widely available and adaptable technologies is critical to the acceptance of the services by the end-users. However, ensuring this acceptance mainly depends on the commitment and capability of the management of the services.

This paper has investigated success- as well as failure factors, and discussed the role of new technologies. The study contributes by providing a comprehensive view of the challenges of AMIS in developing countries and an evaluation matrix (IS-PEM) based on the findings, which together contribute to improving the design of future projects.

References

1. Båge, L.: Rural development: key to reaching the Millennium Development Goals. Agriculture in the Commonwealth (2004)
2. Danielson, A.: When Do the Poor Benefit From Growth, and Why? Sida, Lidingö (2001)
3. Shepherd, A.W., Schalke, A.J.F.: An Assessment of the Indonesian Horticultural Market Information Service. FAO-the UN, AGSM Occasional Paper No. 8, Rome (1995)
4. Shepherd, A.W.: Market Information Services: Theory and Practices. Agricultural Services Bulletin No. 125, FAO- The UN, Rome (1997)
5. Singh, S.: Selected Success Stories on Agricultural Information System. In: Asia-Pacific Asso65CIATion of Agricultural Research Institutions (APAARI), Thailand (2006)
6. Mabota, A., Arlindo, P., Paulo, A., Donovan, C.: Market Information: A Low Cost Tool for Agricultural Market Development?, Results of Research from SIMA-DEST and Department of Policies Analysis No. 37E, Ministry of Agriculture (MADER), Mozambique (2003)
7. Tollens, E.F.: Market Information Systems in sub-Sahara Africa Challenges and Opportunities. In: The Intl. Assoc. of Agri. Economists Conference, Australia (2006)

8. UN-OHRLLS – United Nations Office of the High Representative for the LDCs, LLDCs and SIDS, http://www.unohrlls.org/en/ldc/related/62/
9. Goodman, L.A.: Snowball sampling. Annals of Mathematical Statistics, 148–170 (1961)
10. MSU - Michigan State University, AMIS-Africa Online, International Department of Agricultural Economics, Development Department of Economics, USA (2009), http://www.aec.42MSU.edu/fs2/test/marketinformation/index.htm
11. Vallée, J.C.L.: Intl. Development Working Papers. Market Information Sources Available through the Internet, Working Paper No. 64, Michigan State University, USA (2001)
12. Awasthi, B.D.: Relevance of Market Information System to Environment Protection. Journal of Agriculture and Environment 8, 46–54 (2007)
13. Roberts, M., Kernick, H.: Feasibility Study for SMS-enabled Collection and Delivery of Rural Market Information. International Development Enterprises (2006)
14. Ferris, S., Engoru, P., Kaganzi, E.: Making Market Information Services Work Better For the Poor in Uganda. Working paper No. 77, CAMA for Smallholders, USA (2006)
15. Jensen, R.: The Digital Provide: Information (Technology), Market Performance, and Welfare in the South Indian Fisheries Sector. The Quarterly Journal of Economics, USA CXXII(3) (2007)
16. Tague, N.R.: The quality toolbox, 2nd edn. American Society for Quality (2005)
17. Changqing, G., Kezheng, H., Fei, M.: Comparison of innovation methodologies and TRIZ. The TRIZ Journal, Issue (September 2005)
18. Clark, G.: The Price History of English Agriculture - 1209-1914. Research in Economic History 22, 41–124 (2004)
19. Nikolov, G., Hughes, D.: Market Information Services in Economies in Transition: The Case of Bulgaria. Journal of Euromarketing 8(3) (2000)
20. Lancaster Farming, Just a phone calls away, p. 120, (October 22, 1977)
21. Lancaster Farming, A new Green Thumb idea, p. 121 (November 15, 1980)
22. FAO, Marketing information systems for non-timber forest products, Community Forestry Field Manuals – 06 (2003)
23. Shepherd, A.W.: Farm Radio as a Medium for Market Information Dissemination. Marketing and Rural Finance Service. FAO, Rome (2001)
24. Shreshtha, K.B.: Agricultural Marketing System in Nepal. Journal on Agricultural marketing, Government of India XLV(4), 42–46 (2003)
25. CTA: Status of ICM and strategic priorities for agricultural and rural development information in Lesotho (2007)
26. Garforth, C.: Agricultural knowledge and IS in Hagaz, Eritrea. FAO, Rome (2001)
27. Islam, S., Grönlund, Å.: Agriculture market information e-service in Bangladesh: A stakeholder-oriented case analysis. In: Wimmer, M.A., Scholl, J., Grönlund, Å. (eds.) EGOV 2007. LNCS, vol. 4656, pp. 167–178. Springer, Heidelberg (2007)
28. Weber, M.T., Donovan, C., Staatz, J.M., 20Dembélé, N.N.: Guidelines for Building Sustainable MIS in Africa, Policy Synthesis, Number 78, USAID, USA (2005)
29. FAO, Proceedings of the Regional Workshop For Strengthening National ICM Focal Units in Near East and North Africa Region Muscat – Oman (January 8-10, 2008)
30. Traoré, A., Dembélé, N.N., Diarra, S.B., Staatz, J.: Role of Information And Communication Tools in Food And Nutritional Security in The ACP Countries. In: CTA International Conference Role of Information Tools in Food Security, Mozambique (2004)
31. MSU- Michigan State University: A Working Demonstration of What Can Be Done. AMIS-Africa Online African Country-Level Agri-Food Market Information Reports, Department of Agricultural, Food, and Resource Economics, USA (2008)

32. Keita, N.: Economic Statistics and Agricultural Policy in African context. In: Intl. Assoc. of Agri. Economists Conference, Australia (2006)
33. Dembélé, N.N., Tefft, J.F., Staatz, J.M.: Mali's market Information System. Policy Synthesis for Cooperating USAID Offices And Country Missions, Number 56 (2000)
34. Maputo: Key Lessons for MIS. In: CTA Conference on role of Information Tools in Food and Nutrition Security in ACP Countries (November 8-12, 2004)
35. Foodnet, Agricultural Marketing: Fact Sheet 3, NADS, Uganda (2006)
36. Mabota, A., Arlindo, P., Paulo, A., Donovan, C.: Market Information: A Low Cost Tool for Agricultural Market Development? Analysis No. 37E, Ministry of Agriculture (MADER), Mozambique (September 23, 2003)
37. Manda, E.: Market IS Role in Agriculture Marketing: The case of Malawi Agriculture Commodity Exchange (MACE). In: AGRA Markets Workshop, Kenya (2009)
38. Agredia: The Neuchâtel Initiative: Review of Experiences of Market Oriented Agricultural Advisory Services (MOAAS), Neuchâtel Group, Switzerland (2007)
39. PDA - Programme de Développement de l'Agriculture: Review of Experiences on Market Oriented Agricultural Advisory Services (MOAAS) in Burkina Faso (2006)
40. Mokitimi, N.: Review of the Performance of the Lesotho Agricultural Marketing. UNISWA Journal of Agriculture 9, 57–66 (2000)
41. Dembélé, N.: Mali's Agricultural Market Watch. ICT U55PDAte, Issue 9, Technical Centre for Agricultural and Rural Cooperation (2002)
42. Carrilho, L., Paulo, A.: Market Information Systems and Partnerships in Mozambique. In: WFP Workshop on Partnerships in Market Analysis for Food Security, South Africa (2007)
43. Koh, D.: Case study: Nokia Life Tools, CNET Asia (October 20, 2009)
44. Sikombe, L.: District Marketing Information System: Experiences from Central Province, Zambia. Center for International Public Enterprise, Mozambique (2004)
45. CIPE: Mozambican Experience with Agricultural Market Information Systems. In: Workshop on Developing Sustainable MIS in Africa, Mozambique (2004)
46. Wichern, R., Hausner, U., Chiwele, D.K.: Impediments to agricultural growth in Zambia. International Food Policy Research Institute, TMD Discussion Papers No. 47, USA (1999)
47. CIAT: MIS and Agricultural Commodities Exchanges. Session 4: Innovation of Market Information Services. Colombia, USA (2005)
48. Diarra, S., Traoré, A., Staatz, J.: Developing Sustainable Agricultural Information Services: Lessons from Mali. Center for International Public Enterprise, Mozambique (2004)

Community-Based E-Government: Libraries as E-Government Partners and Providers

John Carlo Bertot

College of Information Studies
University of Maryland College Park
College Park, Maryland, United States
jbertot@umd.edu

Abstract. In the United States, e-government is a complex mix of federal, state, and local governments; technologies; service paradigms; and policies. There is no single approach to e-government, with a range of e-government applications and set of e-government technologies in effect. Agencies and levels of government have different mandates and approaches regarding e-government, leaving users on their own to identify and resolve their e-government needs. Without a bridge between previously mediated interactions, users often make their way to libraries and rely on librarian expertise to fulfill their e-government needs. This paper explores the ability of libraries and government agencies to collaborate effectively in the provision of e-government to residents and communities in this country, presenting findings from a national survey of U.S. public libraries, and interviews and case sites conducted with 15 public libraries in four states.

Keywords: Libraries, collaborative e-government, e-government partnerships.

1 Introduction

A key focus of e-government development has been on interactions between the government and members of the public, with many agencies now viewing e-government as their primary method for interacting with members of the public [1,2,4,5,6]. Often, users seek access to e-government information to fulfill an important need, such as [7,8]: seeking unemployment benefits and other social services; registering to vote; renewing licenses; applying for jobs; paying taxes; enrolling children in school; applying for citizenship; scheduling appointments; and completing numerous other important federal, state, and local government functions online. Access to e-government is not just an issue of benefit to members of the public through direct services, however, as access to government information and services is a central premise of democracy and an informed citizenry.

A number of individuals, however, lack the means to access, understand, and use e-government. In many locations in the United States, the lack of availability of computers, Internet access, or even basic telecommunications infrastructure serve as barriers to access [26,27], and it is unclear as to whether investments in broadband

M.A. Wimmer et al. (Eds.): EGOV 2010, LNCS 6228, pp. 121–131, 2010.

infrastructure through the American Recovery and Reinvestment Act of 2009 will lead to increased broadband access and adoption. Nearly 40% of U.S. homes lack Internet access, and the percentage of households without Internet access jumps to 62% in rural communities. Among homes with Internet access, 45% lack broadband access, while 10% continue to rely on dial-up Internet service [9,10]. E-government access can be limited by difficulties in searching for and locating the desired information, lack of familiarity with the structure of government, lack of education about e-government, language barriers, and attitudes toward technology and government [11, 12, 13].

At the same time, government agencies increasingly offer their services electronically – in some cases exclusively online. These agencies often direct users to public libraries for help when they need access or assistance [7]. Nearly all state departments of taxation only make printed forms available on request, requiring filers to request forms or access them online – and states and the federal government are strongly encouraging e-filing. Florida requires that individuals apply online for social service benefits from the Department of Children and Families (DCF) through AccessFlorida (http://www.myflorida.com/accessflorida/); and immigrant services (e.g., appointments, applications, status checking - http://www.uscis.gov/portal/site/uscis) are increasingly online processes.

As a result of these gaps and challenges, members of the public seek assistance with e-government in libraries because they [5,7,14,15,16,17,18,19]: 1) lack access to computers and the Internet, which serve as a critical pre-requisite to engaging in e-government transactions; 2) lack the technical skills to use the online services and resources; 3) lack and understanding of civics and are therefore unable to discern between federal, state, or local government services and/or which agencies are responsible for which e-government services; 4) are uncomfortable engaging in online interactions without guidance; 5) are unable to engage in e-government services due to the lack of accessibility and usability of government websites in general and e-government services in particular; 6) often face a range of social barriers to accessing and using e-government services such as trust, language, and culture; and 7) are specifically directed by an agency to obtain assistance from a library as opposed to the actual agency providing the service.

In addition, people with other means of Internet access often still use e-government in public libraries because libraries and librarians have exceptionally high levels of social trust, making their guidance in accessing and using e-government uniquely trusted by residents [18, 20, 21]. Also, persons with Internet access in the home or elsewhere come to the library for assistance with e-government due to librarian expertise and the lack of available assistance from government agencies providing e-government services. For example, Florida's DCF reduced the number of case workers and assistance providers by over 3,000 positions due to its implementation of the AccessFlorida online application system, resulting in near complete lack of available agency staff from which users can seek assistance [15].

In recognition of the reliance of residents on public libraries for e-government access, many federal, state, and local government agencies openly expect public libraries to provide residents with access to and guidance in using e-government, directing residents to the nearest public library for access and assistance [7,14,17,22]. Government agencies indicate that relying on libraries for e-government access and assistance allows agencies to focus on other issues [7,14,20]. Some local governments also engage public libraries to create and maintain the local government websites [17].

Whether viewed as an unfunded mandate or opportunity to extend e-government services through community-based institutions such as the public library, public libraries and governments are defacto collaborators in the provision of e-government services. The central issue, essentially unexplored, is the extent to which formal and deliberative collaborations can serve to create a robust and user-centered approach to e-government services.

2   Methodology and Research Questions

The findings presented in this paper rely on two data collection efforts: 1) a national survey of U.S. public libraries which collected data between September 2009 and November 2009; and 2) U.S. public library site visits and interviews which occurred between June 2009 and November 2009. The research questions that the study explored included: 1) What e-government service roles do public libraries provide to their communities? 2) What partnerships have libraries formed with government agencies in the provision of e-government services? 3) What are the success factors and/or barriers to forming partnerships with government agencies? 4) What are the challenges that libraries face by serving as e-government providers?

In the United States, there are approximately 16,500 public library buildings that are open to the public. Based on geographic dispersion and population service areas, everyone in the United States has access to a public library – though in certain regions such as the Southwest (i.e., New Mexico, Arizona), library facilities can be quite dispersed, requiring individuals to travel long distances to reach a library. Funded by the American Library Association and the Bill & Melinda Gates Foundation, the survey drew a proportionate-to-size stratified random sample that considered the metropolitan status of the library (i.e., urban, suburban, and rural) and state in order to generate both national and state-level generalizeable estimates of public library Internet connectivity and service provision. The 2009 survey is the 12th survey in a series of public library Internet access surveys conducted since 1994. The survey was Web-based, and sampled libraries received an announcement postcard regarding the survey. In all, the survey produced 7,393 responses, for a response rate of 82.4 percent. Weighted analysis is used to generate both state and national estimates. More specific methodology issues are available in [23].

Interviews and site visits were conducted with 15 libraries in four states. In all, the researcher visited 10 libraries and interviewed the library director in five additional libraries. Libraries were selected by geographic region (North, South, East, and West) as well as library characteristics such as metropolitan status (the same measures of metropolitan status used for the survey were used for site visit libraries), library size, number of staff, and known e-government library-agency partnerships. A Web search and literature review was conducted to ascertain the existence of library-government agency collaborative initiatives to the extent possible.

The combined national survey, interview, and site visit approach provided aggregate and generalizeable data regarding public library e-government service provision and challenges, while simultaneously allowing for on-the-ground assessments of library and government collaborative efforts. Moreover, the site visits allowed for an expansion and better understanding of the service context of library-provided e-government services, as the visits occurred during service hours, thus enabling the researcher to observe the services provided to users and the time of service delivery.

3 Findings

Nearly all U.S. public libraries – 99.0% – provide public access to the Internet. Through that access, libraries now devote a large amount of staff effort to education about e-government (see Table 1). In 2009, 78.7% of public libraries provided direct assistance to patrons who applied for or accessing e-government services [28]. This percentage is a major increase in just one year, as only 54.1% of libraries reported providing this direct assistance in 2008 [24]. Along with direct assistance, 88.8% of libraries provided users with as-needed assistance in using and understanding e-government resources. Libraries are often the only places that residents can turn for help, as the public library is the only provider of free public Internet and computer access in 66.0% of communities. Among patrons using e-government in libraries, 52.4% did not own a computer, 42.4% lacked access both at home and at work, 40% were there because access is free, and 38.1% relied on the assistance of librarians [15]. Although a large percentage of libraries indicated that they provided a wide range of e-government services, 20.5% reported that they have partnerships with government agencies and other organizations. But this did represent an increase, as only 13.4% reported such partnerships in 2008 [24].

Libraries, however, met these e-government access and assistance needs in an increasingly difficult service environment:

- Due to the recession, library usage is increasing dramatically, with 75.7% of libraries reporting increased use of their public access workstations since last year, 71.1% reporting increased use of library wireless (wi-fi) services, and nearly 30.0% reporting increased use of library training services;
- Library funding is decreasing due to the recession, with decreases ranging from 1-10% in operating budgets;
- Public libraries report a decrease in service hours, with nearly 25% of urban public libraries reporting a decrease in the hours they are open;
- Public libraries – 58.6% – report that they do not have enough staff to meet patron needs, do not have staff with the necessary expertise (46.0%), and have too few workstations to meet demand (35.5%); and
- The economic downturn is creating an increase in both employment services and e-government services, which go hand-in-hand due to government unemployment social benefits and the need to seek employment in order to move off government benefits.

This context challenges libraries as they provide e-government services without support and a mandate to do so – and yet, it offers an opportunity to engage in more collaborative approaches to e-government that leverage library and government resources.

Table 1. E-Government Roles and Services Provided by Public Libraries by Metropolitan Status

E-Government roles and services	Metropolitan Status			Overall
	Urban	Suburban	Rural	
Staff provide assistance to patrons applying for or accessing e-government services	75.9% (n=1,913)	78.6% (n=3,820)	79.9% (n=5,383)	78.7% (n=11,116)
Staff provide as needed assistance to patrons for understanding how to access and use e-government Web Sites	91.2% (n=2,300)	88.8% (n=4,317)	87.9% (n=5,918)	88.8% (n=12,535)
Staff provide assistance to patrons for understanding government programs and services	45.6% (n=1,149)	45.6% (n=2,215)	40.7% (n=2,742)	43.3% (n=6,106)
Staff provide assistance to patrons for completing government forms	71.4% (n=1,800)	65.2% (n=3,168)	65.1% (n=4,386)	66.3% (n=9,354)
The library developed guides, tip sheets, or other tools to help patrons use e-government websites and services	23.3% (n=588)	18.7% (n=907)	14.2% (n=957)	17.4% (n=2,452)
The library offers training classes regarding the use of government Web sites, understanding government programs, and completing electronic forms	22.9% (n=578)	7.3% (n=357)	4.8% (n=321)	8.9% (n=1,256)
The library offered translation services for forms and services in other languages	11.1% (n=279)	6.6% (n=321)	4.2% (n=280)	6.2% (n=880)
The library is partnering with government agencies, non-profit organizations, and others to provide e-government services	26.4% (n=666)	21.2% (n=1,030)	17.8% (n=1,201)	20.5% (n=2,898)
The library is working with government agencies (local, state, or federal) to help agencies improve their websites and/or e-government services	11.0% (n=277)	8.2% (n=398)	6.0% (n=405)	7.7% (n=1,080)
The library has at least one staff member with significant knowledge and skills in provision of e-government services	31.5% (n=794)	16.2% (n=789)	15.4% (n=1035)	18.5% (n=2,618)
Other	4.8% (n=121)	3.3% (n=159)	4.4% (n=298)	4.1% (n=578)

The site visits and interviews identified and explored a number of library/government agency projects, including:

- The Alachua County Library District in Florida, which partnered with the Florida Department of Children and Families, as well as community organizations, to create The Library Partnership (http://www.acld.lib.fl.us/locations/the-library-partnership). The library provides space within libraries for agencies devoted to child welfare to offer assistance with accessing e-government forms and applications used by the organizations providing services at the center, as well as homework help, GED and literacy classes.

- The Austin Public Library in Texas, which partnered with the U.S. Citizenship and Immigration Services (USCIS) agency to create its New Immigrants Centers to provide resources and support for immigrants. These Centers provide a range of support services in multiple languages, including citizenship courses and test preparation.
- The Hartford Public Library in Connecticut, which partnered with the USCIS to create The American Place to provide resources and support for immigrants, particularly those seeking U.S. Citizenship.
- The public libraries in Georgetown County South Carolina, which collaborated with the state Department of Emergency Management on Web 2.0 materials – including video-game simulations, social media, oral-history video interviews, digital storytelling, and the creation of a digital collection of historic hurricane views – to record the history of Hurricane Hugo (http://georgetowncountylibrary.sc.gov/randompages/hurricane.htm) and help the community respond to emergency situations.

These examples demonstrate just some of the types of collaborations between libraries and government agencies. Table 2 provides examples of additional library-government (and other) e-government collaborations.

Table 2. Sample Public Library-Government E-government Partnerships

Project Title	Partnership	Description
Queens Library Health Link	Queens Library National Institute of Health	Queens Library Health Link program is designed to test the efficacy of a comprehensive participatory research approach to reduce disparities by improving the use of cancer prevention, screening and treatments interventions. In this project, public library branches provide a base for neighborhood organizing, education, data gathering, planning and implementation of local health promotion experiments and dissemination of results, working with 42 of the 63 branch libraries in Queens.
California Health Resources	California Healthcare Foundation; National Network of Libraries of Medicine; Pacific Southwest Region; California Public Libraries	Phase one of a potential multi-year effort to build the capacity of California's public libraries to provide reliable consumer health information. Libraries will also be positioned as model environments supporting healthy lifestyle choices.
Passport Application Acceptance Facility	East Brunswick Public Library and the U.S. State Department	The East Brunswick Public Library is an officially designated passport application acceptance facility with passport processing hours.
Solar Test Bed Project	Fayetteville Public Library; the city of Fayetteville, University of Arkansas; Arkansas Energy Office; American Electric Power; National Center for Reliable Electric Power Transmission; others	The partnership will design, install, and operate a solar-generated energy system to support a test environment for solar-energy products created within the local economy. This project will position the library as the city's incubator for local solar business development and stimulate Fayetteville's fledgling green businesses, as well as promote citizen interest in adopting solar technologies.

The partnerships varied in degree and scope. The Alachua County Library District partnership, for example, was an embedded and integrative partnership. The library served as the central hub of the government service, providing space, librarian expertise, agency expertise, and a range of information support services designed to meet the needs of those seeking e-government services. In this sense, the library and agencies formed a collaborative approach to engaging in e-government service provision and access that maximized the strengths of each partnership participant.

The Austin and Hartford Public Library collaboration differed in nature. Through coordination with USCIS, the libraries assisted USCIS develop a range of informational resources and built services around immigration and citizenship. It is, however, the libraries that provide the training classes and assist the immigrant populations that they serve. The libraries in essence serve as facilitators of immigration and citizenship e-government services.

The South Carolina libraries in Georgetown County collaboration is yet another type of partnership in which the library serves in both a cultural role in terms of historical preservation of government information as well as an emergency response role that facilitates community recovery efforts in the event of an emergency.

Given the limitation of the site visits and the wide range of partnerships and collaborations found, it is clear that collaborations between libraries and government agencies take many forms and can evolve in different ways. There are preliminary indications that there is a continuum of library-government e-government partnerships that require additional exploration.

The site visits and interviews also identified both benefits and barriers to library-government partnerships. Identified benefits included:

- The ability to provide combine services with public access technologies and Internet access, which many of the users lacked elsewhere;
- The ability to embed e-government services within a trusted and neutral community organization such as the public library;
- The ability to create an integrated service environment that cut across multiple agency services and benefits, as individuals often required multiple e-government interactions provided by different levels of government and agencies; and
- The librarian, whom served as an intermediary between e-government services and the user.

Identified challenges included:
- Agencies, due to mandates and service authority constraints, focused on their own services and did not necessarily view the entire e-government spectrum that libraries faced in a public access service context;
- Partnerships are often associated with risk due to public scrutiny, and agencies were loathe to form partnerships and accept the risks that could manifest through partnerships;
- When willing to engage in partnerships, some agencies viewed the library as a means through which to offload agency workload rather than create a truly collaborative e-government service approach; and
- Partnerships were evolutionary in nature, as both libraries and agencies learned over time the best ways to approach their collaborations.

As discussed below, there are benefits, challenges, and issues associated with forging government-library partnerships.

4 Key Issues and Challenges

Key findings from the research studies identified above indicated that there are numerous factors that affect the degree to which a library can successfully provide e-government services, such as staff skills and knowledge, staff time commitments, resource constraints, availability of workstations, and broadband. More specifically, these service challenges included:

- Libraries often lack wide-scale coordination with critical e-government service agencies (e.g., immigration, taxes, health, social services) which users most frequently seek;
- Librarians do not necessarily have expertise in the range of e-government services, resources, or applications necessary for users to access and successfully participate;
- Librarians may not understand the larger policy/governance/jurisdictional context of e-government (e.g., immigration policy; tax law; federal, state, local government);
- Library e-government roles, which can vary from library to library, have yet to be clearly defined and differentiated in light of local situational factors – though some libraries have clearly embraced the e-government service role through innovative practices and support structures;
- Libraries face a range of constraints, including insufficient number of computers to meet patron needs; budgetary, space, and infrastructure challenges; and inadequate bandwidth to meet increasingly bandwidth-heavy e-government services;
- Libraries experienced a significant increase in usage as a result of the recession; and
- Libraries are a service provider at the end of a vast e-government service environment that, at the federal level alone, encompasses more than 30,000 websites and well over 100 million pages [25].

The site visits and interviews provided, however, indications that collaborative e-government, based on agency and library partnerships, can ultimately create a comprehensive community-based approach to e-government service provision.

But these partnerships seem to occur on a continuum from a library simply serving as a public access point to workstations and the Internet all the way to a fully integrated government-library service outlet housed in the library – around which the library builds a range of information and staff support services. Given the exploratory nature of this research, it is not possible to codify or fully determine this emerging collaborative continuum.

The site visits also identified a range of success factors for these collaborations:

- Both the library and the agency saw mutual benefit to entering into a partnership designed to provide collaborative e-government services;

- Agencies viewed the partnerships as ways through which to extend e-government services to the intended service recipients through libraries, rather than as a means to shift service provision costs to libraries;
- Agencies considered the library a true partner and considered librarian feedback regarding e-government service design and delivery;
- Agencies were willing to help librarians better understand the e-government services, resources, and technologies;
- Agencies provided library-specific support (i.e., a separate help e-mail and phone number) through which librarians could contact agency staff for assistance;
- The library considered providing e-government services as part of its mission to serve the public; and
- The library built a support infrastructure (e.g., information resources, technology training, staff assistance) around the e-government services.

These success factors require additional testing and verification through additional research, but seemed to permeate the site visit and interview partnerships.

5 Conclusion

This paper presented the results of a national survey, site visits, and interviews regarding the provision of e-government services in U.S. public libraries. The exploratory research indicated that government-library collaborations can extend e-government services into communities and ensure that e-government services and resources are available to and inclusive of all members of society. The research identified critical roles that public libraries offer to their users, but also identified success factors for successful collaborations between government agencies and libraries. The research also identified, however, a range of challenges that public libraries face as providers of e-government services. Additional research is necessary to more fully understand the complexity, benefits, and challenges to library and government collaborations to promote the adoption and use of e-government services to the greatest extent possible.

Acknowledgment. Funding for this study was provided in part by the American Library Association and the Bill & Melinda Gates Foundation.

References

1. Bertot, J.C., Jaeger, P.T.: User-centered e-government: Challenges and benefits for government Web sites. Government Information Quarterly 23, 163–168 (2006)
2. Bertot, J.C., Jaeger, P.T.: The e-government paradox: Better customer service doesn't necessarily cost less. Government Information Quarterly 25, 149–154 (2008)
3. Dawes, S.S.: Governance in the digital age: A research and action framework for an uncertain future. Government Information Quarterly 26, 257–264 (2009)
4. Ebbers, W.E., Pieterson, W.J., Noordman, H.N.: Electronic government: Rethinking channel management strategies. Government Information Quarterly 25, 181–201 (2008)

5. Jaeger, P.T., Bertot, J.C.: Designing, implementing, and evaluating user-centered and citizen-centered e-government. International Journal of Electronic Government Research (in press)

6. Streib, G., Navarro, I.: Citizen demand for interactive e-government: The case of Georgia consumer services. American Review of Public Administration 36, 288–300 (2006)

7. Bertot, J.C., Jaeger, P.T., Langa, L.A., McClure, C.R.: Public access computing and Internet access in public libraries: The role of public libraries in e-government and emergency situations. First Monday 11(9) (2006),
http://www.firstmonday.org/issues/issue11_9/bertot/index.html

8. McClure, C.R., Jaeger, P.T., Bertot, J.C.: The looming infrastructure plateau?: Space, funding, connection speed, and the ability of public libraries to meet the demand for free Internet access. First Monday, 12(12) (2007),
http://www.uic.edu/htbin/cgiwrap/bin/ojs/index.php/
fm/article/view/2017/1907

9. Horrigan, J.B.: Home broadband adoption 2008: Adoption stalls for low-income Americans even as many broadband users opt for premium services that give them more speed. Pew Internet and American Life Project, Washington, D.C. (2008)

10. Horrigan, J.B.: Obama's online opportunities II: If you build it, will they log on? Pew Internet and American Life Project, Washington, D.C. (2009)

11. Fenster, M.: The opacity of transparency. Iowa Law Review 91, 885–949 (2006)

12. Jaeger, P.T., Thompson, K.M.: E-government around the world: Lessons, challenges, and new directions. Government Information Quarterly 20(4), 389–394 (2003)

13. Jaeger, P.T., Thompson, K.M.: Social information behavior and the democratic process: Information poverty, normative behavior, and electronic government in the United States. Library & Information Science Research 26(1), 94–107 (2004)

14. Bertot, J.C., Jaeger, P.T., Langa, L.A., McClure, C.R.: Drafted: I want you to deliver e-government. Library Journal 131(13), 34–39 (2006)

15. Gibson, A.N., Bertot, J.C., McClure, C.R.: Emerging role of public librarians as E-government providers. In: Sprague Jr., R.H. (ed.) Proceedings of the 42nd Hawaii International Conference on System Sciences, pp. 1–10 (2009) doi:10.1109/HICSS.2009.183

16. Jaeger, P.T.: User-centered policy evaluations of Section 508 of the Rehabilitation Act: Evaluating e-government websites for accessibility. Journal of Disability Policy Studies 19(1), 24–33 (2008a)

17. Jaeger, P.T.: Public libraries and local e-government. In: Reddick, C.G. (ed.) Handbook on research on strategies for local e-government adoption and implementation: Comparative studies, pp. 647–660. IGI Global, Hershey (2009)

18. Jaeger, P.T., Fleischmann, K.R.: Public libraries, values, trust, and e-government. Information Technology and Libraries 26(4), 35–43 (2007)

19. Jaeger, P.T., Langa, L.A., McClure, C.R., Bertot, J.C.: The 2004 and 2005 Gulf Coast hurricanes: Evolving roles and lessons learned for public libraries in disaster preparedness and community services. Public Library Quarterly 25(3/4), 199–214 (2007)

20. Fisher, K.E., Becker, S., Crandall, M.: E-government service use and impact through public libraries: Preliminary findings from a national study of public access computing in public libraries. In: Proceedings of the 43rd Hawaii International Conference on System Sciences, pp. 1–10 (2010)

21. Heanue, A.: In support of democracy: The library role in public access to government information. In: Kranich, N. (ed.) Libraries & Democracy: The Cornerstones of Liberty, pp. 121–128. American Library Association, Chicago (2001)

22. Jaeger, P.T., Bertot, J.C.: E-government education in public libraries: New service roles and expanding social responsibilities. Journal of Education for Library and Information Science 50, 40–50 (2009)
23. Bertot, J.C., Langa, L.A., Grimes, J., Simmons, S.N., Sigler, K.: 2009-2010 Public Library Funding and Technology Access survey: Survey Results and Findings. Center for Library and Information Innovation, College Park (2010), http://www.liicenter.org/plinternet/
24. American Library Association: Libraries Connect Communities 3: Public Library Funding & Technology Access Study 2008-2009. American Library Association, Chicago (2009), http://www.ala.org/plinternetfunding/
25. Evans, K.: E-government and information technology for the federal government. Talk presented at the Center for Information Policy and Electronic Government, University of Maryland (2007)
26. Bertot, J.C.: The multiple dimensions of the digital divide: More than technology 'haves' and 'have-nots'. Government Information Quarterly 20, 185–191 (2003)
27. Bertot, J.C.: Public access technologies in public libraries: Impacts and implications. Information Technology & Libraries 28(2), 84–95 (2009)
28. American Library Association: Libraries Connect Communities: Public Library Funding & Technology Access Study 2009-2010. American Library Association, Chicago, Available when published, http://www.ala.org/plinternetfunding/ (forthcoming 2010a)

Civil Servants' Internet Skills:
Are They Ready for E-Government?

Alexander van Deursen and Jan van Dijk

University of Twente, Department of Media, Communication and Organization,
P.O. Box 217, 7500 AE Enschede, The Netherlands
a.j.a.m.vandeursen@utwente.nl

Abstract. In order to utilize the possibilities of information and communication technology within the public domain and thereby further develop the electronic government, it is necessary that civil servants possess sufficient levels of Internet skills. Higher levels of these skills among professionals in the public sphere might result in better Internet usage, thus improving both productivity and efficiency. Based on results of this research, we can conclude that the levels of operational and formal Internet skills are higher than the levels of information and strategic Internet skills. A main finding is that civil servants do not perform well on higher Internet skills involving information and strategic tasks. The implications of the results are discussed and several policy recommendations to improve digital skill levels of civil servants are given.

Keywords: Internet skills, civil servants, productivity, efficiency.

1 Introduction

In 2007 and 2008, two large scale studies were conducted at the University of Twente to test the level of Internet skills of Dutch citizens [1,2]. To measure these skills, a sequential definition was used accounting both for medium- and content-related Internet skills. The results indicate that the level of Internet skills varies largely between different segments of the Dutch population, and that low levels of these skills hinder an optimal use of the possibilities offered by the Internet. In order to utilize the possibilities of the Internet within the public domain and thereby further develop the electronic government, it is necessary that civil servants possess sufficient levels of Internet skills. Not much is known about the current levels of these skills among public servants. The training of civil servants in basic ICT skills has been identified as a major problem in the development of e-Government [3]. In his Ceremonial speech of CommunicAsia 2000, the Prime Minister mentioned: *"We will equip our public servants with the necessary skills, tools, systems and infrastructure to make them effective workers in the digital economy. Indeed, when the world is marching to Internet speed, our public servants must be able to work at a similar speed or be left behind."*

The Internet plays an important role, both for civil servants that are in contact with citizens through the Internet or for servants that are responsible for current and future developments. Based on the results of the two studies conducted among Dutch

M.A. Wimmer et al. (Eds.): EGOV 2010, LNCS 6228, pp. 132–143, 2010.

citizens, one might question whether civil servants possess the necessary Internet skills. Even though they may be in contact with public electronic services on a daily basis, they might not perform better than ordinary Dutch citizens. In this study, the actual level of Internet skills among different segments of civil servants (including executive employees, policy advisors and administrators) is measured in performance tests. The measured Internet skills are discussed in Section 2. Then, Section 3 describes the method applied, followed by an overview of the findings in Section 4. Section 5 contains the conclusions and policy recommendations.

2 Research Background

The literature concerning Internet skills is not consistent in the terms used and in the underlying concepts applied. The confusion caused by the varied terminologies and meanings might be the cause for a lack of practical implementations and support for all these terms [1]. The development of assessments is hampered particularly by the lack of consensus on what constitutes measurable dimensions [2]. Operational definitions have rarely been defined and most of the Internet skills research applies limited definitions that do not extend beyond so-called 'button knowledge,' not paying attention to the multiple underlying indices. This stipulates the need for more academic research. To encourage research to focus on in-depth skill measurement, Van Deursen & Van Dijk [3,4] elaborated four types of Internet skills. The four Internet skills categories proposed are based on individual abilities. So far, most conducted studies strongly focused on the operation and use of computers and the Internet. Van Deursen & Van Dijk [3,4] proposed the following set of Internet skills:

Operational skills means being able to:

- Operate an Internet browser:
  - o Opening websites by entering the URL in the browser's location bar
  - o Surfing forward and backward between pages using the browser buttons
  - o Saving files on the Hard Disk
  - o Opening various common file formats (e.g., PDF, SWF)
  - o Bookmarking websites
  - o Changing the browser's preferences (e.g., start page)

- Operate online search engines:
  - o Entering keywords in the proper field
  - o Executing the search operation
  - o Opening search results in the search result lists

- Complete online forms:
  - o Using the different types of fields and buttons (e.g., drop-down menus)
  - o Submitting a form

Formal skills means being able to:

- Navigate the Internet by:
  - o Recognizing and using hyperlinks (e.g., menu links, textual links, and image links) in different menu and website layouts
- Maintain a sense of location while navigating the Internet, meaning:
  - o Not getting disoriented when surfing within a website
  - o Not getting disoriented when surfing between websites
  - o Not getting disoriented when browsing through, and opening search results

Information skills means being able to
- Locate required information, by:
  - o Choosing a search system or place to seek information
  - o Defining search queries that focus on the information problem
  - o Selecting information
  - o Evaluating information sources

Strategic skills means being able to:

- Take advantage of the Internet by:
  - o An orientation towards a particular goal
  - o Taking the right action to reach this goal
  - o Making the right decision to reach this goal
  - o Gaining the benefits associated with this goal

This definition was used in the Internet skills studies among Dutch citizens, in which subjects had to complete assignments on the Internet. Using performance tests for measuring Internet skills is much more reliable and valid than using surveys in which subjects are asked to assess their own level of skills [5,6]. In most cases, studies that use surveys provide an exaggerated picture of the actual Internet skill levels. This problem is compounded by the fact that Internet skills, in most cases, are measured very superficially and do not go beyond operational skills. This causes surveys to generate a too flattering picture compared to the actual skill levels. Results of both studies revealed that operational and formal Internet skills were not the most problematic. Rather, information and strategic Internet skills presented the greatest difficulties. The results also revealed that Internet experience only correlated to the level of operational skills, and that older age groups did not perform worse than their younger counterparts with regards to information and strategic skills. As such, the assumption that there would not be a digital skill problem without the presence of an elderly population was tempered.

One might suggest that high levels of information and strategic skills are a necessity for administrators and policy advisors. These skills form part of their ability to define policy and administer the electronic government. For executive employees, high levels of operational and formal skills are a necessity, as they have to work with online applications. Indeed, citizens who have trouble with online public services expect support. Higher levels of Internet skills among professionals in the public sphere might result in better Internet usage, thus improving both productivity and efficiency. Also, one might expect positive effects in public service delivery. The problems described and the proposed definition lead to the first research question:

> *RQ 1: What are the levels of operational, formal, information, and strategic Internet skills of Dutch civil servants?*

To gain a better understanding of the levels of these skills among civil servants, they can be compared to the Internet skill levels of citizens. Other studies that measure Internet skills more profoundly are very rare. It is expected that Internet skills will not be the same among different segments of civil servants. This study distinguishes among two groups of civil servants. On the on hand:

- Administrators that are responsible for political and administrative affairs and for the institution of the public information supply, both internally and externally. They have to decide on the acquisition and implementation of infrastructures, architectures and applications and assess whether these fit within the existing organization or whether they need to be adapted. It is therefore recommended that administrators possess more strategic ICT knowledge and skills.
- Policy advisors in the field of eGovernment that support administrators in decision-making. Policy advisors have to be aware of all possibilities that ICT usage offers to the government.

On the other hand:

- Executive employees that use electronic applications for serving citizens. They need to be able to operate applications for handling forms and transactions. And need sufficient operational and formal skills as well as specific information skills associated with their positions.

Besides these groups of civil servants, gender, education, and age are accounted for, as are Internet experience, amount of time spent on the Internet, using social support, the primary location of Internet use, and socio-economic status, all factors that come forward as an explanation of Internet usage differences [7,8,9,10]. The assumption that Internet skills will not be the same among different segments of civil servants leads to the second research question:

> *RQ 2: Are there significant differences among groups of civil servants and categories of gender, age, educational level attained, Internet experience, amount of time spent weekly on the Internet, help from peers and the primary location of Internet use?*

If answers to these questions reveal that the levels of particular Internet skills among civil servants is not adequate in comparison to their job requirements, the following research question then needs to be answered:

> *RQ 3: How can the level of Internet skills among (particular groups of) civil servants be increased?*

3 Method

3.1 Subjects

During a time period of six months, 98 civil servants were visited and subjected to performance tests. The participating civil servants were selected at departments within executive policy agencies and municipalities that have the most direct contact with citizens. The departments of Social Affairs and Public affairs were selected in the municipalities. Municipalities were randomly selected throughout the Netherlands and their size was taken into account in order to reflect the national distribution in the Netherlands. The heads of the selected departments received a letter signed by the Ministry of Internal Affairs (the sponsor of the study), in which they were invited to take part in a study. The procedure was also explained in the letter. Municipalities that agreed to participate randomly selected six civil servants: three in the Social Affairs department and three in the Public Affairs department. In every department, two executive employees that had direct contact with citizens and one administrator responsible for electronic service delivery were selected. At the executive policy agencies, three administrators and five executing employees were selected. The characteristics of the subjects are summarized in Table 1.The average years of age was 45 (SD = 8.7), average years of Internet experience was 9.0 years (SD = 4.2), and the average amount of hours spent online weekly 9.0 (SD = 13.2).

Executive employees were civil servants that had direct contact with citizens, mainly at the counter. The administrators in most cases fulfilled a management position in the department of Social Affairs or Public Affairs. Some were the head of a section that contained more departments. Policy advisors all had positions in where they directly advised the managers. All subjects directly used the Internet, either at the counter, for defining policy or for advising in the development of electronic services.

Table 1. Sample characteristics of participating civil servants

	n	%
Position		
Executing position	50	51
Administrator	31	32
Policy / Advise position	17	17
Organization		
Municipalities	78	80
Public Affairs	40	51
Social Affairs	35	45
Other	3	4
Executive Policy Agencies	20	20
Education		
Low	15	15
Middle	30	31
High	53	54
Age		
18-29	6	6
30-39	20	20
40-54	59	60
55-80	13	13
Gender		
Male	40	41
Female	58	59

3.2 Technical Specifications

The studies were conducted in the subject's office. For the performance test, a laptop with separate keyboard and mouse was used. The laptop connected to the Internet on a high-speed wireless network. During the study, subjects were allowed to use their choice of browser (Internet Explorer 6, 7 or Mozilla Firefox 3), so that they could replicate their usual Internet use. No default page was set on the browsers and all the assignments started out with an empty page. To ensure that subjects were not influenced by previous users' actions, the browser was totally reset after each session.

3.3 Performance Test Assignments

Eight assignments were prepared, two for measuring operational Internet skills, two for formal Internet skills, two for information Internet skills and two for strategic Internet skills. The assignments were a combination of the assignments used in the two Internet skills studies conducted among Dutch citizens. Some assignments, however, were shortened in order to lower the barrier to participation. A complete session took about one-and-a-half hours.

In the two operational skills assignments, subjects were for example instructed to open and save a PDF file, add a website to the Favorites (or bookmarks), fill out a form, and use a search engine. The two formal Internet skill assignments instructed subjects to look up simple contact details at two governmental agencies that used totally different website layouts and menu structures. Subjects were also asked to follow multiple links, go back to the homepages of websites that were opened in different windows, and inspect different search results after conducting a search operation. The first of the two information skills assignments asked subjects to look up subscription information at the website of a major telecom provider. In the second assignment, a more open search task was given using Google as a departure point: subjects had to look up information regarding minimum wages. The first strategic skills assignment was a follow–up that asked subjects what they would do after being underpaid. In the final strategic skills assignment, subjects were instructed to book a flight-hotel combination that was as inexpensive as possible, accounting for few demands. The appendix contains the full list of the eight assignments that subjects were asked to complete. All assignments were of a closed format (i.e., only one answer or action was correct).

The subjects' performance was measured by their successful completion of assignments and the time (in seconds) they spent on each assignment. Both completion and time required were noted directly. In all of the assignments, the subjects themselves decided when they were finished or wanted to give up. After a specific, ample time period, a deadline appeared when the test leader gently asked the subjects to pass on to the next assignment. However, no encouragements were given, as the pressure to succeed was already higher in a test setting. All subjects completed the assignments in the same order.

Prior to the experiment, a five minute questionnaire was administered to gather personal data such as position within the department, age, gender, education level, Internet experience and information about the frequency and location of the subjects' regular Internet usage.

4 Results

This section starts with a general overview of the completion of the assignment. Subsequently, linear regression analyses are performed for both the number of tasks completed and the time spent on the tasks for each skill in order to identify factors that might influence the level of Internet skills.

4.1 General Overview

The two assignments used to measure operational Internet skills consisted of seven tasks. According to Table 2, the subjects completed an average of 74% of these tasks. The two assignments used to measure formal Internet skills consisted of three tasks, of which the subjects completed an average of 80%. Of the two information Internet skills assignments, an average of 50% was completed. Finally, of the two strategic Internet skill assignments, an average of 30% was completed. The time spent on the assignments differed substantially as depicted in Table 2. Of the seven operational Internet skill tasks, only 14% of civil servants were able to complete all of them successfully. 58 Percent of the civil servants were able to successfully complete all three formal skill tasks, 30% both the information skill assignments and only 9% both of the strategic skill assignments.

Table 2. Average number of tasks completed successfully and average time spend on the tasks

	Average # of tasks completed		Time spent on tasks (seconds)	
	M (SD)	%	M (SD)	Min. / Max.
Operational tasks (7)	5.2 (1.2)	74	314 (108)	97 / 631
Formal tasks (3)	2.4 (0.7)	80	353 (131)	118 / 872
Information tasks (3)	1.0 (0.8)	50	518 (238)	155 / 1200*
Strategic tasks (2)	0.6 (0.7)	30	1242 (486)	216 / 2400*

*Maximum time allowed

4.2 Operational Internet Skills

Table 3. Linear regression results for the # of operational tasks completed successfully and time spent

	Number of Tasks completed successfully		Time spent	
	t	β	t	β
Gender	-.672	-.069	-.078	-.007
Age	-4.035	-.391***	5.098	.463***
Education (low/middle/high)	-1.841	-.215	.488	.054
Internet experience (years)	.490	.047	-.736	-.067
Internet use (hours a week))	1.429	.139	-1.316	-.121
Position (admin. and policy adv./executive)	-3.032	-.343***	2.162	.231*
Participated in an Internet course (yes/no)	-.241	-.023	1.405	.126
Receive help from others (yes/no)	-1.890	-.191	2.125	.200*
Location (at home/elsewhere)	-.070	-.006	.278	.024
Adjusted R^2		.29		.39
F		4.46***		6.15***

*$p<.05$, ***$p<.001$. N=98

As shown in Table 3, age and position are the main predictors for the level of operational Internet skills. They are significant both for the number of tasks completed successfully and the time spent on the tasks. Administrators and policy advisors perform better than executive employees. Receiving help from others was a minor contributor to the time spent on Internet tasks.

4.3 Formal Internet Skills

The two assignments for measuring formal Internet skills consisted of three tasks, of which an average of 2.5 was completed successfully. As presented in Table 4, age and position once again are the main contributors for the number of formal tasks completed successfully and for the amount of time spent on the tasks. Also here administrators and policy advisors perform better than executive employees.

Table 4. Linear regression results for the # of formal tasks completed successfully and time spent

	Number of Tasks completed successfully		Time spent	
	t	β	t	β
Gender	,908	,101	,167	,018
Age	-2,581	-,273***	3,280	,344***
Education (low/middle/high)	-1,420	-,181	-,472	-,060
Internet experience (years)	1,593	,168	1,074	,113
Internet use (hours a week))	,245	,026	-,726	-,077
Position (administrator/executive)	-2,153	-,266*	1,250	,153
Participated in an Internet course (yes/no)	-1,148	-,117	-1,275	-,131
Receive help from others (yes/no)	,268	,029	1,029	,112
Location (at home/elsewhere)	-,928	-,093	,725	,072
Adjusted R^2		.16		.19
F		1.89*		2.22*

*$p<.05$, ***$p<.001$, N=98

4.4 Information Internet Skills

Table 5. Linear regression results for the # of information tasks completed successfully and time spent

	Number of Tasks completed successfully		Time spent	
	t	β	t	β
Gender	-0.36	-.04	2.06	.23*
Age	-1.62	-.17	1.40	.15
Education (low/middle/high)	1.60	.20	-0.70	-.09
Internet experience (years)	0.15	.02	0.25	.03
Internet use (hours a week))	1.99	.21	-1.40	-.15
Position (admin. and policy adv./executive)	-0.64	-.08	1.12	.14
Participated in an Internet course (yes/no)	-0.67	-.07	-0.32	-.03
Receive help from others (yes/no)	-0.06	-.06	0.76	.08
Location (at home/elsewhere)	0.02	.02	0.44	.04
Adjusted R^2		.12		.12
F		2.48*		2.37*

*$p<.05$, N=98

The selection of civil servants was mainly based on their position and department. We did not apply a quota sample for gender, age, and education, which would have made it much harder to find willing civil servants to participate. The drawback, however, is that differences among these groups do not vary greatly. As a result, there are no significant predictors indicated in the regression analyses, as shown in Table 5.

4.5 Strategic Internet Skills

Of the two strategic skill assignments, subjects completed an average of 0.6 assignments. Just like the regression analyses in the prior section, no significant contributors appear, as can be seen from Table 6.

Table 6. Linear regression results for the # of strategic tasks completed successfully and time spent

	Number of Tasks completed successfully		Time spent	
	t	β	t	β
Gender	1.38	.15	2.53	.29
Age	-1.77	-.18	-1.00	-.11
Education (low/middle/high)	1.01	.13	-0.51	-.07
Internet experience (years)	0.52	.05	0.51	.06
Internet use (hours a week))	0.82	.09	0.70	.08
Position (admin. and policy adv./executive)	0.34	.04	-0.90	-.12
Participated in an Internet course (yes/no)	-2.51	-.25	0.74	.08
Receive help from others (yes/no)	-1.31	-.14	-1.73	-.20
Location (at home/elsewhere)	0.13	.01	-1.23	-.13
Adjusted R^2		.12		.14
F		2.41*		2.33*

*$p<.05$, N=98

5 Conclusions and Policy Recommendations

The in this study measured Internet skills should be considered as basic skills that civil servants need in order to work for the electronic government. One might even suggest these skills as a minimum norm, which is also desired for citizens that want to function in contemporary information-based society [11]. Further still, this study did not take into account the wide array of extended ICT knowledge and skills that exists and that is necessary for specific positions. Based on results of this research, we can conclude that the levels of operational and formal Internet skills are higher than the levels of information and strategic Internet skills. The operational and formal Internet skills are not the most problematic; these are the information and strategic Internet skills of which on average not even half of the assignments were completed successfully.

In order to determine whether there are statistically significant differences among gender, age, educational level attained, position (administrator, policy advisor, or executive employee), Internet experience, amount of Internet use, following an Internet course and obtaining help from others, the study took all of these variables into account in regression analyses. The results indicated that age and position appear most important for the civil servant's level of operational and formal Internet skills. Younger civil servants performed better than their older counterparts, and the executive employees performed worse than policy advisors and administrators. With regards to the level of strategic skills, it is harder to point out contributing factors.

The main question that arises from these conclusions is whether the state of affairs hinders further development of the electronic government. As outlined in the first section, the Internet plays an important role for civil servants that are in direct contact with citizens through the Internet or are responsible for current and future developments. All civil servants would benefit from better information and strategic Internet skills. Information skills consisting of selecting search systems, formulating search queries, and selecting and evaluating information sources are necessary in an increasing number of governmental positions and especially among policy advisors. Making use of strategic skills in government positions involves using information as a means in specific services and positions, including information provision, transactions, maintaining contacts, and developing organizational strategies. For executive employees, high levels of operational and formal skills are a necessity, as they have to work with online applications for handling forms and transactions. They also need specific information skills associated with their positions. When these skills are not adequate, more training, or even replacement of the employee, is necessary. Indeed, citizens who have trouble with online public services expect support. According to the results of this research, one might question whether civil servants are able to provide such assistance.

Sufficient levels of Information and strategic Internet skills are important for administrators and policy advisors to form part of their ability to define policy and administer the electronic government. Administrators are responsible for the institution of the public information supply, both internally and externally. They have to decide on the acquisition and implementation of infrastructures, architectures and applications and assess whether these fit within the existing organization or whether they need to be adapted. It is therefore recommended that administrators possess more Internet skills. Policy advisors should support administrators in decision-making and have to be aware of all possibilities that the Internet offers to the government.

It is highly recommended to improve the levels of Internet skills among civil servants, especially the levels of information and strategic Internet skills. It must be stressed that the government is the primary party responsible for the development and possession of these skills among its civil servants. Employers often expect that their employees possess general ICT competency that was learned either at the home or at the school. As such, they assume that employees only need specific training. For instance, more educated employees are expected to possess all necessary Internet skills, which they are not tested for. Civil servants have difficulties using search engines effectively. Knowledge regarding online exchange and cooperation with other companies and citizens is not covered in training programs. It is recommended that the Internet skill levels are tested when hiring new employers, preferably using tests or surveys.

Executive employees should be partly educated in operational and formal Internet skills, just as older administrators and policy advisors. Specific computer courses neglect some elementary operational and formal skills by having too narrow a focus. Executive employees cannot help insufficiently skilled citizens if they themselves only possess elementary knowledge. Administrators and some policy advisors would benefit from training in strategic information management, which is all too often passed to the ICT department. Currently, administrators follow several training programs that neglect information management and focus on financial and juridical affairs or human resource management [12]. Policy advisors would benefit from taking part in training programs for information skills and strategic skills.

References

1. Bawden, D.: Information and Digital Literacies: A Review of Concepts. Journal of Documentation 57(2), 218–259 (2001)
2. Ba, H., Tally, W., Tsikalas, K.: Investigating children's emerging digital literacies. Journal of Technology, Learning and Assessment 1(4), 1–48 (2002)
3. Van Deursen, A.J.A.M., Van Dijk, J.A.G.M.: Measuring Internet skills. International Journal of Human Computer Interaction (in press)
4. Van Deursen, A.J.A.M., Van Dijk, J.A.G.M.: Using the Internet: Skill-related Problems in Users' Online Behavior. Interacting with Computers, 21 (2009)
5. Merritt, K., Smith, D., Renzo, J.C.D.: An Investigation of Self-Reported Computer Literacy: Is It Reliable? Issues in Information Systems 6(1) (2005)
6. Talja, S.: The Social and Discursive Construction of Computing Skills. Journal of the American Society for Information Science and Technology 56(1), 13–22 (2005)
7. Norris, P.: Digital Divide: Civic Engagement, Information Poverty and the Internet Worldwide, Cambridge (2001)
8. Mossberger, K., Tolbert, C.J., Stansbury, M.: Virtual Inequality: Beyond the Digital Divide. Georgetown University Press, Washington (2003)
9. Warschauer, M.: Technology and Social inclusion: Rethinking the Digital Divide. The MIT Press, Cambridge (2003)
10. Van Dijk, J.A.G.M.: The deepening divide. Inequality in the information society. Sage Publications, London (2005)
11. Van Deursen, A.J.A.M., Van Dijk, J.A.G.M.: Improving digital skills for the use of online public information and services. Government Information Quarterly 26, 333–340 (2009)
12. Zuurmond, A.: In Verweij: Bijscholen maar hoe! Digitaal Bestuur Maart 2009 (2009)

Appendix

Assignment 1. (max. 6 minutes) – Operational Internet skills

- Task 1.1: Go to the website of the CBR (www.cbr.nl).
- Task 1.2: Click on the link 'Motor' in the menu on the left. Click on the subject 'Motor and scooter', placed in the column 'Brochures.'
- Task 1.3: Open the brochure 'Motor and scooter.' Save the brochure in the folder 'CBR' in My Documents. Close the brochure.
- Task 1.4: Add the homepage to the Favorites (or bookmarks).

Assignment 2. (max. 5 minutes) – Operational Internet skills.

- Task 2.1: Go to the website of Marktplaats (www.marktplaats.nl). Click the link 'Uitgebreid zoeken.'
- Task 2.2: Complete the fields using the information given.
- Task 2.3: Save the logo of Marktplaats in the upper left corner on the desktop of the computer.

Assignment 3. (max. 8 minutes) - Formal Internet skills.

- Task 3.1: Go to the website of the ANWB (www.anwb.nl). Follow the options Car / Sell / Selling Occasion. Choose the option: 'Selling my car via Auto Trader.'
- Task 3.2: In both windows, go to the homepage of the site opened. Go to the homepage of the Autotrader website in the new window. Go to the homepage of the ANWB in the old window.

Assignment 4. (max. 8 minutes) - Formal Internet skills.

Imagine that you just moved to Nijmegen. You would like to look up the physical office addresses of the following organizations: IB-Groep and UWV.

Assignment 5. T-mobile (max. 10 minutes) - Information Internet skills.

Imagine… 8 months ago you subscribed to a mobile telephone contract with T-mobile. Now you would like to take advantage of the new T-mobile iPhone offer. Answer the following question, using the T-mobile website (www.t-mobile.nl): Is it possible to subscribe to a T-mobile iPhone contract as a continuation of your current subscription?

Assignment 6. Salary (max. 12 min) - Information Internet skills.

Imagine that you are 25 years old. In between September 1st and December 30th you had a full-time job in a factory (40 h/week). Your wage was 1275 euro gross every month. This was not much. Use a search engine (e.g., www.google.nl or the one you use at home) to find out whether you were entitled to a higher salary during this period. (Yes, because the salary was lower than ___ euro./No, because the salary was higher than _ euro).

Assignment 7. Salary (max. 12 min) - Strategic Internet skills.

When your employer paid you too little, what financial recourse do you have can you then personally obtain? Sort this out using the Internet.

Assignment 8. Travelling (max. 25 minutes) - Strategic Internet skills.

Imagine… from March the 7th through the13th of next year you are going on a trip to London with your partner. You would like to book two tickets from a nearby airport (in the Netherlands or just across the border) and a hotel in the centre of London. Find out how much this would cost using the Internet, aiming to identify the cheapest options. Consider flight, hotel and travel expenses to and from the airport in London.

Channel Choice and Source Choice of Entrepreneurs in a Public Organizational Context: The Dutch Case

Jurjen Jansen, Lidwien van de Wijngaert, and Willem Pieterson

University of Twente, Center for e-Government Studies
P.O. Box 217, 7500 AE Enschede, The Netherlands
{j.jansen,l.vandewijngaert,w.pieterson}@utwente.nl

Abstract. Most e-Government research focuses on citizens, the use and effects of electronic channels and services. However, businesses are an important target group for governmental agencies as well. Governmental agencies have a duty to inform businesses and to make this information easy to access. In order to increase accessibility it is important to closely relate to the behavior of users. Therefore, the purpose of the present investigation is to gain insight about the channel and source choice of entrepreneurs in a public organizational context. According to 323 entrepreneurs, who filled out an electronic questionnaire, the internet is the most preferred channel and a search engine is the most preferred source for obtaining governmental information. Business-, entrepreneur- and situational characteristics have, although small, effect on these choices.

Keywords: Channel choice, source choice, entrepreneurs, businesses, public service delivery, vignette method.

1 Introduction

Governmental agencies deliver services to both citizens and businesses. Given the complexities of many businesses it is likely that governmental agencies have more contacts with businesses than with citizens. However, most studies focusing on the use of (electronic) services and/or service channels [e.g. 1, 2-5] are aimed at citizens. It is questionable to what extent the results of studies among citizens are applicable to businesses. Businesses have more complex service interactions and the internet penetration among businesses is higher than among citizens. This, for example, has led to a mandatory electronic tax filing for business in the Netherlands [6]. However, it remains difficult for governmental agencies to reach businesses. Bergers [7], for example, states that governmental information, to a large extent, does not reach the entrepreneur. She states that too little is known about this target group as the most important reasons for this; a client-centered approach is missing.

In order to better direct information to entrepreneurs insight into the channel choice and source choice of entrepreneurs regarding public organizations needs to be obtained. This is the main focus of our paper.

M.A. Wimmer et al. (Eds.): EGOV 2010, LNCS 6228, pp. 144–155, 2010.

2 Public Service Delivery to Businesses

The relationship between governmental agencies and businesses is, in general, relatively complex. This complexity is driven by a number of aspects. First of all, there are more rules and regulations and more contact points as compared to the relationship between governmental agencies and citizens. Second, the playing-field is complex. Entrepreneurs do business with different kinds of (semi) public organizations. This means that public service delivery has a complex and networked nature. Third, the moments of contact are complex. In some cases public organizations have indirect contact with a business, i.e. through intermediaries. This means that some contacts are mediated and some are not. The fourth and last aspect of complexity is the business itself. In some cases the entrepreneur is the business, while in other cases this is the accountant or bookkeeper. The whole makes service delivery to businesses hard to optimize.

Illustrative for this complexity is the limited range of knowledge in this field [e.g. 8]. Not only is the amount of research regarding service delivery to businesses in sharp contrast with research regarding service delivery to citizens, it can also be questioned to what extent the insights about citizens can be applied to businesses.

Public organizations do, however, increasingly feel a need to adopt a more client-centered approach [9]. According to Van Duivenboden and Lips [10] there are three explanations for this. First, changing expectations from businesses, second, a complex societal environment that calls for different ways of direction, and, third, a differentiating offer of public services by using ICTs. Furthermore, according to Jansen et al. [9] this is prompted by ongoing bureaucratic procedures and the increase of abstract and impersonal electronic services and also by society in general which is becoming more complex, dynamic and diverse.

This diversity [see, 9] is based on three types of characteristics, namely: business characteristics, entrepreneur characteristics, and situational characteristics. We believe that these characteristics are important predictors of channel and source choice.

2.1 Business, Entrepreneur, and Situational Characteristics

The first category of characteristics can be defined as demographics. Demographic segmentation holds that people who have the same demographics characteristics, e.g. age and gender, act the same [11].

According to Statistics Netherlands, the number of businesses in the Netherlands in 2008 was almost 800.000. We have chosen to focus our study on small and medium enterprises (SMEs). SMEs, i.e. businesses with 1 - 49 employees, are by far the largest group of businesses in the Netherlands. According to Statistics Netherlands 98% of the businesses can be defined as SMEs.

Besides the demographic characteristics of businesses we also take a look at entrepreneur demographics. According to Statistics Netherlands over two-thirds of the entrepreneurs is male. Furthermore, the entrepreneurs are most found in the age groups 25 to 45 and 45 to 65 years. A small percentage of entrepreneurs is older than 65 and an even smaller percentage is 15 to 25 years. Conclusively, we take a look at the educational level of entrepreneurs.

In addition, we focus on the psychographic characteristics of entrepreneurs. Cahill [12] defines psychographic segmentation as differentiation in activities, interests, opinions, and values. The Technology Acceptance Model, henceforth TAM [13] has been successfully validated by scholars who have tested the model empirically and found that it explained much of the variance between perceived usefulness and perceived ease of use, i.e. attitude, and adoption intentions [e.g. 14, 15-17]. Because of this, the TAM is regarded as a trustworthy tool for predicting the intention to adopt and use (new) technologies. We define attitude as attitude towards governmental information, i.e. the first psychographic characteristic.

Although attitude can be a useful predictor for behavior, we believe behavior can be better predicted by mapping what people actually do. Applying ICTs in service delivery processes is an obvious choice for most public organizations. However, it is not obvious that everyone can make proper use of these electronic services. According to Van Deursen and Van Dijk [18] four types of digital skills determine to what extend one can use these services. These skills are: operational skills, formal skills, information skills, and strategic skills. Although no numbers are known about the digital skills of entrepreneurs we believe that they, like citizens [18], have different skill levels. Therefore, digital skills are the second psychographic characteristics we include in our research.

The final type of characteristics is the situational characteristics. We believe that situational characteristics, often not included in behavior models, are important predictors of both channel and source choice [19, 20]. In this paper we have defined five situational characteristics. The first one is topic. Entrepreneurs may visit different channels or make use of different sources considering the topic. Important and often searched for topics by entrepreneurs are about: starting a new business, personnel, housing, environment, tax, innovation, transaction, and rules and regulations.

The other situational characteristics we define are: type of need, i.e. need to know versus nice to know; level of importance, i.e. high versus low; type of knowledge, i.e. orientation versus specific; and level of urgency, i.e. high versus low.

2.2 Channel Choice and Source Choice

Informing businesses can be done through different service channels. Pieterson et al. [19, p.9] define a channel as "…an access point by which organizations and clients can have contact with each other". According to these researchers channels are used to communicate with clients, facilitate clients with purchases, and offer clients products or services. For this research we define three channels: internet, telephone, and service desk.

Besides channels, entrepreneurs have a whole range of sources to choose from. Based on cluster analysis (see chapter 3), we define five main categories of sources. The main sources are: search engines, portals, governmental agencies, expert organizations, and the personal network of the entrepreneurs.

2.3 Conclusion

In sum, we expect that four groups of factors influence the choice of channels and sources by entrepreneurs, i.e. business characteristics (business size), entrepreneur demographics (age, gender and education), entrepreneur psychographics (attitude towards governmental information), and situational characteristics (subject, type, importance, type of knowledge and urgency).

Using a quantitative study, we will try to answer the question what channels and sources entrepreneurs choose to obtain governmental information and how the four groups of factors affect these choices.

3   Method

The research model provides an overview of the variables that were included in this research project. In the online questionnaire questions were posed regarding personal characteristics such as age and gender, preferences for channels and sources. To assess how different situational characteristics affect channel and source choices, we have used a vignette method (see below). Before the questionnaire was put online it was pretested by three researchers and six entrepreneurs.

In the questionnaire, respondents were presented with a list of fifteen different sources of information from which they could choose to search for information. In order to reduce complexity we used hierarchical clustering. Using an Euclidean distance as a measure of closeness and furthest neighbor to cluster the sources we distinguished five sources of information as presented in section 2.3.

The research population concerned all SMEs in the Netherlands. In order to reach this group we made use of an online panel of a commercial market research company. The panel consisted of 8000 possible respondents.

The questionnaire could be filled in from the beginning of October till the beginning of December in 2009. A relative long period was needed in order to receive enough respondents. In December, an effective response of 4% (N=323) was reached. This low response can be partly explained by the selection criteria. Of the 953 people who accessed our survey 538 did not meet the proper conditions to participate. Despite the low response rate, the final sample provides an adequate representation of the Dutch population of entrepreneurs. Female entrepreneurs are well represented with 35%. The mean age of the respondents is 42. Entrepreneurs with higher education levels are slightly over-represented, while the different kinds of company sizes are well represented.

3.1 The Vignette Method

This research method is also referred to as factorial surveys, vignette studies, policy capturing and conjoint measurement. These methods offer similar, yet more or less unrelated approaches in marketing and product development research and have been around for some time [20]. The methods borrow and adapt the concept of manipulation from the experimental tradition. From the survey tradition they borrow the greater richness of detail and complexity that characterizes real-life circumstances [22]. The basic idea is to present people with contrived hypothetical situations. These situations, scenarios, vignettes or cases are developed by combining characteristics of possible situations as described in the research model. This can be explained the easiest by using an example:

> *Suppose... You are thinking about starting a new business. You know there are a number of legal obligations need to be fulfilled. You have not yet looked into the matter but would like to look for some information. Where and how will you search for information?*

In this hypothetical situation the subject is starting a new business. Furthermore, the situation can be characterized as need to know, orientation and non-urgent. In total, respondents were presented with eight of such situations. Other cases, for example, do not outline a general situation, as above, but also more specific situations in which an entrepreneur has a specific question about a particular scheme.

3.2 Scales and Analysis

The following table shows an overview of the measures used in the study:

Table 1. Variables and measures

Variable	Measure/Description
Business demographics	
size	Number of employees of the firm
Entrepreneur demographics	
Age	Age of the respondent
Gender	Gender of the respondent
Education	Highest level of education of the respondent
Entrepreneur psychographics	
Attitude	Attitude of the respondent towards governmental information
Digital skills	Self assessed level of digital skills
Situational characteristics	
Subject	Starting a new business, personnel, housing, environment, tax, innovation, transaction, and rules and regulations
Type	Need to know or nice to know
Importance	High or low importance of the issue
Type of knowledge	Specific or general (orientation) knowledge
Urgency	High or low urgency

Data are analyzed in different ways. In order to group the different sources we used a cluster analysis using the Ward method [23]. We have used (multi-nominal) logistic regression in order to analyze the impact of the (dichotomous) situational characteristics on channel and source selection and regular (OLS) regression to assess the impact of the other variables.

4 Results

We used a number of items to measure the attitude towards the government. Six items, related to the quality of governmental information were presented to respondents. These items showed a homogeneous picture with a Cronbach's Alpha of 0.84. The average score on each of the items ranged between four and five on a seven point scale, which means that respondents in general were relatively positive about the quality of governmental information.

Similarly, digital skills were measured using four items that expressed different levels of digital skills [18]. Analysis of homogeneity resulted in a Cronbach's Alpha of 0.78. In general, respondents expressed a relatively high level of digital skills with scores between five and six on a seven point scale.

4.1   Channel Choice

The first objective was to gain more insight in the channel choice of entrepreneurs. We asked the respondents what the probability is of choosing each channel. We have done this both directly, i.e. by self-reports (figure 1a), and indirectly, by asking them what they would choose based on the vignettes (figure 1b).

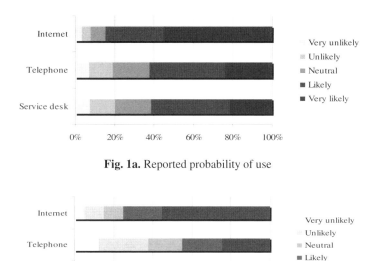

Fig. 1a. Reported probability of use

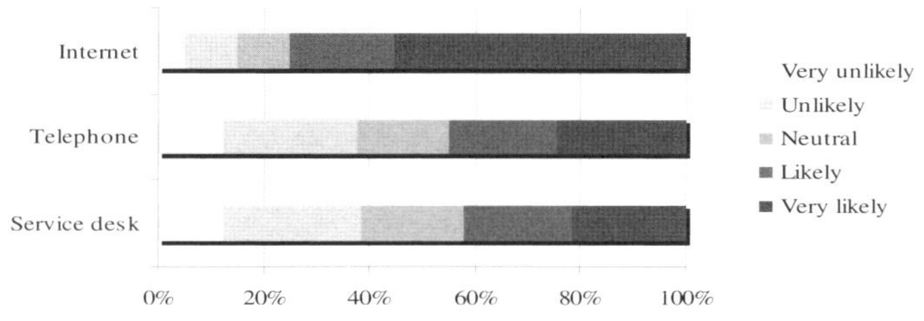

Fig. 1b. Probability of use based on the vignettes

What can be seen from the figures above is that the reported probability differs from the probability based on the vignettes. In general, the internet channel is the most preferred channel. A large majority uses this channel on a monthly basis or more frequent. The preferences for telephone and service desk score lower, especially in the vignettes. About 50% never visits the service desk and 40% just a few times a year. Besides this, entrepreneurs turn out to be real multi-channelers. On average, the respondents make use of three different channels. About one-third has used four channels in 2009.

Regarding the demographic characteristics of businesses we see that larger businesses have a small favor for the telephone compared to internet and service desk. Concerning the demographic characteristics of entrepreneurs we observed two significant results (see the left side of table 2a in the annex). Older entrepreneurs tend to choose the internet channel more often than younger entrepreneurs and male entrepreneurs make more use of the telephone than female entrepreneurs. No significant results were found regarding the service desk. This could imply that the service desk is a suitable channel for everyone.

The psychographic characteristics show also some variation. An increase of the digital skills has a significant effect on the choice of all three channels. This is the highest for the internet channel. Entrepreneurs with a positive attitude towards governmental information also have a preference for internet.

The topics of the vignettes are no great predictor of channel choice. The preference for the service desk, however, shows the most variation. The preference for this channel is the strongest with the topics about personnel and starting a business. The other characteristics of the vignettes do not or hardly influence channel choice. Only small differences were found considering the service desk. When the vignettes dealt with low importance and orientation issues, entrepreneurs slightly, but significantly preferred the service desk as a channel to get information (see the left side of table 2b in the annex).

4.2   Source Choice

The second objective was to gain more insight in the source choice of entrepreneurs. In this section we discuss the relationship between the choices for a specific source based on the characteristics of the vignettes that were presented to the respondents.

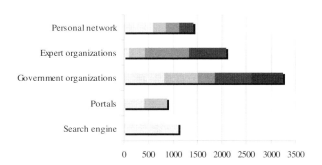

Fig. 2. Source choices of entrepreneurs

Figure 2 shows the number of times that a specific source was mentioned for a specific topic. Most source clusters contain multiple sources. For example, the personal network consists of external advisors, family and friends, internal colleagues, and external colleagues. The search engine is the most used source for searching public information. Also expert organizations, e.g. chamber of commerce and professional associations are important as well as government organizations, like national government and municipalities.

Regarding the demographic characteristics of businesses we conclude from the right side of table 2a in the annex that larger businesses make less use of expert organizations and more use of their personal network as compared to smaller businesses. Concerning the demographic characteristics of entrepreneurs we see that older entrepreneurs use government and expert organizations as a source for information. Younger entrepreneurs rather consult their personal network. Female, and higher educated entrepreneurs consult expert organizations more often as a source for information than male and lower educated entrepreneurs.

The psychographic characteristics show also some variation. Entrepreneurs with a high level of digital skills significantly use search engines and consult government organizations more often than entrepreneurs with less digital skills. When entrepreneurs have a negative attitude towards governmental information, they make significantly more use of their personal network compared to entrepreneurs with positive attitudes towards governmental information.

On the right side of table 2b in the annex it is demonstrated that search engines and portals are used most when entrepreneurs are in need for specific information. Government organizations are accessed in cases of high importance as well as for specific purposes. Expert organizations are consulted when the importance is high and when urgency is high. The personal network is addressed when the importance is high and when entrepreneurs are seeking information about specific issues. Furthermore, we found that search engines and portals are used for all topics. Moreover, portals are used a little less often than search engines as a starting point. Also, entrepreneurs gather information from expert organizations relatively often when the topic is about starting a new business, personnel and tax issues. Government organizations are approached most often when the topics are about environment, transactions, or rules and regulations issues.

5   Conclusion and Discussion

The goal of this study was to gain insight in which channels and which sources entrepreneurs use for public information. In order to reach this goal an online questionnaire was presented to Dutch entrepreneurs containing a vignette method. In total, 323 respondents have fully completed the questionnaire. Based on the response rate and the difficulty to achieve this, we conclude that entrepreneurs are a hard to reach target group for research. Especially immigrant entrepreneurs were difficult to reach with a presence of 3%. Nonetheless, considering the drawbacks of the respondents, they do form a realistic reflection of the entrepreneurial target group. However, the study is limited to the Dutch context and little can be said if the findings would remain valid in other national and cultural contexts.

This brings us to the first research question: which channels and which sources do entrepreneurs use regarding public organizational information? Based on the results we can conclude the following:

1) Entrepreneurs have chosen internet as the most preferred channel to obtain governmental information. Nevertheless, this does not imply that other channels are not used. Therefore, government organizations should still follow multi-channel strategies. This finding is, however, not really surprising. Perhaps the internet as a channel should have been differentiated in different possibilities, like e-mail and chat.

2) Based on the self-reports, entrepreneurs have a strong preference for the internet channel when they are orientating themselves, when they want to know something fast, and when they want to know things about rules and regulations. On the other hand, when they want to know things about which has high importance or about a specific topic, they prefer the telephone or service desk.

3) Based on the vignettes, entrepreneurs still have a strong preference for the internet channel, but the differences are smaller. Surprisingly, the opposite seems to be unfolding. For orientation questions entrepreneurs seem to prefer the service desk. This contradiction can be explained by differentiating between intentional behavior and actual behavior. Whereas self-reports, by stating propositions, reflect intentional behavior, vignettes do a better job in portraying actual behavior.

In the seventies and eighties of the last century scholars believed in the rational model of channel choice. This model was based on the Media Richness Theory [24] and the Social Presence Theory [25]. This model implies that people think rational about their channel choice, based on the characteristics of the channels and the characteristics of the question they have. However, as noted by the Social Influence Model [26] and the Channel Expansion Theory [27], these choices can also be influenced by unconscious variables. This is supported by research of Pieterson [19] who developed a framework for the channel choice of citizens. One of the main predictors in his model is habit.

In the case of the vignettes, entrepreneurs likely revert to their habits, than when asked to think about their behavior. Thus, the vignettes give a more realistic picture of the reality. However, there is a price to pay. Although the situational characteristics have some influence, the explained variance is low. This could, however, be caused by the design of our vignettes. Therefore, a more precise description of different situations should be considered.

4) Regarding the sources, entrepreneurs have a strong preference for search engines like Google to obtain governmental information. However, government organizations as well as expert organizations and to a smaller extent portals can also be considered among the most important sources for searching information. It seems that entrepreneurs rely more on their own skills to obtain governmental information than to obtain it via portals. The question is if this is the most efficient way. When searching for governmental information via portals it is more certain that all relevant information is obtained. Perhaps entrepreneurs should be educated about this? An additional point of discussion is that no attention is paid to traditional offline sources, like telephone books.

The second research question was: to what extent do the four groups of factors affect the channel and source choice of entrepreneurs regarding public organizational information? Based on the results we can conclude the following:

1) Larger businesses make use more of the telephone channel and less of the internet and service desk. Furthermore, they make more use of their personal network and less of expert organizations compared to smaller businesses.

2) Older entrepreneurs make use of the internet channel the most and have more contact with governmental and expert organizations. We expected that younger entrepreneurs would make more use of the internet. A possible explanation for this is that they are well aware of the drawbacks of the internet and therefore make use of

the telephone. Younger entrepreneurs are consulting their personal network more often. Male entrepreneurs make more use of the telephone. Female and higher educated entrepreneurs make more use of consulting expert organizations.

3) When entrepreneurs have a positive attitude towards government information they tend to use the internet more often. Entrepreneurs with a more negative attitude are getting their information from their personal network. When the digital skills of entrepreneurs increase, the preference for all the other channels increases as well, especially for the internet channel. Digital skilled entrepreneurs also make more use of search engines and consult governmental organizations more often.

4) Conclusively, the situational characteristics are no great predictor of channel choice. However, it does have some effect on source choice. Entrepreneurs who are in need for specific information have a strong preference for using search engines and portals. When the information is necessary for specific and highly important topics, governmental agencies are accessed. Expert organizations are addressed when the importance is high and when urgency is high. The personal network is consulted when the importance is high and when entrepreneurs are seeking information about specific issues.

Our study is amongst the first to analyze channel and source choice behavior among businesses. In line with studies among citizens we see that businesses use different channels for different purposes in different situations. However we lack theories that describe or predict how these situational characteristics affect channel and source choice. The variables used in this study might help in building such a theory.

The added value of this research is that it shows that it is possible to explain channel and source choice from situational characteristics in stead of only asking respondents their preferences, e.g. ease of use and perceived usefulness. However, we need to understand more clearly what it is exactly in these situations that explain certain types of behavior. Future research should focus on this.

References

1. Pieterson, W.: Channel Choice; Citizens' Channel Behavior and Public Service Channel Strategy. Faculty of Behavioural Sciences, PhD. University of Twente, Enschede, 302 (2009)
2. Pieterson, W., Ebbers, W.: The Use of Service Channels by Citizens in the Netherlands: Implications for Multi-Channel Management. International Review of Administrative Sciences 74 (2008)
3. Reddick, C.G.: Citizen-Initiated Contacts with Government: Comparing Phones and Websites. Journal of E-Government 2, 27–53 (2005)
4. Reddick, C.G.: Citizen Interaction with E-Government: From the Streets to Servers? Government Information Quarterly 22, 38–57 (2005)
5. Thomas, J.C., Streib, G.: The New Face of Government: Citizen-Initiated Contacts in the Era of E-Government. Journal of Public Administration Research and Theory 13, 83 (2003)
6. Ebbers, W., Pieterson, W., Noordman, H.: Electronic Government: Rethinking Channel Management Strategies. Government Information Quarterly 25, 181–201 (2008)

7. Bergers, A.M.: Communicatie met Ondernemers in het MKB: Een Handreiking voor Communicatie-adviseurs van de Rijksoverheid (Communication with SME Entrepreneurs: Assistance for Communication Advisors of the Federal Government) (2003), http://www.communicatieplein.nl/dsc?c=getobject&s=obj&objectid=143472 (retrieved March 9, 2008)
8. Sadowski, B.M., Maitland, C., van Dongen, J.: Strategic Use of the Internet by Small- and Medium-Sized Companies: An Exploratory Study. Information Economics and Policy 14, 75–93 (2002)
9. Jansen, J., de Vries, S., van der Geest, T., Arendsen, R., van Dijk, J.A.G.M.: The state of client-centered public service delivery in the netherlands. In: Wimmer, M.A., Scholl, H.J., Janssen, M., Traunmüller, R. (eds.) EGOV 2009. LNCS, vol. 5693, pp. 293–304. Springer, Heidelberg (2009)
10. van Duivenboden, H., Lips, M.: CRM in de Publieke Sector: Naar een Klantgerichte Elektronische Overheid (CRM in the Public Sector: Towards a Client-Centered Electronic Government). Holland Management Review 85, 45–57 (2002)
11. Fu, J.-R., Chao, W.-P., Farn, C.-K.: Determinants of Taxpayers' Adoption of Electronic Filing Methods in Taiwan: An Exploratory Study. Journal of Public Information 30, 658–683 (2004)
12. Cahill, D.J.: Lifestyle Market Segmentation. Haworth Press, New York (2006)
13. Davis, F.D.: Perceived Usefulness, Perceived Ease of Use, and User Acceptance of Information technology. MIS Quarterly 13, 319–339 (1989)
14. Adams, D.A., Nelson, R.R., Todd, P.A.: Perceived Usefulness, Ease of Use, and Usage of Information Technology: A Replication. MIS Quarterly 16(2), 227–246 (1992)
15. Szajna, B.: Empirical Evaluation of the Revised Technology Acceptance Model. Management Science 42(1), 85–92 (1996)
16. Venkatesh, V., Davis, F.D.: A Theoretical Extension of the Technology Acceptance Model: Four Longitudinal Field Studies. Management Science 46(2), 186–204 (2000)
17. Venkatesh, V., Morris, M.G., Davis, G.B., Davis, F.D.: User Acceptance of Information Technology: Toward a Unified View. MIS Quarterly 27(3), 425–478 (2003)
18. van Deursen, A.J.A.M., van Dijk, J.A.G.M.: Improving Digital Skills for the Use of Online Public Information and Services. Government Information Quarterly 26, 333–340 (2009)
19. Pieterson, W.: Channel Choice: Citizens Channel Behavior and Public Service Channel Strategy. University of Twente, Enschede (2009)
20. Van de Wijngaert, L., Bouwman, H.A.: Multi-Theory Approach Towards the Adoption, Use and Effects of IT-Services. In: Vishwanath, A., Barnett, G. (eds.) Advances in the Study of the Diffusion of Innovations: Theory, Methods, and Applications (forthcoming)
21. Pieterson, W., Teerling, M., Klievink, M., Lankhorst, M., Janssen, M., Boekhoudt, P.: Multichannel Management: De Stand van Zaken. Multi-Channel Management: State of the Art. Novay, Enschede (2007)
22. Rossi, P.H., Nock, S.S.: Measuring Social Judgments: The Factorial Survey Approach. Sage, Beverly Hills (1982)
23. Ward, J.: Hierarchical Grouping to Optimize an Objective Function. Journal of the American Statistical Association 58, 236–244 (1963)
24. Daft, R.L., Lengel, R.H.: Information richness: A new approach to managerial behavior and organizational design. In: Cummings, L.L., Staw, B.M. (eds.) Research in organizational behavior, vol. 6, pp. 191–233. JAI Press, Homewood (1984)
25. Short, J., Williams, E., Christie, B.: The social psychology of telecommunications. John Wiley, London (1976)

26. Fulk, J., Schmitz, J., Steinfield, C.W.: A social influence model of technology use. In: Fulk, J., Steinfield, C.W. (eds.) Organizations and communication technology. Sage Publications, London (1990)
27. Carlson, J.R., Zmud, R.W.: Channel expansion theory and the experiential nature of media richness perceptions. The Academy of Management Journal 42(2), 153–170 (1994)

Annex

Table 2a. Business and entrepreneur characteristics x channels and sources

OLS Regression	Internet		Telephone		Service desk		Search engine		Portals		Government		Expert		Personal	
R^2	12%		11%		5%		5%		n.s.		7%		13%		10%	
	Beta	t	Beta	t	Beta	t	Beta	t	Beta	t	Beta	t	Beta	t	Beta	t
Entrepreneur demographics																
Age	0.18	2.89**	-0.07	-1.03	0.01	0.22	0.05	0.75			0.15	2.45**	0.21	3.40***	-0.17	-2.64**
Gender	0.00	-0.06	0.18	2.80**	0.05	0.72	0.09	1.47			-0.08	-1.35	-0.12	-2.00*	0.10	1.67
Education	0.06	1.02	-0.04	-0.60	0.12	1.96	0.05	0.75			-0.02	-0.39	0.12	2.08*	-0.11	-1.83
Entrepreneur psychographics																
Digital skills	0.24	4.02***	0.22	3.54***	0.16	2.59*	0.20	3.14***			0.12	1.94*	0.09	1.46	0.08	1.38
Attitude	0.15	2.50**	0.07	1.15	0.02	0.27	0.01	0.15			0.10	1.51	0.03	0.46	-0.17	-2.79**
Business demographics																
Business size	-0.05	-0.90	0.07	1.07	-0.09	-1.51	-0.01	-0.12			0.12	1.87	-0.17	-2.86***	0.19	3.05***

*=p 0.05; **=p 0.01; ***=p 0.00

Table 2b. Vignette characteristics x channels and sources

OLS Regression	Internet		Telephone		Service desk		Search engine		Portals		Government		Expert		Personal	
Cox & Snell R^2	n.s.		n.s.		1%		1%		1%		2%		8%		2%	
Nagelkerke R^2					1%		1%		1%		3%		11%		3%	
	Beta	Wald	Beta	Wald	Beta	Wald	Beta	Wald	Beta	Wald	Beta	Wald	Beta	Wald	Beta	Wald
Vignettes																
Need nice (need=0; nice=1)							-0.06	0.57	0.05	0.31	0.04	0.20	0.01	0.20	0.01	0.02
Importance (low=0; high=1)					-0.12	3.94***	-0.11	2.06	-0.03	0.15	-0.47	30.92***	1.12	180.48***	0.20	5.78*
Knowledge (one=0; spec=1)					-0.10	4.90***	0.28	12.26**	0.36	16.90***	0.37	18.60***	0.11	1.65	0.59	50.65***
Urgency (low=0; high=1)					-0.04	2.04	-0.04	0.29	0.09	1.08	-0.16	3.67	0.40	23.23***	-0.14	2.71

*=p 0.05; **=p 0.01; ***=p 0.00

Measuring and Benchmarking the Back-end of E-Government: A Participative Self-assessment Approach

Marijn Janssen

Delft University of Technology, Faculty of Technology, Policy and Management,
Jaffalaan 5, 2628 BX, Delft, The Netherlands
m.f.w.h.a.janssen@tudelft.nl

Abstract. Measuring e-government has traditionally been focused on measuring and benchmarking websites and their use. This provides useful information from a user-perspective, but does not provide any information how well the back-end of e-government is organized and what can be learnt from others. In this paper a self-assessment instrument for organizational and technology infrastructure aspects is developed and tested. This model has been used to benchmark 15 initiates in the Netherlands in a group session. This helped them to identify opportunities for improvement and to share their experiences and practices. The benchmark results shows that only a disappointingly few investigated back-ends (20%) fall in the highest quadrant. Measuring the back-end should capture both organizational and technical elements. A crucial element for gaining in-depth insight with limited resources is the utilizing of a participative, self-assessment approach. Such an approach ensures an emphasis on learning, avoids the adverse aspects of benchmarking and dispute over the outcomes.

Keywords: e-government, measurement, benchmarking, back-end, self-assessment, group session.

1 Introduction

Electronic Government measurement and benchmarking have gained considerable attention over the recent years. Especially the UN Index, Brown University, Accenture and Cap Gemini surveys have been widely discussed and have stimulated governments to develop their online efforts [1-5]. The basic idea of benchmarking is often to be able to distinct good from bad practices, and provide incentives for improvements. The efforts of these instruments concentrate on measuring the level of e-government in countries or at regional levels to enable comparison. Often, a combination of measurement instruments is employed to accomplish this. These types of instruments access the level of e-government often from the outside, i.e. what is directly observable at the front-end, and often consider the back-end as a black-box. Measurement focuses predominantly on the front (primarily counting the number of services offered) and not on the back-office processes [6]. This is a logical focus when taking the citizens' point of view or from the view of other stakeholders who are not directly interested or involved in improving the back-end. In contrast, public

M.A. Wimmer et al. (Eds.): EGOV 2010, LNCS 6228, pp. 156–167, 2010.

managers and decisions-makers who are interested in improving the back-end have the concern to understand and measure the performance of the back-end. They have a need to have an understanding of the insides of the black-box, not to a level of detail to understand all processes and system components, but at a level of measuring to enable the benchmarking with others and learning from each other's practices. These insights can then be used to improve their own functioning.

The organization of the back-end of government involves many, often heterogeneous types of business processes, software applications and organizational arrangements. A major bottleneck is the lack of a shared infrastructure [7]. This is further complicated due to the many unrelated changes that happened over time. Each government and each department have developed their own systems and processes, which need to be integrated to enable integrated service delivery. Generally it is assumed that transformation of e-government requires new structures based on citizen/business focus and not in a division in functions. The variety in back-ends is even increased due to the stream of new or altered legislations requiring adaptations in the back-end. The diverse landscape and the need for constantly changing this landscape often block the progress towards more innovative solutions. Despite the significance, the measurement of the back-end of e-government has gained limited attention [6].

One reason for the limited attention is the difficulty of measuring and benchmarking in general and the back-end in particular. Measurements and benchmarks have been criticized from various views [8, 9]. The bottom line is that benchmarks are not a reliable way of measuring. Often the focus of measurement is on a generic level at the expense of detailed insights. This might especially hold for the back-end, as the measurement of this is less straightforward than the front-end. The outcomes of the benchmarks might be discussable and the position might be dependent on normative criteria that might not hold in all situations. There exists little agreement on a uniform set of measures [6]. This difficulty might result in the adverse affects that benchmarks might have limited practical meaning, but might have a huge impact on political decision-making [9]. Benchmarking of websites have resulted in a normative view on citizens as customers and have resulted in uncritically copying each other elements [10]. Instead the focus should be on understanding what is needed and the resulting business models capturing the organizing logic that can fulfill this need [11].

In this paper the focus is on the measurement and benchmarking of the back-end of government organizations. The instrument developed and used in this paper is aimed at enabling the self-assessment of the back-end by providing attention to a variety of elements instead of trying to develop a generic, uni-interpretable instrument providing a single outcome. The aim of the instrument is to measure and benchmark the back-end in comparison with others who are involved in the same situation. In this way it should facilitate learning and help to transfer best practices.

This paper is structured as follows. In the next section e-government benchmarking and measurement literature is reviewed. This literature is used as a starting point to develop the back-end measurement and benchmarking model. The research methodology is presented in section three, followed by the measurement model and the findings of the use of the model in a participative session. The findings are discussed and finally conclusions are drawn.

2 Related Literature

There are many stages and growth models in e-governments [12-15]. Although stages and growth models are popular in e-government, these models have not been translated in operational measures for the back-end. There are many other benchmarks available [1-3]. Ojo et al. [16] compare three different surveys, those by the United Nations (UN), Accenture and Brown University to distil out a 'core' set of indicators. Janssen et al. [17] identify 18 benchmarks in four areas e.g. supply studies, demand studies, information society studies and e-Government indicator studies. Kunstelj and Vintar [8] found 41 reports grouped as e-readiness, back office, front office supply, front office demand and effects and impacts. The metrics used concentrate on measuring the level of sophistication, but do not measure the back-end and say little about the effectiveness and level of customer orientation [6]. The European Foundation for Quality Management (EFQM) model has been used for accessing services [18]. EFQM Excellence Model enables managers to effectively self-assess critical performance issues to identify a range of service interrelationships affecting customers [19].

User-centric measuring approaches include functionality, usability and accessibility testing [20]. Functionality is about measuring if the system actually works in the intended behavior, usability is about the way users interact, and accessibility refers to the use by disabled people. The measurement of user satisfaction and perceptions of citizens or businesses is more and more conducted by governments. Although very important, as these approaches take the citizens' perspective into account, the disadvantage of such these approaches for our purposes is that the actual situation is not measured. Instead the experiences as perceived by the citizens/businesses at a certain moment in time are measured. These perceptions might be arbitrarily and can be influenced by other factors, including temporary factors such as mood and attitude, and provide limited insight into how to improve the back-end. A recent example shows that the user satisfaction in a survey increased due to marketing and communication efforts, whereas the actual systems did not change at all (http://www.uwv.nl/overuwv/pers/nieuwsberichten/overzicht2009/). In conclusion, these are not appropriate approaches with which to gauge success of the back-end of e-government.

Bannister [9] provides an overview of the major problems with benchmarking in his paper 'the curse of the benchmark'. He criticizes a number of elements. One of them is the scoring method, as often benchmarks are reduced to a score on a single item. There are usually no fixed or agreed rules for this with result in arbitrary scores. Often proxies are measured, interpretation is ambiguous and there is no framework guiding the interpretation by decision-makers [6, 9]. Also the change of metrics over time and the comparisons of services that might actually not be the same due to difference in legislations and other factors are criticized. Comparison over time requires that metrics are time invariant, which is often not the case. The interpretation of measurements and benchmarks is difficult due to the abstraction and the actual position might tell little about the real performance. Finally, the scope and complexity is criticized by Bannister [9] as many important elements might not become visible. The complexity of the measurement models and the accompanying problems of operationalizing the measures require abstraction that might not prove to be correct.

Much of the critics can be reduced to the measurement methodologies taken in the measurement and benchmarking approaches. Measurement methodologies are guided by cost constraints [9]. As there is no data available that can be directly used, the data should often be collected using limited funds. The limited resources might result in stopping the investigation too early and might results in outcomes that might not be true or only cover the situation partly. There are numerous examples demonstrating this problem. The bottom line is that the available resources constrain the possibilities of benchmarking and influence the validity of the results.

Mosse and Whitley [10] and Janssen [17] suggest that the benchmarking of websites have cultivated a view of citizens as customers and warns against uncritically copying benchmark criteria. This the criticism implied in the title of Janssen et al.'s [17] article: 'If you measure it they will score'. Rightly or wrongly, the benchmarking has distracted the focus of governmental agencies away from a closer examination of the underlying business logics, which is often used interchangeably with the term, business model [11].

3 Research Approach

The goal of this research is to develop an instrument that helps government to assess their back-end and benchmark their situation with other organizations. Bannister [9] argued that a benchmark is a trade-off between cost, scale and quality of information. Due to the limited resources, the need to gain in-depth insight and the aim of helping governments directly, we focus on the use of participative self-assessment approach. The time needed is limited to the session time during which a survey is used to assess the status and the results are discussed to create a benchmark. This instrument was developed in close cooperation with stakeholders and the design was largely determined by their aims and requirements. The aims were to develop a measuring instrument facilitating the insight in the own back-end and provide understanding and improvement directions by benchmarking with others. The requirements on the instrument included simplicity, easy communication and give attention to a broad range of aspects.

The measurement and benchmarking instrument consists of a survey used for self-assessment *and* a group session in which the participants conduct the self-assessment and discuss the results. This instrument was used and tested in a session in which the participants assessed their own situations, discussed their self-assessment with their colleagues in other organizations and identified improvement directions for their own organizations. The session was facilitated by the author and organized by a government representative. The session was held in November 2009 and the participants came from various governmental organizations. Participants included process managers, decision-makers, public managers and administrative staff involved in back-end processes. Other stakeholder groups like citizens, politicians, associations and action groups were not included. In total 25 participants representing 15 back-ends were involved in the group session. During the session the main steps followed were:

1. *Introduction and background*

2. *Measuring the back-end.* All participants were asked to score the back-ends based on the questionnaire representing the constructs of the measurement models. If more than one person represented a back-end, they were asked to fill in the questionnaire independently, then to compare the results, discuss the deviations and then create consensus about the position.

3. *Benchmarking.* Each back-end was positioned on a projection of the matrix as shown in Figure 1. This matrix provides the relative position of the back-end in comparison to the others.

4. *Motivating the position.* Each participant was asked to explain the positioning. This step is aimed at creating a mutual understanding of the reasons for low and high scores. Furthermore, this step can be viewed as a way to validate the scores.

5. *Discussion the results.* All scores were discussed and all participants were requested to explain the scoring on the matrix. Participants having high scores were challenged to briefly share their experiences with others.

6. *Identifying improvements.* Participants were asked to identify improvement directions for their back-end based on the self-assessment. The other participants were asked to provide contact persons of persons from their organizations who would be able to show how this was tackled in their organizations. In this way 'best practices' could be shared.

7. *Closing*

The measurement and benchmarking model and the session findings are discussed.

4 Measurement Model

Our instrument is aimed at measuring the back-end and enabling communication among stakeholders facing the challenge of improving the back-end. These stakeholders are likely to have different competences and knowledge bases, therefore our aim was to visualize the outcomes of the benchmark. We opted for the use of two main criteria consisting of multiple dimensions, as the use of multiple criteria are favored over the use of a single criterion [e.g. 9] and at the same time the results should be easy to visualize and communicate. Instead of trying to compute a final score on a single scale we opted for visualizing based on two variables.

The back-end is in essence a socio-technical system in which administrative processes are supported by information and in which data is stored in software applications. Socio-technical systems are "systems that involve both complex physical-technical systems and networks of interdependent actors" [21 p. 981]. The back-end is an organization consisting of human activities, interactions and communications supported by a digital government infrastructure. The latter provide generic functionalities that are used by large numbers of users [22]. Whereas the organization element refers to the responsibilities, governance mechanisms and administrative processes, the infrastructure elements refers to the business processes supported by applications and a communication network. We follow a socio-technical view on the back-end and use as the two main variables 1) organization and 2) infrastructure.

In general, the front-end includes humans, business processes and facilities that are used to interact directly with citizens and/or businesses, whilst the back-end comprises all that do not directly involve customer interactions. To measure the back-end we investigate the relationships between the back-end departments as well as the relationships between the front-end and back-end.

The supporting technical *infrastructure* needs to be changed to realize and support the e-government ambitions. Infrastructures are often developed over time and consist of applications for processing information, databases for storing information, connections among these components and the network transporting information. This incremental and gradual development underlines the path-dependent nature of infrastructure developments. Decisions in the past influence the current infrastructure. These decisions are not necessarily taken by having e-government purposes into account. In consultation with the participants, the level of infrastructure is measured using the following factors.

- Availability of shared infrastructure
- Openness and interoperability of applications
- Level of systems integration
- Standardization of data and messages
- Generic integration architecture
- Automatic routing of data
- Tracking and tracing and monitoring systems
- Citizens relationship management (CRM) system
- Integral management information

The *organization* part refers to the whole organization of the back-end. This concerns the humans working in the administrative processes, the organization of these processes in service centers, the division of responsibilities, the control of the workload and lead time and governance mechanisms to discuss the status of requests, problems in processing and joint decision-making. Governance mechanisms determine how communication, responsibilities and decision-making structures are formalized [23]. The main variables used are related to the following elements.

- Organizational structure
- Departments are aware of each other processes
- Cross-departmental workflow management
- Governance mechanisms (decision-making structures, responsibilities and communication)
- Readiness
- Knowledge, education and training

The use of the two main dimensions resulted in the creation of four quadrants and each quadrant was given a name. The naming and explanation of the quadrants should help the session participants to give meaning to the position which should improve the interpretation of the right positioning. The following four quadrants were used.

1. *ad hoc*: There is hardly any facilitating infrastructure or coordination of processes.
2. *coordinated*: There is hardly any facilitating infrastructure, but the processes and activities in the front-end and back-end are coordinated. The employees know each other and how to contact each other, but exchange is primarily paper or telephone-based
3. *shared infrastructure*: An infrastructure enabling the integration between the back-end and front-end is available. Information can be exchanged. Nevertheless the processes in the front-end and back-end are not aligned and there is hardly any insight in the status of processes and dependencies.
4. *Orchestrated*: There is both a facilitating infrastructure as well as processes in the front and back-end are aligned. Like in an orchestra both elements function in concert and are harmonious.

The variables of the two dimensions were translated into a self-assessment instrument. The self-assessment instrument was used as part of a group session. The measurement and benchmarking methodology is made up by combining the two instruments.

4 Measurement and Benchmarking Results

The organization and infrastructure dimensions are used to measure and position the case studies. The participants were asked to answer the questions and the positioning consists of the counting of the scores on the constructs mentioned above on the two dimensions. No weighting or other means was used to give more priority to certain factors over other factors. The resulting positions should not be viewed as a hard benchmark, instead it should be viewed as an indication. In total 15 back-ends are positioned as shown in Figure 1. Several back-ends were represented by more than one person. Each of these persons scored their own back-end independently. This sometimes resulted in small deviations in outcomes. These persons were asked to compare their scores and to seek consensus concerning the outcomes. This step was completed within minutes as there were no large deviations. Next the various outcomes were discussed to explain the ranking. This was used as an instrument to validate whether the position was right. There was hardly any surprise concerning the position of their back-end. Most persons were aware of the functioning of their back-end and status in comparison with others. Nevertheless this was viewed as an important step as one person mentioned "*we already knew this, still it is confronting to end-up in the lowest quadrant*". The hope of many persons representing a relatively bad-performing back-end was to gain understanding about how to move forward and their hope was that the benchmark results will help them to get funding to move up.

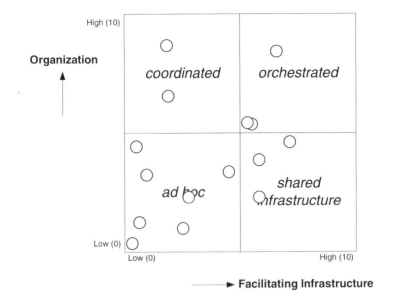

Fig. 1. Measurement and benchmarking outcomes

The results of the benchmark showed that 7 out of 15 (47%) are in the ad hoc quadrant, 3 (20%) are in the orchestrated quadrant, only 2 (13%) are in the coordinated quadrant and 3 (20%) fall in the shared infrastructure quadrant. These outcomes did not really come as a surprise to most participants. One participant indicated '*The front-end has gained a lot of attention and has been leading*'. The developments in the back-end are lagging behind and improvements might be more difficult to realize and might take much longer.

Discussing the Session Results

The results provide no clear indication for whether the infrastructure or organization should be developed first. The participants agreed on the normative starting point that having both a good organization and a good infrastructure is necessary. The plot in Figure 1 provides some indication that both are correlated. The investigation of which type of change strategy was preferred (organization or infrastructure first) resulted in mixed feelings. Although there was no consensus, most participants agreed that the organization development should go hand in by hand with the infrastructure development. Both are necessary to improve the back-end and one cannot do without the other.

The discussion of the results showed that low scores on the *organization* dimension is characterized by many complaints on front-end by back-end. The cause of these complaints is that the back-end was often supplied with low quality of information, and many calls and/or emails from the back-end to the citizen/business are necessary to ensure that the right information is collected. Although we have no direct prove, the impression is that low levels of organization is characterized by duplication of activities, as the back-end and front-end are not aware of each other activities. The problems result in the introduction of duplicate activities.

Organizations having high scores on the organization dimensions had often accomplished a change in their organization structure. The structure is changed from a functional to a customer-oriented organization structure and often service centers are introduced. Furthermore, high scores on the organization dimension were often created by an understanding of processes crossing the various departments which are supported by regular meetings to discuss work-in-progress and problems.

When looking at the *infrastructure* dimensions almost all organization have a basic infrastructure connecting the systems with each other and only a limited number of organizations have integrated their systems. The organizations having high scores on the infrastructure dimension often utilize some kind of broker structure (mid-office) facilitating the data exchange among systems.

None of the investigated back-ends had a single system providing an overview of interactions and history of the citizens/businesses. The lack of a Citizens Relationship Management (CRM) system was viewed as a major weakness for creating integrated service delivery. The departments are not aware of each other interactions with citizens/businesses.

Discussing the Measurement and Benchmarking Approach

The self-assessment instrument and participative session proved to be a useful instrument for measuring and benchmarking the back-end. Most session participants were positive concerning the session and the session results. As one persons stated *"this provides us insight and now I know who to contact to learn from"*. From the other hand, the filling-in of the self-assessment and positioning in the matrix was viewed as difficult. One of the participants commented that the filling in of the self-assessment instrument to position it on the matrix had little value. He argued that the position could be done without using a self-assessment instrument and the subsequent discussion of the results brings the real added value. He suggested creating an easier measurement instrument and using the variables to score the dimensions only as a checklist to understand the score. On the other hand, several participants indicated that the benchmark created by positioning the cases in the matrix should be based on some measurable variables. One of the main problems with the variables used for the self-assessment is the use of objective criteria. The inclusion of normative elements is an essential part of the benchmark in order to give direction and determine the relative position. Normative elements are probably always subject to discussions as it is not likely that all persons agree on all elements. Furthermore the normative base might change over time due to increased understanding. Finally, a good back-end can be organized and realized in different ways.

All participants agreed that participation is an essential ingredient of the measurement and benchmarking exercise. Without a good understanding the benchmarks can easily be misinterpreted and misused. The self-measurement and self-assessment is much dependent on the input and involvement of stakeholders. Non-involved stakeholders might give different meaning to the scores. As such a participative session might be viewed as a sense-making process. This part was favored by the participants as they indicated that the goal of the process is not the ending up of a certain position in the ranking. Instead the goals is to support the improvement of the back-end and the mutual learning to understand what needs and can be done to improve it. Especially the exchange of practices and experiences was found to be valuable and the measurement and benchmarking exercise is a useful means to accomplish this.

The stakeholders did like the visualization of the scores in the quadrants as this provides an indication of the position at first glance. As this was a participant session they were less concerned about the exact position, which they are when they were positioned on the public benchmarks. As one participants phrased *"this benchmark makes it transparent for us, and this might not be the case for the outside world... This cultivates learning instead of copying each other features"*. This avoids the adverse affects of benchmarking that all organizations want to end up in the top 10 or top 3 and start copying each other features. On the other hand this might give no direct external incentives to improve and might not result in attention to attract resources for performing better.

5   Conclusions and Further Research Directions

Measuring the back-end of e-government is a difficult endeavor. First, many technical and organizational elements should be taken into account. The more aspects the more resources are needed and the more difficult comparison is. Second, measurement is further complicated by the heterogeneity of possible back-ends' which are not as homogenous as the front-end. This heterogeneity complicates the calculation of a score to benchmark the relative position. A good back-end can be accomplished in a variety of ways. Third, the performance of back-ends consists of both technology and organizational aspects which need to be both captured. The interplay between these determines the overall performance. These factors complicate the creation of a straightforward benchmark.

The requirements on the benchmarking instrument included simplicity, consume limited resources, measure in-depth, enable easy communication and give attention to a broad range of aspects. Given these requirements a participative self-assessment instrument was developed and employed in a group session. A survey was developed as a self-assessment instrument which was filled in by organizational representatives during the group session. The survey provided the detailed elements and helped to position the own back-end based on two-dimensions. The resulting two-by-two matrix proved to enable easy communication. The stakeholders did like the visualization of the scores in the quadrants as this provides an indication of the position at first glance.

The utilization of the group session proved to be an essential ingredient of the measurement and benchmarking exercise, as this provides the opportunity to gain in-depth insight with limited resources. Furthermore, the group session provided the opportunity to discuss the relative position in detail, explain the position on the benchmark and foster mutual learning and sharing experiences and practices. The use of a group session ensures an emphasis on learning, avoid adverse aspects of benchmarking and dispute over the outcomes.

The self-assessment was viewed a fruitful instrument to assess the status, to compare the own score with the scores of those of the own organizations, and to compare the own position with that of other organizations. This approach is focused on consensus about the position and making the results discussable. This results in the exchange of practices and experiences which facilitates future development of the back-end. Another advantage of utilizing a participative instrument is that it avoids the focus on a single measure, especially discussions broadens the views. Furthermore, there was less discussion about the actual scores, as the score were based on self-assessment. A shared understanding of the scores was created by discussing the arguments and position.

The results show that measuring the back-end should capture both organizational and technical elements. For gaining in-depth insight in the back-end many research challenges remain open. We opted for a participative session utilizing a self-assessment instrument based on the measurement of limited elements. In further research this instrument can be transformed to an instrument that can measure and benchmark without needing a participative session. The number of elements that were measured in this research can easily be extended. We recommend further research in the use of participative sessions as they are less resource intensive. An option can be to develop an online assessment instrument that can be filled in by organizational members and used as an input for discussing the back-end performance and possible improvements. A drawback might be the possible bias and interpretations.

References

1. West, D.M.: E-Government and the Transformation of Service Delivery and Citizen Attitudes. Public Administration Review 64, 15–27 (2004)
2. UNPAN: Benchmarking e-Government - A Global Perspective. United Nations, New York (2002)
3. UNPAN: UN e-government survey 2008: From e-government to connected governance. United Nations, New York (2008)
4. Cap Gemini, E.Y.: Summary Report: Web-based Survey on Electronic Public Services. Report of the First Measurement. Directorate General for the Information Society (2001)
5. Accenture: Governments Closing Gap Between Political Rhetoric and eGovernment Reality (2001)
6. Peters, R., Janssen, M., Engers, T.M.v.: Measuring E-government Impact: Existing practices and shortcomings. In: Janssen, M., Sol, H.G., Wagenaar, R.W. (eds.) 6th International Conference on Electronic Commerce, Delft, the Netherlands. ACM International conference proceedings series, vol. 60 (2004)
7. Bekkers, V.: Flexible Information Infrastructures in Dutch e-governmnet collaboration arrangements: Experiences and policy implications. Government Information Quarterly 26, 60–68 (2009)
8. Kunstelj, M., Vintar, M.: Evaluating the Progress of e-Government. Information Polity 9, 131–148 (2004)
9. Bannister, F.: The curse of the benchmark: an assessment of the validity and value of e-government comparisons. International Review of Administrative Sciences 73, 171–188 (2007)
10. Mosse, B., Whitley, E.A.: Critically classifying: UK e-government website benchmarking and the recasting of the citizen as customers. Information Systems Journal 19, 149–173 (2009)

11. Janssen, M., Kuk, G., Wagenaar, R.W.: A Survey of Web-based Business Models for e-Government in the Netherlands. Government Information Quarterly 25, 202–220 (2008)
12. Andersen, K.V., Henriksen, H.Z.: E-government maturity models: Extension of the Layne and Lee model. Government Information Quarterly 23, 236–248 (2006)
13. Layne, K., Lee, J.: Developing fully functional E-government: A four stage model. Government Information Quarterly 18, 122–136 (2001)
14. Moon, M.J.: The Evolution of E-Government Among Municipalities; Rhetoric or reality? Public Administration Review 62, 424–433 (2002)
15. Klievink, B., Janssen, M.: Realizing Joined-up Government. Dynamic Capabilities and Stage Models for Transformation. Government Information Quarterly 26, 275–284 (2009)
16. Ojo, A., Janowski, T., Estevez, E.: Determining Progress Towards e-Government: What are the Core Indicators? In: Remenyi, D. (ed.) 5th European Conference on e-Government, Antwerpen, pp. 313–322 (2005)
17. Janssen, D., Rotthier, S., Snijkers, K.: If You Measure It, They Will Score: An Assessment of International eGovernment Benchmarking. Information Polity 9e, 121–130 (2004)
18. Shergold, K., Reed, D.M.: Striving for excellence: how self-assessment using the Business Excellence Model can result in improvements in all areas of business activities. The TQM Magazine 8, 48–52 (1996)
19. Jacobs, B., Suckling, S.: Assessing customer focus using the EFQM Excellence Model: a local government case. The TQM Magazine 19, 368–378 (2007)
20. Bertot, J.C., Jaeger, P.T.: User-centered e-government: Challenges and benefits for government Web sites. Government Information Quarterly 23, 163–168 (2006)
21. Bruijn, H.d., Herder, P.M.: Systems and Actor Perspectives on Sociotechnical Systems. IEEE Transactions on Systems, Man and Cybernetics - Part A 39, 981–992 (2009)
22. Janssen, M., Chun, S.A., Gil-Garcia, R.: Building the Next Generation of Digital Government Infrastructures. Government Information Quarterly 26, 233–237 (2009)
23. Weill, P., Ross, J.: A matrixed approach to designing IT governance. MIT Sloan Management Review 46, 26–34 (2005)

Assessing Emerging ICT-Enabled Governance Models in European Cities: Results from a Mapping Survey

Gianluca Misuraca[1,2], Enrico Ferro[3], and Brunella Caroleo[4]

[1] European Commission Joint Research Centre,
Institute for Prospective Technological Studies (IPTS), Information Society Unit, Seville, Spain
{gianluca.misuraca}@ec.europa.eu
[2] Ecole Polytechnique Fédérale de Lausanne (EPFL),
College of Management of Technology, Lausanne, Switzerland
{gianluca.misuraca}@epfl.ch
[3] Istituto Superiore Mario Boella, Technology to Business Intelligence Unit,
Via Boggio 61, 10138 Torino, Italy
{enrico.ferro}@ismb.it
[4] Politecnico di Torino, Department of Production Systems and Business Economics,
Corso Duca degli Abruzzi 24, 10129 Torino, Italy
{brunella.caroleo}@polito.it

Abstract. The paper presents the preliminary results of an exploratory survey conducted by the Information Society Unit of the Institute for Prospective Technological Studies (IPTS) of the European Commission. The main goal of the research is to deepen the understanding of the interplay between ICTs and governance processes at city level in the EU by looking at what new ICT-enabled governance models are emerging in European cities and what are their key socio-economic implications. In this preliminary phase efforts have been directed towards addressing the following research question: *what key city governance policy areas ICTs impact most and what governance changes are driven by ICTs?* This questions have been investigated through a questionnaire based online survey. The evidence collected provided a comprehensive mapping of the use of ICTs in European cities as well as the views of policy makers, city government officials, practitioners and researchers, on the way ICTs are influencing governance processes. The evidence collected shows that new ICT-enabled governance models are emerging, and it allowed to identify the main dimensions of change, drivers, barriers, enablers and characteristics, as well as opportunities, risks and challenges associated with them.

Keywords: ICTs, Governance, Policy Research, Cities, Benchlearning.

Disclaimer: The views expressed in this paper are purely those of the authors and may not in any circumstances be regarded as stating an official position of the European Commission.

M.A. Wimmer et al. (Eds.): EGOV 2010, LNCS 6228, pp. 168–179, 2010.
© IFIP International Federation for Information Processing 2010

1 Introduction

In spatial, economic and cultural terms, the Information Society is dominated by cities and metropolitan regions [1]. Around 70% of all Europeans live in cities. They are throughout recognized as the dominant space of Information and Communication Technologies (ICTs) industries and uses, but they are also the area where most of the poor, the disadvantaged and excluded live. They are the government layer closest to neighborhood and citizen initiatives and local non-government organizations. Furthermore, city governments are in an excellent position to engage in necessary strategic partnerships across the public, private and third sector. Cities can therefore play a key role in the field of ICT-enabled governance, but especially when their capacities are used in an integrated way that allows the highest impact on social cohesion and local economies [2]. In addition to being close to citizens and business, most public services are offered on the city government level; in some EU member states this share amounts to 70% of all public services.

As a matter of fact, based on the analysis of the state of the art of research and practice in this field, it can be observed that while experiments and pilot projects are taking place at different governance level, it is at the city level that the appropriate use and integration of ICTs in the governance mechanisms can support social and institutional innovation, particularly in empowering officials and community representatives; ensuring social inclusion; providing timely, efficient, transparent and accountable services; improving the management of administrative operations; facilitating planning and policy making processes; monitoring and recording political decisions and assessing socio-economic impacts in the municipalities and their locale.

However, while research in the overlapping areas of e-Government, e-Governance, e-Participation and e-Inclusion at city level has been examining mainly the supply side and the sophistication of e-Services offered; reliable data on measuring the effects of ICT-enabled applications on governance processes and the impacts on specific policy areas are lacking, and where existing not yet harmonized, incomplete or difficult to use for comparison in other contexts or at EU level.

For this reason, following a preliminary analysis and consultations with stakeholders, IPTS designed and launched jointly with EUROCITIES a 'mapping survey'[1] in order to identify key city governance policy areas most impacted by ICTs and select significant case studies to be analysed in depth in the following phases of an exploratory research on emerging ICT-enabled governance models in EU cities. .

In this first phase of the research efforts have been directed towards addressing the following research question: *what key city governance policy areas ICTs impact most and what governance changes are driven by ICTs?*

The paper is structured as follows: first of all it outlines the conceptual framework underpinning the research and the methodological approach followed for the survey. The results of the survey and some preliminary conclusions and indications on the future steps of the research are then presented.

---

[1] The survey has been conducted during the period 15 November – 15 December, further extended until 31 December 2009 due to the high interest raised.

2 Conceptual Framework

The notion of urban governance, which is often considered as an alternative to traditional approaches to government (centralised, hierarchical, top-down, bureaucratic) promotes an approach based on public action networks and mechanisms aimed at cooperation, organisation and even integration in the systems and mechanisms of a wide diversity of public and private stakeholders (a polycentric, network-based, horizontal, cross-disciplinary, process-based, bottom-up approach) [3]. There are a number of different theories generally put forward to explain the emergence of the concept of urban governance, according to the various problems and changes in society which the concept attempts to address [4].

Research in this area, however, does not usually consider the impacts of major economic trends and their consequences in terms of the spatial distribution of production factors (capital and workforce) at urban level [5]. Structural analysis of the linkages between the high-value added assets of the digital economy is not considered from most research on urban governance and local development [6].

Considering governance as a multidimensional construct, the focus of our research is instead on the way the different stakeholders interact when introducing ICT-enabled services and innovations in specific policy areas and the way these interactions affect institutions and communities, and the related governance processes. The governance changes under scrutiny are both technologically and socially driven and manifest themselves in new governance models and public management practices, revised institutional processes and organisational structures. In particular, the research is based upon the belief that the socio-economic perspectives, which stand at the interface between analyses of individual behaviour and wider societal structures, are well placed to elucidate the impacts of ICTs on governance.

In the theoretical framework underpinning the research we therefore combine neo-institutionalist perspectives [7] with constructivist approaches to policy and socio-political institutions such as the ones developed by Schmidt [8] and Berger and Luckmann [9]. This is especially useful in investigating how social phenomena develop in the particular social contexts characterized by ICTs [10].

The attention of our analysis is in fact on the way the different stakeholders interact when introducing ICTs in governance systems, the way these interactions affect institutions and communities, and the related decision-making process. Two main issues are specifically investigated: 1) the changes produced by ICTs on the governance processes[2], (e.g. regulatory and legal frameworks, organisational and administrative procedures, roles of various stakeholders involved, etc.) and consequently the effects on decision-making, public management and service delivery; and 2) the socio-economic implications at policy level.

---

[2] We refer here to changes due to ICTs both at inter-administration level and with regard to the relationship between the government and the different stakeholders involved in the specific service, either directly provided by the city government or mediated by other actors as intermediaries.

In brief, the research has a twofold objective. On the one hand, it intends to contribute to inform policy-makers about the implications of change produced by new and emerging ICT-enabled governance models in EU cities and demonstrate evidence of impacts on the specific policy areas under investigation. On the other hand, the research aims also at contributing to consolidate scientific evidence of impacts of ICT-enabled applications on city governance models in the EU.

Therefore, for this research, **governance** is defined as *the process of decision-making and the process by which decisions are implemented and* **ICT-enabled governance**[3] *as 'the use of ICTs to comprehensively: (1) simplify and improve the internal administrative operations of government and their relations with other bodies involved in public management and service delivery; (2) facilitate public service interaction between government, citizens and other stakeholders (legislative bodies, private sector, civil society organizations, self-organised communities), thus enabling better citizen participation and overall monitoring and evaluation of decision-making processes and their implementation; and (3) ensure inclusiveness and equal opportunity for all'* [11]. This concept is to be intended as an 'ideal model' to indicate the comprehensive framework enfolding a broad range of informal and formal descriptions to represent core aspects of the governance process, including policy and decision -making, strategic and operational processes, legal and organisational structures, working practices, inter-actor relationships, and the public service delivery, aiming at creating -in a proactive manner- public value.

3 Methodological Approach

The methodological approach used for the first phase of the research is based on grounded-theory / action research and involved an online survey addressed to city government in Europe in order to identify perceptions on the impact of ICTs on governance. The data collected through the survey have been analyzed using statistical techniques such as clustering and complemented with consultations with stakeholders and a focus group meeting with representatives of city governments and researchers to validate the findings and define the next activities of the research.

The survey gathered 62 answers from cities in 27 European countries, covering 25 EU27 member States plus Croatia and Switzerland. It is therefore highly representative of different governance models and ICT-enabled services currently provided by European cities as the sample includes cities covering about 93% of EU27. In particular, out of the 62 cities respondents to the survey, 44 cities (71%) are 'large cities' (with more than 200.000 citizens). Other respondents to the survey are cities or counties with a smaller or larger population.

Concerning the respondents profile, the distribution looks as follows: 41% (25) are City Government officials (e.g. CIO/Head of IT Departments, etc.); 26% (16) are researchers; 19% (12) are policy or technical advisors, while only 3% (2) are City Manager/Mayor or their representatives (Figure 1).

---

[3] Source: [11], based on: OECD, 2001 and 2006; UNDP, 1997, 2003, 2009; UNDESA, 2007.

4 Survey's Results

Results from the first part of the survey, clearly indicate that respondents consider ICTs are producing changes on governance processes in many respects. About 65% of the respondents have indicated ICTs are producing a significant change on governance processes and 11% even pointed out ICTs are generating very significant change (see Figure 1). These results are of particular significance as there seems to be a strong opinion on the impacting role of ICTs in generating effective change in city governance processes.

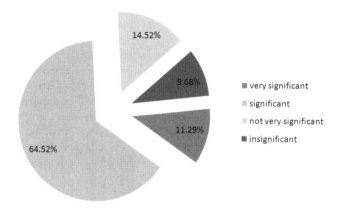

Fig. 1. City Governance changes due to application of ICTs

When analysing more specifically which are the ***policy areas most impacted by ICTs***, a fragmented picture emerges. Rather than on specific policy areas, ICTs seem to impact city governance across the board. Moreover, to better understand in which policy areas these impacts were produced, the order of preference given by respondents for each policy area was analysed. Two messages emerge from figure 2.: information and communication, economic development, energy and environment and healthcare seem to be the most impacted policy areas (if looking at the aggregate of 1st and 2nd choice). At the same time a more generalized and cross-sectional impact seems to be perceived across all policy areas.

The case of Social Inclusion is of particular interest as it does not present any 'first choice' but it is indicated by about 60% of the respondents as a second choice. The policy area of Employment instead has not been indicated by any of the respondents as 'first choice', and it actually presents a limited relative score also as second choice (about 25%), thus making it the domain considered as the less affected by ICTs.

However, it must be considered that responses on some of the policy areas are influenced by the fact that governance systems are different in different countries, and that city government administrative competences and responsibilities are diverse in various governance systems. For example, Employment policies in many cases are not direct responsibility of the city level government.

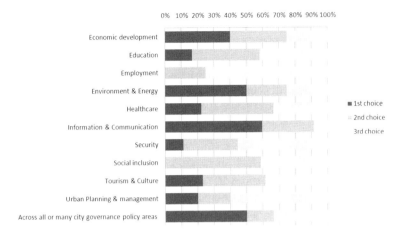

Fig. 2. Policy areas most impacted by ICTs disaggregated according to order of choice

Based on the responses to the survey and on the analysis of the examples provided, it was also possible to make a preliminary categorization of what has changed in the governance process according to respondents (see Figure 3).

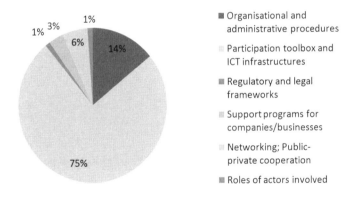

Fig. 3. Effects of ICT-driven changes on governance processes

A large majority of respondents (75%) associated initiatives driven by ICTs with changes in the ICT infrastructure and what can be defined as the participation toolbox, 14% of the respondents indicated ICTs is generating changes in terms of organizational and administrative procedures and a 6% on Networking and Public and Private Cooperation. A limited number of respondents (3%) indicated that ICTs are producing changes in the way of organizing and delivering support programs for companies and to start-up new businesses and only 1% considers that ICTs is changing regulatory and legal framework and the roles of actors involved in the governance process.

Furthermore, focusing on the ***governance function which is impacted most by ICTs***, the survey provides evidence that ICTs are considered to be more impacting at the service delivery level (46% of response rates). However, 34% of response rates indicates that ICTs are also producing significant effects on the decision making process. Impacts on legal and regulatory frameworks directly linked to ICTs are instead more limited, but still counting for 20% of the response rate.

Crossing data between governance functions most affected by ICTs and policy areas, confirms the general sentiment that ICTs impact on governance functions is distributed equally in most policy areas. Some exceptions can be found in the area of Employment, where changes are clearly mainly of legal and regulatory nature.

Interesting are the cases of Urban Planning and Information and Communication which present a quite high impact of ICTs on decision-making process (40%), while the domains of Social Inclusion and Tourism and Culture, in addition to Employment, do not present changes in this function, ICTs impacting only on service delivery and regulatory frameworks. On the contrary, the case of Environment and Energy shows no changes affected by ICTs on legal and regulatory frameworks.

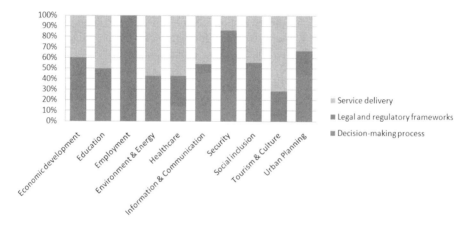

Fig. 4. Governance functions most impacted by ICTs per policy area

Finally, an analysis of the impacts of ICTs in different geographic areas in Europe shows a quite interesting situation (see Figure 5). It seems in fact that while in North Europe ICTs are considered to have a strong impact (with 22% very significant, 73% significant and only 5% not very significant), the situation is much more scattered in other regions. In central Europe, for example, there is almost a balance between the significant impact of ICTs (63%) and the not very significant impact (47%). In the Mediterranean and Eastern Europe areas instead, it seems that ICTs have a less significant impact on changes in the governance process.

This analysis somehow confirms general literature on administrative and cultural traditions of governance models in Europe, where we can see that many factors affecting public administration performance and bureaucratic traditions are based on different governance models.

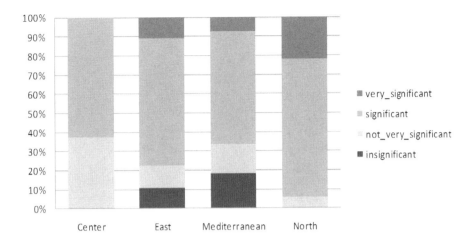

Fig. 5. Impact of ICTs in Europe per geographic areas

The implication of these considerations for the current research is precisely that when defining an ICT-enabled governance model at the level of city government, the administrative traditions and cultural context on which ICTs are applied should also be considered. This is of particular importance when then attempting to assess the changes driven by ICTs through impact assessment. Just to give an example, indicators of cost savings in term of human resources or of improved effectiveness through the redeployment of resources freed-up from the success of an ICT-enabled application (i.e. resources moved to the front-end thanks to efficiency gains in the back-off) must take into account that in certain countries rules and regulations, labour contracts negotiations with public employment trade unions and the likes, can hinder and/or delay the exploitation of such gains. In such instances, a strictly defined indicator of human resources cost saving would find difficulties to be accepted by all European administrations. In the same way, to measure the inter-operability and degree of shared/joined-up services, it is necessary to take into account that the likelihood of reaching such objectives depends also on the governance structure of the state (not only at the city level then) and it is reasonable to assume them to be more difficult to achieve in decentralised and federalist states.

In this connection, the cluster analysis of ICTs impact on governance and policy areas in European cities allowed us to identify 5 clusters (see Figure 6) of which 4 have been considered relevant for the analysis mentioned above (see Table 1).

The cluster analysis was also instrumental to identify possible case studies representatives of different governance models in Europe to be further analysed in depth. It is clear that the clustering, while does not provide us with definitive conclusions about the kind of ICT-enabled governance models in EU cities, will facilitate the next steps of the research in classifying possible impacts of ICTs on city governance models.

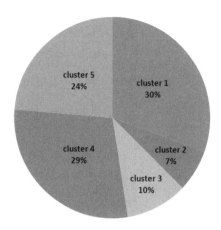

Fig. 6. Clusters of ICTs impact on governance and policy areas in EU cities

Table 1. Description of Clusters of ICTs impact on governance and policy areas in EU cities[4]

1	2	4	5
Overall very significant impact of ICTs on governance and especially on decision-making processes and characterized by changes in ICT infrastructure and participation toolbox, mainly in the policy area of information and communication (e.g. public relations, citizens' participation and engagement)	Overall significant impact of ICTs on governance and especially on service delivery mechanisms and characterized by changes in the policy area of economic development (e.g. industry, business and SMEs, taxation, etc.)	Overall significant impact of ICTs on governance and especially on service delivery mechanisms and characterized by changes in the policy area of information and communication (e.g. public relations, citizens' participation and engagement)	Overall not very significant impact of ICTs on governance, but when impact is present this is especially on service delivery mechanisms and characterized by changes in the policy areas of Urban Planning and Management and Tourism and Culture and manifested by changes in ICT infrastructure and participation toolbox

In addition to the impacts of ICTs on city governance policy areas, the survey was also looking at exploring whether ***new forms of ICT-enabled governance models*** are emerging at city level in Europe. Findings from the survey indicate that the majority of cities (60%) consider new ICT-enabled governance models are emerging, either clearly (15%) or to some extent (45%). However, an important number of respondents (36%) said that 'they don't know', either because it is too early to judge (33%), or in some cases because it is impossible to tell (3%). Only 3% of respondents indicate that no new governance models are emerging due to ICTs. Responses to this part of the survey indicate a very promising perception of the emergence of new ICT-enabled governance models, thus opening up the road for further analysis in this direction.

---

[4] For the cities grouped under Cluster 3, it was not possible to find common characteristics.

Moreover, the survey also collected qualitative examples and statements of city views on emerging ICT-enabled governance models, with specific regard to the main barriers to change and the main foreseeable risks, the main enablers of change and the key characteristics of the new emerging ICT-enabled governance models.

In particular, based on the analysis of the examples provided by cities, it has been possible identify some of the main drivers of change on governance driven by ICTs. These changes are reported here not in order of importance but as a list of key issues, as pointed out by the respondents to the survey.

Drivers of changes for ICT-enabled governance models

1) Efficiency & Effectiveness of public service delivery

2) Quality of public service provision & enhancement of users' satisfaction

3) Trust on public agencies & Citizens' participation in the decision making processes

4) Performance Measurement & motivation of civil servants

5) Reengineering and standardisation of public administration processes;

6) Prioritisation/customisation of public services (focusing on high-impact services and strategic policy areas, and in particular focusing on inclusion)

7) Streamlining governance processes to cope with increased ICT-enabled demand

8) Addressing social and economic needs for increasing growth and quality of life

9) Data sharing based on interoperable platforms

10) Promoting creativity and innovation, building especially on the use of social networking tools and media by young people.

The main barriers to change and risks indicated by respondents are the following:

Barriers to changes and Risks

1) ICT Access for all / digital divide

2) Skills and capabilities (of both users and civil servants)

3) Different levels of competences between various levels of governance (municipal/local, regional, national…) and overlapping responsibilities

4) Resistance to change consolidated bureaucratic management practices

5) Lack of financial and human resources (especially due to high initial costs and need of continuous education and training)

6) Lack of culture and mechanisms for new forms of inter-administrative collaboration and customer-orientation

7) Not appropriate legal and regulatory frameworks

8) Lack of interest/motivation for both politicians and citizens in engaging in dialogue and participation, if not effective

9) Too ICT-driven governance models and lack of business understanding of ICTs in the public sector

10) Security, safety and privacy risks

On the other hand, respondents identified the following as main enablers and opportunities of ICT-enabled governance:

Enablers of changes and Opportunities
1) Reduction of administrative burdens
2) Establishment of effective PPPs
3) Citizens and civil society organisations' engagement and participation
4) Creation of strong and secure interoperability platforms
5) Integration of front and back-office administrative processes
6) Change of behaviour of civil servants
7) Leadership and clear vision
8) Time & economic savings
9) Transparency and accountability
10) General educational and socio-cultural context of reference at city level

Finally, in terms of main characteristics of the emerging ICT-enabled governance models, as pointed out by respondents, the following can be mentioned at this initial state of research:

Characteristics of ICT-enabled governance models
1) Information and data/services sharing based on interoperable, secure and open platforms
2) Better access to all citizens to policy-making processes through citizens' engagement and participation in order to ensure all views are taken into consideration
3) Standardisation of processes and decentralisation of services (including PPPs and outsourcing to civil society organisations and other service providers as mediators)
4) Performance measurement (efficiency and effectiveness) based on result-oriented/customer satisfaction mechanisms of quality control
5) Agile ICT-based and innovative/co-created/co-managed public services

5   Conclusions and Further Research

In conclusion, the analysis of survey results provided a quite comprehensive mapping of the use of ICTs in European cities as well as the views of policy makers, city government officials, practitioners and researchers, on the way ICTs are influencing governance processes. The analysis also provided very useful indication on what new ICT-enabled governance models are emerging, and some preliminary classifications of dimensions of change, main drivers, barriers, enablers and characteristics, identifying also opportunities, risks and challenges.

In terms of **ICT-driven changes**, although most respondents indicate that ICTs are producing significant (65%) or very significant changes (11%), 24% of respondents point out to a limited impact on governance changes due to ICTs. On the one side, in fact, this result brings us to broaden the scope of the analysis to shed lights beyond the technical issues -and difficulties- related to the introduction of ICTs into government systems, on the role of legal, organizational and cultural changes when discussing of

ICT-enabled governance models. On the other side, this further justifies the need of deeper research in this field, in order to better understand the implications ICTs are having on governance at city level, and the drivers of changes in relation to ICT-enabled services and governance innovations.

With specific regard to the **policy areas most impacted by ICTs**, the survey identifies the pivotal role of ICTs for renewing the **Information and Communication** policy activities, and with particular regard to **citizens' participation and engagement**.

However, although the sound sample already may allow to generalize results at EU level and to initiate deeper analysis through case studies, a further effort of analysis of the results of the survey will be conducted to consolidate the findings and substantiate the research dimensions under exploration. In addition to this, and based on the indications emerged from the survey, as well as conceptual work conducted during the next phases of the research a measurement framework will be elaborated by IPTS in collaboration with city government representatives, researchers and practitioners experts in ICT for governance at city level aiming at seeking to capture ICT-driven changes on governance processes in EU cities.

References

1. Graham, S. (ed.): The Cybercities Reader. Routledge, London (2004)
2. Misuraca, G., Ollé Sanz, E.: Exploring ICT-enabled governance models in European cities: a preliminary analysis towards developing a conceptual and measurement policy impact framework. In: Paper submitted to the 10th European Conference on e-Government (ECEG 2010), June 17-18, 2009, University of Limerick, Ireland (forthcoming 2010)
3. Jacquier, C.: Urban Governance: forging a path between complications and complexity. Paper presented at the Towards New Territorial Governance (2008)
4. Perroux, P.: Dictionnaire économique et social Paris: Haitier (1990)
5. EU: Cohesion Policy and Cities: the Urban Contribution to Growth and Jobs in the Regions (known as the Bristol Accord): European Commission (2006)
6. Jouyet, J.P., Levy, M.: L'économie de l'immatériel. La croissance de demain. Report by the Commission on the intangible economy to the French Industry Minister (2006)
7. Hay, C.: Constructivist Institutionalism. In: Rhodes, R.A.W., Binder, S., Rockman, B. (eds.) The Oxford Handbook of Political Institutions, pp. 56–74. Oxford Univ. Press, Oxford (2006)
8. Schmidt, V.A.: Discursive Institutionalism: The Explanatory Power of Ideas and Discourse. Annual Review of Political Science 11, 303–326 (2008)
9. Berger, P.L., Luckmann, T.: The Social Construction of Reality (1966)
10. Misuraca, G.: e-Government 2015: exploring m-government scenarios, between ICT-driven experiments and citizen-centric implications. Technology Analysis and Strategic Management 21(3), 18 (2009)
11. Misuraca, G.: Social Computing and Governance. In: Punie, Y., Lusoli, W., Centeno, C., Misuraca, G., Broster, D. (eds.) The impact of Social Computing on the EU Information Society and Economy, IPTS, JRC, European Commission (2009)

Designing and Evaluating Dashboards for Multi-agency Crisis Preparation: A Living Lab

Nitesh Bharosa[1], Marijn Janssen[1], Sebastiaan Meijer[1], and Fritjof Brave[2]

[1] Delft University of Technology, Jaffalaan 5, 2628 BX Delft, The Netherlands
{n.bharosa,m.f.w.h.a.janssen,s.meijer}@tudelft.nl
[2] Berenschot Groep B.V., Europalaan 40, 3526 KS Utrecht, The Netherlands
f.brave@berenschot.nl

Abstract. Public organizations show growing interest in the development of dashboards that aid relief agency managers in crisis preparation. Yet, there is a dearth of research on the development of such dashboards. This paper discusses the experiences gained from a pioneering Living Lab on the development and evaluation of dashboards for assessing crisis preparedness. In order to evaluate and further improve dashboards, a two-day user-centered gaming simulation was organized with forty relief agency managers. A survey distributed amongst the managers indicates that they were satisfied with the dashboards and intend to use these in practice. However, the managers suggested that the formulation and clustering of the performance indicators requires better alignment with the context of use. One of the main findings is that the high level of uncertainty regarding the final set of performance indicators and the corresponding norms demands flexibility in the dashboard architecture beyond the evaluation stage.

Keywords: Dashboards, Living Lab, crisis preparation, crises management, gaming, simulation, IS success.

1   Introduction

In e-government disparate public agencies have to coordinate their activities with each other horizontally and vertically [1]. Crises preparation and response are a subset of e-government, in which public organizations (i.e., police, fire department and ambulance services) need to coordinate their activities in real-time [2]. As the occurrence and evolution of a crisis cannot be predicted in advance, it is of vital importance to be prepared in order to enable rapid crisis response. This has resulted in an increasing interest in crisis preparedness of the main relief agencies, especially since some of the major crises in the past decade (e.g., 9/11, Katrina, London, Madrid) have exhibited poor crisis preparation. Due to the impact and associated media attention, policy makers cannot afford to say "we were unprepared" anymore to victims and their families in case of a crisis [3]. Hence, relief agency managers are expected to prepare for the eventuality of a crisis by understanding the vulnerabilities of an organization, analyzing the organizational capability to deal with a range of crisis scenarios, and by taking precautionary measures to mitigate the possible risks of being unable to cope with crisis events. In each of these crisis preparation processes,

M.A. Wimmer et al. (Eds.): EGOV 2010, LNCS 6228, pp. 180–191, 2010.

performance indicators (PIs) are considered of major importance [4]. Historically, relief agencies operate in a silo-ed manner and define and use their own set of PIs. They usually focus their PIs on internal processes, clustered in themes such as financial status, human resources, and service delivery.

In general, relief agency managers depend on governmental agencies for their financial resources. Since policy makers usually have a fixed budget for relief agencies, they need to know how to balance financial resources between agencies in order to maintain an overall level of preparedness. For policymakers, PIs are essential for planning crisis preparedness. Yet the current mono-agency sets of PIs do not show the aggregate level of preparedness of the relief services as a whole, which in turn is the criterion by which the public will judge governmental agencies.

Scholars in the domains of strategic management [e.g., 5, 6] have proposed the use of dashboards as instruments for both the clustering and visualization of PIs. A dashboard is "a visual display of the most important information needed to achieve one or more objectives, consolidated and arranged on a single screen so the information can be monitored at a glance" [7, p. 34]. Despite the advantages predicted for organizations when using dashboards [e.g., 8, 9-10], literature on the development of dashboards indicating the level of crisis preparedness on a multi-agency scale is scarce. Instead, most studies are concerned with the appropriateness or success of response activities. Accordingly, the objective of this paper is to present experiences extracted from the development and evaluation of dashboards in practice. The authors pursued this objective by employing a Living Lab approach, in which academics, relief agency managers, and policy makers join forces in order to achieve a common purpose. This paper contributes to existing literature on crisis preparation by presenting experiences extracted from dashboard development and evaluation. In addition, this paper elaborates on the types of dashboard required for crisis preparation in a multi-agency environment.

The next section presents theoretical backgrounds of the dashboard concept. Then, we discuss the Living Lab on dashboard development in The Netherlands, followed by a brief description of the resulting dashboards. Here, we explicitly focus on the design choices and tradeoffs made in this project. Section 4 discusses the setup and results of the dashboard evaluation process, followed by some derived guidelines for developing dashboards for multi-agency crisis preparation. The paper concludes with some conclusions, discussions, and opportunities for further research.

2 A Living Lab for Disaster Preparation

2.1 Background

At the start of 2008, the Dutch parliament finally passed a long debated law mandating the formation of twenty-five multi-agency safety organizations. According to this law, the multi-agency safety organizations that were to be formed would act as the main responsible entities when it comes to crisis preparation and response in the geographic region they covered. This meant that previously autonomous relief agencies, including the police, fire and ambulance services, were now required to collaborate in terms of crisis preparation and response. The law also mandates that the multi-agency safety organizations, needed to conduct crisis preparation activities based on standardized and comparable PIs. In order to comply with the law, five out of twenty-five multi-agency safety organizations went on and agreed to collaborate in the development and use of PIs. The collaboration project was titled 'Aristoteles' (after the Greek Philosopher) and started in August 2008. The main goal of the Aristoteles project was to bring together academia and practitioners in the development and evaluation of dashboards visualizing the state of crisis preparedness in the multi-agency safety organization. Since this project was the first of its kind in the Dutch context, a major part of this project required the collaboration of academia and practitioners. The authors were key members of the project group that decided to follow a Living Lab approach. The next subsection discusses and motivates the choice for this approach.

2.2   A Living Lab Approach to Developing Dashboards

Both researchers and practitioners show increasing interest in the Living Labs approach to innovation and research in complex design environments involving many stakeholders. Yet, this approach is still relatively new, therefore lacking standard and universally agreed upon definitions and instruments. Pallot [11] argues that a Living Lab is neither a traditional research lab nor a "testbed", but rather an "innovation platform" that engages all stakeholders such as end-users, researchers, industrialists, policy makers, and so on at the earlier stage of the innovation process. As such, Living Labs allow stakeholders to experiment with breakthrough concepts and assess the potential value for both the society (citizens) and users that will lead to breakthrough innovations. Lama and Origin [12] describe Living Labs as "a user-centric research methodology for sensing, prototyping, validating and refining complex solutions in multiple and evolving real life contexts." Følstad [13] explained that literature on Living Lab has served to identify two characteristics that discriminate Living Labs from other approaches: (1) Contextualized co-creation: Living Labs supporting context research and co-creation with users, and (2) Testbed association: Living Labs serving as a testbed extension, where testbed applications are accessed in contexts familiar to the users. Living Labs are mostly established through collaboration of private as well as public research partners and can be used with multiple iterations throughout multiple stages of the innovation [14].

The Aristoteles project team decided to employ a Living Lab approach for two main reasons. Firstly, since there were no comparable dashboards for multi-agency disaster preparation in practice, little was known about the specific set of PIs and corresponding dashboards required for the various relief agencies. The project team was convinced that user co-creation, one of the characteristics of Living Labs, would be the most efficient, and yet most effective way to determine the necessary PIs and dashboards. Living Labs can be cost-effective as they avoid making costly changes at a later innovation stage [12, 13]. They also generate better ideas and allow the detection and elimination of the "probably unsuccessful" ideas faster [13]. However, one of the main weaknesses of Living Labs is that they require a lot of time and budget. The second reason for selecting a Living Lab approach is that Living Labs allow for the combination of quantitative and qualitative research methods for data collection. As a Living Lab, the Aristoteles project creates a unique opportunity for researchers to investigate how dashboards can be developed and evaluated in a multi-agency and inter-regional setting. Figure 1 outlines the main phases of the Living Lab.

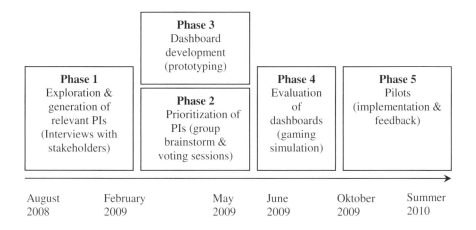

Fig. 1. Phases of the Aristoteles Living Lab

The first phase included semi structured interviews with stakeholders, allowing us to generate a long-list of required PIs. The results of this phase include a spreadsheet with over 500 different PIs gathered from the interviews. After completing phase 1, phase 2 and 3 were implemented in parallel. Having a first idea on the type and categories of PIs that needed to be visualized in the dashboards, the team developed the dashboard alternatives. In the meantime, work was done on reducing the initial long-list of PIs gathered from the interviews. We specially pursued a shortlist of PIs with a specific and concise set of PIs we could visualize in the dashboards. In order to make sure no crucial performance indicators were left out in the shortlist, the stakeholders participated in five brainstorms and voting sessions. Each session included a dozen relief agency managers responsible for crisis preparation for their respective agency. The goal of these sessions was to stimulate the actual users of PIs to prioritize the main PIs they needed for the process of multi-agency disaster preparation. The next sections discuss the resulting dashboard prototypes.

3 Dashboard Prototypes

Dashboards can be designed and tailored to many specific purposes depending on the task to be supported, the context of use and the frequency of use [7]. Moreover, the various data and purposes that dashboards can be used for are worth distinguishing, as they can demand differences in visual design and functionality. The factor that relates most directly to a dashboard's visual design involves the role it plays, whether strategic, tactical, or operational. The design characteristics of the dashboard can be tailored to effectively support the needs of each of these roles. In line with Morrissey [15], our process of tailoring dashboard content consisted of three phases: (1) identifying the main stakeholders; (2) identifying goals and establishing baseline capability for each stakeholder; and (3) selecting strategic, tactical, or operational dashboard content aligned with these goals. While certain differences such as these will affect design, there are also many commonalities that span all dashboards and invite a standard set of design practices. Based on the number of relief agencies and the three levels (strategic, tactical, and operational) that needed to be supported, seven different dashboards were developed. Each dashboard display was adaptable from detailed information (tables, trends) to a more abstract level (traffic lights and speedometer). Table 1 summarizes three types of dashboards we developed: strategic, tactical, and operational level dashboards.

Table 1. Overview of the developed dashboards and targeted users

Dashboard	User	User roles	Dashboard type
1	Fire Department	Second in command, Financial advisor, Human resource advisor	Operational, focused on fire department operations
2	Ambulance services	Second in command, Financial advisor, Human resource advisor	Operational, focused on ambulance services operations
3	Emergency control room	Second in command, Financial advisor, Police department representative	Operational, focused on the multi-agency performance of the control room
4	Crisis management agency	Director of regional crisis management department, Regional Hazard/risk advisor, Human resource advisor	Tactical, focused on the multi-agency performance regarding crisis management
5	Financial board	Director of financial department, Financial advisor, Human resource advisor	Tactical, focused on mid-term financial performance of the multi-agency safety region
6	Board of Commanders	Commanders of the respective relief agencies (five in total)	Tactical, focused on mid-term overall performance of the multi-agency safety region
7	Board of Mayors	Mayors of the respective municipalities (five in total)	Strategic, focused on long-term overall performance of the multi-agency safety region

Table 1 shows that we developed three dashboards for the operational level of the multi-agency safety organization. Each type of dashboard serves a different level and user group with different information needs. For the daily crisis preparation process, the team decided that the absolute values and thresholds per PI, based on averages and norms were more important than trends. The dashboards for the operational level are complementary to each other since they display different sets of PIs. The focus of the operational dashboards is daily use in the crisis preparation process. These dashboards are agency specific in scope and therefore tailored to the core processes of the individual relief agencies. The three dashboards developed for the tactical level of the multi-agency safety organization measure short-term (monthly) trends and progress toward strategic initiatives or specific projects. The audience for these dashboards consists of the directors or commanding officers of the relief agencies. Similar to the operational level dashboards, the tactical level dashboards display detailed PIs that relief agency managers need for performing their daily tasks. The tactical dashboards take advantage of awareness of context and the sophistication of relief agency managers to present significantly more detail without sacrificing comprehension. The emphasis is on highlighting opportunities or identifying risks regarding crisis preparation.

The third type of dashboard was developed for the strategic level stakeholders in the safety region. The following screenshot illustrates this dashboard.

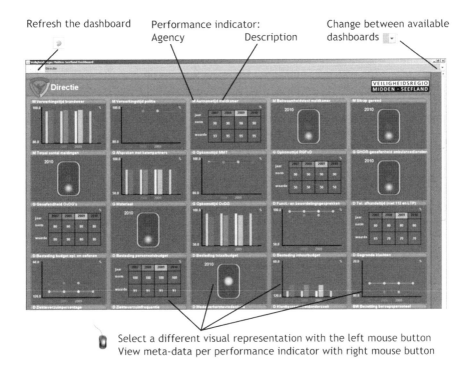

Fig. 2. Screenshot of a dashboard (strategic level)

The strategic level dashboard developed displays aggregated and periodical PIs. The reasoning behind this is that it would be unusual for a top-level manager to use an operational dashboard. The audience for the strategic dashboard consists of the Mayors of municipalities included in the regional multi-agency safety organization. For this audience, graphics summarizing long-term trends are more appropriate than measure showing the day-to-day processes in near real time with the aim of intervening quickly to resolve issues or take advantage of opportunities. The strategic level dashboard was highly summarized, graphical, and less frequently updated since the PIs values represented contained information aggregated over longer periods of time (i.e., yearly values). On this level of crisis preparation, the project team considered the overall performance of the multi-agency safety organization and the trends to be more important than the daily/absolute value of the PIs. Due to the longer time intervals compared to tactical and operational dashboards, the strategic level dashboard was based on various equations and functions that combine the values individual PIs. The strategic dashboards developed also included national, external, trend, and growth measures relevant for the safety region as a whole.

4   Dashboard Evaluation

4.1   Gaming Simulation

The fourth phase of the Living Lab included a two-day gaming simulation with forty relief agency managers. Gaming simulation is an approach often applied for awareness creation and learning in strategic management and policy formulation [16]. However, as demonstrated by Meijer et al. [17] gaming simulation is also very instrumental when it comes to the evaluation of artifacts in semi-realistic environments. The gaming simulation served three purposes. The first and most important purpose was to evaluate the preliminary dashboards in a semi-realistic setting. The second purpose was to extract aspects of the dashboards that required further improvement. Finally, the gaming simulation was also a way to demonstrate the results of the Living Lab to the future users (i.e., relief agency managers) and politicians. The following table outlines the gaming simulation activities.

Table 2. Overview gaming simulation activities

	Period	Main activities
Day 1	Morning	-Introduction to the game (purpose, design etc) -Explanation of the dashboards (types, PIs, buttons etc) -Round 1: prepare a crisis plan for 2010 -Plenary evaluation of round 1 (focus group)
	Afternoon	-Round 2: prepare a crisis plan for 2011 -Plenary evaluation of round 2 (focus group): what needs to be changed to the dashboards for more efficient and effective crisis preparation?
	Evening	-Implementation of the changes suggested by the participants in the dashboards (only by the architects)
Day 2	Morning	-Round 3: prepare a crisis plan for 2013 -Plenary evaluation of round 3 (focus group)
	Afternoon	-Plenary evaluation of the entire game -Fill in the questionnaires

The participants were separated in seven teams each using a different dashboard (see Table 1). Accordingly, the relief agency managers were required to engage in several crisis preparation processes, involving information acquisition, collaboration, planning, and decision-making in a multi-agency setting. The main task of the participants in the gaming session was to develop a crisis preparation plan, either for their agency or for the safety region. In order to develop such a plan, each participant needed PIs (provided in the dashboards) and context information (simulated by the facilitators). Depending on the agency of the participant (fire department, ambulance services etc) and the level of crisis preparation (operational, tactical and strategic) each participant interacted with a different dashboard. The context and drivers for the crisis preparation plans were simulated based on a predefined script, instructions, and paper messages. The session simulated several potential crisis events that have occurred or may still occur in a hypothetical safety region, each requiring multi-agency crisis preparation. During the gaming simulation, the qualitative and quantitative data gathering instruments resulted in data that is discussed next.

4.2   Qualitative Dashboard Evaluation: Findings of the Focus Group Sessions

Focus groups reflected on the experience with the dashboards during the gaming simulation. The data generated was of a qualitative nature. A list of observations recorded by the facilitators stimulated the participants to share their opinions about the dashboard they used for crisis preparation. The first focus group session (after round 1) was dominated by discussions surrounding the graphical user interface (GUI) of the dashboards. While the majority of participants were positive on the GUI design, some participants pointed to the problem of information overload and complexity due to the "many performance indicators on a single screen." The second focus group session (after game round 2) was focused on the structure of the PIs in the dashboards. More specifically, the participants reflected on the alignment of the PIs to the actual process of crisis preparation. In several cases, the participants suggested that the sequence of the PIs needed to be changed in accordance to the actual process of crisis preparation for their respective agency. Moreover, some participants mentioned that the dashboard developers did not accurately understand the individual sub processes of crisis preparation. Since the alignment of PIs to the sub-processes was important, the facilitators sketched a more accurate framework of the sub processes together with the participants. Based on the resulting framework, several elements of the dashboards were restructured before the start of round 3 on day 2 of the gaming simulation. The final focus group session took place after round 3. During this focus group, the strengths, weaknesses, opportunities, and threats (SWOT) of using the developed dashboards were discussed using a SWOT analysis. While the majority of participants acknowledged the value of dashboards for multi-agency disaster preparation, there were some mixed feelings regarding the standardization and enforcement of these dashboards across all the safety regions in the Netherlands. The issue here was that none of the safety regions in the Netherlands were the same or comparable in terms of capacity for handling crises. Moreover, every safety region faces different risks and potential crisis. Hence, the thresholds for the PIs needed to include a correction for several characteristics of a safety region, including the size, risks profile, and capacity of that specific region.

4.3   Quantitative Dashboad Evaluation: Findings from Questionnaires

In order to capture some quantitative, user generated data from the evaluation of the proposed dashboards, we employed questionnaires. Our purpose with the survey was to collect data on the individual level of satisfaction with the dashboards, their ability to aid in crisis preparation, and the intention of the individual participants to use the dashboards in practice. We administered short (one page, single sided) paper questionnaires at the end of the gaming simulation (day 2). We employed questionnaire items from two theoretical models that explain the satisfaction and success of technology: (1) the Information Systems Success (ISS) model by Delone and Mclean [18] and (2) the Technology Acceptance Model (TAM) [19]. Both ISS and TAM contain well agreed upon and frequently tested questionnaire items for evaluating information systems. The items listed in table two were measured using a seven-point Likert scale ranging from 1= strongly disagree to 7 = strongly agree. We analyzed the questionnaire data in order to obtain a picture of the satisfaction with and the intention to use dashboards. SPSS 17.0 yielded frequency tables, means (average values), and standard deviations for respondents' answers on the 7-point scale. The analysis provided an insight into the numbers of respondents associated with different values for a variable (criterion), the average value for each criterion—which could be considered an indication of the weight attached by the respondents to each of the different criteria used in performance evaluation—and the dispersion of the respondents' answers. Table 3 summarizes the questionnaire items and findings (n=22).

Table 3. Some questionnaire items and scores (measured using a 7-point Likert scale)

Nr	Construct	Item Question	Mean	Standard deviation
1	Collaboration1	The dashboard stimulated me to collaborate with the other domains in the safety region.	4,77	1,152
2	EaseofUse1	It would be easier if the PIs are clustered according to the primary processes of my organization.	5,55	1,605
3	EaseofUse2	The user interface (screen, buttons) was intuitive and easy to use.	5,48	1,167
4	TaskSupport1	The information provided via the dashboard was relevant (directly useable for executing my tasks).	4,82	1,332
5	TaskSupport2	Use of the dashboard leads to information overload (too much information)	3,43	1,502
6	TaskSupport3	The dashboard was stable and always available	4,68	1,249
7	Useability1	The information provided via the dashboard was easy to understand	4,86	1,283
8	Useability2	The refresh frequency of the dashboard was insufficient (yearly instead of monthly).	4,91	1,477
9	Useability3	For improved usability, the indicators on the dashboard need to be clustered in themes.	6,41	0,734
10	Preparation1	The information provided via the dashboard helped me to prepare for crisis response.	4,86	1,246
11	Preparation2	The dashboard provided me with valuable information for executing my individual tasks.	4,45	1,625
12	Preparation3	The dashboard provided me with valuable information for our group tasks.	5,18	1,140
13	Satisfaction1	I am satisfied with the dashboard.	4,86	1,153
14	Satisfaction2	I believe that the adoption of the dashboard would lead to improved crisis response.	5,64	.848
15	Intention2use1	In the future, I would like to use the dashboard in practice.	5,95	.653
16	Intention2use2	I will use the dashboard in the future, but only if it is used in other safety regions.	3,91	1,998
17	Usefulnnes1	The dashboard fulfilled my information needs.	3,82	1,259
18	Usefulness2	My information needs were beyond the information provided via the dashboard.	5,36	1,049
19	Usefulness3	The capability to add or remove indicators improves the usefulness of the dashboard.	6,18	.795

In total 22 out of the 27 (81%) participants remaining at the end of the second gaming-simulation day returned a completed questionnaire. From this sample, four respondents represented the fire department, four the medical services, three the emergency control room, three the central financial department of the safety region, three the Crisis Management Planning Centre, two the Safety Region management and three the Board of Directors (the Mayors). The questionnaire contained nine constructs.

The results of the questionnaire indicate that the relief agency managers found that the dashboard did improve their ability to prepare for a crisis. Items number 5 (task support), 11 (preparation) and 16 (intention to use) show the largest standard deviation in respondent scores. From the scores in the table we can conclude that the operators of the dashboards were not only satisfied with the dashboards, but also found the dashboards useful when preparing for a crisis. The majority of respondents have also indicated that they intent to use the dashboard in the future (if they were to be implemented). Based on the results of the questionnaire (high scores on usefulness, organizational impact, task-support and intention to use), we regard the dashboards developed accepted from a TAM perspective and successful from an ISS perspective.

5   Conclusion and Discussion: Experiences from the Living Lab

The main deliverable of the Aristoteles Living Lab is a set of seven dashboards for multi-agency crisis preparation. Key in the development of these dashboards was user co-creation, a process in which (future) users of the proposed dashboards were actively involved in a Living Lab. This paper contributes a description and discussion of a real-world development trajectory that, due to its explorative nature, required several research stages with professionals. The findings from both the qualitative and quantitative evaluation suggest that users were overall satisfied with the dashboards and show intention to use these in practice. Moreover, the majority of participants felt the dashboard did help them prepare for the eventuality of a crisis during the gaming session. Yet, the participants in the gaming simulation phase of the Living Lab suggest that the formulation and clustering of the performance indicators require better alignment with the context of use. We consider this alignment as one of the major challenges for further research, especially since the process of crisis response is very difficult to capture and specify in a general workflow.

Even though we collected both qualitative and quantitative data on the value of the proposed dashboards allowing us to triangulate some of our findings, the relatively small number of participants in the evaluation phase limits us in generalizing our findings. Having acknowledged this limitation, a Living Lab does allow synthesizing some experiences in the development of dashboards for disaster preparation. The experiences include the design trade-offs that need to be made by dashboard architects and are outlined in the Table 4. For scholars, these experiences may be used to formulate more specific propositions and hypotheses for future research. For practitioners, these experiences may be used as guidelines for developing dashboards. One of the main experiences is that the high level of uncertainty regarding the final set of performance indicators and the corresponding norms demands flexibility in the dashboard architecture beyond the evaluation stage.

Table 4. Experiences gained from the Living Lab

Experience	Trade-off	Explanation
Maximize stakeholder involvement	Speed of dashboard development process versus level of commitment	Involving all stakeholders in the Living Lab might reduce the speed of this process since each stakeholder has its own goals and (technical) preferences. Yet, it is crucial not to neglect the wishes of stakeholders who might lobby against the proposed dashboards.
Maintain open and flexible (fluid) dashboards for user co-creation	Hard coded versus flexible dashboards	In contrast to traditional system design processes, user co-creation requires flexible dashboards, PI sets, and thresholds (underlying performance norms) even during the evaluation phase.
Communicate problems in PI formulation	Granularity: detailed or abstract PIs?	For user co-creation, dashboard architects need to communicate problems regarding the PI formulation and evaluation process.
Generate "look & feel" moments in the Living Lab	Dry runs or live runs?	Organize real life sessions (i.e., using focus groups and gaming simulations) to allow users to obtain a practical understanding of the implications of PI.
Show intention to accommodate suggestions	Closed or fixed dashboards?	User co-creation demands that the feedback and suggestions of stakeholders is implemented as soon as possible. This highlights user involvement in the dashboard development process.
Allow customization of dashboard representations	Options for GUI personalization by the user: fully or non-customizable interfaces?	Users should be able to choose the style of visual representation (bar charts, graphs, numeric tables) depending on the task at hand (i.e., work flow management data, payroll, human resources, material management).
Predefine the level of information load per PI according to roles and tasks	High or low-level information accuracy?	Too little information may lead to insufficient task support whereas too much information may lead to information overload. Consequently, dashboards should help relief agency managers by providing only the necessary information, but also attracting the attention to information easily ignored.

Based on the experiences listed in Table 4, we conclude that the development of dashboards is a difficult endeavor as it requires a constant balancing act on trade-offs. The Living Lab involves several stakeholders that co-decide about the trade-offs, and consequently construct the project specific benchmark for success. Moreover, previous research has not reported comparable dashboard development efforts that we could draw upon. We found that the Living Lab approach was useful for the development and evaluation of dashboard involving many stakeholders. User co-creation, one of the main characteristics of Living Labs, was particularly important in the dashboard design and evaluation process. User co-creation was particularly instrumental for dealing with uncertainty regarding dashboard elements, PIs, thresholds and so on. Users in the Living Lab appreciated the interaction between the various stakeholders, the use of prototypes, and the look and feel experiences generated during the gaming simulation. As such, we recommend the use of Living

Labs in e-government when dealing with these types of complex problems involving many actors and uncertain (future) user needs.

References

1. Layne, K., Lee, J.: Developing fully functional E-government: A four stage model. Government Information Quarterly 18, 122–136 (2001)
2. Bharosa, N., Janssen, M., Groenleer, M., van Zanten, B.: Transforming crisis management: field studies on network-centric operations. In: Wimmer, M. (ed.) DEXA EGOV 2009. LNCS. Springer, Heidelberg (2009)
3. Boin, A., 't Hart, P., Stern, E., Sundelius, B.: The Politics of Crisis Management: Public Leadership Under Pressure. Cambridge University Press, Cambridge (2005)
4. Carter, N., Klein, R., Day, P.: How organisations measure success: The use of performance indicators in goverment. Taylor & Francis Group, Routledge (1995)
5. Clarke, S.: Your Business Dashboard: Knowing When to Change the Oil. The Journal of Corporate Accounting & Finance 16, 51–54 (2005)
6. Adam, F., Pomerol, J.C.: Developing Practical Decision Support Tools Using Dashboards of Information. In: Burstein, F., Holsapple, C.W. (eds.) Handbook on Decision Support Systems, vol. 2, pp. 151–173. Springer, Heidelberg (2008)
7. Few, S.: Information Dashboard Design: The Effective Visual Communication of Data. O'Reilly Media, Inc., Sebastopol (2006)
8. Dover, C.: How Dashboards Can Change Your Culture. Strategic Finance 86, 43–48 (2004)
9. Gitlow, H.: Organizational Dashboards: Steering an Organization Towards its Mission. Quality Engineering 17, 345–357 (2005)
10. Resnick, M.L.: Situation Awareness Applications to Executive Dashboard Design. In: 47th Annual Conference of the Human Factors and Ergonomics Society, pp. 449–453 (2003)
11. Pallot, M.: The Living Lab Approach: A User Centred Open Innovation Ecosystem. In: Webergence Blog, vol. 2010 (2009)
12. Lama, N., Origin, A.: Innovation ECOSYSTEMS: Services engineering & living labs a dream to drive innovation? (2006)
13. Følstad, A.: Living labs for innovation and development of information and communication technology: A literature review. The Electronic Journal for Virtual Organizations and Networks 10, 99–131 (2008)
14. Erikkson, M., Niitamo, V.P., Kulkki, S.: State-of the-art in utilizing Living Labs approach to user-centric ICT innovation - a European approach (2005)
15. Morrissey, R.: Tailoring Performance Dashboard Content. Business Intelligence Journal 12 (2007)
16. Duke, R.D., Geurts, J.: Policy games for strategic management. Dutch University Press, Amsterdam (2004)
17. Meijer, S.M., Hofstede, G.J., Omta, S.W.F., Beers, G.: The organization of transactions: research with the Trust and Tracing game. Journal on Chain and Network Science 8, 1–20 (2008)
18. Delone, W., McLean, E.: Information Systems Succes: the quest for the dependent variable. Information Systems Research 3, 60–95 (1992)
19. Davis, F.D.: User acceptance of information technology: system characteristics, user perceptions and behavioral impacts. International Journal of Man-Machine Studies 38, 475–487 (1993)

Automatic Generation of Roadmap for E-Government Implementation

Mauricio Solar, Daniel Pantoja, and Gonzalo Valdés

Universidad Técnica Federico Santa María (UTFSM), Chile
{msolar,daniel.pantoja,gvaldes}@inf.utfsm.cl

Abstract. Evaluating readiness of individual public agencies to execute specific e-Government programs and directives is a key ingredient for wider e-Government deployment and success. This article describes how the e-Government Maturity Model (eGov-MM) identifies specific areas in which public agencies should focus improvement efforts. eGov-MM is a capability maturity model, that identifies capability levels for each critical variable and Key Domain Areas, proposes a synthetic maturity level for institutions, and automatically generates the roadmap for each evaluated public agency. In this article, the automatic generation of the proposed roadmap is detailed.

Keywords: e-government, roadmap, capability, maturity model.

1 Introduction

The eGov-MM model (e-Government Maturity Model) [1] is a model to measure public institutions readiness to manage and implement e-Government. It considered several information sources [2, 3, 4, 5, 6, 7] in its initial formulation summarized in [8]. The model was piloted with seven (initially 9) public agencies, and a tuned version was generated which incorporates the participants' feedback and an eGov implementation *roadmap* for each evaluated public agency. An associated self-assessment Web tool was also built and similarly validated [9].

eGov-MM is not only a diagnostic tool, but also a generator of improvement *roadmaps*. The model proposes concrete *roadmaps* for capability improvement, i.e. directives about where the organization financial and human resources should be canalized to improve its capability to carry out eGov initiatives. This *roadmap* is automatically generated.

Section 2 describes the eGov-MM, its main characteristics, objectives and how an organization maturity is evaluated; Section 3 explains the design of the automatic generator of *roadmaps*; Section 4 presents the results and analysis; and Section 5 summarizes and concludes.

2 Model of Capabilities and Maturity

One goal of the eGov-MM is to generate *roadmaps* for progressive evolution of capabilities and maturity. To this end, first we describe the generic model used to

M.A. Wimmer et al. (Eds.): EGOV 2010, LNCS 6228, pp. 192–203, 2010.

define the capability levels for each model variable; then we describe the relation between variables capabilities and their respective Key Domain Areas (KDAs); and finally we describe how the organization maturity is determined from its KDA capabilities.

2.1 Capability and Maturity Levels

The capability is a measurement of the state of each KDA that contributes to support the organization development. The capability of a KDA is determined using the capability level (CL) of each of its Critical Variables, i.e. what is really evaluated is the capability of these variables to satisfy certain requirements. The capabilities of the critical variables are weighed according to their importance to give a final KDA CL.

The CL of a KDA and its critical variables determine the organizational maturity level (ML). The ML is a property of the organization as a whole; each ML corresponds to a predetermined configuration of KDAs in predefined CLs. The model allows, once the current ML is assessed, to identify the states required to advance to a higher level and propose a "*roadmap*" to improve the organization.

2.2 Generic Capabilities Model

For each KDA there is a measurement scale from 1 to 5, associated with a generic qualitative capabilities model that ranges from "*initial capabilities*" to "*integrated capabilities*"; the values are shown in Table 1.

Table 1. Capacity levels of the maturity model

Capacity Level	Description
Level 1: Initial capabilities	There is evidence that KDA has been recognized and needs to be approached
Level 2: Developing capabilities (repeatable but intuitive)	There is no formal training or procedures spreading, and the responsibility to follow them falls to each individual
Level 3: Defined capabilities	The procedures are not sophisticated, but are the formalization of existing practices
Level 4: Managed capabilities	Established standards and norms are applied through the organization. Tools are mainly automated.
Level 5: Integrated capabilities (Optimized)	Procedures have become best practices, and continuous improvement is applied

The capability levels of each KDA are built from the levels of their variables. For each level, several aspects are considered (incrementally in each level): awareness; human resources training; communication; procedures and practices; compliance of standards and norms; tools and automation; and involvement and responsibility.

2.3 Relationship between Capability Variables and KDAs

The capability level (CL) of a KDA is generally the average of the CLs of its critical Variables V_i. To accommodate eGov strategies or country development levels with different variables relevance, weights are used for each variable group. Thus, the *CL* of a KDA is the *weighted average* of the *CLs* of its variables V_i (see Eq. 1).

$$CL_{KDA} = \frac{\sum_{i=1}^{n} CL(V_i) * W_i}{100}$$

(Eq. 1)

The weights W_i used in the first model applications (pilot and initial massive application) are shown in [9].

2.4 Organizational Maturity Model

Maturity is a property of the organizational unit as a whole, and the maturity level (*ML*) is obtained from the KDA capacity levels that the unit has. Thus, each *ML*:

- Frames a set of KDAs for a given *CL*.
- Establishes equivalence among eGov implementation maturity of units.

There are several options to determine an organization maturity, namely:

1. Minimum *CL* among all KDAs
2. Average *CL* of all KDAs
3. Predetermined KDA configuration, using a set of values for all KDAs in model.
4. Configuration of high-priority KDAs, using a set of *minimum* values for all KDAs in the model.

The last criterion (Configuration of high-priority KDAs) was adopted in eGov-MM [9]. The organization *ML* is determined (Eq. 2) by a set of values for all KDAs in the model.

$$ML_1 = \text{Conf}_1(CL(\text{KDA}_1), \dots, CL(\text{KDA}_i))$$
$$ML_2 = \text{Conf}_2(CL(\text{KDA}_1), \dots, CL(\text{KDA}_j))$$

(Eq. 2)

$$\dots$$
$$ML_5 = \text{Conf}_5(CL(\text{KDA}_1), \dots, CL(\text{KDA}_k))$$

This mechanism was selected for eGov-MM for its flexibility to allow graduating progress according to specific eGov strategies, since it only requires to fixing a minimum set of KDAs that are important for a given *ML*; development criteria and rates for other KDAs are left to the organization. The actual criteria to use can be extracted from domain specialists or agencies leaderships; e.g. from phrases such as:

- "Maintaining enterprise architecture is an advanced issue, which allows aligning business objectives and computer networks … and thus should not be requiring nor evaluating for lower *MLs*…"
- "It is very important to start by aligning the IT, eGov and of business strategies … this should be required even for lower *MLs*".

3   Design of the Automatic Generator of *Roadmaps*

Roadmaps play a leading role in the continuous improvement cycle proposed by the model, since they constitute the direct recommendations to advance to a higher level of maturity.

It is therefore, fundamental for the design of a *roadmaps* system to consider the challenge it implies to automatically generate recommendations, and in particular for this model, it has a high complexity standard since the system must consider strategic aspects that will indorse an optimum upgrading through the maturity levels (*ML*).

3.1   Previous Considerations

To guarantee that the *roadmaps* automatically generated by a system are optimum, 4 key factors must be considered: bounding KDAs; variables weight; load balance; and "almost" variables, hereunder detailed.

Bounding KDA

The first factor is to generate *roadmaps* for those KDAs that are bounding the upgrading to the next level of maturity. This means to only generate *roadmaps* of the areas that do not accomplish with the *CL* necessary for the next *ML*. This consideration is because in most of the cases there will be *CLs* of the KDAs that will meet with the requirements of the next *ML* and only a few that are limiting the advance.

Variables Weight (W_i)

This is a high relevance factor, since the fundamental basis of the quality or the optimization of the *roadmaps* system lies in the weight of the variables, W_i.

Considering that the variables have a weight W_i that represent their importance within the KDA, it is fundamental to mathematically control the supply to the *CL* of the KDA represented by the increase of the *CL* of that variable.

In most of the cases, following this logic, it will be only necessary to increase the *CL* of an amount of variables less than the total quantity of the area in order to obtain the increase of a *CL* of the total KDA.

Load Balance

This factor establishes that *roadmaps* must generate an advance with homogeneity along the *CLs* of the variables of the institutions' KDAs. The basis of this factor is a contradictory concept in the short term, but fundamental in the long term, since the maturity levels implicitly involve a homogeneous advance through the *CLs* of the KDAs, and furthermore, in practice the differences between *CLs* of the same area variables create withdrawing behaviors from the optimum management.

"Almost" Variables

Another fundamental factor that must be taken in consideration in the system design are the "almost" variables that allow a variable – in spite of having the same *CLs* of the *roadmaps*. These variables classification correspond to those that although they are in a certain *CL*, they meet with the conditions required of a higher *CL*. This is a common case since in spite of the quality of the *CL* classification by variable, reality is always more complex, and another can be closer to upgrading to the next level.

In the design context of the *roadmaps* system, these variables must be favored in fair conditions with respect to other variables, since its increase of *CL* will require less effort that a common variable.

3.2 Algorithm Logic of the Automatic *Roadmaps*

Automatic *roadmaps* generation algorithm logic developed considers all the key factors above mentioned to assure that the generated *roadmaps* are the best recommendations so the institution can accomplish the next *ML*. This logic is divided basically in the following 5 main stages.

3.2.1 Determination of Limiting KDAs

This phase is based on one of the 4 key factors to be considered, which postulates that in most of the cases the institution can be limited to upgrade to the next ML for only a few KDAs and not for the total of them.

Therefore, the first step of the algorithm consists in identifying the KDAs that are limiting the upgrading, so as to later only generating *roadmaps* in these areas.

In case none of the KDAs of the institution meet with the *CL* of the following *ML* all the KDAs are considered limiting KDAs.

3.2.2 Definition of the Levels That the Limiting KDA Must Increase

This step is in charge of the immediate management of a technical problem, that is to say, that the limiting KDAs could need to increase more than one *CL* so the organization will increase only one *ML*. Because of this, the second stage of the algorithm consists in reviewing how many *CLs* must increase each area so as to allow the upgrading of the institutions to the next *ML*.

However, the *CL* of the KDA is obtained by means of a weighting of the *CLs* of the variables (Eq. 1), which eliminates the decimal component of the final result. Therefore, in most of the situations there is a remainder of the percentage of the *CL* of the area that must be considered to optimize the *roadmaps* generation.

For example, Table 2 shows a KDA with its corresponding *CLs*.

Table 2. Capability level of variables into a KDA

KDA	V_i	W_i	CL
Vision,	Communication to stakeholders	25	2
Strategies	Strategies Alignment	15	1
and	High Management Commitment	30	1
Policies	Resources Asignment for eGov	30	1

Applying equation 1 for the calculation of the *CL* of the KDA, the results of Eq. 3 shows that the KDA "*Vision, Strategies and Policies*" is in a *CL* 1, but has a 25%

capability from the second level, therefore, *roadmaps* are optimum, they just must increase the *CL* of the area in a 75% and not in a 100%.

$$CL_{KDA} = \frac{50 + 15 + 30 + 30}{100} = \frac{125}{100} = 1.25 \qquad \text{(Eq. 3)}$$

3.2.3 Identification of the "almost" Variables by Area

This step of the algorithm is directly related to one of the key factors mentioned before, "almost" variables. It is known that these variables are of great importance within the *roadmaps* generation, positions that will be preferential when generating them, since the increase of a *CL* from an "almost" variable requires less effort than a normal one needs. Specifically in this step each variable of a KDA is analyzed so as to recognize if it is an "almost" variable or not; also, a record is saved with the total amount of "almost" variables of the KDA.

3.2.4 Classification of the Problem of the *Roadmaps* Generation

This step is one of the most important of the *roadmaps* generation algorithm, since it is in this step where the logic to be used when generating the *roadmaps* of each KDA in an optimum manner is decided.

The classification of the problems is carried out based on two parameters: levels quantity that the KDA must upgrade to increase the *ML* of the institution and the amount of "almost" variables contained in Table 3.

Table 3. Problems classification of the *roadmaps* generation

Increase of the *CL*	"Almost" Variables
1	All
1	Non
1	Some
More than 1	All
More than 1	Non
More than 1	Some

3.2.5 Calculation of the *Roadmaps* According to the Type of Problem

The last stage of the *roadmaps* algorithm consists basically in the *roadmaps* generation according to the logic associated to the type of problem defined in the preceding step, which was classified at the same time, as per the information obtained from the first steps.

Although there are 6 classifications of different problems, it has been decided that only 4 logics of *roadmaps* generation are enough for the solution of all the cases; the 4 logics associated to the types of problems are hereunder detailed:

- **One *CL* and only "almost" variables:** Solves the homonymous problem; the characteristics of this problem assure that the increase of the *CL* required will be achieved in the worst of the cases, increasing all the variables of the KDA.

Since all the variables are essentially "almost" type, the increase of the *CL* in any of them require the same effort, therefore, as from this point of view no variables priority exist.

The logic that solves the problem consists of, in first instance identifying the best *CL* contribution of the KDA generated by the increase of a *CL* of one (or more than one) variable that together with the remaining of the *CL* of the KDA could achieve to carry into effect the KDA to the next level. Once detecting what variables will be increased of level, the optimum *roadmaps* will be those that will promote the development of the characteristics of the next *CL* of these variables.

- **One *CL* and none "almost" variable:** Solves the homonymous problem, the characteristics of the problem establish that no priority exists between additional variables to the contribution that each one of them provides to the increasing of the *CL* of the KDA.

  The challenge of this problem lies in the fact that no guarantee exists that all the variables can go through the next level (one of those can be in the maximum level), therefore the algorithm must be able to find the best combination of variables (that will produce the highest contribution to the *CL* of the KDA), and *CLs* that each one must increase, so together with the remains of the *CL* of the KDA they will be able to upgrade the KDA to the next level. The optimum *roadmaps* will be assigned to promote the development of the next *CL* of these variables.

- **One or more CLs and some "almost" variables:** Solves the problems "*one CL and an 'almost' variable*" and "*more than one level and some 'almost' variable*". The reason by which a same logic involves these two problems is that to the principal reasoning the amount of *CLs* that the KDA must increase is indifferent because, as the preceding case, it is not possible to assure that all the variables of the KDA could increase the level (any of them could be in its maximum level) so the algorithm must be able to find the best combination of variables (that will produce the biggest contribution to the *CL* of the KDA) and *CLs* that each one must increase, so together with the remaining of the *CL* of the KDA they can achieve to upgrade to the next level the KDA.

  Unlike the preceding case, in this one it an additional priority to the contribution that each variable performs exists, and it is present in the "almost" variables, since the increase of levels of these variables, require less demand.

  Therefore, the process of generating the *roadmaps* must choose the variables (favoring the "almost" variables and the weight balancing) and the amount of *CL* that each one must increase, that perform the best contribution to the *CL* of the KDA.

- **More than one *CL*, and none or all of the "almost" variables:** Solves the problem "*more than one CL and not any 'almost' variable*" and "*more than one level, and only 'almost' variables*". The reason by which a same logic involves the two problems is that the characteristics of these two problems are similar, in both cases all of the variables have the same priority (except for the contribution) and the fact that all the variables can upgrade their *CL* is not guaranteed (any of them can be found in the maximum level). For this reason the *roadmaps* algorithm must be able to find the best combinations of variables (those that will produce the highest contribution to the *CL* of the KDA), and *CLs* that each one must increase, so together with the remaining *CL* of the KDA they can move the KDA to the next level. The optimum *roadmaps* will have to promote the development of the established *CL* characteristics that must be achieved by these variables.

3.3 Implementation of the Automatic *Roadmaps* Algorithm

Implementation of automatic *roadmaps* generation algorithm has been integrated to the web system of the evaluation and diagnosis of the maturity model and ICT use capability in public agencies. In this way, *roadmaps* are instantly established when the questions associated to each variable are answered.

```
Central Algorithm of the Roadmap
{
 bounding_areas ← areas that bound the next ML
 For each (bounding_areas)
 {
   CL-KDA ← CL of a KDA
   cl ← Levels to be incremented in the KDA
   V_area[] ← List of variables in a KDA sorted by descending weight
   CL_dec ← CL not rounded of the KDA (decimal)
   IF (cl == 1)
   {
     For each V_area[]
       IF (verify_almost(V_area) == true)
       almost_var[] ← V_area
     IF (count(almost_var[]) == count(V_area[]))
     roadmap ← best_contr_all_almost(V_area[], CL_dec);
     IF (count(almost_var[]) == 0)
     roadmap ← best_contrib_zero_almost(V_area [],CL_dec);
     IF (0 < count(almost_var[]) < count(V_area[]))
     roadmap ← best_contr_some_almost(V_area[],CL_dec, almost_var[])
   }
   IF (cl > 1)
   {
     For each V_area[]
       IF (verify_almost(V_area) == true)
       almost_var[] ← V_area
     IF (count(almost_var[])==count(V_area[]))OR(count(almost_var[])==0)
     roadmap ← best_contrib_cero_all_almost_2(V_area[],CL_dec, c_level)
     IF (0 < count(almost_var[]) < count(V_area[]))
     roadmap ← best_contr_some_almost(V_area[],CL_dec, almost_var[], cl)
   }
 print(roadmap)
}
```

Automatic calculation of the *roadmaps* is divided in two parts: a central algorithm in charge of the general management and a specific function dedicated to each of the 4 logics described above. Above you can see the central algorithm for the *roadmap* and below one of the 4 functions assigned to manage each of the logics.

```
function best_contr_all_almost(V_area, CL_dec)
{
 delta_capacity_necessary ← (floor(CL_dec)+1)-CL_dec
 delta_comparative ← 0
 levels_to_rise ← 1
 for each V_area
 {
   IF (V_area → level_capacity_question < 5)
   {
     delta_comparative += V_area → weight/100
     roadmap ← array(levels_to_rise, V_area)
   }
   IF (delta_comparative > delta_capacity_necessary)
   return roadmap
 }
 return 0
}
```

4   Results and Analysis

The model was applied to a small set of public agencies as a validation mechanism, but in this section we present the results of applying the eGov-MM and its automatic *roadmap* generator tool to one public agency; it describes the main sample characteristics, the results of capability measurement for the sample, and the generated *roadmaps*.

The *ML* obtained by the reported agency was the minimum level (Level 1). This reality priori disagrees with what was observed and expected, so, in order to understand the result obtained, a deeper analysis should be carried on.

CL by Area
The *CLs* of the areas are found mainly in the two first levels. There are areas with a higher *CL* (level 3) that is worth to mention: "Performance management", "Infrastructure and eGov Tools", and "Change management".

These higher capacity levels are mainly possible because the agency has demonstrated that a suitable infrastructure was prepared in order to improve the quality of their services, and that an adequate management and control of the functionaries and of the work they carry on was also considered.

Furthermore, it is remarkable one area that is in a high *CL* (level 4), "Inter-operability Practices". This area reflects the agency understanding about the importance of working with other agencies in an integrated manner, and they have also completely assumed the challenge that interoperability brings both, at the institutional and technical level.

CLs by Variable
At variables level reality is similar; the *CLs* are mainly distributed in the two first levels. Those areas that accomplish a higher *CL* are homogeneously supported by the *CL* of their variables.

It is interesting the case of 3 variables that accomplish the maximum *CL*: "Basis Infrastructure Hardware/Software", "Institutional Interoperability" and "Customers' satisfaction".

In outline it can be observed that the public agency has prepared an adequate interoperability platform to their initiatives of electronic government.

They fully meet with their task of knowing the necessities and requirements of the citizens and have disclosed the importance of counting with interoperability services so as to be related to other agencies and improving the quality and access easiness to the services that the agency offers.

Roadmaps

As above was mentioned, the calculation of the *ML* depends on a pre-established definition of the *CLs* by area for each real level and the proximity of the following *ML*.

The web system of evaluation and diagnosis of the Maturity Model and Capability of the ICT use in public agencies points out that the organization is in level 1 for 3 KDAs, that is to say, there are 14 KDAs that meet with the *ML* 2, and only 3 that do not.

The 3 KDAs that are bounding the advance to the next *ML* are: "IT Management and Organization", "Regulations Compliance", and "Human Capital".

Also, 2 of these 3 bounding areas are very close to upgrading their *CL*, so moving the agency to the next *ML* is a task almost easy to carry on. Considering that it is only limited by 3 areas, and because 2 of the 3 areas have variables that are at just one step of upgrading to the next *CL*, in consequence, the area is very close to its upgrading to the next *CL*.

Roadmaps automatically generated by the system indicate that for the institution to accomplish *ML* 2, it has only to meet with the requirements of Table 4.

Table 4. *Roadmap* automatically generated

IT Management and Organization (amount of levels to increase: 1)
IT Infrastructure Planning (amount of levels to increase: 1)
• IT Unit is incorporating the IT Infrastructure Planning activities but only to a tactical level
• IT Unit has developed a documented Infrastructure Plan but it is not consistently applied
• Staff of the IT Unit have accomplished the planning skills but not in a structured way
Regulations Compliance (amount of levels to increase: 1)
Internal Regulation (amount of levels to increase: 1)
• The High Board already defined or is analyzing the mechanisms to be endowed of a diffusion strategy of the internal regulations, to facilitate the eGov initiatives.
Human Capital (amount of levels to increase: 1)
Management of eGov Competences (amount of levels to increase: 1)
• The model that allows a Management based on the Competences integrates the competences definitions that the eGov requires for all the roles.

Regarding the agency, the conclusion is that, although it obtained a minimum *ML* it is very close to accomplishing the next level. Also, according to the *CLs* of the variables and areas obtained by the agency, it is observed that an adequate interoperability platform exists for the development of the ICT use, besides, there is an excellent identification of the citizens' needs, and the new technological developments receive from the high commands the basic minimum necessary support. However, the vision and strategy of the ICT use is limited, no clear planning of the path to follow in the use of them exists. Therefore, generated *roadmap* is in accord with the institution's reality.

5 Conclusions

The information provided by the Maturity Model is useful in taking decisions with respect to the ICT strategy and direction, and is a feedback tool for the institution management which, as a consequence allows the generation of a continuous improving cycle when discovering the areas that are developed according to the institutions' reality and those that do not.

The model not only performs this measuring, but also generates the *roadmaps* necessary to follow, so as to accomplish the next maturity level in the best way. These are automatically generated as soon as changes in measuring are carried on, so it is assured that no efforts or resources are wasted in variables of areas that do not have an impact in the short or medium term within the organization.

Roadmaps algorithm was developed to be adapted to any situation that could show up when applying the model to the organization; it goes beyond the detail level of variable to consider also the characteristics of each variable.

In this way it is guaranteed that the generated recommendations are the best in relation to the minimum effort to obtain the maximum level, both in capacity and maturity, but furthermore it should guarantee that the institution will develop itself as a balanced organization in the three areas.

The algorithm works correctly and it is integrated to the application of evaluation and diagnosis of the Maturity Model and Capability of the ICT use in public agencies.

As a future work, it would be interesting to add the possibility of addressing the focus to the *roadmaps* generation, so as to allow that the upgrade through the maturity levels do coincide with short term goals. In this way it would be possible that the model will not only lead institution to a higher maturity level through the shortest path, but will also do it through the shortest path that will meet with the short or medium term targets of the IT strategies put into action by the institution.

Thus, eGov-MM is not only a diagnostic tool, but also a generator of improvement *roadmaps*. Government has a methodological and technological tool to measure status and improvement of eGov implementation by specific public agencies.

References

1. Iribarren, M., Concha, G., Valdes, G., Solar, M., Villarroel, M., Gutiérrez, P., Vásquez, A.: Capability Maturity Framework for e-Government: A Multi-dimensional Model and Assessing Tool. In: Wimmer, M.A., Scholl, H.J., Ferro, E. (eds.) EGOV 2008. LNCS, vol. 5184, pp. 136–147. Springer, Heidelberg (2008)
2. Andersen, K.V., Henriksen, Z.H.: E-government Maturity Models: Extension of the Layne and Lee Model. Government Information Quarterly 23, 236–248 (2006)
3. Cresswell, A., Pardo, T., Canestarro, D.: Digital Capability Assessment for e-Government: A Multidimensional Approach. In: Wimmer, M.A., Scholl, H.J., Grönlund, Å., Andersen, K.V. (eds.) EGOV 2006. LNCS, vol. 4084, pp. 293–304. Springer, Heidelberg (2006)

4. Layne, K., Lee, J.: Developing Fully Functional e-Government: A Four Stage Model. Government Information Quarterly 18, 122–136 (2001)
5. Wimmer, M.A., Tambouris, E.: Online One-Stop Government: A Working Framework and Requirements. In: Proc. of the 17th IFIP World Computer Congress, pp. 117–130. Kluwer Academic Publishers, Boston (2002)
6. Esteves, J., Joseph, R.: A Comprehensive Framework for the Assessment of e-Government Projects. Government Information Quarterly 25, 118–132 (2008)
7. Al-Khatib, H.: A Citizen Oriented E-government Maturity Model. Brunel University, Londres (2009)
8. Valdes, G., Iribarren, M., Concha, G., Solar, M., Visconti, M., Astudillo, H., Villarroel, M., Gutiérrez, P., Vásquez, A.: Identifying relevant National e-Government Implementations for an Emerging Country: A Selective Survey. In: Ferro, E., Scholl, H.J., Wimmer, M.A. (eds.) EGOV 2008. LNCS, vol. 5184, pp. 141–149. Springer, Heidelberg (2008)
9. Solar, M., Astudillo, H., Valdes, G., Iribarren, M., Concha, G.: Identifying Weaknesses for Chilean e-Government Implementation in Public Agencies with Maturity Model. In: Wimmer, M.A., et al. (eds.) EGOV 2009. LNCS, vol. 5693, pp. 151–162. Springer, Heidelberg (2009)

Success of Government E-Service Delivery: Does Satisfaction Matter?

Parmita Saha[1], Atanu Nath[2], and Esmail Salehi-Sangari[3]

[1] Division of Industrial Marketing, E-Commerce, and Logistics, Luleå University of
Technology, Sweden
Department of Marketing, University of Surrey, Surrey, gu2 7xh, United Kingdom
p.saha@surrey.ac.uk
[2] Department of Marketing, University of Surrey, Surrey, gu2 7xh, United Kingdom
a.nath@surrey.ac.uk
[3] Division of Industrial Marketing and Entrepreneurship, Institute of Industrial Economy and
Organisation, The Royal Institute of Technology, Sweden
Division of Industrial Marketing, E-Commerce, and Logistics, Luleå University of
Technology, Sweden
ess@ltu.se

Abstract. For measuring e-government success a well-founded theory is important which can help governments to improve their services and identify how effectively public money is spent. We propose using citizen satisfaction as a measure of e-government success, as well as explore its relationships with e-government service quality. Three hypotheses have been formulated to test the model. For empirical estimation, the data used in this study was collected form Sweden. An online survey was conducted using systematic sampling among the municipalities in Sweden, 425 valid responses were received. The measures of each variables selected in this article were mainly adapted from related previous studies. Efficiency, privacy, responsiveness and web assistance were selected as e-service quality dimensions. Actual usages were measured by three items- Frequency of usage, Diversity of usages and Dependency. Confirmatory factor analyses were conducted to confirm the factor structures. The analysis shows that 43% of the variance among the factors of e-service quality, and usage is explained by citizen satisfaction. We found e-service quality has a relation with citizen satisfaction considering four dimensions of service quality. Efficiency, responsiveness and web assistance were found to be of more importance compared to privacy in determining e-service quality. Use was found to be positively and significantly related to citizen satisfaction. The results should contribute towards understanding of the key issues that influence citizens' needs and level of satisfaction with the tax services and help improve the service delivery process. Further research is suggested to explore other quality dimensions such as system and information quality.

Keywords: e-service quality, e-government success, satisfaction, e-tax.

M.A. Wimmer et al. (Eds.): EGOV 2010, LNCS 6228, pp. 204–215, 2010.

1 Introduction

Explosive growth of information and communication technology has had an impact on government activities, which allows for service delivery to the citizen electronically. The aim of this initiative is to deliver better services to the citizens and communities through information and communication technology (ICT), especially through the Internet (Blakeley and Matsuura, 2001). The emergence of e-government has molded the use of information and communications technology; and albeit with varying degrees of success, has transformed the public sector from being "inward looking and administration-focused" to becoming outward looking with a focus on service delivery (Connolly & Bannister, 2008).

In order to provide e-government initiatives both national and regional governments have made serious investments in terms of resources, personnel and time and they believed that it will improve the quality of services of government for citizens. These indicate citizens could access a public service electronically; citizen could navigate through a number of public services and agencies electronically and access the most current information on services, regulations, procedures, forms, etc (Buckley 2003). Government organizational units are increasingly seeking ways to encourage citizens to use online modes of service delivery. To do so, it is imperative that such bodies take stock of the dimensions of website service excellence, to fully utilize the potential of such services and also to improve both its adoption by the citizenry as well as the level of satisfaction with public administration (Connolly & Bannister, 2008).

For measuring e-government success a well-founded theory is important that can help governments to improve their services and identify how effectively public money is spent (Peters, Janssen & Engers, 2004). Lihua & Zheng (2005) identified e-government performance as a dependent variable that includes service level to constituents and operational efficiency. It is important to have certain standards to measure the e-government success since transition from traditional government to e-government remains complicated and difficult (Hu, Xiao, Pang, Xie, 2005).

Services literature has focused on the measurement of perceived quality, satisfaction of complex multi-service organizations (Peters, Janssen & Engers, 2004). Bigné et al., (2003) identified the concepts of perceived quality and satisfactions are two of the fundamental pillars for evaluation for multi-service organization. They mentioned that measurement of perceived quality and satisfaction are more complex in multi-service organizations, where the customer has access to several services. It is necessary to take into consideration the overall perceived quality for measuring the quality of such integrated service. In private sector the bulk of service quality literature tends to originate in the profit-oriented contexts (Collins and Butler, 1995). Based on the variables identified by Parasuraman et al., (1988) which are tangibility, reliability, responsiveness, confidence and empathy, Bigné et al. (2003) used the scale to determine the perceived quality of the core services of hospitals, and universities. Buckley (2003) identified key issues in determining service quality in the public sector. Hazlett and Hill (2003) discussed the current level of government measurement. They mentioned the fact that government's two central aims, one being high quality customer service and the other being value-for money, could potentially be in conflict. In recent years, a number of researchers have focused their studies on the application of marketing and of the concepts of perceived quality and satisfaction to public services and in higher education (Bigné *et al.*, 1997; Kanji and bin Tambi, 1999; and in health Bigné *et al.*, 1997; Eckerlund *et al.*, 2000). The assessment of service quality has been relatively less studied with respect to public services and most studies have focused on mainly two sectors health and education for assessing service quality. It is necessary to explore a different method of service quality evaluation of public services in the light of e-government success measurement (Ray & Rao 2004).

Thus, the purpose of this study is to identify the factors affecting e-government success. Success factors are to be identified through applying service quality constructs which help assess the level of satisfaction of the recipients of such services.

2   Theoretical Background

The main elements of government E-service delivery include: electronic delivery of all appropriate government services; access to information about government services; electronic payment and a government-wide intranet for secure online communication. Web based e-government services can be defined as "the information and services provided to the public on government web sites (Wang et al., 2005). Improving customer satisfaction; development of strong relationship with customers and business partners; and the reduction of the service delivery costs are the main reasons for development of government e-services. For the delivery of government services the main strategy is to design a customer friendly website and to increase the collaboration between the government agencies for share information about the customer (Guo & Raban, 2002).

2.1   Citizen Satisfaction

Government has the prospective to increase citizen satisfaction with government by utilizing the information and communication technology properly, specially the internet. This improved channel of communication ensures the accessibility and completeness of government information and service delivery in a more convenient way. Citizen satisfaction with e-government services is related with citizen's perception about online service convenience (transaction), reliability of the information (transparency) and engaged electronic communication (interactivity) (Welch, Hinnant & Moon, 2004). Kelly & Swindell (2002) defined Service out put as performance measurements and service outcomes as citizen satisfaction.

2.2   Measuring E-Service Quality

E-service quality has been studied less in the public sector (Buckley, 2003). Kaylor et al. (2001) highlight that existing research in the area of e-government focuses more on standards-based scenarios; in other words, an ideal scenario of service delivery. However, they point out that the realities that develop as the solutions are implemented are often different from an ideal situation; they state that looking only at standards does not provide us with enough insight into problems with specific functions and services as they are implemented in municipal Web sites. Based on the variables identified by Parasuraman et al. (1988) tangibility, reliability, responsiveness, confidence, and empathy, Bigné et al. (2003) used the scale to determine the perceived quality of the core services of hospitals and universities. Ray & Rao (2004) identified service quality dimensions regarding a property tax payment system implemented by the municipal corporation of the city of Ahmedabad, Gujarat, India. They classified service quality dimensions into three broad categories. These are, service level expectations, Empowerment, and Anxiety reducing.

Zeithaml et al. (2000) developed e-SERVQUAL for measuring e-service quality. Through focus group interviews, they identified seven dimensions of online service quality: efficiency, reliability, fulfillment, privacy, responsiveness, compensation, and contact. They identified four dimensions, efficiency, reliability, fulfillment, and privacy, to form the core e-SERVQUAL scale that is used to measure customer perceptions of service quality delivered by online retailers. Parasuraman et al. (2005) developed an e-core service quality scale (E-S-QUAL) for examining Web site service quality in which 22 item scales were developed covering four dimensions to measure the service quality delivered by Web sites. These four dimensions are efficiency, fulfillment, system availability, and privacy. Connolly & Bannister (2008) examined the dimensions of Web site service quality in the context of filing tax returns in Ireland using E-S-QUAL. Their study indicates the applicability of the SERVQUAL survey instrument in the context of government e-tax service, and it improved the understanding of the e-government service environment. We have chosen to conduct this study in Sweden since it is one of the leading countries in the Western world that has pro-actively engaged in incorporating e-governance strategies extensively. E-tax services run by Skatteverket is a primary example of such strategies being put in action. In Sweden every year approximately 6.5m paper based version of tax forms are sent out among the Swedish citizen for tax filing purpose. Citizen can file tax through the Internet by using a "soft electronic ID,using a pin and pass word provided by the Tax board. Citizens also can use Tax board's telephone services or via sms. According to the Skatteverket's figures (Skatteverket pressmeddelande, 2009-05-06) over half the citizenry required to pay taxes are choosing to do so online. During the tax year 2008-2009, 3.9 million people filed their tax declarations electronically. This is a 9% increase over the previous year. 1.46 million, or 37% of online tax payers chose usage of a security code when filing taxes through the internet, whereas 24% chose to use a software based "e-legitimation" or electronic ID. This is in contrast to 2006-2007, when the total number of taxpayers who utilized electronic method of tax payment was 3,103,031; out of which 1,657,848 were women, and 1,445,183 were men. Thus, about 45% of the tax paying population used the electronic payment facilities, and 55% used a paper based declaration. The number shows an increase of over half a million users who have started using an electronic method over the previous year.

2.2 The Proposed Model and Research Hypotheses

User satisfaction was identified as a significant measure of information system success (DeLone & McLean 1992) and quality constructs and system used are identified as a critical success factors (Liu & Arnett, 2000). We propose that E-government success can be determined by the citizen satisfaction, perceived service quality and usage of the system.

"E-Service Quality is the extent to which a Web site facilitates efficient and effective shopping, purchasing and delivery of products and services" (Parasuraman et al., 2005). Based on this definition we defined e-government service quality as "the extent to which a website facilitates efficient and effective delivery of public services including information, communication, interaction, contracting and transaction to citizens, business partners, suppliers and those who are working in the government sector. A number of studies identified the determinant of satisfaction. Service quality has been found to be an important input to customer satisfaction (Caruana 2002). Cronin and Taylor (1992) originally hypothesized that satisfaction is an antecedent of service quality, their research with a multi industry sample showed, in a LISREL analysis, an opposite relationship. Service quality appears to be only one of the service factors contributing to customers' satisfaction judgments (Cronin and Taylor, 1992; Ruyter et al., 1997; Spreng and Mackoy, 1996). A number of academics such as Parasuraman et al. (1985, 1988); Grönroos (1984); Johnston (1997) and others have tried to identify key determinants by which a customer assesses service quality and consequently results in satisfaction or not. Roca et al., (2006) have also found the significant relationship between service quality and satisfaction in their study.

DeLone and MacLean (2004) included service quality in their original IS success model and they mentioned that service quality have a direct effect on user satisfaction and use. Use and user satisfaction are inter related with each other. To measure e-commerce system success Molla and Licker (2001) proposed customer satisfaction as a dependent variable and they proposed use has an impact on satisfaction. Researchers often measure breadth of use to measure the degree to which the system is used as a task. From the perspective of a system, breadth refers to the number of features used in the system (Burton-Jones and Straub 2004). Wang et al., (2007) proposed e-learning system success model. In their model they mention six factors that assess e-learing system success. According to their study service quality has a positive effect on use and satisfaction. Usage of the system has an impact on satisfaction and satisfaction has a relation with usage of the system. There are three aspects to e-service quality: user-focused, user satisfaction; outcomes (Buckley 2003).

Based on this discussion the following hypotheses have been formulated:

H1: *Government e-service quality is positively related to user/citizen satisfaction.*
H2: *Government e-service quality is positively related to actual usage*
H3: *Actual usage is positively related to user/citizen satisfaction.*

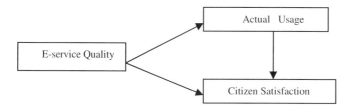

Fig. 1. Proposed model for the study

3 Empirical Methodology

The data used to in this study were collected form Sweden. The questionnaire used in the survey was pre-tested prior to data collection. An online survey using a web based questionnaire with both Swedish and English versions was conducted using systematic sampling among the municipalities in Sweden. 425 valid responses were received. Criteria for selecting these respondent was familiarity with using the Swedish online tax payment system and familiar with the tax web site for getting different services, such as information search, filing tax return, registration etc. Efficiency, privacy, responsiveness and web assistance were selected as e-service quality dimension. All the items to measure these dimensions were selected from the previous research done by Zeithaml, Parasuraman, and Malhotra (2000, 2002, 2005); Xie, Tan & Li (2002); Collier and Bienstock (2006).

Actual usages were measured by three items- Frequency of usage, Diversity of usages and Dependency. All the item were selected from previous studies done by Thompson, Higgins & Howell (1991); Wang, Wang & Shee (2007); Rai, Lang & Welker (2002); Goodhue & Thompson (1995). Five items were selected for measuring citizen satisfaction were derived from study conducted by Cronin, Brady & Hult (2000); Luarn & Lin (2003); Roca, Chiu & Martinez (2006).

4 Data Analysis

In order to establish the internal consistency of the measurement instruments, reliability analysis was conducted by calculating coefficient alpha, also known as Cronbach's alpha to measure the internal consistency of the measurement scale. All the items are found to be reliable since the values are above the recommended level of 0.7. Cronbach's alpha of the scales Efficiency (.909) and satisfaction (.959) showed excellent internal consistency. Other three items- Web assistance (.873), privacy (.835) showed very good internal consistency of the scales. Coefficient alpha of Actual Usage (.756) and Responsiveness (.770) showed good internal consistency of the items. In order to further examine the factor structure of the 29- item instruments exploratory factor analysis was conducted. The factor loading of the item responsiveness 1 is low and less than 0.5, it was removed from the list to measure e-service quality. Other two success factors: citizen satisfaction and actual use are clearly defined with high loading.

4.1 Confirmatory Factor Analysis (CFA) to Confirm the Factor Structure

Based on hypothesis testing, CFA is used to find out to which degree the different assumed variables measure a certain factor.

According to Janssens (2008) all the latent variable measures must have a high loading (>.50) and must me significant (critical ratio= C.R. = t-value> 1.96). In Table 1, it shows that all of the unstandardized loadings (regression weights) differ significantly from zero. In the critical ratio column, all the values are over 1.96. Except one item priv 2 all the loadings are acceptable since all these are more than .50. In order to improve the model fit, item priv 2 was removed.

Table 1. E-Service quality constructs

Structural relation	Regression weight	Standard error	Critical ratio	Standardized regression weights	squared multiple correlation
Eff ← eSQ	1.000			.718	.515
Res ← eSQ	.902	.100	9.021	.763	.582
Wass ← eSQ	1.056	.106	9.971	.829	.687
Priv ← eSQ	.291	.088	3.311	.198	.039
Eff3 ← eff	1.000			.855	.731
Eff2 ← eff	1.069	.048	22.334	.885	.783
Eff1 ← eff	1.117	.053	21.256	.849	.720
Res4 ← res	1.000			.666	.443
Res3 ← res	1.148	.079	14.553	.884	.781
Res2 ← res	1.062	.075	14.220	.828	.685
Wass2 ← wass	1.000			.870	.756
Wass1 ← wass	1.110	.062	17.971	.887	.787
Priv4 ← priv	1.000			.808	857
Priv3 ← priv	1.118	.068	16.359	.926	857
Priv1 ← priv	.728	.052	13.998	.656	.430
Chi-square = 87.473, p = .000					
Model	RMSEA	CMIN/DF	GFI	AGFI	CFI	TLI	IFI
Default model	.053	2.187	.964	.940	.982	.975	.982
Saturated model			1.000		1.000		1.000
Independence model	.334	48.271	.381	.257	.000	.000	.000

There are different criteria to determine the overall fit of the models. The goodness of fit index (GFI) should be greater than .90 and the adjusted goodness of fit index (AGFI) preferably greater than .80. In this case GFI is .964 and AGFI .940 which means both values are greater than cut-off point. Two reliable indicators are the Tucker-Lewis Index (TLI) and Comparative fit index (CFI) which should preferably be greater than .90. In this case TLI and CFI are .975 and .982 which is more than acceptable level. The RMSEA value is .053 which indicates a good fit. Hu and Bentler (1999) place the cut-off value at .06, whereas Browne and Cudeck (1993) assert that values less than or equal to .05 indicate a good fit and values up to .08 indicate an acceptable fit.

Table 2. Satisfaction constructs

Structural relation	Regression weight	Standard error	Critical ratio	Standardized regression weights	squared multiple correlation
scsat2 ← Csat	1.000			.830	.689
Scsat3 ← Csat	1.121	.042	26.479	.948	.899
Scsat4 ← Csat	1.021	.043	23.701	.890	.792
Scsat5 ← Csat	1.087	.042	26.141	.941	.886
Chi-square = 9.653, p = .008					
Model	RMSEA	CMIN/DF	GFI	AGFI	CFI	TLI	IFI
Default model	.095	4.827	.989	.947	.996	.987	.996
Saturated model			1.000		1.000		1.000
Independence model	.821	287.111	.334	-.111	.000	.000	.000

All standardized regression weight values are high, at over .70, and the critical ratios are over 1.96. Goodness of fit index (GFI) value is .989, and average goodness of fit index (AGFI) is .947. Both values indicate very good model fit. The CFI (.996), TLI (.987), and IFI (.996) also indicate good model fit. The RMSEA (.095) and CMIN/DF (4.827) values are acceptable.

Table 3. Model specification and hypothesis testing

Structural relation	Regression weight	Standard error	Critical ratio	Standardized regression weights	squared multiple correlation
AU←eSQ	1.666	.549	3.031	.314	.098
Eff←eSQ	3.292	.903	3.646	.755	.571
Priv←eSQ	1.000			.217	.047
Res←eSQ	2.767	.772	3.583	.753	.567
Wass←eSQ	3.153	.865	3.647	.795	.632
Csat←eSQ	1.852	.551	3.360	.374	.426
Csat←AU	.401	.051	7.840	.430	
Eff3←Eff	1.000			.853	.728
Eff2←Eff	1.068	.048	22.311	.883	.779
Eff1←Eff	1.124	.053	21.384	.852	.726
Priv4←Priv	1.000			.809	.655
Priv3←Priv	1.113	.068	16.434	.924	.853
Priv1←Priv	.728	.052	14.021	.657	.432
Res4←Res	1.000			.660	.436
Res3←Res	1.158	.080	14.431	.885	.783
Res2←Res	1.074	.076	14.125	.831	.690
Wass2←Wass	1.000			.865	.748
Wass1←Wass	1.122	.063	17.840	.892	.795
Au1←Au	1.000			825	.680
Au2←Au	.791	.067	11.788	.692	.479
Au3←Au	.753	.070	10.829	.611	.373
Csat5←Csat	.928	.035	26.439	.938	.881
Csat4←Csat	1.033	.027	38.504	.891	.795
Csat3←Csat	.943	.030	31.526	.948	.898
Csat2←Csat	1.000			.836	.698
Chi-square = 423.212 , p = .000					

Model	RMSEA	CMIN/DF	GFI	AGFI	CFI	TLI	IFI
Default model	.074	3.306	.907	.875	.942	.930	.942
Saturated model			1.000		1.000		1.000
Independence model	.279	34.031	.311	.230	.000	.000	.000

Model fit indicates a good fit. GFI is .907 which is good and greater than cut-off point and AGFI .875 which is also acceptable. Two reliable indicators are the Tucker-Lewis Index (TLI) and Comparative fit index (CFI) which should preferably be greater than .90. In this case TLI and CFI are .930 and .942 which is more than acceptable level. The RMSEA value is .074 which indicates acceptable fit. From the analysis, we can see that 43% of the variance among the factors of e-service quality, and usage is explained by citizen satisfaction. E-service quality is positively and significantly related to citizen satisfaction, with a path estimate of .37, critical ratio of 3.360, and significance at less than a p < 0,001 level. Therefore, the hypothesis is supported. The relationship between e-service quality and use is found to be significant, with the path value of .314 and a critical ratio of 3.031. Thus, the hypothesis is accepted. Use is positively and significantly related to citizen satisfaction at significance level less than <0.001, with a path value .43, and a critical ratio is 7.840. Therefore the hypothesis is supported. From the structural equation analysis, we found that all the hypothesized relationships are supported by the empirical data.

5 Discussion and Implications

The aim of the present study is to identify success factors for e-service delivery. For doing that we used e-service quality and use as an antecedent of citizen satisfaction. Based on result of empirical analysis all three hypotheses have been accepted.

In this study, Citizen Satisfaction was considered as an indicator of success of government e-tax service delivery, the assumption being that if citizens are satisfied with using this service, then that implies the service is successful. From the analysis of data, it was found that the variance explained by factors leading to citizen satisfaction is 43%. Previous studies considered user satisfaction as a success measure in information system success, e-commerce success, and Web site success (DeLone & McLean, 1992, 2004; Seddon and Kiew, 1996; Rai, 2002; Crowston et al., 2006).

We found e-service quality has a relation with citizen satisfaction considering four dimensions of service quality. Previous literature also suggested that Service quality is important antecedent to user satisfaction (Kettinger and Lee, 1994, 1997; Pitt et al., 1995; Caruana, 2002; Cronin and Taylor, 1992; Grönroos, 1984; Johnston, 1997).These four dimensions are efficiency, privacy, responsiveness and web assistance That means citizens consider these as important factors when they are using government e-services. Efficiency, responsiveness and web assistance are more important compared to privacy in determining e-service quality. Citizens are more concerned about how effectively and efficiently they can use this kind of website, what kind of support they can receive when they are filing their tax return. Privacy dimension was not found to be a very important. A reason behind this could be since this is a government website, the citizen believes that a government organization will maintain citizens' privacy and will not abuse citizen information for any commercial purposes, as might be the case for an industrial or commercial organization. According to the DeLone McLean IS success model, use is an important dimension of success and we also found evidence of it from our empirical data analysis. According to the analysis of empirical data we found the relationship between usage and satisfaction. That means increase usage of the system will also increase the level of citizen satisfaction.

The first and foremost contribution of this study is identifying success factors of government e-service delivery that is developed in the context of the e-tax filing system in Sweden. Secondly, the result indicates that information system (IS), e-commerce, and marketing theory are applicable in the government to citizen (G2C) area; more specifically, government e-tax service delivery.

These findings have led this research to stress the need to focus on the factors that work behind the scenes in the satisfactory provisioning of this service to citizens as well as the need and means for measuring such satisfaction. Along with the theoretical contributions, there are some practical implications of the research findings. It is important for the practitioner such as tax authorities and other government organizations that are involved with the delivery of e-services, to be aware of the factors that contribute towards the future maintenance of the quality of the e-government services. The results can help the tax authority to identify the key quality criteria for the e-tax service web sites that are valued by citizens. The results will also help the tax authority to understand the key issues that influence citizens' needs and level of satisfaction with this service.

6 Limitations and Suggestions for Future Research

Based on our empirical analysis we found satisfaction to be an important factor for success and satisfaction is determined by service quality and uses of the services. But results also indicate that there are additional factors that determine satisfaction since variance explained by factors leading to citizen satisfaction is 43%. The study only included service quality; further study can explore other quality dimensions- system quality, information quality and other success factors. Tax payment was the study context, but other studies can be done in the context of other web based government services like e-health, renewing driver's license, voting on the Internet etc.

References

Bigné, E., Moliner, M.A., Sánchez, J.: Perceived quality and satisfaction in multiservice organisations: the case of Spanish public services. Journal of Services Marketing 17(4), 420–442 (2003)

Blakeley, C.J., Matsuura, J.H.: E-government: An engine to power e-commerce development. In: Proceedings of the 2nd European conference on e-government, Dublin, Ireland, pp. 39–48 (2001)

Booze Allen Hamilton consulting report on world-wide best practice in e-government, commissioned by the UK Cabinet Office (2005)

Buckley, J.: E-service quality and the public sector. Managing Service Quality 13(6), 453–462 (2003)

Burton-Jones, A., Straub, D.W.: Reconceptualizing System Usage: An Approach and Empirical Test. Information Systems Research 17(3), 228–246 (2006)

Caruana, A.: Service Loyalty-The effects of service quality and the mediating role of customer satisfaction. European Journal of Marketing 36(7/8), 811–828 (2002)

Centeno, C., Van Bavel, R., Burgelman, J.C.: A Prospective View of e-Government in the European Union. The Electronic Journal of e-Government 3(2), 59–66 (2005)

Collier, J.E., Bienstock, C.C.: Measuring Service Quality in E-Retailing. Journal of Service Research 8, 260 (2006)

Connolly, R., Bannister, F.: eTax Filing & Service Quality: The Case of the Revenue Online Service. In: Proceedings of World Academy of Science, Engineering and Technology, April 2008, vol. 28 (2008) ISSN: 1307-6884

Cronin, J.J., Brady, M.K., Hult, T.M.: Assessing the Effects of Quality, Value, and Customer Satisfaction on Consumer Behavioral Intentions in Service Environments. Journal of Retailing 76(2), 193–218 (2000) ISSN: 0022-4359

Cronin, J.J., Taylor, S.A.: Measuring service quality: a re-examination and extension. Journal of Marketing 56(3), 55–69 (1992)

Crowston, K., Howison, J., Annabi, H.: Information systems success in free and open source software development: Theory and measures. Software Process: Improvement and Practice (Special Issue on Free/Open Source Software Processes) (in press)

DeLone, W.H., McLean, E.R.: Measuring e-Commerce Success: Applying the DeLone & McLean Information Systems Success Model. International Journal of Electronic Commerce 9(1), 31–47 (2004)

DeLone, W.H., McLean, E.R.: Information system Success: The quest for dependent variable. Information system research 3(1) (1992)

Eckerlund, I., Eklöf, J.A., Nathorst-Böös, J.: Patient satisfaction and priority setting in ambulatory health care. Total Quality Management 11(7), 967–978 (2000)

Goodhue, D.L., Thompson, R.L.: Task-Technology Fit and Individual Performance. MIS Quarterly 19(2), 213–236 (1995)

Grönroos, C.: A service quality model and its market implications. European Journal of Marketing 18(4), 36–44 (1984)

Guo, X., Lu, J., Raban, R.: An Assessment of the Characteristics of Australian Government E-service Websites. Collaborative Electronic Commerce Technology and Research (2002)

Hair, J.F., Babin, B., Money, A.H., Samouel, P.: Essentials of Business Research. John Wiley & Sons, Inc., Chichester (2007)

Hazlett, S.A., Hill, F.: E-government: the realities of using IT to transform the public sector. Managing Service Quality 13(6), 445–452 (2003)

Janssens, W., Wijnen, K., Pelsmacker, P.D., Kenhove, P.V.: Marketing Research with SPSS. Prentice-Hall, Englewood Cliffs (2008)

Johnston, R.: Identifying the critical determinant of service quality in retail banking: importance and effect. International Journal of bank marketing 15(4), 111–116 (1997)

Kanji, G.K., A. bin Tambi, A.M.: Total quality management in UK higher education institutions. Total Quality Management 10(1), 129–153 (1999)

Kaylor, C., Deshazo, R., Van Eck, D.: Gauging e-government: a report on implementing services among American cities. Government Information Quarterly 18, 293–307 (2001)

Kelly, J.M., Swindell, D.: Service Quality Variable Across Urban Apace: First Steps Toward a Model of Citizen Satisfaction. Journal of urban affairs 24(3), 271–288 (2002)

Kettinger, W.J., Lee, C.C.: Perceived service quality and user satisfaction with the information services function. Decision Sciences 25(5/6), 737–766 (1994)

Lihua, W., Zheng, Q.: Internet use and e-government performance: a conceptual Model. In: Ninth Pacific Asia Conference on Information Systems, PACIS, Bangkok, Thailand (2005)

Li, Y.N., Tan, K.C., Xie, M.: Measuring web-based service quality. Total Quality Management 13(5), 685–700 (2002)

Liu, C., Arnett, K.P.: Exploring the Factors Associated with Website Success in the Context of Electronic Commerce. Information & Management 38, 23–33 (2000)

Luarn, P., Lin, H.: A customer loyalty model for e-service context. Journal of Electronic Commerce Research 4(4) (2003)

Molla, A., Licker, P.S.: E-Commerce system success: An attempt to extend and respecify the DeLone & McLean model of IS success. Journal of Electronic Commerce Research 2(4) (2001)

Parasuraman, A., Berry, L.L., Zeithaml, V.A.: Refinement and Reassessment of the SERVQUAL Scale. Journal of Retailing 67(4), 420–450 (1991)

Parasuraman, A., Zeithaml, V.A., Malhotra, A.: E-S-QUAL: A Multiple-Item Scale for Assessing Electronic Service Quality. Journal of Service Research 7(3), 213–233 (2005)

Parasuraman, A., Zeithaml, V.A., Berry, L.L.: SERVQUAL: a multiple item scale for measuring consumer perceptions of service quality. Journal of Retailing 64, 12–40 (Spring 1988)

Peters, R.M., Janssen, M., Van Engers, T.M.: Measuring e-Government Impact: Existing practices and shortcomings. In: ICEC'04, sixth International Conference on Electronic Commerce (2004)

Pitt, L.F., Watson, R.T., Kavan, C.B.: Service Quality: A measure of information systems effectiveness. MIS Quarterly (June 1995)

Rai, A., Lang, S.S., Welker, R.B.: Assessing the Validity of IS Success Models: An Empirical Test and Theoretical Analysis. Information Systems Research 13(1), 50–69 (2002)

Ray, S., Rao, V.: Evaluating Government Service: A customers' Perspective of e-Government. In: Proceedings of the 4th European Conference on E-Government, Dublin, Ireland, June 17-18 (2004)

Roca, C.J., Chiu, C.-M., Martinez, F.J.: Understanding e-learning continuance intention: An extension of the Technology Acceptance Model. International Journal of Human-Computer Studies 64, 683–696 (2006)

Ruyter, K.D., Bloemer, J., Peeters, P.: Merging service quality and service satisfaction. An empirical test of an integrative model. Journal of Economic Psychology 18(4), 387–406 (1997)

Seddon, P.B.: A Respecification and Extension of the DeLone and Mclean Model of IS Success. Information System Research 8(3) (1997)

Seddon, P.B., Kiew, M.Y.: A partial test and development of Delone and Mclean's model of is success. Australian Journal of Information system (AJIS) 4(2) (1996)

Spreng, R.A., Mackoy, R.: An empirical examination of a model of perceived service quality and satisfaction. Journal of Retailing 72(2), 201–214 (1996)

Thompson, R.L., Higgins, C.A., Howell, J.M.: Towards a Conceptual Model of Utilization. MIS Quarterly 15(1), 125–143 (1991)

Wang, Y.S., Wang, H.Y., Shee, D.Y.: Measuring e-learning systems success in an organizational context: Scale development and validation. Computers in Human Behavior 23, 1792–1808 (2007)

Wang, L., Bretschneider, S., Gant, J.: Evaluating Web-based e government services with a citizen-centric approach. In: Proceedings of the 38th Hawaii International Conference on System Sciences 2005 (2005)

Welch, E.W., Hinnant, C.C., Moon, J.M.: Linking Citizen Satisfaction with E-Government and Trust in Government. Journal of Public Administration Research and Theory 15(3) (2004)

Hu, Y., Xiao, J., Pang, J., Xie, K.: A research on the framework of e-government project success. In: Seventh international conference on electronic commerce, ICEC, Xian, China (2005)

Zeithaml, V.A., Parasuraman, A., Malhotra, A.: A Conceptual Framework for Understanding e-Service Quality: Implications for Future Research and Managerial Practice: Working paper, Marketing Science Institute, Report Number 00-115, Cambridge, MA (2000)

Zeithaml, V.A., Parasuraman, A., Malhotra, A.: Service quality delivery through web sites: a critical review of extant knowledge. Journal of the academy of marketing science 30(4) (2002)

Emerging Barriers in E-Government Implementation

Spyros Angelopoulos[1], Fotis Kitsios[2], Petros Kofakis[3], and Thanos Papadopoulos[4]

[1] Information Systems and Management Group, Warwick Business School,
The University of Warwick, Coventry, CV4 7AL, UK
spyros.angelopoulos.09@mail.wbs.ac.uk
[2] Department of Technology Management, University of Macedonia,
Loggou-Tourpali, 59200 Naousa, Greece
kitsios@uom.gr
[3] KP Research & Consultancy, P.O. Box 3138, 10210 Athens, Greece
kofakis@gmail.com
[4] Knowledge and Information Systems Management Group, Centre for Operational Research,
Management Science and Information Systems (CORMSIS), School of Management,
University of Southampton, SO17 1BJ Southampton, UK
a.papadopoulos@soton.ac.uk

Abstract. This study presents the outcomes of a qualitative case study of implementing e-government Information Systems within the national digital strategy in a governmental organisation, following action research. The results show that although e-government is a socio-technical process and has to accommodate the views of all stakeholders, this is questioned in practice. No matter if e-government needs to be a tool for decentralisation and democratisation, this scope may be rendered futile due to the fundamental role of the political support required to secure future funds for implementation. While focusing on the changes in business processes that have to be considered by governmental institutions to successfully implement e-government, the need for a holistic model, which can embrace the back- and front- office, and be linked to the real citizens' needs, arises.

Keywords: e-government, public sector organisation, digital strategy.

1 Introduction

E-government is a phenomenon of an era that e-business is becoming vital in both the private sector and in the governmental institutions. It utilises Information and Communication Technologies (ICT) in order to accomplish reform by fostering transparency, eliminating distance as well as other divides, and empowering people to participate in the political processes that affect their lives. Hence, it is regarded as a fundamental enabler of greater citizen involvement in civic and democratic matters in the sense of direct democracy as the one practiced in the city-states of ancient Greece [2].

The use of ICT as a tool for change in the structures and processes of governmental organizations and the subsequent attempt to enable the exchange of information

M.A. Wimmer et al. (Eds.): EGOV 2010, LNCS 6228, pp. 216–225, 2010.

amongst citizens, businesses and government may result in improved efficiency, convenience as well as better accessibility of public services. Ubiquity postulates the omnipresence of networking; an unbounded and universal network [3]. Therefore, ample and ubiquitous access to ICT is essential for uniform and consistent diffusion of innovation. This, however, can only be implemented through the sharing of ICT resources across governments and their citizens. Hence, the implementation of e-government as a means for facilitating information and knowledge exchange amongst all the aforementioned stakeholders remains a challenge.

The structure of the paper is as follows: after a discussion of the barriers of the e-government concept, the paper explicates the methodological and conceptual rectifications utilised to address the issue of under-specification in the e-government literature. A case study was followed in a Governmental Organization (GO)[1] to enhance the understanding of e-government policy processes and actors and correlate e-government to mainstream public administration research. The implementation of Information Technology (IT) projects in the public sector involves multiple stakeholders, such as administrators, policy-makers and the end-users. Defining the intentions and responsibilities of different stakeholders within a national digital strategy can become a really difficult task and differences in their agendas may eventually render the project futile. The uniqueness of the case study lies in studying and discussing issues related to e-government implementation at the highest decision level. The last section discusses these issues and concludes the paper.

2   Barriers in E-Government Implementation

Research in the past has investigated issues in respect to the implementation of e-government using diffusion models. For instance, by using Diffusion Theory [25], studies have focused on the adoption of IT in the public sector [5], [14], [22], [23] suggesting *inter alia*, that the size of administration and professionalism are the primary determinants of the adoption of computer technology. Rogers [25] presents five categories of determining variables for the rate of adoption: perceived attributes of the innovation, type of innovation decision, communication channels, nature of the social system and extent of the change agent's promotion efforts. Choudrie and Lee [9] found that the use of broadband connection within government departments and agencies improved the QoS and encouraged previously bureaucratic organisations to re-engineer the way services are delivered to citizens. However, no single diffusion model best explains all cases [22].

The Information Systems (IS) Success Model [11] and the Technology Acceptance Model (TAM) [10] suggests another means to study the implementation of e-government by measuring perceived usefulness and perceived ease of use influence one's attitude towards system usage. The success factors presented in TAM have to do mainly with the acceptance of organisational software, but have been tested for various users and types of systems [30] [31], and user adoption of e-commerce [15], [21]. However, TAM constructs represent the subjective user assessments of a system and may not be representative of its objective acceptance [6].

---

[1] The name of the Organization is not revealed for confidentiality reasons.

Barriers, however, to the success of IS and e-government concern, for instance, the high cost or the low security of the needed infrastructure and can impede its implementation and adoption. The integration of various IT applications and components inside and outside the organisational boundary remains costly and time-consuming due to the heterogeneity of the computing environments involved in public-sector organisations [26]. Literature (e.g. [4], [12]) agrees that governments face a shortage of technical infrastructure. This shortage presents a significant barrier in the development of the capabilities of government organisations to provide online services and transactions.

A frequently cited barrier in the literature seems to be the need for security and privacy in an e-government strategy [15]. The shortage of IT skills is also a barrier, which contends many challenges regarding the efficiency of a public administration to provide innovative e-government services [8], [18]. Finally, a major barrier to the adoption and implementation of e-government is funding [18], which also relates to the business procedure of government, management strategy and organisational culture [19].

Organisational barriers relate to structural issues such as fragmentation, poor relations and communication between the functional departments, and an acceptance of the strategic benefits of new initiatives by the senior management (e.g. [1]). Nevertheless, despite the existing literature on the implementation of e-government, there is a need for more research to be conducted. Scholars of the discourse have not shed enough light on the development of new services in e-government [2]. Various initiatives investigate the application of quality management principles to the delivery of public e-services [17], but manifold problems related to their quality still exist [13].

The relevant literature is limited on studying the outcomes of projects and hence the political processes underlying e-government development [32]. The major issue is the definition of procedures and data that need to be exchanged at different phases of the process. If these procedures are well defined, then ICT could be applied successfully; and *vice-versa*, the application of ICT reinforces the use of good practices and standardisation of the e-government implementation process. Therefore, amongst the major questions is to grasp the meaning of e-government and uncover the problems that can emerge during the implementation of a project. To answer this, the authors set out to investigate a case study in GO. Before embarking on the discussion of the case, in the next section the research methodology is explicated.

3 Research Methodology

To deal with the research question as outlined in the previous section, this study followed a qualitative case study strategy. Semi-structured interviews were scheduled with the system users, the managers and the governmental leadership of the GO. Thirty interviews were conducted, recorded and transcribed verbatim. The duration of the interviews was about forty-five minutes on average. The themes covered the implementation strategy of e-government and also questions regarding the meaning of e-government for each of the interviewees, the agency and citizens. Action research was chosen as the method for the study [7].

Data analysis involved three activities, namely data reduction, data display, and conclusion drawing and verification [20]. Initial codes were assigned to the transcripts based on description; interpretive codes were assigned, later transformed refined into pattern codes (*ibid*). Themes and patterns emerged and were further refined in the process.

4   Implementing E-Government Project

The decision for the implementation of e-government within the GO was taken when the need for a more efficient and effective way of implementing directives and policies occurred. The constant increase in paper documents describing activities and actions to be taken and the time wasted in locating these documents; in addition to further external information needed from other governmental organisations along with internal information from various departments, led to this decision. Before that, the life cycle of a certain issue could begin from a particular document that would be forwarded to specific persons or services for 'execution'. Any immediate action would result in a new document. The completion of all these actions would lead to the objective, which described a final document.

However, one of the most intriguing aspects of the project was the fact that it entailed various stakeholders from various departments. End-users, managers and the board of directors were to be involved. They all had different agendas as well as different timetables, and thus the system had to accommodate their different views. Hence, the complete definition and formal analysis of the existing situation, the priorities, the workflow, the tracing and control of all the activities and procedures were challenges in the study.

The implementation team, consisted of inter-organisational consultants and academic researchers, set out to record the end-user requirements. They had to deliver a definition of the system documents and describe the workflow states specific to the board of directors. The system would ensure the tracking and control of all respective issues and activities. Selected users should be trained in the use of the system, and IT experts would support them.

The analysis showed that six types of activities need to be considered, and in particular those regarding procedures and activities analysis and related to the creation of subject matter, data structures and information; activities regarding the collection and preparation (data entry) or data in the system; those that had to do with the infrastructure of the project, as well as those with application development and the integration of IS. Finally, the last part of the implementation process included the training of all the end-users.

5   An Overview of the IS from a Technical Perspective

The development of the IS was a demanding application in the fields of information collection and processing. Due to time and budget constraints it was decided to use open standards, which would allow the interoperability of the application and dependent services. There are several benefits embedded in the use of open-source systems and the most important is that they are developed with the use of non-proprietary tools. Working in such environments would eliminate the danger of 'lock-in' with specific vendors or software packages. The code of open-source systems could be obtained for free and any commercial support associated with the product would be typically comparable or cheaper than other solutions available in the market. Furthermore, active communities of developers support the open-source solutions. The combination of open platforms and simplicity of customization made integrating open-source content management systems (CMS) with other software considerably easier. Last but not least, most open-source solutions also make use of newer technology [24] with all positive or negative consequences that this may imply.

In the specific project, the requirements and the restrictions set for such an application included an open architecture independent from proprietary systems, which would include capabilities of constant development, update, and extension. The need for the cost to be kept at low levels, since external governmental funding had not been secured and it was only through non-finite internal funding channels that the project could be based on. The system had to be user-friendly and to have a unified, platform-independent user interface. Ubiquitous, easy and direct access to the system without any geographical limitations was the final objective.

The solution made use of distributed systems and intranet. In other words, a Web Server was installed as a central access point for all functions. The basic components of the system therefore were the Web Server, Document Management and Retrieval System, Database server, Project Management System, and a Workflow Management System. Additionally, from the discussion with the end-users, their requirements included a graphical representation of the achievement of the objectives, the progress of all issues and activities as well as resource information; features that would enable them to set activities, actions, duties and timetables for members of the organisation as well as to review activities or actions, request and receive reports from involved parties, analyse and check different scenarios for timetable comparison, and allocate human and financial resources. Finally, the system should set new activities or issues and distribute them to the involved parties or authorities. As part of the system implementation, this study continues with the description of two examples of the use of the system, which reflect real-world case studies of the organisation.

5.1 Workflow Example 1: Research Institute Foundation

Among the several responsibilities that rely on the duties of GO is the process of National Research Institute Foundation. Therefore, the first example needs to deal with the required workflow for such a task to be properly completed within the new system. Twenty-one steps, all of them inextricably tied on the process, part the process of foundation. All steps are listed bellow followed by a visual representation of the workflow. The authors feel that the chosen simple and visual way of presenting the framework serves best the study as a whole (Figure 1).

5.2 Workflow Example 2: Legislation Process

Processing of new laws is one of the major duties of GO. Legislation processes are marked by original and ongoing negotiations, which tend to be critical to the definition of the political community as well as the development and operation of the

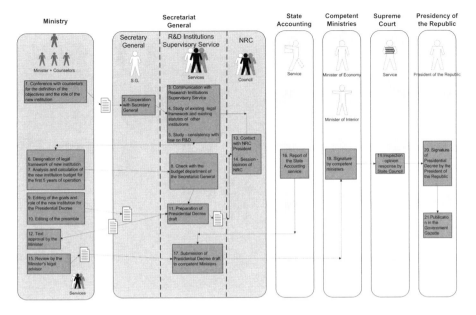

Fig. 1. Workflow of Research Institute foundation case study

constitution, requiring habits of dialogue and compromise [19]. There is often no closure to the constitution-making process [29] and in this context the participation of citizens plays a centric role. Countries with decentralized power tend to be less corrupted [28] and that is the main reason why several developed countries around the world have marked the end of an era and the beginning of new one, under the hegemony of new social forces [19]. Democracy implies the existence of a political community, and as such constitutions followed social forces that promoted democracy; they did not create them from scratch. Therefore, the second example needs to deal with the required workflow for a new law to be properly implemented. Fifteen steps, all of them inextricably tied on the legislation process, part the procedure. All steps are listed bellow followed by a visual representation of the workflow. The visual presentation of the framework enhances this study as a whole (Figure 2).

The implementation took place considering the aforementioned steps after consultation with the users of the system. The steps were to be followed after the system was finally implemented. The aim of the system was to save time and money in three ways: firstly, decisions would be taken on the spot and sent electronically to the corresponding stakeholders; any modifications would be sent immediately for 'execution'; and thirdly, since every decision would be kept electronically, savings would occur in terms of paper use, as well as the GO would eventually go 'greener'.

However, despite the aim of the board of directors and the implementation team to have everything in place, two unexpected events took place, which postponed the implementation. The first had to do with the different agendas of stakeholders that came to the foreground, soon after the system was designed. Senior managers perceived IS/IT in the public sector not as a tool for democratisation and decentralisation but rather as a utility, and their influence was reflected on the budget

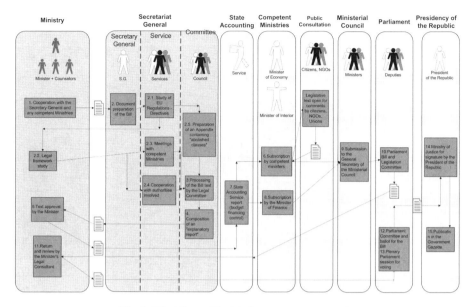

Fig. 2. Workflow of legislation process case study

of the project, where the cost for implementation was dramatically reduced. Moreover, the end-users treated the IS as a potential enemy which could effectively change their way for completing their tasks. Their different agenda compared to the agenda of the board and the governmental leader of GO and the futile attempts to reach consensus brought the project to a permanent standstill. Furthermore, the involved stakeholders had different workloads; this acted as a hindrance mechanism to the implementation. It was really difficult to take them away from their everyday duties and train them to adapt to the new system. The second event was also an outcome of the period in which the implementation took place. Shortly after the user requirements and the implementation process started, the tenure of the governmental lead came to an end and any attempt to reform the GO was cancelled.

6   Discussion and Conclusion

E-government is considered to be one of the key contributors to the development of an information society and governments around the world have seen its rapid evolution when there is an integrated approach to planning and implementation of public sector reform. However, the application of ICT in e-government should not be considered as an end in itself. The case study has shown that even if there is political will to implement e-government, the different stakeholder agendas may render it futile. This study has not focused on the role of the heterogeneity of the computer environments involved in public-sector organisations [27], and suggested that e-government is not simply the use of IT for delivering services to the citizens; instead, the turbulent political environment in which e-government needs to operate plays an important role.

The success of e-government is dependent on the deeper recognition of complex political and institutional environments in which it is going to operate [32]. Indeed, this was evident in the case from the fact that when the tenure of the governmental lead came to an end, the project was cancelled. It was not, thus, dependent on IT skills [18] or specific software since open source products were chosen. It was, however, dependent on funding (*ibid*) –related to organisational culture [19]– which stopped after the political support was removed. Hence, to secure the success of future e-government projects, funding may not be directly related to political support. Projects that are important for improving the efficiency of decision-making and improvements in everyday working practices would be implemented, irrespectively of any changes in the political / governmental leadership.

Additionally, this study makes a case for the changing agendas of the participating stakeholders. In particular, the initial support of the stakeholders, replaced in the later stages of the project due to changes in their working practices indicates that the managerial concern needs to be focused not only on the acceptance of the strategic benefits of new initiatives by the senior management [1], but also by end users, since the investment aims at modernising the organization at all levels [16].

As an addition to the current status of e-government, future work needs to answer the dilemma whether e-government is really a tool for decentralization and democratization or the result of a socio-technical process towards a new model of public administration; an answer will boost the evolution of e-government and provide citizens with effective access to better quality services. Finally, one of the basic concerns is business process management in governmental institutions to successfully implement e-government principles. Therefore, future research needs to focus on a holistic model, which can embrace the back- and front-office, and be linked to the real citizens' needs.

References

1. Aichholzer, G., Schmutzer, R.: Organisational challenges to the development of electronic government. In: 11th International Workshop on Database and Expert Systems Applications. IEEE Computer Society, Los Alamitos (2000)
2. Angelopoulos, S., Kitsios, F., Papadopoulos, T.: Identifying Critical Success Factors in e-Government: A New service development approach. Transforming Government: People, Process and Policy 4(1), 95–118 (2010)
3. Angelopoulos, S., Kitsios, F., Babulak, E.: From e to u: Towards an innovative digital era. In: Kotsopoulos, S., Ioannou, K. (eds.) Heterogeneous Next Generation Networking: Innovations and Platform, pp. 427–444 (2008)
4. Bourn, J.: Better Public Services Through E-Government. The National Audit Office, London (2002)
5. Brudney, J., Selden, S.: The adoption of innovation by smaller local governments: the case of computer technology. American Review of Public Administration 25, 71–86 (1995)
6. Carter, L., Belanger, F.: The utilization of e-government services: citizen trust, innovation and acceptance factors. Information Systems Journal 15, 5–25 (2005)
7. Checkland, P.: Systems Thinking, Systems Practice. Wiley, Chichester (1981)

8. Chen, Y., Gant, J.: Transforming local e-government services: the use of application service providers. Government Information Quarterly 18(4), 343–355 (2001)

9. Choudrie, J., Lee, H.: Broadband development in South Korea: institutional and cultural factor. European Journal of Information Systems 13(2), 103–114 (2004)

10. Davis, F.: Perceived usefulness, perceived ease of use and user acceptance of information technology. MIS Quarterly 13, 319–340 (1989)

11. DeLone, W.H., McLean, E.R.: Information systems success: The quest for the dependent variable. Information Systems Research 3(1), 60–95 (1992)

12. Dillon, J., Pelgrin, W.: E-Government/Commerce in New York State, Office of Technology, New York, NY (2002)

13. EU DG Information Society.: Top of the Web: user satisfaction and usage survey of e-government services, DG Information Society, European Commission (2004),
    `http://www.eprocnet.gov.ie/other-documents/`
    `topofthewebsurveyresults.pdf/`

14. Elliman, T., Irani, Z., Love, P.E.D., Jones, S., Themistocleous, M.: Evaluating e-government: Learning from the Experiences of Two UK Local Authorities. Information Systems Journal, special issue on e-Government 15, 61–82 (2005)

15. Gefen, D., Pavlou, P.A., Warkentin, M., Rose, G.M.: EGovernment Adoption. In: The Proceedings of the Eighth Americas Conference on Information Systems (2002)

16. Hackney, R., Jones, S., Irani, Z.: eGovernment Information Systems Evaluation: Conceptualising 'Customer Engagement'. In: eGovernment Workshop, eGOV'05 (2005)

17. Halaris, C., Magoutas, B., Papadomichelaki, X., Mentzas, G.: Classification and Synthesis of Quality Approaches in e-Government Services. Internet Research 17(4), 378–401 (2007)

18. Heeks, R.: Understanding e-Governance for development, The University of Manchester, Institute for Development Policy and Management: iGovernment Working Papers Series, Number 11/2001 (2001),
    `http://unpan1.un.org/intradoc/groups/public/`
    `documents/NISPAcee/UNPAN015484.pdf`

19. Lenk, K., Traunmuller, R.: A framework for electronic government. Paper Presented at 11th International Workshop on Database and Expert Systems Applications. IEEE Computer Society, London (2000)

20. Miles, M.B., Huberman, A.M.: Qualitative Data Analysis: An Expanded Sourcebook. Sage, Thousand Oaks (1994)

21. Moon, J., Kim, Y.: Extending the TAM for a worldwide-web context. Information and Management 28, 217–230 (2001)

22. Moon, J., Norris, D.: Does managerial orientation matter? The adoption of reinventing government and e-government at the municipal level. Information Systems Journal 15, 43–60 (2005)

23. Norris, D.F., Campillo, D.: Factors Affecting Innovation Adoption by City Governments: The Case of Leading Edge Information Technologies, Maryland Institute for Policy Analysis and Research. University of Maryland, Baltimore, MD, USA (2000)

24. Robertson, J.: Open-source content management systems (2004),
    `http://www.steptwo.com.au/files/kmc_opensource.pdf` (June 22, 2005)

25. Rogers, E.: Diffusion of Innovations, 4th edn. Free Press, New York (1995)

26. Simon, H.A.: Administrative behavior, 3rd edn. The Free Press, New York (1976)

27. Themistocleous, M., Irani, Z.: Evaluating Enterprise Application Integration Technologies: A Novel Frame of References. European Journal of Operational Research (2002)

28. Tsai, J.H.: Political structure, legislative process, and corruption: comparing Taiwan and South Korea, Crime, Law and Social Change (2009) doi: 10.1007/s10611-009-9188-y
29. Tully, J., Chambers, S.: Contract or Conversation? Theoretical Lessons from the Canadian Constitutional Crisis, Politics and Society 26(1), 143–172 (1998)
30. Venkatesh, V., Davis, F.: A theoretical extension of the technology acceptance model: four longitudinal field studies. Management Science 46, 186–204 (2000)
31. Venkatesh, V., Morris, M.: Why don't men ever stop to ask for directions? Gender, social influence, and their role in technology acceptance and usage behaviour. MIS Quarterly 24, 115–139 (2000)
32. Yildiz, M.: E-government Research: Reviewing the Literature, Limitations, and Ways Forward. Government Information Quarterly 24, 646–665 (2007)

Rituals in E-Government Implementation: An Analysis of Failure

Rahul De' and Sandeep Sarkar

Indian Institute of Management Bangalore
{rahul,sandeeps08}@iimb.ernet.in

Abstract. This paper presents a case analysis of a failed e-government implementation in a developing country context. The project involved constructing a large system for a central government department in India. After seven years and a few million rupees in costs, the project was terminated. Prior research in failed information systems implementations has highlighted many issues, most of which are now part of software project management literature. With e-government systems, though scientific project management is diligently applied, failure rates are very high, particularly in developing countries. The analysis in this paper suggests that though issues of lack of user involvement, inadequate delegation, and improper planning are responsible, the important causes are the rituals that management enacted, that had overt rationality but buried agendas.

Keywords: e-Government, system implementation, failure, developing country, India.

1 Introduction

E-government systems constitute a priority for many governments of developing countries as a means to reform and modernise governance. This priority has ingrained into policy and led to massive allocation of funds for computerisation. Government departments take pride in their computerisation efforts, and their ability to stay 'ahead' of their manual-only counterparts. E-government is built for two kinds of situations - those that are internal to departments and those that are public-facing to provide some service for citizens at large. The effort to computerise, in a developing country like India, has included both types of systems.

This effort, though, comes at a price: many projects fail and constitute a waste of money and personnel time. Some researchers report that the failure rates in developing countries are quite high, to the extent of more than 80% of projects being total or partial failures [8,9]. It is thus important to understand why projects fail and what measures can be taken to eliminate or reduce such failures.

This paper examines a failed e-government project in India. The project was intended to build a financial management system for a large government department of the central government of India. The project lasted about seven years, from initiation to its final closure.

M.A. Wimmer et al. (Eds.): EGOV 2010, LNCS 6228, pp. 226–237, 2010.

On the surface, the project appears to reflect the classic problems of project failures anywhere - top-down push without much stakeholder buy-in; conflicting and un-clear goals; inadequate risk assessment and contingency planning; unclear delegation; and poor vendor management. However, a deeper analysis reveals that there are strong issues emanating from the culture and practices of government departments of developing countries and the project management failures are but a symptom of the deeper issues.

This paper proceeds as follows: the following section reviews the literature in e-government in developing countries and also the Information Systems literature on project implementation failures. The main research question is identified, and the methodology followed in this research is discussed. This is followed by a description of the case data after which an analysis is presented. The paper concludes with a discussion of issues in failed e-government projects.

2   Background and Literature Review

E-government in developing countries started with the computerisation efforts for building applications within departments, or e-government systems, that were implemented with the direct assistance of developed nations or multi-lateral funding agencies. These efforts date back to the 60s and 70s, and were few and restricted to well-known data crunching operations such as the census or tax processing. The emphasis on public facing systems grew with the advent of the public Internet in the 90s and the spread of connectivity across developing countries.

Research in e-government systems in developing countries has mainly focussed on identifying successful projects that can be replicated [11], or on evaluation of such systems to see if they are indeed realising the intended impacts (or understand what the impacts are) [12,14,15]. There are few papers that closely examine failures, to understand what went wrong and why, and what lessons can be learned. This paper addresses such a gap in the literature.

Failures in information systems implementation is an area of study that has received much attention [6,7,10]. The research in these papers sought to explain failures, and consequently point to how success could be achieved. Large system implementations were deeply complex and required planning of every possible detail. This was treated in a technical project planning manner, with the evolution of the field of software engineering and software project management. However, despite the detailed planning, systems implementations still failed and this led to research uncovering issues of politics [13], democracy [5], user participation and conflict [2], and control [3], amongst others.

The research does differentiate between project implementation failure issues during the course of the project, from failures happening after the project is complete and implementation is being undertaken in the organisation. The difference between the two is subtle but important. E-government systems are affected by both kinds of problems. In this paper the focus is on the former.

The nature and priorities of project management issues for e-government projects are different from private sector or profit-seeking firms. The issues have to do with the manner in which projects are conceptualised, the manner in which they are funded, the role of various department heads and functional heads, the duration of project managers with the project, and the entrenched problems of power, control and resistance [17].

One issue of particular interest is that of the rituals of project management that some stakeholders enact [16]. Rituals are perfunctory duties that employees and stakeholders of the organisations perform in order to satisfy the needs of project management techniques and guides. Rituals take the form of setting targets, team formation, requirements analysis, and so on, however the stakeholders often have no interest in seeing the project through in this manner, and often have alternative, personal agendas.

In theory, rituals in organisations serve to confirm and consolidate organisational practices, or serve to suppress conflict and control [1]. Further, rituals also enable sense-making of social processes [4].

The bureaucracy in developing countries is often a structure that wields immense power and plays an important role in the implementation of systems. For countries such as India, the bureaucracy is structured as a strict hierarchy, with an elite core of civil servants at the top, supported by cadres of the lower bureaucracy at the state and district levels. The upper bureaucracy retains centralised control over all sanctions of resources [18]. Further, they are held on very short tenure at their respective positions, and are invariably rotated at least every three years.

3   Research Question and Methodology

This paper examines the problem of system implementation failure, but from the context of an e-government system in a developing country. The context of a developing country and e-government system is sufficiently different from the context of similar studies of system implementation failure in private, profit-seeking firms. This implicit assumption drives the research question for this paper:

> What are the principal causes of system implementation failure in e-government projects in developing countries? How do factors such as stakeholder goals, power, politics, and rituals enable these causes?

The methodology followed for this paper is that of case study research [19]. This methodology is considered appropriate as the research is exploratory. The study consists of 22 interviews of project staff belonging to a large Indian government department, where an IT implementation was under way. The interviews were of system implementers, project team leaders, user staff, unit heads, vendors, and top management of the department. Each interview lasted for a duration of 30 - 60 minutes. Project documents were sought and collected, wherever possible.

In the following section the case data is presented as an independent narrative, followed by the analysis. This separation enables an independent verification of the analysis.

4   The Case Data

The case concerns the efforts of a department (referred to as the Department), of a large Ministry of the Central Government of India, to implement an information system. This department provides financial services to all the organisations under the administrative control of the Ministry. The functions of the Department involve assimilation and processing of a large volume of data, mostly financial. The Department oversees the fiscal management of a budget of approximately USD 39,260 million (at 2009 prices). As paymasters to approximately 1.7 million personnel located across the country, the Department has to ensure accuracy of payment and audit of the same. Another major task of the department is pension sanction, payment and grievance redressal where it oversees pensionary benefits to approximately 2.2 million retired personnel - an activity that is fraught with political risks. With major capital acquisitions for modernization of the Ministry being a priority, and an emphasis of the government on austerity and prudent financial management, the Department plays an important role.

The Department has a history of automation of its work processes, started in the 1970s. By the mid-1990s, a realisation of technical obsolescence had set in, also arising out of issues of depleting manpower, increased transactions, increased expectations of the clients (who had carried out extensive automation of their own work processes), as also technical problems such as data inter-operability. In 2002 the Department launched an ambitious automation project (henceforth referred to as the Project) aimed at a total online integrated computerisation of all functions. The Project was sanctioned as a major e-Government initiative in 2004 at a total cost of Rs 420 million (USD 9.1 million), to be completed by 2007.

The Project was the brain child of a very senior officer of the Department (called the Charismatic Leader) who, though not occupying the top rung, was influential enough to push for this project. He created a band of followers, mainly officers from the middle management, who would fulfill the development and implementation of this information system project.

Initially, Study Groups were constituted for major functional areas of the Department. These groups, led by a Branch Head and comprising of 3 - 4 officers, looked into the areas currently automated, the weaknesses in them and made suggestions for the future. Since all functions of the Department were proposed to be automated, and there were common areas of work in different offices, the evolved approach was that such common functions would be developed only once in the project. The constitution of the groups was decided by the Charismatic Leader. Based on the recommendations of these study groups - which came in by mid 2003 - unique functionalities of various offices were treated as separate 'systems' to be developed. These were again divided into (a) Main systems - which comprised of the core functions of an office and (b) Plug-in systems - which consisted of functions common across one or more offices. As the software development was to be outsourced, one or more systems were clubbed into a single "Lot" based on common functions. By the third quarter of the 2003-04, the Vision Document - outlining the design and project management techniques - was sent out.

Project Teams - comprising of domain experts and users of the particular function that was to be automated - were created on site, in field offices, and were tasked with aiding the implementation at the respective locations. The overall control and coordination of the project - including issues of software development, hardware procurement, tendering, manpower training and placement - was made the responsibility of another body called the Project Steering Group (PSG) which was located at the Headquarters. The PSG and Project Teams were staffed by a few officers (middle management) handpicked by the Charismatic Leader. There were two visible faces of PSG whom we call the Lawyer and the Engineer. The PSG and the Project Teams drew their authority and mandate from the Charismatic Leader. In fact certain middle level officers - particularly the Lawyer and the Engineer - had direct access to him.

The Project created a lot of enthusiasm and expectation in the Department in the initial stages. A lot of training - from basic computer literacy to advanced Java - was imparted; computer hardware and networking equipment was procured; test data was created and so on. The Project was looked upon by some of the personnel as a means of freeing them from the drudgery of routine financial tasks that their charter of duties entailed. Some of the Project Leads and younger officers got down to delivering the goals set by the Charismatic Leader. Recalled an earlier Project Lead: "This was the first time when we were given the mandate to think to suggest and change procedures, documents and work flow - something which we had so far accepted as a given. We felt that as the inheritors of the department, we owed it to ourselves to set up this automation project and carry it to finality. It would have only helped us in the long run".

After the study group submitted their reports - where they had collected input requirements from the functional heads of the field sites - the policy for managing the project left out the Branch Heads from the major decision areas. Most of the decision rights lay with the Headquarters and in particular with the Charismatic Leader and the PSG. Having decided on the policy, the implementation aspects were left to the middle management officers who were charged to deliver by making them the Project Leads. The Project Teams (in the field) had direct reporting access to the PSG (at the headquarters), who in turn reported (informally) to the head of the Department.

Echoing these issues, a senior (now retired) officer, who headed one of the largest field offices of the Project, said: "The Branch Heads seem to have been left out of the loop in arriving at the system design and the prioritization of the functions that would form a part of the projects applicable to their own offices. The Project Teams used to interact directly with the PSG, take their instructions from them and move onto their implementation. The Branch Head would come to know if the Project Lead chose to inform them or if he took pains to learn so by himself. This did cause alienation amongst the senior officers in the field who felt that they were not considered fit to be consulted. The PSG had become all powerful."

Realizing this disconnect the Headquarters in March 2006, fearing a lack of ownership of the project amongst the top officers, solicited their involvement. The same retired officer said: "Yes they did try and involve the Branch Heads, but by that time the basic design, architecture and priority of development had already been developed, contracts with software vendors entered into and there was little scope to make any changes. The realization came a bit too late."

Between September 2003 and mid-2006, the User Requirements and Specifications (URS) were firmed up and written by the Project Teams. Based on the clubbing of Lots, tendering action for software development began and contracts entered into. While the process of sending Requests-for-Proposals began in mid 2004, the first contract was signed in March 2005 and the last one in March 2007.

By the first quarter of 2006, Charismatic Leader had left the Department and moved onto the Ministry, and his direct intervention in the affairs of the Department declined.

After the retirement of the successor of the Charismatic Leader, in mid 2007, the resources that were being committed to the project began to decline. The IT setup in the Headquarters office - of which PSG was a part - began to shrink and officers were posted out, and the posts were never filled. Said the Lawyer: "In the field the early Project Leads who shared the vision of the Project started to move out. In some cases they were replaced by officers who did not own up the project. Though we requested for changes, none took place."

When the successor to the Charismatic Leader retired, while work progressed on some Lots, the ones tendered out initially started experiencing problems. Differences arose between the Project Teams and vendors at the testing stage. The failure of one firm, which had been awarded contracts for four systems, to deliver the project milestones complicated things further as the performance of the first tendered lots were being watched keenly in order to establish benchmarks for the remaining ones. While there appeared to be issues of vendor inefficiencies, voices of dissent over inadequate resources, lack of authority and frequent changes in the composition of Project Teams, began to emerge from the field Branch Heads. Issues of improper planning were raised mainly by the new officers who replaced some of the ones who were moved out of the Project Teams. Realizing that there would be substantial time and cost overruns, the Department - now under a new Department Head - moved the Ministry for an extension. This was granted in September 2007 as a result of which the cost was now pegged at Rs 500 million (USD 10.87 million) and the project was given a new deadline of December 2009.

The Project was seen as highly centralized, with too many decisions taken at the headquarters. The uniformity and standards (in project conceptualization, URS writing, etc) that the Headquarters and PSG had envisaged, as an efficient project development technique, began to be seen as a covert act of centralization. One of the senior Branch Heads went on to say: "This centralization of procedures and processes does not give leeway to design and develop the application as per our needs."

By the third quarter of 2007, when a new set of officers arrived at the Headquarters the voices, on the viability of the approach towards automation of all functions at one go (as against an incremental development process) and the lack of authority given to field offices and the Project Teams, became shriller. A senior officer, who had been part of one of the original project development teams of the 1980s (called the Pioneer) said: "We should have learnt from our past experience that a big bang approach, as evident in the Project, does not work...."

Many of the respondents indicated that adequate and requisite inputs had not been provided during the design of the project. This had to do with the non-involvement of business/process owners (the 'non IT personnel' as dubbed by most officers) in the initial design. The general feeling that had begun to emerge was that the approach adopted in the Project was esoteric, not-workable and certainly not in tune with the ground realities.

Concerns were also being voiced by some of the Branch Heads over the adverse fallout of the project on their regular functions as the members of the Project Teams were unable to devote more time towards their regular duties due to their preoccupation with the Project. They made no bones about their displeasure on the additional work entrusted to their subordinates. The views of a senior (now retired) field Branch Head: "I have to take care of my bread and butter functions first - I am paid for that. Everything else can wait. I cannot afford to have my officers devote a major portion of their working time to one project and neglect the core functions of the office in the process."

The vendors also started complaining of non-cooperation by the Project Teams. Scope creep and a lack of ownership - manifested primarily in the unavailability of Project team members and a hesitation to sign (on reports etc) - were reported by them. Often the vendors used to take their problems and complaints directly to the PSG who, at Headquarters level, was responsible for management of the contracts. Their intervention to sort out the issues between the vendors and the Project Teams were seen as bullying tactics by the latter and consequently resisted. In their eagerness to push the project and to adhere to the deadlines, the PSGs efforts in this direction were seen as siding with the vendors, by the Project Teams, and resented as acts of unwarranted intrusion into the domain of the latter. An officer who had headed one of the Project Teams earlier said: "Instead of understanding our problems and helping us resolve them, at the behest of PSG we were often hauled up for delaying the project. Headquarters does not have a clue on project management. There is no forum to resolve issues."

One official report, on the problems in the project, also highlights this issue. Opined the Pioneer: "There is a lot of alienation amongst the field officers and especially the Branch Heads. When project problems were reported to the PSG - the body responsible for coordination issues - one usually got an advice to sort out issues at their own end."

When these issues were posed to the Lawyer and the Engineer they pointed out that they had taken pains to understand the problems on the ground by not only studying each URS in detail but had made many trips to most field sites to resolve issues and had, in their opinion, made substantial progress. The Engineer was also said: "We never acted as bosses from Headquarters office. We tried to keep all communication channels open and were very open and receptive to the ideas and concerns of the field offices...."

While they did admit that there may have been flaws in the project management plan, the Lawyer and the Engineer were of the opinion that these could have been corrected if the top management had really owned up to it. As an issue that was close to their functional area, they pointed to the hesitation to deploy more manpower to the project and to ensure their permanence - at Headquarters as well as in the field.

Things were difficult in most of the field offices. One official report points out that: "Principles of sound IT Project Management have not been adopted for executing the Project, rather the Project [was] implemented under the normal bureaucratic manner. The (Project Leads) were not given adequate authority to discharge day to day responsibility."

By the end of 2007, the enthusiasm of the early days had been overtaken by a despondency and a tendency to stay away from the project or at best letting it run its own course. A feeling had developed that even after so much effort (and time and money) none of the systems were near completion.

The situation for the Project got worse in 2008. There were immense delays in the project milestones, in all the Lots. None of the original members of the Project Teams, and most of the Branch Heads, to whom references had been made in 2006, were in their respective positions anymore. On top of this, the Central Government in India announced new pay and other entitlement structures for its employees in September 2008. This came as a nail in the coffin for most of the Lots in the project. The basis for calculation of various allowances (pay, pension etc) were radically altered necessitating large scale changes in the software logic. This effectively put a major portion of the project on hold as, irrespective of the stage of the earlier development, the project stages from URS onwards needed to be revisited.

In November 2008, the Department set up a committee to review the project. The committee - comprising primarily of officers who had proposed alternate project management approaches - sought comments and views of all the Branch Heads, whose offices were the declared project development sites. The Lawyer and the Engineer were however not consulted. The committee came to the conclusion that the project was a partial failure and there was a need for closure of some of the Lots. The Department issued termination notices for the four chosen Lots in August 2009.

By this time, the setup in the headquarters IT division of the Department had been changed. Both the Lawyer and the Engineer had been transferred out in the first quarter of 2009 and a new set of officers had come in. Interviews with them revealed that one of the top priorities, at that time, was to short-close most of the contracts and to rethink the automation project. Thus the need to automate to improve service delivery had come a full circle since its inception in 2002.

5   Analysis

The Department is a microcosm of the larger Government and bureaucratic structure in India. It is highly compartmentalized in its functions and has a layered structure. While most of the lower grade personnel are recruited into the clerical grade and then make the slow climb up the hierarchy, the officers, a minority recruited from the Civil Services or promoted from the lower ranks, are generalists but have the largest decision rights in the functioning of their offices. While there is specialization in the lower cadres, the structure is highly formalized and bound by rules and procedures, some dating back to the pre-Independence era. The decision making process on major issues is highly centralized.

5.1   The Overtly Rational

The case shows a preponderance of behaviours by the leading participants in the project that is described as "overtly rational" by Robey and Markus (1984). These are behaviours and actions taken by the project leaders that were meant to conform to project management procedures. Hindsight shows that these actions could not have achieved what they were supposed to achieve, however well they may have been executed, owing to the particular context of the organisation and its composition.

Project Management Structure: The Charismatic Leader created project teams and the PSG, staffed with the Lawyer and the Engineer, to create a clear and unambiguous decision hierarchy for the project. Tasks were identified and allocated, and the plan for activities, reporting relationships, and responsibilities was laid down. There was enthusiasm for the project and the roles assigned - as one project lead stated "... this was the first time when we were given the mandate to think to suggest and change procedures...."

However, the data shows that this structure clearly violated the norms of strict hierarchy, and, in fact, by-passed the Branch Heads altogether although they had the most authority as the users. The reporting relationships in the team enabled those junior to the Branch Heads to report directly to the PSG or to the Charismatic Leader. When it became clear that this short-circuit in the hierarchy was becoming a problem, another overtly rational activity was undertaken - that of including the Branch Heads in the decision making. However, by this time the design had been formalised and fixed, leaving no room for any serious inputs by the Heads.

Project Execution: The project leadership empowered the teams to handle the execution tasks. This was done formally, with a clear delegation of tasks. The execution initially proceeded well, with considerable motivation from the PSG and the team. Vendors were to deliver on the Lots and these were to be tested and verified by the teams. This was the overtly rational behaviour.

The execution of the project was prioritised by the central leadership, with some choices left to the teams. The teams later complained that they "...were not given adequate authority to discharge day to day responsibility" while working on the project. Vendors were not managed, and were left to deal with scope creep and lack of ownership on their own. The staff rotation, which was routine and well known, was not accounted for and many staff who left were not replaced.

After the Charismatic Leader and his successor moved on, or retired, the project execution seems to have collapsed almost entirely. The centralised control had snapped and the remaining power structures were not up to the task.

The Worldviews: The Charismatic Leader had envisioned the project with a certain worldview. It was to be conceived and executed on a grand scale, covering a wide swathe of functions and branches of the Department. In 2002, this was not a far fetched idea in India. The Indian IT industry was strong and well known as being highly competent. Much larger projects had been initiated in other government departments, and some had been delivered successfully. So the plan of a "big bang" approach had merit and overt rationality.

In the later stages of the project, the new team of leaders who took over the reins differed with the grand implementation idea, and were of the view that the project would have been better implemented in stages, a tactic the Department had been successful with in the past. This was a worldview and a vision of project management that was in stark contrast with the overt rationality of the Charismatic Leader and his team.

5.2   Rituals

Rituals are powerful and central to the Indian ethos. Their practice has the legitimacy and sanction similar to that of religious observance. They are the core of ceremonial behaviour and reflect a rationality that has an inherent, implied logic that is not expressed and is rarely explained. The rituals enacted in the project had a similar tone - though they purported to correspond to a rationality of scientific project management. Teams were formed, designs were made, plans were drawn up with the overt rationality of objective and scientific actions. This is re-affirmed by the official committee that reported principles of scientific management had not been followed and the project was "...implemented under the normal bureaucratic manner."

When the emergent problems challenged the rationality, the response was to re-affirm the plans, and devise further rituals as recompense. Project teams were hauled up when there there slippages in deadlines, without any investigation. The ritual of decentralised control was enacted and teams were told to "... sort out issues at their own end."

These rituals enabled the team at headquarters to retain strong control over all aspects of the project - from initiation, funding, planning, design, to execution. An overt rationality of scientific management masked these rituals and enabled them to be played out without active resistance from other stakeholders [1]. It is important to note that the power play inherent in the rituals was designed to control the implementation process, and legitimate it, thus subverting the possible power inversions that could result after the system was available and in use.

Rituals uphold values of 'scientific management,' and 'efficiency,' and 'effectiveness' and are endemic in government departments. They mask the underlying power plays and manoeuvrings that are constant and pervasive in all e-government projects. With systems implementations being undertaken at such a large scale in developing countries, it is imperative that such phenomenon are understood.

6   Conclusions

The system implementation project initiated by the Department in 2002 was terminated in late 2009; most of the vendors were relieved, and all the participants moved on. The system cost the government a few millions, and thousands of person hours of effort. The committee that had been set up to examine the problems with the project did create a valuable report that included lessons on project management. The personnel who had participated in the project had gained from their experience. Barring the last two positive outcomes, overall the project was a failure.

The phenomenon of rituals examined in this paper is not easy to uncover and establish. A question that arises from this research is how rituals can be identified in projects? A related question is how the overtly rational actions can be delineated from those required for the success of the project? One answer to these questions may be found in the possible predictors of problems and project failure - creation of parallel structures of governance that undermines the existing hierarchy; conducting a requirements analysis without including important stakeholders; using an approach to systems development that is at odds with the familiar methods used in the organisation; and shifting project execution responsibility to those without a buy-in to the project.

The method followed in this research was that of interviewing participants during the course of the project, albiet towards the end. Interviews, of a cross-section of the stakeholders, about the goals and intentions of actions taken during the project, the meaning of certain practices of project management, and the conflicts that arose within the organisation, led to uncovering the rituals enacted. This method is a first attempt to understand rituals in e-government projects, and future work will address the deeper issues of interpretation of the interview data.

References

1. Anand, N., Watson, M.R.: Tournament rituals in the evolution of fields: The case of the grammy awards. The Academy of Management Journal 47(1), 59–80 (2004)
2. Barki, H., Hartwick, J.: Interpersonal conflict and its management in information system development. MIS Quarterly 25(2), 195–228 (2001)
3. Baronas, A.M.K., Louis, M.R.: Restoring a sense of control during implementation: How user involvement leads to system acceptance. MIS Quarterly 12(1), 111–124 (1988)

4. Bell, C.: Ritual: Perspectives and Dimensions. Oxford University Press, Oxford (2009)
5. Bjerknes, G., Bratteteig, T.: User participation and democracy: A discussion of Scandinavian research on system development. Scandinavian Journal of Information Systems 7(1), 73–98 (1995)
6. Bostrom, R.B., Heinen, J.A.: MIS problems and failures. a socio-technical perspective: Part i: The causes. MIS Quarterly 1(3), 17–32 (1977)
7. Ginzberg, M.: Early diagnosis of MIS implementation failure: Promising results and unanswered questions. Management Science 27(4), 459–478 (1981)
8. Heeks, R.: Information systems and developing countries: Failure, success, and local improvisations. The Information Society 18, 101–112 (2002)
9. Heeks, R.: Most eGovernment-for-development projects fail: How can risks be reduced? iGovernment working paper series, IDPM, University of Manchester (2003)
10. Keil, M.: Pulling the plug: Software project management and the problem of project escalation. MIS Quarterly 19(4), 421–447 (1995)
11. Krishna, S., Walsham, G.: Implementing public information systems in developing countries: Learning from a success story. Information Technology for Development 11(2), 1–18 (2005)
12. Madon, S.: Evaluating the developmental impact of e-governance initiatives: An exploratory framework. The Electronic Journal of Information Systems in Developing Countries 20(5), 1–13 (2004)
13. Markus, M.L.: Power, politics, and MIS implementation. Communications of the ACM 26(6), 430–444 (1983)
14. Parthasarathy, B.: Information and communication technologies for development: A comparative analysis of impacts and costs from India. Tech. rep., International Institute of Information Technology, Bangalore (2005)
15. Prakash, A., De', R.: Importance of developement context in ICT4D projects: A study of computerization of land records in India. Information Technology & People 20(3), 262–281 (2007)
16. Robey, D., Markus, M.L.: Rituals in information system design. MIS Quarterly 8(1), 5–15 (1984)
17. Silva, L., Hirschheim, R.: Fighting against windmills: Strategic information systems and organizational deep structures. MIS Quarterly 31(2), 327–354 (2007)
18. Vanaik, A.: The Painful Transition: Bourgeois Democracy in India. Verso, New York (1990)
19. Yin, R.K.: Case Study Research: Design and Methods. Applied Social Science Research Methods Series, vol. 5. Sage Publications, Thousand Oaks (2003)

E-Governance - A Challenge for the Regional Sustainable Development in Romania

Mihaela Mureşan

Dimitrie Cantemir Christian University, Splaiul Unirii 176, Bucharest, Romania

Abstract. The paper addresses specific issues of the local governance in its transition to the knowledge society and the web based processes. The innovative e-Governance approach creates a new regional framework for changing the process of the sustainable strategy design and implementation, from a system-oriented to an actor-driven one, focusing on the development of two ways online channels for supporting the pro-active citizens' behavior and their involvement in the consultation and decisional processes. The solution, based on web 2.0 technologies, integrates e-Knowledge, e-Consultation and e-Voting tools in a regional portal, facilitating the bottom-up decision-making processes. The regional virtual portal provides simultaneously a quantitative approach represented by the information concerning the regional opportunities and possible evolution trends, based on advanced modeling tools and set of indicators, and, complementary, a qualitative approach using various tools for the direct expression of the specific actors' opinions, creating a holistic image on the regional development.

Keywords: regional e-Governance, e-Participation, e-Knowledge, regional strategy.

1 Introduction

The paper emphasizes the role of the advanced interactive web services provided by a virtual platform, as a single point of access, for the regional governance and the regional actors, aiming at designing and implementing coherent regional sustainable strategies. This approach is in line with the actual public administration reform and its transition to the knowledge society and the e-Governance paradigm. The regional development is the main driver for increasing the competitiveness and attending the goals of the Lisbon Strategy. In order to be responsive to the European priorities, as part of the European Union, Romania intensifies its efforts for accelerating the decentralization in the public administration, which is a relative recent process. In addition, due to the actual complexity of the socio-economic context, to the challenges of the global knowledge economy and to the negative effects of the financial crisis, it is a real need of coagulating all the intellectual resources for finding appropriate solutions for the positive evolution of the region. Consequently, strengthening and enlarging the regional partnership, and integrating the regional knowledge and expertise resources, for creating a holistic approach related to the

M.A. Wimmer et al. (Eds.): EGOV 2010, LNCS 6228, pp. 238–250, 2010.

regional strategy design, become the main priorities of the Romanian local governance. The paper presents the specific issues of the Romanian development region Bucharest-Ilfov and the solutions proposed by the research team for creating the framework of the regional actors' participation in the regional planning process and increasing the local administration factors' capacity to reach tangible and appropriate decisions.

This paper aims to present an innovative view related to the transition to e-Governance by consultative and decisional online processes (e-Participation), focused on the regional strategy design and implementation, as a solution for increasing the public engagement of the citizens around the issues that affect their lives. Moreover, the solution includes also e-Knowledge tools for the acquisition of data and knowledge related to the regional development and for the presentation of the analysis results in real-time, in order to create a realistic image of the opportunities and challenges at the regional level. Integrating the e-Knowledge and e-Participation tools in a virtual regional platform creates a single access point to the information and to the interactive dialogue between the regional actors and the regional public governance.

The new Web 2.0 technologies have a major contribution for the development of the two ways online channels, supporting the active dissemination and use of the information, and the citizens' involvement in the public administration decision-making processes. The paper presents the e-Knowledge and e-Participation tools integrated in a virtual regional platform, as major components of the regional e-Governance.

2 Regional Strategy Design as a Participative and Iterative Process

The research contextualizes the challenges for Romania taking into consideration the specific situation of the transition from a centralized to a decentralized governmental system. The actual Romanian legislation creates the frame for the design of the regional development strategy, enabling wide participative processes, taking into consideration the European Cohesion Policy, as well as the main challenges of the decentralization and the new created Romanian territorial structures (the eight development regions). The Romanian legislative framework stipulates the procedures and the main workflows in designing the regional strategy. The institutional infrastructure for the new territorial structures (development regions) is represented by the eight regional development agencies, non-governmental entities providing public services and cooperating with the public local and central administration. This new institutional infrastructure and the challenges of becoming a member of the European Union lead to a wide re-engineering process for the public administration entities.

2.1 Main Workflows of the Regional Strategy Design

According to the actual legislation, the public administration is involved in and has the responsibility for the design of the regional strategy, as a participative and iterative process. The whole process of the design of the regional strategy for the 2007-2103 period and the main interactions among the actors involved are illustrated in the Fig. 1. The coordination of the regional strategy design represents the responsibility of the Council for the Regional Development (CRD), the main decisional actor at the regional level, integrating representatives of various public administration entities. The Council also coordinates the activity of the regional development agencies (RDA) and validates the final version of the strategy. Creating the regional partnership represents the responsibility of the regional development agencies, which are also in charge with the design of the regional strategy, coordinating the activity of the Committee for the Design of the Regional Strategy (CDRS). The CDRS is responsible with the consultation process, creating the opportunities for the wide regional debate among the main regional stakeholders: representatives from the central and public administration, socio-economic entities, high education institutions, research centers etc.

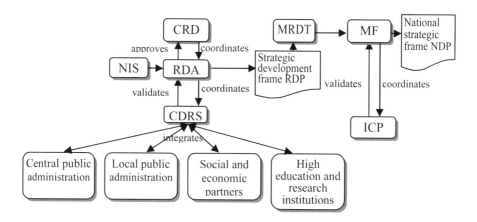

Fig. 1. Main workflows for the design of the regional strategy

A key role plays the National Institute for Statistics (NIS), providing the main information for a quantitative analysis. The regional strategy represents the basis for the elaboration of the Regional Development Plan (RDP), including concrete measures for the implementation of the strategy. The Ministry for the Regional Development and Tourism (MRDT) has the responsibility for the design of the RDP, integrating the regional strategic frames. The RDP represents the main input for the design of the National Development Plan (NDP), under the coordination of the Inter-institutional Committee for the National Plan (ICP), which acts under the direct supervision of the Ministry of Finance (MF).

The results of the desk research and of the direct observation of the process carried out in Bucharest-Ilfov (2005-2007) suggest that the process has integrated various activities focusing on information provision, design, deliberation, consultation and approval, but without a wide representativeness, which was limited to some reduced focus groups debates, not even focused on specific issues. Moreover, it has been observed the lack of the citizens' participation to these activities, the inhabitants of the region being not directly involved or well represented by the non-governmental organizations. In conclusion, the analysis of the real implementation of the legislative framework concerning the regional development strategy design in Romania revealed a gap between rhetoric (the legislation framework) and reality, such as the lack of a consistent dialogue between the local governance and the regional actors, including the inhabitants of the region.

2.2 Citizens' Interest Related to the Regional Strategy Design in the Bucharest-Ilfov Region

In order to refine the results of the research, a survey was organized in the Bucharest-Ilfov region, aiming at identifying the citizens' perceptions and opinions related to the regional strategy design. The main objective of the pilot survey is represented by the identification of the citizens' interest and wiliness to participate to the regional strategy design process. The main hypothesis of the survey are: (1) the majority of the inhabitants of the Bucharest-Ilfov region have not informed about the process of the regional strategy design; (2) the majority of the inhabitants of the Bucharest-Ilfov region would like to be involved in the process of the regional strategy design.

The questionnaire used was framed, with clearly formulated questions, so everybody could understand them, without any shadow of a doubt and with no ambiguities. The majority of the questions are closed, not leaving any room for personal subjective interpretation. The logical approach of the questions and the scale used to assess the answers aim to allow the ordering, centralizing and handling of data using statistical methods and IT programs. The sample was represented by 150 persons, all residents of the Bucharest-Ilfov region (126 persons from Bucharest – 84% and 24 from Ilfov – 16%). Aiming at conclusive results, a heterogeneous sample was random selected including a diversity of profiles, concerning the age, education, profession, occupation or socio-economic status. The respondents have been selected from a regional stakeholders' database, representing the main domains of the activity of the Bucharest-Ilfov region (47.3% in economic and financial area; 7.4 % in socio-political area; 13.3% in educational area; 6% in health area; 9.1% in public sector and 14.2 in other sectors). The distribution of the sample related to the age revealed that the majority of the respondents were under 45 years , i.e. 90% (30% in the group 18 – 25 years old; 25,3 in the group 26 – 35 years old and 30,7% in the group 36 - 45 years old) and only 10% were in the group of 46 to 60 years old. The analysis of the sample emphasizes also that the majority of the respondents were high qualified from the

Table 1. Summary of the answers to the main questions of the pilot survey

Questions	YES	NO
Participation to the RS design 2005-2007	6.7%	93.3%
Interest to know about the RS	84.7 %	15.3%
Knowledge about the RS design process	15.3 %	84.7 %
Knowledge about the actual RS	15.3 %	84.7 %
Interest to participate to the future RS design	64.0 %	36.0 %
Interest to have information about possible regional development scenarios	88.0 %	12.0 %

point of view of the education level and of the professional status. The majority of the persons participating in the survey were graduated (64,7%) and the rest of the people (35,3%) had attended the upper secondary education. This stands for an important asset concerning the capacity of the respondents to have a consistent contribution related to the sustainable regional strategy design.

The process of the design of the regional strategy was conducted during 2005-2007, and the interviews have been organized in February-March 2008. The main questions of the interview focused on the knowledge about the regional strategy, the design process and also about the interest to participate in the future to the similar processes and to be informed about the results, as illustrated in the table 1.

The analysis of the answers to the main questions confirmed the hypothesis of the survey, demonstrating that the majority of the citizens of the Bucharest-Ilfov region were not involved in the process of the strategy design (93.3%) and moreover, they had no information about the strategy itself and about its design process (84.7%).

In the same time, the respondents were interested to have information about the regional strategy (88%) and also to be involved in the design process (64%). The 10 persons involved in the regional strategy design (6.7%), acted as representatives of the public administration (7 persons – 4.7%) and NGOs (3 persons – 2%). Nobody declared the involvement as simple citizen, which confirmed the initial hypothesis (1). In addition, the respondents also confirmed the utility of the virtual platform for the information delivery and for the online processes of consultation and deliberation: 53% considered the virtual platform very useful, 39% useful and only 8% not so useful. The survey demonstrated the citizens' increasingly demand to be informed and to take part in decision-making processes (hypothesis 2).

Beyond these conclusions the survey revealed also the need of tools and mechanism to increase the accessibility to public information and to provide the opportunity of an effective public engagement. The development of the adequate framework for the e-Participation and the implementation of the appropriate principles for the public engagement will contribute to avoid the citizens' lack of trust in policymakers and policy and will build a real regional consensus, facilitating also the implementation of the regional strategy.

3   Regional E-Governance for the Strategy Design

In accordance with the European framework, the Romanian procedure for the strategy design needs the support and participation of the various actors in a formal or informal way, in order to support the decision-making for public policy purposes at any stage of the policy lifecycle [13]. As the conclusions of the direct observations, desk research and the results of the survey demonstrate, the regional stakeholders' involvement was very low. Therefore the involvement of the citizens in the strategy definition, with a consultative and decisional role, should be one of the major concerns of the Romanian local government for the future.

The solution proposed, i.e. a virtual regional platform supporting the participation of the citizens to the regional strategy design, offer a balanced approach for the decision–making process and the public engagement of the citizens. The openness of the public administration [10] and the extended use of the ICT tools, namely the

Internet, increase the opportunities of creating interactive space between citizens and political actors [14]. This new approach, defined broadly as e-Democracy, generated wide debates among researchers and practitioners, concerning both conceptual and pragmatic sides of the e-Democracy and its place in the transition from e-Government to e-Governance.

3.1 E- Governance versus E- Government

There are various definitions for the e-Government concept adopted by the European Commission or the World Bank, such as: "The use of information and communication technologies in public administration combined with organizational change and new skills in order to improve public services and democratic processes and strengthen support to public policies" [7]; and also: "e-Government is the use of information technology to support government operations, engage citizens, and provide government services" [3].

The e-Governance concept introduces a wider perspective, being defined in terms of the interaction between the citizens and the representatives of the public authorities for defining, adopting and implementing policies. The fulfillment of this ambitious goal involves a complex process for translating the research results and advanced knowledge into practical applications, which enables transformational changes based on technology, as mentioned at the Ministerial Conference in Lisbon, 2007 [17]. Beyond the intensive knowledge use and technological approach, the e-Governance involves also, on one side, major structural changes for the public administration and the governance of the society [8], and on the other side, the citizens and various stakeholders' pro-active behavior in the framework of the policies design, approval and implementation. In this perspective, the concept of e-Democracy refers to "the possibility to develop the influence and participation of the public in the political sphere" [11], using advanced and efficient online interaction channels. As the pioneer researcher in the area, Jane E. Fountain, emphasized, this is "not only a question of improving efficiency" [8], by reducing the bureaucracy and enhancing the workflows, but mainly a change in mentality from both sides: government and citizens. As the European Commission outlines, "the pressure on public administration is so great that improving existing routines with the help of ICT alone is not enough; progress also requires more innovative approaches" [6]. In addition to the increased global competition, the democratic deficit and the ageing population, the actual financial crisis creates new challenges for the governmental entities consisting in the need of more efficient and effective strategic solutions. Thus, it is crucial to create a framework for an efficient cooperation within the governmental area and between the public authorities and the citizens, and all the entities which can support the decision-making processes, in order to integrate as many views and ideas as possible, aiming at addressing the actual challenges.

3.2 E-Participation - Main Support for the E-Governance

The e-Participation tools stimulate the democratic engagement, facilitating the online consultation (e-Consultation) and voting services (e-Voting). Despite the need of the public involvement in the policy design and implementation, the observers of the

European e-Consultation processes noticed that the citizens' initiatives "have been poorly and arbitrarily integrated in the respective policies they intend to inform" [14]. The fact that the regional actors' initiatives are rarely included in the policies developed creates the regional actors' inertial behavior. Therefore, the stimulation of the regional actors' pro-active attitude represents one of the major challenges as a success factor in the e-consultation process, relying on basic principles [16], consisting in: taking into consideration the real needs of the regional actors, promoting a culture of sustained engagement, increasing the inclusion and the demographic diversity, supporting and encouraging the wide participation, creating an open, and transparent environment based on trust, ensuring a real impact of the participatory efforts. In addition, the intensive use of the Internet at individual level, as well as the facilities of the web 2.0 technologies create new opportunities related to the attractiveness of the virtual environment and its flexibility. The use of a virtual regional platform, due to its synchronous and asynchronous interactions through two ways communication channels, provides the adequate solution for networking the governmental entities and implementing adequate tools (e-Knowledge, e-Practice, e-Consultation), for ensuring the efficient interactions within the governmental area, and also for promoting the community building and the dialogue with the citizens and other stakeholders.

3.3 E-Consultation and E-Knowledge Tools of the Regional Virtual Platform

Meanwhile the e-Consultation process becomes a popular approach in the European space, for the active civic engagement in policy-making, in Romania it is a real need for promoting these concepts and creating the adequate infrastructure and web tools. In the previous planning process for the period 2007-2013, the citizens have not been involved, and only partially experts and representatives of various organizations took part in the debates. Consequently, one of the main results of the research project consists in designing the virtual regional platform, including e-Knowledge and e-Participation tools, in order to enlarge the regional partnership and to increase the interactivity between the citizens and the local governance entities. It has been noticed that the effectiveness of this process depends on different major factors, such as: the determination of the regional actors to participate in the process, the capacity of the citizens to provide a consistent input for the decision makers, and the political will to integrate the outcomes of the e-consultations in the regional strategy design.

3.4 E-Knowledge Tools of the Regional Virtual Platform

Another critical issue is represented by the capability of the stakeholders to be involved as contributors to the strategy design. For this purpose, a regional knowledge base is designed and implemented as a repository of valuable knowledge and information related to the regional development trends, models and scenarios. The accessibility to this information, the simulations, the benchmarking and the various scenarios offer a scientific frame for a better understanding of the possible evolution of the region and a holistic approach related to the sustainable regional development. The platform, through its specific e-knowledge tools, supports the quantitative approach and provides valuable information for all the regional actors. The main indexes and set of indicators implemented through the regional virtual platform are represented by the: Sustainable Development Indicators (10 Themes, 3 levels) – Eurostat, National Institute for Statistics (Theme 1–8); Composite index for monitoring Lisbon strategy – European Commission; Sustainable Society Index (SSI) - Geurt van de Kerk; regional innovation performance index (RIPI) – European Commission; Environmental Performance Index (EPI) - Columbia University and Yale University; human development index (HDI) – United Nations Development Program. The research team has also proposed a composite index integrating the index for the personal development, the index for the quality of the environment, the index for the social environment and the index for the economic development. The quantitative analysis is based on these various indexes, facilitating the appropriate evaluation of the region results compared with other similar European regions and with other Romanian regions. The information provided integrating four axes: human development, environment protection, economic and social development illustrates the positioning of the region in the European and national space, identifying the future trends in the regional sustainable development (Fig. 2). The e-region platform, as a specific knowledge integrator and generator at the regional level, has as main functions: the acquisition of relevant knowledge and data; the analysis and data processing using various mechanism for specific benchmarking, trends identification, and foresight exercises.

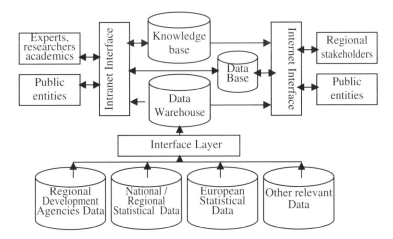

Fig. 2. Generic architecture for the e-Knowledge tool for the sustainable regional strategy design

The sustainable models, the data analysis and the interpretation of the data contribute to the generation of various scenarios, as embedded knowledge, representing important tools for the decisional process of the identification of the objectives and priorities for the regional development on medium- and long term. The open access to the knowledge and information creates the premises for the regional actors to better understand the possible regional evolution. In this case, the regional stakeholders are well informed, have access to scientific analysis and their opinions could be more consistent and coherent. The decision makers could benefit from a holistic approach based on the effectiveness of the synergy between quantitative and qualitative perspectives of the analysis. The use of the e-Knowledge tools in conjunction with the e-Participation ones represents also the innovation introduced in the design of the regional virtual platform.

3.5 E-Participation Tools of the Regional Virtual Platform

The collaborative environment provided by the virtual platform, such as forum and virtual debates, will support also the wide interactions among specialists, citizens and local government representatives on a realistic and scientific base, aiming at identifying the objectives and the priorities for the regional development. The new generation of user-friendly digital tools and various communication channels support the facile interactivity of the regional actors, contributing to strengthen the regional partnership and to increase the synergy between the quantitative and qualitative analysis. As the European Commission emphasizes, "the discussion forums need to be better run and followed-up" [5], and, in this way, the effectiveness of the two-ways communication with the citizens will be enhanced. The various surveys and e-consultations sessions ensure the synergy between the quantitative and the qualitative views related to the perspectives of the regional development, facilitating the identification of the major development directions. In this case, the importance of the citizens, as major contributors, will increase and it is obvious that the decision-makers will be more sensitive to the outcomes of the e-consultation process. This approach ensures a more accurate ex-ante evaluation of the regional strategy, increasing the quality of the process and of the outcomes provided. An important step after the e-consultation and virtual debates is represented by the e-voting phase for selecting the objectives and priorities identified and even validating the final version of the regional strategy. In this case, the citizens, with their opinions and views are integrated in the design process of the strategy and also in the final phase of its approval. The participative process ensures the accuracy of the analysis and the consensus building related to the future development of the region, and accordingly represents a guaranty for the further involvement of the regional stakeholders during the implementation process. The organizations and the citizens have the opportunity to participate in the ongoing processes and further to observe their implementation. This approach increases the transparency of the process of the regional strategy design and implementation, which stands for main goal of the European Union [15]. In this perspective, the platform provides the facilities of an e-barometer, as a democratic-centric regional driver, used for gathering and analyzing the local/regional actors' satisfaction, in order to improve the local/regional development strategy and its design and implementation processes.

The e-Participation "offers citizens a greater share in political discourse and the ability to contribute with their own ideas, suggestions, and requests" [12], creating the e-Governance framework. The citizens have the opportunity to become contributors to the regional strategy design, melting their expertise and perception into the regional intellectual capital. The local administration could take advantage of this important unexploited potential, enhancing the local governance act. "The usability of the applications, tools, channels and devices through which e-Participation will take place in virtual space, need to be designed properly to support the citizens in this regard" [12]. In the same time, it is important to mention that the effectiveness of the e-Participation process, as component of the e-Governance, represents not only the reflex of the technological approach, but also a major mentality change for both sides: governance and regional actors.

Analyzing the state of the art related to regional virtual platform and e-Governance, we identified various European initiatives such as digital business ecosystems [1] and regional internet community portals [9], which are business oriented portals networking the business entities and have not the goal to bridge the public administration with the regional actors, especially the citizens, in order to create a democratic process for the development of public policies. Another important contribution in the area is represented by the eDemocracy.org, founded by Steven Clift, an important and enthusiastic sustainer of the e-Governance doctrine. We took advantage of the positive experience of the Steven Clift, shared in a generous way: "To build e-participation momentum, citizens need to experience results they can see and touch. By investing in transferable local models and tools, more people will use the Internet as a tool to strength their communities, protect and enrich their families and neighborhoods, and be heard in a meaningful way." [2] The ten steps proposed by Steven Clift [2] for building the e-Democracy represent a valuable guide concerning the "web based systems for supporting the decision-making at governmental levels" [13].

On one side, the regional stakeholders are stimulated to have a pro-active behavior in a structured manner through the e-region platform, so that their opinions could influence the regional decision-makers. On the other side, the participants in the process will be stimulated to be contributors as well for the knowledge base (new models, indicators, specific detailed information, refined analysis and scenarios etc) and also for the qualitative approach, i.e. expressing their personal perception on the regional sustainable development. For this purpose, the participants are invited to interact online with the public governance representatives, through various instruments.

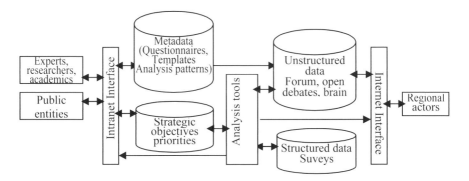

Fig. 3. Generic architecture for the e-Consultation

The e-Consultation process integrates different tools for collecting as much information as possible, in order to build a holistic view on the regional development opportunities, aiming at adopting the best policies for the positive evolution of the region. The e-Consultation process (Fig. 3) is structured in phases, from the identification of the ideas, design of the regional strategy, consensus building, until the final step of the approval of the designed strategy. The first phases are based on gathering the regional actors' opinions through open forum debates and online brainstorming sessions. The second phase consists in filling in various sets of questionnaires, aiming at gathering the information related to the regional stakeholders' perception and satisfaction regarding their own life, the regional environment, the social and economic context. The results of the surveys are automatically processed and the centralized data and their interpretation are available for all the regional stakeholders, including public entities. Beside the formal interaction through various surveys, the citizens have the opportunity to participate also in an informal way, contributing with their suggestions to the debates and consultation processes. The e-region platform functionality supports also the iterative process of the identification of the objectives and priorities for the sustainable regional development, providing adequate tools for e-voting, in order to select the appropriate targets and to ensure a holistic and efficient approach for the future development. The platform facilitates the open interaction of the main regional actors, including the decision-makers during the successive refinement of the regional strategy. The final objectives and priorities will be selected by open online vote. This approach supports the community consensus building related to major issues of the region and its future development, according to the regional actors' interest.

4   Conclusions

According to the new citizen-oriented governance paradigm, the articulation of the e-Knowledge and e-Participation tools supports the binomial analysis of both quantitative approach, represented by the information concerning the regional opportunities and possible evolution trends, and qualitative approach, using various tools for the direct expression of the regional actors' opinions. The e-region platform creates the virtual environment and the specific tools supporting the scientific and realistic approach of the regional strategy design. The innovative solutions supporting the transition to the e-Governance at the regional level in Romania provides the adequate instruments to strengthen the regional partnership and to coagulate the regional intellectual capital in order to cope with the complexity of the actual development challenges. The main findings introduced by the research project are represented by the improvement of the scientific base of the regional strategy design and by the efficient interaction of the regional/local public entities with the stakeholders. This innovative approach represents a qualitative change for the regional governance, involving major changes in the policies design process. The decisions makers, represented by the various regional or central entities will have at their disposal accurate information, including the feedback obtained from the regional actors, in order to improve the regional policies. The acceptance and the implementation of such a platform is part of a wider process of the transition to the e-Governance. The platform articulates functions and components such as the regional knowledge repository and generator, and the e-Participation and e-Voting tools, creating the premises for bridging the gap between local governance and the regional actors. The platform offers also a solution for the decentralization process, which represents a real challenge for the Romanian local administration. This represents an efficient way to involve citizens and organizations in the regional development, as a knowledge based process. The design and the implementation of the regional/local strategy becomes an efficient and more realistic bottom-up process, integrating the best experiences and practices and better responding to the local needs. In this inclusive and democratic view, everybody, regardless of the socio-economic background, is given an equitable playing role in the design of the regional strategy, being part in the e-Governance process.

Acknowledgments. The innovative solution represents the results of a Romanian research project: "Regional Knowledge Management Architecture for the regional sustainable strategy development" (KnowHowReg), funded by the Romanian National Authority for Scientific Research, through the National Council for Higher Education and Research. We would like to thank all of our contributors to the progress of our research.

References

1. Ceclan, M., Ceclan, R.: Digital Business Ecosystems a model for regional development & knowledge economy, Electra, Bucharest (2008)
2. Clift, S.: Ten Practical Online Steps for Government Support of Democracy – By Steven Clift (2007), http://www.eDemocracy.org
3. Dawes, S.: Governance in the information age: a research framework for an uncertain future. In: Proceedings of the 2008 international conference on Digital government research, Montreal, Canada, pp. 290–297 (2008)
4. European Commission: Growing Regions – Growing Europe. Fourth Report on Economic and Social Cohesion, Brussels (2007)
5. European Commission: Communicating about Europe via the Internet, engaging the citizens, SEC(2007)1742, Brussels, pp. 9–12 (2007), http://ec.europa.eu/dgs/communication/pdf/internet-strategy_en.pdf
6. European Commission: Working Paper on eGovernment Beyond 2005 – An overview of policy issues, Information Society Directorate-General, eGovernment Unit (2004)
7. European Commission: The role of eGovernment for Europe's future, European Commission, COM (2003) 567 (2003)
8. Fountain, J.E.: Building the Virtual State. In: Information Technology and Institutional Change. Bookings Institution Press, Washington (2001)
9. Gengatharen, D.: Interpreting the success and failure of regional internet community portals in promoting e-commerce adoption by SMEs: A cultural perspective. Journal of Systems and Information Technology 10(1), 56–71 (2008)
10. Lenk, K.: Electronic Government als Schlüssel zur Innovation der öffentlichen Verwaltung. In: Lenk, K., Traunmüller, R. (eds.) Öffentliche Verwaltung und Informationstechnik - Perspektiven einer radikalen Neugestaltung der öffentlichen Verwaltung mit Informationstechnik, Schriftenreihe Verwaltungsinformatik, vol. 20, pp. 123–142. R. v. Decker's Verlag, Heidelberg (1999)

11. Nordfors, L., Ericson, B., Lindell, H., Lapidus, J.: - Gullers Grupp: Government of Tomorrow - Future Scenarios for 2020, Vinnova Report VR 2009:28, Vinnova, pp.15 (2009)
12. Scherer, S., et al: Usability Engineering in e-Participation. European Journal of ePractice 7 (2009), http://www.epractice.eu/en/document/
13. Smith, S., Dalakiouridou, E.: Contextualising Public (e)Participation in the Governance of the European Union. European Journal of ePractice 7 (2009), http://www.epractice.eu/en/document/
14. Tomkova, J.: E-consultations: New tools for civic engagement or facades for political correctness? European Journal of ePractice 7 (2009), http://www.epractice.eu/en/document/
15. Winter, A.: Die österreichische Verwaltung im Internet. In: Reinermann, H. (Hrsg.) Regieren und Verwalten im Informationszeitalter: Unterwegs zur virtuellen Verwaltung, pp. 170–185. R.v. Decker, Heidelberg (2000)
16. Core Principles for Public Engagement (2009), http://www.thataway.org/files/ Core_Principles_of_Public_Engagement.pdf
17. 4th Ministerial eGovernment Conference (2009), http://egov2007.gov.pt/

Towards a Roadmap for User Involvement in E-Government Service Development

Jesper Holgersson[1], Eva Söderström[1], Fredrik Karlsson[2], and Karin Hedström[2]

[1] University of Skövde, Högskolevägen, SE-541 28 Skövde, Sweden
{eva.soderstrom,jesper.holgersson}@his.se
[2] MELAB, Swedish Business School at Örebro University, SE-701 82 Örebro, Sweden
{fredrik.karlsson,karin.hedstrom}@oru.se

Abstract. New technology means new ways of both developing, providing and consuming services. In the strive for government organizations to build and maintain relationships with its citizens, e-presence is highly important. E-services are one way to go, and it has been argued that user participation is an important part of developing said services. In this paper we analyze a selection of user participation approaches from a goal perspective to see how they fit in an e-government service development context., In doing so, we identify four challenges that need to be addressed when including users in the development: 1) Identifying the user target segment, 2) Identifying the individual user within each segment, 3) Getting users to participate, and 4) Lacking adequate skills.

Keywords: E-services, E-government, E-service development, User participation.

1 Introduction

New technology enables a broadened choice of how to deliver services, and electronic services (e-services) have become an increasingly adopted channel [1]. Today, this channel is an important part of implementing e-government strategies. When e-services are introduced as part of the e-government concept they are often viewed as a way to automate internal, manual, processes [2]. In other words, they are driven from the government perspective, and user considerations have been given less attention.

Recent studies [3] have shown that increased attention to users' (citizens, public authorities, or businesses using the e-service) needs bring positive effects when e-services are deployed. This confirms earlier research about user involvement [4] and is not surprising. User involvement has been treated extensively in information systems (IS) literature [4], and there are several well known approaches, such as Participatory Design (PD) [5], User Centered Design (UCD) [6] and User Innovation (UI) [7]. Each of these can be viewed as a design theory [8], with associated design principles or design goals, for how to take users' needs into consideration during development. However, as discussed by [9] and [10] these theories are introduced in new settings as the information systems field moves forward, settings that was not considered when the theories evolved. Consequently, e-service development can be

M.A. Wimmer et al. (Eds.): EGOV 2010, LNCS 6228, pp. 251–262, 2010.

viewed as such a new setting. It is therefore natural to investigate if it is possible to apply them when developing e-government services. This paper aims to analyze the three mentioned user participation approaches in e-government service development from a goal perspective, in order to identify challenges for user participation in development. Awareness of the challenges is important in order to increase citizen inclusion, as well as the chances of mutual gain from development. Inclusion may also increase democratic principles, and enable the development of more usable and valuable e-government services.

The paper is structured as follows. In the second Section we outline our research design and analytical framework. In the third Section we identify requirements on e-government service development. Sections four and five contain the analysis, where we map the requirements to the goals behind the user participation approaches. Finally, the paper ends with short conclusions concerning the challenges identified and reflections on future research.

2 Research Design

In this paper we view user participation approaches from a design science perspective [11], where each approach represents a design theory. This means each approach has been devised through a goal-oriented design activity [12], where certain design goals were set out. Hence these design goals or principles tell us what can be achieved with that particular approach, which can be compared with the requirements that are found about e-government service development. To achieve this end we need an analysis framework that can reconstruct the design principles of each design theory. Therefore, we have chosen the framework laid out in [13] to analyze the rationale, or the goals, behind each approach.

The framework in Fig. 1 is depicted as a Unified Modelling Language-class diagram. It consists of three classes: method fragment, goal and values, and between these we find a number of named associations. The method fragment concept refers to a description of a systems development method, or any coherent part thereof [14]. According to [15] method fragments can be studied on five different levels of granularity: method, stage, model, diagram, and concept. Method addresses a complete method for systems development, for example, Rational Unified Process. Concept on the other hand is the smallest part of a method, representing a single construct in the method.

Each method fragment is anchored in goals and values. These are often referred to as the method's perspective [16] or argumentative dimension [17]. Goals reflect the method designer's intentions with the method, what that the method user will be able to achieve when using it – in other words, the design goals. Since a method can have several goals, these goals can either support or contradict each other. In addition, a goal is based on one or more values, which are ideals held by the method designer. The principle about achievement and contradiction applies here as well, where values in a method can support or contradict each other.

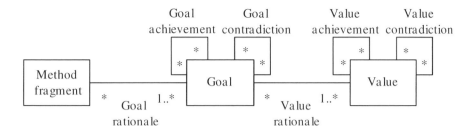

Fig. 1. Method rationale framework [13]

Our data analysis was done in three steps, where the last two steps form an iterative pattern. The first step concerns elicitation of the requirements of e-government service development. This step is based on existing research on e-government service and was presented in Section 2. The second step, presented in Section 4, consists of a reconstruction of the design goals behind each of the selected user participation approaches. In order to make the methods more comparable we have used goals graphs, using a unified notation, inspired by Yu [18]. We have selected goals put forward as important in literature. As we are interested in the challenges to fulfil these goals we have decided not to include values in the analysis. Subsequently, we do not question the goals and the values as such, rather investigating the problems of fulfilling them in an e-government service development context.

All methods consist of a large number of goals if the analysis is done at a low granularity level. However, since we are interested in a strategic discussion concerning the applicability of these approaches we view the selected approaches as one stage in a development method. According to Brinkkemper's [15] typology of method fragments, a stage addresses "a segment of the life-cycle of the information system," for example, design. Therefore, we have investigated high-level goals to see how well they support the requirements of e-government services development.

The third step focuses on analysing the possibilities to fulfil the goals that we have identified for each user participation approach. In Section 5, we have mapped the identified requirements to the design goals. With this basis we have identified challenges with meeting certain requirements.

3 E-Government Service Development

Many governments wish to improve their service to citizens and companies by becoming more flexible in a dynamic and changing environment [19]. Today, web-based technologies, such as e-services [1, 20], offer new opportunities for governments to communicate with citizens and businesses. These technologies are efficient alternatives to the traditional physical channels. But development of e-government services is a complex endeavor. Many of these services have to be offered more all less universally to all citizens [21] in order to fulfill normative values such as democracy and individual human rights. Hence, identifying relevant e-government services and eliciting valid systems requirements for these broad target groups are challenging [22]. Also, development often includes integration of different government entities, which results in complex solutions [23].

Normative and legal values are embedded in the actions performed by public administrations [24]. For example, in Sweden they are referred to as a "public ethos" that shall govern the actions of the civil servants. The public ethos is based on democracy and human rights, striving for the legal rights of the individual [25]. As e-government concerns the development of information systems (IS) for the public sector, the IS supporting e-government services, should be developed with particular attention to the values and goals related to the public ethos, such as using ICT as a tool to support increased citizen participation in democratic processes [2, 26]. Business values are also included in the Swedish public ethos [25], meaning that public administrations should take into account economic values such as functionality, productivity and efficiency [27, 28].

Development of e-government services has, as mentioned, traditionally focused on automating internal manual business processes [2]. Attention has been on possible efficiency generated by the e-service, and not on users [29]. At best, user needs have been guessed and not thoroughly analyzed [30]. However, the role of the user is now shifting towards active user participation in various forms [31]. It is evident that active user participation increase the likelihood of positive effects on service use, not only from the providing authority's point of view but also from the user's [32, 33]

Table 1. Requirements on e-government service development

Requirement	References
To develop e-services that are *relevant* to the users	[21, 22]
To develop e-services that are *useable*	[29, 30, 32, 33]
To develop e-services that are *efficient* for the government	[2, 25, 27, 28]
To develop e-services that *supports democracy*	[2, 25, 26]
To employ an *efficient and democratic development process* for the government	[25, 27]

To summarize, the interest for applying user participation approaches in e-government service development is growing. At the same time we can also identify (at least) five requirements that are important during development of e-government services. These requirements, which are central to the analysis in this paper, are summarized in Table 1.

4   User Participation Approaches

There are numerous approaches for how to incorporate users in the development process. A closer look at these approaches reveals many shared characteristics. In this paper, we focus on three such approaches: Participatory Design (PD), User Centered Design (UCD), and User Innovation (UI). We have chosen these three approaches for two reasons; (a) they are commonly mentioned in research literature; and (b) they are focused on user participation, but from different perspectives. The analysis maps out, and relates, the design goals of each approach, which enables comparison of the three. Each goal is first given a design approach identifier (PD, UCD and UI respectively), and then a goal identifier (G1, etc.)

4.1 Participatory Design

PD represents "*a rich diversity of theories, practices, analyses, and actions, with the goal of working directly with users (and other stakeholders) in the design*" [34pp. 25]. The overall goal is usable and accepted ICT systems (PD-G1 in Fig. 2). PD stems from basic democratic principles: people affected by a decision or change should be able to influence it (PD-G2). Another important PD aspect is that users or user representatives (PD-G3) must actively contribute (PD-G4) in analysis, design, prototyping and implementation of an information system [35]. Furthermore, the importance of designers and users working together is emphasized [5] (PD-G5). Both roles are equally important and must take responsibility for the project outcome. The designer needs knowledge about the information system setting (PD-G7) and the user needs knowledge about technical possibilities and restrictions (PD-G6). Kensing & Blomberg [35] state three basic PD requirements, the users must: have access to relevant information; have the possibility to take an independent position to the problem dealt with; and participate in decision making.

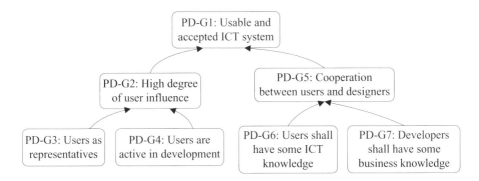

Fig. 2. Goal analysis for Participatory Design

4.2 User Centered Design

UCD emphasizes that the system purpose is to serve the user, not to use a specific technology or be an elegant piece of programming [6]. User environments must therefore be understood and considered when designing systems [36]. In Fig 3, we express this as UCD-G1. Better user theories will allow designers to build more usable interfaces and systems [37]. Work organization must hence be analyzed beyond traditional task analysis to incorporate social and organizational contexts that influence the users' operations [37]. The user needs should dominate the interface design, and the interface needs should in turn dominate the remaining systems design

[6]. This is illustrated as UCD-G2 in Fig. 3. From the beginning, UCD did not involve users actively even though user needs were imperative. Now, user participation is essential in the early project phases, with a focus on requirements analysis [38]. If users are to have any impact, they must provide information that is appropriate to particular stages of the development. Developers therefore need extensive business knowledge (UCD-G5). User participation for partially finished products is only worthwhile if changes and modifications can be made at this stage [38]. It is, however, possible to include users to assess if user requirements are met. In summary, in UCD, users are rather passive and act as advisors, only having moderate influence on the development per se (UCD-G4); thus designers have the design responsibility (UCD-G3).

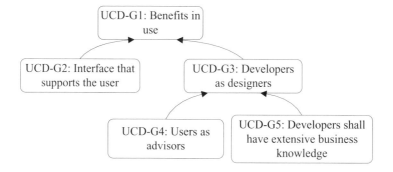

Fig. 3. Goal analysis for User Centered Design

4.3 User Innovation

UI is focused on innovations made by users. As shown by UI-G1, in Fig. 4, the overall goal is to provide 'innovative systems functionality.' Users are the source for innovation and design rather than organizations, [7, 39]. UI is based on the concept of lead users that capture ideas (UI-G2), which are transformed into full-blown solutions in collaboration between users and developers (UI-G5). Typically, lead users are the ones who perform product and service innovations; they identify the problems (UI-G3) as well as the design solution (UI-G4). A lead user is considered to be a user of a certain application or product [39].

Using lead users in design differs from other approaches in the sense that the lead users themselves try to design products and services that satisfy their needs. Subsequently, they are responsible for problems and solutions (UI-G6). This means that lead users own the design, even if developers build the solution (UI-G7). This may lead to innovative ideas and solutions compared to other approaches, since lead users are free from the limits of regular designers. Focusing on typical users, rather than lead users, is not optimal when working with fast moving fields such as IS, were time of development may result in obsolete applications and products. In this case working with lead users to identify novel needs that have not yet been discovered by the general public may prove to be beneficial [7, 39, 40].

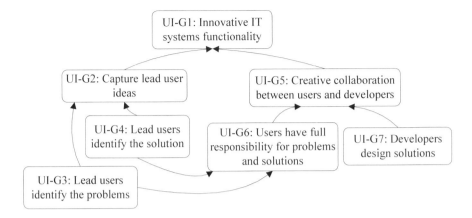

Fig. 4. Goal analysis for User Innovation

5   Design Goal Challenges for User Participation

We emphasize that user participation is important, and may provide beneficial results [3]. However, user participation approaches are associated with potential challenges that need to be addressed. In this Section, each approach is analyzed separately, using references to the goals in Fig. 2 to 4 and keywords from the five requirements in bold style.

5.1   Challenges with Participatory Design

PD aims for collaboration, and interactive development between developers and user representatives. The question is, however, how to create a development environment that emphasizes and encourages collaboration and interactivity. It is generally difficult to attract users to participate in e-service development, and even more difficult when the users are external. It is also difficult to ensure that all participants have sufficient knowledge and "speak the same language." Still, user participation is a must according to PD in order to develop *relevant* (PD-G3, PD-G4, PD-G7) and *usable* e-government services (PD-G4, PD-G6) that *support democratic processes* (PD-G1).

Efficiency is a keyword for government, both concerning the resulting e-services and the *development process* itself (PD-G7). Using the e-service will only be efficient if the surrounding work processes are streamlined, often a neglected aspect. The systems development method requires a suitable set of method fragments selected for the situation, which in turn requires developers to critically review the potential method fragments. Basic skills and domain knowledge is imperative, but not given. *Democracy* (PD-G5) concerns how the government can communicate with the users and encourage them to put their opinions forward, as well as how to ensure participation across citizen groups in a *democratic development process* (PD-G3). The resulting e-service should foster inclusion of as many citizen groups as possible, and the risk is always that one or more groups feel left out.

5.2   Challenges with User Centered Design

UCD aims to consider users and their environment during systems development. The user group is dispersed, which makes it difficult firstly to satisfy everyone's needs and thus make the e-services *relevant* (UCD-G4), and to find a language that enables communication about requirements and needs. Getting users to take on the advisory role is not trivial either. One question is thus how to attract potential advisors and how to acquire knowledge from users. A related challenge concerns *usability* of the e-services (UCD-G2, UCD-G4), in particular when developing an interface that supports all citizen groups.

Much like PD, *efficiency* in both e-services and the *development process* is difficult and requires the right tools (UCD-G5). Work processes must be identified and adjusted, but this is often a sensitive process. There are also great demands on the developers, since they must know not only the application environment, but also the users and their needs since the these are not active themselves during development. UCD also shares the challenges when working with *democratic* principles as PD does (UCD-G4, UCD-G5).

5.3   Challenges with User Innovation

UI is focused on the users being the driving force in development. The most difficult problem is to identify lead users in society. It is only then that lead user ideas can be captured, which affects *relevance* of the e-government services (UI-G2). However, these users should also want and have time to participate in and even lead e-government service development. Furthermore, it is difficult to identify what a lead user *is* in a particular situation, and also what is required by that user. Regardless of user innovativeness, can they speak for the entire user (citizen) spectrum? The answer affects broad acceptance and *usability* of the solution (UI-G4). The e-services are intended for use within government organizations, and are hence also part of their work processes. Hence, can and should lead users judge how *efficient* (UI-G6, UI-G7) a solution is for the government organization. One main point in UI is that users drive the *development process* (UI-G6, UI-G7). It is not certain, however, that these users are experienced in developing e-government services, and they may therefore have problems expressing ideas and solutions.

Most users live in a world where *democratic* principles are important and drive the society. In this case, both the e-services (UI-G4) and the *development process* (UI-G2) are concerned. Even so, lead users may firstly not be representative for the public in general, and there is no guarantee that their ideas and solutions put democratic principles before personal needs.

6   Summarizing Analysis

As Sections 5.1 to 5.3 express, one challenge is to identify a clear user target segment. PD is working with user representatives (PD-G3), UCD with user advisors (UCD-G4), and UI builds on lead users (IU-G2). Hence, the users have to be representatives, advisors, or lead users for a larger group. However, demarcating such a target group is not easy. Many e-government services have to be offered more or less universally to all citizens [21]. Targeting "all" users in an entire population is a daunting task, which seems very hard to accomplish. In other words, one challenge is the dispersed target segment faced during development of e-government services.

All three approaches are also anchored in the assumption that individual users in the target group can be identified, and that these users can represent a larger user group (see for example PD-G3, UCD-G4, and UI-G2). However, most users are external, residing outside the governments organizational boundaries [41]. Consequently, it becomes more complicated to address appropriate users for participation in the development process, especially if we have to address individual citizens. A second challenge is, therefore, to identify individual users within the target segment.

The three user participation approaches range from active to passive participation. Both in PD and UI, the user is supposed to take active part in development (PD-G4, UI-G3, UI-G4), while in UCD, the user has a more passive role as advisor (UCD-G4). This means that the user often must be persuaded to participate and in the case of UI to have the ownership of the design (UI-G6). This is a major challenge, since the users most often are external to the government organization, and participation is based on free will. Internal users can be obliged to participate in development activities and may also see benefits with new functionality more clearly [42]. Accordingly, all three approaches have to face the challenge on how to attract external users to participate, where UI is the most demanding approach.

Development of e-government services is a complex endeavor. These artifacts often inherit a complex architecture from back-office systems, with a high number of relations and dependencies. This complexity is often invisible to the user and it is questionable to require that users should have such knowledge. When considering the design goals of our three approaches we see that they demands business knowledge to different degrees. Most demanding is UI, since the user is responsible for identifying the solution (UI-G6, IU-G7). In order to do that one is required to have extensive knowledge of what is possible to achieve. Least demanding is UCD, where the users have a more passive role and the developers have the business knowledge. Hence, skill inadequacy is the fourth challenge depending on the user's role in the design theories.

7   Conclusions

The importance of user involvement has been stressed in recent e-government research. Therefore, we have in this paper analyzed three user participation approaches, Participatory Design, User Centered Design and User Innovation, in e-government service development from a goal perspective. In doing so, we identified four challenges when including users in development: (1) Identifying the user target segment, (2) Identifying the individual user within each segment, (3) Getting users to participate, and (4) Lacking adequate skills.

Traditionally, users have not been included in the e-government service development process [43]. However, e-presence and highlighted democratic principles that new technologies bring increase the need for government organizations to interact with citizens and enable their voices to be heard to a different extent than today. User participation generally produces better results in terms of, for example, more usable e-services. Government organizations should therefore be interested in adopting user participation in their e-government service development processes. They should also pay close attention to the challenges and allocate appropriate resources for dealing with them before they become problems.

The shift to user participation in e-government service development calls for future research into the structure and composition of a roadmap for said participation. For example, how shall ideas for new or improved services be captured? How shall ideas be prioritized and selected? And how can selected ideas be sufficiently detailed to allow for effective development? Our future research aims to develop a roadmap that is empirically grounded, and which is simple to adopt, use, and learn. It needs to be comprised of a set of methods fragments with concrete advice on how to apply them in an e-government service development setting. In this context, it is relevant to consider incorporating research on virtual or social communities, and in what way these phenomena alter or affect e-government service development.

References

1. Rowley, J.: An analysis of the e-service literature: towards a research agenda. Internet Research: Electronic Networking Applications and Policy 16, 879–897 (2006)
2. Asgarkhani, M.: The effectiveness of e-Service in Local Government: A Case Study. Electric journal of e-government 3, 157–166 (2005)
3. Melin, U., Axelsson, K., Lundsten, M.: Talking to, not about, Entrepreneurs – Experiences of Public e-service Development in a Business Start Up Case. In: Cunningham, P., Cunningham, M. (eds.) eChallanges, pp. 383–390 (2008)
4. Cavaye, A.L.M.: User participation is systems development revisited. Information and Management 28, 311–323 (1995)
5. Schuler, D., Namioka, A.: Participatory Design Priciples and Practicies - Preface. In: Schuler, D., Namioka, A. (eds.) Participatory Design Principles and Practicies, Lawrence Erlbaum Associates Inc., London (1993)
6. Norman, D.: Cognitive engineering. In: Norman, D. (ed.) User-Centered System Design: New Perspectives on Human Computer Interaction, pp. 31–65. Lawrence Erbaum Associated, London (1986)
7. Hippel, E.: Lead Users: A Source of Novel Product Concepts. Management Science 32, 791–805 (1986)
8. Hevner, A.R., March, S.T., Park, J., Ram, S.: Design Science in Information Systems Research. MIS Quarterly 28, 75–105 (2004)
9. Holmström, H.: Virtual Communities as Platforms for Product Development: An Interpretive Case Study of Customer Involvement in Online Game Developmen. In: International Conference on Information Systems 2001 (ICIS 2001), New Orleans, Louisiana, USA (2001)
10. Hansson, C., Dittrich, Y., Randall, D.: How to Include Users in the Development of Off-the-Shelf Software: A Case for Complementing Participatory Design with Agile Development. In: Annual Hawaii International Conference on System Sciences 2006 (HICSS 06), vol. 8. IEEE Computer Society, Los Alamitos (2006)
11. Gregor, S., Jones, D.: The Anatomy of a Design Theory. Journal of the Association of Information systems 8, 312–335 (2007)

12. Friedman, K.: Theory construction in design research: criteria, approaches, and methods. Design Studies 24, 507–522 (2003)
13. Ågerfalk, P.J., Wistrand, K.: Systems Development Method Rationale: A Conceptual Framework for Analysis. In: Proceedings of the 5th International Conference on Enterprise Information Systems (ICEIS 2003), Angers, France (2003)
14. Harmsen, F.: Situational Method Engineering (1997)
15. Brinkkemper, S., Saeki, M., Harmsen, F.: Meta-Modelling based assembly techniques for situational method engineering. Information Systems 24, 209–228 (1999)
16. Brinkkemper, S.: Method engineering: engineering of information systems development methods and tools. Information and Software Technology 38, 275–280 (1996)
17. Jayratna, N.: Understanding and evaluating methodologies. McGraw-Hill, London (1994)
18. Yu, E.: Modeling Organizations for Information Systems Requirements Engineering. In: The IEEE International Symposium on Requirements Engineering, San Diego, USA (1993)
19. Klievink, B., Janssen, M.: Improving Integrated Service Delivery: A Simulation Game (2009)
20. Goldkuhl, G.: Socio-instrumental service modelling: An inquiry on e-services for tax declarations. In: Persson, A., Stirna, J. (eds.) PoEM 2009, vol. 39, pp. 207–221. Springer, Stockholm (2009)
21. Henriksen, Z.H.: The diffusion of e-services in Danish municipalities. In: Traunmüller, R. (ed.) EGOV 2004. LNCS, vol. 3183, pp. 164–171. Springer, Heidelberg (2004)
22. Lenk, K.: Electronic Service Delivery – A driver of public sector modernization. Information Polity 7, 87–96 (2002)
23. Layne, K., Lee, J.: Developing fully functional E-government: A four stage model. Government Information Quarterly 18, 122–136 (2001)
24. Cordella, A., Willcocks, L.: Outsourcing, bureaucracy and public value: Reappraising the notion of the "contract state". Government Information Quarterly 27, 82–88 (2010)
25. Odell, M., Hellberg, L.: Government Decision: Mission to initiate a project concerning a public ethos. Swedish Ministry of Finance (2009) (in Swedish)
26. Kangas, J., Store, R.: Internet and teledemocracy in participatory planning of natural resources management. Landscape and Urban Planning 62, 89–101 (2003)
27. Editorial Board. Government Information Quarterly 23, CO2–CO2 (2006)
28. Watson, R.T., Mundy, B.: A strategic perspective of electronic democracy. Communications of the ACM 44, 27–30 (2001)
29. Anthopoulos, L.G., Siozos, P.S., Tsoukalas, I.A.: Applying participatory design and collaboration in digital public services for discovering and re-designing e-Government services. Government Information Quarterly 24, 353–376 (2007)
30. Jupp, V.: Realizing the vision of e-government. In: Curtin, G., Sommer, M., Sommer-Vis, V. (eds.) The world of E-Government. Haworth Press (2003)
31. Lindblad-Gidlund, K.: Driver or Passenger? An analysis of Citizen-Driven eGovernment. In: Wimmer, M.A., Scholl, H.J., Ferro, E. (eds.) EGOV 2008. LNCS, vol. 5184, pp. 267–278. Springer, Heidelberg (2008)
32. Andersen, V.K., Medaglia, R.: eGovernment Front-End Services: Administrative and Citizen Cost Benefits. In: Wimmer, M.A., Scholl, H.J., Ferro, E. (eds.) EGOV 2008. LNCS, vol. 5184, pp. 148–159. Springer, Heidelberg (2008)
33. Carroll, J.M., Rosson, M.B.: Participatory design in community informatics. Design Studies 28, 243–261 (2007)
34. Muller, M.J., Kuhn, S.: Participatory design. Communications of the ACM 36, 24–28 (1993)

35. Kensing, F., Blomberg, J.: Participatory design: Issues and Concerns. Computer Supported Cooperative work 7, 167–185 (1998)
36. Hooper, K.: Architectural design: An anology. In: Norman, D. (ed.) User-Centered System Design: New Perspectives on Human-Computer Interaction, pp. 9–23. Lawrence Erlbaum Associated, London (1986)
37. Bannon, L.: Issues in Design: Some Notes. In: User-Centered System Design: New Perspecives on Human-Computer Interaction, pp. 27–29. Lawrence Erlbaum, London (1986)
38. Noyes, J., Barber, C.: User-Centered design of systems. Springer, London (1999)
39. Hippel, E.: New Product Ideas from Lead Users. Research Technology Management 32, 24–27 (1989)
40. Herstatt, C., Hippel, E.: Developing New Product Concepts Via the Lead User Method: A Case Study in a "Low Tech Field". Journal of Product Innovation Management 9, 213–221 (1992)
41. Axelsson, K., Melin, U.: Citizen Participation and Involvement in eGovernment Projects – An emergent framework. In: Wimmer, M.A., Scholl, H.J., Ferro, E. (eds.) EGOV 2008. LNCS, vol. 5184, pp. 207–218. Springer, Heidelberg (2008)
42. Albinsson, L., Forsgren, K.: Co-Design Metaphors and Scenarios - Two Elements in a Design Language for Co-Design. LAP, Kiruna (2005)
43. Axelsson, K., Melin, U.: Talking to, not about, citizens – Experiences of focus groups in public e-service development. In: Wimmer, M.A., Scholl, H.J., Grönlund, Å. (eds.) EGOV 2007. LNCS, vol. 4656, pp. 179–218. Springer, Heidelberg (2007)

ICT Diffusion in an Aging Society: A Scenario Analysis

Enrico Ferro[1], Brunella Caroleo[2], Marco Cantamessa[2], and Maurizio Leo[2]

[1] Istituto Superiore Mario Boella, Technology to Business Intelligence Unit,
Via Boggio 61, 10138 Torino, Italy
enrico.ferro@ismb.it
www.enricoferro.com
[2] Politecnico di Torino, Department of Production Systems and Business Economics,
Corso Duca degli Abruzzi 24, 10129 Torino, Italy
{brunella.caroleo,marco.cantamessa,maurizio.leo}@polito.it

Abstract. The relevance of Information and Communication Technologies (ICTs) is progressively increasing in every aspect of modern life. At the same time, the aging trend most European countries are experiencing, may significantly impact on their absorptive capacity of innovation, which is a key determinant of socioeconomic development, with deep policy implications for both the private and the public sector. The aim of this paper is thus to investigate the relationship between age and technological diffusion. The analysis is performed using the Internet as a case study, combining agent-based simulation with classical statistical analysis. Three different demographic scenarios are considered, representing different geographical areas as well as possible alternative futures. The results obtained show that the age factor and the demographic trends exert a significant influence on both the dynamics and length of the diffusion process.

Keywords: diffusion of innovation, aging, policy, agent-based simulation, ICT governance.

1 Introduction

The diffusion of Information and Communication Technologies (ICTs) in nearly every crevice of society has significantly increased and extended the importance of network externalities deriving from the use of compatible technologies by critical masses of users. Furthermore, ICT diffusion has contributed to render the competitiveness and equality of socioeconomic systems strictly dependent on their capacity to absorb innovation and fruitfully put it into practice.

At the same time, the aging trend present in European societies is bound to pose significant challenges to the process of innovation adoption and use. This trend is currently particularly severe. As an example, in Italy (one of the "eldest" European countries) the percentage of people over 65 as of 2008 is equal to 20% and is expected to reach 35% by 2050 [1].

Technological paradigms are, in fact, highly intertwined with users' generations, whose ability to migrate across them is significantly influenced -among other factors- by

M.A. Wimmer et al. (Eds.): EGOV 2010, LNCS 6228, pp. 263–274, 2010.
© IFIP International Federation for Information Processing 2010

age, and this is particularly true for innovations that are related to knowledge and cognition [2]. If the demographic distribution of a population WAS in steady state, technology diffusion processes, though dependent on age, would be independent from the distribution. However, when the demographic distribution does change, it is likely that this will affect technology diffusion processes. In such scenario, national and regional governments might have to deal with unprecedented challenges requiring a profound rethinking of the policy and strategic approaches so far implemented. The situation thus calls for a deep understanding of the problem dynamics and dimensions, necessary to identify timely policy responses and the minimization of errors.

This paper presents the results of the first phase of the I-PAS project financed by Regione Piemonte (IT) on 'Innovation Policies for an Aging Society'. The main objective of such project is to investigate the influence of the aging trend on the innovation absorption capacity of a socioeconomic system, and to identify the most suitable policy responses. A decision support tool will be developed allowing to test different policies, thus resulting in more informed political choices. The present article constitutes a preliminary contribution to the achievement of such objectives, starting to investigate the relationship between demographic trends and the corresponding evolution of diffusion phenomena.

The research question, object of the present paper, can be summarized in: "*what will be the impact of demographic changes on technology adoption?*". Answering this question represents a first step to assess policies to make timely and more informed choices on which course of action to take.

Different demographic scenarios are considered, in order to represent three main trends currently present worldwide (Figure 2):

— Setting 1, *aging* societies: populations experiencing a heavy aging trend, i.e. aged people is going to constitute the prevailing part of the population (e.g. Italy, Germany, Japan);
— Setting 2, *middle-aged* societies: populations in which the middle-aged demographic distribution will expand, becoming dominant (e.g. India);
— Setting 3, *young* societies: populations in which the aging phenomenon is going to be only slightly present (e.g. sub-Saharan countries), thus going to be mainly composed by young cohorts.

The change of technological adoption is simulated through agent-based modeling, in order to overcome the limits of "traditional" analytical models in the treatment of complex dynamic systems. The results of the simulation are subsequently explored via statistical analyses in order to obtain a flexible yet robust methodology.

The article is structured as follows: in the next Section a literature review on technology diffusion related to the aging issue is proposed; Section 3 presents demographic data and trends; an example of technology diffusion data related to age is given. In Section 4, three demographic settings are introduced: simulation parameters and assumptions are described and results are then discussed. Finally, conclusions are drawn and some implications for further research and practice are discussed.

2   State of the Art

The demographic change due to an increase of the elderly population represents a well-known phenomenon currently experienced in many countries [3, 4].

Over the last decade, the core of the literature dealing with the aging of societies has mainly focused on welfare state systems. To exemplify, Casey [5] discussed the possible impacts of aging on expenditure and fiscal pressures. Anderson [6] studied the effects of population aging on retirement policies, as well as on health spending and on workforce composition, seeking to identify policy actions useful to face the phenomenon.

More recently, the issue of aging has been embraced by the European Commission as part of its eInclusion policy. This resulted in a number of studies and projects mainly focused on understanding how ICT could improve the life of elderly people [7, 8]. Nevertheless, little attention has so far been paid to the aggregate effect of aging on the innovation absorption performance of a socioeconomic system.

The role of innovation as a major driving force in economic growth and social development has been in fact repeatedly recognized over the last decades. Technological progress has been found to be responsible for up to one half of the growth of a country economy [9].

Looking at the literature on diffusion of innovation, the role of age in technological adoption is not clearly defined. As Rogers wrote [10], "about half of the diffusion studies on the relationship of age and innovativeness show no relationship, a few found that earlier adopters are younger, and some indicate they are older". However, no empirical evidence is provided in Rogers' book. In addition, this literature strand mainly refers to types of innovation that may be considered significantly different in terms of preconditions for adoption from Internet related technologies (e.g. cognitive skills, IT literacy, language barriers in accessing a significant portion of the content available for non-English speaking users, etc.). For this reason, it is probably the right time to reconsider investigating this relationship to shed some light on the potential impacts that the ageing of societies could exert on countries' ability to absorb innovation.

In this respect, the strand of literature focusing on digital divide has provided useful insights on the differences among generation in the adoption and usage of ICTs [11-14]. This in an attempt to foster a higher level of eInclusion that is considered to be instrumental to increase social cohesion, quality of life and the diffusion of complementary activities such as eGovernment, eParticipation and eCommerce. As a matter of fact, while eGovernment is establishing as the most important public sector reform strategy, age is a factor which may strongly affect its usage [15].

The contribution that this paper intends to bring to the existing body of knowledge on this topic is threefold. Firstly, an investigation of the relationship between Rogers' categories of adopters for Internet related technologies. Secondly, a better understanding of the diffusion process within age classes in terms of innovation and imitation. Thirdly, a dynamic assessment (through agent-based simulation) of the future impact of the aging societies on their ability to absorb innovation.

3 Data and Demographic Trends

As introduced in Section 1, the aging phenomenon is going to represent one of the main socioeconomic challenges in the next decades. As an example, Figure 1 shows the comparison of the old-age dependency ratio in some World countries in 2010 and 2050 [16]; this indicator represents the number of people aged 65 and over as percentage of labor force (aged 15-64); for instance, Japanese and Italian old-age dependency ratios will double.

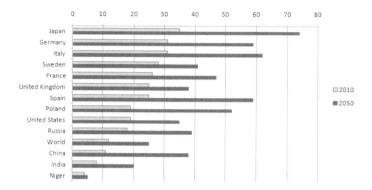

Fig. 1. Old-age dependency ratios in 2010 and 2050 in some World countries (source: United Nations, 2009)

The aging trend is noticeable also in the population pyramid shift that some countries are experiencing (Figure 2): on the one hand, the declining birth rate is going to reduce young generations consistency, and on the other hand the postponement of decease age will increase life expectancy. Even the migratory flows (accounted for in the demographic projections shown in Figure 2) seem not to exert any significant offsetting effect.

In order to analyze the relationship between the aging trend and technological adoption, the process of Internet diffusion has been used as a case study.

Although age may by no means be considered as the only determinant of Internet access and usage (as a matter of fact, education and income have also been proven [13, 14] to exert a significant influence), the next section will attempt to investigate and isolate the influence that the age variable may exert on Internet adoption, setting the stage for the simulation of alternative scenarios aimed at testing the impacts of three different demographic trends on innovation absorptive capacity of a given socioeconomic system.

3.1 Internet Penetration Data by Age Groups: The Case of Germany

Figure 3 shows the data on the diffusion of Internet technology in Germany from 1997 to 2008, considering each age group separately [17]. It is interesting to map this pattern of diffusion within the different age groups against the well-known

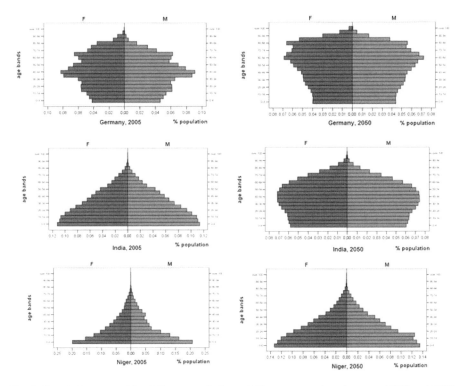

Fig. 2. Population pyramids of Germany, India and Niger: comparison between 2005 and 2050 (source: United Nations, 2009)

categorization of adopters by Rogers [10] in order to understand the distribution of Internet innovators and laggards as a function of age. To this aim, an estimate of earlier data (since 1990) by a logistic regression has been necessary to analyze the distribution of the first stage of diffusion (innovators).

The resulting composition of Rogers' categories for Internet diffusion divided by age groups is summarized in Figure 4. Some important considerations may be put forward:

- innovators are constituted almost exclusively by the active population (20-59 years old); it is likely that, in the first stages of diffusion, people began using the Internet because it was a necessity connected to work; furthermore, Internet connections were quite expensive, and only people with a substantial income were able to afford it;
- for subsequent categories (early adopters and early majority) the Internet diffused among younger people, becoming both an entertainment tool and a useful support for education;
- the number of elder people using Internet is increasing though penetration in the over-60 population is lower than 30%, and the threshold defining *laggards* (84% of total population) has not been reached yet.

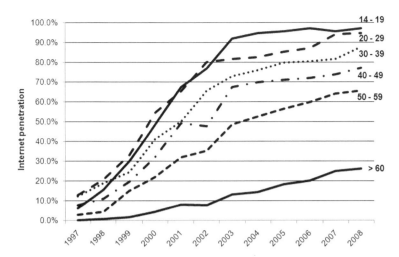

Fig. 3. Internet penetration by age in Germany, 1997 – 2008 (source: ARD/ZDF-Onlinestudie, 2008)

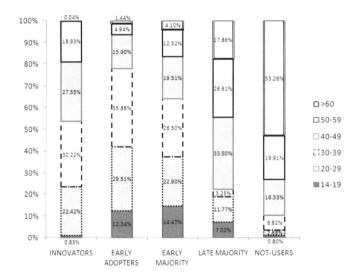

Fig. 4. Composition of Rogers' categories by age for Internet technology

Other interesting results emerge by identifying the Bass model parameters [18] of the diffusion curves for each age group (Table 1); innovation (p) and imitation (q) parameters have been estimated using a non-linear regression model [19] and neglecting inter-group imitative effects.

Not surprisingly, given the strong network externalities present in Internet technology, the diffusion process appears to have been strongly affected by an imitative effect and especially in the youngest population (14 – 19). Interestingly enough, both parameters substantially differ from one age group to another.

Table 1. Estimates of Bass parameters for each age group

	Innovation parameter (p)	Imitation parameter (q)
14 – 19	0.0360	0.7579
20 – 29	0.1111	0.2746
30 – 39	0.0970	0.1790
40 – 49	0.0828	0.1345
50 – 59	0.0522	0.1350
> 60	0.0098	0.1610

Once identified the main parameters involved in the diffusion of Internet technology as a function of age, it is possible to analyze how the technology adoption will evolve in different demographic scenarios.

4   Scenarios and Simulations

Three settings (Figure 2) have been considered to represent the situation that different countries in the world could face in the future from a demographic perspective.

- The first scenario (*aging* societies) corresponds to the case of low birth rates and low death rates, peculiar of the population pyramids of developed countries. The parameters of this setting refer to Eurostat data about Germany in 2007 [1] and may be considered representative of other countries (such as Italy, Japan and Spain) affected by both current and future aging of the population.
- The second scenario (*middle-aged* societies) corresponds to the situation which countries characterized by high birth rates and low death rates could experience in the near future, such as India and Latin America. The parameters of this setting refer to India [16].
- The third scenario (*young* societies) corresponds to the case of high birth and death rates, peculiar of the population pyramids of most developing countries, such as African Sub-Saharan ones. The parameters of this setting refer to Niger [16].

Annual death rates and birth rates for each setting are summarized in Table 2 and 3, respectively.

Table 2. Annual death rates for each setting

	Setting 1: *aging* societies	Setting 2: *middle-aged* societies	Setting 3: *young* societies
0 – 14	0.04 %	0.30 %	1.67 %
15 – 19	0.02 %	0.17 %	0.41 %
20 – 29	0.04 %	0.25 %	0.87 %
30 – 39	0.06 %	0.38 %	1.21 %
40 – 49	0.18 %	0.59 %	1.66 %
50 – 59	0.50 %	1.38 %	2.50 %
> 60	3.55 %	5.49 %	5.94 %

Table 3. Annual birth rates for each setting

	Setting 1: *aging* societies	Setting 2: *middle-aged* societies	Setting 3: *young* societies
Birth rate	0.83 %	2.30 %	5.41 %

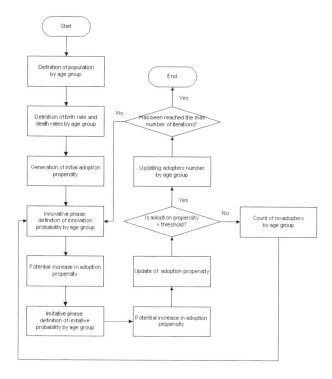

Fig. 5. Flowchart of the agent-based simulation

For each scenario, 15 simulation runs have been performed, in order to have statistically significant outputs; the duration of a single simulation run corresponds to a period of 30 years (equivalent to 1600 time buckets).

The flowchart of the simulation is represented in Figure 5 and is based on the progressive growth of an "adoption propensity" by each individual – affected by exogenous and imitative effects – until an "adoption threshold" is reached. Age of each agent is deterministically updated as time goes by. The adoption threshold is kept fixed for the whole duration of the simulation; this hypothesis is valid if the difficulty of accessing the technology can be supposed to be constant during the entire time horizon. Future work will be performed in the case in which the adoption threshold varies in time. This would allow studying cases in which adoption becomes easier (e.g. if price tends to decrease) or more difficult (e.g. if it becomes more difficult to switch from an established to a new paradigm) as time goes by.

4.1 Simulations Results

Figure 6 represents the output of simulations referred to the first scenario (aging societies) and projecting into the future the diffusion processes presented in Figure 3.

This plot depicts the diffusion processes among the different age ranges and shows the persistence of an adoption gap between people aged over 60 and the rest of the population.

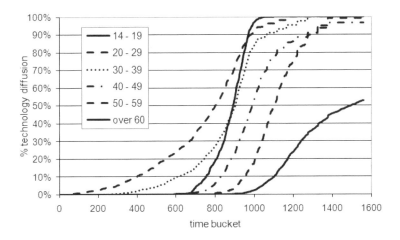

Fig. 6. Results of the simulation for Scenario 1: technology diffusion for each age group

The digital gap of people aged over 60 is more noticeable in comparison with the correspondent demography (dashed line in Figure 7).

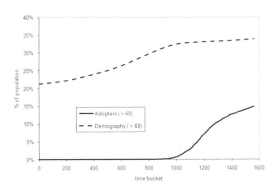

Fig. 7. Adoption of people aged over 60 in Scenario 1, compared with the demography

Due to lack of space available, we do not present detailed results for the other two settings. Figure 8 compares the diffusion curves of the three demographic scenarios over a thirty-year period for a possible future technology. *All the other variables being equal except for age* (therefore not accounting for, e.g., the socio-economic context of each country), technology diffusion in aging societies (setting 1) is slower than in younger ones. In addition, using the concept of S-time-distance proposed by Sicherl [20], the time advantage between middle-aged/young societies and aging ones at the end of the simulation may be quantified in 9 years.

This is probably due to the composition of non- or late adopters of the technology, which are concentrated in the elder population; since diffusion seems to propagate similarly in scenario 2 and 3, and since in such settings the proportion of people aged over 60 is quite similar, it is likely that the factor that influences the most the process of technology diffusion is the portion of people aged over 60 in the population, and not the composition of the remaining population. This information could be precious for policy makers, highlighting the concept that they should design and address specific policies to the elderly.

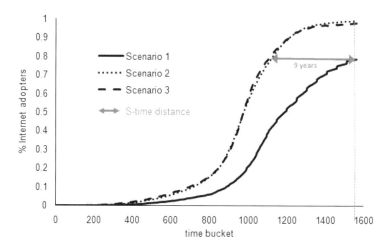

Fig. 8. Diffusion curves corresponding to the three scenarios

5 Conclusions

This paper intended to present the results of the preliminary work conducted in the context of the I-PAS project. The analysis mainly focused on better understanding the relationship between age and technology adoption. This was done in an attempt to assess the relevance of the aging trends on the diffusion processes of future technologies and, more in general, on the innovation absorptive capacity of socioeconomic systems. To this aim three sets of analyses have been performed, using the Internet as a case of study.

Firstly, the diffusion process present inside each age group has been studied revealing that age impacts on both its innovative and imitative aspects. The word-of-mouth effect appears to be the most relevant across all age groups and to exert a strong influence on youngest people (14-19). A significant role of the imitative effect may also be found in the eldest portion of population (over 60). Furthermore, the distribution of age groups inside Rogers' categories has been analyzed, showing a higher concentration of over 60 among laggards (currently non-users). This represents an indication of the reduced propensity of this age group towards the adoption of innovation.

Secondly, the process of Internet diffusion for the "European" setting has been projected in the future through an agent-based simulation. The results obtained show that the eldest portion of the population (over 60) most likely will not become adopters for a long period, if at all.

Finally, the "European" *aging* scenario has been compared to other two demographic settings (*middle-aged* and *young* societies). This comparison allowed us to understand that the most influencing factor is the proportion of people aged over 60 in the population (as a matter of fact, the diffusion processes for other two scenarios do not show any significant difference). This translates into a potential digital gap between aging and younger societies, quantifiable –at the end of the time horizon- as a S-time distance of 9 years or a difference in penetration equal to about 20% (Figure 8).

When developing policies for the diffusion of a technology (such as the Internet), policy makers should therefore take into account the age factor, since it is one (obviously not the unique) relevant factor in the diffusion process. It is therefore of primary importance that policy makers become aware of which aging scenario they will have to face, and design and shape their actions accordingly.

Concluding, the results presented in this paper constitute a stepping stone for further investigation. Further research will be necessary in order to understand if and how these conclusions may be extended to other types of technologies. Future work will be directed towards the identification and simulation of alternative policies that may help reducing the impact of aging on the innovation absorptive capacity of a socioeconomic system. The comparative assessment of the effectiveness of alternative policy actions will in fact be instrumental to allow policy makers to timely respond to the challenges posed by the aging of society through more suitable and informed choices.

References

1. Eurostat, `http://ec.europa.eu/eurostat/`
2. Venkatesh, V., Morris, M.G., Davis, G.B., Davis, F.D.: User acceptance of information technology: Toward a unified view. MIS Quarterly 27(3), 425–478 (2003)
3. Morgan, L.A., Kunkel, S.: Aging, Society, and the Life Course. Springer, New York (2007)
4. Cockerham, W.C.: This Aging Society. Prentice Hall, New Jersey (1996)
5. Casey, B., Oxley, H., Whitehouse, E.R., Antolín, P., Duval, R., Leibfritz, W.: Policies for an Ageing Society: Recent Measures and Areas for Further Reform. OECD Economics Department Working Papers 369, OECD Economics Department, no. 369 (2003)
6. Anderson, G.F., Hussey, P.S.: Population Aging: A Comparison Among Industrialized Countries. Health Affaire 19(3), 191–203 (2000)
7. European Commission: ICT & Ageing: Users, Markets and Technologies (2009), `http://ec.europa.eu/information_society/activities/einclusion/library/studies/docs/ageing_ict_good_1.pdf`
8. European Commission: Seniorwatch 2 - Assessment of the Senior Market for ICT Progress and Developments (2008), `http://ec.europa.eu/information_society/activities/einclusion/docs/swa2finalreport.pdf`

9. Schacht, W.H.: Industrial Competitiveness and Technological Advancement: Debate Over Government Policy. The National Council for Science and the Environment (2000)
10. Rogers, E.M.: Diffusion of Innovations. Free Press, Glencoe (1962)
11. Ferro, E., Helbig, N.C., Gil-Garcia, J.R.: The Digital Divide Metaphor: Understanding Paths to IT Literacy. In: Wimmer, M.A., Scholl, H.J., Grönlund, A. (eds.) EGOV 2007. LNCS, vol. 4656, pp. 265–280. Springer, Heidelberg (2007)
12. Selwyn, N.: The information aged: A qualitative study of older adults' use of information and communications technology. Journal of Aging Studies 18(4), 369–384 (2004)
13. Ferro, E., Dwivedi, Y.K., Gil-Garcia, J.R., Williams, M.D.: Handbook of Research on Overcoming Digital Divides: Constructing an Equitable and Competitive Information Society. Information Science Reference, IGI Global (2009)
14. Norris, P.: Digital Divide: Civic Engagement, Information Poverty, and the Internet Worldwide. Cambridge University Press, Cambridge (2001)
15. Niehaves, B., Becker, J.: The Age-Divide in E-Government - Data, Interpretations, Theory Fragments. In: Oya, M., Uda, R., Yasunobu, C. (eds.) Towards Sustainable Society on Ubiquitous Networks, vol. 286, pp. 279–287. Springer, Boston (2008)
16. United Nations, Department of Economic and Social Affairs, Population Division, `http://esa.un.org/unpp/`
17. ARD/ZDF-Onlinestudie, by van Eimeren, B., Frees, B.: Internetverbreitung: Größter Zuwachs bei Silver Surfern. In: Media Perspektiven, S. 332, pp. 330–344 (July 2008)
18. Bass, F.: A new product growth model for consumer durables. Management Science 15(5), 215–227 (1969)
19. Srinivasan, V., Mason, C.H.: Nonlinear Least Squares Estimation of New Product Diffusion Models. Marketing Science 5(2), 169–178 (1986)
20. Sicherl, P.: Analysis of Information Society Indicators with Time Distance Methodology. Journal of Computing and Information Technology 13(4), 293–298 (2005)

What Is the Issue with Internet Acceptance among Elderly Citizens? Theory Development and Policy Recommendations for Inclusive E-Government*

Bjoern Niehaves and Ralf Plattfaut

Westfälische Wilhelms-Universität Münster, European Research Center for Information Systems, Leonardo-Campus 3, 48149 Münster
{bjoern.niehaves,ralf.plattfaut}@ercis.uni-muenster.de

Abstract. Digital divide is still a big topic in information systems and e-government research. In the past, several tracks and workshops on this topic existed. As information technology and especially the internet become more and more important governments cannot ignore the fact that elderly citizens are excluded from the benefits related to internet usage. Although e-Inclusion programmes and initiatives changed over the years and, moreover, although the amount of e-Inclusion literature is constantly growing, there is still no thorough understanding of potential factors influencing private internet usage. Hence, in this study we identify important influencing factors based on the literature on technology acceptance and digital divide. We develop a model based on these factors and test it against comprehensive survey data (n=192). Our theoretical model is able to explain more than 70% of the variation in private internet usage. We derive policy recommendations based on the results and discuss implications for future research.

Keywords: Digital Divide, e-Inclusion, UTAUT, Quantitative Study.

1 Introduction

Today's western societies face two common trends: First, today's societies around the world tend to "age" or "grey" [26]. The share of population older than 65 years is 15.9% and will rise up to 25.9% by 2050. Second, the importance of information, information processing, and communication is constantly growing. This phenomenon has been condensed to the term information society [34, 15].

Societal aging bears several risks for an information society. On the one hand, an increasing share of elderly citizens results in problems for local governments such as fiscal stress and increasing expenditure on health care or pensions [19]. On the other hand, large parts of the population are excluded from the information society. They neither have access nor skills to use modern media like the internet. A digital divide among on-liners and non-liners exists [22]. Especially senior citizens are often excluded from modern technology [6, 4].

---

* The authors are grateful to the financial support of this research by the Volkswagen-Foundation.

M.A. Wimmer et al. (Eds.): EGOV 2010, LNCS 6228, pp. 275–288, 2010.

However, governments want to make use of the growing importance of ICT. Especially local authorities can enhance the effectiveness and efficiency of their processes and organisational structure using ICT and, by this, lever their productivity to a new level (electronic or transformation government [31]). Moreover, government agencies can provide their services "online" and support them by means of ICT. However, in a digitally divided world the non-liners are excluded from the benefits of ICT supported governmental services. The European Union recognised both the importance of ICT and the existence of a digital divide. Therefore, the ministers of the member states of the EU called for an inclusive information society and declared to focus on multiple goals to reach this aim [21]. This was also captured by the cabinet office of the United Kingdom which called for tackling "overall issues of digital inclusion" [9] and works "towards achieving equitable access to new technology and remove the barriers to take-up" [10]. Both define electronic inclusion (e-inclusion) as an integral part of (especially local) governmental policies.

Projects to bridge the digital divide have a long history. First generation projects included grants to provide more senior citizens with computers [16], free internet access at local libraries or comparable centres, as well as internet courses specially designed for elderly people [32]. However, technology acceptance research suggests several other barriers that could be tackled by governmental e-inclusion projects. The Unified Theory of Acceptance and Use of Technology (UTAUT) suggests that next to Effort Expectancy, which is tackled by internet courses, and Facilitating Conditions, which are (among others) established through the provision of access, Performance Expectancy and the social milieu play an important role in explaining usage behaviour. Hence, it is doubtable whether the mere provision of computer courses or free internet access are sufficient to reach an inclusive information society. Moreover, there is the possibility that the group of non-liners is fragmented and that different measures should be established for different groups. Hence, this study aims at clarifying the following research questions:

RQ1 How can we explain the private internet usage and non-usage of senior citizens?

RQ2 What are important factors for senior citizens' usage and non-usage of the internet?

RQ3 Does an extension of UTAUT using more moderating variables from the digital divide literature provide a benefit in explaining private internet usage among the elderly?

RQ4 What can practitioners learn from a more comprehensive view on senior citizens' internet usage?

To answer this question, we quantitatively study the citizens of age 50 or higher in a medium-sized city in Western Europe. We created a questionnaire based on the theoretical background of the UTAUT [47] and the Digital Divide literature [48, 45, 2, 5]. This questionnaire was handed out to more than 3,000 randomly chosen inhabitants. In sum, we received 192 questionnaires from respondents aged 50 or higher. For data analysis, we use the partial least squares (PLS) method [35].The paper is structured as follows. In the next section, we will present some theoretical background. Afterwards, we will develop our research model based on the UTAUT and Digital Divide literature. In section four, we will present our research methodology in detail. The results are presented in section five. We will discuss them in terms of relevance for theory and practice in section six. The last section is concerned with limitations, conclusions, and future research.

2   Theoretical Background

E- and T-government have been established as a main concept in government change processes and integrates technical, social, and organisational themes [31, 42]. Being ready to change and improve has become a necessity for public administrations in order to cope with increased demands in a complex change environment. Exploitation of benefits realised by electronic government (e-government) is the essential part of this strategy. Being part of this agenda, in its transformation government implementation plan, the Cabinet Office [10, page 4] acknowledges that the exploitation of the full potential of electronic service delivery includes making wider use of online provision in order to make services more accessible to the public (see for instance, online centres [9, 36]). However, research discusses age-related factors and demographic trends that might counteract these efforts. Societal aging is a major demographic trend in industrialised societies. Hauser & Duncan [28, p2] define demography as "the study of the size, territorial distribution, and composition of population, changes therein, and the components of such changes, which may be identified as natality, mortality, territorial movement (migration), and social mobility (change of status)." Three major factors constitute the development of demography: a) fertility, b) mortality, and c) migration. In this context, especially fertility and mortality have undergone significant changes in most industrialised countries over the last decades. On the one hand, fertility has been declining due to, for instance, changed life models or family planning [38]. On the other hand, regarding mortality, life expectancy has increased substantially because of, e.g., improved medical care. For instance, between 1995 and 2003, life expectancy at birth in European countries, now being 78 years on average for men and 83 for women, went up by an average of 3 months each year for men and 2 months for women [17]. As a consequence, societal aging (synonym: population aging) has established itself as a long-term trend that will continue for generations to come. Demographic projections indicate that the group of 65 years and older will continue to constitute a growing share of population. For instance, at present, 14 of the world's 15 "oldest" countries in terms of percentage of people aged 65 or older, are in Europe, while Japan heads this ranking [40]. In 2050, for the European Union (EU) the population share of those aged 65 and more is projected to increase to 29.9% and for Japan to 39.6%. Similarly, in the United States (USA) and Canada, the population share of those aged 65 and more, is estimated to increase to 21% and 23.7% respectively. While the demographic trend of societal aging is particularly distinct in more developed nations, less and least developed nations also share this general tendency.

Societal aging poses challenges to the development of t-government and e-inclusion strategies. One of these challenges is the (here: age-related) digital divide [45, 2, 5, 3], in this context understood as an emerging polarisation phenomenon in society, creating a gap between those who do have access to and use the potentialities of ICTs, and those who do not [18]. The demographic gap refers, amongst others, to the fact that senior people often do not use ICT on a regular basis [6, 39, 5]. The reasons for this gap results from a multitude of challenges which senior people often face. These include for instance isolation, physical disabilities, or low retirement pension [33]. Disabilities can debar people from actively using information technology. For the usage of online services the most important disabilities to consider are visual handicaps, cognitive defects and limitations of motor skills. Geographical differences refer to gaps in ICT usage between different regions. Socio-economic gaps include differences in occupation, income and education whereas ethnical and cultural gaps identify barriers in the ICT usage of migrants and ethnical minorities. Here, e-inclusion focuses on the elimination of these barriers for the use of ICT. The declaration of Riga gives the following definition of E-inclusion: "'eInclusion' means both inclusive ICT and the use of ICT to achieve wider inclusion objectives. It focuses on participation of all individuals and communities in all aspects of the information society. E-inclusion policy, therefore, aims at reducing gaps in ICT usage and promoting the use of ICT to overcome exclusion, and improve economic performance, employment opportunities, quality of life, social participation and cohesion." [21, p. 1] The main focus of e-inclusion is on creating accessible services over ICT. This effort can be divided into accessibility and usability aspects [33]. Accessibility means the possibility for handicapped people to access the relevant service (e.g. Braille support). Usability focuses on the user-friendliness of a web-service (e.g. easy discovery and fast navigation within a website [20]).

3 Research Model

Against the background of our research objective, our research model is informed by two streams of research: acceptance and use of technology as well as digital divide research. As for research on acceptance and use of technology, Venkatesh et al. [47] undertake a comprehensive comparison of theories in this field in order to develop their UTAUT. The authors provide evidence that, for the case of information technology acceptance, their model shows best explanatory power, comparing with, for instance, the theory of reasoned action [24, 23], the technology acceptance model [13], or the theory of planned behaviour [43]. Therefore, we will apply UTAUT for explaining behavioural intention towards personal use of the internet (BI) as well as for explaining use behaviour regarding personal internal usage (USE). Here, Venkatesh et al. [47] provide evidence for the influence of the following independent variables: Performance Expectancy (PE), Effort Expectancy (EE), Social Influence (SI), and Facilitating Conditions (FC). As for the representation of the digital divide perspective, four additional variables were included in our model: education [45,2,5], gender [27,7,2,5], income [48,7,2,5], and migration background [2,5]. Here, we argue – in line with other studies – that these factors moderate the relationships described in the original UTAUT model.[1]

---

[1] Please contact the author for information on the constructs, questions, measures, and their roots.

According to studies of technology acceptance, specifically UTAUT, and taking into account digital divide research, we formulate the following hypotheses in order to explain behavioural intention towards personal use of the internet:

1) On the influence of Performance Expectancy:

H1a: Performance Expectancy will positively influence Behavioural Intention.

H1b: The influence of Performance Expectancy on Behavioural Intention will be moderated by education, gender, income, and migration background (digital divide variables).

2) On the influence of Effort Expectancy:

H2a: Effort Expectancy will positively influence Behavioural Intention.

H2b: The influence of Effort Expectancy on Behavioural Intention will be moderated by education, gender, income, and migration background (digital divide variables).

3) On the influence of Social Influence:

H3a: Social Influence will positively influence Behavioural Intention.

H3b: The influence of Social Influence on Behavioural Intention will be moderated by education, gender, income, and migration background (digital divide variables).

As for the explanation of internet personal use behaviour we formulate the following hypotheses based on Venkatesh et al. [47] as well as digital divide research:

4) On the influence of Behavioural Intention:

H4:   Behavioural Intention will positively influence Use Behaviour.

5) On the influence of Facilitating Conditions:

H5a: Facilitating Conditions will positively influence Use Behaviour.

H5b: The influence of Facilitating Conditions on Use Behavioural will be moderated by education, gender, income, and migration background (digital divide variables).

We assume that the original UTAUT has significant power to explain variations in behavioural intention towards personal internet use and in use behaviour. Moreover, we assume that taking into account insights from digital divide research, specifically variables such as education, gender, income, and migration background, will further increase the explanatory power of the model. We thus seek to apply UTAUT for studying personal internet usage and to extend the model by integrating insights from digital divide research.

4   Research Methodology

Data collection phase. Before the data collection phase, we constructed a questionnaire according to the research model presented above. Here, we applied well established constructs and items for measurement. Also, we conducted a pilot study with 7 respondents for the purpose of questionnaire validation. It led to positive feedback and did not result in any changes in the set of questions, items, or constructs. The questionnaire was used to gather data within a medium-sized city located in Europe between September and October 2009. We employed a multi-channel strategy to reach the respondents: We contacted 100 people via phone and 1500 via mail (both randomly chosen). Moreover, we placed additional 1,500 questionnaires at the cities' town-hall and local libraries. Potential respondents were assured of the confidentiality of their responses. Furthermore, we raffled three material prizes among all respondents. Thanks to an active involvement of the mayor our study found good coverage in the local media. Thus, we received 518 questionnaires (192 from respondents of age 50 or higher). An additional non-response analysis did not reveal any biases.

Data analysis phase. The structured data was first analysed using SPSS 17.0.0. Here, we selected only data records from respondents of age 50 or higher (senior citizens) which led to 192 cases. To further analyse our dataset, we employed the partial least squares (PLS) path modelling algorithm as it is suitable for data sets with lower than 200 cases [35, 38]. The software package to support this was SmartPLS [41]. Except internet usage (formative measurement), all constructs were modelled using reflective indicators (cf. [47]; for a detailed discussion on formative versus reflective indicators, cf. [14]). The data used incorporates some missing values (Average of 2 per case). These missing values were treated using the mean replacement algorithm [1]. In the analysis phase we compared two different models, one without moderating effects and one with moderation through variables from the digital divide knowledge base. This data analysis procedure allows us to evaluate the above stated hypotheses.

Sample Demographics. Our sample consists of data of 192 senior citizens. The mean age of the respondents was slightly above 62. They spent on average 11.6 years in school or university which proves a decent education. Concerning gender, our sample is almost equally distributed (51.56% were female). The income variable shows the most missing values (52). However, we can observe quite high incomes for the sample population (Table 1). Moreover, sample demographics show that the number of people with migration background is rather low. 98% of the respondents have the citizenship of the country studied and 97% are native speakers of the corresponding language. Hence, it is quite difficult to analyse any results related to migration background.

Table 1. Demographics of the analysed sample

Question	N	Min	Max	Mean	Std. Dev.
AGE (in years)	192	50,00	83,00	62,3385	8,41371
EDU (in years of education)	180	0	20	11.63	3.853
INC (0 = less than 1000€; 1 = between 1000€ and 2000€; 2 = between 2000€ and 3000€; 3 = more than 3000€)	140	0	3	1,83	,952

5 Results

We will present our results derived using the above mentioned methodology in a three-stepped approach. First, we will study the validity of our constructs (outer model) using standardised measures [7,46,47]. Second, we will present the inner model: the paths and their coefficients in both models (with and without moderating digital divide variables). Third, we will present and compare the coefficient of determination of both models.

Outer Model. We measured the internal consistency reliability (ICR) of all latent variables using Cronbach's Alpha. Generally, an ICR above .9 is considered as excellent, one between .7 and .9 as high, one between .5 and .7 as moderately high, and one between .5 as low [30]. The reliabilities in the presented study are comparably high, only social influence is in the high moderate area. The high ICRs show that the items measure the corresponding construct. All correlations between the constructs were lower than the square roots of the shared variance between the constructs and their measures in every case. According to Fornell and Larker [25] this supports convergent and discriminant validity.[2] We employed a bootstrapping method (500 iterations) using randomly selected sub-samples to the significance of our PLS model. Analysing the item loadings, we could generally observe that our latent variables are measured by the corresponding items. All items except PE4 and FC4 have comparably high item loadings (Table 2). However, analysing the average variance extracted in all cases shows that our constructs can be considered valid [30].

Table 2. Item Loadings (with moderator effect – significance of items is stable)

LV	Item	Loading	LV	Item	Loading
PE	PE1	.8910***	BI	BI1	.9301***
PE	PE2	.8190***	BI	BI2	.8323***
PE	PE3	.7681***	BI	BI3	.9235***
PE	PE4	.3629***	USE	USE01INFO	.5894
EE	EE1	.8473***	USE	USE02COMM	.2515
EE	EE2	.8244***	USE	USE03BUSI	.1113
EE	EE3	.8142***	USE	USE04BANK	.1475
EE	EE4	.7042***	USE	USE05HEAL	.0582
SI	SI1	.6820***	USE	USE06TOUR	.0829
SI	SI2	.5839***	USE	USE07GOVE	.0556
SI	SI3	.5977***	USE	USE08EDUC	.0217
SI	SI4	.7666***	USE	USE09SOCI	.0147
FC	FC1	.8779***	USE	USE10GAME	-.0678
FC	FC2	.8835***	USE	USE_PRI_MINPERW	.0744
FC	FC3	.8887***	MIG	LANGUAGE	.9507***
FC	FC4	.2518*	MIG	NATIONALITY	.9530***

a) USE was measured in a formative way, therefore we present the corresponding weights.
b) Education, Income, and Gender were measured with one variable.

Inner Model. In the first model without moderator effects (UTAUT), all paths have to be proven significant using the bootstrapping method (Table 3). We observed a high influence of Performance Expectancy on Behavioural Intention and of

---

[2] Data for the measurement model estimation can be found in the Appendix for review purposes only.

Behavioural Intention on USE. The other path coefficients are comparably low. However, as the analysis suggests that every considered path is correct, we did not drop any for the second model with moderator effects.

In the second model (UTAUT and digital divide variables), several relationships were moderated by education, gender, income, and migration background. By this, 16 interaction terms were added to the analysis. The moderator variable migration background was added; however, as the sample population shows almost no migration background the related results are not interpretable. Bootstrapping suggests that only a minority of all paths used is significant. This is due to the high amount of moderating constructs in the model and can be ignored [47]. However, some path coefficients are high and will be further analysed in the discussion section.

Table 3. Path Coefficients

Dependent Variable: BI	without moderator effects	with moderator effect	**Dependent Variable: USE**	without moderator effects	with moderator effect
R²	.5181	.6378	R²	.7120	.7440
PE	.4651***	.0867	BI	.7065***	.6469***
EE	.2106**	.3892	FC	.1770**	.1274
SI	.1947***	.2223	EDU		-.0243
EDU		-.2678*	GEN		-.2206
GEN		.1682	INC		.0320
INC		-.0519	MIG		-.0679
MIG		-.0741	FC*EDU		.1265
PE*EDU		.6236*	FC*GEN		.3307*
PE*GEN		-.0502	FC*INC		.0471
PE*INC		.0394	FC*MIG		-.1191
PE*MIG		.0989			
EE*EDU		-.2068			
EE*GEN		.1472			
EE*INC		.0536			
EE*MIG		-.1460			
SI*EDU		.1354			
SI*GEN		-.1956			
SI*INC		-.0600			
SI*MIG		-.0736			

Coefficient of Determination. The coefficient of determination (R^2) is defined as the proportion of variability in the data explained by the statistical model (and not by random error terms or not included constructs). The original UTAUT achieved an R^2 for BI between .51 and .77 and for USE between .41 and .52 [47]. Our analysis already shows a high coefficient of determination of .5181 for BI and .7120 for USE in the first model without moderating effects. In the second case with moderating effects we can even observe higher R²-Values for both BI (.6378) and USE (.7440). Thus, the model combining UTAUT and Digital Divide is able to explain more of the variance in usage behaviour of senior citizens (Table 3).

6 Discussion

Outer Model. As shown above, all constructs are valid which is in line with the theoretical foundation. However, the UTAUT-originating construct Social Influence has an ICR of .59. This is only considered moderately high by Hinton et al. [30]. Further theory development could try to find better fitting items, for instance by including items from the Model of Adoption of Technology in Households [8].

Inner Model and Hypotheses. The results for the paths' coefficients of the inner model can be mapped with the hypotheses mentioned in section 3. Especially the path coefficient of the moderating digital divide variables are of high interest.

- The expected performance of internet usage is the main driver for elderly citizens. With the highest path coefficient of all, performance expectancy has high influence on the internet usage. Therefore, governments aiming at an inclusive information society should evaluate their e-inclusion t-governmental strategies with special regards to raising the positive expectations of senior citizens. Thus, our analysis confirms hypothesis H1a. The influence of Performance Expectancy on Behavioural Intention is highly positive moderated by education. Especially for higher educated seniors the expected performance is a good predictor for the intention to use the internet. Other moderator variables provide only marginal powers of explanation. Hence, our analysis partially confirms hypothesis H1b.
- The influence of Effort Expectancy is overestimated. Although Effort Expectancy does significantly influence Behavioural Intention in a high positive way, it is not among the main drivers for internet usage. Apparently, Effort Expectancy is overestimated as its influence is not as high as expected. However, the analysis partially approved our hypothesis H2a. The relationship between Effort Expectancy and Behavioural Intention is moderated by education and gender. On the one hand, especially for less educated people, the expected effort is of high importance for their Behavioural Intention. On the other hand, the same fact holds true for men. The influence of other moderator variables is low. Therefore, our analysis partially validates the hypotheses H2b.
- Social factors influence Behavioural Intention. The impact of Social Influences on Behavioural Intention is comparable to the one of Effort Expectancy. Thus, hypothesis H3a can be regarded as partially confirmed. Moreover, our analysis shows that especially women are influenced by their social milieu with the path coefficient for the corresponding moderator variable at -.1956. The second moderator variable influencing the importance of social factors is education. Highly educated senior citizens are more influenced by their social setting than less educated ones. Thus, hypothesis H3b can be regarded as partially confirmed.
- The influence of Behavioural Intention on actual internet usage is high. In both models tested, the influence of the intention to use on the actual use is both high and significant. Thus, we can regard the hypothesis H4 as proven.

- Facilitating Conditions is not the main driver for internet usage. Our analysis provides evidence that the impact of Facilitating Conditions on actual usage is not as high as expected. Material access as part of facilitating conditions is neither the only nor the main driver for internet usage as the corresponding path coefficient is the lowest of all construct related path coefficients in the whole model (ad H5a). However, the impact of Facilitating Conditions is highly moderated by education and gender. Apparently, especially for well educated men, facilitating conditions are crucial for internet usage.

Model Comparison. Both presented models explain the variance of private internet use significantly. Our quantitative analysis shows that the fusion of UTAUT and Digital Divide constructs provides great value in predicting both the intention to use and the use of the internet in a private manner. We can show that a model that integrates both approaches is better than a model building on the original UTAUT-constructs only. However, the UTAUT has to be proven as valuable for predicting private internet usage.

Our results bear several implications for practice. Today's local government use ICT to lever their organisation and processes to a more effective and efficient level in terms of e-government or t-government. However, to make their ICT supported governmental services accessed by everyone they need to bridge the digital divide.

- As Performance Expectancy is the main driver for behavioural intention to use the internet local authorities should think about the communication and marketing of benefits of internet usage in general and the usage of ICT supported governmental services (t-government) in special to elderly citizens. Here, especially more educated citizens can be reached.
- So far, a lot of courses to provide the right skill set to elderly citizens have been initiated or supported by local governments. However, the study shows that the influence of Effort Expectancy is comparably low. Authorities should evaluate their undertakings in terms of computer courses and especially focus on less educated persons.
- Decision makers should also think about working on the social environment of their inhabitants and, e.g. address strong disseminators enrooted in the corresponding milieu. One idea would be to train local opinion leaders to use the internet and give them the opportunity to talk about their path to becoming "experts" on the local radio.
- The silver bullet of local governments to bridge the digital divide has been to provide internet access to excluded groups. However, our study suggests that this approach is outdated: Material access as part of facilitating conditions is neither the only nor the main driver for internet usage. The corresponding path coefficient is the lowest of all construct related path coefficients in the whole model. Apparently, pure material access is not the crucial factor any more. Local authorities should therefore rethink their engagements in this direction in order to make their ICT supported services used by everyone.

7 Conclusion

This paper examines influencing factors for senior citizens' use of the internet for private purposes. We present a research model and develop a corresponding questionnaire based on technology acceptance and digital divide research. Our 2009 survey yields 192 responses from senior citizens (age 50 yrs and above). The resulting dataset was analysed using PLS path modelling [41]. Our results suggest that UTAUT is particularly useful for analysing private internet usage achieving an R^2 as high as .7120. We also found that the main driver for senior citizens internet usage is performance expectancy: The higher the expected performance or utility, the higher the intention to use the internet. Drawing from digital divide research, we extended the UTAUT-model by four additional variables that are hypothesised to mediate original UTAUT-relationships. Including interaction terms, we observed that e.g. especially for women the social influence through their corresponding milieu is extremely important and that men are more influenced by the facilitating conditions. All in all, our extended model is able to explain as much as 74% of the variation in internet usage and, therefore, is better than the original UTAUT model for this specific purpose. We thus provide evidence that the inclusion of digital divide constructs yields greater explanatory power than UTAUT constructs only.

However, our study is beset with certain limitations. First, the total population studied did not include many people with migration background (only 3% of the respondents). Therefore, we could not well interpret the results on the influence of this specific variable. Moreover, our study was carried out in a specific region in Western Europe. We believe that our results will, to a great extent, hold true in other settings as well. Future research could aim at testing this assumption by carrying out a comparable study in other national/social/cultural settings. In addition, longitudinal studies could show the development of private internet usage and its influencing factors among senior citizens over time and could thus be regarded another potentially fruitful avenue for future research. Other future research could cover the matching of existing local government e-inclusion projects with the given explaining variables: Which projects contribute to performance or effort expectancy, how is social influence stimulated and how can facilitating conditions be improved? Which projects address the needs of specific groups (see digital divide variables) best? Such overview, we believe, could be very valuable but does not yet exist to our knowledge. As for future theory development, we were able to explain the largest share of variance in private internet usage among senior citizens by employing nine variables, taken from technology acceptance and digital divide research. Here, we believe, further testing of influencing factors, for instance psychological variables (e.g., the Big Five, cf. [12]) could still increase explanatory power.

References

1. Afifi, A.A., Elashoff, R.M.: Observations in Multivariate Statistics: I. Review of the Literature. Journal of the American Statistical Association 61(315), 595–604 (1966)
2. Agerwal, R., Animesh, A., Prasad, K.: Social Interactions and the "Digital Divide": Explaining Variations in Internet Use. Information Systems Research 20(2), 277–294 (2009)

3. Al-Shafi, S., Weerakkody, V.: Understanding Citizens' Behavioural Intention in the Adoption of E-Government Services in the State of Qatar. In: European Conference on Information Systems, Verona, Italy (2009)
4. Becker, J., Niehaves, B., Bergener, P., Fielenbach, K., Räckers, M., Weiß, B.: The Digital Divide in E-Government - A Quantitative Analysis. In: Proceedings of the IADIS International Conference e-Society, Algarve, Portugal, pp. 337–344 (2008)
5. Bélanger, F., Carter, L.: The Impact Of The Digital Divide On E-Government Use. Communications of the ACM 52(4), 132–135 (2009)
6. Brandtweiner, R., Donat, E.: Digital Divide in Austria - Any Reasons for Enthusiasm? The Case of Austria. In: Proceedings of the 20th Bled eConference – eMergence: Merging and Emerging Technologies, Processes and Institutions, Bled Slovenia, June 3-6 (2007)
7. Brown, S.A., Venkatesh, V.: Model of Adoption of Technology in Households: A Baseline Model Test and Extension Incorporating Household Life Cycle. MIS Quarterly 29(3), 399–426 (2005)
8. Brown, S.A., Venkatesh, V., Bala, H.: Household technology Use: Integrating Household Life Cycle and the Model of Adoption of Technology in Households. The Information Society 22, 205–218 (2006)
9. Cabinet Office: Transformational Government – Enabled by Technology. Strategy Document, London, UK (2005)
10. Cabinet Office: Transformational Government – Implementation Plan, London, UK (2006)
11. Compeau, D.R., Higgins, C.A., Huff, S.: Social Cognitive Theory and Individual Reactions to Computing Technology: A Longitudinal Study. MIS Quarterly 23(2), 145–158 (1999)
12. Costa, P.T., McCrae, R.R.: Revised NEO Personality Inventory (NEO-PI-R) and NEO Five-Factor Inventory (NEO-FFI) professional manual. Psychological Assessment Resources, Odessa (1992)
13. Davis, F.D.: Perceived usefulness, perceived ease of use, and user acceptance of information technology. MIS Quarterly 13(3), 319–339 (1989)
14. Diamantopoulos, A., Siguaw, J.A.A.: Formative versus Reflective Indicators in Organizational Measure Development: A Comparison and Empirical Illustration. British Journal of Management 17(4), 263–282 (2006)
15. Duff, A.S., Craig, D., McNeill, D.A.: A note on the origins of 'information society'. Journal of Information Science 22(5), 122–171 (1996)
16. Eastman, J.K., Iyer, R.: The elderly's uses and attitudes towards the internet. Journal of Consumer Marketing 21(3), 208–220 (2004)
17. EHEMU: Are we living longer, healthier lives in the EU? European Health Expectancy Monitoring Unit Technical report 2, Montpellier, France (2005), http://www.hs.le.ac.uk/reves/ehemutest/pdf/techrep20507.pdf
18. European Commission: eInclusion@EU: Strengthening eInclusion & eAccessibility across Europe. Analytic framework - eInclusion and eAccessibility priority issues (2004a)
19. European Commission: The impact of ageing on public expenditure: projections for the EU 25 Member States on pensions, health care, long-term care, education and unemployment transfers (2004-2005), European Commission, Brussels (2006)
20. European Commission: Top of the web. User Satisfaction and Usage Survey of E-Government services, Kopenhagen (2004b)
21. European Union: Riga Ministerial Declaration (2006), http://ec.europa.eu/information_society/events/ict_riga_2006/doc/declaration_riga.pdf

22. Ferro, E., Gil-Garcia, J.R., Helbig, N.: The Digital Divide Metaphor: Understanding Paths to IT Literacy. In: Wimmer, M.A., Scholl, J., Grönlund, Å. (eds.) EGOV 2007. LNCS, vol. 4656, pp. 265–280. Springer, Heidelberg (2007)

23. Fishbein, M., Ajzen, I.:: Belief, attitude, intention, and behaviour : An introduction to theory and research. Addison-Wesley Pub. Co., Reading (1975)

24. Fishbein, M.: Attitude and the prediction of behaviour. In: Fishbein, M. (ed.) Readings in attitude theory and measurement, pp. 477–492. Wiley, New York (1967)

25. Fornell, C., Larker, D.F.: Evaluating Structural Equation Models with Unobservable Variables and Measurement Error: Algebra and Statistics. Journal of Marketing Research 18(3), 382–388 (1981)

26. Fougère, M., Mérette, M.: Population ageing and economic growth in seven OECD countries. Economic Modelling 16, 411–427 (1999)

27. Gilly, M.C., Enis, B.M.: Recycling the Family Life Cycle: A Proposal for Redefinition. Advances in Consumer Research 9, 271–276 (1982)

28. Hauser, P.M., Duncan, O.D.: The Study of Population. An Inventory and Appraisal, Chicago (1959)

29. Henseler, J., Fassott, G.: Testing Moderating Effects in PLS Path Models: An Illustration of Available Procedures. In: Handbook of Partial Least Squares: Concepts, Methods and Applications in Marketing and Related Fields. Springer, Heidelberg (2009)

30. Hinton, P.R., Brownlow, C., McMurvay, I., Cozens, B.: SPSS explained. Routledge Inc., East Sussex (2004)

31. Irani, Z., Elliman, T., Jackson, P.: Electronic transformation of government in the U.K.: a research agenda. European Journal of Information Systems 16, 327–335 (2007)

32. Kiel, J.: The digital divide: Internet and e-mail use by the elderly. Medical Informatics & the Internet in Medicine 30(1), 19–23 (2005)

33. Kraner, S.: Bridging the Digital Divide in E-Government, Zürich (2004)

34. Machlup, F.: The Production and Distribution of Knowledge in the United States. Princeton University Press, Princeton (1962)

35. Marcoulides, G.A., Chin, W.W., Saunders, C.: A Critical Look at Partial Least Squares Modeling'. MIS Quarterly 33(1), 171–175 (2009)

36. Milner, H.: UK online centres: Transformational Government for the Citizen. Research report, Sheffield, UK (2009)

37. Moore, G.C., Benbasat, I.: Development of an Instrument to Measure the Perceptions of Adopting an Information Technology Innovation. Information Systems Research 2(3), 192–222 (1991)

38. Morgan, S.P., Hagewen, K.J.: Handbook of Population (2006)

39. Niehaves, B., Becker, J.: The Age-Divide in E-Government - Data, Interpretations, Theory Fragments. In: Proceedings of the 8th IFIP Conference on e-Business, e-Services, and e-Society (I3E 2008), Tokyo, Japan, pp. 279–287 (2008)

40. Population Reference Bureau: World Population Data Sheet 2006, Washington, DC (2006), http://www.prb.org/pdf06/06WorldDataSheet.pdf

41. Ringle, C.M., Wende, S., Will, S.: SmartPLS 2.0 (M3) Beta, Hamburg (2005), http://www.smartpls.de

42. Smith, P.: A Blueprint for Transformation. E-Government Bulletin (2006), http://www.cio.gov.uk/documents/news/pdf/ABlueprintForTransformation.pdf

43. Taylor, S., Todd, P.A.: Understanding Information Technology Usage: A Test of Competing Models. Information Systems Research 6(4), 570–591 (1995)

44. Thompson, R.L., Higgins, C.A., Howell, J.M.: Personal Computing: Toward a Conceptual Model of Utilization. MIS Quarterly 15(1), 124–143 (1991)
45. van Dijk, J.A.G.M.: Digital divide research, achievements and shortcomings. Poetics 34(4-5), 221–235 (2006)
46. Venkatesh, V., Brown, S.A., Maruping, L.M., Bala, H.: Predicting Different Conceptualizations of System Use: The Competing Roles of Behavioural Intention, Facilitating Conditions, and Behavioural Expectation. MIS Quarterly 32(3), 483–502 (2008)
47. Venkatesh, V., Morris, M.G., Davis, G., Davis, F.: User Acceptance of Information Technology: Toward a Unified View. MIS Quarterly 27(3), 425–478 (2003)
48. Wagner, J., Hanna, S.: The Effectiveness of Family Life Cycle Variables in Consumer Expenditure Research. Journal of Consumer Research 10, 281–291 (1983)

Design of an Open Social E-Service for Assisted Living

Gustaf Juell-Skielse and Petia Wohed

Stockholm University
{gjs,petia}@dsv.su.se

Abstract. E-government has emerged as one of the most promising means to reform the public sector. E-government is now being used to improve services for assisted living. The purpose of assisted living services is to provide ways for elderly people to continue to live at home. However, these services require formal decisions by local government officials. Therefore Swedish municipalities aim to move control toward citizens to reduce authoritative barriers and to simplify administration. In this paper we report experiences from developing an open social e-service for assisted living[1]. The major objectives are to relocate control to the citizen and to establish a highly integrated and efficient administrative process. It is designed to meet legal requirements of the Swedish Social Services Act. In order to achieve the objectives several process innovation techniques have been applied. During the design process we experienced several legal, organizational and technical challenges which we report in this paper.

Keywords: assisted living, e-government, e-services, social services, street-level bureaucracy.

1 Introduction

Assisted living services are becoming more and more important due to the increased share of elderly in the population of Western countries. In 2020 the share of older people in Europe will be almost doubled compared to 1960 [1]. Assisted living services can increase the quality of life by helping elderly to live in their homes longer and to stay integrated in social life [1]. In addition, the costs for assisted living services are significantly lower than the costs of providing special housing [2].

In Sweden, services for assisted living are usually administrated and provided by the social services committee of the municipality where the person resides. Although few applications for assisted living services are rejected, they require extensive investigations and formal decisions by local government officials. Therefore, Swedish municipalities consider to provide assisted living services in a more open and efficient manner. In addition, Swedish municipalities aim to utilize e-government technology, e.g. e-services. Through open social e-services the fundamental idea is to move decision control closer to the citizen, to increase service access and transparency and to decrease service administration.

---

[1] This is not to be confused with Google open social initiative.
http://code.google.com/apis/opensocial/

M.A. Wimmer et al. (Eds.): EGOV 2010, LNCS 6228, pp. 289–300, 2010.
© IFIP International Federation for Information Processing 2010

In this paper we report experiences from developing open social e-services. During the design process we experienced several legal, organizational and technical challenges. More specifically we report:

- A design of an open social e-service for assisted living.
- Potential benefits of introducing open social e-services in the administration of assisted living services.
- Challenges during design and development of the open social e-service for assisted living.

The design of the open social e-service for assisted living will serve as a proof-of-concept and a foundation for future development. The potential benefits will serve as variables for measuring costs and benefits of open e-services for assisted living. By solving some of the challenges the reported work paves the way for e-government initiatives in the social services area. Other challenges provide valuable input to make future development of e-services more effective.

The paper is structured as follows. In section 2 we present the assisted living service for which we design an open social e-service solution. In addition we discuss assisted living services and frameworks for process innovation, benefits analysis and e-government challenges. In section 3 we cover the method used in our research. Section 4 presents the results: design of an open social e-service solution, analysis of potential benefits and experienced challenges. In section 5 we conclude the paper with a suggestion for future work.

2   Extended Background

In this section we present the assisted living service for which we design an open social e-service solution. In addition we discuss frameworks for process innovation, benefits analysis and e-government challenges, which are used in the design of the open social e-service.

2.1 E-Government Case Description

Sweden is currently ranked as the leading country in e-government readiness [3]. Järfälla is one of Sweden's 290 municipalities and located 20 kilometers Northwest of Stockholm. With 65.000 inhabitants it is, by Swedish standards, a relatively large municipality. An important responsibility for the municipality is to provide assisted living services for elderly and disabled citizens. The Järfälla Social Service Council care for approximately 1.540 elderly and 860 disabled citizens [4]. The cost for social services in Järfälla is somewhat lower than the Swedish average. The net annual cost per capita for care of elderly and disabled are 9.446 SEK as compared to the Swedish average of 13.172 SEK.

Assisted living services include both technological and organizational-institutional innovations to enhance the autonomy and quality of life of elderly people and to decrease the cost for elderly care [1]. The assisted living services which are subject to be offered as open social e-services in the municipality of Järfälla are emergency help telephone service, part-time successors and companions [5]. Emergency help telephones provide around the clock in-door emergency treatment assistance which means that the citizen can get in contact with care personnel in case of emergency. Part-time successors provide in-door autonomy enhancement services to relieve relatives from the responsibility of taking care of the elderly or disabled under shorter time periods. Companions provide outdoor autonomy enhancement and comfort services for people who find it hard to get to and from activities, such as hair-dressing and social events.

The administrative process for providing emergency help telephone service was selected for developing an open social e-service. There were several reasons behind this decision: First, an emergency help telephone service is often the first social care service that a person applies for. Second, most of the applications for emergency help telephone services are accepted. Third, the application process for emergency help telephone services has recently been thoroughly analyzed and simplified by Järfälla municipality. Fourth, the administrative process for handling applications for emergency help telephone services could serve as a benchmark for several other services.

2.2 Process Innovation Techniques

In e-government, information and communication technology is used to improve government processes. Davenport [6] identifies nine different ways in which information and communication technology can be used to improve processes. In turn, these process improvements can generate quality improvements, time reductions and economic benefits. Mansar and Reijers [7] categorize successful process redesign heuristics, such as control relocation, contact reduction, control addition, case types, exception, task elimination, task automation and integrative technology. *Control relocation* [8] is when controls are moved towards the customer. Control relocation is used to reduce back-office administration and errors. For example, control is relocated when citizens are empowered to perform their own investigation on which a formal decision on assisted living services is made. Errors can be reduced by digitally collecting application data at the source, e.g. letting citizens fill out electronic application forms. *Contact reduction* [9] is when contacts with customers and third-parties are reduced. For example, telephone contacts confirming the receipt of applications are replaced by immediate electronic confirmations. *Control addition* is when completeness and correctness is checked at the information source [10]. It is used to reduce rework. In e-services, controls are usually included in electronic forms used to collect data. The redesign heuristic *case type*, is used to reorganize processes, e.g. when a set of tasks are broken out of a larger process and combined into a process of its own [11]. *Exception* is when handling of exceptions is isolated into separate process flows [11]. *Task elimination* is when unnecessary tasks are removed from the process. *Task automation* is when manual tasks are automated [12]. It is used to decrease execution time and cost. *Integrative technology* is when technology is used to eliminate physical constraints in a process [6].

2.3 Benefits Analysis of E-Government Initiatives

Benefit analyses are used to evaluate effects, potential and actual, of process improvements, e.g. enabled by investments in e-government technology. Gupta and Jana [13] suggest a combination of hard and soft methods to evaluate e-government initiatives. By doing so, multiple views and multiple skills are engaged in balancing the needs of being rigorous enough in the analysis with the needs to be flexible in order to be relevant for different stakeholders. A specific method for benefits evaluation of IT-investments and process changes is Peng [14]. Peng is widely used in both the private and the public sector. The method consists of ten steps, and ideally it involves users and managers as well as functional and technical specialists from the organization. Benefits are identified in workshops and organized in an objectives structure that depicts the relationships between benefits, process changes and IT functionality. All benefits are expressed in financial terms although the intention is not to achieve accounting precision. In order to validate the results, the benefits are classified as direct, indirect and intangible benefits. Identification of IT-costs is supported by a pre-defined list of costs and types. Finally, the net value of the benefits and costs are calculated and managers responsible for the realization of the benefits are appointed.

2.4 Expected Challenges

Municipalities that introduce e-government face a number of challenges. Gil-Garcia and Pardo [15] have organized e-government challenges reported by several authors in five challenge categories: information and data quality, information technology, organizational and managerial, legal and regulatory as well as institutional and environmental. Typical data related challenges include insufficient quality of data, lack of data and inconsistencies of data. Information technology challenges are for example the incompatibility between older and newer system approaches, i.e. universal systems and component-based or service oriented systems [16]. Examples of organizational and managerial challenges include diversity of the organizations involved in e-government initiatives and conflicting goals within government organizations [3]. Legal and regulatory challenges include the need for adapting laws and regulations to new technologies, e.g. electronic identification and digital archiving. Institutional and environmental challenges include for example privacy concerns as well as policy and political pressure.

3 Method

In this paper, the goal is to move control toward citizens and to simplify administration in social services, i.e. assisted living services. We use design research [17, 18, 19] to seek for new solutions based on advances in information technology. Design research is an area within the IS-field that intervenes to create alternative futures instead of studying the past to discover truth.

We went through the following steps to develop the open social e-service. First an as-is analysis of the current process was performed. A number of workshops and in-depth interviews were carried out to gather information about the existing process and related sub-processes. Representatives for all roles involved in the current process participated in the workshops, i.e. local government official (LGO), accounting assistant, emergency group (a sub-supplier), and installer (a sub-supplier to the emergency group). The discussions were steered to retrieve the different process steps, the responsible actors and the data processed at each step. The processes were documented in YAWL [20]. For the resource and data perspectives additional visualization techniques were used. YAWL was chosen because it is a powerful process modeling language with an open source supporting environment. It is based on results from the Workflow Patterns initiative (www.workflowpatterns.com) and supports a wide variety of patterns compared to other business process management systems [21, 22]. For our project, it was essential to evaluate the applicability of an open source business process management tool.

At the end of the as-is analysis a prototype in YAWL of the main process was demonstrated to the work group as a process validation means. After that a performance analysis was carried out, i.e. the execution time of the individual tasks was measured or estimated[2] and documented. Finally, the handling of a pilot case of the emergency telephone application was video recorded and the movie was used by the project team to validate the as-is process among the municipal executives.

The results of the as-is analysis were: (a) process models for: the emergency help telephone application and installation process and the two related processes, i.e. periodical re-investigation and prolongation of the service subscription as well as cancellation of the service; (b) a list of problems caused by limitations in or the utilization of the current IT-system identified during the analysis.

In parallel with the as-is analysis, an investigation was initiated on the legal issues related to the transformation of the service to an open social service. For this the Department of Law at the University of Lund was consulted. Three alternatives from a legal point of view were outlined and evaluated from three perspectives: process-changes, technical impact of the proposed solution and benefits. One of these alternatives was selected for implementation by Järfälla Social committee.

Based on the as-is analysis, and the results from the legal investigation a to-be process was designed together with the work group established earlier. The group was first presented with a prospective solution through a small theatrical sketch. This prospective solution was our revision of the current process so that 1) the problems identified in the as-in process were solved and 2) the benefits of e-services technology added to the process (e.g. relocation of the application registration task from a local government official to a citizen). A prototype in YAWL for the designed solution was then developed and demonstrated to the work group for validation. In parallel, work with the interface design for the e-service was carried out.

4   Results

The goal is to design an open social e-service for assisted living services. The objectives are to move control closer to the citizen and to reduce bureaucracy. Control

---

[2] A telephone call with the citizen is an example of a task for which the performance time was estimated. As the conversation time may vary significantly between different citizens an estimated average was agreed upon.

can be moved closer to the citizen by the use of interactive e-services and increased transparency. Bureaucracy can be reduced by eliminating formal decisions and decreasing administrative tasks, such as manual data entry and manual case filing.

4.1 Design of the Open Social E-Service

Three different alternatives to an open social e-service were identified.

- Open for anyone
- Open with eligibility criteria
- Open after general approval

Open for anyone is a fully open service with no municipal decision making where citizens pay a fee for service provisioning. Open with eligibility criteria is a service open to citizens which meet pre-defined eligibility criteria. Open after general approval is a service open to citizens who already have received a municipal approval for social services. Based on the approval, these citizens can then order a number of available assisted living services based on his or her perceived needs.

The first solution *Open for anyone* was found to be complicated from a legal standpoint. The social services act requires that decisions are made on an individual level in order to provide documentation, to provide the possibility to file legal claims against the decision and to provide a basis for communication to the individual. Further, the social service council requires formal and individual decisions in order to document information about individuals that is used for future care decisions and for providing statistics to the government. In addition, the county council has recently criticized a number of municipalities providing emergency alarms as open services without formal decisions [23]. The city council's view is that emergency alarms ultimately are care services due to the life saving actions that may be provided in case of an alarm. The second solution *Open with eligibility criteria* was legally acceptable if the decision is taken based on a number of clearly defined eligibility criteria and that the individual could be satisfactorily identified. If the citizen does not meet the eligibility criteria a manual application process should be initiated. Given these circumstances, a formal decision could be automated. In the third solution *Open after general approval* the citizen is offered a selection of living assistance services based on an initial formal decision. The citizen can then choose one or more living assistance services from this selection of services over a period of time. Järfälla Social committee decided to go for the second solution "Open with eligibility criteria".

The administrative process for the open social e-service was detailed according to the solution "Open with eligibility criteria", see Figure 1. The process starts with a citizen filling out an electronic application and submitting it to the municipality. The application form contains the citizen's personal and contact data, information of the citizen's health situation that may be of importance when providing the living assistance service, as well as data for a number of prerequisites and eligibility criteria defined by Järfälla Social Committee [24], see Figure 2. The prerequisites aim to make clear the necessary conditions, e.g. that the citizen is able to use the emergency help telephone equipment. In addition, there are two eligibility criteria: perceived insecurity and perceived risk of falling. A citizen is eligible for the emergency help telephone service if at least one of these criteria is met.

An individual and automated decision is made based on the input provided for the prerequisites and eligibility criteria. In case the criteria are fulfilled, the application is approved, the citizen notified, and installation organized and carried out, see Figure 1.

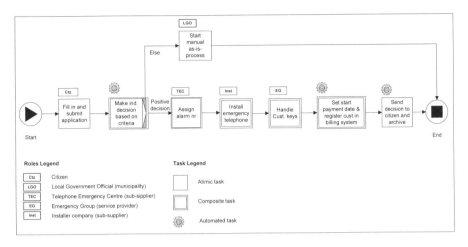

Fig. 1. The to-be administrative process for the open social e-service

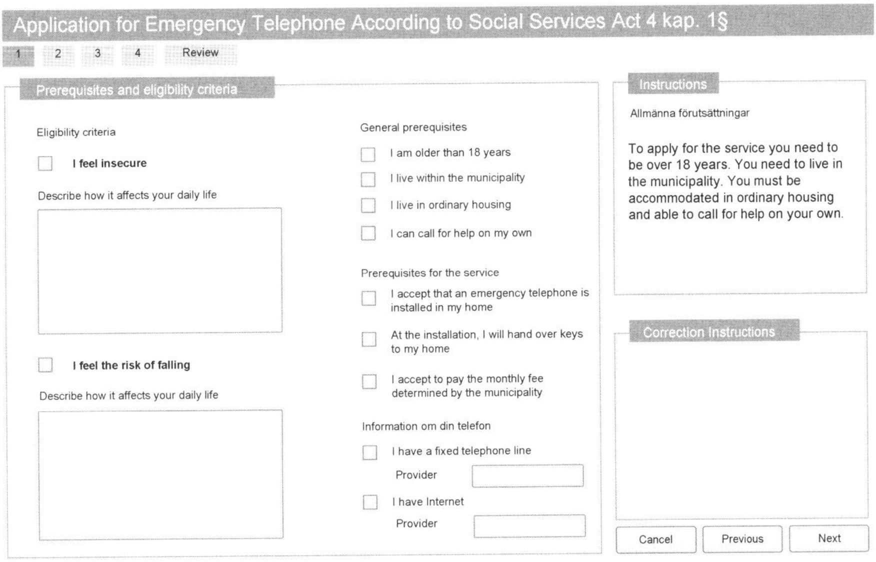

Fig. 2. Application form including prerequisites and eligibility criteria [26]

First an alarm number is assigned to the citizen by the Telephone Emergency Center (TEC). TEC is a national organization providing the technical infrastructure for directing emergency calls from citizens to different emergency groups. When a citizen has received an alarm number, installation of the emergency telephone equipment can take place. Installation is organized and carried out by a third party provider, in the model referred to as Installer. During the installation, keys to the citizen's home are collected (so that help can be provided even if the citizen is not able to open the door). The keys are handed over to the Emergency Group (EG) where they are allocated to a storage space and kept in a secure way. Finally, start date for the service is derived (usually the same as the installation date), citizen added to the billing system and informed about the start of the service and payment date.

As nearly all of the applications today result in approvals, the expectation is that the process proposed in Figure 1 will be used for most of the applications in the future. However, a fundamental standpoint is that negative decisions shall never be automated. For this reason, if a citizen does not fulfill the prerequisites and eligibility criteria, the case will be handled manually.

4.2 Analysis of Potential Benefits and Use of Process Innovation Techniques

The potential benefits of the administrative process for the open social e-service are expressed as a reduction in work time. The total potential benefits are estimated, using Peng (see section 2.3), to between 53 and 69 minutes per case. This is an effect of the process redesign heuristics (see section 2.2) applied to the to-be administrative process. The potential benefits and applied redesign heuristics are presented in Table 1. In the first task *Fill in and submit application* control is relocated to the citizen by letting the citizen perform her own investigation through the use of an electronic form where required information is made explicit and input data controls are added. Integrative technology is used by a workflow system supporting the administrative process from start to end. In the second task *Make individual decision based on criteria* the decision task is automated for approved cases. Approval is based on

Table 1. Potential benefits and applied process redesign heuristics

Task	To-be	Applied process redesign heuristics	Potential benefits (minutes of work time)
1	Fill in and submit application	Control relocation, Control addition, Contact reduction, Integrative technology	17-22
2	Make individual decision based on criteria	Integrative technology, Task elimination, Task automation, Exception	8
3	Assign alarm number	Task automation, Control relocation, Integrative technology	5
4	Install help telephone	Integrative technology	3-5
5	Handle citizen keys	Task automation, Integrative technology	3
6	Set start payment date and register in billing system	Task automation, Case type, Integrative technology	11-15
7	Send decision to citizen and archive	Task automation , Integrative technology	6-11

prerequisites and eligibility criteria. The case is redirected to an exception handling process if the prerequisites or eligibility criteria are not met. In the tasks 3-7, task automation and integrative technology are applied in the same fashion. In the third task *Assign alarm number* control is relocated to a third-party service supplier. In the sixth task *Set start payment date and register citizen in billing system* a service fee decision is automated and tasks related to reduction service fee applications are broken out into a separate process. In summary, the use of an e-service in combination with a workflow system will have a significant impact on the administrative process. Since a large number of tasks are relocated, eliminated or automated work organization will change.

4.3 Experienced Challenges

Several challenges were experienced during the design and development of the open social e-service for assisted living: conflict of interests, technological incompatibility, lock-in relationship with IT-suppliers.

Conflict of Interests. There are two groups of interests. On the one hand there are the director of the Social Services Committee and the local government officials. On the other hand there are the middle managers reporting to the director and responsible for managing the work of the officials.

The director and the officials see opportunities in relocating control toward citizens. This means that citizens instead of local government officials become responsible for decision making and for providing input data. The director argues that open social e-services support Järfälla's aim to become more open and transparent to citizens. The director refers to changes in other areas of social services where it has been possible to successfully remove decision making, e.g. simple home maintenance assistance for elderly citizens, such as change of light bulbs. The officials want to remove administration from their duties and through open social e-services they become no longer active in the operative process.

The middle managers are hesitant to relocate control toward citizens. They want to keep decision making since individual decisions make it possible for municipalities to collect social information about individuals. Middle managers argue that emergency help telephone services differ from simple home maintenance assistance services due to the caring nature of emergency help telephone services. It is also the city council's view that emergency help telephone services ultimately are care services due to the life saving actions that may be provided in case of an alarm [23]. In addition, the National Board of Health and Welfare requires municipalities to provide statistics about assisted living services which is simplified through the availability of individual social information.

We believe that the above conflict of interests depends on that open social e-services challenge the current way control is exercised within the Social Services Committee. Today, control and implementation of policies is to a large extent exercised by local government officials. They are so called street-level bureaucrats [25, 26] that exercise a large amount of influence over how public policy is actually carried out. When local government officials are removed from the administrative process and the daily exercise of policy implementation the demands on middle management will increase.

The challenge was initially managed by conducting an in-depth analysis of the legal issues of providing different solutions to open social e-services and then to request a formal decision by the Social Services Committee on which solution to choose.

Technological Incompatibility. The current information system package lacks workflow capabilities. It is built on a database using forms to create, read and update information. The only means to signal hand-over between roles in the organization are changes in case status. This means that it is difficult to build on this application when integrating the administrative process further.

The challenge was managed by letting the IT-supplier conduct a pre-study of how to communicate with the e-service front-end (My Pages) and to implement changes necessary to realize the to-be process. If the criteria could be handled separately and disconnected from the web form and the decision logic in the workflow then the e-service would be more or less transparent to all application processes in most municipalities.

Lock-in Relationship with IT-suppliers. The current information system used by the Social Services Committee, Procapita, is built using a two-tier technical architecture: database and application. The database is owned by the municipality of Järfälla but the operations and maintenance is outsourced to the IT-supplier that owns the application Procapita. The agreement between Järfälla and the IT-supplier does not allow for other applications to create or update data. Also, it is not allowed to change the structure of the database. This has the effect that IT-related changes have to involve the IT-supplier which is costly and often time consuming. Even small changes can be very difficult to realize.

To manage this challenge, the project has tried to involve the IT-supplier in the development process. Since Procapita is an information system used by a majority of Swedish municipalities, the support for open social e-services may potentially be used by a large number of municipalities.

5 Epilogue

In this paper we set forth to design an "Open Social e-Service" for assisted living services. The administrative process for the emergency help telephone in the municipality of Järfälla was analyzed and redesigned. Several best practices for process innovation were used to relocate control towards the citizen and to eliminate tasks and manual work in the current administrative process. The design was demonstrated in a YAWL-prototype. Potential benefits were analyzed from the perspective of the municipality and the service provider. Challenges experienced during the work were reported and analyzed.

We conclude that a major challenge with open social e-services is the transition from the current way of how control is exercised by the local government officials within the Social Services Committee to a new way of how control is shared by citizens and middle management within the Social Services Committee. We also conclude that for the open e-service to be applicable to other domains and municipalities, it is important to manage decision criteria separately. Hence, a second design iteration should consider separation of concerns [27].

The service is currently under implementation and will be evaluated through tests and analysis of actual benefits achieved. Verification, acceptance and usability tests are planned for second half of 2010. Benefit analysis are planned to be carried out in 2011 using an approach combining Peng and Value modeling [28, 29].

Acknowledgements

We would like to thank the participants in the project "Open Social e-Services" in the municipality of Järfälla. We would also like to thank Prof. Titti Mattsson and Dr. Vilhelm Persson from the Department of Law at Lund University for contributing their legal expertise to the case study reported here. This study was partly funded by Vinnova, the Swedish Governmental Agency for Innovation Systems [30].

References

1. Steg, H., Strese, H., Hull, J., Schmidt, S.: Europe is facing a demographic challenge Ambient Assisted Living offers solutions (2005),
   http://www.aal169.org/Published/Final%20Version.pdf
2. Hjälpmedelsinstitutet: Stora skillnader i kostnad mellan hjälpmedel och särskilt boende (2009) (in Swedish),
   http://www.hi.se/sv-se/Pressrum/Pressmeddelanden-2009/
   Stora-skillnader-i-kostnad-mellan-hjalpmedel-och-sarskilt-
   boende/
3. United Nations, UN E-Government Survey 2008: From E-Government to Connected Governance, United Nations, New York (2008)
4. Järfälla Municipality, http://www.jarfalla.se
5. Helfrich, J.: Projektbeskrivning Öppna Sociala e-Tjänster ver.3.6.(2008) (in Swedish),
   http://www.jarfalla.se/upload/Omsorg%20och%20std/socialtjnst/
   Rev_Projektbeskr_inovat_ver36-1.pdf
6. Davenport, T.H.: Process Innovation, Reengineering Work through Information Technology. Harvard Business School Press, Boston (1993)
7. Mansar, S.L., Reijers, H.A.: Best practices in business process redesign: validation of a redesign framework. Computers in Industry 56(5), 457–471 (2005)
8. Klein, M.: 10 principles of reengineering. Executive Excellence 12(2), 20 (1995)
9. Hammer, M., Champy, J.: Reengineering the corporation: a manifesto for business revolution. Harper Business Editions, New York (1993)
10. Poyssick, G., Hannaford, S.: Workflow reengineering. Adobe Press Editions, Mountain View (1996)
11. Reijers, H.A.: Process Design and Redesign. In: Dumas, M., van der Aalst, W., ter Hofstede, A. (eds.) Process-aware information systems: bridging people and software through Process Technology, pp. 207–233. John Wiley & Sons Inc., Chichester (2006)
12. Peppard, J., Rowland, P.: The essence of business process reengineering. Prentice-Hall Editions, New York (1995)
13. Gupta, M.P., Jana, D.: E-government evaluation: a framework and case study. Government Information Quarterly 20(4), 365–387 (2003)
14. Dahlgren, L.E., Lundgren, G., Stigberg, L.: Make IT profitable: PENG - A practical tool for financial evaluation of IT benefits. Ekerlids Förlag, Stockholm (1997)

15. Gil-Garcia, J.R., Pardo, T.A.: E-government success factors: Mapping practical tools to theoretical foundations. Government Information Quarterly 22, 187–216 (2005)
16. Erl, T.: Service-Oriented Architecture: Concepts, Technology, and Design. Prentice Hall, Englewood Cliffs (2005)
17. March, S., Smith, G.: Design and Natural Science Research on Information Technology. Decision Support Systems 15, 251–266 (1995)
18. Hevner, A., March, S., Park, J., Ram, S.: Design Science in Information Systems Research. MIS Quarterly 28(1), 75–105 (2004)
19. Peffers, K., Tuunanen, T., Rothenberger, M.A., Chatterjee, S.: A design science research methodology for information systems research. Journal of Management Information Systems 24(3), 47–77 (2008)
20. YAWL: Modern Business Process Automation: YAWL and its Support Environment. Springer, Heidelberg (in press)
21. Russell, N.: Foundations of Process-Aware Information Systems. PhD Thesis, Queensland University of Technology, Brisbane, Australia (2007)
22. Wohed, P., Russell, N., ter Hofstede, A.H.M., Andersson, B., van der Aalst, W.M.P.: Patterns-based evaluation of open source BPM systems: The cases of jBPM, OpenWFE, and Enhydra Shark. Information & Software Technology 51(8), 1187–1216 (2009)
23. Uppsala County Council: Trygghetslarm i ordinärt boende. Länsstyrelsens meddelandeserie, 2008:18 (2008) (in Swedish) ISSN 1400-4712
24. Arvidsson, E.: Kriterier för trygghetstelefon som öppen tjänst inom handikappomsorg och äldreomsorg (2009) (in Swedish),
    `http://www.jarfalla.se/upload/Politik/Social/2009%20handling`
    `ar/2009-04-23/`
    `16.1%20Tj%C3%A4nsteskrivelse%20trygghetstelefoner%20kriterie`
    `r%20f%C3%B6r%20%C3%B6ppen%20tj%C3%A4nst.pdf`
25. Lipsky, M.: Street-level Bureaucracy: Dilemmas of the Individual in Public Services. Russell Sage Foundation, New York (1980)
26. Verva: Styrning för ökad effektivitet, 2007:12 (2007) (in Swedish)
27. Hürsch, W.L., Lopes, C.V.: Separation of Concerns. Technical Report NU-CCS-95-03, Northeastern University, Boston (1995)
28. Juell-Skielse, G., Perjons, E.: Improving E-Government through Benefit Analysis and Value Modeling. In: 33rd Annual IEEE International Computer Software and Applications Conference, pp. 332–339. IEEE Computer Society, Los Alamitos (2009)
29. Juell-Skielse, G., Perjons, E.: Improving E-Government through Benefit Analysis and Value Modeling. In: 4th International Conference on Research Challenges in Information Science, pp. 437–445. IEEE Computer Society Press, Los Alamitos (2010)
30. Vinnova: Öppen Socialtjänst (2008) (in Swedish) ,
    `http://www.vinnova.se/misc/VINNOVA-projekt/Projekt-`
    `Listhuvud/17573/`

How to Develop an Open and Flexible Information Infrastructure for the Public Sector?

Erik Hornnes[1], Arild Jansen[2], and Øivind Langeland[1]

[1] Agency for Public Management and eGovernment Post Box 8115 Dep., 0032 Oslo, Norway
[2] Section for eGovernment, Department for Private Law, University of Oslo, Norway

Abstract. In line with a number of other countries, Norway has decided to base their ICT solutions in the public sector on a common ICT architecture. This article discusses some challenges related to this work. The theoretical basis for the discussions is our understanding of information infrastructures, which we claim offers a fruitful perspective to the building of ICT architectures. Of particular relevance is its installed base: the history of technical and non-technical components that determines its further development. We argue that an ICT architecture for the public sector should be seen as an important element of a government information infrastructure. However, it has to be adapted to other principles and fulfil a wider range of needs than traditional types of infrastructures, including the specific political, regulatory and organizational context that it targets

Keywords: ICT architecture, information infrastructure, installed base, IT governance.

1 Introduction

The Norwegian government, like governments in many other countries, is facing great challenges in their efforts to improve service provision to the citizens and the private sector at large. One important challenge is to overcome the obstacles created by the highly fragmented public sector, and as the result, a silo-organization of its information systems. Modern eGovernment services require IT-solutions whereby information can be easily accessed and transferred between agencies and across sector-based boundaries. As a response, many countries have defined more coherent strategies for developing their ICT-solutions designed to simplify information exchange and interaction between public agencies in order to provide better services to citizens and businesses in a coordinated and user friendly manner. One common component in many of these strategies is to build a common ICT-architecture as a framework for their eGovernment solutions (see e.g. Janssen and Hjort-Madsen 2007, Liimatainen 2008). However, such efforts imply technical, as well as organizational and, not least, legal challenges. It also includes measures that have been proposed in the past, however without having succeeded (e.g. Heeks 2006). We do believe that the chances for success are greater now than in the past, since there is a much stronger understanding on the political level, which manifests itself, for example, through the strong focus

M.A. Wimmer et al. (Eds.): EGOV 2010, LNCS 6228, pp. 301–314, 2010.

among the EU members[1]. However, we argue that a major challenge is to build an adequate information infrastructure that can constitute an open and flexible foundation for new eGovernment services, and that the design and implementation of a government ICT-architecture must be an integral part of that work.

Thus, from both a theoretical and a practical point of view, we need a better understanding of the type of "artefact" this government ICT-architecture should be. Still, eGovernment as a research field is in its early stage (see e.g. Grønlund 2005, Grønlund & Andersson 2006, Heeks & Bailur 2007, Scholl 2009), and the broader IS research field is able to capture the variety and complexity in the public sector only to a limited extent. This implies that we lack an adequate conceptual framework that can describe the different types of systems and solutions we find in the public sector, not least ICT-architectures. A traditional perspective has been to see ICT as a toolbox, implying that the user can select the appropriate tool for a specific task and use it, having full control. This is in contrast to the machine perspective, characterized by "something" determining how a production process unfolds and requiring the operator to carry out specific operations as mandated by the machine. It seems rather evident that none of these perspectives are fruitful as analytical tools for understanding ICT-architectures. No single entity can control an ICT-architecture, nor does an architecture imply a determining machine.

In their seminal paper "*Desperately Seeking the 'IT' in IT Research—A Call to Theorizing the IT Artifact*" Orlikowski and Iacono (2001) argue that we need a better conceptualization of the information technology (IT) artefact. Based on a review of a number of published articles, they discuss different categories of IT, where their "ensemble view" seems to be a valuable contribution to understanding the nature of an ICT-architecture. But it does not capture all its dimensions, neither its socio-technical character nor its installed base; that is, the history of technical and non-technical components that determines its further development. We do not claim that an ICT-architecture on its own will constitute an information infrastructure. We will, however argue that an information infrastructure perspective can be fruitful when analysing the different properties of an ICT-architecture. This will also make visible some of the barriers that are linked to the implementation of an ICT-architecture in the government. The article will discuss the following research questions:

1. In what manner is the perspective of information infrastructures relevant for the building of an ICT-architecture in the public sector?
2. How do we conceptualize the installed base of an ICT architecture?
3. What specific characteristics are important for such information infrastructures?

1.1 Our Research Approach

This study is based on an inductive approach where the aim is to contribute to an increased theoretical understanding of the kind of infrastructure needed to support the provision of electronic services to citizens. Our theoretical point of departure is from information infrastructures (Weill and Broadbent 1988, Shapiro and Varian 1999,

---

[1] See the Fifth ministerial eGovernment conference 19 - 20 November in Malmö,
    `http://ec.europa.eu/information_society/activities/`
    `egovernment/conferences/past/malmo_2009/index_en`

Hanseth and Lyytinen 2004) and from management control and technological drift (Ciborra 2000, 2002). Our main empirical base is the ongoing work to realize an ICT-architecture in Norway, which we believe is representative of similar efforts in many other countries. Our data collection and analysis comprises analysis of documents, including descriptions of planned and finished eGovernment projects. The proposal for a Norwegian Common ICT architecture, along with all remarks to that report, as well as the budget documents and "assignment letters" etc. have been particularly relevant. Furthermore, we have participated in open hearings and meetings that have been organized in relation to this work in Norway.

The next chapter will briefly present the basic ideas of ICT-architecture, illustrated by current work in the Norwegian government. Chapter 3 provides the theoretical framework, followed by our analysis, findings and our conclusions with suggestions for further research.

2   What Is an ICT Architecture for the Public Sector?

As part of public modernization plans in many countries, governments seek to offer citizens and businesses seamless online services by improving horizontal and vertical relationships and linking independently developed processes and information systems. Current efforts are focused on coordinating the projects and providing a framework that will function as an umbrella for explaining the relationships among the projects. These kinds of frameworks are often denoted as *national enterprise architecture* (NEA); see, for example, Janssen and Madsen (2007). The Norwegian government has also defined a common ICT-architecture (Report to the Storting no.17: 2006-07). Facing the reality that the Norwegian public sector (as many others) is a collection of a large number of independent and heterogeneous organizations, having different business processes and information systems, this architecture aims at ensuring interoperability, avoiding duplication of efforts and enabling reuse of existing ICT-based services and solutions.

Even though the Norwegian architecture has been designed in a national context, its overall principles are based on a service-oriented framework, heavily influenced by the work in Denmark and other countries. Its overall, layered structure is illustrated in figure 1. The business layer at the bottom consists of the different government agencies and their ICT solutions. The middle layer provides shared services that may be relevant to many or all eGovernment services, such as an identification and authentication solution, etc. in order to enable the reuse of ICT-services (DIFI 2009). The presentation layer at the top enables citizens and businesses to interact with the electronic services provided by the different government agencies. This layered structure makes it much more flexible and robust with respect to future changes in the different layers, since a change in one layer will not impact on another layer. This assumes that the layers are loosely coupled and that they make use of open and standardized interfaces, preferably through the use of open standards.

The Norwegian government has defined seven architectural principles: service orientation, interoperability, availability, security, openness, flexibility and scalability. Other countries such as Denmark and Sweden operate with similar sets of architectural principles.. Although the principles are somewhat differently described, their

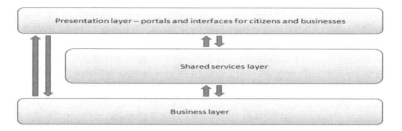

Fig. 1. Generic government ICT architecture

goal is also to provide a unified framework for the national ICT architecture in question. Denmark has defined nine architectural principles[2] (IT- og Telestyrelsen 2009). Sweden has defined six architectural principles (Verket för förvaltningsutveckling 2008). In the Netherlands, their architectural program is based on adopting one part of the Zachman framework, and includes a large number of principles (Janssen and Hjort-Madsen 2007). In these countries, the use of the national architecture is based on a sort of voluntarism, in the sense that each individual agency may decide not to use the principles if there are good reasons for not doing so. However, there is substantial pressure to accommodate to the national framework.[3] We also find similar approaches in countries like the UK and the US. However, as we argue below, these are minor differences at a detailed level, and the relevance of an information infrastructure perspective is not dependent upon the type of architecture as such. The overall scope and design of the architecture is more important, i.e. that the architecture is open and accessible to all relevant stakeholders and that it is sufficiently flexible to support the diversity of ICT – systems and services that are continuously evolving.

Although these different ICT-architectures do share many characteristics with enterprise architectures (EAs), there are nevertheless many differences. EAs lack a universally accepted definition (Rohloff 2005); a common understanding, however, is that it "identifies the main components of the enterprise, its information systems, the ways in which these components work together in order to achieve defined objectives and the way in which the systems support business processes". Weill (2007) defines an EA as "*the organizing logic for business processes and IT infrastructure reflecting the integration and standardization requirements of the firm's operating model*", which implies that it involves redesigning the business. Architectures aim at creating some kind of coherence and structure in a chaotic environment through the use of systematic approaches.

Our argument, in line with Janssen and Hjort-Madsen (op.cit. p 2), is that national (government) ICT-architecture differs from EA in that "*architecting public sector involves designing public administrations to reflect the political and public managers'*

---

[2] The Danish principles address topics such as information security, flexibility, user orientation, modularization and loose coupling etc, while the Swedish architecture addresses topics such as information security, clearly defined interfaces, standardization, universal design etc.

[3] There are still differences between the national policies. While the Norwegian approach implies that an agency has to explain why they choose not to apply these principles, the Danish policy is primarily driven by incentives and non-mandatory principles, and the Dutch policy primarily aims at guiding and stimulating the individual agencies to adopt best practice.

decisions at a strategic level in operational activities and decisions". Public administration must be seen as a collection of a large number of heterogeneous organizations having different business processes and information systems which constitute their "installed base" of technical, organizational and legal elements. Ross (2003) criticized enterprise frameworks for taking a technologist view and claimed that such frameworks do not highlight the role of institutions and capabilities critical to enabling the governance, adoption and diffusion of an EA, a viewpoint we fully support. Our point of departure here is that there exist a number of different national EA-like initiatives having different ambitions and scope, but having some common features in that they are designed to support advanced eGovernment services that span different agencies and sectors. In this respect they need a foundation of technical and non-technical elements that correspond to infrastructures, in line with Janssen and Hjort-Madsen (2007, p5-6). Below we will discuss a "generic" government information infrastructure, as a kind of basic kernel for the individual ICT-architectures.

3   ICT-Architecture in an Information Infrastructure Perspective

The term information infrastructure was introduced in the early 1990s, usually by reference to Al Gore's political initiative to build a global information network in the US. Important contributors to the development of the information infrastructure theory, among others, have been Hanseth and Monteiro (1996), Weill and Broadbent (1998), Hanseth and Lyytinen (2004). This perspective has proved fruitful in the analysis of a number of cases, including the description of complex technical systems (Ciborra 2000, 2002), with links to standardization processes (Braa et al. 2007).

Hanseth and Lyytinen (2004) define an information infrastructure (II) as: *"a shared, evolving, heterogeneous installed base of IT capabilities among a set of user communities based on open and/or standardized interfaces"*. We find many similarities when comparing this definition with the basic principles of an ICT-architecture; it has to be shared by all its users by being accessible and open to a broad community of users and interests; it has to be continuously evolving, flexible and scalable in order to meet new requirements etc.

By the installed base we mean the history of its technical and non-technical components that determines its further development, that is, the interconnected practices and technologies that are institutionalized in the organization (Hanseth, Ciborra and Braa 2001). One thus needs to understand what the installed base in the public sector comprises, and what implications it might have for the development work. One important part is all the legacy systems; which are often based on proprietary technical solutions, old data formats and non-standard databases. Although many of them are technically outdated, they represent a lot of invested "capital" and are linked to work routines and organizational practices. The legal framework itself is another essential part of the installed base, which in many ways implies substantial challenges both in terms of implementation of the technical solutions and its governance and control. First of all, it constitutes the overall (political) setting for the use of ICT in the public sector, that is the overall principles for governance management. Secondly, it amounts to the logic of a number of systems that are being used in decision making. These systems cannot be changed without revising the corresponding regulation. Furthermore, many of the eGovernment solutions are linked to specific regulations that may include legal definitions which are not, however, consistent across government, making interoperability difficult. Furthermore, the public sector is diverse and manifold in many ways; it includes a large number of agencies that are independent each with its own responsibilities and decision-making power. Furthermore, it is continuously being reformed, and new laws and regulations are being implemented consecutively. We thus define the installed base in a specific government as *"the history of technical, organizational and legal components, including work routines, practices and even social and cultural structures that influence how the ICT systems in government are being used"*. This installed base is neither static nor controlled by a single authority, and it will include multiple local architectures and the specific ICT-solutions that are being developed and maintained at various levels in the public sector.

4   What Type of Infrastructure Is Needed in the Public Sector?

Even though it seems evident that modern governmental electronic services need an information infrastructure, the type of infrastructure this may be is not obvious, nor the requirements it should meet. Hanseth and Lyytinen (2004) present a simple taxonomy for IIs. Using the scale and scope of the II as the main classification criterion they distinguish between three types of vertical II's: 1) universal service infrastructure, 2) business sector infrastructure, and 3) corporate information infrastructure. A *universal service infrastructure* is designed for all types of users and applications, based upon a set of international standards. Internet is the most typical example. Second, a *business sector infrastructure* is designed for specific groups of users, and offers specialized transactions- and data exchange services (e.g. the finance industry, car industry etc). Thirdly, their *corporate infrastructure* offers information- and transaction services for its internal users and its partners, which has a limited focus and may be based on specialized standards and services.

Although information infrastructures for the government share many of the characteristics of these different types of II's, such as being heterogeneous and containing many standards and many service providers, there are also quite a few differences. Although a government II will span a large and heterogeneous group of users, that is, public agencies, citizens, businesses, suppliers etc., it will be more limited than a universal II designed to support potentially any application, service or user. Another important difference is the presence of legal regulations in the installed base of a government II. The principle of legality is an important factor in modern government, implying that legal regulations must always be taken into account.

In the same way it can be argued that an II for the government will resemble some of the properties of a corporate II, e.g. regarding its more limited scope and appliance. It is also possible to determine more specific guidelines and directions related to architecture and technical systems. On the other hand, an II for the government will have greater diversity than a corporate II since it will include a large number of state agencies and municipalities which to a large extent are independent, in that each institution has its own specific responsibility and decision authority. Furthermore, while a private company may define its own standards, the government has to pay attention to precompetitive measures and secure an open and accessible public sector. It could also be argued that a government II bears some resemblance to a business sector II;. However, a business sector infrastructure will be more restricted than the government infrastructure, with regard to purpose, functions and methods of use. The table below summarizes these four categories of II's and their characteristics[4]:

Table 1. Different types of information infrastructures and their characteristics

Types\n\nQuality	Universal II	Business sector II	Corporation II	Government II
Shared (by)	Potentially any application, service or user on earth.	Primarily companies within the sector (including their employees), but also customer and suppliers.	Primarily units and employees within the corporation, but also suppliers, customers and partners.	Primarily public agencies along with suppliers to and users of the public services
Evolving	By adding services and computers to the network since the first data network was established	By exchanging new types of information among the users and by involving more organizations.	By integrating more applications with each other, by introducing new applications	By adding new services, exchanging new types of information and integration of new applications
Hetero-geneous	Many sub infrastructures, different version of standards, service providers, etc.	Multiplicity of competing and overlapping subinfrastructures, standards, service providers, etc.	Multiplicity of applications and subinfrastructures, users, services etc.	Includes many sector-wise infrastructures, multiplicity of applications and various types of standards
Installed base	The current Internet, applications integrated with it, users and use practices	All current integrated services, their users and developers, and the practices they are supporting and embedding.	All current applications and their users and developers, and the working practices they support and embed	Legal regulations, politics, administrative practices, legacy systems, etc

We will thus argue that it will be fruitful to introduce this new category: an (e)*Government information infrastructurs,* denoted GII. Our definition of the objective of a GII is that it *"should include the technical, organizational and legal structures that are required to enable and support ICT-solutions in the public administration to operate as intended".* This approach would correspond to the definition introduced by Tilson and Lyytinen (2009, p2), which states that infrastructures are *"the basic physical and organizational structures needed for the operation of a society or enterprise".* Our definition is based on normative criteria since it describes what goals must be fulfilled in order to be included in a GII, rather than describing what specific characteristics that must be met. This definition is somewhat "vague", but it reflects the basic nature of infrastructures; they cannot be conceived as static and well-defined., but continuously changing and expanding. Just as we cannot consider the public administration as a single "body", it follows that we cannot perceive a government II as merely a single entity, but rather as several (sub) infrastructures related to the different levels and the different sectors. This implies that a GII must be perceived as a diverse collection of elements that grows through an evolutionary harmonization and coupling of different sub-infrastructures, which implies the coupling of the different installed bases that are already part of the public administration today.

---

[4] This table is based on table II in Hanseth and Lyytinen (2004), but expanded with a fourth category:Government II (GII).

In addition to the characteristics described in the table, there are also other characteristics, as its dynamics, the stakeholders and strategy for governance, that illustrate the differences between them and why it is reasonable to introduce GII as a fourth category.

The dynamics and drivers in a GII will primarily be agency needs and it will thus be shaped by political directions and signals. This is different from the other types of IIs, in view of the fact that a universal II is technology and user driven, while a business sector II is user driven and shaped by the requirements from the civil society, and that a corporation II is driven by business needs of the corporation. A GII will comprise a wide range of stakeholders, including citizens, businesses, agencies, NGO's, suppliers and politicians. This, however, represents a more "focused" group of stakeholders than for a universal II, which comprises all types of users and use patterns. But it is clearly a larger and more heterogeneous group of stakeholders than for both business and corporate IIs, which are typically limited to the stakeholders within the businesses and industries.

Not least, the strategy for governance is different. In the context of a GII strategy will mainly manifest itself through political governance, legal regulations and principles for the public administration, including the perspectives of democracy and rule of law. This is in contrast to e.g. a universal infrastructure, where the emphasis is put on international consensus. We also find that the governance structure and use of policy instruments in the public sector differ from what we find in private corporations as well as in business sectors. In particular, a corporate infrastructure may appear more coherent in that it can apply more powerful means of co-ordination without having to allow for influence from the environment, which the government, on the other hand, is obliged to accommodate. As a contrast, the government acts both as a service provider and as an authority that must exercise control and ensure common values and civil rights, which in turn implies that a government II must also exhibit other characteristics. An important element of a governance strategy for a GII will furthermore be to overcome the barriers represented by the silo organization in the public sector when developing new eGovernment services.

One may ask to what extent it is fruitful to introduce this new type of information infrastructure. The contrary would be to claim that since its installed base does not fit into existing categories, one should rather accept that an information infrastructure perspective does not add much insight when it comes to government ICT architecture, and that it may even be counterproductive since it offers misleading associations. Such arguments should be taken seriously, and an II perspective is not the only relevant perspective to be applied in the analysis of government ICT architectures. However, we will argue that an II perspective will help us to identify both similarities and differences, and in this way create a basis for a better understanding of what government ICT architectures should be and should not be. Not least we should carefully examine what lessons can be learned from other II projects when it comes to design and not least management of complex ICT architectures.

Implications of an Infrastructure Perspective for Designing ICT Architectures

Previous experiences from building infrastructures clearly reveal that they cannot be constructed in the same way as traditional information systems. Hanseth and Lyytinen (op. cit, p 208) points out that IIs are large and complex, evolving over a heterogeneous set of communities and components; they need to adapt to both functional and technical requirements that are *unknown* at the time of designing, and they are commonly designed as extensions to, or improvements on, the existing installed base with heterogeneous, diverse components that are not under the control of a single authority or designer. The implication of this view on ICT architectures is to admit that the complexity and diversity of the public sector cannot be resolved, but has to be accepted and handled in constructive ways. It thus follows that ICT-architectures cannot be designed and built through a top-down process-reengineering approach. Rather the opposite, whereas they are meant for a variety of users and types of usage implying an abundance of user requirements and external conditions, they have to be adopted and adapted in a step-wise, bottom-up strategy, thus corresponding to the building of infrastructures (see e.g. Ciborra 2000, 2002). For a GII this means that the strategy for development will be driven by the needs of the different public agencies along with requirements from citizens and private sector users. It is therefore particularly important that government ICT-architectures are adapted not only to existing technical components, but also to institutions and capabilities critical to the governance, adoption and diffusion of them (Ross, 2005).

The proposal for the Norwegian ICT-architecture is based on a layered structure, which is in line with central principles of object-oriented system architecture. This also resembles service-oriented architecture. Hanseth and Lyytinen (2004) also demonstrate a similar strategy in the design of infrastructures by decomposing a complex infrastructure into a set of simpler ones which offer only one type of functionality. This type of *horizontal* decomposition is equivalent to the use of abstraction principles applied in software engineering. According to Hanseth and Lyytinen (ibid) an infrastructure may be split into an application infrastructure and an underlying support infrastructure, where the latter is split into a transport- and service infrastructure such as we find in the Internet architecture. A similar approach of layering information infrastructures is applicable for a GII. This means that a government information infrastructure will consist of a basic infrastructure, a service infrastructure and an application infrastructure, cf. figure 2. The basic infrastructure will contain generic shared services, while the application infrastructure will contain specialized shared services based on the generic ones. Examples of such services are shared handling of registries, shared metadata and the generation of electronic forms. This implies that the

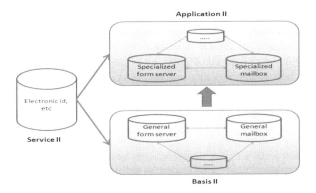

Fig. 2. Layering of infrastructures – the case of Norwegian ICT-architecture

generic, shared services of the basic infrastructure will offer a minimum of functionality, which most of the stakeholders will find useful and valuable. Additional functionality that is not offered by the generic shared services may be implemented by building specialized services in the application infrastructure on top. Both types of services may utilize the shared services in the service infrastructure, for example electronic ID.

4.1 Legal Regulation – Also a Catalyst for New Services in the Public Sector?

Traditionally, laws and regulations are regarded as barriers against development of eGovernment. Legal regulation, however, may also be seen as a catalyst in the public sector, because new laws and regulations can help facilitate the penetration of new ICT solutions. An example in Norway is the introduction of the eGovernment administrative rule[5], which has accelerated the development and use of secure electronic communication services in the government. The Norwegian Freedom of Information Act is yet another example, prescribing that all Norwegian ministries, directorates and authorities make their mail records publicly accessible on the Internet.

Similarly, new common components may be introduced through a "bootstrapping" strategy, because a legal regulation identifies and creates requirements that must be fulfilled. On the other hand these requirements may be demanding to implement, due to old systems and practices. Bootstrapping means "to promote or develop by initiative and effort with little or no assistance" (Hanseth & Aanestad 2001). Hanseth & Lyytinen (2004) propose some simple design principles: i) design initially a service that takes the desires of chosen user groups into account; ii) draw upon existing installed bases where this is advantageous; iii) expand installed base by persuasive tactics in order to gain sufficient momentum (critical mass of users); iv) make the solution as simple and modular as possible, especially in order to avoid future lock-ins.

We have seen that such a strategy has been successful in a Norwegian context, for example the Norwegian State Educational Loan Fund has succeeded in providing new eGovernment services to a limited user group. The need for financial support in order to pursue studies has motivated their customers to use the electronic services for identification and authentication. Thus, the fact that most of them are young and educated implies that they have the skills to take the authentication service into use (Lånekassen 2008). Although their interests as users were limited, by using a part of the ICT-architecture they will contribute to increasing the value of the entire infrastructure through the mechanism denoted as *positive network externalities* (Weil and Broadbent 1998, Hanseth & Aanestad 2001). A similar mechanism was crucial when the first version of the Norwegian portal *Altinn*[6,] a common portal for public reporting in Norway, was introduced and has subsequently proved to be successful.

---

[5] The rule, enacted by the Public Administration Act (1967), regulates how electronic communication in government can take place and requires agencies to respond to electronicl enquiries in a similar way.

[6] Altinn is a common portal for public reporting to the government in Norway. It started out as a project between two ministries and three agencies to help businesses report accounting records to the government, but it is currently used by more the 25 different agencies in their dialogue with a large variety of private businesses and organizations. It has undergone an evolutionary process and has been adopted and adapted throughout the Norwegian Government.

This illustrates that ICT solutions, when made simple at the outset, can be further developed and adapted in the long run to accommodate continual shifts in requirements and needs. A prerequisite is that ICT solutions are designed with sufficient flexibility so as to handle changes after the solutions have been taken into use. This flexibility is twofold and consists of both *change and use*. The *change* perspective emphasizes that a standard [in the infrastructure] may be replaced by another (more appropriate) standard, without entailing high costs and uncertainty. Examples here are how standards have been replaced on the Internet at various layers. The *use* perspective emphasizes that the infrastructure must allow for usage in different ways and for different purposes. Again, Internet is the best example, but new mobile communication platforms are also used today for many different types of applications. These two perspectives are related in the sense that increased flexibility in usage will entail a lesser need for change flexibility and vice versa. In practical terms it means that a generically designed ICT-architecture will have a lesser need for flexibility to changes than an ICT-architecture that is designed in a more specialized and narrow manner. In this way, an open and flexible infrastructure will help to overcome many of the obstacles caused by the information silos in the public sector.

5 Concluding Remarks

We have demonstrated that it can be fruitful to apply an information infrastructure perspective when designing a government ICT-architecture in order to understand its scope, variety and dynamic nature. We have defined a new type of infrastructure, an eGovernment information infrastructure that will include essential components of the ICT-architecture. When comparing the characteristics of an eGovernment ICT-architecture with different types of (conceptual) information infrastructures described in the literature, we find a number of similarities, but also differences, which can help us to identify important factors for the successful planning, implementation and management of an ICT-architecture. In particular, we have illustrated that it can help us to understand the complexity of the installed base, and how to handle it in a constructive way, for example through bootstrapping and cultivation approaches. We emphasize that such work is not primarily a technical design task, but must include ongoing organizational, legal and cultural reform processes on various levels in the government. Thus, our understanding is in line with Bygstad's (2008) conclusion that *"it is fruitful to regard information infrastructure as an ICT-based organizational form"*, which represents an important contribution to understanding what kind of role and ICT-architecture may play in the public sector. An important implication of this view is that an ICT-architecture cannot be designed and implemented in a top-down manner, but has to evolve through dynamic, iterative and also, to some extent, experimental development processes. Janssen and Hjort-Madsen, 2007, p 2) claim that ICT-architectures are often initiated at the political levels and diffused using different governance mechanisms. A government ICT-architecture is meaningless if it is not adopted and used by public agencies.

Although some of our discussions have been based on the specific characteristics of the Norwegian public sector and its proposed ICT-architecture, we maintain that our arguments are applicable to a large extent to similar work being done in other national governments. However, it is necessary to understand the significance of the specific political, regulatory and organizational context which is defined by the constitutional framework, the political setting and the current organizational practices in each country.

Our discussions furthermore illustrate that ICT architectures, by definition, are not neutral, universal, or given, but designed according to specific purposes and underlying interests and norms. This is above all related to the overall policies in general and in particular to how one wishes to control the development of eGovernment in the different countries. Thus it has significance for both the use and effects of the ICT-architecture. Furthermore, they are woven into a given socio-technical reality in a political, organizational and institutional context that cannot be overlooked. They are neither static nor closed, but rather, they grow out of organizational practices and a political setting that will change over time in interaction with its environment.

Finally, we do not deny that other conceptualizations of ICT-architectures can be fruitful, such as, for example, Orlikowski and Iacono's (2000) "ensemble view", but we believe that the addition of an infrastructure perspective is useful. We fully support their concluding statement that *"the lack of theories about IT artefacts, the ways in which they emerge and evolve over time, and how they become interdependent with socio-economic contexts and practices, are key unresolved issues for our field and ones that will become even more problematic in these dynamic and innovative times"*. More research on the different types of ICT artefacts in eGovernment solutions is highly needed.

References

Braa, J., Hanseth, O., Mohammed, W., Heywood, A., Shaw, V.: Developing Health Information Systems in Developing Countries. The Flexible Standards Strategy. MIS Quarterly 31(2), 381–402 (2007)

Bygstad, B.: Information infrastructure as organization. A critical realist view. In: Twenty Ninth International Conference on Information Systems (ICIS 2008) (2008)

Ciborra, C.: A Critical review of the literature on the Management of Corporate Information Infrastructures. In: Ciborra, et al. (eds.) From control to drift. Oxford University Press, Oxford (2000)

Ciborra, C.: The labyrinths of information. Challenging the wisdom of systems. Oxford University Press, Oxford (2002)

Grönlund, Å.: State of the Art in E-Gov Research: Surveying Conference Publications. International Journal of Electronic Government Research 1(4), 1–25 (2005)

Grönlund, Å., Andersson, A.: e-Gov Research Quality Improvements Since 2003: Electronic Government. In: Wimmer, M.A., Scholl, H.J., Grönlund, Å., Andersen, K.V. (eds.) EGOV 2006. LNCS, vol. 4084, pp. 1–12. Springer, Heidelberg (2006)

Hanseth, O., Monteiro, E.: Information Infrastructure development. The tension between Standardization and flexibility. In: Science, technology and Human Values vol. 21(4) (1996)

Hanseth, O., Lyytinen, K.: Theorizing about the Design of Information Infrastructures: Design Kernel Theories and Principles. Sprouts Working Papers on Information Systems, http://sprouts.aisnet.org/124/1/040412.pdf

Hanseth, O., Aanestad, M.: Bootstrapping networks, communities and infrastructures. On the evolution of ICT solutions in health care (2001), `http://heim.ifi.uio.no/~oleha/Publications/On%20the%20evoluti on%20of%20telemedicine%20networks4.pdf`

Hanseth, O., Ciborra, C., Braa, K.: The Control Revolution. The EPR and the side effects of globalisation. The Data Base for advances in Information Systems 32(4), 34–46 (2001)

Heeks, R.: Implementing and managing eGovernment. Sage, London (2006)

Heeks, R., Bailur, S.: Analyzing e-government research: Perspectives, philosophies, theories, methods, and practice. Government Information Quarterly 24(2), 243–265 (2007)

Janssen, M., Hjort-Madsen, K.: Analyzing enterprise architecture in national governments. In: Proceedings of the 40th HICSS'07 (2007), `http://www2.computer.org/portal/web/csdl/doi/ 10.1109/HICSS.2007.79`

Liimatainen, K.: Evaluating Benefits of Government Enterprise Architecture (2008), `http://www.iris31.se/papers/IRIS31-059.pdf`

Ministeriet for videnskab, teknologi og utvikling: Hvidbok om IT-arkitektur (2003), `http://www.itst.dk/arkitektur-og-standarder/publikationer/ arkitekturpublikationer/hvidbog-om-it- arkitektur/Hvidbog_om_IT-arkitektur.pdf`

Orlikowski, W.J., Iacono, C.S.: Desperately Seeking the "IT" in IT Research—A Call to Theorizing the IT Artifact. Information Systems Research, INFORMS 12(2), 121–134 (2001)

Rohloff, M.: Enterprise architecture: Framework and methodology for the design of architecture in the large. In: European Conference on Information Systems (2005)

Ross, J.: Creating a strategic IT architecture competency: Learning in stages. MISQ Quarterly Executive 2(1), 31–43 (2003)

Shapiro, C., Varian, H.R.: Information rules: a strategic guide to the network economy. Harvard Business School Press, Boston (1999)

Scholl, H.J.: Profiling the EG Research Community and Its Core. In: Wimmer, M.A., et al. (eds.) EGOV 2009. LNCS, vol. 5693, pp. 1–12. Springer, Heidelberg (2009)

St.meld. nr. 17: Eit Informasjonssamfunn for alle Fornyings- og adm.departementet (2006-2007)

Tilson, D., Lyytinen, K., Sørensen, C.: Desperately seeking the infrastructure in IS research: Conceptualization of "Digital Convergence" as the co-evolution of social and technical infrastructures. In: Proceedings of the 43rd Hawaii International Conference on System Sciences—2010 (2008)

Verket för förvaltningsutveckling: Nationellt ramverk för interoperabilitet (2008)

Weill: Innovation information systems. What do the most innovative forms in the world do? Presentation at Sixth e-Business Conference, Barcelona (2007) `http://www.iese.edu/en/files/6_29338.pdf`

Weill, P., Broadbent, M.: Leveraging the New Infrastructure: How Market Leaders Capitalize on Information. Technology. Harvard Business School Press, Boston (1998)

Internet References

Fad, Felles IKT-Arkitektur for offentlig sector (2008), `http://www.regjeringen.no/nb/dep/fad/dok/horinger/horingsdoku menter/2008/horing-felles-elektronisk- tjenesteytin.html?id=518980`

Difi: Overordnede IKT-arkitekturprinsipper for offentlig sektor (2009),
  http://www.difi.no/IKT-arkitekturprinsipper_BHNq1.pdf.file
IT- og Telestyrelsen: It-arkitekturprincipper (2009),
  http://www.itst.dk/arkitektur-og-standarder/arkitektur/
  arkitekturkrav/5539-ITST-10_it-principper_K8.pdf
Lånekassen (2008): Årsrapport (2007),
  http://www.lanekassen.no/upload/Arsrapport/2007/Lanekassens%2
  0arsrapport%202007.pdf
Altinn: Om Altinnsamarbeidet (2006),
  https://www.altinn.no/upload/3/OmAltinnforetater_sept06.pdf

Interoperability in Public Sector:
How Use of a Lightweight Approach Can Reduce the Gap between Plans and Reality

Svein Ølnes

Western Norway Research Institute
P.O. Box 163, N-6851 Sogndal, Norway
svein.olnes@vestforsk.no
http://www.vestforsk.no

Abstract. Better interoperability between systems, vocabularies, and organizations is considered necessary to most public organizations in order to better meet the demands from the users. The rapid growth of the Internet has been a driving force for both the user expectations and the enabling of such exchange. But succeeding with interoperability initiatives is hard, and the risks of failing are high, mostly because the expectations are too high and the inherent challenges are often underestimated. Many interoperability projects are over-specified and their findings are under-implemented.This paper discusses the challenges of interoperability in public sector and argues for a lightweight approach in order lower the gap between plans and reality. The Los system is illustrated as an example of this lightweight approach to interoperability.

Keywords: eGovernment, interoperability, semantics.

1 Introduction: What Difference Interoperability Can Make

This paper discusses challenges to making public websites, and especially municipality websites, easier to use by improving their basic structure and at the same time be able to interoperate with other websites. The ICT system *Los* is described as an example of a lightweight approach to interoperability that is also based on a "bottom-up" approach of designing a shared, controlled vocabulary.

First we take a look at an example showing the immediate internal benefits of using a shared controlled vocabulary like *Los*. If we do a search for 'waste' ('søppel' in Norwegian') on the website of the two biggest municipalities in Norway, Oslo and Bergen, this is what we get:

The search for 'søppel' gives the user a link to the theme 'renovasjon' ('waste handling') which is the official term used by the municipality. But 'søppel' is what most users likely will search for. The municipality's own waste management company BIR is also high on the list of results. In addition, when the user clicks on the term 'Renovasjon', she also gets relevant information from the central authorities regarding this term. This information covers laws and other regulations that affect the particular service. These external links are maintained by the Los system and the

M.A. Wimmer et al. (Eds.): EGOV 2010, LNCS 6228, pp. 315–326, 2010.

Fig. 1. Search for 'søppel' ('waste') on the municipality of Bergen's website (thematic search) as of March 2010

individual Los users (mostly municipalities) do not have to worry about it since the information on the municipality's website will be automatically updated.

The same search on the municipality of Oslo's website, gives this result:

Fig. 2. Search for 'waste' ('søppel') on the municipality of Oslo's website, March 2010

The result of the search on Oslo's website gives the user a seemingly random article which happens to mention 'søppel' but is far from leading the user to the core service of waste handling. It is also quite old, as the rest of the returned articles on the first result page. The user is left confused and there is really no clue where to get more information, whether Oslo municipality's own information or relevant information from governmental bodies.

The improvements in internal information retrieval is important, but even more important is the provision of links to relevant external sources. Bergen will automatically get links to relevant governmental resources regarding the specific term (in this case handling of waste) from the Los system.

2 Interoperability

The examples shown in the introduction point first of all to the need for a well formed internal information architecture. A good information architecture is necessary in order to help users find what they look for. But it is not sufficient in order to make the individual website interoperable with other websites. In order to achieve interoperability there has to be agreed upon standards and terms or concepts.

Interoperability means the enabling ability of information and communication technology (ICT) systems and of the business processes they support to exchange data, and to enable them with the sharing of information and knowledge [1]. The Swedish public agency, Verva adds to this definition that this must be enabled without the need for any special efforts [2].

The European Commission, through their programme IDABC[1], further split interoperability into three layers in the first version of the European Interoperability Framework, EIF [1]: organizational interoperability, semantic interoperability, and technical interoperability

In the EIF 2.0 draft IDABC [3] puts forward this definition of interoperability:

"Interoperability is the ability of disparate and diverse organisations to interact towards mutually beneficial and agreed common goals, involving the sharing of information and knowledge between the organizations via the business processes they support, by means of the exchange of data between their respective information and communication technology (ICT) systems."

Scholl [4] says that interoperability in essence leads to extensive information sharing among and between governmental entities. However, the obstacles, which prevent a rapid progress in that direction, are not merely technical. In fact, the technology side may prove the least difficult to address, while the organizational, legal, political, and social aspects may prove much more of a challenge.

The extraordinary growth and success of the Internet, and especially the web, has been a key driver in the need for interoperability. With Internet, communication has become a central part of almost every ICT system. And, because Internet represents an open platform, a heterogeneous digital environment has become the norm and not an exception.

In a more closed environment it was easier to look at information exchange as a bilateral challenge that could be solved between pairs of systems, one at the time. XML, the standard syntax for information exchange on the Net, was at first seen as the solution to the interoperability challenges before it was recognised as only the technical part of the interoperability stack. The agreement on using XML as the container of information did not solve the fundamental problems of interoperability. To say that different systems can communicate because they use XML is similar to saying that since you use the Latin alphabet you will be able to communicate. The

---

[1] IDABC is a Community programme managed by the European Commission's Directorate-General for Informatics. IDABC stands for Interoperable Delivery of European eGovernment Services to public Administrations, Business and Citizens.

meaning of the communication is vastly underestimated. As Harris et al. [5] states "..
these technologies will not be effective unless the meaning of the tabs, data items, and
models of data are properly described, coordinated, communicated, and reused
between designers, developers, and users of the information systems".

Slowly, the challenges of interoperability are beginning to be fully understood, and
there is a general acceptance in most governments, for the need of common
frameworks to resolve this complex issue. Most European countries have
implemented Governmental Interoperability Frameworks and they rely heavily on the
recommendations in EIF coupled with the Service Oriented Architecture (SOA)
described by OASIS[2] [6] among others.

In Norway, the Ministry of Government Administration and Reform has proposed
an interoperability architecture for public sector in which the SOA principles are at
the core [7]. The follow-up of the proposal has yet to be outlined, but a central part of
the proposal is the idea of shared components. Public sector agencies should strive to
build applications using shared components in order to facilitate openness and reuse.
The use of open standards and open source software are also key parts of the
architecture.

3 Challenges to Achieving Interoperability

Going back to the definition of interoperability from the European Commission and
Verva, it means the ability of ICT systems (and the business processes they support)
to exchange data and to enable the sharing of information and knowledge without any
specific prearrangement. The "specific prearrangement" means that if a specific
interoperability process functions between organisations A and B, it should also
function between organisations A and C without any further amendments.

That does not mean that there is no prearrangement necessary. There is
prearrangement necessary to facilitate interoperability between systems and
processes. Primarily, the interoperability process involves the use of standards.
Standards are agreements on terms, concepts and techniques (syntax), and are
prerequisites for multilateral information exchange. These types of standards are what
David and Greenstein [8] call compatibility standards and are separated from two
other kinds of standards; the reference and the minimum quality standards. For the
discussion of interoperability, only the compatibility standards are relevant.

The techniques or syntax part of standard agreements is the technical layer of the
interoperability model. XML can serve as a good example of technical interoperability
standards. The XML specification says how to format the code in your mark-up
language and has a strict syntax definition contrary to HTML. But the name of the tags
is at the discretion of the developer to define. That means that XML is a very good
bearer of information where the names of tags have been agreed upon.

But, even if you have agreed that a specific XML should contain the tag <name>,
there will probably be questions of how to interpret it. Is it both the first and the last

---

[2] Organization for the Advancement of Structured Information Standards is a not-for-profit
consortium that drives the development, convergence and adoption of open standards for the
global information society.

name or just either one of them? Should, it be written with the last name first? And it gets worse! Consider the tag <address>. Is it visiting address? Is it postal address? What information should it contain?

Clearly, agreeing on terms and thus moving up to the semantic layer, is not enough either to avoid ambiguity. To avoid, or at least reduce, ambiguity there is a need to define the terms and concepts and there is also often a need to describe the relation between concepts. In other words there is a need for an ontology. Ontology is a wide term and in the ICT domain it is often common to distinguish between ontologies with a small or big 'o' [9].

Ontologies come in many flavours, from the simple controlled vocabulary to complex OWL models. The most familiar ontologies are taxonomies, hierarchical structures which essentially only have the relations 'broader' and 'narrower'. Thesauri go a bit further and expand the list of relations beyond mere hierarchical ones. Relations like 'Use', 'Used for', and 'Related Term' are added. But still there is only a finite list of relations.

If we want to create relations freely, the only possibility is to use semantic technology. Using semantic technology, you are no longer restricted to a set of given relations but can create them as you wish. The structure is no longer hierarchical as in a taxonomy and (partly) a thesauri, but a graph structure.

There are currently two standards for semantic technology; the RDF/OWL (Resource Description Framework/Web Ontology Language) suite from W3C [10] [11], also called semantic web, and the ISO 13250 Topic Maps standard [12].

Worldwide the semantic web standard from W3C draws the main attention, but in Norway the situation is special because of a very strong hold for Topic Maps. The latter is due to the relatively large Topic Maps community. Key developers of the Topic Maps standard are also Norwegian and they hold important positions as senior developers and architectures in major ICT consultancies. As a result, there exist several ready semantic solutions for Topic Maps, especially software supporting portal implementations, in contrast to the semantic web where lack of customer ready software currently is the Achilles heel.

Having the technology in place, the next challenge is to map information to the ontology of some kind. This task is difficult even if the ontology is as simple as its taxonomy.

Accepting that interoperability is more than agreeing on a common syntax (like XML), the next challenge is not to be overwhelmed of the complexities and almost try to encompass the whole world in the system model. The risk of doing things overly complex is just as serious as underestimating the challenges of interoperability. Many systems fall victim to the danger of being over-specified and under-implemented. The clue is, to strike the right balance between accepting a complex challenge and seeking the simplest possible solution to the specific problem.

The development of the European Interoperability Framework from version 1.0 to the proposed version 2.0 can serve as an illustration of how interoperability issues often tend to get overly complex. In the EIF 1.0, the famous and much cited three-layer model with organizational, semantic, and technical interoperability was introduced. The framework was well received and many national interoperability frameworks (NIF) were developed on the basis of EIF.

In the proposed 2.0 version [3] the original three-layer model has been expanded to five layers. Also, two additional dimensions have been introduced to capture standards and interoperability chains.

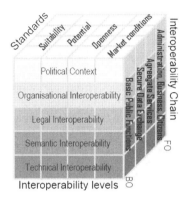

Fig. 3. The new interoperability model proposed in the EIF 2.0 draft (BO is Back Office and FO is Front Office)

What used to be a simple model has become a complex one and it is necessary to ask whether this really adds to the understanding of the interoperability issue in itself. Interoperability is complex but we should use models to simplify complex things, not make them more complex.

The introduction of new interoperability levels can be fruitful in order to reveal hidden knowledge or structures. The addition of a legal interoperability level was first seen in the Swedish report on a national framework for interoperability by Verva [2]. However, the political context should probably be seen as an implicit part of lawmaking. After all laws are the instruments enabling the transformation of political ideas into action.

As the challenges of interoperability finally seem to be fully understood, the huge gap between plans and reality in this field is also recognized [13]. Codagnone and Wimmer found that although a lot of attention has been paid to interoperability from the EU member states, the gap between intentions as expressed in various ICT plans and the actual achievements were assessed as very high.

Lowering the huge gap between plans and reality calls for the highlighting of good practices showing what is achievable with relatively low complexity. The Norwegian information sharing system Los is one of these examples and is explained in detail below.

4   Los – A Lightweight Approach to Interoperability

Los is the name of a system enabling seamless exchange of information between public organisations. The information exchange is based upon a list of keywords describing public services. At present the system is mostly used by municipalities in their information portals, as shown in the introductory chapter. The name Los means a pilot at sea (a navigator) in English and refers to easier navigation to public sector information and services.

4.1 The Los Information Architecture

Los is a controlled vocabulary with terms describing public services. The vocabulary is organized as a thesaurus following the ISO 2788 standard for monolingual thesauri construction [14] and the broader terms suggest a two-level navigation structure, shown in the figure below. To each preferred term a number of *help words* are attached. Help words are synonyms, expired terms, and so on; generally all the terms that are *not preferred*.

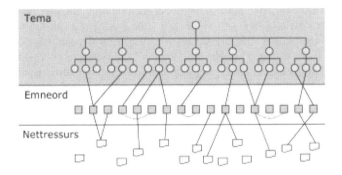

Fig. 4. The Los information architecture. "Tema" is the two-level thematic structure, "Emneord" are the topic words (terms), and "Nettressurs" are the information resources linked to the topic words.

The Los thesaurus was developed by doing a thorough examination of public websites and how they presented their information about their services [15]. Municipalities were also asked what services was most sought after by the users, and search logs, especially the search log at www.norge.no, were studied to identify the words used by the users when searching for public services.

Los has been available from 2007 and almost 100 municipalities have implemented it in their local portals. The key to this uptake is that the vendors of public sector portals have been interested in the project and implemented support for it in their portal systems. Through the key vendors of municipality portal system Los is therefore available to 80-90 % of the municipalities in Norway, although only a third of these have actually started using it.

4.2 Classification and Categorization

Los is a system for categorizing information about public sector services. The categorization process involves annotating information resources with Los topic words. The right words can be found either by browsing the Los structure or by browsing or searching the combined topic words and help words.

The users will meet Los either through navigating the structure itself or by searching and hitting a keyword or help word, as shown in the introduction chapter.

The concepts classification and categorization are often used interchangeably. Since both concepts deal with organizing information they are often mistaken for being synonymous. But as Elin K. Jacob [16] points out there is a difference between the two concepts, and to quote Jacob it is "a difference that makes a difference".

According to Jacob traditional classification is characterized by rigor in that it mandates that an entity either is or is not a member of a particular class. The fact that the classes are mutually exclusive and non-overlapping makes the system itself stable. This contrasts to the system of categorization where nonbinding associations between entities are drawn. Unlike classification these associations are not based on a set of predetermined principles, but on the simple recognition of similarities that exist across a set of entities. This makes categorization a flexible but also unstable system.

The figure below shows some of the principle differences between classes/classification and categories/categorization from the municipality sector. The predefined classes in our example are 'Person', 'Service', and 'Institution' are all relevant building blocks in an ontology describing a municipality. But of course it is only a small part of this ontology. The hierarchical structure often associated with classes and classification is not shown here, but it is easy to imagine both 'Institution' and 'Service' as top nodes in a taxonomy (e.g. the class 'Service' could have a subclass of 'Educational services' and so on).

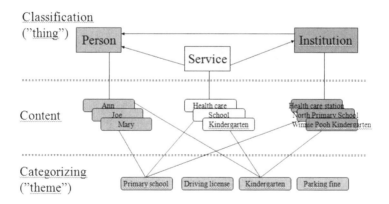

Fig. 5. Classification and categorization

The categorization part on the other deals with keywords that can be attached to content regardless of the class it belongs to. One keyword can easily be attached to different content and thus different classes. . But this "meeting" of classification and categorization is not troublefree. It is in some senses different worlds meeting, and often colliding. However, they can play together if we regard the differences and turn them into strengths.

The classification and categorization concept division can also be found in today's main approaches to semantic technology. The semantic web, represented by the W3C standards rdf and owl is tightly coupled with the classification system in classes being the main concept and taxonomy structures denoting subclasses.

The other standard for semantic technology is Topic Maps. Although Topic Maps can be used to model typical classification systems, modelling using this standard normally tends to lean much on the categorization system. The reason for this can be that Topic Maps comes from the domain of library information science while semantic web has its roots in mathematics and logics [17].

Los is about categorization and therefore is only part of the answer to building a complete ontology for a municipality web portal. Los has to be integrated into a richer ontology in order to make the most out of it

4.3 Information Resources, Not Services

A very important aspect of Los is the underlying semantics and the description of the key concepts. Los does not link to services but to information about services, whether they are electronically available or not. This distinction between *services* and *information that describes services* is very important in order to get a coherent semantic system where definitions of concepts are clear and unambiguous. The problems that can occur with unambiguous definitions were encountered during the test phase when the Los ontology met the ontology for the Bergen municipality web portal. It became clear that the municipality of Bergen, as one of the pilot users of Los, used a different definition of *service* than Los and that caused failures in the information integration process.

The following example can illustrate the difference between a service and a resource describing the service. Kindergarten is a service from the municipality (or a private company). Providing an online application form for kindergarten does not mean that there is an online service for kindergarten. The kindergarten is still the same physical thing, the online application form is not the service. There is considerable confusing and misuse of terms in regard to this. In our daily speaking we understand each other even if we are not very precise, but for a semantic system it is of utmost importance to clarify the terms and use them in a precise way.

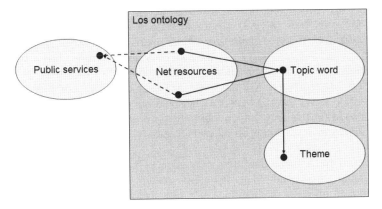

Fig. 6. The general Los ontology. Notice the distinction between services and information about services. Los is about the latter.

4.4 Lightweight Approach to Information Sharing

As shown in the introduction chapter Los is well suited to improve the information architecture on a public website. But the real value in the system lies in the ability to share information across organizations and across sectors. Los comes with an extensible collection of governmental resources annotated with the Los vocabulary. A subscriber to Los will automatically get access to these resources and can use the structure and vocabulary to adjust it to own information. By annotating one's own information the organization using Los can combine local and central information structured according to the predefined vocabulary. The result is that external links will be automatically linked and updatet and there is no maintenance for the organization.

The vocabulary with the corresponding resources can be fetched from the Los hub by queries following the REST principle [18]. This way the information sharing process is completely open and foreseeable.

A local municipality using Los can share its annotated resources with others using the lightweight publishing protocol Atom [19]. Los resources are described using Qualified Dublin Core [20], but due to the dumbing-down principle the reader of the RSS based Los-information can skip all the DC details it does not understand and just show the known RSS elements.

Locally annotated Los resources are also expected to be expressed in the original document using Qualified Dublin Core. This way also systems not knowing of Los can make use of some of the added metadata. This way Los will also add value to the current intiatives for increased publishing of open data from public sector.

5 Conclusions and Further Research

Common guidelines are necessary to achieve interoperability. The proposed common architectural framework for public sector in Norway states that every (digital) service established should be designed for interoperability [7]. Interoperability is one of seven proposed principles laid down for the architectural framework, with the service-oriented approach as the overlaying principle.

But the report says little about how to achieve interoperability although it should be mandatory for every new (digital) service to at least discuss the needs and the possibilities. At the same time the challenges of interoperability can seem daunting to most organizations and this can itself delay the necessary development.

In the meantime, waiting for such guidelines, it is important to shed light on good practices like Los. It represents a lightweight approach to interoperability that is valuable as a way to lower the gap between plans and reality in interoperability. The immediate challenge for this and similar solutions, once they are fully implemented, is to open up and harmonise with each other and other initiatives both in public and private sector.

There is a need for a more thorough evaluation of interoperability projects or initiatives to better understand what the main challenges are. It would also be interesting to look at different methodological approaches in the these projects; i.e. a "top-down" or a "bottom-up" approach.

Another interesting research issue is how lightweight approaches fit together with the more demanding interoperability initiatives and frameworks.

It would also be interesting to look at the use of Los from a municipality's perspective and whether it has improved user satisfaction and reduced the need for physical contact or telephone or email contact with the municpality's administration.

References

1. IDABC: European Interoperability Framework for Pan-European eGovernment Services v. 1.0, Luxembourg (2004),
   http://ec.europa.eu/idabc/servlets/Doc?id=19529
2. Verva: Nationellt ramverk för interoperabilitet Stockholm (2008),
   http://verva.24-timmarswebben.se/upload/
   verksamhetsstod/presentation-hearing.pdf
3. IDABC: European Interoperability Framework for Pan-European eGovernment Services, v. 2.0 draft, Luxembourg (2008),
   http://ec.europa.eu/idabc/servlets/Doc?id=31597
4. Scholl, H.J.: Interoperability in E-Government: More than Just Smart Middleware. In: Proceedings of the 38th Annual Hawaii International Conference on System Sciences (HICSS'05), HICSS - Track 5, vol. 5, p. 123 (2005)
5. Harris, S., Gibbons, J., Davies, J., Tsui, A., Crichton, C.: Semantic Technologies in Electronic Government. In: Janowski, T., Pardo, T. (eds.) ICEGOV 2008, Cairo, December 2008, pp. 45–51. ACM Press, New York (2008)
6. OASIS: Reference Model for Service Oriented Architecture (2006),
   http://docs.oasis-open.org/soa-rm/v1.0/soa-rm.pdf
7. Ministry of Government Administration, Reform and Church Affairs: Felles IKT-arkitektur i offentlig sektor. Oslo (2007),
   http://www.regjeringen.no/upload/FAD/Vedlegg/
   IKT-politikk/Felles_IKT_arkitektur_off_sektor.pdf
8. David, P.A., Greenstein, S.: The Economics of Compatibility Standards: An Introduction to Recent Research. Economics of Innovation and New Technology 1(½) (1990)
9. Daconta, M.C., Orst, L.J., Smith, K.T.: The Semantic Web – A Guide to the Future of XML, Web Services, and Knowledge Management. Wiley Publishing, Inc., Indianapolis (2003)
10. W3C: RDF Specification Development (2004), http://www.w3.org/RDF/#specs
11. W3C: OWL Specification Development (2004),
    http://www.w3.org/2004/OWL/#specs
12. ISO: Topic Maps. ISO 13250:2003 (2003),
    http://www.iso.org/iso/iso_catalogue/catalogue_tc/
    catalogue_detail.htm?csnumber=38068
13. Codagnone, C., Wimmer, M.A. (eds.): Roadmapping eGovernment Research: Visions and Measurestowards Innovative Governments in 2020. Guerinoni Marco (2007) ISBN 978-88-95549-00-2
14. ISO: ISO 2788:1986: Guidelines for the establishment and development of monolingual thesauri (1986),
    http://www.iso.org/iso/iso_catalogue/catalogue_tc/
    catalogue_detail.htm?csnumber=7776

15. Ølnes, S.: Nye LivsIT – Forslag til ny informasjonsstruktur for LivsIT. VF Report 2-2005 Vestlandsforsking, Sogndal (2005),
    http://www.vestforsk.no/www/download.do?id=547
16. Jacob, E.K.: Classification and Categorization: A Difference that Makes a Difference. Library Trends 52(3), 515–540 (winter 2004)
17. Pepper, S.: The TAO of Topic Maps. Finding the Way in Age of Infoglut. In: XML Europe 2000, Paris (2000),
    http://www.gca.org/papers/xmleurope2000/papers/s11-01.html
18. Fielding, R.T.: Architectural Styles and the Design of Networked-based Software Architectures, Dissertation for the degree of PhD, University of California, Irvine (2000),
    http://www.ics.uci.edu/~fielding/pubs/dissertation/top.htm
19. IETF: The Atom Publishing Protocol, RFC 5023 (2007),
    http://bitworking.org/projects/atom/rfc5023.html
20. Dublin Core Metadata Initiative: The Dublin Core Metadata Element Set (2008),
    http://dublincore.org/documents/dcmi-terms/

Dynamic Public Service Mediation

Wout Hofman and Mark van Staalduinen

TNO, P.O. Box 5050, 2600 GB, The Netherlands
{Wout.Hofman,Mark.vanStaalduinen}@tno.nl

Abstract. This paper presents an approach to dynamic public service mediation. It is based on a conceptual model and the use of search and ranking algorithms. The conceptual model is based on Abstract State Machine theory. Requirements for dynamic service mediation were derived from a real-world case. The conceptual model and the algorithms are developed and implemented by a proof of concept for this case. This model is build on existing means for sharing public services, which would enable migration of existing applications to our proposed approach. The conceptual model is compared to other models for service mediation to illustrate differences and identify similarities.

Keywords: public services, service discovery, abstract state machines, WSMO.

1 Introduction

Over the past decades, services have become important [1]. The service economy refers to the services sector, but it is also applicable to governments. Many government organizations have defined and published their services on the Internet. Interoperability of these public services is of importance to the EU (European Union) market [2]. Standards are being set, both at European [3] and national level [4] and have been developed in EU funded projects [5]. Earlier research indicated that discovery of these public services does not satisfy citizens and organizations requirements [6], and therefore it requires new strategies.

One of the strategies is 'life events' for service discovery (see for instance [7]). A complicating factor is that life events are containers, e.g. 'birth', 'marriage', and 'decease', whereas the relevant services for a specific event may be provided by different government organizations. In addition, it is impossible to capture each real-world event by a life event. Furthermore, each organization still offers its particular services without taking into account the relations with services of other organizations. Thus, it is difficult for a citizen to discover the complete set of services that matches with his requirement.

This paper investigates the issue of public service discovery and mediation. The main objective of our solution is dynamic mediation of a user his goal with public services. First, the conceptual model is introduced. Thereafter, the service discovery algorithms are discussed. These are based on natural language and search technology. Subsequently, a dynamic interaction model is introduced to support interactive mediation of requirements and services. A realistic case is used to validate this model. Based on the model and the use-case a proof of concept has been constructed.

M.A. Wimmer et al. (Eds.): EGOV 2010, LNCS 6228, pp. 327–338, 2010.

Furthermore, the proposed conceptual model is compared with existing approaches. Finally, conclusions are drawn, and recommendations for further research are made.

2 The Conceptual Service Model

This section introduces a model for service discovery to create the public service experience. This solution is part of a larger model for enterprise interoperability [8]. First, the overall model is introduced. Thereafter, the different concepts of the model are given.

2.1 The Model

Figure 1 shows the model and its concepts for public service discovery. It allows a user to formulate in natural language his goal, which is a real world event. Processing of this event leads to a dynamic interaction model that flexibly composes a selection of services that are required to achieve a user's goal.

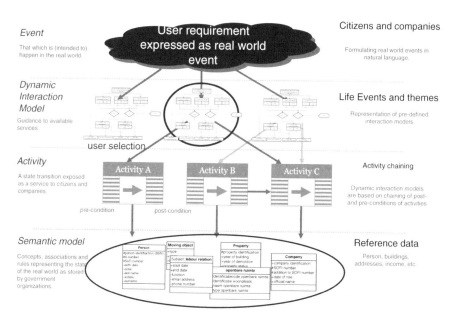

Fig. 1. The overall model

'Event, 'activity' and 'reference data' are the basic concepts of our model. These concepts are presented hereafter. The 'dynamic interaction model' is part of the mediation process, and therefore it is discussed in the next section.

In general, a public service should not only specify what a government organization does, but also how this can be achieved, e.g. the interaction choreography, durations, and other process characteristics [18]. These aspects of a 'service' are not within the scope of this paper. It focuses on the concept 'activity' to represent the behavior of a service.

2.2 Event

There are many definitions of 'event', e.g. from different perspectives. We will use a philosophic approach: 'an event is an operation on an object with given properties at a specific time or within a time interval' [20]. Events can be intentional, e.g. taking a holiday, or not, e.g. a tornado. Not all real world events are of interest to government organizations. In the context of this paper, an event can be a trigger to a user to initiate an activity with one or more government authorities with a specific goal: the event has already happened in the real world and needs to be administrated by a government authority, e.g. 'birth' and 'unemployment', or a user intends to execute an event for which permission of a government authority is required, e.g. 'building a house' or 'transportation of livestock to another country'. Intentional events that need registration or permission can also take place without permission in which case we call it fraud, theft or another form of crime. Each event could result in related services, e.g. 'birth' and 'unemployment' lead to financial support by a government ('child benefit' and 'unemployment benefit' respectively). Events requiring permission can be performed as soon as permission has been given. Note, that it is never sure that they also are actually executed (e.g. it is never sure that a house will also be built based on the granted permission). For this reason, government organizations have inspections that ensure that these events are executed according to the granted permission.

2.3 Activity

Like 'event', there are many definitions of 'activity', e.g. 'the intentional behavior of and actor to achieve a certain goal' [21]. An activity can be initiated by a user based on an event that has occurred or is to occur. In the context of this paper an activity can be performed by a government authority to handle the (intended) real world events triggered by a user. Activities are provided by government organizations and have to be matched with a user's representation of 'event'. Activities have the same properties as a state transition [9]:

- *Pre-condition*: (complex) Predicates that must all be true before an activity can be executed.
- *Post-conditions*: The actual result of the execution of an activity. This result is defined as the state in case of an activity that is executed successfully.
- *Firing rules*: The (ordered) set of rules that are executed when the pre-condition is met and results in a post-condition. In an administration of an authority a firing rule actually changes the state of the representation of the operation.

From a service mediation viewpoint, a firing rule is not of interest. It is the objective to retrieve the complete set of services to achieve the user his goal. This set is determined by chaining activities using the pre- and post-conditions.

Pre- and post-conditions are expressed as the state space represented by the reference data. These abstract specifications are determined by means of logical expressions. These activities are specified by civil servants who do not understand the formalization of the pre- and post-conditions. An abstract specifications is also not sufficient for service mediation, which requires user interaction (e.g. 'Do you have a parking permit?' in case parking is only allowed with a permit in a particular area).

An important issue is activity chaining to discover related services during mediation. Chaining means the discovery of activities with a post-condition that met unsatisfied pre-conditions. This paper shows a practical case to obtain a parking place for a physically disabled person. This example requires a parking permit, which is another activity that results in granting this permission. That latter activity has 'granting parking permission' as a post-condition.

A method should be developed to establish links based on a formal specification of pre- and post-conditions that could be defined by civil servants. This method is left for further research, while this paper shows the result that is achieved if this method would be defined. The model is tested using the following specification of an activity (Figure 2 shows the representation of 'activity'):

- An activity has a name, a description, one or more pre-conditions, and a post-condition.
- A pre-condition, which is repeatable and represents a predicate, has a description, a question, an input state, and potential a validation service (which is not required from a conceptual point of view). The input state is used for linking and the validation service calls a web service in case the input state is not specified.
- A post-condition has a description and a resulting state that could be linked to an input state.

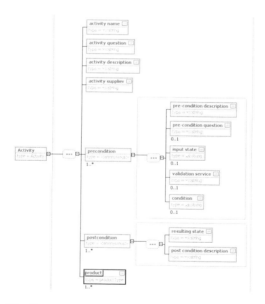

Fig. 2. The structured representation of an 'activity'

The representation of an 'activity' (Figure 2) is an extension of the XML structure of the shared public services [4]. The XML element 'productType' is defined in [4]. The figure also shows that an activity can identify more than one product, which reflects the situation that (Dutch) governments have defined products for individual events [8]. The figure shows the XML elements 'input state' and 'validation service', which are obsolete in case formal expressions are used for modelling pre- and post-conditions. Each question has to be answered by a user during interaction to select a proper (set of) activity. However, the answers to these questions have to be validated by the pre-condition of an activity based on the actual data provided by a user after selecting that activity. Data provision and validation is outside the scope of this paper.

2.4 Reference Data

This section presents a brief outline of reference data as contained by government organizations. It actually contains the administrative description of real world state as perceived by government organizations. The complete set with reference data is complex and large. Examples of reference data are 'natural persons', 'buildings', 'organizations' and associations between these concepts like 'person' to 'address', and 'address' to 'building'. Figure 3 shows a draft of the reference data modelled using a UML (Universal Modelling Language, [19]) class diagram. It shows the complexity of the state determined by government organizations.

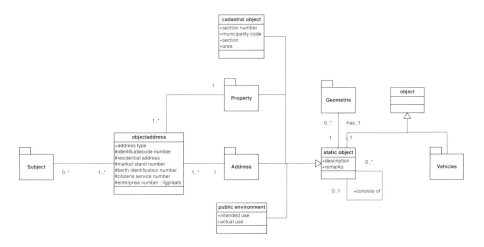

Fig. 3. Overview of reference data

3 Service Mediation

This section presents functionalities to determine the service mediation process. It is determined by a self-learning search algorithm and the construction of dynamic interaction model based on activity chaining.

3.1 Self-learning Search Technology

In general, a user is perfectly able to formulate his/hers particular goal using natural language. The objective is to match this goal to the correct service. This process is called mediation [10]. The match can be performed in a variety of ways. The field of text analytics provides solutions like language model-based text retrieval (e.g. [13]), syntactic analysis (e.g. [12]), and information ranking approaches that learn how to rank candidate answers to questions (e.g. [11]).

Our solution to query-answer matching consists of a mixture of language modelling and ranking techniques. First, a document index is constructed for a set of activities using commonly available index engines like Lucene ([14]) or Lemur (http://www.lemurproject.org/). Using such an engine, the formulated query is matched with candidate activities. If the description of a query is too short, character n-gram indexing can be of use to generate sufficient textual material for matching. Under this type of representation, words in both user events and indexed documents are split into overlapping sequences of characters, e.g. {cha, har,ara,rac,act,cte,ter}. The benefits of character n-grams in retrieval are well-known (e.g. [15]).

The candidate activities are subsequently presented to a user. If a user selects one of the answers, then it is assumed that this is the correct activity for his event. This selection is used to derive an improved ranking (see e.g. [16]). A Ranking Support Vector Machine (R-SVM) is trained using this feedback, which is used for re-ranking the results of the retrieval engine in subsequent passes. The R-SVM can be supplied with specific kernels geared towards bag-of-word representations, such as geodesic kernels (e.g. [17]). Using this approach, the performance of service mediation improves using the user feedback during its usage (the latter is tested with limited interaction tests).

3.2 Dynamic Interaction Model for Service Mediation

A dynamic interaction model supports user interaction based on selections made by a user, instead of having predefined interaction models that serve as a navigation structure, e.g. life event based navigation. Both a dynamic interaction model and its predefined version are decision trees. A dynamic interaction model meets all possible user requirements supported by government services, which is not feasible by a static, predefined model. Dynamic interaction models are constructed by chaining activities based on an activity selected by a user with the self-learning search techniques.

There are two important aspects for the construction of dynamic interaction models. First, the application of AND and OR operators as pre-conditions:

- AND indicates that two or more pre-conditions can be satisfied by two or more post conditions of other activities, e.g. a 'drivers licence' and a 'parking permit' is required.
- OR indicates that if one or more pre-conditions are not satisfied, then the activity can not be executed. The OR construction is also used to select one of the options of a set given using a pre-condition.

Second, identical pre-conditions of relevant activities should appear once in the interaction model. By backward chaining from pre-conditions of an activity selected by a user, a complete list of activities is constructed and identical pre-conditions should be mentioned once. We will illustrate this mechanism using in our practical case.

4 Model Validation with a Practical Case

The case, which is a view of reality for the sake of our proof of concept, considers a physically disabled citizen who wants a reserved parking place near his or her door. In that particular area, a parking permit is required. Furthermore, a special card for parking on parking places for handicapped persons is required. In this particular case, parking permits are issued by the parking authority, handicap parking cards by a municipal social security authority, and an handicap parking place by a third department. Thus, there are at least three authorities involved. The legal aspects for arriving at a collaborated decision by these authorities are not discussed even as the orchestration of selected services. This paper focuses on service discovery and mediation. First, this section describes chaining of the relevant activities. Second, it presents the dynamic interaction model. Finally, some screenshots of the proof of concept are shown.

4.1 Activities

The case considers chaining of the following activities:
- a parking place reserved for handicapped drivers,
- a handicap parking card,
- a parking permit.

4.1.1 Backward Chaining of Relevant Activities

Activity chaining includes the complete set of activities to achieve a user his goal. The complete chain of activities is constructed dynamically based on linked pre- and post-conditions. Since, pre-conditions are linked to post-conditions, it could be considered as a step backwards. For this reason, this chaining approach is called backward chaining. Figure 4 visualizes this process to obtain a parking place for a physically disabled citizen.

Fig. 4. Backward activity chaining for user requirement 'handicapped parking place'

This figure shows that authentication by DigiD is used for a number of activities. Second, it shows that having a car and a driver's licence are required for a parking permit. These are obtained using different activities. Furthermore, it shows additional activities like 'driver's license registration', 'examination', 'person registration' and 'car registration'. Thus, a network of activities is obtained to describe this 'simple' case. As 'car registration' and 'examination' require an activity performed outside the scope of the government, the pre-condition of these two activities cannot be satisfied during user interaction. Thus, these activities are not considered for this case. As stated before, the questions are used for user interaction and the answers will be validated by actual data offered by a user to execute an activity.

4.1.2 Parking Place for Disabled Persons

A parking place for disabled persons can only be used by persons with a handicap parking card. To be able to request such a parking place, several pre-conditions need to be met. These pre-conditions are given by:

1. The person needs to have valid identification means of the set {drivers license, passport, digital authentication mechanism}. In our proof of concept, we use the Dutch digital authentication mechanism: DigiD. The address of the person should be equal to the one retrieved by DigiD.
2. There should be sufficient parking space in the neighborhood to reserve a handicapped parking place. The related question is: 'Is there sufficient parking space near the place you live?'
3. The person should have a valid driver's license. The question is: 'Do you have a valid driver's license?'
4. The person should have a car. The question is: 'Do you have a registered car?'
5. The person should have a handicap parking card. The question is: 'Do you have a handicap parking card?'
6. The person should have a parking permit. The question is: 'Do you have a parking permit?'

An interesting extension on this model is the following. If web services are available that connect to public registers, then a number of questions in the interaction model could be answered automatically. For example, a check could be performed, whether the authenticated person has a driver's license.

4.1.3 Handicap Parking Card

A handicap parking card is required to park a vehicle on a parking place reserved for disabled persons in the Netherlands. It is recognized as a valid document by all parking authorities in the Netherlands. To request this card, the following pre-conditions should be satisfied:

1. The person should have a DigiD authentication.
2. The person should have a valid driver's license. The question is: 'Do you have a valid driver's license?'
3. The person should have a car. The question is: 'Do you have a registered car?'

4.1.4 Parking Permit

A parking permit issued by the relevant authority for a particular area. It is only used to park a vehicle in that particular area and cannot be used in other areas. To request a parking permit, the following pre-conditions should be satisfied:

1. The person should have a DigiD authentication.
2. The persons should live in the municipality for which a parking permit is requested. A validation for this address could be identified using DigiD.
3. The person should have a valid driver's license. The question is: 'Do you have a valid driver's license?'
4. The person should have a car. The question is: 'Do you have a registered car?'

4.2 Constructing the Dynamic Interaction Model

A dynamic interaction model is based on backward chaining of activities. First of all, a user should select the activity that fulfills his goal. A dynamic interaction model is constructed using this choice as figure 5 presents. The interaction model shows that although the three activities described before have identical questions, these questions appear once. Furthermore, the questions that can not be satisfied by another activity to achieve a user his goal appear first.

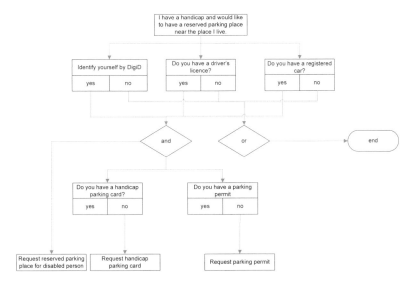

Fig. 5. The dynamic interaction model that is constructed after selection of 'parking place for disabled persons'

4.3 Proof-of-Concept

The Proof-of-Concept visualizes service discovery and mediation using the proposed techniques, e.g. the XML structure of activities and the shared product catalogue. It starts with the formulation of an event using natural language. Thereafter, a user receives a list with activities that could possibly satisfy the goal of a user with respect to the event. By improving the ranking, it is the aim to have the most suiting activity for a particular goal at rank one. It is possible to select multiple activities. The state of the user is determined by exploiting the scope of the selected activities based on a dynamic interaction model of selected activities. Finally, a set of one or more services is presented that should be executed to achieve the user his goal.

5 Discussion on Alternative Methodologies to Model Public Services

Our conceptual model is based on the theory of Abstract Service Machines (ASM, [9]). A similar approach is taken by Web Service Modeling Ontology (WSMO, [10]), that is also based on ASM. WSMO defines 'capability', which is identical to our concept of 'activity'. WSMO defines service discovery and mediation as matching a customer requirement expressed as a goal with one or more capabilities offered by a service provider. However, both 'capability' and 'goal' should be expressed formally with identical pre- and post-conditions. It cannot serve as the basis for dynamic service mediation. Furthermore, capability chaining is not specified in WSMO [10].

Public services are formally specified in for instance WSMO-PA (WSMO for Public Administration, [5]). WSMO-PA specifies data requirements for public services, e.g. the requirement of identification with a valid document, like passport or driver's license, or another digital means. We have shown that these requirements depend on pre-conditions of activities, such that they could be derived from these pre-conditions. This topic is left for further research.

6 Conclusions and Further Research

This paper presented a conceptual model for public service discovery and mediation. The case, presented in section 4, showed that our conceptual model can be practically deployed. This is further illustrated using our proof of concept. Our conceptual model and software that supports this model has several advantages:

1. It is not required to construct decision trees manually to achieve a user his goal using public services. These are generated dynamically.
2. Our ranking algorithm learns from users with similar goals to show the best matching activities first. Learning from user feedback improves the system.
3. The conceptual model is build upon existing standards used by Dutch government organizations, which makes migration easier.

We are convinced that our approach leads to systems that are adaptive to changes in laws and regulations with lower costs for specification and maintenance, while it is provides a simple and accessible interface to end-users. However, the approach still needs further research in the following areas:

- A business case needs to be constructed to show the advantages of the proposed approach compared with existing approaches. Such a business case should be based on improved user experience. This improvement needs to be tested for more cases, also to validate and possibly refine the model.

- Research questions regarding the conceptual model are:

    o Dynamic backward chaining of activities on a formal description of pre- and post-conditions to support scalability.
    o The ranking algorithm may be extended by creating so-called personae: users that have similar traits e.g. shared customer.

- Operational questions are:

    o Tooling that can be used by civil servants with limited knowledge of formal specification technologies like ASM.
    o Efficiency improvement by derivation of semantic models out of existing data models.
    o A methodological aspect is integration of distributed development of these semantic models by various government organizations responsible for particular laws and regulations.
    o We have only given a partly model of reference data. It needs to be refined and extended to include all relevant data maintained by government organizations, e.g. educational data and patient data.

Acknowledgments

We would like to thank our colleagues Stephan Raaijmakers, Joost de Wit, and Corne Versloot for their work on the realization of the proof of concept. Furthermore, we would like to thank Harrie van Houtum (IND – Dutch Immigration Service) for introducing the concept 'dynamic interaction model', ICTU for providing the product feeds, and GovUnited for offering their platform to perform tests.

References

1. Heineke, J., Davis, M.: The emergence of service operations management as an academic discipline. Journal of Operations Management 25, 364–374 (2007)
2. European Interoperability Framework for Public Services (version 2.0). In: European Commission – IADBC (2009)
3. Discovery of and Access to eGovernment Resources – part 1 to 5, CWA 15971-1, CEN (2009)
4. van der Wijst, L.: Sharing Government Services, version 2.11 (May 2009) (in Dutch)
5. Wang, X., Vitvar, T., Peristeras, V., Mocan, A., Goudos, S., Tarabanis, K.: WSMO-PA: Formal specification of Public Administration Service model on Semantic Web Service Ontology. In: Proceedings of the 40th Annual Hawaii International Conference on System Sciences (2007)
6. van der Geest, T., Klaassen, R., Karreman, J.: Public information discovery – search strategies of citizens, University of Twente (2005) (in Dutch)
7. OneStopGov home page, http://www.onestopgov-project.org

8. Hofman, W.J.: Concepts of enterprise interoperability. In: ICSOFT 2010 (2010) (for review)
9. Börger, E.: High Level System Design and Analysis Using Abstract State Machines. In: Proceedings of the International Workshop on Current Trends in Applied Formal Method: Applied Formal Methods, October 07-09, pp. 1–43 (1998)
10. Fensel, D., Kerrigan, M., Zaremba, M. (eds.): Implementing Semantic Web Services – the SESA framework. Springer, Heidelberg (2008)
11. Verberne, S., Van Halteren, H., Theijssen, D., Raaijmakers, S., Boves, L.: Evaluating Machine Learning Techniques for Re-ranking QA Data. In: Proceedings Workshop Learning to Rank for Information Retrieval, SIGIR 2009, Boston, USA (2009)
12. Mittendorfer, M., Winiwarter, W.: Exploiting syntactic analysis of queries for information retrieval. Data & Knowledge Engineering 42(3), 315–325 (2002)
13. Hiemstra, D.: Using language models for information retrieval. PhD Thesis, University of Twente (2001)
14. Gospodnetic, O., Hatcher, E., McCandless, M.: Lucene in Action, 2nd edn., June 28, p. 475. Manning Publications (2009)
15. McNamee, P.: Character N-Gram Tokenization for European Language Text Retrieval. Information Retrieval 7(1-2), 73–97 (2004)
16. Joachims, T.: Optimizing Search Engines Using Clickthrough Data. In: Proceedings of the ACM Conference on Knowledge Discovery and Data Mining (KDD). ACM, New York (2002)
17. Raaijmakers, S., Kraaij, W.: Polarity Classification of Blog TREC 2008 Data with a Geodesic Kernel. In: Proceedings TREC 2008, Gaithersburg, USA (2008)
18. OWL-S, Semantic Markup for Web Services, W3C member submission (2004)
19. Fowler, M.: UML Distilled, A brief guide to the standard object modeling language, 3rd edn. Addison-Wesley, Reading (2004)
20. Kim, J.: Supervenience and Mind: Selected Philosophical Essays. Cambridge University Press, New York (1993)
21. Bratman, M.E.: Faces of Intention. Cambridge University Press, Cambridge (1999)

Enabling Interoperability of Government Data Catalogues

Fadi Maali[1], Richard Cyganiak[1], and Vassilios Peristeras[1,2]

[1] DERI, National University of Ireland, Galway
[2] Greek National Center for Public Administration and Decentralization
{fadi.maali,richard.cyganiak,vassilios.peristeras}@deri.org

Abstract. Opening public sector information has recently become a trend in many countries around the world. Online government data catalogues with national, regional or local scope act as one-stop data portals providing descriptions of available government datasets. These catalogues though remain isolated. Potential benefits from federating geographically overlapping or thematically complementary catalogues are not realized. We propose an RDF Schema vocabulary as an interchange format among data catalogues and as a way of bringing them into the Web of Linked Data, where they can enjoy interoperability among themselves and with other deployed datasets. The vocabulary's design was informed by a survey of seven data catalogues from five different countries, and has been verified by unifying four data catalogues to allow cross-catalogue queries and browsing.

Keywords: Government Catalog, RDF, Vocabulary, Interoperability, Linked Data.

1   Motivation

"Open Data" and "Open Government"—these terms describe a recent trend towards more openness and transparency in government that is both demanded by advocates in the public and embraced by some administrations. As a part of this trend, information that was previously inaccessible to the public is increasingly opened up, often using the Web [4,5,1]. This development promises social benefits through increased transparency and openness; economic benefits and private sector cost savings through realising the full potential of data that has already been produced as part of the administration's day-to-day operations and paid for by the taxpayer; and to enable the provision of new innovative services that the government cannot or will not provide [10].

Data catalogues such as data.gov in the US[1], data.gov.uk in the UK[2], CA.gov Data in California[3], the New York City Data Mine[4], and the London Datastore[5]

---

[1] http://www.data.gov/
[2] http://data.gov.uk/
[3] http://www.ca.gov/data/
[4] http://www.nyc.gov/html/datamine/
[5] http://data.london.gov.uk/

M.A. Wimmer et al. (Eds.): EGOV 2010, LNCS 6228, pp. 339–350, 2010.

have recently appeared as one-stop web portals that facilitate access and increase findability of such data by providing lists of government datasets along with metadata such as name of the publishing agency, file format, geographic coverage, and category of the dataset. Catalogues differ in scope (national, regional, local) and in operator (official or citizen initiatives). The phenomenon of the data catalogue, including its history and public policy environment, is studied in [13].

Public sector data ranges from census data to lists of locations of fire hydrants. On the technical side, it may take the form of office documents (PDF, Excel); geographical data (ESRI shape files, KML files); statistical data (SDMX, PC-Axis); developer-oriented XML files or web service APIs; and web sites with wizards for searching complex databases.

It is common for the data catalogues themselves to be available not just as a web site, but also in some format that is amenable to machine processing, such as CSV, RSS feed, or embedded RDFa markup. This enables bulk processing of datasets, automated checks for updated data in applications, and refined search over the often thousands of catalogue records.

In this paper, we propose a standardised interchange format for such machine-readable representations of government data catalogues. The adoption of such a format—either directly by the catalogue operators, or through wrappers that convert from the currently available machine-readable formats to the proposed standard—has several benefits:

1. Embedding machine-readable metadata in web pages increases findability by next-generation search engines.
2. Decentralised publishing: Individual agencies could publish separate catalogues, which could be aggregated into national or supra-national (e.g., EU-wide) catalogues.
3. It enables federated search over catalogues with overlapping scope, such as the catalogues for San Francisco, California, and the entire US.
4. Application developers can benefit from one-click download and installation of data packages into local databases.
5. Manifest files with accurate dataset metadata are crucial in efforts towards archiving and digital preservation of valuable government datasets.
6. Software tools and applications, such as improved search and data visualisation interfaces, can be built to work with multiple, or even across, catalogues.

An interoperability format for data catalogues becomes particularly interesting when the catalogued datasets are also amenable to machine processing. Our effort is therefore well aligned with the increased exploration and adoption of the Linked Data technology stack in government data publishing [7,8,11].

Defining an interoperability format for data catalogues is challenging. Catalogues differ widely in their scope, terminology, provided metadata fields, and the quality and amount of structure in the collected dataset descriptions. To clarify the requirements and guide the design of the interoperability format, we undertook a survey of seven existing data catalogues. We report on the results in Sect. 2. Section 3 presents our proposed interoperability format, the *dcat* RDF vocabulary. Section 4 reports on a feasibility study that unifies the contents of four data catalogues. Section 5 discusses related work, and Sect. 6 concludes and reports on ongoing work within the W3C towards broader adoption and standardisation of *dcat*.

2   Survey of Data Catalogues

Most government data catalogues are in beta version and under constant development, so rather than conducting a comparative study, the goal of our analysis was to identify commonalities and overlap in the structure, and to document challenges and practices in this new and rapidly evolving area. We believe that this analysis is timely and that it can guide future initiatives towards setting up new data catalogues.

The goal of the survey was to ensure that our model reflects the reality of current data catalogues. The model must cover what's available in the catalogues, without requiring investments in new data acquisition or manual data cleanup. This encourages quick uptake and lowers the cost of adoption. After listing the surveyed catalogs (Sect. 2.1) and reporting on general characteristics of the catalogues (Sect. 2.2), we thus examine their structure to identify common metadata fields, to determine which ones should be treated as required, recommended and optional (Sect. 2.3). As several of the use cases listed in Sect. 1 require accessing and processing of the actual data files, we examine download links in Sect. 2.4.

The survey was done by first importing the studied catalogs into a relational database, which required development of a custom importer or screen-scraper for each catalog. SQL queries were executed against the database in order to study the completeness and consistency of values within each metadata field. This was combined with study of the catalogue websites and additional documentation on the catalogues' metadata schema where available. Manual inspection of all datasets was used to determine the availability of direct download links.

2.1   Catalogue Selection

For our analysis we select seven catalogues from five different countries:

1. *data.gov*: A catalogue of machine readable datasets generated by the Executive Branch of the US Federal Government.
2. *data.gov.uk*: A catalogue of UK governmental data.
3. *data.govt.nz*: A directory of publicly-available New Zealand government datasets.
4. *data.australia.gov.au*: The home of datasets created by different Australian government agencies.
5. *datasf.org*: A clearinghouse of datasets from the City of San Francisco.
6. *data.london.gov.uk*: An initiative by Greater London Authority (GLA) to release as much of the data that it holds as possible.
7. *statcentral.ie*: Provides information about official statistics produced by Ireland's government departments and state organisations.

This selection was chosen to include a range of different kinds of catalogues. All the major national catalogues available at the time of writing were included. Two local catalogues (SF, London) are included as representatives of smaller-scale catalogues. We made sure that some catalogues overlap in their geographical coverage (US and SF; UK and London). Finally, statcentral.ie was included as the "home catalogue" of the authors, and because of its focus on statistical data, a mature discipline with well-established metadata management practices.

2.2 General Characteristics

Size. The size of a catalogue here refers to the number of datasets it includes. This is an indicator of limited value which we present just to enable broad comparison, as there exists no consensus on the definition of dataset. For example, "2005 Toxics Release Inventory data for Texas" and "2006 Toxics Release Inventory data for Texas" may or may not be considered a single dataset. Most of the catalogues are constantly updated, so the numbers are only valid at the time the data was collected (January 2010).

Machine-readability. The data catalogue itself is considered "data" and should be published as structured data, so that third parties can extract information about the datasets [7]. This is achieved in one of the following ways:

- *RDFa*, a syntax for embedding structured RDF data in HTML pages.
- As described in [14], *feeds* can serve not just as a notification mechanism but also as persistent access points.
- A machine-readable version of the catalogue (usually CSV or XML) is listed as a dataset within the catalogue, e.g., *data.gov* dataset #92.

Table 1 summarizes size and machine-readability of the studied catalogues.

Table 1. General characteristics of catalogues

Catalogue	Size	Machine readability
data.gov	1320	CSV
data.gov.uk	2879	RDFa, CSV
data.govt.nz	251	Feeds
data.australia.gov.au	69	RDFa
datasf.org	132	–
data.london.gov.uk	189	–
statcentral.ie	227	–

2.3 Dataset Metadata

Next, we examine structure, consistency and availability of the metadata that makes up the catalogues. A detailed analysis of metadata quality in government catalogues is out of the scope of this paper. We focused on identifying metadata properties that are used consistently across different catalogues, and on understanding the level of control applied to the values of various metadata fields.

Metadata structure. We looked at what properties are used to describe each dataset. Table 2 summarizes common properties used across the studied catalogues. We find that, although widely different terminology is used to label metadata fields, close examination reveals large overlap in the used fields.

Table 2. Metadata structure of catalogues

	General – title	description	publisher	frequency	release date	update date	temporal coverage	geographic coverage	license	data dictionary	granularity	metadata update	Categorization – theme	tags/keywords	Access – dataset URL	format	size	Other – references and citation	quality characteristics	data collection charact.
data.gov	Y	Y	Y	Y	Y	Y	Y	Y		Y	Y		Y	Y	Y	Y		Y	Y	Y
data.gov.uk	Y	Y	Y	Y	Y	Y	Y	Y	Y		Y		Y	Y	Y	Y		Y	Y	
data.govt.nz	Y	Y	Y		Y				Y				Y	Y	Y	Y				
data.australia.gov.au	Y	Y	Y	Y	Y	Y	Y	Y	Y	Y	Y	Y	Y	Y	Y	Y	Y	Y		Y
datasf.org	Y	Y	Y	Y	Y		Y			Y			Y	Y	Y	Y				
data.london.gov.uk	Y	Y	Y	Y	Y	Y	Y	Y	Y		Y	Y	Y	Y	Y	Y		Y		
statcentral.ie	Y	Y	Y	Y	Y	Y	Y	Y		Y	Y	Y	Y	Y	Y	Y		Y	Y	Y

Metadata consistency. In Table 3, we summarize the findings on metadata consistency on a qualitative scale. Date fields are considered consistent if they follow consistent syntactical format within a catalogue. Other properties are considered consistent if their values are drawn from a fixed set of options (controlled vocabulary). Absence of such control is evident when multiple values refer to the same entity, e.g., "U.S." and "United States". Many catalogs do not even maintain syntactical consistency of date values.

Metadata availability. Providing a sparse set of property values, where the value is often missing or has an uninformative value like "not specified", adversely affects the usefulness of metadata. Table 3 shows the percentage of availability of values for a set of common properties across catalogues.

Dataset categorization. All catalogues use both themes (broad catagories, usually functional domains like *Education* or *Health*), and tags or keywords to categorize datasets. Table 3 shows that while themes are always chosen from a controlled vocabulary, tags are not. Themes enable intuitive browsing of datasets and give an instant overview of the available data in a catalogue. A sufficient description of a catalogue should clearly distinguish themes from keywords.

Table 3. metadata consistency and availability. +,= and – represent high, medium and low consistency. Numbers represent the percentage of datasets in a catalogue for which the metadata attribute is specified.

	Metadata consistency							Metadata availability				
	geographic coverage	temporal coverage	frequency	release date	update date	theme	tags	geographic coverage	release date	license	frequency	tags
data.gov	–	–	–	–	–	+	–	95	79		99	100
data.gov.uk	+	+	–	=	=	+	–	99	52	100	52	94
data.govt.nz				+		+	–		100	98		100
data.australia.gov.au	–	=	=	+	+	+	=	81	70	93	8	68
datasf.org		–	+	–		+	–		100		38	100
data.london.gov.uk	+		+	–	+	+	–	93	95	91	94	62
statcentral.ie	+	–	–	+	+	+	–		100		100	100

2.4   Dataset Accessibility

Catalogues do not always provide direct download links for datasets. The data might be available only after accepting a click-through license, or there might be a splash page that lists the parts of a multi-file download, or data access might require use of a web service[6]. While direct download links are available for virtually all datasets in *data.london.gov.uk* and for 95% in *data.gov*, they are provided only for about 10% in *datasf.org* and 7%[7] in *data.gov.uk*. A vocabulary should support a distinction between direct and indirect download links as this is required for scenarios that involve bulk processing of datasets.

Catalogues provide data in different formats. While some of them are machine-readable, others are not (e.g., PDF, HTML wizards). The format of datasets is very important to mashup developers and for bulk processing of the data and should be explicitly expressed.

3   The *dcat* Vocabulary

Based on the survey described in the previous section, we have developed an RDF Schema vocabulary that allows the expression of data catalogues in the RDF data model. We have chosen RDF because (i) most of the use cases considered in Sect. 1 involve querying of aggregated data, which is well-supported

---

[6] E.g. NextMuni XML data at datasf.org is available as RESTful web service:
http://www.datasf.org/story.php?title=nextmuni-xml-data

[7] Because of the large size of the catalog, we examined only a random sample of 75 data.gov.uk datasets.

in RDF; (ii) re-use and extension of existing metadata standards such as Dublin Core is straightforward in RDF; and (iii) for compatibility with Linked Data [8]. The use of more expressive formalisms such as OWL ontologies was considered unnecessary because the goal is not domain modelling or reasoning, but interoperable data exchange. Classes and properties from existing vocabularies, especially Dublin Core, were re-used whenever possible[8]. Here we will briefly describe the vocabulary's main classes, as shown in Fig. 1. Full documentation is available online[9].

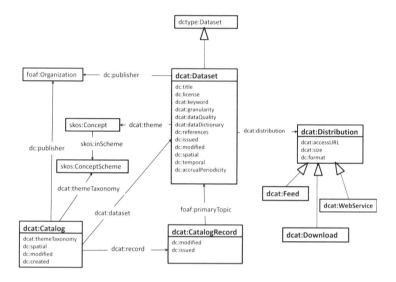

Fig. 1. Overview of the *dcat* vocabulary

dcat:Catalog. A Catalog represents a collection of dataset descriptions. A Catalog does not own or provide the actual datasets, but provides a structured description of them. Properties used to describe Catalog include `dcat: themeTaxonomy, dc:modified, dc:issued, dc:publisher` and `dc:spatial`.

dcat:Dataset. A Dataset represents a collection of data which is published or will be published. Properties used to describe Dataset include `dcat: theme, dcat:keyword, dcat:granularity, dcat:dataDictionary, dcat: dataQuality, dc:modified, dc:issued, dc:license, dc:publisher` and `dc:references`.

dcat:CatalogRecord. One source of ambiguity in catalogues results from the absence of clear distinction between a dataset and its corresponding description in the catalogue. For example, does the "last update" refer to the actual data of the dataset or to its description in the corresponding catalogue?

---

[8] In accordance with RDF conventions, we use *QNames* to identify terms. Terms beginning with *dc*: are part of Dublin Core, terms beginning with *dcat*: are defined in our vocabulary. Other prefixes have their conventional meaning.

[9] http://vocab.deri.ie/dcat

Having a stand-alone entity for a catalogue record resolves this ambiguity and allows adding further description about the metadata provided by the catalogue for a specific dataset. Properties used to describe `CatalogRecord` include `foaf:primaryTopic`, `dc:modified` and `dc:issued`.

dcat:Distribution. A `Distribution` represents the availability of a dataset in a particular format. `accessURL` property refers to the dataset location. `Download`, `Feed` and `WebService` refine `Distribution` to indicate availability in those forms. Properties used to describe `Distribution` include `dcat:accessURL`, `dcat:size`, `dc:format`.

Dataset Categorization. The `theme` and `keyword` properties describe categorization of datasets. It is recommended to use a controlled vocabulary or taxonomy described using SKOS for the theme. Cross-catalogue browsing by theme can be enabled by mapping the local scheme to standardized schemes such as the SDMX List of Subject-matter Domains[10] or the Integrated Public Service Vocabulary (IPSV)[11].

4   Feasibility Study

To verify our claim that different catalogues can be rendered in the *dcat* vocabulary, we applied the vocabulary to represent the *data.gov, data.australia.gov.au, data.london.gov.uk* and *datasf.org* catalogues in RDF[12]. After importing the catalogues into a relational database, we used D2R Server[13] for generating RDF data. D2R Server also provides a SPARQL endpoint for querying the data and an HTML interface for browsing. D2R Server's basic out-of-the-box Linked Data enabled web interface, without any customisation, already provides functionalities that are not available on many of the catalogue websites, such as browsing by category/keyword and browsing by agency.

Figure 2 shows an RDF snippet describing a *data.gov* dataset and its availability as a downloadable XML file. We use the Turtle RDF syntax.

Figure 3 shows a SPARQL query to retrieve all datasets about health which have XML distribution, and the results of the query[14]. Results come from both *data.london.gov.uk* and *data.gov*. Such cross-catalogue queries are enabled by the common representation in RDF.

The data can be enriched by linking it to other available Linked Datasets, to enable further useful queries and navigation vectors. Figure 4 shows a SPARQL query that retrieves all *data.gov* datasets published by an agency having a budget of more than 50 billion. Budget information is obtained from DBpedia[15].

---

[10] `http://sdmx.org/wp-content/uploads/2009/01/03_sdmx_cog_annex_3_smd_2009.pdf`

[11] `http://www.esd.org.uk/standards/ipsv/`

[12] `http://lab.linkeddata.deri.ie/govcat/`

[13] `http://www4.wiwiss.fu-berlin.de/bizer/d2r-server/`

[14] Queries can be tested at `http://lab.linkeddata.deri.ie/govcat/snorql/`

[15] `http://dbpedia.org/About`

```
:data.gov/dataset/1263 a dcat:Dataset ;
     dc:title              "FinancialStability.gov TARP..." ;
     dc:accrualPeriodicity "approximately twice weekly" ;
     dc:modified           "2009-12-04"^^xsd:date ;
     dc:publisher          :data.gov/agency/Department_of_the_Treasury ;
     dc:temporal           "October 2008 - present" ;
     dcat:dataDictionary   <http://www.financialstability.gov/impact/...> ;
     dcat:granularity      "Financial transactions" ;
     dcat:distribution     :data.gov/1263/distribution/2566 ;
     dcat:keyword          "tarp", "cbli" ;
     dcat:theme            :data.gov/category/banking_and_insurance ;
     foaf:homepage         <http://www.data.gov/details/1263> .


:data.gov/1263/distribution/2566 a dcat:Download ;
     rdfs:label            "text/xml distribution of FinancialStability" ;
     dc:format             "text/xml" ;
     dcat:accessURL        <http://www.financialstability.gov/impact/cbli.xml> ;
     dcat:size             [ dcat:bytes 4 ] .
```

Fig. 2. Sample RDF description of a dataset

```
SELECT DISTINCT ?title ?url
WHERE {
        ?dataset a dcat:Dataset;
        dct:title ?title;
        dcat:theme ?theme;
        dcat:distribution ?distribution.
        ?distribution dcat:accessURL ?url;
        dct:format ?format.
        ?theme skos:prefLabel ?themeLabel.
        FILTER regex(?themeLabel, "health", "i").
        FILTER regex(?format,"text/xml")
}
```

title	url
"Census 2001 Key Statistics 08: Health"	<http://data.london.gov.uk/datafiles/demographics/census-2001-ks08-borough.xml>
"Census 2001 Key Statistics 21: Long Term Illness"	<http://data.london.gov.uk/datafiles/demographics/census-2001-ks21-borough.xml>
"Legal Abortion Rates"	<http://data.london.gov.uk/datafiles/health/abortion-legal-rates-pct.xml>
"Alcohol Related Hospital Admissions"	<http://data.london.gov.uk/datafiles/health/alcohol-admissions-borough.xml>
"Crime Attributable to Alcohol"	<http://data.london.gov.uk/datafiles/health/alcohol-crime-borough.xml>
"Land Transport Deaths due to Alcohol"	<http://data.london.gov.uk/datafiles/health/alcohol-deaths-transport-borough.xml>
"Hazardous, Harmful and Binge Drinking Rates"	<http://data.london.gov.uk/datafiles/health/alcohol-drinking-rates-borough.xml>
"Alcohol Related Hospital Admissions Indicators"	<http://data.london.gov.uk/datafiles/health/alcohol-indicators-borough.xml>
"Alcohol Related Mortality"	<http://data.london.gov.uk/datafiles/health/alcohol-mortality-borough.xml>
"Births and Fertility Rates"	<http://data.london.gov.uk/datafiles/health/births-fertility-rates-borough.xml>
"Births with Low Birthweight"	<http://data.london.gov.uk/datafiles/health/births-low-weight-borough.xml>
"Births by Birthplace of Mother"	<http://data.london.gov.uk/datafiles/health/births-mother-birthplace-borough.xml>
"Benefit Claimants due to Alcoholism"	<http://data.london.gov.uk/datafiles/health/claimants-alcoholism-borough.xml>
"Working Age Disability"	<http://data.london.gov.uk/datafiles/health/disability-working-age-borough.xml>
"MyPyramid Food Raw Data"	<http://www.cnpp.usda.gov/Innovations/DataSource/MyFoodapediaData.zip>

Fig. 3. SPARQL query across catalogues, with results

```
SELECT ?title
WHERE {
     :data.gov dcat:dataset ?dataset.
     ?dataset dc:title ?title;
     dc:publisher ?agency.
     ?agency dbpedia:budget ?budget.
     FILTER (?budget>50000000000)
}
```

Fig. 4. SPARQL query integrating an external dataset (DBpedia)

5   Related Work

We identify related work in the areas of catalogue aggregation, metadata standards for documents, and from the linked data field. We briefly discuss these efforts below.

Following the need for horizontal access to federation of catalogues, efforts to aggregate catalogues started to emerge recently, most notably Guardian's *World Government Data site*[16] and Sunlight Labs' *National Data Catalog*[17]. However, lack of a standardised model obliges these solutions to rely on coding a custom importer per catalogue. Imported catalogues are then translated to some proprietary unified model defined for the federated catalogue. This limits flexibility, reusability and extensibility as it substantially increases the required effort for each new catalogue addition.

Many metadata standards for document description already exist, like e-GMS [2] and AGLS [3]. These standards were motivated by the concerns of document management, so they closely resemble the widely-used Dublin Core standard. Such standards provide rich properties for resource description but would require subsetting or other additional guidelines before they can be used to describe data catalogues.

The Linked Data community has developed a number of vocabularies for the description of datasets. VoiD [6], SCOVO [12] and SDMX-RDF [9] are RDF vocabularies for the description of RDF datasets and statistical datasets, respectively. They are not intended for describing other kinds or formats of datasets and hence are not applicable to data catalogues, but can be used in conjunction with *dcat* to provide more detailed descriptions of applicable datasets. A simple RDF vocabulary for the description of data catalogues has been defined at CTIC[18], but unlike *dcat* it just defines 2 basic classes and no metadata fields. Sunlight Labs also suggests a list of common properties to use for dataset description[19]. This list is not defined in any standard way, limited to datasets description and not comprehensive.

---

[16] http://www.guardian.co.uk/world-government-data

[17] http://nationaldatacatalog.com/

[18] http://data.fundacionctic.org/vocab/catalog/datasets.html

[19] http://sunlightlabs.com/blog/2010/drafting-guidelines-government-data-catalogs/

Koumenides et al. [13] also approach the problem of integrating data catalogues using RDF, and contribute an in-depth review of the literature and public policy setting that surrounds the data catalogue phenomenon. They convert a number of data catalogues to RDF and compare them both quantitatively (e.g., growth over time) and qualitatively (e.g., by visualisation via tag clouds), but do not continue their work to tackle the problem of developing a unified RDF vocabulary.

As already discussed, our proposed solution goes beyond the state of the art as a) it takes into account and reuses many terms of the vocabularies mentioned above, b) extends their catalogue representation by a richer description of not only datasets but also of catalogues and data files, c) presents a formal description of a data catalogue in RDF, d) enables a single importer to be used to import all catalogues that support the format, e) makes the federation process loose and easy to participate as the individual catalogue owners need only to map their metadata fields to *dcat*.

6 Future Work and Conclusion

We proposed the *dcat* RDF vocabulary as an interchange format to enable standardised description of government data catalogues as part of the nascent Web of Data. To identify the most relevant concepts to include in such vocabulary, we analysed a number of existing data catalogues. We have also demonstrated how our vocabulary can be used to allow cross-catalogue querying and browsing over four major data catalogues.

Besides refining the *dcat* vocabulary and validating it against more catalogues, particularly interesting areas for future work include the exploration of dcat's potential for improved user interfaces over integrated catalogues in situations where structural information about the datasets is available, e.g., for datasets in RDF format, or highly-structured statistical and geographical datasets; and as a driver for discovering cross-links between datasets within a catalogue and to linked datasets elsewhere on the Web.

The operators of data catalogues tend to aggressively pursue an agenda of openness and are technologically sophisticated. Many more data catalogues are likely to appear in the near future. We believe that the cost for implementing *dcat* is low, especially when deployed as embedded RDFa. We therefore expect that *dcat* can play an important role in facilitating wider re-use of government data. To achieve this goal, the W3C's eGovernment Interest Group has set up a task force to support the further development and deployment of *dcat*[20]. A first successful outcome is the adoption of *dcat* on the `data.gov.uk` site[21]

Acknowledgements

The work presented in this paper has been funded in part by Science Foundation Ireland under Grant No. SFI/08/CE/I1380 (Lion-2) and the European Union under Grant No. 238900 (Rural Inclusion).

---

[20] `http://www.w3.org/egov/wiki/Data_Catalog_Vocabulary`
[21] `http://data.gov.uk/blog/project-update`

References

1. C. European Parliament, "Directive 2003/98/ec on the re-use of public sector information" (2003)
2. e-Government Metadata Standard, version 3.1, Cabinet Office, e-Government Unit, UK (2006)
3. AGLS Metadata Standard, National Archives of Australia (2008),
   `http://www.agls.gov.au/documents/terminology/`
4. Open Government Directive. Memorandum for the heads of executive departments and agencies, office of Management and Budget, Washington, D.C. (2009)
5. Putting the frontline first: smarter government. UK Government (2009),
   `http://www.hmg.gov.uk/media/52788/smarter-government-final.pdf`
6. Alexander, K., Cyganiak, R., Hausenblas, M., Zhao, J.: Describing linked datasets. In: WWW 2009 Workshop: Linked Data on the Web, LDOW 2009 (2009)
7. Bennett, D., Harvey, A.: Publishing open government data. W3C working draft, World Wide Web Consortium (2009), `http://www.w3.org/TR/gov-data/`
8. Bizer, C., Heath, T., Berners-Lee, T.: Linked Data: The story so far. International Journal on Semantic Web and Information Systems (IJSWIS) 5 (2009)
9. Cyganiak, R., Field, S., Gregory, A., Halb, W., Tennison, J.: Semantic statistics: Bringing together SDMX and SCOVO. In: Proceedings of the Linked Data on the Web Workshop (LDOW 2010), Raleigh, NC (April 2010)
10. Dekkers, M., Polman, F., te Velde, R., de Vries, M.: MEPSIR: Measuring european public sector information resources. Final report of study on exploitation of public sector information. Tech. rep. (2006),
    `http://ec.europa.eu/information_society/policy/psi/docs/pdfs/`
    `mepsir/fin%al_report.pdf`
11. Ding, L., DiFranzo, D., Graves, A., Michaelis, J.R., Li, X., McGuinness, D.L., Hendler, J.: Data-gov Wiki: Towards Linking Government Data. In: The 2010 AAAI Spring Symposium on Linked Data Meets Artificial Intelligence (2010)
12. Hausenblas, M., Halb, W., Raimond, Y., Feigenbaum, L., Ayers, D.: SCOVO: Using statistics on the web of data. In: 6th European Semantic Web Conference, ESWC 2009 (2009)
13. Koumenides, C., Alani, H., Shadbolt, N.: Global integration of public sector information. In: Proc. of WebSci10 (2010), `http://journal.webscience.org/303/`
14. Wilde, E., Kansa, E., Yee, R.: Web Services for recovery.gov. Tech. Rep. 2009-035, UC Berkeley School of Information (October 2009)

Knowledge Sharing in E-Collaboration

Neil Ireson and Gregoire Burel

University of Sheffield, UK

Abstract. For eCollaboration to be effective, especially where it attempts to promote true collective decision-making, it is necessary to consider how knowledge is shared. The paper examines the knowledge sharing literature from the perspective of eCollaboration and discusses the critical challenges, principally the motivation of knowledge sources and maintenance of semantics, and describes how techniques and technologies can be employed to alleviate the difficulties. The paper concludes with an example of how such technologies are being applied for Emergency Response, to facilitate knowledge sharing both amongst the citizens and between the citizens and organisations.

Keywords: eCollaboration, knowledge sharing, emergency response.

1 Introduction

Knowledge sharing is an activity where agents (individuals, communities or organisations) exchange their knowledge (information, skills or expertise). It is intrinsically linked to the knowledge management process, which can be broadly characterised by four activities, the: creation, storage and retrieval, transfer and application of knowledge. Whilst knowledge sharing is fundamentally concerned with the transfer activity, it cannot be isolated from the other activities: the complete sharing process involves the externalisation of their knowledge by the source (often referred to as knowledge capture), the transmission of that knowledge, and finally the internalisation of the knowledge by the recipient. Therefore any methodology concerning knowledge sharing must also consider the wider knowledge management activities.

The majority of the knowledge sharing research and practice has focused on the sharing within and between professional organisations, however more recently there has been an increasing realisation that organisations can exploit the potential benefits offered through harnessing the power of the users to which they provide products and services. The catalyst for this new model of interaction between organisation and users (i.e. customers of businesses, citizens or service-users of public bodies) has been the development of Web 2.0 technologies, such as: online social-networking, content-sharing, wikis and blogs.

The traditional interaction model, whereby any information provided by users is anonymously absorbed into the organisation, and organisations broadcast to all users regardless of individual needs, is giving way to a complex web of interactions, where information relevant to the organisation is communicated amongst

M.A. Wimmer et al. (Eds.): EGOV 2010, LNCS 6228, pp. 351–362, 2010.

individuals and groups, and between those individuals and groups and the organisation itself. The most common form of benefit to be derived from users is via user-feedback on the products/services provided by organisations, either as simple ratings or more qualitative assessment. However it is also possible that, rather than users just providing a reaction to the organisations activities, they can be pro-actively engage in the decision-making processes that determine how an organisation's activities are carried out. Users can act as information-gathers, determining the nature, extent and importance of issues and opportunities faced by the organisation. For example, The Ben & Jerry's Facebook page[1] has nearly 1 million fans who have created new flavours, determined by interactive polls, Johnson & Johnson's set up the Baby Center[2], the Webs number one global interactive parenting network, where they can engage their consumers and curate conversations to solicit information on given topics, and possibly most famously the use of collaborative technologies during the Obama presidential campaign [1].

In essence organisations utilising technology that makes it easy for like-minded individuals to connect and collaborate around the topics (both personal to professional) they care about. However there are inherent issues in ensuring that this more direct engagement of users satisfies both organisation and citizen requirements. Organisations require accurate, coherent, objective information, upon which to base their decision-making, however the subjective and conversational nature of citizens' input means: it can contain personal references; stated facts may be speculative, incomplete or simply incorrect; some citizens may even seek to provide deliberately misleading information; and, as organisations do not control the content of user communication, much of the information will not be of interest to the organisation. Therefore the organisations need to employ technologies to translate the copious quantities of unstructured conversational data into accurate, coherent, objective, structured information: in effect, to determine the signal from the noise. In addition, if organisations are to truly engage in a two-way dialogue with users then it is necessary for them to determine the information that is of interest to the users. To maintain an effective relationship with users, organisations should respect users' limited attention by minimising the amount of irrelevant information they communicated.

Organisations wishing to take advantage of their users are therefore forming a new model of knowledge; rather than explicitly being held within an organisation, knowledge is seen as a systemic property of people in "communities of practice", i.e. groups with shared interests who will benefit from collaboration and sharing knowledge. Information is not only held within formal documents and systems, but also in dialogues amongst groups of people. In this view, knowledge is both individual and collective, and it has crucial implications for an organisation's knowledge management practices. In this context, communities of practice generally, and knowledge-building communities specifically, form the arena for the creation and dissemination of knowledge.

---

[1] http://www.facebook.com/benjerry Accessed 14/12/09.
[2] http://community.babycenter.com/ Accessed 14/12/09.

The majority of the work which considers knowledge sharing in eGovernment does so from the perspective of either intra- or inter- organisational sharing, or how such technologies can improve the communication from organisations to citizens, Vitvar et al [2] provides a collection of recent work in these areas. The potential benefits which can be derived from the use of user-generated content in eGovernment has been recognised [3,4], however the work neither systematically considered the issues in terms of the knowledge sharing literature nor implements and evaluates the suggested solutions.

2   Knowledge Sharing Context

In order to develop the correct knowledge sharing methodology, and technologies, to apply in a given scenario it is necessary to consider the application context. In eCollaboration, as the requirements upon the degree of engagement increase: from information gathering through consultation to systems which attempt to promote true collaboration and collective decision-making, the challenges upon efficacious knowledge sharing will increase. In Cummings' extensive survey of the literature on knowledge sharing [5] he identifies five primary contexts that can affect knowledge sharing, these are:

- **Relational** — The relationship between the source and the recipient, i.e. their distance in: physical, social, cultural, educational, etc. terms.
- **Knowledge** — Assessed accordingly to: ***explicitness***, i.e. the extent to which knowledge is able to be expressed, codified and transmitted through in formal language; and ***embeddedness***, i.e. the extent to which it is possible to isolate the package of knowledge to be shared, or whether that knowledge is embedded within the source (people, products, tools, routines, etc.).
- **Recipient** — Ability of to successful receive and internalise the shared knowledge, determine by their: motivation, learning capacities, intent, knowledge experience, collaborative experience, retentive capacity and culture.
- **Source** — The sources knowledge-sharing capability, i.e. the ability to explicitly communicate credible and comprehensible knowledge.
- **Environmental** — The broader environment in which the sharing occurs, which has a vicarious effect upon the impact of the other contexts.

Applications which facilitate eCollaboration are fundamentally focused on exploiting the ability to share knowledge between organisations and their community of users, as well as within the community of users. As the target community expands and users become more diverse, the relational context of the sources and recipients weakens. The complexity of the knowledge will vary according to the degree to which the user is allowed, and expected, to express their mind: from simple ratings provided in petitions through questionnaires to open dialogues where users can freely express their thoughts, feelings, experience and opinions. Where knowledge is contained within such conversational data it is necessary to consider the extent to which the knowledge is embedded within the dialogue, in order to ensure that it is shared as an interpretable package. It should also be noted that when packaging (codifying) the knowledge it is possible to *over* codify the knowledge, for example if imperfection in the knowledge exist at the source this should not be hidden by codification. Also there may be a trade-off between the recipients ability to consider knowledge in its fully codified form and their need for timely knowledge, this is particularly likely if the recipients context is such that they have limited resources to spend on sharing activities.

3   Motivation for Knowledge Sharing

To develop a effective knowledge sharing system it is essential to consider the motivation of the users to share their knowledge. In fact, a user-centred design philosophy may argue that unless the technology employed fosters users' motivations, or at least does not actively hinder them, it is unlikely to function effectively. Broadly there are two types of motivation: intrinsic (self-oriented motives) — self expression, personal development, utilitarian motives, economic motives and knowledge efficacy; and extrinsic (external-oriented motives): social affiliation, enhance reputation, social ranking, competition, reciprocity, expected economic and organisational rewards.

There are a myriad of factors, both personal traits and the characteristics of the task, which influence any individual's motivations to act, and a single individual's motivations will vary over time. Studies into group dynamics tend to indicate that each member of the group takes into account what others are doing [6], and have done [7], before deciding to act (i.e. they are extrinsically motivate). Although other research argues that rational actors will contribute if their efforts are cost-effective, that is, if they know (or think they know) they can "make a difference", then they will contribute regardless of others in the group [8]. This self-efficacy, or belief that one's actions have an effect, does seem to motivate sharing in online environments [9,10] and has been indicated as an important factor to consider in the decision to participate in a democratic process [11]. Although there will not be a single type of motivation for all users of an eCollaboration system, in organisations there is an expectation of some extrinsic reward for any knowledge shared, whilst in community-based systems, incentives become less significant thus the intrinsic motivation to participate and share knowledge becomes more important [12].

4   Knowledge Sharing in a Community of Practice

As was stated in the introduction, eCollaboration is primarily concerned with facilitating knowledge sharing in Communities of Practice (CoP), where a CoP can be characterised as an informal network of individuals who share a common set of information needs or problems. The challenge is to support such communities and make them effective; provided them with knowledge management tools to allow more natural, intuitive and efficacious access to knowledge. In order to consider the systematic factors which influence knowledge generation and sharing in CoP, the C4P framework is adopted[13]. This posits that knowledge is generated and shared when there is purposeful conversation around content in context. C4P is shorthand for content, conversation, connections, (information) context, and purpose. These elements comprise a non-linear system that occurs in a CoP. It is assumed that the more these elements are present in any community, the more likely and effective the knowledge generation and sharing will be. The following sections will provide a critical assessment the C4P elements, in terms of how they impact upon a knowledge-sharing community. This allows the focusing of context and motivation factors towards more pragmatic considerations of an eCollaboration system.

4.1   Content

Content, i.e. the contributed information: text, images, videos, etc, satisfies a number of purposes in a CoP, it: is an explicit container for the information (and knowledge) available; is an asset to attract member by providing immediate value; defines, implicitly, the domain of interest; and provides the basis for conversations. Whilst it is desirable to build a system which solicits members to provide content, quality and not quantity is the key measure, i.e. content must be relevant, accurate and coherent. Certain extrinsic rewards, such as: social interaction ties, reciprocity and identification, increase an individual's quantity of shared knowledge but not necessarily its quality [14], and in fact may have a negative impact [15].

The generation of quality content is one of the fundamental challenges of eCollaboration, and is obviously a prerequisite to having effective knowledge sharing. It is generally the case that the minority of community members provide the majority of content, for example in Wikipedia 2.5% of registered users contributed 80% of all the content [16]. There have been numerous studies into how to motivate quality content contributions, including those specific to online communities. Whilst the research does not result in a clear "best practice" list of techniques to employ in all circumstances, the most important factors are generally given as: age, socio-economic status, gender, proficiency and familiarity [17]. It is therefore necessary to consider the nature of the users to determine the likely interaction with the system the users will exhibit, in order to maximise the quality of their contribution.

Research shows that one of the key ways to stimulate content contribution is to receive feedback (i.e. replies, reviews, ranking), however it also points out that feedback is more likely if the contributor is engaged with the community [18,19], this leads to difficulties in soliciting contributions from newcomers. It is therefore beneficial, especially for newcomers, that knowledge capture services guide uses to generate messages which are more likely to stimulate feedback, i.e. ones which are short, on-topic, asking questions and using less complex language. In addition it is advisable for newcomers to introducing themselves to the community via autobiographical testimonials [18]. Newcomers are also unwilling to contribute if the do not fully understand how to use the technology [19], therefore the system should be simple to learn and use, it is also necessary to ensure suitable access is provided, as people can choose (perceived) ease of access over content quantity/quality when selecting an information source [20].

4.2 Conversation

The conversations in the system are the primary means by which knowledge is shared. Where conversation which is focused on a piece of quality content is likely to build upon the knowledge embedded with it, and as long as the content is relevant to the CoP purpose the conversation is likely to be as well. If there is a strong and clear sense of shared purpose then it becomes more likely that everyone involved understands that the goal of every conversation is to support that purpose, and not change the topic or thread. The challenge is to provide such focused conversations that draw out meaningful knowledge (signal), rather than aimless chat (noise). However not all conversation will be directly toward the purpose of the CoP, and therefore it may be necessary for organisations to guide them, for example by asking for clarification or providing further information about of points of interest. Providing such feedback, including even being given specific and challenging goals, has been shown to stimulate individuals contribution [17].

To facilitate sharing it is necessary to provide support for the nature of online conversation. The individual needs to maintain continuity and comprehension of the flow of a conversation even when it is disjointed. Generally this is achieved by archiving the conversion threads (as with forums and blogs), however when revisiting conversations users' comprehension is aided by allowing the focusing on specific user (or group of users), time or spatially related input.

4.3 Connections

Connections (which can be seen as a strong relational context) foster the development of trust and common goals. Whilst previous work which suggests that developing such connections requires rich interpersonal interactions and a shared history [21], recent studies have shown that even with impersonal sharing processes users perceived their actions as being a social act [15]. Individuals may be willing to share their personal knowledge due to strong feelings toward the virtual community, without necessarily trusting other members in the virtual community [14]. Therefore, rather than connections amongst individuals, it is the connection to the community as a whole which may be just as influential on the motivation to share knowledge.

In addition whilst connections build trust, trust does not necessarily impact upon of knowledge sharing, it is arguable that trust is not crucial unless individuals have a degree of risk (possible cost) in sharing knowledge. One cost which can cause a hesitation to contribute is the fear of criticism, or of misleading the community members (not being sure that their contributions are important, or completely accurate, or relevant to a specific discussion), therefore members must feel safe from personal attack [22], which can be provided by moderation, either by an assigned moderator or by the community as a whole.

4.4   Information Context

Information context is the who, what, where, when, why, and how that facilitates the interpretation of the knowledge by the recipient and thus enables them to determine the relative merits of the knowledge to them and their situation, and eases its internalisation and reuse. It should also be emphasised that knowledge sharing is not content sharing, rather it is the ability to share the knowledge embedded within content which the technology aims to facilitate. If the context of the information within the content is relatively explicit, or the sender and receiver share a conceptual understanding of the content, then sharing the content may be sufficient to also share its embedded knowledge. However if this is not the case addition information (context) must also be provided with the content. It can consist of information about the knowledge provider, or the knowledge itself, e.g. links to related material and previous uses of the knowledge.

4.5   Purpose

It could be said that the shared purpose of a CoP is its defining characteristic, and that the community content, conversations, connections and context are both guided by and defined by its purpose. The community may well have some explicitly stated purpose (or vision) and ideally it's actual purpose, the one defined by the communities members and their actions and interactions, will be congruent with that: as a shared purpose is seen to promote quality sharing, and also reduce the quantity of off-topic exchanges [14]. The a key to the success of knowledge sharing in a CoP is that personal purpose should match the group purpose [23]. One of the main determinants of both quantity and quality of knowledge sharing appears to be the expectations of successful community-related goals [9], however if these conflict with an individual's personal goals then that can have a negative impact upon the quantity of knowledge sharing [14].

5   Technological Support for Knowledge Sharing

An organisation's need for knowledge management and sharing tools that foster collaboration becomes even more important when the required information is outside of organisations: within the wider community. Knowledge tools can enable or reduce the time taken in searching, browsing and interpreting documents to find out how they are related to one another and thus locate the similarities and differences among pieces of information. Exposing the implicit information structures can allow otherwise isolated information to be placed into a meaningful context and thus help users manage information (and knowledge) more efficiently. The recent technologies employed to facilitate knowledge sharing in eCollaboration can be broadly encapsulated by the Web 2.0 technologies, that is, those technologies used by: forums, blogs, new feeds, wikis, etc. This section considers how such technologies are employed to aid the knowledge sharing activity and how incorporating Semantic Web technologies (sometimes termed Web 3.0) can be used to further enhance the effectiveness of Web 2.0 technologies for knowledge sharing.

Web 2.0 technologies primarily improve knowledge sharing by: lowering temporal and spatial barriers between the knowledge source and recipient; providing some degree of dialogue management between a potential multitude of sources and recipients; and improving access to information, i.e. easing the storage, retrieval and transfer of knowledge artefacts, i.e. the documents (notes, emails, images, etc.) which implicitly or explicitly contain the knowledge. However simply providing the ability for this interaction to take place has limited value if it ignores when and how the quality of knowledge sharing will be enhanced [23]. Whilst Web 2.0 technologies can aid communities in the construction of a collaborative information pool, the information it contains can be of varying quality and have multifarious expressions. This leads to difficulties when attempting to share the knowledge and develop a collective understanding, especially when the community is made up from diverse individuals, with different: cultural backgrounds, education, experience, expertise, etc. where there is an increased likelihood of a variety of expressions and terminology which require some degree of tacit knowledge to interpret the meaning.

In terms of the C4P framework discussed above Web 2.0 technologies readily enhance the ability to: store, retrieve and transfer content; facilitate conversation between temporally and spatially disparate groups of individuals; and managed the network of links between connected individuals. However they do not inherently provide means to store, retrieve and transfer the context of the information, and without this such technologies provide means for information exchange and social interaction leading to content rather than knowledge sharing. In order for knowledge sharing to take place, and the community to develop a collective understanding, the technologies should also provide a means for the knowledge, which resides in its member and is implicit in the content they share, to be made explicit, to ensure that the intended meaning (semantics) of the knowledge is maintained. Existing solutions to this problem can be classified into three main approaches [24]: internalisation, socialisation and externalisation.

With internalisation approaches the shared information context is contained within the community dialogues: held in the blogs, mailing lists, bulletin boards, discussion forums, etc. This presumes that the information context is expressed by community members, which requires a community motivated towards question answering. Relying on such approaches means there is no structure or standard in how the information context is expressed and thus retrieval of the context is potential difficult and arduous, thus useful knowledge can easily be lost. The socialisation approach aims at supporting the sharing of knowledge through linking of individuals likely to share an understanding. Thus, the technology provides some shared space where contextually related users (e.g. concerned with the same issue or working on same task) can exchange knowledge and engage with each other. The externalisation approaches aim to develop an explicit model of shared conceptualisations, known as an ontology, which provide a formal description of concepts and the relationships between them.

Ontologies provide an abstract, simplified (possibly incomplete) view of a domain and therefore a means to explicitly represent the context of information: modelling the semantics (meaning) of information in a way both processable by computers and usable for the communication of meaning between human users. They have been identified as particularly applicable to addressing the issues, discussed above, which effect sharing in CoP, such as: missing or imperfect conceptual models, unclear system boundaries, and heterogeneous representations [25]. Ontologies provide the ability to organise knowledge into a more controllable form and can be used to determine the relative importance, context, significance and association between pieces of information. This can enable CoP engaged in tasks with ad hoc interactions, between diverse individuals, to organise the knowledge artefacts into the predefined conceptual classes of the ontology, allowing more efficacious access to knowledge.

6   E-Collaboration Ontology

This section briefly describes the key concepts of an eCollaboration ontology called CURIO (Collaborative User Resource Interaction Ontology)[3]. In effect it represents the world view of eCollaboration information and provides a pragmatic combination of the formal ontologies used for describing the knowledge areas. A full description of the Ontology is beyond the scope of this paper (however the full specification is available on the website), the following briefly describes the five key concepts:

Resource: The ontology is articulated around the concept of Resource, which can be defined as an abstract piece of information or anything that can be inserted in the system by a user. The ontology distinguishes two main Resource types that are the focal concepts containing the information of primary interest to the users, Document and Thread, see below. Each Resource can possess a number of properties, such as: a title, a date of creation, a description, a creator, a set of tags, etc. Additionally, each Resource may be subscribed by any user of the system through the use of a *ResourceFeed*, this mechanism allows a user to be notified when a resource changes. In addition a Resource can be associated with a localisation, which provides temporal and spatial information.

Document: Documents are any media (i.e. text, images or audio) content which is provided by the user, they are pieces of information that can be: used as evidence to induce, describe and define a Thread; associated to Users (as a creator or modifier), and assigned a number of Tags.

Thread: A Thread acts as a container describing how resources are combined into coherent structures, e.g. Events or Arguments. Thus all the information (resources and users) related to a given Thread are linked with an instance of

---

[3] http://purl.org/net/curio/ns# Accessed 14/12/09.

a Thread. In addition threads are composed into structures to express their interrelationships, this composition can be a simple subsumption (i.e. a global thread with a number of sub-threads) or may involve more complex relationships based on causality and correlation.

User: The representation of a user includes the ability to express their personal details, preferences and profile their interests.

Tag/Comment/Rating: Tags can be either free-text or related to some tag hierarchy (taxonomy or ontology) that provides a stable, dereferencable identifier for the concept expressed by the Tag. In addition to tagging, it is possible to attach a (textual) Comment and (numeric) Rating to a Resource. Such concepts are key to providing the ability to effective retrieve information via browsing and searching.

7   Knowledge Sharing in Emergency Response

The techniques and technologies described above have be applied in developing an Emergency Response (ER) system that combines organisation and citizen information to improve situational awareness and thus the decision-making process. The nature of such an eCollaboration application means the citizens engaged in the system may not have a strong relational context, simply being brought together by happenstance. Initially the requirements for both the organisational professionals were gathered and compared, to ensure these are satisfied, in general there was a correlation between the information needs of these two groups, although citizens expressed a stronger desire for social information and professionals had more strict non-functional requirements. Both groups basically expressed a need for factual (temporal, spatial and topic related) information [26]. In the ER domain there is also a need for timeliness of information in order to react to critical incidents as quickly as possible.

The system allows users can log in with federated identities, such as OpenID[4], which allows new uses to import their personal information, thus can enabling newcomer introduction. In addition a user profile is used to direct their attention to content which is likely to be of interest. As users add content (Documents) into the system they receive automatic suggestions to tag (or locate) their content, encouraging them to provide a more systematic encoding of their content. The uploaded information is then automatically organised into Threads (incidents/events) which can be validated and augmented by the ER professionals. This process of combining evidence provides reinforcement to increase confidence in the citizens' information. Users can add further information to Threads and also subscribed to them, to receive notification of changes and thus promote further contributions.

The information in the system can be accessed via the ontological concepts, the information can be viewed on maps and timelines and can be filtered according to user type (i.e. citizen or professional), or the associated tags, descriptions

---

[4] `http://openid.net/` Accessed 14/12/09.

and comments. Therefore it is possible to develop an overall situational awareness as the incident/event information is added to the system and to focus in on particular information (in a locality or related to a given topic) which is of interest to the user. The evaluation of the initial prototype with both citizens and ER professional indicates that such codification of knowledge improves the ability to quickly and accurately evaluate the information available in assessing the location and severity of incidents.

8   Conclusions

In order for effective eCollaboration it is necessary to consider how knowledge can be effectively shared, both amongst citizens and between those citizens and organisations. This task poses challenging difficulties, as the individuals involved may: be from diverse backgrounds; have no previous relationship; lack common understanding; provide varying quality input; and have disparate information needs. By examining the literature in the context of eCollaboration two critical factors emerge: the need to motivate users to contribute their knowledge and need to codify that knowledge to enable its interpretation and reuse. To address these issues the use of Web 2.0 and Web 3.0 techniques is proposed, and shown to provide potential benefit in the development of situational awareness for Emergency Response.

Acknowledgments. This work has been supported by the European Commission as part of the project WeKnowIt (FP7-215453).

References

1. Kes-Erkul, A., Erkul, R.E.: Web 2.0 in the process of e-participation: The case of organizing for america and the obama administration. Working Paper 09-001, National Center for Digital Government (October 2009)
2. Vitvar, T., Peristeras, V., Tarabanis, K. (eds.): Semantic Technologies for E-Government. Springer, Heidelberg (2010)
3. Krogstie, J.: Citizens, from consumers to prosumers: e-government services typologies revisited. In: Proceedings of the NordicCHI'06 Workshop User Involvement and representation in e-Government projects (2006)
4. Zappen, J.P., Harrison, T.M., Watson, D.: A new paradigm for designing e-government: web 2.0 and experience design. In: Proceedings of the 2008 international conference on Digital government research, pp. 17–26 (2008)
5. Cummings, J.: Knowledge sharing: A review of the literature. Technical report, The World Bank Operations Evaluation Department (2003)
6. Granovetter, M.S.: The strength of weak ties. The American Journal of Sociology 78(6), 1360–1380 (1973)
7. Macy, M.W.: Chains of cooperation: Threshold effects in collective action. American Sociological Review 56(6), 730–747 (1991)
8. Oliver, P.E., Marwell, G.: The paradox of group size in collective action: A theory of the critical mass. ii. American Sociological Review 53(1), 1–8 (1988)

9. Benbunan-Fich, R., Koufaris, M.: Motivations and contribution behaviour in so-cial bookmarking systems: An empirical investigation. Electron. Market. 18(2), 150–160 (2008)
10. Chen, I.Y.L., Chen, N.S.: Kinshuk: Examining the factors influencing participants knowledge sharing behavior in virtual learning communities. Educational Technology and Society 12(1), 134–148 (2009)
11. Cruickshank, P., Smith, C.F.: Self-efficacy as a factor in the evaluation of e-petitions. In: Parycek, A. (ed.) Proceedings of EDEM 2009 - Conference on Electronic Democracy, pp. 223–232. Austrian Computer Society, Vienna (2009); Written as part of the EuroPetition project
12. Palmisano, J.: A motivational model of knowledge sharing. In: Burstein, F., Holsapple, C.W. (eds.) Handbook on Decision Support Systems, vol. 1, pp. 355–370. Springer, Heidelberg (2008)
13. Hoadley, C.M., Kilner, P.G.: Using technology to transform communities of practice into knowledge-building communities. SIGGROUP Bull. 25(1), 31–40 (2005)
14. Chiu, C.M., Hsu, M.H., Wang, E.T.G.: Understanding knowledge sharing in virtual communities: an integration of social capital and social cognitive theories. Decis. Support Syst. 42(3), 1872–1888 (2006)
15. Peddibhotla, N.B., Subramani, M.R.: Contributing to public document reposito-ries: A critical mass theory perspective. Organization Studies 28(3), 327–346 (2007)
16. Tapscott, D., Williams, A.D.: Wikinomics: How Mass Collaboration Changes Ev-erything. Portfolio Hardcover (2006)
17. Beenen, G., Ling, K., Wang, X., Chang, K., Frankowski, D., Resnick, P., Kraut, R.E.: Using social psychology to motivate contributions to online communities. In: CSCW '04: Proceedings of the 2004 ACM conference on Computer supported cooperative work, pp. 212–221. ACM, New York (2004)
18. Arguello, J., Butler, B.S., Joyce, E., Kraut, R., Ling, K.S., Rosé, C., Wang, X.: Talk to me: foundations for successful individual-group interactions in online com-munities. In: CHI '06: Proceedings of the SIGCHI conference on Human Factors in computing systems, pp. 959–968. ACM, New York (2006)
19. Burke, M., Marlow, C., Lento, T.: Feed me: motivating newcomer contribution in social network sites. In: CHI '09: Proceedings of the 27th international conference on Human factors in computing systems, pp. 945–954. ACM, New York (2009)
20. Mann, T.: Library research methods: a guide to classification, cataloging and com-puters. Oxford University Press, New York (1993)
21. Nahapiet, J., Ghoshal, S.: Social capital, intellectual capital, and the organizational advantage. Academy of management review, 242–266 (1998)
22. Ardichvili, A., Page, V., Wentling, T.: Motivation and barriers to participation in virtual knowledge-sharing communities of practice. Knowledge Management 7(1), 64–77 (2003)
23. Hendriks, P.: Why share knowledge? the influence of ict on the motivation for knowledge sharing. Knowledge and Process Management 6, 91–100 (1999)
24. Novak, J., Wurst, M.: Supporting knowledge creation and sharing in communi-ties based on mapping implicit knowledge. Journal of Universal Computer Science 10(3), 235–251 (2004)
25. Stuckenschmidt, H., van Harmelen, F.: Information Sharing on the Semantic Web. Springer, Heidelberg (2004)
26. Lanfranchi, V., Ireson, N.: User requirements for a collective intelligence emergency response system. In: Proceedings of 23rd BCS HCI Group Conference (HCI 2009), September 2009. British Computer Society, Cambridge (2009)

Digital Certificate Management for Document Workflows in E-Government Services

Florin Pop, Ciprian Dobre, Decebal Popescu, Vlad Ciobanu, and Valentin Cristea

Computer Science Department, Faculty of Automatic Control and Computers
University POLITEHNICA of Bucharest, Romania
{florin.pop,ciprian.dobre,decebal.popescu,vlad.ciobanu,
valentin.cristea}@e-caesar.ro

Abstract. This paper presents a proper solution for a medium enterprise or public institution that enables easier management of the digital documents library and eases the common document workflows. The main problem addressed by the proposed project is the complexity of document workflows in public administration. Documents that need to be filled out and signed are always around us and often can cause problems and delays when poorly managed. With its characteristics, our solution eliminates all the inconvenient of the document workflows helped by the document library and workflows, while keeping the security part, now represented by hand signatures with the implementation of the digital signatures. The main benefit it brings to the client is that it automates the signing and approval process to any kind of document it uses inside or outside the company. The signature system allows signing on multiple levels (counter-signatures) and multiple signatures per level (co-signatures) for perfectly mimicking a plain document.

Keywords: e-Government, Electronic Services, Digital Certificate, Document Workflows, Public Key Infrastructure.

1 Introduction

In our days information security is a very delicate matter because more and more information is sent electronically and some of it requires special handling and quality standards. Public Key Infrastructures (PKI) offer the services required to meet those security and quality standards required [1]. PKI based applications bring those services to the end users enabling them to use digital documents as securely as old, plain authenticated documents.

The strength and security offered by system using PKI is proven by the multiple examples of existing solutions that are built the same way and are around us for some time. When reading an email you can be very sure that you are reading exactly what the other person wrote before hitting the send button, or you can be sure that no other person but you has read the information, features enabled by the PKI products, the user digital certificates. When accessing an online-banking account to operate a payment or money transfer or simply when buying anything on the internet, you are sure that your most sensitive credit card information is secure, thanks to the PKI

M.A. Wimmer et al. (Eds.): EGOV 2010, LNCS 6228, pp. 363–374, 2010.

enabled SSL certificates. When enabling a VPN connection to a remote place, all the network traffic flow is encrypted using digital certificates [2]. All the above examples stand as proof that the PKI is a viable option for our design [3].

For a public institution, implementing the proposed solution would certainly bring a boost in quality services. Currently, most trips to a public institution are viewed as a nightmare mostly because of the confusion around all the paperwork that needs to be filled out, the tight schedules of the institutions employees or even the waiting time at the counter especially around certain deadlines (income declaration deadline). Enabling citizens to digitally fill out all paperwork with good guidance and examples all available at a public digital library would help everyone a lot [4]. From the institution's point of view it would mean less paper document handling, susceptible loosing or damaging, less people at the counter bringing important cost savings.

For an enterprise, implementing the solution enables better management for internal documents. Again, dealing with digital versions of a document is much desirable than handling paper documents that are very prone to being lost, damaged and even forged [5]. Digital signatures evolved to a point where it is easier to forge a hand signature than forging a digital signature produced even by a medium security PKI environment in the same time eliminating the human factor in deciding if the signature is indeed authentic. Last but not least there is a small ecological point of view in the entire project by reducing paper usage in the company.

The rest of this paper is structured as follows. We first present the related work and critical analysis of similar solutions. In the next section we present implementation details of the pilot solution, presenting the technical issues and solutions. Next we present several obtained results and, in the final section, we give the open issues, improvements, future development and conclusions.

2 Related Work

In this section we present results for a solution similar to what we are trying to develop. We also present some options for a PKI deployment and compare them with Microsoft Certificate Services from Windows 2003.

Microsoft Office SharePoint Services (MOSS). This is the big brother of the actual chosen solution [6]. Unlike it, MOSS is not free and the extra features it brings do not compensate for the extra cost and complexity increase of both deploy and manage. One of those features that we could have been interested in would be the integrated document approval workflow and form providing out-of the-box solution for the main type of workflow needed in our application. However, being only able to work with .doc files represents a very big draw-back and ultimately led to not choosing this solution. A critical analysis of MOSS is presented in Table 1.

OpenSSL. It is an open source project, focused on developing a free, open, toolkit for SSL and TSL protocols and cryptography. At the core of the toolkit stands the "openSSL" command line application [7]. Even if it's not featured as a CA, "openSSL" can provide the services of a Certification Authority with the help of the integrated cryptographic library: Creation and management of public/private keys, creation of X.509 certificates, CRL files and PKI cryptographic operations (see Table 2) [8].

Table 1. Critical analysis of MOSS

Plus	Minus
Easy and quick to implement (out-of-the-box solution)	Only works for "Doc" documents.
Good workflow management, alerting and task management	Not free, unlike the simpler version SharePoint Services
	A lot more complex and more complicated to use.

Table 2. Critical analysis of OpenSSL

Plus	Minus
Free to use.	Designed and optimized for SSL and TSL protocols
Open Source	No user interface, hard to manage.
Still under development, offers not regular but often updates.	No OCSP supported
	Not really designed to be used as a CA in a PKI environment.
	Cannot deploy multiple tier architecture.

CertSign certificates and signing application: CertSign is a company that offers digital certificates for any person that wants a digital identity. Included in their offerings package there is an application that can be used for digital documents management. Implementation of this pseudo-solution in an enterprise would mean buying certificates from CertSign for every employee and use the application to perform operations on digital documents. In Table 3 there is a list with the summarization of this solution, pointing out the strengths and weaknesses.

Table 3. Critical analysis of CertSign

Plus	Minus
Good, secure PKI, trusted.	No workflow management
Good application for document signing, producing signatures in well known formats (PKCS#7) that can be processed with any other application	Expensive to implement and maintain (certificates need to be renewed annually at a certain price)
Offers certificates on USB tokens – provides good security	No control over issued certificates

CryptoBOT e-Workflow: This is a commercial application part of a bigger solution, also including a signing application (e-Crypt) and a Certification Authority server. It also works with other externally issued certificates. The e-Workflow solution is composed from two main components: *the server component* that is simply an application running on a designated computer that listens for workflow requests and *forward alerts to users* that need to take action in a workflow. Also interacts with the database for logging [9]. The client part is a more complex application where the user logs in and can see a list of documents and running workflows. The application seems complicated and difficult to use and manage and does not have an attractive look and feel. The critical analysis is presented in Table 4.

Table 4. Critical analysis of CryptoBOT e-Workflow

Plus	Minus
Can sign and integrate any type of document in a workflow	Server component is a simple desktop application.
Can define levels of urgency to documents in a workflow	Client application is difficult to use, does not have an attractive look and feel
Ability to insert comments along with the signature using the e-Crypt application	The alerting system is not based on email but on alerts being sent from the server to the client application, requiring the client app to be started at any time.
	Only works with e-Crypt application forcing you to buy the whole package.
	Saves the signature files in a proprietary format thus not allowing the signatures to be verified and validated outside the environment.
	As the web-site shows, it appears the solution has not been updated for a long time.

EJBCA. Another open source PKI Certificate Authority built on J2EE technology. It is advertised as a strong, flexible, high performance CA with a lot of features, ready to be implemented. One of the greatest advantages of EJBCA is that it is platform independent, being built on J2EE [10]. Also it supports most cryptographic algorithms and formats for certificates, revocation lists and it supports OCSP responders [11]. Actually, this is a very good alternative to Microsoft's Certificate Authority and could be a valid option in our infrastructure if the client requires it. The main problem with it, and the reason that we could chose Microsoft over it, is that being an open source project, there is no real official support or security patches that can be produced in little short time in case of an emergency.

Table 5. Critical analysis of EJBCA

Plus	Minus
Free to use	Management is done with a web application that depends on a web server.
Open source	No official tech support
Implemented as PKI in some word-class enterprises.	

3   Public Key Infrastructure Architecture

In this section is presented the proposed PKI architecture including both the hardware structure, with network design and components, and the software that all relies on. The target market for this project is made up by medium-large companies or public institutions that need or want to upgrade their digital document handling capabilities by proving means to safely and securely process documents without printing them. No doubt that every deployment site has a computer network in place and most probably has a way of managing users and services in that network and it is likely that it uses an Active Directory to achieve that.

As stated above, the solution focuses on providing digital signatures and/or encryption to internal or external documents, thus there is only one scope for all certificates issued and only a few types of certificates to be issued. Considering this information the best architectural decision would be in favor of a two-tier Certification Authority (CA) architecture consisting of one Root (Self-Signed) CA and one Issuing (Subordinate) CA. The layer missing is the policy layer, which is encapsulated in the Root CA. Three-tier architecture would have had sense if different issuing policies were needed: Issuing certificates for employees for internal use such as domain authentication requires a different policy than issuing certificates for clients and internal staff for document signatures and communication, resulting in a 3-tier architecture with one policy CA for each scope. If dealing with a larger scale institution multiple Issuing CA's can be added to the PKI for load balancing or availability issues.

Certificate Services relies on Active Directory Domain Services (AD DS) [12] providing multiple services such as: storage of configuration information, certificate publishing, and policy and authentication base. Even though it is possible to deploy the PKI in a non AD environment (by using only stand-alone CAs) it s highly discouraged, as it lowers the security standards. Certificate Services will work on most AD environments.

If the client's network does not contain an AD then we will deploy a single-forest, single-domain AD based using 2 Domain Controllers (Main and Backup). However if the company already has an AD environment, there are several cases we need to take into consideration. The simplest situation is a one-forest, one-domain AD, in which we simply deploy our CAs in the existing domain. Next, for a single-forest, multi-domain case, we need to decide, after consulting with the IT manager, where to deploy the CA. The most difficult scenario is the multi-forest, multi-domain AD, where we need to deploy one CA for each forest in the domain because the Enterprise CA cannot issue certificates to users outside the domain.

A very important point in the infrastructure's design is the physical foundation it has, the actual network that links all the systems and components together. The proposed network design consists of 3 separate sub-networks that define the modules described above. Security is the first and most important aspect when implementing the PKI (see Figure 1).

The attention has to be set on the CA network because it holds the most important piece of information: the Root Authority Private Key. The Root CA system is connected only to the Issuing CA (or CAs if more issuing CAs are used). The link is temporary and is used only when the Issuing CA has to renew the authority certificate or when the Root has to issue the Certificate Revocation Lists. Attached to the Root CA is the Hardware Security Module (HSM) [13], a piece of hardware specifically designed to safely store the Authority private key. The same module can be used for private key archiving, mandatory when the PKI is issuing encryption certificates. Other security measures regarding the Root CA range from disconnecting the server from the network to locking the physical machine locked in a safe, depending on the security needs of the particular implementation.

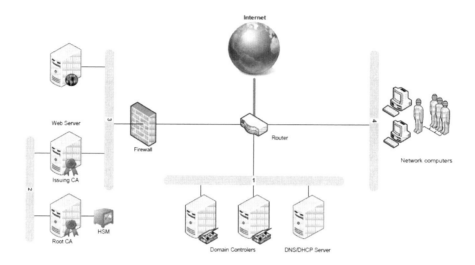

Fig. 1. Solution network design

Along with the CA computers, the sub-network could contain an IIS driven web-server responsible with certificate and Certificate Revocation List (CRL) distribution and certificate enrollment. Most interesting task is the certificate web enrollment scenario. This allows certificate issuing using Microsoft provided API using a customizable web page. This feature is active and usable by default when deploying Issuing CA server. It is not uncommon that the IIS server to be installed on the same machine as the Issuing CA, but for some cases, the separate machine is recommended.

The entire sub-network is protected by a hardware firewall, blocking all incoming connections excepting certificate or certificate validation requests. Requests for certificate enrollment are permitted only from private hosts and only for the specific computer running web certificate enrollment. The firewall becomes a single point of failure in this scenario but problems resulted by a failure can easily be overcome. If the firewall fails, two important services cannot be fulfilled by the CA network: certificate enrollment, certificate validation and distribution. First problem is easily solved by manually issuing a certificate based on a certificate request file and using the integrated Certificate Services administration console available on the Issuing CA server. Access to certificate distribution and revocation lists can be quickly regained if 2 separate machines are used for the Issuing CA and IIS server, and it's done by simply connecting the IIS server directly in the domain network. However, make sure to disable web enrollment (do not allow issuing certificates using web pages) while outside the protected network (see Figure 2).

If extreme security is needed, and if certificate issuing is not required to be real-time a different issuing method could be employed. This implies using a second web server, placed in the AD or services network, with the sole responsibility to receive the user requests for certificates, named Registration Authority (RA).

The users apply for a new certificate using the pages offered by the server. Upon completion, the server will create a certificate request and stores it. At specified time intervals, the Issuing CA polls the RA for the certificate requests, processes the requests internally and issues or denies the certificates. They are sent back to the RA and the users can pick up their certificates. The main advantage of this solution is that it offers further protection to the CA network by configuring the firewall to deny all packets originating from outside the CA network unless they are a response to a CA started connection.

Fig. 2. External enrollment method

Main elements in the network are the Domain Controllers that make up the Active Directory environment. Using a single domain controller would create a very disruptive single point of failure, in a place where down-time is not acceptable as all security policies, user accounts, network services are provided by the domain controllers. The easiest and cheapest way to reduce the risk of failure in this area is creating and maintaining a second, backup domain controller. Other services such as DNS, which are required by AD, will be installed in the network, if not already present in the institution.

The proposed architecture and network design benefits from two main architectural characteristics: Modularity and Extensibility. It is modular as it can be easily integrated in any network design the client might have, and it's extensible because it allows for quick upgrades or additions to any component.

4 A Pilot Implementation

Deploying the some of the basic components such as the domain controller, DNS server DHTP server or IIS server, from the proposed design is a common, if not trivial, task for all system administrators.

We propose an implementation totally based on Microsoft solutions. Before choosing it we carefully analyzed the pros and cons of it because this is a major architectural decision that would be hard to change.

The main disadvantage identified is that all components of the infrastructure are sealed (not open-source) and most of them require licensing (they are not free). On the other hand, being a security related project, it is important to keep up to date with any improvements or upgrades that appear in the field. Microsoft's constant development and upgrades of its products along with a high variety of good technical documentation are very good reasons to choose it. The good part about paying for it is that along with the product, you are also offered official support and guidance that can be extremely useful in emergency cases. Also the fact that a lot of companies use Microsoft technologies for they IT infrastructure made a decisive point in choosing Microsoft as a base for the infrastructure.

At the base of the PKI there is the "Certification Services" component from Windows 2003 Server. Certificate Services provides customizable services for issuing, managing and revoking digital certificates.

Even if it might seem like a trivial task, deploying a certificate authority requires several steps of planning and configuration even before installing begins. As the base operating system has been settled to Windows 2003 Server, we now know need to plan for the characteristics of the authority we are deploying.

After the installation is complete, we must check that everything is ok and complete the server's configuration by reviewing and updating registry information. All the steps for this configuration can be done via the CAs graphical interface, but using command line commands, enables building a batch that creates a good automation for a future configuration. The most important settings that are applied in this step are the CRL Distribution Points (CDP) and Authoritative Information Access (AIA) locations. The information will be added as an extension to every certificate issued by the Root CA, enabling end-applications using the certificate to locate the required information about the CRLs and parent Certificates. All commands are sent using the "certutil.exe" command line utility using the "–setreg" modifier.

```
certutil -setreg CA\CRLPublicationURLs
1:%windir%\system32\CertSrv\CertEnroll\%%3%%8%%9.crl
15:ldap:///CN=%%7%%8,CN=%%2,CN=CDP,CN=Public Key Services,CN=Services,%%6%%10
6:http://portal.cad-ca.net/crls/%%3%%8%%9.crl

certutil -setreg CA\CACertPublicationURLs
1:%windir%\system32\CertSrv\CertEnroll\%%1_%%3%%4.crt
3:ldap:///CN=%%7,CN=AIA,CN=Public Key Services, CN=Services,%%6%%11
2:http://portal.cad-ca.net/crls/%%3%%8%%9.crt
```

The commands above use define 3 locations for CDP and AIA parameters. Contents for each location is defined using a number resulted from binary representations of different types. The actual location address is defined after the ":" symbol and uses %x variables, which take their values according to the Certificate Services root certificate name and Active Directory names.

An Issuing certificate authority, unlike the Root Authority does not self-sign the base certificate. It uses a certificate signed by the parent authority (the Root CA in our case), thereby being granted the full trust of the Root authority.

The installation of the second and last CA server in out PKI, the Issuing CA consists of the same steps as the installation of the Root CA in consequence we not repeat them. There are however some subtle differences in the configuration process that we highlight and most important there is an additional step required for finishing the installation.

Only one additional step required in the post-installation configuration, consisting in creating a script that issues the Certificate Revocation Lists and then deploys them to all CRL distribution points defined. Deployment to active directory is made automatically when issuing them so in our case we still need to make them available on the website as stated in the configuration. To manage this with a script we need a public share on the web server. With the share in place, the script would look like the one presented below:

```
certutil -crl

copy /y %windir%\system32\certsrv\certenroll\*.cr? C:\_CA-Services\CertROOT

copy /y %windir%\system32\certsrv\certenroll\*.cr? \\portal\certificates
```

After all configuring of the CA is finished; we can start to plan for managing it. A great tool to quickly asses the PKI status is "PKI Health" available on Windows 2003 Resource kit available for free download on Microsoft's site. After installing it, it can be run with the command "pkiview.msc" from the Run menu. A healthy PKI should look something like the picture below.

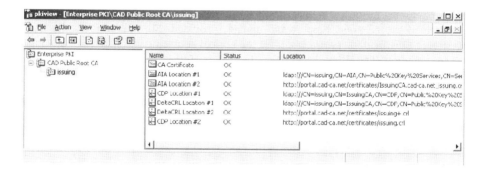

The application verifies if all the CA's in the organizations are working properly and if all CRL files are available at each location specified.

Another issue to be taken care of is configuring the CA for key archival in case of issuing certificates for key agreement purpose (data encryption). This is important because a lost private key will render all encrypted documents useless because there is no other way to decrypt them. In order to activate key archival, you need to create a Key Archival template, a Key Archival Manager and issue a certificate. The certificate is then set as Key archival certificate for the issuing CA enabling users who request encryption certificates to apply for key archival.

5 Open Issues

For Digital Certificate Management the open issues refer to main possible extensions of our application.

Security updates and improvements

Security is a sensitive matter and has to be treated with care. For the PKI area, improving the security policies for the CA basic functions, writing and maintain the practices to be followed in any situations should be under constant watch.

Better key archival methodology

When a PKI starts issuing certificates for encryption purposes it is mandatory that proper private key archival to be set up. The PKI currently employs basic key archival for those certificates but this is a certain area that could be improved.

Add OCSP responder support

The PKI currently relies on CRL for certificate status distribution which has some major disadvantages. Adding OSCP support would greatly improve this area. A good option to take into account could be the migration of the Issuing CA to Windows Server 2008 that has an integrated OCSP responder.

Analyze migration of Certificate Services to Windows 2008

The reasons of choosing Microsoft's platform for the PKI implementation is represented by the good support and updates provided. So, migrating to the latest version of Certificate Services would be the normal course of action. We already have the first white ball to Windows 2008 in the matter of the default OCSP responder but before making this important step all scenarios must be carefully analyzed.

Implement customized portal to issue certificates online

Issuing certificates online is a good feature of the current solution. But, the default user interface enabling the online certificate issuing could use a nice redesign so creating a new web-site, maybe integrated in the SharePoint portal could be a good future improvement point.

Automatic CRL issuing and distribution batch

The PKI administrator is now responsible with issuing the CRL certificates every time they are close to expiration and publish them to all CDP locations. The job is already half automated in the fact that all the operations are gathered in a command batch. To make it complete, a time schedule component should be added to the batch in order to remove all human factor from the equation. Having expired CRL's will cause all certificate validation to throw an error, stating that they cannot evaluate the certificate's validity, so the problem of always issuing timely CRL's is almost of critical importance.

6 Conclusions

We presented in this paper a solution that enables easier management of the digital documents library and eases the common document workflows. This solution can be used for public administration institution and for business environment. The document workflows in public administration are complex and the documents need to be filled out and signed are always around us and often can cause problems and delays when poorly managed.

The proposed solution eliminates all the inconvenient of the document workflows helped by the document library and workflows, while keeping the security part, now represented by hand signatures with the implementation of the digital signatures.

We consider that implementing the solution in a public institution would greatly improve the quality of services offered by eliminating the high waiting times for signatures and validations that increases dramatically with the number of people involved. Also, the project could improve document travel times, rendering document mailing useless in the same time as winning points for being a green project because it reduces the paper consumption.

The main benefit it brings to the client is that it automates the signing and approval process to any kind of document it uses inside or outside the company. The signature system allows signing on multiple levels (counter-signatures) and multiple signatures per level (co-signatures) for perfectly mimicking a plain document.

The future work can be oriented on security updates and improvements, better key archival methodology, analyze of migration to Certificate Services in Windows 2008, and implement customized portal to issue certificates online.

Acknowledgments

The research presented in this paper is supported by E-CAESAR, Centre for Advanced Studies on Electronic Services (http://www.e-caesar.eu), as a part of the project *EU-Services Directive for Romania - Point of Single Contact*.

References

1. Price, G.: Public Key Infrastructures: A research agenda. J. Comput. Secur. 14(5), 391–417 (2006)
2. Bou Diab, W., Tohme, S., Bassil, C.: Critical VPN security analysis and new approach for securing VOIP communications over VPN networks. In: Proceedings of the 3rd ACM Workshop on Wireless Multimedia Networking and Performance Modeling, WMuNeP '07, Chania, Crete Island, Greece, October 22, pp. 92–96. ACM, New York (2007)
3. Staff 2009. E-Government Developments. IWAYS 32(3), 136–187 (2009)
4. Chou, C., Cheng, W.C., Golubchik, L.: Performance study of online batch-based digital signature schemes. J. Netw. Comput. Appl. 33(2), 98–114 (2010)
5. Zhao, C., Gao, F.: The business process model for IT service management. WTOS 7(12), 1494–1503 (2008)
6. Antonovich, M.: Office and SharePoint 2007, User's Guide: Integrating SharePoint with Excel, Outlook, Access and Word (Pro). APress (2008)

7. Haron, G.R., Siong, N.K., Bee, T.F.: Translation of RFC 3820 to software codes using OpenSSL primitives. In: Sahni, S.K. (ed.) Proceedings of the Fourth IASTED international Conference on Advances in Computer Science and Technology, International Association Of Science And Technology For Development, Langkawi, Malaysia, April 02 - 04, pp. 109–114. ACTA Press, Anaheim (2008)

8. Nambiar, V.P., Khalil-Hani, M., Zabidi, M.M.: Accelerating the AES encryption function in OpenSSL for embedded systems. Int. J. Inf. Commun. Techol. 2(1/2), 83–93 (2009)

9. Sun, H., Ding, Y.: An Adaptable Method of E-Workflow Composition Based on Distributed Awareness. In: Ma, Y., Choi, D., Ata, S. (eds.) APNOMS 2008. LNCS, vol. 5297, pp. 503–506. Springer, Heidelberg (2008)

10. Pantaleev, A., Rountev, A.: Identifying Data Transfer Objects in EJB Applications. In: Proceedings of the 5th international Workshop on Dynamic Analysis, International Conference on Software Engineering, May 20 - 26, p. 5. IEEE Computer Society, Washington (2007)

11. Muñoz, J.L., Esparza, O., Forné, J., Pallares, E.: H-OCSP: A protocol to reduce the processing burden in online certificate status validation. Electronic Commerce Research 8(4), 255–273 (2008)

12. Policelli, J.: Active Directory Domain Services 2008, How-To. 1st. SAMS (2009)

13. de Souza, T.C., Martina, J.E., Custódio, R.F.: Audit and backup procedures for hardware security modules. In: Proceedings of the 7th Symposium on Identity and Trust on the internet, IDtrust '08, Gaithersburg, Maryland, March 04 - 06, vol. 283, pp. 89–97. ACM, New York (2008)

Software Reuse in Local Public Bodies: Lessons Learned in Tuscany

Vincenzo Ambriola and Giovanni A. Cignoni

Dipartimento di Informatica, Università di Pisa
Largo B. Pontecorvo, 3 – I-56127 Pisa – Italy
{ambriola,cignoni}@di.unipi.it

Abstract. In the last years, in Italy, *software reuse* has become an e-government hot topic. In this context, reuse is intended as the large scale adoption of software applications developed by local and independent initiatives. Due to the large autonomy of Italian local public administrations, reuse is preferred to centralized development of applications. The paper presents the experience of a three years regional project to manage and enforce reuse in Tuscany. The main result of the project is a *model for reuse* that emphasizes freedom to develop and freedom to adopt. The implementation of the model is based on a *reusable application repository* that lists and certifies software products that are available for reuse.

Keywords: software reuse, regional policies, application repository.

1 Introduction

IT developers are well aware about *reuse* of software components and libraries. They usually share the idea that the practice of reuse is strongly related to the achievement of economical, organizational, and product quality goals. In other words, software reuse is a mature domain with well known and assessed benefits.

In Italy, in the last years, software reuse has become an *e-government* hot topic, adding a new flavour to the meaning of the term. In this context, reuse aims to the large scale adoption of software products which have been locally and independently developed by (or for) public administrations (PA's). These software products are autonomously developed by initiative either of a single PA or of a small group of PA's. In this context, reuse is an interesting issue for private companies too. Usually, local IT companies are involved in implementation, technical support, and services supplied to public bodies. Sometimes, IT companies drive the development of software products with direct investments.

This paper describes the *model for reuse* developed for the Tuscany Region and currently adopted and enforced by a regional law. Section 2 introduces the characteristics and the needs of the Italian local PA's. Section 3 describes the reuse model and its implementation as a *reusable application repository* where reusable products are listed and described along three different dimensions: *availability*, *requirements*, and *quality*. The next sections present the details of the model according to this three

M.A. Wimmer et al. (Eds.): EGOV 2010, LNCS 6228, pp. 375–386, 2010.

dimensional approach: legal availability (Section 4), functional and technological requirements (Section 5), assured quality for reusability (Section 6). Section 7 presents the results of the experimentation of the model, since its introduction in late 2007 to now.

2   The Italian Context and the Tuscany Region Actions

In Italy, between 2000 and 2006 there has been a large financial investment aimed to introduce and exploit information technology in the PA's. In this period, usually called the "first phase of (Italian) e-government", more than 130 projects have been proposed by local PA's and financed by national programmes. In addition to the national initiative, a relevant number of other projects has been started and completed, some financed by regional programmes (36 in Tuscany), others as autonomous investments of local PA's.

A major characteristic of this phase was autonomy (a severe observer may say anarchy). Although national and regional programmes gave some directions, local PA's were completely autonomous in developing their technological solutions. This was a natural consequence of the large administrative autonomy that Italian local PA's have for political, historical, and cultural reasons. As it is easy to argue, in many cases autonomy is a source of difficulties and inefficiencies. However, autonomy is a fact that cannot be changed and that is not worth to discuss here. In the case of e-government, autonomy caused a scattered innovation, a large set of software applications, and, among these, a high level of replication.

For these reasons, after the first phase of e-government, reuse of developed applications has been identified as a way to:

- spread innovation to cover the whole Italian territory,
- enforce selection and integration between applications to decrease replication.

In this perspective, reuse is one of the principal guidelines of the Italian "second phase of e-government", currently on-going. As part of this strategy, reuse is ruled by the Italian law: every PA is required to make its owned software products available to any other PA's that request them.

Today there are many initiatives for promoting reuse in central and local Italian PA's. Details can be found at the National Centre for Information Technology in Public Administration, officially called *DigitPA* [1].

In Tuscany Region software reuse is part of the strategies for supporting innovation for local PA's. In 2005 the role of reuse has been formalized by a regional law that fosters the creation of a *Competence Centre* in charge of providing research and services. In May 2006, Tuscany Region has published a call for starting the *Regional Competence Centre for Reuse* (in Italian, *Centro Regionale di Competenza per il Riuso* or, in short, CRC.R [2]). In December 2006, this project has been assigned to the University of Pisa.

In November 2007 the first proposal of a model for reuse [3] was released and an experimental reusable application repository was set up. In December 2008 the experimentation phase ended and the model proposed by CRC.R was acknowledged and formally recognized in another regional law [4]. In July 2009 the model and its implementation were declared stable and Tuscany Region published a public call to assign the services for the management of the repository to an industrial supplier. The selection ended in late 2009 and the supplier is currently starting its services. Today, the model for reuse presented in this paper is a running reality.

3 The CRC.R Model for Reuse

The notion of software reuse belongs to Software Engineering since it was founded at Garmisch-Partenkirchen 40 years ago [5]. Today, *reusability* is a software property, defined by the standard IEEE 610 [6] – which is stable since 1990. The reuse process is the subject of another standard, IEEE 1517 [7]. The *reusable assets model* proposed by OMG [8] is the reference framework for describing reusable software objects, both components and complete products. In particular, the OMG model deals with the need of *listing* and *describing* software components in order to retrieving them and to make convenient their selection, use, change, and evolution.

Listing and describing are two foundational aspects of the model for reuse proposed by CRC.R. The model is based on a *shared portfolio of software applications*. Reuse of applications and their natural selection are enforced by publishing their characteristics on the portfolio.

To be effectively reusable, applications have to show specific characteristics. Our model identifies these characteristics along three different dimensions:

- *availability* for reuse, that copes with legal issues and reuse agreements;
- *requirements*, both functional and technological;
- *quality*, intended as assurance of good reusability characteristics.

The proposed model can be viewed as a specialization of the well grounded general OMG model based on listing and describing reusable assets. The shared portfolio of software applications is implemented by a web tool: the *Reusable Application Repository* (RAR) that provides the listing facility.

Listing a product in a publicly browsable repository makes the potential reusers aware about its existence. The next step is to make the interested reusers able to evaluate the product. Description along the three dimensions fulfils this goal and specializes the OMG general model according to the needs of our particular context.

Availability may seem obvious: the presence of a product in the repository should be in itself a condition of its availability. In practice, however, there are several degrees of availability. For instance, availability varies with respect to freedom to modify and redistribute the product, or with respect to the kind of bureaucracy that is needed to actually get the product. In the worst case, reuse may involve the adoption of services that can be provided by a unique industrial supplier.

Product features are the characteristics usually published in a repository for reuse. In this context, *requirements* have the classical meaning intended in software engineering: the requirements that the product fulfils (and not, as in standard commercial practice, the requirements that must be satisfied to install the product). Requirements must be declared in a way that eases comparison with other solutions, both on functional and technological perspectives. The former is related to the core needs of potential reusers. The latter is related to compatibility with already available platforms in the installation environment, like hardware, networking, operating systems, database servers, web servers, and so on.

The decision to invest in a reusable product is difficult. A detailed and fair presentation of product requirements is needed to ease the evaluation made by the potential reuser itself, but it is not sufficient. Some advice is needed from a trusted third part. The third dimension of the model, *quality*, fulfils this goal providing incremental certifications of product quality with respect to reusability characteristics.

To make practically viable the evaluation of reusable assets along the three dimensions of the model we implemented three different kinds of tools:

- licenses, to set public references for reuse agreements;
- specification schemas, to define a common grid to declare requirements;
- certification process, to express quality for reuse with respect to given criteria.

Figure 1 shows a graphical representation of the model. In the next sections we discuss in details the three central concepts of the shared portfolio and their implementation in the RAR.

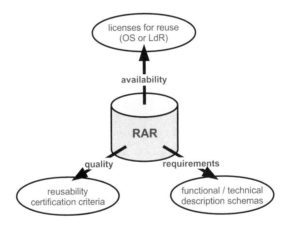

Fig. 1. The three dimensions of product description in the RAR

A last issue that the model must cope with is management of the reuse process among PA's in the Tuscany Region. In few words, reuse is promoted by building, managing, and rationalizing the portfolio of reusable applications of local PA's.

The regional level is a natural choice for implementing and managing the portfolio. From a quantitative perspective, it is large enough to make possible good rates of reuse with perceived benefits. From a functional point of view, software needs of the local PA's often depend on regional issues like laws, policies, and development programmes.

In a nutshell, governing reuse means a "well tuned development" of the portfolio that can be achieved by making systematic diffusion, selection, evolution, and integration of software products. A well tuned portfolio concurs to obtain the following benefits:

- scale economy in the development and management of software products;
- open market for services in support of products, competition among suppliers;

- better integration among services and applications;
- homogeneous and qualitatively selected services for PA's and citizens.

The portfolio must be functionally complete and technologically updated. It must be directly controlled by the local PA's that manage the development of products by means of reuse communities. IT companies participate to this development, either as providers of services or as co-investors.

The reuse community associated to a product is made of PA's and IT companies. While PA's manage the overall life of a product, IT companies are in charge of providing technological services and competences. Being the software products shared among customers, suppliers have to compete among them, and competition may only be based on economical efficiency and technological skills. In this perspective, our model aims at innovation both in the public and in the private sector.

4 Availability

As already stated, in general, there are several degrees of availability. The Italian context makes the issue even more complicated. According to the Italian law [9], a PA that owns a software application must provide it (with no charge) to any other PA that requests it for reuse. Thus availability seems granted. In practice, however, details of availability are ruled by licenses and agreements. And details often matter.

The most common solution implies that each reuse instance is formalized by a contract subscribed by the PA that owns the product and the PA that requests it for reuse. A standardization of this approach was proposed at national level, making available a common template. However, in practice the actual contracts modify, even substantially, the template clauses: the meaning of "reuse" changes drastically among products and even between distinct reuse instances of the same product. Moreover, this "availability on request" is a severe limitation to the practice of reuse: formalizing a contract each time produces a bureaucratic impedance to reuse.

A simpler and more practical solution is to release a product using licenses that explicitly guarantee its availability for reuse. The licences are few, written once and for all, they are public, and cannot be modified. Products can be securely distributed because they are protected by well known licenses. European Union Public License [10] or other Open Source (OS) licenses [11] are natural and for many reasons, auspicious choices to release products for reuse. CRC.R suggests them as a first choice.

However, considering what is required by the Italian law for reuse, it appears that OS licenses are more "open" than requested. This causes some fear and inertia by PA's. In particular, the chance that a product owned and paid by a public body may be used by anyone for profit (as many OS licenses grant) is interpreted by many legal officers as a bad use of public resources. In order to take into account these concerns, we defined an ad hoc *License for Reuse* (LR) [12].

The first goal of the LR is to make software products easy to reuse. The owner, by means of the license, makes available a product in all its components: source code, configuration data, executables, initial contents, documentation for developers, system administrators, and users. The first advantage is simplification: reuse no more requires an explicit request, an agreement to be reached, and a contract to be signed.

The second goal of the LR is to grant the maximum level of openness with respect to all misuse concerns. The product is fully available for evaluation by potential re-users and for study by suppliers, thus guaranteeing a fair competition between IT companies interested to provide assistance and development services. LR allows all subjects (public and private) to modify a product and to realize derivative products.

The LR protects the product against actions which are perceived as inappropriate for products developed with public funds. To avoid the product from being improperly marked in terms of ownership, LR states that all contributions to realize and evolve the product must be recognized, with a clear evidence of the period of their execution and their specific nature. In order to avoid uses of a product that could be out of the scope defined by Italian law, LR does not allow private companies to use it for internal applicative purposes or for providing commercial services in ASP mode.

To maintain availability for reuse, LR states that a derived product can be distributed if and only if it is released with the same license. Moreover, in an attempt to preserve quality, LR states that derived products can be distributed only if they are not been *degraded* in reusability. In principle, it may be hard to prove degradation of software quality. In the case of reuse, however, many cases of degradation are easily identifiable: introduction of dependencies from proprietary components, limitation of functionality, limitation of supported platforms, documentation out of sync.

Last but not least, the LR is not a translation of another license stemmed from a different juridical context (like many OS licenses), since it has been written with an explicit reference to the Italian law. This aspect, that at a first glance can be considered marginal, is actually of great relevance for Italian PA's.

Although LR shares many characteristics with other OS licences, it is worth to say that it is not an OS license: licensed products cannot be used by private companies and the non-degradation clause may be interpreted as a limitation to the freedom to modify a product. However, we believe that, even as a "less open" version of an OS license, LR can be effective to spread fundamental OS principles: availability of code and documentation, freedom to change, co-operative development, competition based on technological competence, product life cycle management in charge of the whole stakeholders community (users and developers).

In conclusion, availability of products must be defined by shared and efficient means. OS licenses are a good choice. Where PA's have concerns, the LR fills the gap. In any case, OS licenses, LR, common templates for reuse agreements, custom agreements, are different levels of availability that the RAR made manifest. Besides being a practical solution, the LR also meets the goal to mark a reference for the highest level of availability for reuse before OS licenses.

5 Requirements

The RAR is the tool that makes visible the characteristics of products that belong to the application portfolio. By browsing the RAR, local PA's can verify the convenience of adopting an existing software product before deciding to invest in the development or the acquisition of another one with the same functionality.

The description of the product characteristics must satisfy two needs: searching the products that fit the needs of a PA and selecting the best one in terms of convenience of reuse. The RAR dimension about requirements copes with the need fulfilment issue. Product requirements includes:

- *functional description*; the product must be clearly identified in terms of offered functionalities;
- *documentation*; product documentation must be available including manuals, software architecture, protocols, programming interfaces, test results, and so on;
- *platform dependence*; all dependencies relative to hardware, system and base software, libraries, web services, and the like must be explicitly stated.

To maximize the chance to compare products, requirements are given according to predefined glossaries and ontologies, which cover several level of functionalities, types of documentation and platform components types and versions. Only at the very last level of details, and just for additional documentation purposes, it is possible to fill free text fields or to add links to external documents.

Glossaries and ontologies are managed by CRC.R: they can be dynamically updated to satisfy the needs of the products listed in the RAR. The concept of shared portfolio means that the procedure to describe products requirements is shared too. This solution leads to a common description framework that enhances a fair and objective comparison among products. Managing the requirement description schema is a continuous and demanding task since currently it counts about 300 base functionalities organized in 30 classes. This effort is essential if we want to maintain a fair and shared base for describing and comparing reusable products.

When a public body decide to enrol a product in the RAR we require that a *product manager* be in charge of its evolution. The product manager has access to the RAR and is – formally – committed to a defined role, which includes:

- to fill and keep updated in the RAR all the fields of the product description;
- to give full support to reusers, even potential ones, for the evaluation of the product, providing access to further documentation and demo's.

Since the role of the product manager is demanding, it can be played by several professionals sharing or dividing their competencies. In our model, the role has been defined in order to foster the reuse of a product. Actually, a product that is not supported by human resources adequate to fill its description and to keep it up-to-date, is not reusable. The behaviour of a product manager is a good measure of the support given to a product and, thus, it is a practical indicator of its reusability.

Forcing the commitment of the product manager is a way to implement the notion of *product community*. The PA that originally developed and offered a product for reuse is naturally inclined to lead the community and to provide real resources to promote the reuse of *its* product. We believe that, for PA's, this strategy is politically rewarding. From another perspective, IT companies can invest in the support of a product to gain visibility and show competencies that can be useful for the bidding procedures that assign services and development activities.

6 Quality

The CRC.R identified a process of governing reuse that makes systematic availability, diffusion, selection, evolution, and integration of software products belonging to the shared application portfolio. LR and OS licenses satisfy the availability goal, product requirements description satisfies the diffusion goal. To fully cope with the selection issue the RAR provides a flexible *certification schema*.

Convenience of reuse of a given product is strictly related to assessment and visibility of its quality. Pragmatically, a product is economically convenient if, in addition to satisfying the functional needs of a PA, it is:

- technologically at the state of the art,
- fully documented,
- independent from specific infrastructures (or providers),
- capable to attract a user community that can share experiences and sustain its development.

The RAR description schema already eases autonomous evaluation of these characteristics. In addition, the RAR offers a certification process that implements fair product quality evaluation against common and – again – shared *criteria*.

To guarantee fair, efficient, and timely evaluation of the criteria for all the products enrolled in the RAR, the certification process is completely automatic. Criteria are coded in a set of predicates defined on the fields of the product descriptions. Predicates are periodically evaluated as batch processes (in practice every night). Automation is possible because descriptions of the products are given with respect to predefined glossaries and ontologies. Of course, the validity of a certificate relies on the accuracy of the data in the product description. Here it is worth to remember that description data are formal declarations expressed by a product manager which is committed to a well defined role.

Certification criteria can be tuned according to different perceptions of quality. For software products in general and, in particular, in the perspective of reuse, quality assessment changes in time and may depend on many factors:

- internal needs of PA's;
- services that have to be implemented, by law or by choice;
- availability of new technologies;
- changes in the hardware and software platforms;
- policies for the development of the information society.

The predicate mechanism gives a high degree of freedom in the definition of the criteria. Multiple sets of criteria may be active at the same time. Each set corresponds to a *certificate*, i.e. a symbol that identifies a quality or a group of related qualities of product that are important to highlight for the sake of reuse. For instance, it is possible to define criteria that:

- match the presence of a minimal set of functionalities for products that declare to belong to a given category;
- check the availability of important piece of documentation like licenses and manuals for users and technicians;

- count the number of declared reusing PA's to evaluate the product against a threshold of proven reusability.

The certification mechanism was designed by keeping in mind the flexibility needed to implement what was described as a "well tuned development of the shared portfolio". The initial set of products candidate to be enrolled in the RAR were quite far from having reusability qualities. On the other hand, being severe was not a good choice to start the reuse process. The adopted solution, that strongly relies on the certification mechanism, is to initially build certificates that can highlight the few qualities that somewhere are present. The severity level of certificates will increase in the future and will be used jointly with funding programmes promoted by Tuscany Region. For instance, a product may access a programme if it already has a given certificate or if the funded project aims to improve the product to a higher certificate. In other words, certification is a tool to foster competition and selection among the products of the RAR.

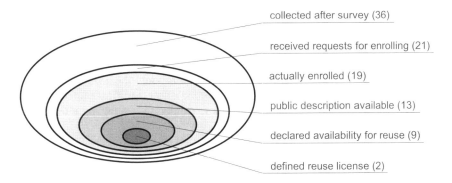

collected after survey (36)

received requests for enrolling (21)

actually enrolled (19)

public description available (13)

declared availability for reuse (9)

defined reuse license (2)

Fig. 2. The actual state of products today in the RAR

7   Results and Lessons Learned

In December 2006, when the CRC.R project started, a survey was made to collect a list of potentially reusable products. The survey started considering the set of projects funded by the Tuscany Region during the so called first phase of e-government, but it was – and still is – open to other contributes. In about three years of activity a total of 36 products were investigated. The results, in terms of products listed in the RAR today, are graphically summarized in figure 2.

To be enrolled in the RAR a product must submit a formal request. All 36 products which emerged from the survey were heartily invited to apply. However, only 21 actually showed up (and 2 of them did not finalize their application).

1st *lesson*: many public bodies are not ready to support reuse of their products.

Once enrolled, the product manager has to describe the product. The description may require some time and a bit of interaction with CRC.R to learn glossaries and ontologies and, maybe, trade modification and extensions of the shared sets. During the process, to avoid publication of partial data, the product is shown in the RAR in a "closed" state. Of the 19 enrolled products only 13 terminated the process and were opened to public.

2nd lesson: moving along the requirement dimension is difficult.

Looking at the 13 products with open descriptions, the current state of affairs is not encouraging yet. Functional descriptions are in general complete, but documentation and platform dependencies are often incomplete and sometimes missing. It is also a source of concerns the fact that, despite explicit evidence of incompleteness, the managers nevertheless decided to open the product to the public.

Moreover, we found some critical issues related to the declaration of availability for reuse. Of the 13 open products, 9 formally declared their availability, but under particular conditions which, unfortunately, were not specified. Only 2 products had a clear specification of terms and conditions. In many cases, problems about availability of a product were due to contracts with suppliers or project partners that were signed years ago, without taking into account future reuse.

3rd lesson: moving along the availability dimension is even more difficult.

The certification criteria actually in place are very forgiving: the mechanism is not yet used at its full power, and in practice the exploiting of the certification features of the RAR was postponed. From a practical point, simply by asking requirements and availability we triggered a severe selection.

Selection is a good thing, especially when it prevents future investments in badly supported products. However, many PA's were disappointed by this cruel reality and there are concerns about the opportunity to release official evaluations, especially when evaluations are mostly negative.

4th lesson: moving along the quality dimension is, at the moment, almost impossible.

Just by looking at these results one is inclined to conclude that reuse in Tuscany is an *impossible mission*. There are, however, a number of encouraging signals.

First of all, albeit the severe and demanding approach, in the first years of experimentation, our model attracted some new products. Considering the 13 opened products, 4 are new with respect to the initial set and are the outcome of independent projects. We believe that the candidate area for reuse is larger than expected and that the portion outside the regional programmes can express a significant number of products (about one third of the "good" ones).

It is proved that difficulties about availability of the product for reuse can be solved. One of the two products that clearly state terms and conditions for reuse has reached this result by exploiting the consultancy services of the CRC.R. The case was quite complex: the product was the result of several supplies for a PA, the ownership of the product moved from a private company to another; all parties have to agree about a license. The mediation of the CRC.R was needed to set a number of meetings and to prepare few formal agreements. At the end, a little effort and the general willingness to make the product available for reuse achieved the improvement goal.

From a more technical point of view, functional and technical descriptions of the product were demonstrated feasible too. Actually, products reached full descriptions whenever product managers (and the PA's they represent) were truly committed to invest a reasonable effort to retrieve their documentation and to interact with the suppliers to gather the needed information.

8   Conclusions

In Italy there are examples of different approaches to the promotion and management of reuse. For instance, several other Regions decided to adopt centralized solutions by setting up public owned software houses in charge to develop "standard" application portfolios. Examples in this direction are, for instance, from Piedmont [13] and Latium [14].

However, in Italy local PA's have large autonomy, in part granted by law and in part due to a deep rooted cultural attitude. The strategy adopted by Tuscany Region conforms to this situation: in the model proposed by CRC.R the Region acts as a "soft" coordinator of the application portfolio of its local PA's. The model developed and implemented by CRC.R was successful. With respect to the goal of enforcing selection among products, the three dimensions approach highlighted defects in the products that severely reduced their number. In few, while remarkable, cases it was also demonstrated that targeted product improvement, for instance along just one dimension, is feasible at reasonable costs.

Being the content and the evolution of our shared portfolio driven by natural selection more than by centralized decisions, we can say that the model fully respect *freedom to develop*: new (and hopefully improved) products will arise when the RAR will show the need for them. Moreover, to grant wide freedom to develop and distribute derived products, preference is given both to our LR or to any OS licence.

To respect the *freedom to reuse* by local PA's, the description and the certification schema allows a fair comparison among products, leading to responsible and well-aware choices for reusers. The preferred licenses concur to the capability to evaluate, study, and test products without explicit requests and before signing any contracts.

The model proposed by CRC.R has some costs: on the part of PA's and IT companies, to promote and support reuse of their products; on the part of the management of the RAR, since it requires some effort and high skills.

Costs have their part on the severe selection the products were forced to. However, selection was expected. We consider selection necessary and, by far, preferable to a huge catalogue of ghost products with confused descriptions and unreliable support. Costs are also a clear indication that investments to build reusable products need to be sponsored by regional programmes which have to recognize and award the products able to sustain comparison and selection.

References

1. DigitPA, National Centre for Information Technology in Public Administration, http://www.cnipa.gov.it/
2. CRC.R, Regional Competence Centre for Reuse, http://www.crcr.toscana.it/

3. Ambriola, V., Cignoni, G.A.: A Regional Experiment to Govern Reuse in Local Public Bodies. In: Proceedings of the 2nd International Conference on Methodologies, Technologies and Tools enabling e-Government, MeTTeG (2008)
4. Tuscany Regional Law 5913/2008: Istruzioni per le modalità del riuso di applicazioni e prodotti di amministrazione digitale nell'ambito della Rete Telematica Regionale Toscana e per la gestione del Catalogo Regionale per il Riuso (in brief, Instructions for reuse of software products and for management of the Regional Catalog of Reusable Products)" (2008)
5. Naur, P., Randell, B. (eds.): Software Engineering. In: Proceedings of NATO Science Committee Conference (1968)
6. IEEE, Std. 610.12: Standard Glossary of Software Engineering Terminology, Institute of Electrical and Electronics Engineers (1990)
7. IEEE, Std. 1517: Standard for Information Technology – Software Life Cycle Processes – Reuse Process, Institute of Electrical and Electronics Engineers (2004)
8. Reusable Asset Specification v. 2.2, Object Management Group (2004)
9. Italian Law 07/03/2005 n. 82: Codice dell'Amministrazione Digitale (Codex of digital administration) (2005)
10. European Commission: European Union Public License, IDABC, EUPL v. 1.1 (2009)
11. Open Source Initiative: List of Open source Licenses, http://www.opensource.org/
12. Cignoni, G.A., Ambriola, V., Flick, C.: Licenza di Riuso v. 1.00 (Reuse License), CRC.R, Dipartimento di Informatica, Università di Pisa (2008)
13. CSI Piemonte, http://www.csipiemonte.it/en
14. LAit, http://www.laitspa.it/

From Bureaucratic to Quasi-market Environments: On the Co-evolution of Public Sector Business Process Management

Bjoern Niehaves and Ralf Plattfaut

Westfälische Wilhelms-Universität Münster, European Research Center for Information Systems, Leonardo-Campus 3, 48149 Münster
{bjoern.niehaves,ralf.plattfaut}@ercis.uni-muenster.de

Abstract. Business Process Management (BPM) can be viewed as a set of techniques to integrate, build, and reconfigure an organization's business processes for the purpose achieving a fit with the market environment. While business processes are rather stable in low-dynamic markets, the frequency, quality, and importance of process change amplifies with an increase in environmental dynamics. We show that existing designs of public sector BPM might not be able to cope with the mounting frequency and quality of business process change. Our qualitative in-depth case study of a local government suggests that a major cause for such misfit lies in ineffective organizational learning. We contribute to the literature by applying the Dynamic Capability framework to public sector BPM in order to better understand shifts in market dynamics and their consequences for BPM effectiveness. Practitioners find a proposal for identifying, understanding, and reacting to a BPM-misfit and for developing effective BPM strategies.

Keywords: Public Sector, Business Process Management, Dynamic Capabilities, Resource-Based View, Qualitative Study.

1 Introduction

In the last decades, the environment of public sector organizations has shifted towards being quasi-market. In the 1980s a plethora of reform approaches, especially New Public Management (NPM), was geared towards putting the public sector in a market-like state. NPM constitutes a policy to create and to enhance the cost efficiency of governmental organizations as well as to create competition between public bodies. Numerous other drivers have amplified this development: the financial crisis puts high stress on local governments and forces them to compete with other municipalities for tax-payers and job-creating companies. Even the "death" of organizations is possible, mainly in terms of full depopulation or annexation. As a result, the environment of local governments has become increasingly dynamic and has undergone the major shift from "bureaucratic stability" to an, at least, medium dynamic quasi-market environment [7, 9, 27].

Business process change is a key concept in E-Government and public sector reform [36, 20, 25, 31, 2, 32, 24], yet initiatives regularly remain less successful than

M.A. Wimmer et al. (Eds.): EGOV 2010, LNCS 6228, pp. 387–399, 2010.

predicted. It appears to have established as common sense that municipalities need to reevaluate their business processes: cost-cutting, especially in times of the financial crisis, citizen and service quality-orientation, electronic government [25, 2], transformational government [15], and other reform concepts have called for a program of business process change in public organizations [31]. Most recently, for the case of European governments, the EU Service Directive requires the establishment of a single point of contact for all administrative services and provides yet another major impulse for business process change [38]. Despite repeated large efforts in practice and back-up from academia, ad hoc business process change initiatives show little sustainability and long-term success often lacks behind the grand expectations. Instead, "Neo-Weberian bureaucracies" [27] have established and the reform pendulum appears to swing back [3]. Against this background, we need theories which could be utilized to guide the development of BPM strategies in a shifting and increasingly dynamic market environment, such as the public sector?

Dynamic capabilities theory would view this problem as a mismatch between environmental requirements (based on markets dynamics) and an organization's institutionalized capability to change. Long-term competitive advantage is assumed not to lie in the stable resource configurations of an organization, but in its capacity to change [35]. Here, Dynamic Capabilities represent an organization's specialized set of resources and the firm's ability to integrate, build, and reconfigure operational capabilities for the purpose achieving a fit with the market environment. Business Process Management (BPM), understood as a Dynamic Capability, is especially concerned with integrating, building, and reconfiguring an organization's business processes for this purpose.

The advantageousness of BPM as a Dynamic Capabilities depends on the market environment. In a relatively static environment, business process change could be accomplished through the tacit accumulation of experience and sporadic acts of creativity: Ad hoc change. In such situation, investing resources into a large BPM apparatus appears to be unnecessary and far too costly [43]. While we observe a major shift of market dynamics from bureaucratic stability to a more dynamic quasi-market environment in the public sector, we start our investigation based on the assumption that public administrations did not cope with that environment change, that ad hoc business process change efforts are (still) the standard practice and that effective Dynamic Capabilities, BPM, are not yet successfully established. We assume further that 2nd order learning capabilities ('Do we manage our business processes effectively?', in contrast to 1st order learning capabilities: 'Are our business processes effective?') have not been developed and that, as a result, decisions on the establishment of BPM are not well informed, are lagged, and render many business process change efforts insufficient in terms of a market misfit.

Our paper is structured as follows: First, we will build a theoretical foundation, especially drawing from the Resource-Based View, and conceptualize BPM as a Dynamic Capability. The presentation of our research questions and hypotheses is followed by a discussion of the research methodology applied. Case study insights will be laid out and discussed in the light of implications for theory and practice. The last sections are concerned with limitations, future research, and conclusions.

2 Theory Background

2.1 Resource-Based View and Dynamic Capability Framework

The Resource-Based View of the firm describes organizations as collections of distinct resources and procedures. The term Resource-Based View of the firm (RBV) was coined by [39] and is widely and increasingly used in the IS domain to explain how information systems relate to the strategy and performance of an organization [37]. An organization is viewed as a collection of resources, while these are understood as "anything which could be thought of as a strength or weakness of a given firm." [39, p. 172] Resources consist of both capabilities and assets while capabilities can be regarded as repeatable patterns of actions [37] or coordinated set of tasks [13] – both: processes – that utilize assets as input [1, 13]. However, the RBV has been criticized for under-emphasizing market dynamics. For instance, Eisenhardt & Martin (2000) make the argument that long-term competitive advantage does not lie in stable resource configurations, but in the ability of a firm to adapt these to changing market environments. This argument applies best to dynamic market environments where there is "rapid change in technology and market forces, and feedback effects on firms" [35, p. 512].

Dynamic Capabilities aim at aligning resources with a changing market environment. While the dynamic capability framework is becoming increasingly important to E-Government [19] as well as public sector research [12], scholars have originally differentiated two types of capabilities from one another: (1) Operational Capabilities are geared toward the operational functioning of the organization [43]. In this paper, we will understand *Operational Capabilities* as the ability of an organization to perform a coordinated set of tasks, utilizing organizational assets, for the purpose of the operational functioning of the firm (cf. [43, 40, 13]). (2) Dynamic Capabilities, on the other hand, have been conceptualized by Teece et al. [35, p. 516] as "the firm's ability to integrate, build, and reconfigure internal and external competences to address rapidly changing environments." Other conceptualizations emphasize the nature of these capabilities, "a learned and stable pattern of collective activity through which the organization systematically generates and modifies its operating routines in pursuit of improved effectiveness." [43, p. 340] Some authors stress the hierarchical relationship between the two types of capabilities: "Dynamic capabilities build, integrate, or reconfigure operational capabilities." [13, p. 999] In this paper, we will thus understand *Dynamic Capabilities* as the firm's ability to integrate, build, and reconfigure operational capabilities for the purpose achieving a fit with the market environment.

The advantageousness of Dynamic Capabilities depends on the market environment. Dynamic Capabilities typically require long-term investments and commitments of specialized resources [40, p. 993], they create costs. Helfat & Peteraf [13, p. 1002] find: "Improvements in the functioning of a capability derive from a complex set of factors that include learning-by-doing of individual team members and of the team as a whole, deliberate attempts at process improvement and problem solving, as well as investment over time." However, in a relatively static environment change of operational capabilities could be accomplished through the tacit accumulation of experience and sporadic acts of creativity: ad hoc change. Here, Dynamic Capabilities appear to be unnecessary, and if developed may prove too costly to maintain [43, p. 340]. "Learning, change, and adaptation do not necessarily require the intervention of 'dynamic' capabilities as intermediaries." [13, p. 998] The alternative of change in Operational Capabilities through institutionalized Dynamic Capabilities is thus non-institutionalized ad hoc change (1st order learning mechanisms; see Figure 1; BPM-relevant concepts are already included (in brackets) while being referred to later).

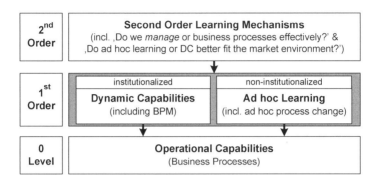

Fig. 1. Dynamic Capabilities and Learning (adapted from [43])

2.2 Business Process Management as Dynamic Capability

BPM is a key concept in E-Government Research. The approach has its roots in Business Process Reengineering (BPR) and Total Quality Management (TQM). On the one hand, the concept of BPR emerged within a Massachusetts Institute of Technology's management research program that examined the role that IT would play in organizations in the 1990s [26]. While both BPR and TQM have in common the focus on improving organizational processes, TQM on the other hand is considered a rather incremental, evolutionary approach aiming at continuous improvement [14]. However, most literature in business process research recognizes that both concepts have to be viewed as complementary integral parts of a process-oriented strategic management system [4, 5, 6, 11, 14]. Against this background, BPM can be viewed as a management approach that applies concepts of both punctuated and incremental change. BPM can be seen as a set of recurring projects that aim at the continuous change of organizational procedures (for focus on change aspects see, for instance, [18], [21], [30]). The focus of BPM projects can range from purely organizational to more technical perspectives [28, 33], the latter especially in the course of information systems (IS) implementations (for an overview on the relationship between IS and process innovation see [34]). Against this background, business process management became a key concept in E-Government research [31, 2] and has been intensively discussed, for instance, at the international conferences on Electronic Government (EGOV, for instance, [36, 20, 25, 32, 24].

BPM can be viewed as a Dynamic Capability. On the one hand, literature discusses a plethora of concrete Dynamic Capabilities, such as product development [8, p. 1106], alliancing [43, p. 347], acquisition [8, p. 1109], and research & development [43, p. 340]. Moreover, a bundle of Dynamic Capability examples relate closely to

BPM, for instance developing manufacturing processes [8, p. 1110], "restructuring" [43, p. 340], "re-engineering" [43, p. 347], quality improvement [43, p. 347], and the ability to adapt "operating processes through a stable activity dedicated to process improvements" [43, p. 340]. On the other hand, process-oriented literature views BPM as "a structured approach to analyze and continually improve fundamental activities such as manufacturing, marketing, communications and other major elements of a company's operation" (for example, [42, p. 64]). Further, a business process is "converting inputs into outputs. It is the way in which all the resources of an organization are used in a reliable, repeatable and consistent way to achieve its goals" (for example, [42, p. 64]). Against the background of these noticeable commonalities, we review BPM from a Dynamic Capability perspective, including a re-understanding of operational capabilities as business processes: we define *Business Process Management* as a set of techniques to integrate, build, and reconfigure an organization's business processes for the purpose of achieving a fit with the market environment. Here, a *business process* refers to the performing of a coordinated set of tasks, utilizing organizational assets, for the purpose of the operational functioning of the firm. BPM is thus not identical with the concept of Dynamic Capabilities, but it is, among others, one Dynamic Capability. The argument is that there are several other functions (Dynamic Capabilities), such as R&D or alliancing, which are (traditionally) not covered by BPM. As a result of reviewing BPM in the light of this theoretical perspective, we are able to build upon and embrace the vocabulary, rich theory, and comprehensive findings of the Dynamic Capability framework for studying and explaining the discussed public sector BPM issues.

3   Research Question and Hypotheses

This paper seeks to address the following research questions while building on the Resource-Based View and Dynamic Capability framework:

(1) How developed is BPM as a dynamic capability in local governments? Here, we aim to explore whether BPM is more or less effective with regard to the purpose of achieving a fit with the market environment and how well the set of techniques to integrate, build, and reconfigure an organization's business processes is established.

(2) Does the existing BPM (or does it not) fit the market environment? We study if a match between BPM as a Dynamic Capability and the quasi-market environments of the public sector exist. The results of the first research question are reflected against (shifting) dynamics in the environment of local administrations. We assume that there will be a market-BPM-misfit due to a dynamic capability adaption lag.

(3) In case of a market-BPM-misfit in local governments, why does it exist? We assume a misfit between environmental dynamics and public sector BPM as a result of 1) organizational culture, 2) deficient organizational learning, especially 2nd order learning (see again figure one), and 3) financial and regulatory restrictions. Our first hypothesis is based on an expected lag in the perception of decision makers: on the basis of a history characterized by bureaucratic stability, decision makers might expect only little change or dynamics in the future. Zollo & Winter [43, p. 346] argue, decision makers might put "different bets [...] on the strategic importance of change in the future", based on their past experiences in a then stable bureaucratic environment.

The second hypothesis proposes that local government organizations feature deficient learning mechanisms that prevent the creation of dynamic capabilities. Business processes are still changed in an ad hoc manner (1st order learning). As a result of only little organizational skills in establishing dynamic capabilities, 2nd order learning capabilities ('Do we manage our business processes effectively?' or 'Do ad hoc learning or Dynamic Capabilities better fit the market environment?') have not been developed and that, as a result, decisions on the establishment of BPM are not well informed which leads to suboptimal results. Our third hypothesis is based on the idea that local governments might find that building BPM as a Dynamic Capability was not affordable. This may be due to the financial situation (especially in the recent financial crisis) and/or due to public sector regulations resulting from the financial situations: budget consolidation plans, for instance, often allow only material investments (such as bridges, buildings etc.) and not in IT, human resources, or organizational/process improvement.

4   Research Methodology

Method Selection and Case Setting. In order to test our research model, we chose to conduct an in-depth case study and to tie in with the rich tradition of qualitative IS research (for instance, [17, 22]). The organization studied is a local government in the western part of Germany. With more than 6,000 employees working in about 50 departments, the organization is one of the larger public bodies in Germany. The organization department is formally responsible for BPM activities which are typically associated with re-engineering and/or IT implementation. With a budget deficit of more than 100 Million Euros, the financial situation of that local government is severe. On the one hand, top management expects BPM to contribute to consolidating this deficit, to cut costs and to improve efficiency. On the other hand, the organization faces other challenges, such as E-Government or the EU service directive [38] which require BPM to contribute to achieving major structural changes and increased effectiveness.

Data Collection. The period of intensive data collection lasted from October 2009 to December 2009, with a prior wave serving the purpose of selecting adequate cases studies with regard to the research question (June 2009 to September 2009). We employed multiple data collection methods in order to exploit the synergetic effects of combining them via triangulation [16, 41]. Three sources of evidence are included in our analysis: focused individual interviews (primary method), direct observations, and documentary information.

- Focused Individual Interviews. The primary sources of evidence are interviews with the key actors in the organization's BPM efforts. Ranks of interview partners included, for instance, head BPM unit, head IT department, head organization department, as well as members of quality management, accounting and others. When contacting our case study organization, we were directed to a contact person, habitually the one formally responsible for BPM. Being the first experts interviewed, they connected us with other significant actors in each setting. Regarding the interviewee selection, we thus followed a purpose-driven snowball sampling approach [29]. As a result, twelve interviews were conducted leading to a total of

1,250 minutes of interview time, and more than 94,000 words of transcript. An interview thus lasted more than 1 hour in average.

- Documentary Information. Several materials produced by or about the organization were incorporated as supplementary source of evidence. For instance, business process documentation, organization charts, press articles, internet sources, research reports, project documentations, minutes of project meetings, or other reports helped us to reconstruct the case study setting in great detail.
- Direct Observations. We were able to directly observe the settings and relevant events throughout a total of 16 site visits. This included, for instance, observing the working procedures and analyses of BPM tools applied. These direct observations yielded additional understanding of the case study setting.

Data Analysis. A total of more than 20 hours of interviews, equating to 94,430 words of transcript, were included in the analysis. As initial step, the first two authors coded the data individually for any relation to the variables of our hypotheses, while all interview data was reviewed in the light of available documentary information and of direct case observations. Afterwards, the resulting coded data were contrasted among the first two authors' perspectives. In case of unresolved differences, the third author was consulted. Then, the codes were interpreted and structured with the help of the theoretical framework. Here again, if no consensus was achieved among the first and the second author, the third party was involved for conciliation. The interpretation of data and refinement of theory elements were highly recursive and formed a continuous interplay [23]. Such approach yielded the advantage that, both, the authors' understanding of the case findings as well as the refinement of theory gradually improved. A set of questions was presented to the interviewees and was then followed by a comprehensive open discussion.

5 Findings

The study yielded the following major findings: (1) Shift of Market Dynamics: Our study suggests an increase of environmental dynamics. In the past, local governments faced a rather stable bureaucratic environment in which competition between administrations was uncommon. Therefore, there was no need for changing the government's resource configuration. However, since the advent of NPM the environment became increasingly dynamic and developed towards a "quasi-market" [7, 9]. Especially the EU services directive has been a main driver for competition and dynamics. This directive is one reason why "*we should not forget that local administrations are competitors*", as a middle manager in our case put it. Subsuming, the politically desired shift towards higher dynamics was realized and is recognized by a large share of the organization's middle management.

(2) Market-BPM-Misfit: Local governments did not react on the shift in market dynamics and did not adapt their BPM adequately. From a theory point of view, a sustained increase in market dynamics should lead to the introduction of Dynamic Capabilities, here BPM. More dynamic markets demand for more frequent business process change, and such change is of greater strategic relevance. However, our case shows that only a small part of the organization posses the necessary knowledge to adequately react on the dynamic shift. BPM initiatives are either still in the very early

phases or have already failed. Until now, our case organization shows only a very few adapted business processes and no institutionalized BPM capabilities. One department (independently) started a BPM project and purchased a BPM tool while the formally responsible department is still planning to kick-off "their" BPM project. Only through our study, BPM managers got to know that the BPM suite they are planning to purchase is the very same already introduced in the other department. Moreover, the majority of departments and divisions yet ignore the topic of process change. As a result, we could not find an integrated BPM strategy, although the reform pressure is very high for our case organization. A middle manager (organization department) stated that *"We are still at the very beginning; so far, we did neither touch our processes nor change our organizational structure."*

(3) Organizational Culture: Although there was basic agreement on the increase in market dynamics, we could not observe large commitment. Many employees regard change as *"not my business"*, as it was said by one interviewee. Moreover, our data suggests that the culture of the organization is locking the organization in the status-quo – or even striving for the status-quo ante. Although the need for change is well recognized, little change has effectively happened. As for the case of the EU service directive, the organization was aware of it since 2004. The final implementation was due by end of 2009, but the case organization is still struggling with the implications: Necessary changes of business processes are not fully implemented or lived.

(4) Organizational Learning: Organizational learning would be a key issue in implementing BPM that fits the changing environment. Parts of the administration studied acknowledged the importance of training and learning-before-doing. However, there is no comprehensive BPM-related training or program established yet. Still, multiple employees are trained in rather obsolete techniques while maintaining outdated qualification schemata. Hence, the administration is yet in the beginning. However, some middle managers already acknowledge the problem of missing know-how. Moreover, they anticipate that this problem is growing due to the demographic change in the workforce of the organization. In the past, several reforms, e. g. in the local government reform 1967-1978 where municipalities were incorporated by others, led to an increase of dynamics as well. However, the case organization anticipated that the phase of increased dynamics would only be short-term. Thus, they changed their processes, i.e. their operational capabilities, in an ad-hoc manner, often with the help of external consultancies. Hence, neither 1st nor 2nd order learning capabilities exist: The local government studied does not employ adequate measures to learn new methodologies and capabilities to face the rising dynamics in its environment.

(5) Financial and Regulatory Restrictions: Several financial issues prevent the case organization to build up BPM for institutionalizing process change. Due to the financial crisis and the structural change of the economy, the local government faces severe financial problems. So far, it has to follow a strict budget consolidation plan which impedes new investments in IT or in human resources. Hence, managers and employees acknowledge that the financial situation is a great barrier to adopting BPM and to adapting both the Operational and the Dynamic Capabilities to the changed environment: *"We should do more, but this is impossible due to our budget situation"* and *"Our financial situation is a huge constraint for introducing BPM"* were statements by two of the middle managers. The financial situation is a significant problem

for building Dynamic Capability for business process change. A structural problem results: Immediate investments would be advantageous, but are not possible today.

6 Discussion

Implications for theory. Our findings both answer the research questions and confirm – at least partially – the hypotheses stated above. Both literature and our study reveal that the dynamic of the environment of local government has shifted in the near past. Local administrations nowadays face a more and more market-like setting – a quasi-market. Hence, theory suggests that investing in dynamic capabilities (here: BPM) is necessary to constantly adapt the operational capabilities to the environment. However, we can observe that, at least for the case of BPM as a dynamic capability, this investment has not been accomplished so far: The case study data suggests that the administration studied has not implemented BPM as a dynamic capability yet. These results give answers to the research questions 1 and 2: First, we found that BPM is not developed to a great extent. In fact, the organization is still at the very beginning. Second, our assumption of a misfit between BPM and the environment has been confirmed. However, our study also reveals that adaption to environmental changes has happened in the past. Then, several occasions led to peaks in market dynamics. The environment of local public sector organizations stayed comparably low-dynamic, but, e. g. through the above mentioned annexation reform, a peak of dynamic occurred. The organization had to react on a peak with process changes. These process changes occurred, though with a small lag of time, with the help of ad-hoc 1st order learning mechanisms or the use of consultancy services. Both options are valid reactions on the change of market dynamics. However, in today's situation of a persistent market dynamic shift, we observe both a lagged and a less intense reaction in form of process change. Although theory suggests that institutionalization of dynamic capabilities in terms of BPM is a necessary reaction to a sustained market dynamic shift, the case organization stays in the old pattern and tries to adapt business processes using ad-hoc measures (see Figure 2). These findings help to answer the third research question (Why does a BPM-market-misfit exist?) where we posed three hypotheses. First, the usage of old behavioral patterns is well documented in the literature on BPM in public sector organizations [10]. The culture of the organization is not ready for change and hinders the institutionalization of Dynamic Capabilities as decision makers put wrong bets on the importance of change [43]. Second, the organization neglected the necessity to install learning-before-doing for BPM. New methodologies are not incorporated which hinders the development of BPM: Business processes are still changed in an ad hoc manner (1st order learning). Third, the organization faces financial stress. As BPM is not regarded as high priority there is a tendency to cut down necessary change projects. Also, an organization-wide BPM strategy is considered too costly. Thus, the organization's only measure to change processes is to stay with ad-hoc learning mechanisms as even external consultants are not affordable. To sum up, all three reasons play together and result in a misfit of market dynamics and BPM as Dynamic Capability.

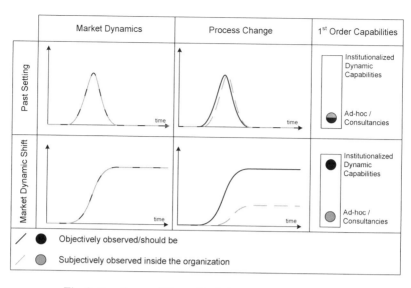

Fig. 2. Reaction on different Variations in Market Dynamics

Further contributions to theory result from our conceptual work. BPM can be understood as a Dynamic Capability in terms of an extended RBV while business processes can be seen as Operational Capabilities applied by an organization to "make a daily living". A business process is a coordinated set of tasks, utilizing organizational assets, for the purpose of the operational functioning of the organization. BPM is an institutionalized first order capability: A set of techniques to integrate, build, and reconfigure the organization's business processes for the purpose of achieving a fit with the environment. Thus, BPM consists of the resources held in stock in order to be able to change the organization. The way BPM is established in an organization depends, as costs come into play, heavily on the dynamics in the environment. A high-velocity market demands a different BPM organization than, e. g., a medium-dynamic market. We showed that this perception is valid by employing it in the public sector. Moreover, with this contribution we elaborate on market dynamics shifts. In our setting, the environment of the organization studied became more dynamic and this resulted in a need for changes of the dynamic capability.

Implications for practice. Local administrations should assess and evaluate their BPM with the background of the corresponding market environment. So far, reform policies seem to be not successfully implemented. Apparently, local governments did not react on the persistently changed dynamics in their market environment. However, as theory suggests they should build up the Dynamic Capability of BPM in order to adapt their business processes to fit the setting. As a first step, a reflection on BPM activities of local administrations seems to be considerable as this would shed some light on the status-quo (2nd order learning). A BPM maturity assessment [28], extended to understanding of market environments, could help to show potential paths towards a more market-adequate BPM.

Limitations. Our results are limited by certain factors. First, we studied only one local administration. Thus, it could be difficult to generalize from this setting to other organizations in other sectors or regions. However, we believe that the organization studied is typical for many western local governments and that its situation can, therefore, be transferred rather well. While we acknowledge that other countries and cultural communities will face different problems, the consideration of the issues mentioned in this study provides a first valuable starting point.

Future research. Both our limitations and contributions show potentially fruitful areas for future research. First, future research could strive for comparing our results with other public sector organizations and, thus, help to make the results generalizable. Second, future studies could transfer our results into other sectors: Viewing BPM as a Dynamic Capability helps to understand, explain, and address the misfit of organizational BPM and the environment. Third, studies could enhance the understanding of BPM as a Dynamic Capability. One example is to study related concepts as workflow management or enterprise content management in the DC framework.

7 Conclusion

We set out to understand BPM as a Dynamic Capability (in the notion of the RBV) as means to adapt an organization's business processes to its environment. We especially focused on the influence of market dynamics on BPM and, moreover, on shifting market dynamics. We posed hypotheses why public sector BPM does not fit the corresponding environmental demands. In order to evaluate our hypotheses, we conducted an in-depth qualitative case study in a local administration. This case study suggested a market dynamic shift. Moreover, we could show that a misfit between BPM as a Dynamic Capability and a dynamic environment exists: The organization studied did not institutionalize BPM to a sufficient extent. We could confirm all three hypotheses: Apparently the organization neglects a long-term market dynamic shift, has not built adequate 1st and 2nd order learning capabilities, and is financially stressed so that projects to build BPM are cut down. Our results might potentially be generalized to local administrations in western countries.

References

1. Amit, R., Shoemaker, P.J.H.: Strategic Assets and Organizational Rent. Strategic Management Journal 14(1), 33–46 (1993)
2. Becker, J., Algermissen, L., Niehaves, B.: A procedure model for process oriented e-government projects. Business Process Management Journal 12(1), 61–75 (2006)
3. Christensen, T., Lægreid, P.: Transcending new public management: the transformation of public sector reforms. Ashgate Publishing (2007)
4. Corbitt, G.F., Christopolus, M., Wright, L.: New Approaches to Business Process Redesign - A Case Study of Collaborative Group Technology and Service Mapping. Group Decision and Negotiation 9(2), 97–107 (2000)
5. Davenport, T.H.: Need radical innovation and continuous improvement? Integrate process reengineering and TQM, Planning Review 21(3), 6–12 (1993)

6. De Bruyn, B., Gelders, L.: From TQM to BPR – Two case studies in personnel administration. International Journal of Production Economics 50(2-3), 169–181 (1997)

7. Dunleavy, P., Hood, C.: From old public administration to new public management. Public Money & Management 14(3), 9–16 (1994)

8. Eisenhardt, K.M., Martin, J.A.: Dynamic Capabilities: What are they? Strategic Management Journal 21(4), 1105–1121 (2000)

9. Ferlie, E., Pettigrew, A., Ashburner, L., Fithgerald, L.: The New Public Management in Action. Oxford University Press, Oxford (1996)

10. Gulledge, T.R., Sommer, R.A.: Business process management: public sector implications. Business Process Management Journal 8(4), 364–376 (2002)

11. Harrison, D.B., Pratt, M.D.: A methodology for reengineering businesses. Planning Review 21(2), 6–11 (1992)

12. Harvey, G., Skelcher, C., Spencer, E., Jas, P., Walshe, K.: Absorptive capacity in a Non-Market Environment: A knowledge-based approach to analyzing the performance of sector organizations. Public Management Review 12(1), 77–97 (2010)

13. Helfat, C.E., Peteraf, M.A.: The Dynamic Recource-Based View: Capability Lifecycles. Strategic Management Journal 24, 997–1010 (2003)

14. Hung, R.Y.-Y.: Business Process Management as Competitive Advantage: A Review and Empirical Study. Total Quality Management 17(1), 21–40 (2006)

15. Irani, Z., Elliman, T., Jackson, P.: Electronic transformation of government in the U.K.: a research agenda. European Journal of Information Systems 16(4), 327–335 (2007)

16. Jick, T.D.: Mixing qualitative and quantitative methods: triangulation in action. Administrative Science Quarterly 24, 602–611 (1979)

17. Kern, T., Willcocks, L.: Exploring relationships in information technology outsourcing: the interaction approach. European Journal of Information Systems 11(1), 3–19 (2002)

18. Kettinger, W.J., Teng, J.T.C., Guha, S.: Business Process Change – A Study of Methodologies, Techniques, and Tools. MIS Quarterly 21(1), 55–80 (1997)

19. Klievink, B., Janssen, M.: Realizing joined-up government - Dynamic capabilities and stage models for transformation. Government Information Quarterly 26(2), 275–284 (2009)

20. Kubicek, H., Millard, J., Westholm, H.: Methodology for Analysing the Relationship between the Reorganisation of the Back Office and Better Electronic Public Services. In: Traunmüller, R. (ed.) EGOV 2003. LNCS, vol. 2739, pp. 199–206. Springer, Heidelberg (2003)

21. Lyytinen, K., Newman, M.: Explaining Information Systems Change: A Punctuated Socio-Technical Change Model. European Journal of Information Systems 17(4), 589–613 (2008)

22. Mingers, J.: The paucity of multimethod research: a review of the information systems literature. Information Systems Journal 13(3), 233–249 (2003)

23. Myers, M.D.: Qualitative Research in Information Systems. MIS Quarterly 21(2), 241–242 (2008)

24. Niehaves, B., Malsch, R.: Democratizing Process Innovation? On Citizen Involvement in Public Sector BPM. In: Wimmer, M.A. (ed.) EGOV 2009. LNCS, vol. 5693, pp. 245–256. Springer, Heidelberg (2009)

25. Palkovits, S., Wimmer, M.: Processes in e-Government - A Holistic Framework for Modelling Electronic Public Services. In: Proceedings of the 2nd International Conference on E-Government, Prague, Czech Republic (2003)

26. Peppard, J., Fitzgerald, D.: The transfer of culturally-grounded management techniques: the case of business process reengineering in Germany. European Management Journal 15(4), 446–460 (1997)

27. Pollitt, C., Bouckaert, G.: Public management reform: a comparative analysis, 2nd edn. Oxford University Press, Oxford (2004)

28. Rosemann, M., de Bruin, T., Power, B.: A model to measure business process management maturity and improve performance. In: Jeston, J., Nelis, J. (eds.) Business Process Management, pp. 299–315. Butterworth Heinemann, Burlington (2006)

29. Salganik, M.J., Heckathorn, D.D.: Sampling and Estimation in Hidden Populations Using Respondent-Driven Sampling. Sociological Methodology 34(1), 193–240 (2004)

30. Sarker, S., Sarker, S., Sidorova, A.: Understanding business process change failure: An actor-network perspective. Journal of Management Information Systems 23(1), 51–86 (2006)

31. Scholl, H.J.: The dimensions of business process change in electronic government. In: Huang, W., Siau, K., Wei, K.K. (eds.) Electronic government strategies and implementation, pp. 44–67. Idea Group Pub., Hershey (2004)

32. Scholl, H.J., Fidel, R., Liu, S.M., Paulsmeyer, M., Unsworth, K.: E-Government Field Force Automation: Promises, Challenges, and Stakeholders. In: Wimmer, M.A., Scholl, J., Grönlund, Å. (eds.) EGOV. LNCS, vol. 4656, pp. 127–142. Springer, Heidelberg (2007)

33. Stohr, E.A., Zhao, J.L.: Workflow automation: Overview and research issues. Information Systems Frontiers 3(3), 281–296 (2001)

34. Tarafdar, M., Gordon, S.R.: Understanding the Influence of Information Systems Competencies on Process Innovation: A Resource-Based View. Journal of Strategic Information Systems 16(4), 353–392 (2007)

35. Teece, D.J., Pisano, G., Shuen, A.: Dynamic Capabilities and Strategic Management. Strategic Management Journal 18(7), 509–533 (1997)

36. Traunmüller, R., Wimmer, M.: Directions in E-Government: Processes, Portals, Knowledge. In: Proceedings of the International Workshop On the Way to Electronic Government in Conjunction with DEXA, Munich, Germany, September 3-7, pp. 313–317. IEEE Computer Society Press, Los Alamitos (2001)

37. Wade, M., Hulland, J.: Review: The Resource-Based View and Information Systems Research: Review. Extension and Suggestions for Future Research, MIS Quarterly 28(1), 107–142 (2004)

38. Weber, I., Sure, Y.: Towards an Implementation of the EU Services Directive with Semantic Web Services. In: 12th International Conference on Business Information Systems, Poznan, Poland, pp. 217–227 (2009)

39. Wernerfelt, B.: A resource-based view of the firm. Strategic Management Journal 5(2), 171–180 (1984)

40. Winter, S.G.: Understanding Dynamic Capabilities. Strategic Management Journal 24(7), 991–995 (2003)

41. Yin, R.K.: Case Study Research: Design and Methods. Sage Publications, London (2003)

42. Zairi, M.: Business process management: a boundaryless approach to modern competitiveness. Business Process Management Journal 3(1), 64–80 (1997)

43. Zollo, M., Winter, S.G.: Deliberate learning and the evolution of dynamic capabilities. Organization Science 13(3), 339–351 (2002)

Process and Data-Oriented Approach for Bundling Corporate Reporting Duties to Public Authorities – A Case Study on the Example of Waste Management Reporting

Armin Sharafi, Petra Wolf, and Helmut Krcmar

Technische Universität München, Chair for Information Systems I17, Boltzmannstr. 3,
85748 Garching bei München, Germany
{armin.sharafi,petra.wolf,krcmar}@in.tum.de

Abstract. Recent bureaucracy cost surveys identify the issue of high financial burdens on government authorities and businesses. These burdens are often caused by a large number of regulations. Therefore, the purpose of process bundling is to redesign Business-to-government processes in a way that eliminates redundant contacts, but still fulfils all reporting duties. The application of our bundling approach shows benefits by replacing similar reporting duties. One possibility to do so is to reuse available data on the business side for numerous duties. This research illustrates an approach for identifying opportunities for data reuse and thus to reduction of bureaucracy costs. The case study applies this approach for environmental reporting duties. After surveying reporting duties in Germany, similar reporting duties with overlaps concerning their content and process were selected. Finally, opportunities for data reuse were derived and implemented.

Keywords: eGovernment, process bundling, data reuse, reporting duties, bureaucracy costs.

1 Introduction

In the fall of 2008, the Federal Statistical Office in Germany identified 9.324 reporting duties between businesses and government in Germany. The expenses on the business side for complying with these duties are measured by using the *Standard Cost Model (SCM)* [1, 2]. The SCM "is designed to measure the administrative consequences for businesses. Today, it is the most widely employed method to do so" [2]. According to the SCM report, the German economy is charged with an annually amount of approximately 47.6 billion Euros, with 22.5 billion Euros due to national regulations and approximately 25 billion Euros based on EU- and international regulations [1]. As a result, businesses are dissatisfied with public administrations. They accuse their local as well as national government for being insufficiently transparent and following antiquated structures [3]. It is considered indispensable to counteract this appearance by reorganizing current administrative processes [4]. Lenk

M.A. Wimmer et al. (Eds.): EGOV 2010, LNCS 6228, pp. 400–411, 2010.

for example [5] states "without process reorganisation it is impossible for information technology to provide help, regarding quality improvement and more efficiency […]" (translated from German into English). As a prerequisite for efficient eGovernment, process integration therefore attempts to achieve common process objectives like simplifying and speeding up administrative procedures, improving quality, enabling new tasks or the extension of opportunities for democratic participation [5]. In order to exploit potentials for modernization, it is necessary to examine underlying processes of Business-to-government (B2G) contacts like reporting duties [6]. Only focusing on organisation-wide processes can enable aspired customer orientation [7].

Since process reorganisation and process integration have already proved powerful approaches to improve efficiency in the industry domain, they are also applied to the public administration domain. The goal is to lower bureaucratic expenses, especially for businesses. Therefore, we analysed the area of environmental reporting duties in order to identify B2G-process structures which might benefit from process bundling. This led us to the following research question: What different types of reporting duties exist in the area of waste disposal management and how can they be bundled? At the same time, the underlying processes will not be modified in their nature. The intention of the process bundle construction can be summarized by contributing to the public welfare (lower bureaucracy costs), improving transparency and protecting the environment from unnecessary pollution.

The paper is structured as follows: Chapter two describes the approach for B2G-process analysis and process redesign. Afterwards, chapter three introduces the application domain environment by giving some facts about the waste disposal sector and illustrating three *environmental reporting duties*: the *German electronic waste notification system (eANV),* the *electronic pollutant release- and transfer register (E-PRTR)* and *the environmental statistic report.* We propose these processes for bundling. Chapter four illustrates the application of the approach in the investigated domain. The emphasis is on the content and the data flow between businesses and administration. At the end of this section we show, how the three processes can be bundled by reusing reporting data generated in one process. In section five and six, our findings are discussed and implications for further research are derived.

2   Method and Approach

We conducted a case study on environmental reporting duties of companies. This was done to identify groups of processes, which might be suitable for bundling. The aim is to provide a more efficient way of reporting a specific type of environment data to government. For being able to decide on "bundling candidates", it was essential to define how B2G processes should be integrated. Based on the assumption that there are many groups of similar reporting duties - referring to the data being reported - criteria for bundling were chosen to measure similarity of reporting duties. This includes their structure and data content.

The applied approach adopts basic ideas and principles from well-established models used for business process management and reengineering within the industry sector [8] [9] [10]. Each approach aims at integrating processes and is mostly composed of four steps. Gaitanides [8] distinguishes between the steps *process identification, process analysis, process design* and *process implementation*. He describes the objectives of a goal-oriented management of the value-added chain (process bundle) regarding quality, time, costs and customer satisfaction. Geier [10] illustrates his procedure model by enumerating the steps *determination of project objectives and content, analysis of the current situation, development of a target concept and implementation*. Becker et al. [9] try to improve the existing process organisation constantly and incrementally through their concept of "Continuous Process Management". This concept is organized through a cyclic arrangement of its sub processes *executing phase, analysis, goal-redefinition phase, modelling phase and business process reengineering phase* [9]. To sum up, first the approaches aim at identifying relevant processes as input for further detailed analysis. The *process analysis* achieves a more detailed structuring of the main process by identifying sub-processes. The following step attains a target *concept or design of a new process bundle*. This is built up from the examined single processes by meeting the main reengineering goals like e.g. improvement of the chronological and logical order. The step *implementation* gives advice how to realize the desired construction [11].

Following the illustrated approaches, we identified basic structures of each model and designed an analysis approach. It is customized for its application to domains, which are characterized by a high number of reporting duties (e.g. environment). The approach is structured as follows (see Fig. 1) [12]:

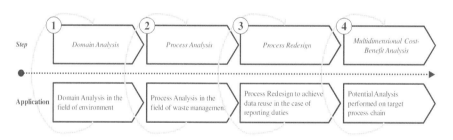

Fig. 1. Process model for process redesign for reporting data reuse (Source: own illustration based on [12])

The derived approach consists of four successive steps. Firstly, it is necessary to define and to analyse the environment of the considered domain (Domain Analysis). Results are B2G processes, which might benefit from bundling. In the second step, selected processes have to be analysed in detail (Process Analysis). This is carried out to prove how they might be redesigned to achieve a more efficient state. Step three points out the issue to redesign processes in order to reuse reporting data (Process Redesign). In the final step, it is important to evaluate the potential benefit of the redesigned process (Multidimensional Cost-Benefit Analysis). Details of the individual steps are described in the course of the following case study.

3 Application Domain Environment

3.1 Industry Sector Waste Disposal

This chapter gives some facts to get in touch with the domain waste disposal in Germany. Today, the waste disposal sector covers about 240.000 employees and a volume of about 50 billion Euro [13]. Since year 2000, the quantity of dangerous waste raised from 15 to 20 million tons a year. Therefore, 250.000 companies and 320 authorities create and deal with round about 10.000 records of proper waste management, 3 million data sheets and 14 million dock receipts concerning the waste notification system [13]. According to the Federal Statistical Office, 214 reporting duties were identified, including the identified processes in the Domain Analysis, concerning the industrial sector "wastewater, waste and miscellaneous waste disposal" [14]. Through a detailed consideration of each duty regarding corresponding bureaucracy, it is possible to allocate specific costs to 177 reporting duties. Summed up, these processes cause bureaucracy costs of 176,947 million Euro [14]. This amount demonstrates the relevance to measure cost reduction. After a brief explanation of 3 processes analysed in our case study, the Process Analysis explores the listed processes in more detail. The goal is to identify concrete links as possibilities to combine them to integrated process bundles [12].

3.2 German Electronic Notification System (eANV)

All involved actors (producer and transporter of waste, waste disposal contractor, authority) have to fill out the "waste data sheet". Besides data about type and quantity of waste, it also contains further data about participating waste disposal partners and the actual transaction [15]. This includes the collection, transport and disposal of waste with an obligation to keep records for the disposal of dangerous waste [16]. So, every involved actor has to keep certain regulations which dictate to create, complete or store corresponding waste data sheets [15]. According to this, many procedures seem to appear regularly with almost the same task. The content of the forms is quite similar, although there are different formats (paper based forms etc.), levels of detail and partially different addressees. The electronic waste notification system (eANV) will soon be introduced in Germany (legislative basis § 45 Abs. 2 KrW-/AbfG). The currently non-automated procedure of the waste notification system often causes redundancies, inconsistencies concerning the data collection and as a result avoidable administrative costs. In order to reduce the appearing paper logistics, eANV aims at substituting paper forms through an electronic way of data registration. The technical infrastructure for running eANV is provided through a central platform. It enables a uniform nationwide data exchange between all involved actors [16]. This will contribute to improvements of the organisation of the nationwide waste disposal and to reduce data exchange efforts [17].

3.3 E-PRTR

The aim of the introduction of the European Pollutant Release and Transfer Register (E-PRTR) is to contribute to transparency and public participation in environmental decision-making [18]. The E-PRTR contains important environmental data from industrial facilities within the EU. It replaces and improves upon the previous European Pollutant Emission Register (EPER). The new register contains data, annually reported by some 24.000 industrial facilities covering 65 economic activities across Europe, including several industry sectors like waste and waste water management [18]. Each facility which fulfils certain criteria (e.g. exceedance of determined threshold values) has to report to E-PRTR including data about the amounts of pollutant releases to air, water and land as well as off-site transfers of waste and of pollutants in waste water from a list of 91 key pollutants. Data are mostly reported annually by the respective facility to responsible authorities [18]. The technical support is a nationally data acquisition software (BUBE), which is used by the operator to transfer reportable data online to PRTR, followed by automated transmission [19]. This reporting duty is important for our considerations, because waste producers and waste disposal contractors have to notify type and amount of waste.

3.4   Environmental Statistic Report Waste Disposal

According to the German environmental law (UStatG) § 1, statistics have to be raised for purposes of environmental policies and fulfilling European and international reporting duties. UStatG § 2 demands for statistics which include inquiries about waste disposal, waste which has to be proved for disposal, disposal of certain waste (UStatG § 5), etc. Especially concerning the waste disposal, § 3 paragraph 1 registers data from involved facilities requiring admissions for disposing waste. That is why for example type, amount, nature and origin of the handled waste have to be reported every year. Number, type and location of the facility have to be reported every two years to the responsible authority. The same companies (waste producers and waste disposal contractors) are obliged to report. This is just a small excerpt of the UStatG to display the content of the considered law and its resulting reporting duties [12]. In order to enable electronic processing of reporting duties, the need for an online-available reporting system arised. Therefore, the *eSTATISTIC.core* system was built up in 2005, developed by national statistical agencies. It provides the possibility for companies and authorities to report automatically data online [20].

4   Application of the Analysis Approach

The following sections describe the four phases of the approach in detail as well as its application in our use case.

4.1   Domain Analysis

The development of the Domain Analysis was inspired by the Needs Driven Approach (NDA) [21]. NDA aims at analysing and representing collaboration, for example by identifying involved actors, interactions, tasks or examining legislative frameworks, work processes, used tools or data storages [21]. In this case, the NDA is used to collect B2G contacts in the domain environment. This is required to identify similar reporting duties as a basis for bundling. The Domain Analysis is important, because following steps are based on its results [22]. In order to identify domain knowledge within the Domain Analysis, a feasibility study [12] developed an approach to identify and collect reporting duties and B2G processes. This includes the completion of four steps called *task analysis, (high-level) work process analysis, interaction analysis* and *selection of candidates for the process analysis* [12].

First of all, the *task analysis* delimits the field of investigation and identifies reporting duties. Therefore, we studied legislative specifications concerning information and licensing requirements related to environmental protection or environmental authorities. To gain necessary domain knowledge, we used sources like process descriptions (e.g. eGovernment sites), legal documents (e.g. reporting forms) and regulations (e.g. government service catalogues), organisational and task plans, workflow diagrams, descriptions of the IT architecture as well as reports concerning the fulfilment of the designated reporting duties. The result is a list of B2G processes.

In the course of the *work process analysis,* we categorized identified B2G processes according to their structure or process type (reports, applications, data requests). Further, they were classified referring to their content - i.e. type of substance being reported on (e.g. waste, waste water) and object of reporting (e.g. quantity, pollutants) - on the basis of a domain model for environment compliance [23]. Finally, we ended up with a systematized composition of the investigated processes.

Thirdly, the *interaction analysis* aims at identifying all actors involved in a B2G contact. It is based on the analysis of documents, especially legislative specifications and forms used in the domain environment.

Step four, the *selection of candidates for the Process Analysis,* uses previous results to select suitable bundling candidates for the design of efficient eGovernment processes. All processes are filtered according to certain attributes (similarity of actors and structure), until a set of processes remains [25].

At the beginning of the research, relevant data about the regarded domain were collected. Relevant in this case are e.g. involved actors on the business side, involved authorities, data to be supplied by the business side, type and frequency of reporting duty, medium, interface and information system for data transfer, legal basis and bureaucracy costs of analysed B2G reporting duties. The collection of relevant data is often difficult, because sub-processes are mostly supported by different IT-systems with different actors and institutions involved in the process. Additionally, most information sources are not digital. That's why problems concerning format inconsistencies occur [9].

According to the analysis phase of the "Continuous Process Management" process [9], collection of required information includes three steps: Firstly, data sources for domain information need to be identified, accompanied by the provision of a corresponding access to the implied information. Secondly, gathered data has to be prepared for its syntactical suitability, for example, to obtain a common data format (e.g. XML). The last step proves the semantic correctness of the collected information. This is done to get an information base, which is suitable for following process evaluation [9]. As a result, the analysis in the field of environment identified 339 processes between business and administration [24]. The structured collection of these processes in a process data library allowed us to select processes for bundling by means of specific criteria (e.g. common laws, involved actors) [25]. Fig. 2 represents a part of the library.

No.	Processes domain environment	Classification			Involved actors (business)			Involved actors (government)			Legislative basis
	name of process/ reporting duty	type (request/re-port/no-tification)	type of substance	object	producer	transporter	waste disposal contractor	Licensing authority waste	Licensing authority for facility	State Office for Statistics	
34	waste report to PRTR (Pollutant Release and Transfer Register)	report	waste	quantity, type of waste	X		X		X		European PRTR Regulation (E-PRTR-VO VO 166/2006 EU)
89	environmental statistic report waste disposal	report	waste	quantity, type of waste			X			X	German Environmental Statistical Law(UStatG)
239	verification about the disposal of (dangerous) waste	notifiation	waste	quantity, type of waste	X	X	X	X			Ordinance on Waste Recovery and Disposal Records (Nachweisverord nung - NachwV)

Fig. 2. Process data library – part of the resulting list through the Domain Analysis (Source: own illustration according to [12])

By using these criteria, it was possible to form groups with content-related similarities. Those similarities can occur e.g. in form of concerned type of substance, involved actors or corresponding reporting period etc. The largest group - referring to the type of substance to be reported on - turned out to be reporting duties concerning the waste disposal management sector. Three of them deal with type and quantity of waste and are therefore similar in their content. All characteristics mentioned before help to determine a pre-selection of processes. Analogies regarding the classification through certain criteria, like type of substance or regulations by law as well as the consideration of the results of a document analysis, result in a small variety of adequate process bundling candidates. This includes *eANV, E-PRTR* as well as *environmental statistic report.*

4.2 Process Analysis

The Process Analysis investigates selected processes. The purpose is to reveal possibilities for their integration towards desired process bundles. This step is also based on principles of the NDA, e. g. by performing *(detailed) work processes* and *tools employed* [21]. In addition, the Process Analysis uses the concept of standardized data profiles to enable a structured procedure. This allows an examination of regarded processes according to predefined characteristics.

The *(detailed) work process analysis* aims at identifying starting points and requirements for the integration towards process bundles through a detailed functional description. Techniques used for that purposes are interviews and business process analysis with a functional as-is profile. At the same time, the process costs are analysed according to the SCM model. Besides this, the degree of routine (number of possible appearances) and the complexity concerning the number of possible variants or length of the process will be recorded.

The *analysis of the used tools* identifies the current IT support including the analysis of interfaces for data exchange as well as transport protocols and data formats. Information required for the Process Analysis comes from legal regulations, public documents, product and system descriptions, interfaces specifications and interviews [12]. Detailed descriptions of processes form the starting point for the following construction of process bundles. Identified processes are analysed regarding their organisational, technical and legal characteristics to derive bundling requirements. The outcome of the Process Analysis consists of three current state profiles. Their investigation (concerning possibilities for connecting them by comparing attributes) ends in a target state profile. The functional conception explores factual requirements, whereas the technical conception examines relevant criteria out of the field information and communication technology [12].

4.3   Process Redesign for Reporting Data Reuse

The proposed procedure of redesigning is inspired by the well-established "Structured Analysis" by DeMarco [26] which contains methods for an analysis of systems. Comparable approaches exist by Ross and Schomann [27] or Mac Menamin [28]. Following their guidelines, the current state of a system has to be raised through an analysis of existing processes and systems first. Secondly, necessary changes have to be defined to develop the desired model [26]. The goal is to replace the redundancy of reporting duties through the reuse of available data. According to [29], process bundling is concerned with changing or redirecting flow of data between activities without changing the actual content of the data.

Every facility producing or dealing with dangerous industrial waste has to report data according to the *eANV*, *PRTR* and *environmental statistic report waste disposal* to the responsible authority (see Fig. 3). The linkage between environmental statistic report waste disposal and eANV takes place through aggregation of reportable data, involved actors which occur in form of the waste disposal contractor and content of the reportable data. The combination of PRTR and the statistic report waste disposal can also be implemented through aggregation of reportable data, involved actors in form of waste producer and waste disposal contractor and content of the report. From the functional point of view, the realization of the process redesign intends to automatically accumulate data.

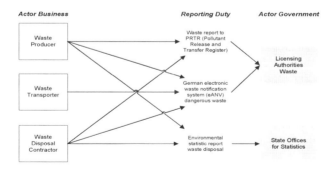

Fig. 3. Three reporting duties of companies (Source: own illustration)

Fig. 4 illustrates the data flow between eANV, PRTR and statistical reports as well as the integrated data flow between all involved actors. This BPMN process model shows the combined and integrated overall process. The data of the *verification conducted on hazardous waste (eANV) report* is used to generate the *PRTR report* of the producer and the waste disposal contractor. The eANV data are also used for the preparation of *statistical reports* of both actors. All reports will then be sent in a further step to the appropriate authority. The goal of the design of the technical implementation is to provide as much support as possible for the economy to fulfil reporting tasks demanded by government.

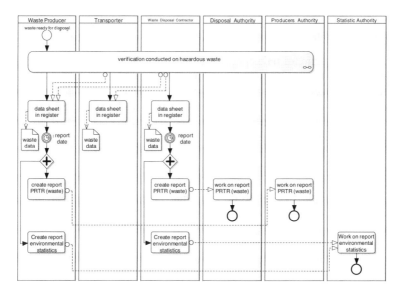

Fig. 4. Target process bundle PRTR – eANV – environmental statistic report (Source: own illustration according to [12])

Finally, the benefit of bundling is analysed by the use of the Multidimensional Cost-Benefit Analysis. The objectives of the procedure are summarized as reduction of the administrative expense for businesses as well as improvement of data quality. The process bundling simplifies the procedure of reporting data to responsible authorities. Actually, different reporting duties with similar content are often processed in different divisions of a company. This separate processing of data leads to unsatisfactory results in the form of inconsistent reports and resulting contradictions. Through reuse of data, reliability of reported data will be improved and fault rates reduced. Although SCM is not able to give evidence about the detailed saving potential, according to estimations of experts, the proposed approach will pay off. Therefore, it is qualified to reduce bureaucracy costs. But a point of criticism concerning the SCM is that it is not a method to calculate actual administrative costs, but rather delivers estimates, using mean values. So, highly efficient or inefficient procedures will not be taken into account. As a result, the appliance of the SCM can provide distorted results [30]. To obtain actual data, it is necessary to perform benchmarks including all companies [31]. Furthermore, there is no statement expressed about the benefit but about costs [32].

5 Conclusion

Companies suffer from high bureaucracy costs incurred by reporting duties to authorities. This paper describes the application of an approach for process bundling, in order to reduce efforts for businesses. The main target in this case was to bundle several individual processes by reusing reporting data. The application of the approach is illustrated in form of a case study. It is based on and developed by the consideration of common principles of process management and reengineering. The appliance in the selected domain demonstrates a way to reduce bureaucracy costs, as well as to achieve common eGovernment objectives. Individual processes were integrated, which provides advantages such as reduced costs, transparency and higher efficiency. The appliance of the approach in this case was possible because of many overlaps between reporting duties. First, we conducted a Domain Analysis to identify reporting duties in the domain and to filter relevant and similar ones for bundling. The next step (Process Analysis) explored selected processes in detail according to defined characteristics. Then, suitable reporting duties are redesigned with the goal to replace redundancies of reporting duties through the multiple use of available data (Process Bundle Determination). Finally, we evaluated the benefit of the reporting duty bundle to derive the potential of the combined process. The use of the approach also showed the necessity for iterative customizations to meet the requirements of the domain. We identified three reporting duties dealing with data about waste and consolidated them into one integrated process. This illustrates potential to contribute to the reduction of bureaucracy costs.

6 Outlook

Despite of some restrictive factors (application of the approach in only one domain), the model represents its potential by the combination of several suitable processes in order to reduce bureaucracy costs. This is getting more and more important to consolidate public finance and to improve the capacity to act through more flexibility [4]. Since the approach has been applied in the domain environment, the applicability in other areas is not verified yet. This is necessary to draw conclusions about the generalization of the approach. The applicability of the model has to be examined in terms of e.g. simplicity and quality. For that matter it is required to consider which criteria may be used for a bundling of processes. Likewise, it is important to elicit which procedure is applicable to derive process criteria and their relationships for the regarded domain. Furthermore, feasibility of integrated processes as a result of the approach has to be examined. This also applies to potential savings indicated in this paper. Last but not least, it is sensible to review the completeness of the approach. Therefore further research is planned to implement a bundle of reporting duties between business and administration.

Acknowledgments. We would like to thank the German Federal Ministry of the Interior for their support and funding of the research project.

References

1. Statistisches Bundesamt Deutschland, Zu viel Bürokratie?,
   `http://www.destatis.de/jetspeed/portal/cms/Sites/destatis/In`
   `ternet/DE/Content/Publikationen/STATmagazin/Sonstiges/`
   `2009__08/PDF2009__08,property=file.pdf` (cited 15.02.2010)
2. O.A., Standard Cost Model Manual,
   `http://www.oecd.org/dataoecd/32/54/34227698.pdf` (cited 18.02.2010)
3. Rodenhagen, J., Diekhans, B., Rieckmann, P.: Prozessmanagement im Kontext des E-Government 2.0 - Einsatzfelder, Rahmenbedingungen, und aktuelle Maßnahmen. Praxis der Wirtschaftsinformatik 265, 36–50 (2009)
4. Bundesministerium des Innern, E-Government 2.0 - Das Programm des Bundes,
   `http://www.cio.bund.de/cae/servlet/contentblob/63262/publica`
   `tionFile/4016/egov2_programm_des_bundes_download.pdf`
   (cited 11.02.2010)
5. Lenk, K.: Notwendige Revisionen des Geschäftsprozessdenkens. In: Wimmer, M. (ed.) Impulse für eGoovernment: Internationale Entwicklungen, Organisation, Recht, Technik, Best Practices, Österreichische Computer Gesellschaft, Wien, pp. 61–71 (2002)
6. Becker, J., Algermissen, L., Niehaves, B.: Vorgehensmodell zur Selektion von eGovernment-Prozessen. eGovernment-Präsenz Fachzeitschrift des Kompetenzzentrums Uni Münster 4 (2004)
7. Beyer, L.: Reengineering. In: Blanke, B., Bandemer, S., Nullmeier, F., Wewer, G. (eds.) Handbuch zur Verwaltungsreform, Opladen, pp. 118–126 (2001)
8. Gaitanides, M.: Prozessorganisation - Entwicklung, Ansätze und Programme des Managements von Geschäftsprozessen. Verlag Franz Vahlen, München (2007)
9. Becker, J., Kugeler, M., Rosemann, M.: Prozessmanagement. Springer, Heidelberg (2008)
10. Geier, C.: Optimierung der Informationstechnologie bei BPR-Projekten. Deutscher Universitäts-Verlag, Wiesbaden (1999)
11. Schulze, G.: Bürokratie- und Regulierungskosten in der chemischen Industrie - Potenziale zu ihrer Reduktion. Verband der chemischen Industrie, Frankfurt am Main (2009)
12. Wolf, P., Sharafi, A., Krcmar, H., Guenther, H., Komm, M., Ortmann, E., Schäfer, M.: Machbarkeitsstudie Prozessketten Umwelt. Lehrstuhl für Wirtschaftsinformatik, TU München, Siemens IT Solutions and Services, Berlin (2009)
13. Viola, G.: Behörden und Unternehmen entlasten - Bürokratiekosten senken,
    `http://www.egovernment-computing.de/`
    `index.cfm?pid=7476&pk=202981&print=true&printtype=article`
    (cited 11.02.2010)
14. Statistisches Bundesamt, WebSKM,
    `https://www-skm.destatis.de/webskm/online` (cited 12.02.2010)
15. Landesamt für Natur Umwelt- und Verbraucherschutz Nordrhein-Westfalen,
    `http://www.lanuv.nrw.de/abfall/abfstroeme/einzelentsor.htm`
    (cited 12.02.2010)
16. Zentale Koordinierungsstelle der Länder, `http://www.zks-abfall.de`
    (cited 15.02.2010)
17. Abfallüberwachungssystem ASYS, `http://www.asysnet.de/` (cited 09.02.2010)
18. PRTR: Schadstofffreisertzungs- und Verbringungsregister,
    `http://www.prtr.bund.de` (cited 11.02.2010)
19. BUBE-Online, `http://home.prtr.de/index.php?pos=el_prtr/bube/`
    (cited 09.02.2010)

20. eSTATISTIK.core, `http://www.statspez.de/core/` (cited 10.02.2010)
21. Schwabe, G., Krcmar, H.: Piloting Socio-Technical Innovation. In: European Conference on Information Systems, Wien (2000)
22. Krallmann, H., Schönherr, M., Trier, M.: Systemanalyse im Unternehmen. Oldenbourg Verlag, München (2007)
23. Krcmar, H., Dold, G., Fischer, H., Strobel, M., Seifert, E.: Informationssysteme für das Umweltmanagement - Das Referenzmodell ECO-Integral, München, Wien (2000)
24. Bundesregierung: Informationspflichten der Wirtschaft, `http://www.bundesregierung.de/Content/DE/StatischeSeiten/Bre` `g/Buerokratieabbau/zahlen-und-fakten-zum-` `buerokratieabbau.html` (cited 08.02.2010)
25. Wolf, P., Jurisch, M., Krcmar, H.: Analyse und Design von Prozessketten. Fachtagung Verwaltungsinformatik (FTVI), Koblenz (2010)
26. DeMarco, T.: Structured Analysis and System Specification. Yourdon Press, New York (1978)
27. Ross, D., Schoman Jr., K.: Structured analysis for requirements definition. IEEE Transactions on Software Engineering (1977)
28. MacMenamin, S., Palmer, J.: Strukturierte Systemanalyse. Hanser (1988)
29. Jurisch, M., Wolf, P., Krcmar, H.: Toward a formal approach to process bunding in public administrations. In: EGOV 2010. Springer, Berlin (2010)
30. den Butter, F., de Graaf, M., Nijsen, A.: The Transaction Costs Perspective on Costs And Benefits of Government Regulation. Tinbergen Institute Discussion Papers (2009)
31. Staatssekretariat für Wirtschaft SECO: Messung der Bürokratiekosten der Mehrwertsteuer - Gesetzgebung auf Basis des Standard-Kosten-Modells, `http://www.seco.admin.ch/themen/00374/00459/02118/index.html` `?lang=de&download=NHzLpZeg7t,lnp6I0NTU04212Z6ln1acy4Zn4Z2qZp` `nO2Yuq2Z6gpJCEfHx9fGym162epYbg2c_JjKbNoKSn6A` (cited 19.02.2010)
32. Slodowicz, J., Zenhäusern, P., Vaterlaus, S.: Verwendungsmöglichkeiten des Standard-Kosten-Modells - Eine Analyse des schweizerischen Kontexts. Plaut Economics, Olten (2007)

Toward a Formal Approach to Process Bundling in Public Administrations

Marlen Jurisch, Petra Wolf, and Helmut Krcmar

Technische Universität München, Chair for Information Systems I17, Boltzmannstr. 3,
85748 Garching bei München
{marlen.jurisch,petra.wolf,krcmar}@in.tum.de

Abstract. Excessive information and data exchanges between companies and public administrations create a need for the bundling of processes. Process bundles are created whenever cross-organizational processes are combined or interlinked. While a considerable amount of literature addressing the process of reorganizing, optimizing, or reengineering processes exists, much less is known about concrete approaches which facilitate the identification of suitable process bundles. This paper presents a review of identification criteria relevant for process bundling. Our literature review is deliberately broad, encompassing work in the fields of process management, reengineering, and E-Government. The analysis discloses that the plain focus on secondary process identification criteria (e.g., inefficiencies and redundancies) neglects to assess if the processes actually fit together. Premised on these results, we synthesize the insights from the cited literature into a methodological intermediary step to support the purposeful elicitation of bundling candidates.

Keywords: process bundling, business-to-government, process identification.

1 Introduction and Context

Municipalities are confronted with constant cost and performance pressures. More so, citizens and businesses demand increased customer orientation and an integration of their needs. This entails a change in how public administrations deliver their services and processes, e.g.: availability of services (e-services), quality of services, timeliness of service delivery, etc [1]. Nowadays, process changes triggered by cost and performance pressures are often driven by technology. Nonetheless, quality and service goals will not be achieved by the mere introduction of technology [2]. The uninterrupted execution of public services coupled with the simultaneous increase in customer orientation, requires an automation of the underpinning public service processes. The optimization of public service processes demands an identification of suitable bundling candidates. For the bundling of processes the identification and selection of appropriate processes is particularly crucial. Yet, this identification of suitable process bundling candidates has proved to be rather complex in practice [3]. Even though most of the existing literature addresses the reorganization, optimization or the reengineering of business processes, very little work has been dedicated to the

M.A. Wimmer et al. (Eds.): EGOV 2010, LNCS 6228, pp. 412–423, 2010.

actual identification of suitable process bundles. This state of affairs led us to the following research question: *What are the criteria for the identification of suitable process bundling candidates?*

The question of "how" to model processes and technical procedures for implementing business process improvements in organizations has been addressed in the literature [4] [5]. Further, several methods, techniques, and tools have been developed and implemented to support process oriented reorganizations within companies [1] [6]. In recent years, process improvement efforts were also undertaken in the area of public administration. Within the context of public institutions, the discussion of public process improvement is often limited to the provision of online services and public administrations' internet portals [7]. In the business domain, an abundance of different business process improvement methodologies exist but only a selected few of these focus specifically on process optimization in public institutions [1] [6]. The theoretical and practical knowledge acquired within the private sector on process improvement has been insufficiently translated and applied into the public sector. Further, the urgent practical challenges faced in the public sector with regards to process improvement have, so far, not been adequately addressed by the relevant academic disciplines. In order to identify a holistic set of criteria for the identification of public service process bundles it is necessary to review common business process improvement methodologies.

We begin this paper by delineating the term process bundling and the undergirding reasons for bundling processes in public administrations. This is followed by a presentation of the method we used for reviewing the relevant literature. We then analyze this literature and synthesize the results into a methodological intermediary step. Finally, we discuss our findings, outline avenues for future research, and suggest implications for practice.

2   Process Bundles in Public Administrations

2.1   What Is Process Bundling?

Bureaucracies are characterized by intense flows of information. Over 90% of all administrative processes are information-processing in nature [8]. Due to their large and often redundant number of functions and functional departments, public institutions are likely to be affected by excessive information and data exchanges across functional departments and with companies. This situation is caused by the fundamental principles of traditional public administrations: bureaucracy, hierarchical organization, bureaucratic delivery, politics/administration dichotomy, etc. [9]. Common business concepts such as value creation, competitive edge, or profit maximization [10] are typically not the foci of public administrations. Rather, public administrations are concerned with the process and delivery of public services to citizens, businesses, and to other governmental institutions. As a result, processes in public institutions need to be understood as reporting duties on the basis of legal requirements [3]. Thus, public service processes are concerned with monitoring compliance to legal regulations and the execution of public services. Public service processes involve a large number of recurrent activities [1] [11], extensive integration of customers, and numerous points of interaction [5]. The excessive information and data exchanges in the public sphere create a fertile ground for the bundling of processes.

From a customer perspective, process bundles are created whenever cross-organizational processes are combined or interlinked either organizationally or technically with the objective to create a coherent data base. Hence, a *process bundle*, within the remit of public administrations, constitutes the purposeful alignment of separate activities, and accordingly processes, along a well-defined value chain [12]. Let us take the example of a real-estate loan award. Throughout this award process the bank needs to maintain contacts with numerous public institutions which do not necessarily have a technically supported infrastructure and are often dependent on manual labor (i.e., fiscal authorities, notary, land registry, bankruptcy court, etc.) [13] [14]. The bundling of these activities through technical interlinking would result in the uninterrupted and efficient execution of the loan award process. According to this understanding, process bundling is concerned with changing or redirecting the flow of information between activities without changing the actual content of the information.

2.2 Reasons for Bundling

The concept of bundling processes or services is neither new nor revolutionary. Particularly in the service domain, bundling has been on the research agenda for over a decade. Streamlining public service processes also implies streamlining their output, which are in fact, the delivered services. To support our arguments presented in this paper, we would like to draw on some of the knowledge of the service domain on bundling.

Our review of the literature on the service domain disclosed that the rationale behind bundling varies in complexity. Nevertheless, two reasons prevail - increasing profits and saving costs. Due to their nature and tasks, municipalities are non- profit oriented. Hence, increasing profits does not provide an adequate reason to support process bundling in public administrations. Saving costs, on the other hand, is a persistent issue and fundamental aspect of the operation of public institutions. The omnipresent financial restrictions forces municipalities to operate cost-efficiently and customer-oriented. The German government, for instance, anticipates cutting the costs of bureaucracy by over 15% through the implementation of process bundling [15] and the streamlining of processes is expected to result in faster through-put times of administrative procedures. It has been proposed that cost savings can occur through a joined transaction of the bundle components and their joined distribution [16].

Another reason for process bundling is to ease the interaction of public authorities with businesses through the synchronization and integration of processes and IT-applications. To accomplish this, legal regulations and public service processes need to be revised critically and, if necessary, adjusted [15]. If employed successfully, process bundling yields the electronic and uninterrupted processing of public service processes. Therefore, existing bureaucratic structures need to be reassessed with the aim of creating more effective and flexible organizations via process bundling.

3 Methodology Used for the Literature Review

The literature review comprised two phases: identification and analysis. In the identification phase we identified and selected research studies which discussed process identification criteria. We assembled a comprehensive collection of publications representing the main body of knowledge in this area. The analysis entailed a careful scrutiny of publications to unveil patterns of commonly addressed research themes.

3.1 Identification of Relevant Literature

Most process reorganization or optimization approaches include a phase for tackling the identification of processes [1] [17-21]. The identification of the right bundling candidates is crucial to the success of process-optimizations and reorganizations [17] [18]. The bundling of inadequate processes could have extensive implications on the organization's operating capabilities. Frequently, process reorganization or optimization projects are burdened by a plethora of information which makes it difficult to identify suitable process bundling candidates. The potential measures are not only numerous (see table 1), but some of them are difficult to operationalize in public administrations. Consequently, purposeful bundling requires a set of well-defined identification criteria.

The identification phase commenced with an initial search for publications relevant to process identification and several sources were consulted for this search. The most important sources were academic books, journals and conference proceedings. The search mechanism included identification of keywords such as process identification, integration, selection, and modeling. As a result, we identified an initial set of 36 relevant publications. We then screened this initial set of publications to select the most significant ones. The screening was conducted on the basis of the quality of the research studies, their relevance to process identification, and their citation frequency. The screening cycle yielded a final set of 15 key research studies which represent the basis of the literature review.

3.2 Structuring the Review

Criteria for the identification of process integration candidates are both abundant and diverse (see table 1). As suggested in the literature [19], we implemented a concept-centric literature review. Based on this review, we conceptualize that the majority of relevant process identification criteria can be categorized according to the following three identification principles: (1) performance, (2) process integration, and (3) complexity (see table 1). These three categories are not mutually exclusive.

4 Analysis - Identification of Process Bundling Candidates

A plethora of diverse approaches for improving processes exists in various disciplines. Information systems, industrial engineering, operations research, and management accounting are among the disciplines represented [17]. In the following, we present the results of the literature analysis structured according to these three categories.

Table 1. Principles of process identification

Principle	Criteria	Source
Performance	Through-put time, costs (of bureaucracy), quality, customer satisfaction, value proposition	[1] [5] [11] [18] [20] [21] [22] [23] [24]
Process integration	Information flow, degree of information integration, timeliness, access, granularity, transparency	[5] [24] [25] [26] [27] [28]
Complexity	Number of cases, exceptions, special cases classification of actors	[20] [21] [27] [29]

4.1 Performance Indicators

Parameters assessing the process' performance and efficiency were among the most frequently listed. Nearly all process reorganization and optimization approaches depict criteria influencing the performance of a process. Gaitanides [21] asserts that optimization potentials can be identified through the analysis of simple data parameters such as through-put time, costs, and quality. Through-put time analyzes the processing time, the transfer time, and the holding time of a process. The primary goal is, of course, the frictionless organization of processes. Therefore, holding times need to be reduced, and unproductive times need to be detected and eliminated. The identification of cost intensive and "non-value" adding processes is the key objective of the cost assessment [21]. Higher costs are often caused by redundancies and inefficient workflow between activities. However, obtaining accurate data on costs is often a troublesome and enormous effort [22]. Various authors have discussed the importance of assessing the costs and time consumed by the execution of a process [1] [18] [20] [22] [24]. According to Wolf et al. [11] the identification of processes in public administrations should focus on those processes which produce the highest costs. The Federal Statistical Office, for instance, assesses the expenses for the processing of businesses-to-government (B2G) contacts on the basis of the standard cost model [30]. The corresponding data can be extracted from a public database. Various studies have assessed the costs of bureaucracy for specific industries (e.g., chemical industry [31]).

Quality, as discussed by Gaitanides [21], measures the error rate of products or services. Quality in this understanding is a measurement for the performance of process outputs, which are either products or services [18]. For tangible process outputs such as products the error rate is rather easy to assess. Gaitanides [21] fails to explain how the error rate should be measured in regard to services. Some researchers have attempted to define specific measures of service quality, i.e.: reliability, responsiveness, empathy, assurance, and tangibles [32]. Customer satisfaction is often clearly correlated with process quality. Therefore, customer satisfaction constitutes another key indicator for process performance [18].

Within the context of customer satisfaction Gaitanides [21] introduces the concept of value orientation. Value orientation focuses on the affiliation of processes to value chains from the customer's perspective [20] [21]. This approach assesses the individual value proposition of each activity to the entire value chain. Thus, all activities of a process must provide value to the production and/or delivery of the product to the customer. Activities that do not support a value chain are either redundant, inefficient, not purposeful, or not profitable [21]. The value proposition should be defined from the customer's perspective.

4.2 Process Integration Indicators

As organizations look to improve business processes, an important initial step is to understand the flow of information associated with the processes. Most public service processes stretch across different functional departments. Therefore, they often split across individuals and across time [24]. The flow of information is interrupted whenever information and data are not available at the required time in a sufficiently detailed manner. Consequently, information integration focuses on facilitating the seamless flow of information. The degree of information integration investigates how informational resources transfer across technical and organizational borders [5] [25]. Even though information integration constitutes the basis for integrated processes, it is not the only supposition for "fully integrated business processes" [24]. Other factors, such as the structure or non-ambiguity of data, can be equally influential.

The notion of timeliness in regard to information transfer becomes evident whenever one understands that process integration necessitates information integration. Timeliness assesses if the information is up to date [26] and available at the beginning of an activity. This understanding of timeliness assumes that information is accessible. Accessibility, in turn, implies that data need to be accessible from any point within the process [26]. The access to information needs to be dependable, convenient, and easily manipulated [28]. Additionally, information needs to be available at the right level of granularity. All information exchanged within the process has to be provided at the right level of detail [24] [26]. Appropriate granularity enables the elimination of extraneous activities that would be required to decompose or summarize the information. The last element concerns the transparency of information. The concept of transparency refers to the ease by which information is passed from one activity to another one [24] and implies a shared understanding of models and structure. According to Aubert et al. [26], there are two ways to achieve transparency; first, through translation among several "languages" or, second, through standardization. Hence, in regard to the transparency of a process, the level of standardization should be analyzed as well.

4.3 Complexity Indicators

At their initiation most processes are usually quite simple [20] but often grow considerably more complex over time. The more cases, variants, or actors that are involved, the more complex the process grows. Complexity indicators commonly disclose processes that can be simplified through integration.

Organizational complexity is generally examined from two perspectives: the company's side or the customer's side [29]. The latter plays a more prominent role in public reorganizations and optimizations since public service processes are characterized by a high degree of customer integration. The number of cases also increases complexity; for every service delivered on the municipality side there is a user on the citizen side [29]. A high number of user groups yield higher variants within and between the cases. In other words, complexity can be analyzed by the number of steps required to perform a process [27]. When integrating B2G processes, it appears critical to identify processes which affect the same group of users. The identification of users on the business side needs to be based on the type of business affected by the public service process and the role of the users' needs to be identified. Process bundling is generally desirable in areas distinguished by high case volumes and the same group of users. The reorganization or optimization of processes exhibiting a small number of cases, and therefore little complexity, is not desirable [29].

4.4 Discussion of Findings

The analysis of the literature review disclosed that there are at least three major principles (e.g., performance, process integration, and complexity) which support the elicitation of process bundling candidates. As mentioned, these three categories are not mutually exclusive. For instance, if a company embarks on a process reorganization project, performance indicators might be just as important for the identification of integration candidates as complexity or process integration indicators. However, none of the process reorganization and optimization concepts discussed above provide insights on how to prioritize the various criteria. Within this study we identified approximately 16 different criteria for the elicitation of bundling candidates. The analysis of all 16 indicators will not be feasible and purposeful in practice and more criteria might exist that we did not cover in our literature review. Therefore, it is extremely important to provide practitioners with guidelines on how to purposefully identify bundling candidates.

Our literature analysis also showed that the identification of adequate candidates for purposeful process bundling is not as straightforward as it may sound. Particularly within the complex setting of public institutions the existing set of identification criteria can be rather misleading. Current approaches to process identification promote a bottom-up identification of potential bundling candidates. These approaches start the identification process by choosing one or a selected number of processes that exhibit the greatest malfunctions. Accordingly, the improvement process always has one specific process as a starting point without providing a holistic picture of the process landscape. Process bundling is essentially concerned with changing or redirecting the flow of information between activities without changing the actual content of the information. In order to identify inefficiencies between processes one needs to study the corresponding information flow [25]. But none of the previously mentioned identification criteria support the comprehensive screening of several hundred public service processes. Based on the existing approaches, screening all public processes would be extremely time consuming and cost intensive. A top-down identification approach is needed within the public sphere in order to investigate the complex information flow between functional departments and companies and to identify relevant bundling candidates. Despite the abundance of existing identification criteria, we posit that the current set of criteria does not suffice and a top-down identification approach is necessary.

5   Synthesis – Introducing a Methodological Intermediary Step

Within this section, we synthesize the analysis of the identified literature into a proposal for a methodological intermediary step in process bundling. This intermediary step addresses primarily the identification of B2G contacts. B2G contacts are commonly characterized by a higher degree of frequency and repetitions than citizen-to-government (C2G) contacts. The processing of B2G contacts requires a considerable amount of time and resource capacities in companies which in return leads to higher costs of bureaucracy. By optimizing B2G processes, monetary and efficiency benefits can be achieved for both sides: companies and public administrations.

We propose that the identification and analysis of public service processes needs to encounter a top-down perspective. Tailoring the identification of processes to a superordinate principle (e.g., content, context, or business event) would yield a more anchored approach and account for the top-down perspective. We therefore propose a methodological intermediary step that promotes first a focus on primary process bundling principles and then on the commonly known identification criteria. In this view, primary principles are to be considered before secondary ones (see figure 1). Primary bundling principles assess the similarity or complementariness of the future process bundles in regard to their content, context, or a specific business event. It is crucial to understand that only one primary principle at a time can be pursued [11]. For instance, either the shared content or the shared context of processes can serve as the basis for further analysis. Processes with a similar or complementary content, even across departments, can then be analyzed in regard to their performance, efficiency, and complexity. The content and context based bundling principles stem from the feasibility studies [3] [13] funded by the German Federal Ministry of the Interior in 2009.

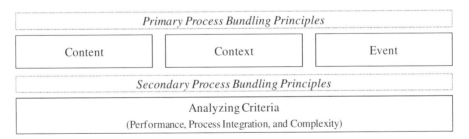

Fig. 1. Primary and secondary process bundling principles

5.1   Context Based Bundling

Various value adding and support processes exist within companies that have multiple interfaces with public administrations. For instance, the award of a property credit exhibits contacts to the local tax office, the notary, the land registry office, and the bankruptcy court [13]. The context based bundling principle aims at guarantying the seamless flow of business processes and B2G contacts are bundled along the process flow. The key integration criterion for context based bundling is the affiliation of B2G contacts to business processes or process clusters. Subsequently, the identification of processes depends on their value adding context. There are various examples on how to identify bundling candidates based on their context affiliation. For instance, [13] examine B2G contacts of financial service providers on the basis of an industry specific process landscape. The affiliation of B2G contacts to the same process cluster within the process landscape is used as an initial identification criterion. This context based affiliation helps the researcher in the identification and selection of process bundling candidates. In short, the context based bundling aims at identifying B2G contacts on the basis of their affiliation to a business process or cluster. Hence, this bundling principle necessitates the mapping of B2G to affiliated processes.

5.2 Content-Based Bundling

Currently, the contacts of German companies with public administrations are characterized by a plethora of similar reporting and notification duties. The content-based bundling principle assumes that these similar reports and notifications can be bundled based on their compatible content [3]. The content-based bundling principle aims at reducing the efforts needed to produce these reports and notifications while simultaneously guaranteeing and potentially increasing their quality. Content-based bundling focuses on exposing data and content redundancies between B2G processes. In this view, content and structural similarities of B2G processes are crucial for the purposeful identification of bundling candidates [3]. In order to efficiently bundle B2G contacts according to the content principle, the following conditions have to be fulfilled: (1) the contents of the processes exhibit a certain degree of similarity or redundancy, (2) the same user group, or companies respectively, have to be affected by the B2G contacts, (3) the direction of the information flow has to be congruent (e.g., in all cases from businesses to public administrations) [3]. These three conditions assure that synergies are used purposefully.

5.3 Event-Based Bundling

The event-based bundling principle assumes that certain business events recur in the life cycle of a company. These specific business events determine when companies need to get in touch with public administrations [33]. Examples of such events in the life cycle of a company are the registration of a business or the merger with another company. Both events force the company to get in touch with multiple functional departments in the public administration. The idea is to streamline these event-based B2G contacts in order to reduce processing errors and efforts on the side of the company. The bundling of business event contacts could potentially result in one government point of contact for the company. Event-based bundling is also discussed within the service domain where components are bundled based on their affiliation to a specific event. The event-based bundling principle has its theoretical foundations in the concept of one-stop government. One-stop government also assumes that information can and should be structured according to certain life events (*Lebenslage*).

6 Conclusion

From our research we have determined that the combination of primary and secondary process bundling principles posits a collectively exhaustive lens for the purposeful identification of B2G processes. We employed a rigorous procedure that generated the identification and analysis of 36 scholarly articles and books. These literature sources provided evidence that secondary identification principles are commonly comprised of performance, process integration, and complexity indicators. The mere employment of secondary identification criteria does not yield purposeful bundles of public service processes. The proposed methodological intermediary step which introduces content, context, and events as primary process bundling criteria fills this gap in current process identification research.

As practitioners look to improve public service processes, our research suggests that they should first focus on primary process bundling principles (e.g., content, context, and event). These principles would enable them to identify what processes can be bundled together while simultaneously providing insight on potential areas for improvement. Secondary process bundling principles support the elicitation of concrete weaknesses and discontinuities within and between processes. The introduction of public service process bundling is expected to reduce the amount of recurrent activities within public administrations. We suspect that the bundling of service processes will lead to fewer points of contact between businesses and public administrations which would in turn lead to cost reductions for both involved parties.

Multiple directions for further research exist. First, the purposeful identification of process bundling candidates remains ill-defined and should be exposed to more structured scrutiny. Second, the newly developed primary bundling principles need to be analyzed and further validated. Third, the transferability of bundling principles for the analysis of C2G contacts needs to be investigated.

Acknowledgments. We would like to thank the German Federal Ministry of the Interior for their support and funding of the research project.

References

1. Scheer, A.-W., Nüttgens, M., Zimmermann, V.: Business Process Reengineering in der Verwaltung. In: Scheer, A.-W., Friedrichs, J. (eds.) Innovative Verwaltungen 2000, pp. 11–29. Wiesbaden, Gabler (2000)
2. Brüggemeier, M., Dovifat, A., Lenk, K.: Open Choice: Improving Public Sector Performance with Process Reorganization Methodology. In: Wimmer, M.A., Scholl, H.J., Grönlund, Å., Andersen, K.V. (eds.) EGOV 2006. LNCS, vol. 4084, pp. 186–194. Springer, Heidelberg (2006)
3. Wolf, P., et al.: Machbarkeitsstudie Prozessketten Umwelt. In: Lehrstuhl für Wirtschaftsinformatik, TU München, Siemens IT Solutions and Services, Berlin (2009)
4. Seethamraju, R., Marjanovic, O.: Role of process knowledge in business process improvement methodology: a case study. Business Process Management Journal 15(6), 920–936 (2009)

5. Becker, J., Algermissen, L., Niehaves, B.: Organizational Engineering in Public Administrations – A Method for process-oriented eGovernment projects. In: Proceedings of the ACM Symposium on Applied Computing (2004)
6. Becker, J., Algermissen, L., Niehaves, B.: A procedure model for process oriented e-government projects. Business Process Management 12(1), 61–75 (2006)
7. Lenk, K.: Notwendige Revisionen des Geschäftsprozessdenkens. In: Wimmer, M.A. (ed.) Impulse für e-Government: Internationale Entwicklungen, Organisation, Recht, Technik, Best Practices, pp. 61–71. Österreichische Computer Gesellschaft, Wien (2002)
8. Zahlen, O.A., Bürokratieabbau, F.z.: (2009), http://www.bundesregierung.de/Content/DE/StatischeSeiten/Bre g/Buerokratieabbau/zahlen-und-fakten-zum- buerokratieabbau.html (cited February 15, 2010)
9. Hughes, O.E.: Public Management and Administration. 3rd edn., Palgrave Macmillan, New York (2003)
10. Porter, M.E.: Competitive Strategy. Free Press, New York (1980)
11. Wolf, P., Jurisch, M., Krcmar, H.: Analyse und Design von Prozessketten. In: Fachtagung Verwaltungsinformatik (FTVI), Koblenz (2010)
12. BMI, Bund Online 2005: Abschlussbericht - Status und Ausblick, Berlin (2006)
13. Fröschle, N., et al.: Machbarkeitsstudie Entwicklung von Prozessketten zwischen Wirtschaft und Verwaltung: Finanzdienstleistungen. Fraunhofer eGovernment Zentrum, Stuttgart (2009)
14. Sharafi, A., Wolf, P., Krcmar, H.: Process and data-oriented approach for bundling corporate reporting duties to public authorities - A case study on the example of waste management reporting. In: EGOV 2010. Springer, Lausanne (2010)
15. Innern, B.d. (ed.): BMI, E-Government 2.0 - Das Programm des Bundes. Bundesministerium des Innern, Berlin (2006)
16. Geng, X.S., Stinchcombe, M.B., Whinston, A.B., Hendershott, T.: Product Bundling. In: Hendershott, T. (ed.) Handbook of Economics and Information Systems, pp. 499–525. Elsevier, Amsterdam (2006)
17. Davenport, T.H.: Process Innovation: Reengineering work through information technology. Harvard Business School Press, Boston (1993)
18. Davenport, T.H., Beers, M.C.: Managing information about processes. Journal of Management Information Systems 12(1), 57–80 (1995)
19. Webster, J., Watson, T.R.: Analyzing the past to prepare for the future: writing a literature review. MIS Quarterly 26(2), xiii–xxiii (2002)
20. Hammer, M., Champy, J.: Reengineering the Corporation: A Manifesto for Business Revolution. HarperBusiness, New York (1993)
21. Gaitanides, M.: Prozessmanagement. Konzepte, Umsetzungen und Erfahrungen des Reengineering. Hanser Fachbuch, München (1994)
22. Harrington, H.J.: Business process improvement: the breakthrough strategy for total quality, productivity, and competitiveness, 23rd edn. McGraw-Hill, New York (2007)
23. 1021, D.-P., Verfahrensmodell zur Gestaltung von Geschäftsprozessen der öffentlichen Verwaltung - Wandel von der funktionalen zur prozessorientierten Verwaltung. 2003: Berlin
24. Berente, N., Vandenbosch, B., Aubert, B.: Information flows and business process integration. Business Process Managament Journal 15(1), 119–141 (2009)
25. Klischewski, R.: Information Integration or Process Integration? How to Achieve Interoperability in Administration. In: Traunmüller, R. (ed.) EGOV 2004. LNCS, vol. 3183. Springer, Heidelberg (2004)

26. Aubert, B.A., Vandenbosch, B., Mignerat, M.: Towards the Measurement of Process Integration. In: Cahier du GReSI (2003)

27. Shostack, L.: Service positioning through structural change. Journal of Marketing 51, 34–43 (1987)

28. Strong, D.M., Yang, W.L., Wang, R.Y.: Data quality in context. Communications of the ACM 40(5), 103–110 (1997)

29. Becker, J.: Referenzmodellierung: Grundlagen, Techniken und domänenbezogene Anwendung. Physica-Verlag, Heidelberg (2004)

30. O.A., Einführung des Standardkosten-Modells Methodenhandbuch der Bundesregierung. Statistisches Bundesamt, Wiesbaden (2006)

31. Schulze, G.: Bürokratie- und Regulierungskosten in der chemischen Industrie - Potenziale zu ihrer Reduktion, Frankfurt am Main, Verband der Chemischen Industrie e.V. (2009)

32. Zeithaml, V.A., Berry, L., Parasuraman, A.: The Behavioral Consequences of Service Quality. Journal of Marketing 60, 31–46 (1996)

33. von Lucke, J.: Hochleistungsportale für die öffentliche Verwaltung. Joseph Eul Verlag GmbH, Lohmar (2008)

Designing Quality Business Processes for E-Government Digital Services

Flavio Corradini, Damiano Falcioni, Andrea Polini,
Alberto Polzonetti, and Barbara Re

Computer Science Division – School of Science and Technologies
University of Camerino
62032 – Camerino (MC), Italy
`firstname.lastname@unicam.it`

Abstract. Research works and surveys focusing on e-Government Digital Services availability and usage, reveal that often services are available but ignored by citizens. In our hypothesis this situation can be justified since defined service delivery processes do not sufficiently take into account social aspects and mainly focus just on technical aspects. Domain knowledge, related to how delivering high quality e-Government Digital Services, remains in most of the case in the mind of e-government stakeholders.

To address these issues we have developed a quality framework to assess delivery process strategies of services. Moreover we have introduced a user-friendly approach permitting to assess, using formal verification techniques, a delivery process with respect to the defined quality framework. The approach has been also implemented in a plug-in for the Eclipse platform and it has been applied to real case scenarios from the Public Administration domain.

In this paper we report and discuss the results we obtained from the conducted experiments. First of all the experiments provided encouraging results confirming that the approach we developed is applicable to the e-government domain. Moreover we discovered that delivery processes, defined for the services under study, reach low quality marks with respect to the framework.

1 Introduction

The e-government domain is characterized by the involvement of many stakeholders with different interests and competences. Among the others we can list citizens, civil servants, managers and politicians. Each of them provides multiple viewpoints on Public Administrations (PAs) needs, objectives and qualities. So for a politicians the objective is to maximize PA efficiency providing services that are highly used at minimum costs, where for citizens the objective would be to maximize service availability and usability leaving aside possible costs. Nevertheless if we consider the current situation of e-Government Digital Services (GDSs) we can say that services are available but not highly used. So the effort

M.A. Wimmer et al. (Eds.): EGOV 2010, LNCS 6228, pp. 424–435, 2010.
© IFIP International Federation for Information Processing 2010

of the politicians toward the introduction of ICT technologies in the PA did not get really good results.

Our opinion here is that, in the development of GDSs, the focus has been put too much on technological aspects, where requirements coming from social and antropological domains have been too often ignored. As a result services are available and often they rely on advanced technologies, nevertheless they are not used since citizens do not grasp the advantage of using it, and in particular in less urbanized areas, they feel more confortable in accessing services via traditional channels. Certainly the digital divide contributes to such a situation. Nevertheless our impression, corroborated by an informal investigation among the people working in our department and with high ICT skills, is that other important factors strongly contribute to the underlined scenario.

In our view it is important to concentrate on aspects and requirements that are not only technological. Therefore, structuring the delivery process of a GDS just replicating the process already in place in the PA could pose some issues, not leading to the expected results. For instance it is necessary to consider that interacting with the PA via an eletronic mean does not bring the same level of trustworthiness with respect of an interaction mediated by the civil servant. This aspect should be certainly considered when structuring the delivery process of a GDS.

Therefore in the delivery of a GDS at least two different kinds of knowledge need to be codified. The first concerns the specific service to be provided to the citizens. This is may be less critical since directly relates to the service that is under development. The second knowledge is instead more general and refers to any kind of service developed within the domain and in particular it can relate to social and anthropological aspects. Both aspects are equally important to derive highly used services. In this line we have defined a quality framework [1] which classifies the delivery process of a GDS. The framework intends to codify properties that a general delivery process of a GDS should satisfy. So in order to increase trustworhiness the framework requires that some kind of transparency on the process execution evolution is implemented. This functionality would permit to the citizen requiring the service to obtain feedbacks and to observe how the service he/she requested is progressing. This will obviously result in an increased trust.

Certainly the codification of domain and quality requirements can per se provide a useful tool to Business Process (BP) analysts. Nevertheless it turned out that the requirements constituting the framework could be translated in temporal properties. Therefore we implemented a tool [2] permitting to automatically verify and classify, applying model checking techniques, that a designed GDS delivery process satisfies the properties defined in the quality framework. Correspondingly it ranks the process with respect to the different levels defined in the framework.

In this paper we discuss on the importance of codifying the different kinds of knowledge and at the same time of having tools supporting such an activity. Moreover we report on experiments we conducted applying the framework and using the corresponding tools on real GDS delivery processes implemented by a local administration. In particular in the next section we report on related works, and then in Section 3 we discuss about knowledge codification in the e-Government domain. Section 4 introduces a tool supporting BP analysis and Section 5 shows how the approach and the tool have been applied in practice. Finally Section 6 draws some conclusions and opportunity for future work.

2   Related Works

The importance of fully functional e-government characterized by vertical and horizontal integration is clearly discussed in [3]. From our point of view the real benefits which e-government promises can be reached when system integration is implemented. The introduction of BP specification can contribute to such integration. Indeed BP potentialities and capabilities are relatively unexplored in e-government. An interesting survey dealing with issues in the application of BPs to e-government can be found in [4]. As far as we know the most comprehensive discussion on e-government business models is proposed by Janssen and Kuk [5]. In this work the authors address the importance of cross-organizational service delivery and propose a framework for studying e-government business model which involves design and implementation of digital services toward the delivery to citizens. Our contribution considers the role of business model as addressed by Jansen and Kuk and it introduces characteristics that are directly process related considering an automatic and systematic approach toward BP improvement and e-government integration.

For what concern the application of mature formal techniques in applied fields of study such as e-government literature shows a quite wide interest. A first discussion on the topic can be found in [6]. This paper is the result of a tutorial-workshop event on technological foundations of e-governance. Our paper contributes to the outcome of the event exploring and validating how model checking can be applied to evaluate service quality.

Other proposals provide user-friendly techniques hiding the complexity of formal languages and tools. A recent survey on Business Process verification provides an interesting classification of proposed techniques [7]. There are for instance interesting approaches aiming at making model checking accessible to a large audience even for people that are not trained in formal techniques [8] [9] [10] [11] [12] [13]. Hovever in most of the case they lack of a domain-dependent requirements framework for BP evaluation and the verification step just considers typical properties such as deadlock, and liveness. Moreover, in most of the case proposed approaches need stand alone tools (for BP modelling, mapping and verification). Such tools can be used only by people with wide technical background. Our contribution provides an integrated development environment for GDS design so that such issues can be solved.

To the best of our knowledge our approach is the first attempt, within the e-government domain, that tries to provide an easy to use environment both for BP design and BP evaluation with respect to a precisely defined quality framework.

3   Domain Knowledge Codification and Verification

Providing successful GDS is a quite complex task. Requirements come from many different sources and the implementation often foresee the interactions of many different PAs. Technically GDS are modeled and implemented using notations and tools based on the Business Process concept. "*A Business Process is a collection of related and structured activities undertaken by one or more organizations in order to pursue some particular goal . Within an organization a BP results in the provisioning of services or in the production of goods for internal or external stakeholders. Moreover BPs are often interrelated since the execution of a BP often results in the activation of related BPs within the same or other organizations*" [14]. In addition to the BP concept Business Process Management (BPM) supports BP experts providing methods, techniques, and software to model, implement, execute and optimize BPs which involve humans, software applications, documents and other sources of information [15].

Unfortunately too often BP analysts in the e-governement domain mainly focus on requirements concerning the specific service under development and forget to consider general requirements coming from the e-government application domain. Moreover, modeling BPs is in general a time-consuming and error-prone activity. Therefore, techniques which help organizations to implement high-quality BPs, and to increase process modeling efficiency have become an highly attractive topic both for industries and for the academy. As illustrated in the following our approach contributes to this topic providing a method, and supporting tools, to codify domain knowledge and to use such knowledge in the verification of a defined BP.

3.1   Domain and Quality Requirements

Domain requirements intend to highlight aspects of a particular application domain that are tipically not know to BP and technical experts, and that are instead quite obvious for domain experts. Missing to report domain requirements generally results in a project failure or in low quality systems. The discovery of domain requirements is particularly critical in the e-government domain where the software to implement is directed to citizens with ample differences in the capability of operating with Information and Communication Technologies (ICT), and in the distrust they have with respect to such technologies. In developing services for the PA becomes then mandatory to consider and codify requirements aiming at removing such possible hurdles in service acceptance. Nevertheless such knowledge is not in the mind of BP or technical experts. Instead it can be provided by people with expertise in social and anthropological fields, that then have to be involved in the requirements discovery phase, and helped in expressing the requirements they think the software system should satisfy. The framework we have defined have been developed taking into account these aspects. For further detail on its definition we refer to [1].

The defined framework considers the following dimensions:

1. *Coordination* is a four level requirement concerning the capability of two or more Public Administrations to work together to accomplish common goals, through the delivery of a service to a citizen and using ICT technologies.
2. *Control* is a four level requirement concerning the activation policies suitable to drive the GDS delivery from its start to the final fulfillment.
3. *Sharing* is a two level requirement that refers to the way in which the PA handles and shares citizen data with other administrations in order to participate in the delivery of a specific GDS.
4. *Transparency* is a three level requirement able to drive the ability of the administration to make citizens aware of the delivery process, improving citizens' perceived trust.
5. *Inclusion* is a three level requirement that considers the ability of the administration to provide service to the citizens considering the diversity.

The framework we defined can be considered just a possible example and certainly other set of general domain requirements for GDS can be identified.

3.2   E-Government Digital Service Specification

The knowledge related to the delivery, as for other aspects, of a specific e-Government Digital Service should codified via a participative approach where every stakeholder contributes with his/her viewpoint. In fact in the general case a GDS can involve many different PAs that will assume different roles within the resulting BP. Furthermore there are many stakeholders, such as politicians, that are interested in the GDS development even though they do not directly participate to its execution. Collecting all the requirements can be a quite difficult task and the requirements directly related to the specific GDS under development have to be complemented with those related to the domain as we discussed above.

Given the inherent complexity of GDS related BPs, it becomes particularly important to provide and set up mechanisms and tools permitting to support the various BP design activities. Particularly interesting is the possiility of applying automatic verification approaches to assess if high level requirements are satisfied by the BP specfication.

As it will be illustrated in the next section for the case of GDS delivery processes, we provide a tool encompassing different BPM activities. In particular the domain quality framework described above has been codified as assertions and it is possible to automatically check their validity on BPs under development.

4   Quality of GDS Delivery Processes

Starting from domain knowledge, the introduction of an approach and a supporting tool permitting to formally and automatically assess the quality of a designed BP, with respect to the defined quality requirements, is an interesting challenge to be addressed. In this section we outline the main elements of the defined user-friendly approach permitting to assess, using formal verification techniques, a GDS delivery process with respect to the defined quality framework.

4.1 Technical Background

Different classes of languages to express BPs have been investigated and defined. Among the others Business Process Modeling Notation (BPMN) [16] is certainly the most used language in practical context also given its intuitive graphical notation. Nevertheless BPMN does not have a precisely defined semantic. For this reason, and in order to permit formal verification we defined a mapping of BPMN constructs to CSP processes [17].

CSP is an event based notation primarily aimed at describing the sequencing of activities within a process and the synchronization (or communication) between different processes. Events represent a form of co-operative synchronization between CSP processes and the environment. Both the processes and the environment may influence the behavior of the other by enabling or refusing certain events or sequences of events.

Formal verification is the act of proving or disproving the correctness of a system with respect to given properties. Many different approaches are available, nevertheless our interest is mainly in model checking techniques [18], which consist in a systematic, and when possible exhaustive, exploration of an operational model to verify if it satisfies a set of given properties. Many model checking tools have been proposed and developed in the literature. In our work we integrate the PAT model checking [19] due to its flexibility and since it uses the CSP formalism as input language.

4.2 BP4PA from an Approach to a Tool Chain

The use of formal mechanisms to verify properties of complex BPs has been already advocated by other authors (see for instance [11]). Our work aims at providing to BP and domain experts the power of formal verification techniques still allowing the use of graphical notation with which they are already acquainted. The approach, which is sketched in Figure 1, relies on the following three main steps: (i) Business Process *specification* and quality requirements selection via a user-friendly notation as already introduced in the Section 3; (ii) *Mapping* of a process specification and of a set of quality requirements to CSP processes and to a set of goals, respectively; (iii) Formal *verification* of defined processes with respect to specified set of requirements (goals).

In case the verification phase ends highlighting some problems, i.e. at least one of the property defined by domain experts results to be violated, the process should be restarted.

For what concerns the precise semantic a GDS specification we have defined a mapping of BPMN elements to CSP processes. Our mapping covers all the core BPMN elements and almost all the elements introduced by the OMG notation.

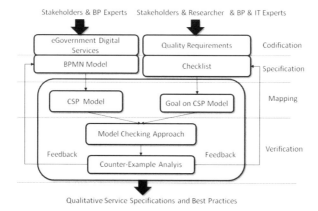

Stakeholders & BP Experts   Stakeholders & Researcher & BP & IT Experts

eGovernment Digital Services   Quality Requirements   Codification

BPMN Model   Checklist   Specification

CSP Model   Goal on CSP Model   Mapping

Model Checking Approach

Feedback   Counter-Example Analyis   Feedback   Verification

Qualitative Service Specifications and Best Practices

Fig. 1. BP4PA - The Proposed Approach

Few constructs dealing with transactions, such as compensation events and cancel events, or time have been kept outside. Main reason for this choice is that they are seldom used in practice [20] at least in the e-Government domain. The mapping has been defined according to the following general principles:

– Each BPMN graphical object included within a pool is formally represented by a CSP process or a parallel execution of generated CSP processes - we name such process *Element CSP*.
– Each pool is mapped to a parallel composition of *Element CSP* processes with barrier synchronization. In this case no message exchange will be observable - we name such process *Private CSP*.
– The whole process results from the parallel execution of the *Private CSP* processes including their interactions implemented via messages exchange - we name such processes *Abstract CSP*.

Due to lack of space we do not detail each mapping rule and we refer to [21] for a wider discussion.

Moreover we defined additional constraints on the definition of the BP both to make the verification step easier, and to make BP specifications clearer. So for instance loops can be introduced only using the specific BPMN constructs. Implicit loops are not admitted. Somehow this constraints ban sort of `goto` statements from the specification. Moreover another constraint requires that tasks receive or send messages but they cannot do both things. BPs modeled according to the defined constraints can be mapped into CSP models to be successively processed by the model checker.

In addition to the BPMN constructs also the quality framework described in Section 3 has been mapped to a formal notation. All the qualities, in the framework we have defined, turned to be expressible as temporal properties. The verification phase is based on model checking techniques. Reachability analysis is applied in order to assess whether the goals that are generated from the properties specification are fulfilled or not.

The formal verification approach is supported by a plug-in (Business Processes for Public Administrations - BP4PA) available for the Eclipse Framework that can be freely downloaded at the BP4PA web page. The plug-in permits to have a fully integrated and user friendly environment which supports domain experts both in the BP specification phase, and in the verification phase. In particular our plug-in is integrated in an Eclipse extension such as the BPMN modeler, and it uses the functionalities of the PAT model checker [19]. The CSP model is derived taking advantage of the Eclipse Modeling Framework (EMF) which is a powerful mechanism available within the Eclipse platform to define meta-models. EMF, together with other frameworks enabling the graphical rendering of the BPMN constructs, is at the base of BPMN modeler. Therefore through EMF, and its API, it is possible to interact with the defined BPMN model to retrieve the list of elements which have been included within a BPMN specification. In this way it is possible to implement a simple parser that for each BPMN element generates the corresponding CSP code, using in our case the syntax of the PAT model checker, and according to the mapping rules. Similarly the code generation includes the specification of variables enabling the checking of relevant quality requirements. After that the transformation of the BPMN specification to the corresponding CSP model has been carried on the verification step can take place. To make also this step easier we integrated the PAT model checker within the Eclipse framework. As a result the whole tool-chain is integrated in a unique integrated development environment. The techniques we used to implement the framework make easy its extension with new properties.

5   BP4PA in Place

Thanks to a close cooperation between our research group and a local Public Administration we applied our approach as well as the tool in practice.

5.1   General Considerations

As for any approach using model checking techniques it is important to check if the state explosion phenomenon could hinder its applicability to real case study. In our case we experimented with ten real processes and all of them have generated relatively small state sets. In particular the experiments we have conducted using a desktop PC equipped with a Core 2 Duo 2,20GHz and 4GB RAM, have highlighted that defined BP can be checked with respect to the properties included in the framework in less than 60 minutes, for the most complex BP scenarios. Moreover the most complex BP generated a state space of around three millions states. This data seems to support the idea that in the current status (i.e. complexity of BP processes in the e-government domain, mapping we have defined and quality properties to be checked) the approach is applicable in real

Table 1. Experimental Results

Service Name	Num. of States	BPMN elem.	Coord. (sec)	Control (sec)	Sharing (sec)	Transp. (sec)	Inclusiv. (sec)
Car registration	3.065.595	66	1629,18	3254,22	3280,48	1631,28	4896,25
Passport Request	735.785	68	594,28	596,08	2368,12	590,17	1777,94
Enrollment in education	44.963	45	33,88	100,85	67,75	33,50	100,59
Declaration to police	32.333	43	14,14	19,60	27,60	13,70	41,17
Social Contribution	19.398	42	18,59	19,51	38,35	10,37	28,68
Social security benefits	14.295	43	10,12	9,89	9,93	4,90	14,69
Job search	4.044	31	3,36	4,68	3,03	1,50	4,52
Health-related services	2.451	36	1,98	1,84	1,78	0,88	2,62
Public libraries	333	18	0,28	0,12	0,07	0,06	0,17
Customs declaration	204	20	0,20	0,11	0,10	0,05	0,14

scenarios and can be a useful support for the BP designer. In Table 1 we report a part of the conducted experimental results. It refers to EU based service in line with Italian law and our local scenario.

The study has also highlighted that all the defined BPs reach low quality levels for all the quality dimensions in the framework. Given that the studied services are seldom used by citizens the defined framework does not contradict itself. Considering transparency, that may be is the most intuitive dimension in the framework, the tool reported that no information were provided, through a message flowing from the PA to the citizen, between the start and the end of the process.

Starting from the evalutation of the processes reported by BP4PA we started to revise the various BPs in order to derive BPs getting higher marks.

5.2   Moving Service

The approach has been used to improve the delivery process associated to the moving service. This is part of the wide area of cooperation among civil registration services. The service permits to an Italian citizen, which has to move to a different municipality, to be registered, to get updated certificates and any other service regardless of its new geographical location. In particular the service under analysis supports in the most comfortable way the registration of a new address, delivering at the same time the request for updating relevant information reported in the driving license. Moreover such service supports the alignment of the information in all the Public Administration offices dedicated to trace moving of citizens.

As many other GDSs, the moving service foresees the interactions of many stakeholders. In particular: (i) The municipality where citizens has to be registered. This can be further decomposed in registry office, local police office and tax office (ii) The Home Affairs Minister deputed to collect and to maintain up to date the information related to citizens using the INA/SAIA infrastructure (iii) Tax Office is the national organization in charge of controlling the status of the

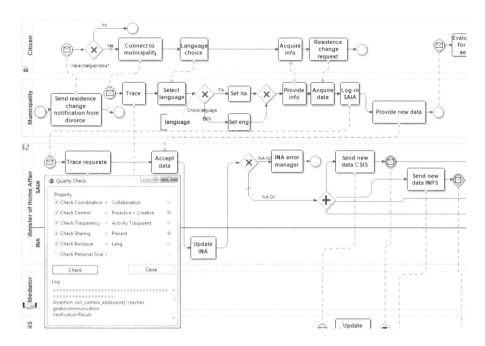

Fig. 2. BP excerpt for the Moving Service - improved version

Italian citizens with respect to tax obbligations (iv) CISIS (Italian inter-regional center for information, statistical and geographical systems) is the association of regional authorities which, among a list of several activities, has to collect all the information requested for statistical purposes (v) INPS is responsible of the pension system. It is deputed to collect and maintain up to date the information related to the social citizens status (vi) Transport Office is the national association devoted to control the traffic for what concerns driving licenses and policies.

The GDS is implemented roughly applying a six-steps process: (i) The citizen asks for activating and accessing the moving service. It is worth mentioning that the access can be provided at the municipality office or via Web when suitable authorizations and authentications mechanisms are set; (ii) The registration municipality collects the information from the citizen; (iii) The registration municipality sends such data to the Home Affair Minister via the SAIA infrastructure; (iv) The Home Affairs Minister is deputed to collect and to maintain up-to-date the information related to citizens; (v) The Home Affair Minister communicates the updating data to de-registration municipality the Tax and Transport Office, and INPS so that citizens data are updated; (vi) The Home Affair Minister communicates the data, relevant for statistical purpose, to the CISIS.

After the first codification the BP4PA tool has been applied, and it returned low marks with respects to the different dimensions of the quality framework. Based on the resulting feedbacks the moving service has been improved and the resulting BP is shown in Figure 2 (for space reason we report only an excerpt of the BP to give an idea of its complexity). Improvements are based on the interpretation of the framework properties as implementation patterns to follow in order to get higher evaluation marks. Nevertheless we have to consider that in general higher level of the quality framework subsume higher investments from the PA. In general terms the starting BP reached bad quality levels in all the dimensions but the sharing one. The improvement intervention aimed at introducing, feedback messages directed to the citizens, messages between the involved administrations to improve their ability to cooperate via electronic means, the possibility of activating the service as result of the access to related services such as request to services related to marriage life events, and finally the provisioning of the service through different channels, profile and languages in order to improve inclusiveness.

6   Conclusions and Future Work

Exploiting domain knowledge in this paper we have introduced a user-friendly approach implemented in a plug-in for the Eclipse platform. It permits to assess, using formal verification techniques, a delivery process with respect to a defined quality framework. A discussion on the results we obtained from the conducted experiments is also reported. The general outcome is that (i) formal verification is mature enough to be introduced and applied in the field of study; (ii) delivery processes, defined for the services under study, reach low quality marks with respect to the defined framework; and (iii) proposed approach can be a useful mean to improve the quality of BP related to GDS delivery.

For the future we intend to continue the evaluation applying the framework to other scenarios. Moreover the extension of the framework is one of the research line in which we have started to work trying to identify additional interesting requirements related to the delivery of GDSs. We also intend to extend the study to BPs related to other GDS aspects and PA activities. In particular we started to investigate how to automatically assess if a BP can be put in place given constraints related to the resources available within a public office.

Acknowledgements

The authors would like to thank Regione Marche local public administration for the cooperation and for partially funding this research. A particular thanks to the offices of "P.F. Sistemi Informativi e Telematici".

References

1. Corradini, F., Hinkelmann, K., Polini, A., Polzonetti, A., Re, B.: C2ST: a quality framework to evaluate e-government service delivery. In: 8th International Conference EGOV 2009, Proceedings of ongoing research, project contributions and workshops, Linz, Austria, pp. 74–84 (2009)
2. Corradini, F., Polini, A., Polzonetti, A., Re, B.: Business processes verification for e-gov service delivery. Information Systems Management journal (to appear)

3. Layne, K., Leeb, J.: Developing fully functional e-government: a four stage model. Government Information Quarterly 18(2), 122–136 (2001)
4. Janssen, M., Kuk, G., Wagenaar, R.W.: A survey of web-based business models for e-government in the netherlands. Government Information Quarterly 25(2), 202–220 (2008)
5. Janssen, M., Kuk, G.: E-government business models for public service networks. International Journal of Electronic Government Research 3(3), 54–71 (2007)
6. Davies, J., Janowski, T., Ojo, A.K., Shukla, A.: Technological foundations of electronic governance. In: Janowski, T., Pardo, T.A. (eds.) ICEGOV. ACM International Conference Proceeding Series, vol. 232, pp. 5–11. ACM Press, New York (2007)
7. Morimoto, S.: A survey of formal verification for business process modeling. In: Bubak, M., van Albada, G.D., Dongarra, J., Sloot, P.M.A. (eds.) ICCS 2008, Part II. LNCS, vol. 5102, pp. 514–522. Springer, Heidelberg (2008)
8. Wong, P.Y.H., Gibbons, J.: A process-algebraic approach to workflow specification and refinement. In: Lumpe, M., Vanderperren, W. (eds.) SC 2007. LNCS, vol. 4829, pp. 51–65. Springer, Heidelberg (2007)
9. Dijkman, R.M., Dumas, M., Ouyang, C.: Formal semantics and analysis of BPMN process models using petri nets. Online (2007)
10. Ye, J., Sun, S., Song, W., Wen, L.: Formal semantics of BPMN process models using YAWL. In: 2007 Workshop on Intelligent Information Technology Applications, vol. 2, pp. 70–74 (2008)
11. Wynn, M., Verbeek, H., van der Aalst, W., ter Hofstede, A., Edmond, D.: Business process verification - finally a reality? Business Process Management Journal 15(1), 74–92 (2009)
12. Farrell, A.D., Sergot, M.J., Bartolini, C.: Formalising workflow: a CCS-inspired characterisation of the YAWL workflow patterns. Group Decision and Negotation 16(3), 213–254 (2007)
13. Zhao, L., Li, Q., Liu, X., Du, N.: A modeling method based on CCS for workflow, pp. 376–384 (2009)
14. Lindsay, A., Downs, D., Lunn, K.: Business processes–attempts to find a definition (Special Issue on Modelling Organisational Processes). Information and Software Technology 45(15), 1015–1019 (2003)
15. Harmon, P.: Business Process Change - A guide tor Business Manager and BPM and Six Sigma Professionals. Horgan Kaufmann, San Francisco (2004)
16. White, S.A., Miers, D.: BPMN Modeling and Reference Guide Understanding and Using BPMN. Future Strategies Inc. (2008)
17. Hoare, C.A.R.: Communicating Sequential Processes. Prentis (2004)
18. Clarke, E.M., Grumberg, O., Peled, D.A.: Model Checking. In: Hardcover (2000)
19. Sun, J., Liu, Y., Dong, J.S.: Model checking CSP revisited: introducing a Process Analysis Toolkit. In: Margaria, T., Steffen, B. (eds.) ISoLA 2004. Communications in Computer and Information Science, vol. 17, pp. 307–322. Springer, Heidelberg (2008)
20. zur Muehlen, M., Recker, J.: How much language is enough? Theoretical and practical use of the business process modeling notation. In: Bellahsène, Z., Léonard, M. (eds.) CAiSE 2008. LNCS, vol. 5074, pp. 465–479. Springer, Heidelberg (2008)
21. Re, B.: Quality of Digital e-Government Services. PhD thesis, School of Advances Studies – University of Camerino (2010)

Author Index

Printing: Mercedes-Druck, Berlin
Binding: Stein+Lehmann, Berlin